VOLUME

13

L—Lyre
pages 1-344

Compton's
Encyclopedia

and Fact-Index

F.E. Compton Company

Division of Encyclopaedia Britannica, Inc.

THE UNIVERSITY OF CHICAGO
COMPTON'S ENCYCLOPEDIA IS PUBLISHED WITH THE EDITORIAL ADVICE
OF THE FACULTIES OF THE UNIVERSITY OF CHICAGO

"Let knowledge grow from more to more and thus be human life enriched"

PHOTOS: Row 1: (left) Katherine Young; (right) Sven Samelius. Row 2: (right) Anthony Bannister—Natural History Photographic Agency. Row 3: (far left) *United Air Lines Mainliner;* (center) John H. Gerard. Row 4: (center left) Art Resource. Row 5: (far right) EB Inc.

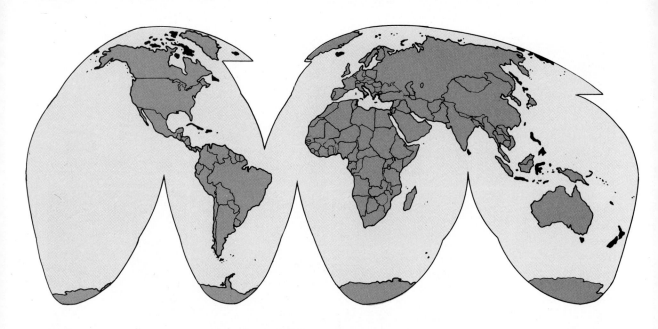

HERE AND THERE IN VOLUME 13

From the A-1 satellite to the zygote cell, thousands of subjects are gathered
together in Compton's Encyclopedia and Fact-Index. Organized
alphabetically, they are drawn from every field of knowledge. Readers who
want to explore their favorite fields in this volume can use this subject-area
outline. While it may serve as a study guide, a specialized learning
experience, or simply a key for browsing, it is not a complete table of contents.

EXPLORING VOLUME 13

What is the common name for the device that produces light amplification by stimulated emission of radiation?   54.

How was Queen Elizabeth I's collar involved in England's foreign relations?   15.

Name the African city that was once a major outlet for Portugal's slave traffic.   327.

Which plant can reproduce in three different ways?   262.

In which country did the children's stories about Babar the elephant originate?   247, 255.

Babar kisses them affectionately and hurries off with them to buy them some fine clothes.

What was the first country to gain independence through the United Nations?   190.

How were the Hawaiian Islands formed?   90.

How do two different kinds of organisms live together so intimately that they seem to be a single plant?   191.

Which French king became too fat to mount his horse?   304.

How did the leopard get its name?   135.

Who was the architect who pioneered the concept of vertical environments with his Marseilles project?   114.

How does the lamprey kill its prey?   26.

Photo Trends

From the article LIBERTY, STATUE OF

The letter L

probably started as a picture sign of an oxgoad, as in a very early Semitic writing used about 1500 B.C. on the Sinai Peninsula (1). A similar sign (2), denoting a peasant's crook, is found in earlier Egyptian hieroglyphic writing. About 1000 B.C., in Byblos and other Phoenician and Canaanite centers, the sign was given a linear form (3), the source of all later forms. In the Semitic languages the sign was called *lamedh,* meaning "oxgoad."

The Greeks first gave the sign some unbalanced forms (4) and renamed it *lambda.* Later they formed their sign symmetrically (5). The Romans adopted the earlier Greek forms (6). From Latin the capital letter came unchanged into English.

In late Roman times the small handwritten "l" was developed from the capital by rounding the lines. Later a form with an open loop in the vertical stroke was developed (7).

© Walter Frerck—Odyssey Productions

Construction workers build a nuclear power plant
in southern Texas near Bay City.

LABOR. In the most general sense labor means
work. Young children know that when they grow up
they will get a job, earn money, and use that money to
live. This appears to be a basic fact of life, as basic as
growing up itself. Actually, however, this form of
earning a living, exchanging hours of work for money, has become common only within the last 200
years. Such paid employment is called wage labor, a
narrower meaning of the word labor.

Work in Pre-Industrial Society

Primitive peoples live in small groups. Everyone
does some of the work needed to survive: hunting,
food gathering, making clothes and tools, cooking,
caring for babies, and so on. Not everyone does the
same work. Young adult males do different things
than do boys and old men. In most primitive societies
women have different tasks from those of men. Precisely what work is "men's work" and "women's
work" differs from one group to another, though
there are some tasks that almost universally fall to
one sex; for instance, the feeding of young children.
Individuals have little choice—they do the work that
is traditional for their age and sex.

Another ancient means of organizing work, or of
deciding who will do which jobs, is slavery. Slavery
first appeared about 4500 BC in Egypt, Mesopotamia,
and Anatolia. Slaves were fundamental to the economies of two great ancient societies—Greece and
Rome. At the height of the Roman Empire in the second century AD, between 30 and 35 percent of the people in Italy were slaves. After that time slavery became less common, but it had a major resurgence
between 1550 and 1888 when black Africans were
forced by Europeans to work as slaves in North and
South America.

Slaves worked at all kinds of tasks, but the majority did heavy or menial labor such as farming, building roads, rowing ships, doing housework, and working in mines. Slaves who did not work as they were
told were punished.

At the end of the Roman Empire, another way of
organizing work, serfdom, became dominant. Serfdom lasted in Western Europe for more than 1,000
years and survived even longer in Eastern Europe.
Serfs were farm workers who were obliged to work a
certain number of days per week for the lord of the
manor on which they lived. In exchange for their
work serfs were granted the right to farm small pieces
of land for themselves.

Serfs had rights that slaves lacked. They could not
be sold, so they did not live in fear of being separated
from their families. They also did not have to obey
every whim of their lord; they had certain required
tasks, but they could not be made to do just anything.
On the other hand, serfs were not free. They could
not leave the manor on which they were born, and
they could not change their employment. Like slaves,
they did not receive money wages for their labor.

In the towns of medieval Europe a different system
prevailed. Artisans who produced cloth, shoes, armor, and similar items were organized into guilds.
Each guild set standards regarding the quality of the
product and the conditions of work in the trade, such
as the hours of work, vacations, and so on. Guilds had
three kinds of members—apprentices, journeymen,
and masters. Apprentices lived with a master and
worked without pay for several years to learn the
trade. After a fixed period apprentices became journeymen, skilled workers who were paid a wage in
exchange for a certain number of hours of work.
Eventually many journeymen could expect to become
masters, or employers. In this way they differed from
most modern wage earners. (*See also* Guilds.)

By 1500 much had changed in Western Europe. In England in particular, many serfs had gained their freedom and had become independent. They paid rent for their land but were free to move to other places and to take any job they could find. These peasants grew food to feed their families and sold the excess to others who needed it.

The Industrial Age

Between 1750 and 1830 the Industrial Revolution transformed life in England. Many factories were built—at first in the textile industry and later in other industries. Wage labor, in which the factories hired employees and paid them for the number of hours worked, became more common.

Unlike slaves or serfs, wage laborers can choose their jobs and change their place of employment—they are mobile. Such mobility is desirable in a growing, changing, industrial economy. An employer establishing a new business benefits because he can get workers simply by offering wages somewhat above those paid elsewhere, and the workers benefit because they get the higher wages.

Wage labor also permits more personal freedom than earlier systems of organizing work. Workers who are unhappy with their jobs can quit; serfs and slaves could not. Wage laborers, however, cannot be sure of having work. They must sell their labor to survive, and at times employers have no need to hire them. Unemployment poses a major social problem in societies based on wage labor.

Wage labor, along with division of labor, has produced large increases in productivity, or the amount each worker can produce. Division of labor means that each task is divided into many small chores, and a separate worker is assigned to each chore. Apparently this increases productivity because workers can do one small thing rapidly, and time is not lost switching from one task to another. Division of labor also increases the possibility of a machine's doing a single part of a task, and the use of machines greatly increases productivity.

Life in early factory towns was appalling. Sewage ran down open ditches at the sides of muddy roads, transmitting disease. Some families slept eight to a windowless room in which the ceiling was so low that an adult could not stand. In 1840 life expectancy for a laborer in industrial Liverpool was only 15 years; this contrasted sharply with 38 years in the nonindustrial district of Rutland.

Many factories operated from sunrise to sundown. This meant that in the summer workers, including young children, worked 14 hours per day. During the Industrial Revolution children and women made up 77 percent of the textile industry work force because they could be paid far less than adult men.

Eventually public outcry and pressure from unions led to the passage of legislation that corrected the worst abuses of the factory system. Just as importantly, the higher output per worker brought about by industrialization eventually raised living standards. As cloth became cheaper, for example, workers could afford to buy more clothes. Standards of living rose in England, especially after 1840.

Industrialization occurred later in the United States than in England. Working conditions were somewhat better in the United States, though child labor, recurring unemployment, low wages, and long hours also accompanied industrialization.

The United States passed federal legislation in the 1930s to set minimum wages, to establish maximum hours of work without the payment of overtime rates, to regulate the employment of children, and to provide income for unemployed and retired workers.

With increasing industrialization, types of jobs changed dramatically. The number of jobs for office workers, managers, and professional workers began to grow rapidly in the late 1800s. This was because large corporations that required professional managers and complicated record-keeping replaced small businesses. Such occupations are still increasing.

Employment also grew rapidly in service industries—those that produce intangibles like insurance, banking services, health care, and education—and in those that sell the goods produced elsewhere. The number of agricultural workers, on the other hand, declined dramatically as the 20th century progressed. Manufacturing employment was fairly stable at around 25 percent of the total, but that has dipped in recent years.

The proportion of women in the labor force, those working outside the home or who are looking for work, has increased rapidly. In the early 1980s more than 60 percent of all women aged 18 to 54 were in the labor force. Since 1964 discrimination against female and minority employees has been against federal law in the United States. Both groups, however, continue to earn considerably less on the average than do white males with the same education and experience. Another United States law regarding work is the Occupational Safety and Health Act of 1970, which regulates unsafe working conditions.

Since the Industrial Revolution many changes have occurred in the kinds of jobs and workers and the laws governing work. Manufacturing employment is expected to decline with increasing use of robots and automated production systems. Robots can be reprogrammed to do different things, so they increase the number of operations that can be mechanized. The dominant form of work, however, is still wage labor, and it would take changes of a kind impossible to foresee before this element of modern life is transformed. (*See also* Labor Movements.)

BIBLIOGRAPHY FOR LABOR

Fogel, Robert and Engerman, Stanley. Time on the Cross: the Economics of American Negro Slavery (Little, 1974).

Hobsbawn, E. J. Industry and Empire, vol. 3 of The Pelican Economic History of Britain (Penguin, 1970).

Stellman, Jeanne. Women's Work, Women's Health: Myths and Realities (Pantheon, 1978).

Terkel, Studs. Working: People Talk About What They Do All Day and How They Feel About What They Do (Pantheon, 1974).

LABOR AND INDUSTRIAL LAW. All of the laws regulating the conditions under which employees work for employers are called labor and industrial law. Examples of the types of issues regulated by labor and industrial law are: hours of labor, child labor, minimum wage, workers' compensation, unemployment insurance, worker safety and health, disability compensation, the rights of collective bargaining by labor unions, and the social security system (*see* Social Security).

While governments have seen fit to legislate in these and other areas, many of the laws are no more than general guidelines. The specifics are frequently left to arrangements between employers and employees within a given company or industry. For instance, government may legislate a 40-hour workweek, but this does not prevent a company from spreading the 40 hours over six days. Nor does it hinder an industry from offering overtime employment, providing wages meet agreed-upon standards.

History

Work has been regulated by governments for many centuries. From the ancient world until the 19th century, slave systems were strictly regulated by both laws and custom. In some countries, such as India, certain castes, or classes, of people were not permitted to engage in some kinds of work. In Europe beginning in the Middle Ages, guilds of tradesmen and apprentices were strictly regulated by society (*see* Apprenticeship; Guilds).

Modern labor law has its origins in the Industrial Revolution that began in England and Europe in the 18th century and spread to the United States and other nations later. There is a crucial difference between the older laws on work and modern labor codes: the earlier work laws were passed by government for the benefit of the state, of employers, and of owners of slaves; the modern codes, originating mostly in the 19th century, have been passed largely for the benefit of workers and all of society.

The reason for this difference is that, as the Industrial Revolution was gaining momentum, there arose in Western Europe and North America a variety of political and economic theories—including anarchism, communism, liberalism, and socialism. These theories, though they differ on many matters, all sprang from the desire for greater political and economic democracy for the masses of people. At the same time, a philosophical movement called the Enlightenment propagated many new ideas concerning the rights of mankind in relation to the state. (The American Declaration of Independence is one of the best statements of Enlightenment principles in this regard.) The American and French revolutions, with their declarations of rights, did much to spread the notion that individuals have certain rights that governments must honor. (*See also* Anarchism; Bill of Rights; Communism; Liberalism; Socialism.)

In this new, more democratic political setting, it became increasingly obvious to many people that the combinations of government and those with great wealth would not look out for the interests of workers unless pressured to do so. Hence, there emerged the first attempts to organize workers into labor and trade unions to exert just such pressure on politicians and employers. For a century or more, these attempts at unionization were regarded by governments as criminal conspiracies (*see* Labor Movement). Gradually, aided by the efforts of liberal politicians and the enlightened self-interest of employers, unions began to gain recognition. Their demands for better working conditions, shorter hours, and social welfare began to be met.

The first major labor law, the Health and Morals of Apprentices Act, was passed by Great Britain in 1802. Other European nations passed similar legislation in the next few decades. The first legal limitation on the working hours of adults was passed in Switzerland in 1848. Germany pioneered in the field of health insurance, workers' compensation, and old-age pensions during the 1880s, when Otto von Bismarck was chancellor. Compulsory arbitration in labor disputes was introduced in New Zealand in the 1890s. Limitations were put on the working hours of children in India in 1881, but similar legislation for adults was not passed until 20 years later.

Most of these laws were designed to meet specific situations in particular localities. The notion of generalized labor laws to cover virtually all the aspects of the employer-employee situation did not emerge until after World War I. In the United States there was virtually no labor legislation of any consequence, except for limitations on hours of work, until the worst of the Great Depression was over in the 1930s. The first comprehensive labor code was promulgated in France between 1910 and 1927. The Mexican Constitution of 1917 and the German Weimar constitution of 1919 both contained extensive formulations about the conditions of labor. Departments or ministries of labor were established to administer labor legislation in Canada in 1900, in France in 1906, in the United States in 1913, in the United Kingdom in 1916, and in Germany in 1918. Such departments were established in most industrialized nations thereafter and in the newly independent countries in Africa and Asia in the 1940s and 1950s.

The Essentials of Labor Law

Apart from the fairly complex matter of government social insurance programs (*see* Social Security), labor and industrial law deals with the following categories: employment, employee-employer relationships, wages and salaries, working conditions, occupational health and safety regulations, and labor-management relations. Because the variety of workers in an advanced society is so great, there are also numerous laws pertaining to specific occupations, such as mine workers, agricultural and migrant laborers, transportation workers, and government employees. Certain categories of personnel, such as managers and part-time workers, are frequently not covered by labor statutes except in the most general way. The same is true for armed forces personnel.

Employment. On Jan. 11, 1944, President Franklin D. Roosevelt, in his annual message to Congress, stated what has come to be called an "economic bill of rights." He urged, among other things, that all people be guaranteed "the right to a useful and remunerative job in the industries or shops or farms or mines of the nation." This speech symbolized a shift in public policy that had been taking place since the onset of the Great Depression both in the United States and in the rest of the industrialized world. In the earliest stages of the Industrial Revolution, the concern of employers had been to find enough workers. Later the problem became finding solutions to cases of massive unemployment during economic panics and depressions. The new approach has expressed itself in the efforts of government and the business sector, working together, to create job opportunities, forecast labor needs, set up worker recruitment centers, and provide vocational and apprenticeship training. Taken together, these combined efforts are called a full-employment policy.

Employee-employer relations. This general-sounding term has its basis in the older master-servant contract that existed before the Industrial Revolution. Today it includes such issues as hiring policy, promotions, transfers, and termination of employment. Fair-employment-practice laws that bar discrimination in hiring because of race, sex, or religion are examples of modern legislation in this area.

Wages, salaries, and other remuneration. This area of labor law covers all the aspects of how workers are rewarded for their labor. Included are minimum wage laws, fringe benefits, cost-of-living increases, and laws protecting workers from forced wage deductions. Many of these matters are decided in collective bargaining between unions and companies. The laws provide general guidelines within which such collective bargaining takes place.

In modern highly industrialized nations, the issue of fringe benefits has grown in importance to rival the basic matter of salaries. In the late 20th century, workers may have paid vacations, pension plans, life and health insurance, paid personal days off from work, and reimbursement for job-related schooling. With the greater number of women in the work force, some companies have started providing day-care centers for children.

Conditions of work. This aspect of labor law originated in laws to limit the hours of work, eliminate child labor, and protect women in the work force. In today's industrial societies the scope of such laws has broadened considerably and shifted its emphasis. There is now much concern with vocational training, career guidance, and job placement, as economies shift from industrial bases to sophisticated technology or service-related enterprises.

The former emphasis on protective legislation for women has become outmoded. Limitations on kinds of jobs and hours of work for women have come to be regarded as discriminatory. More recent laws focus on equal pay for equal work, equal employment opportunities, and adequate maternity protection.

Working conditions have also been improved by legal provisions allowing for at least one day off per week. This principle has been amplified by legislation granting annual vacations and holidays with pay.

Health and safety regulations. This vital area of labor law is one of the most recent to develop. It began with prescribing elementary safety rules for work in mines and for other extremely hazardous jobs. It has since spread to cover a great range of industrial processes and other occupations. Statutes are concerned not only with accident prevention and building safety but with workers who are exposed to radioactive materials, poisons, lead, asbestos, and chemicals with potentially harmful effects. In the United States, these laws are enforced by the federal Occupational Safety and Health Administration. Many states have similar enforcement agencies.

Labor-management relations. Some of the earliest labor laws were those granting legal status to labor unions. The scope of these laws has also broadened considerably to include guarantees of collective bargaining between companies and unions, worker participation in management, work rules, and the prevention and settlement of labor disputes— particularly when they result in strikes or lockouts. There is, in the United States, a considerable body of law, as well as many judicial decisions, in this area of labor law. The two major labor laws are the National Labor Relations Act of 1935 (the Wagner Act) and the Labor Management Relations Act of 1947 (the Taft-Hartley Act).

The International Labor Organization (ILO)

Founded in 1919 as an adjunct to the League of Nations, the International Labor Organization today works as a specialized agency in concert with the United Nations. The purpose of the ILO is to formulate international standards for the betterment of working and living conditions. These standards are submitted to member nations for ratification, and, once the standards have been adopted, they are considered to be binding upon those nations that ratify them. The ILO also publishes labor statistics and does research on labor and management relations, unemployment and underemployment, working conditions, technological change, economic development, and international economic competition.

Since World War II and the breakup of the old colonial empires, the membership of the ILO has become predominantly the developing countries of what is called the Third World. Hence the emphasis of the ILO has shifted to problems of human rights, technological assistance, and economic development. In the early 1980s the ILO had a membership of 145 nations. Member states are represented at the ILO's annual International Labor Conference by government representatives and nominees from businesses and labor organizations.

Women in London carry sandwich-board signs in 1935 protesting wage cuts outside the House of Commons.

LABOR MOVEMENTS.

LABOR MOVEMENTS. The term labor movement is often applied to any organization or association of wage earners who join together to advance their common interests. It more broadly applies, however, to any association of workers by geographical area, trade or industry, or any other factor. While labor unions have been the almost exclusive center of the modern labor movement in the United States, in Western Europe, and in many other countries, the term labor movement has come to embrace labor-oriented political parties as well as labor unions, usually combined in a loose alliance. (*See also* Labor.)

Beginnings of Trade Unions

There are records of fragmentary instances of collective labor action such as strikes as far back as the ancient world, and medieval workers undertook some protective collective labor activities. But a labor movement in the sense of an organized and continuous effort by wage earners to improve their standard of living is a relatively recent event in human history. Only when workers, in the words of labor historians Sidney and Beatrice Webb, "passed into the condition of lifelong wage-earners, possessing neither the instruments of production nor the commodity in the finished state," would substantial, permanent associations of employees emerge.

Such economic conditions emerged with the growth and triumph of market civilization and the Industrial Revolution. It was primarily in the 18th and 19th centuries in England and, beginning a bit later, in the United States that lasting trade unions were established.

This article was contributed by Everett M. Kassalow, Professor of Economics and Industrial Relations, University of Wisconsin; Senior Specialist in Labor, Library of Congress; and Research Director, Industrial Union Department, AFL-CIO.

First Unions in the United States

Contrary to popular opinion, it was not among the employees of the first factories of the Industrial Revolution that such durable associations of wage earners arose. It was rather among such skilled craft workers as printers, woodworkers, shoemakers, and metalworkers. The skilled journeymen—trained craft workers who worked under the supervision of a master with hopes of becoming masters themselves—felt the first loss as they passed into a permanent wage-earning status instead of independence. Such journeymen found themselves increasingly at the mercy of the growing power of merchant capitalists who invaded local community markets and threatened the living standards of craft workers by offering products produced elsewhere at lower cost.

City craft unions. These unions of skilled craft workers were confined to particular cities such as Philadelphia, Boston, New York City, Pittsburgh, Baltimore, and Providence. It was only later, when markets grew even more, that permanent links were established and national unions of printers, metalworkers, and the like were established. These early unions sought to limit the length of the work day and to establish uniform wage scales for their members.

The 1830s were a period of rapid growth for these early American unions, and by the middle of that decade combinations of unions in a number of cities were joining together to form central, city-wide union bodies. Early efforts to establish a national organization were generally unsuccessful.

Decline. The great depression of 1837 struck down much of this early movement. Cuts in wages and campaigns against unions by employers, assisted by the courts, undermined what had promised to become a significant economic and political force.

Throughout the 19th and 20th centuries, the ups and downs of the business cycle have influenced labor movements in the United States. The expansion of economic activity—bringing with it growth in the demand for labor—creates conditions favorable to union organization and to demands of wage earners for improved living standards. Correspondingly, significant economic decline weakens the position of workers and labor unions and often leads to a greater emphasis on government solutions to labor's problems. (*See also* Business Cycle.)

National unions emerge. A new tide of industrial prosperity in the late 1840s and early 1850s helped revive the labor movement. The great expansion of United States' markets then and in the period of the Civil War created a new economic environment for unionism. To deal successfully with employers, many unionists found they had to "match" this new national market with national unions. The National Typographical Union, for example, was established in 1850, soon followed by separate national unions of moulders, machinists and blacksmiths, stonecutters, and hat finishers. During the Civil War additional national unions were established, including those of carpenters, bricklayers, and cigar makers.

Alongside national unions there continued to be many local unions whose operations were confined to a single city. By the end of the Civil War, virtually every major city had a city-wide assembly representing unions from all crafts and trades.

The NLU. It was on the basis of these local assemblies and some of the national unions that the National Labor Union (NLU) was established in 1866. This organization was primarily interested in broad social reform and political objectives. It was dedicated to the promotion of consumer-producer cooperation and to the elimination of the wage system itself. It also supported restriction of immigration, limitation of public lands to actual settlers, establishment of a Department of Labor in the federal government, and an eight-hour work day.

Black workers assumed growing importance after emancipation in the Civil War. The NLU made a conciliatory gesture to black workers and suggested that they form their own labor unions to cooperate with white labor. Most NLU efforts to establish cooperation failed. The organization also became enmeshed in campaigns for political and money reform and other issues that were not among labor unions' immediate concerns. The NLU expired in 1872. The great depression of 1873 dealt organized labor another blow, and within a few years many of the national labor unions were swept away.

Knights of Labor. After the depression several national unions were gradually reconstructed, and a more general organization, the Noble Order of the Knights of Labor, came into existence. Founded in Philadelphia in 1869 as a secret organization, the Knights combined both skilled and unskilled workers behind a plan for broad reform. This included the eight-hour work day, abolition of child labor, public ownership of utilities and railways, and support of corporations for production and distribution of goods. The Knights gradually expanded from Philadelphia into a national organization and grew rapidly in the late 1870s and early '80s. Although the Knights sought to combine both unskilled and skilled workers, their efforts at political and social reform were viewed with skepticism by the national unions of skilled craft workers who were more interested in practical, day-to-day economic objectives.

Having entered the national field, the Knights won a series of victories that climaxed with a successful strike in 1885 against the Wabash Railroad, which was controlled by the financier Jay Gould. The efforts of the Knights to combine unionism and radical social reform began to meet increasing resistance. Moreover, the rising tide of immigration into the country made efforts to organize skilled and unskilled workers more difficult.

The AFL. The return of prosperity strengthened the national unions of skilled workers. In 1881 they established the Federation of Organized Trades and Labor Unions of the United States and Canada, which in 1886 became the American Federation of Labor (AFL). Although the AFL included political demands in its platform, it was largely controlled by the national unions of skilled workers and was devoted to practical union objectives. A basic principle was the safeguarding of its affiliates' individual autonomies and jurisdictions.

The unions of the AFL placed great emphasis on written collective agreements, including the closed shop, in which only union members are permitted to work. The AFL unions also insisted that members pay relatively high dues, and many of them established insurance and strike benefits. They came to be characterized by job consciousness as opposed to class consciousness. While the AFL grew slowly, it wrested the leadership of American labor from the Knights of Labor by the 1890s.

The IWW. The AFL repelled the challenge of the Industrial Workers of the World (IWW), which attempted to unionize workers of major industries into one big industrial union for the revolutionary purpose of overthrowing capitalism and replacing it with workers' self-management. The IWW scorned the written collective agreement as giving in to capitalism, and it fixed members' dues and initiation fees at low levels to avoid creating a bureaucratic structure. Although the IWW gained some strength and led several spectacular strikes before and just after World War I, its radical program and tactics did not attract a permanent following among American workers, and it dwindled by the 1920s.

Western Europe

In the decades in which the AFL took form, European labor on the Continent was establishing significantly different labor movements. Largely as a result of feudal traditions and institutions, European workers lacked the basic political and social freedoms—voting rights, equality before the law, and the right to move from job to job. In addition, many European workers and their children did not have the right to free public education.

Labor political parties. When European labor formed its organizations in the closing decades of the 19th century, it also supported labor, or socialist, political parties to bring about social and political emancipation. In almost every European country, there was a virtually united labor movement that combined unions with a socialist political party.

It was largely a result of the European labor movement that workers gained the right to vote, free public education was established, and full citizenship rights were granted before World War I. These successes reinforced the loyalty of European workers to their unions and socialist parties. Political-legislative action to improve wages, hours, and working conditions came to be as readily employed as was union action. Marxism became less important as the guiding philosophy as workers became more integrated into their own societies.

United States After World War I

Under the leadership of the AFL, American unionism remained largely confined to skilled craft workers, though unions organized along industrial lines in coal mining, breweries, and clothing and paper manufacturing were affiliated with the AFL. Unsuccessful efforts were made by the AFL shortly after World War I to organize workers in several mass production industries, especially in steel and meat packing. Strong opposition from employers, often aided by the government, caused union membership to decline from its immediate postwar peak of five million to three million by the end of the 1920s. Employers used such tactics as the yellow-dog contract in which job seekers were not hired unless they pledged not to join unions. Employers also used labor spies to report union activities, and employees sympathetic to unions were often fired. Some companies established their own employer-controlled unions to forestall outside union organizing. It was common for employers to seek court injunctions to halt strikes on the grounds that they were a threat to property.

The Great Depression and the New Deal. The Great Depression, which struck at the end of 1929, further weakened unions. But the same depression unleashed powerful changes that helped to give birth to a great upsurge of unionism. Traditional social and economic ideas about the inviolable rights of employers and their economic property came under serious reconsideration. Congress, under the leadership of President Franklin D. Roosevelt, enacted many far-reaching economic and social reforms as part of the New Deal. Notable among these reforms were sweeping changes in the laws regulating labor unions and their rights to organize.

Emergence of a national labor policy. Prior to the 1930s the United States lacked a comprehensive labor policy. In the first half of the 19th century, employers frequently resorted to the courts—under common law proceedings—to halt union actions, including strikes. Often the courts held unions to be conspiracies in restraint of trade and restrained them from any effective action. Although the conspiracy doctrine was overturned by the courts by the middle of the century, employers used such laws as the Sherman Anti-Trust Act to persuade the courts to halt union activities. On occasion they even compelled union officials to pay damages to employers. In some labor disputes state governors, and occasionally the federal government, used the national guard to halt strikes. Toward the end of the 19th century, employers' most effective tactic to halt union action was to seek an injunction; usually the judge did not even hear the union's side of the case.

Public opinion began to turn more favorable to labor unions, and in 1932 the Norris-La Guardia Act was passed. It severely limited use of court injunctions in labor disputes, and it outlawed the yellow-dog contract. Finally in 1935 the National Labor Relations Act was passed, as part of the New Deal legislation, clearly establishing workers' rights to form unions without interference from employers.

The CIO. A wave of union growth occurred as unions took advantage of the changed climate of opinion as well as the new legislation. At the center of this wave of organization stood the newly formed Congress of Industrial Organizations (CIO), led by John L. Lewis (*see* Lewis, John L.).

The AFL had largely ignored mass production workers in the 1920s. Lewis and other labor leaders proposed great new organizing drives to build industrial unions that would embrace all employees—skilled and unskilled—in the steel, auto, rubber, and other major industries. When his proposal was rejected by the traditional craft unions in control of the

UNION GROWTH IN SEVEN COUNTRIES

COUNTRY	1948		1968		1979	
	UNION MEMBERSHIP*	PERCENT OF WAGE FORCE†	UNION MEMBERSHIP	PERCENT OF WAGE FORCE	UNION MEMBERSHIP	PERCENT OF WAGE FORCE
United States	14,319	29.7	20,721	29.3	22,807	24.9
Germany, West	5,076	33.5	7,040	35.8	9,217	39.2
Australia	1,456	54.5	2,191	51.1	2,775	52.8
Sweden	1,549	66.5	2,303	77.8	3,124	89.1
Denmark	777	51.9	1,150	61.2	1,686	75.7
Norway	–	–	719	61.8	1,043	62.9
Great Britain	9,363	45.2	10,200	44.0	13,498	55.8

*Union membership in 000's. †Percent refers to union membership as a percentage of the wage and salary force in each country.
Source: George Bain and Robert Price, 'Profiles of Union Growth' (Basil Blackmill, 1980), and further data supplied by correspondence from the authors.

EB Inc.

Wide World

Rhode Island state troopers attempt to break up a textile-workers strike (left) in 1934. I. W. Abel, president of the United Steelworkers, receives a contract from a negotiator (right) in 1965.

AFL, Lewis set up a special committee in 1936 to perform this task. For taking this action his union, the United Mine Workers of America, and those of his collaborators were expelled from the AFL. The CIO was formally established in 1938.

The organization of steel, auto, rubber, and thousands of other mass production workers went forward at a tremendous pace. In general, newly chartered unions of the CIO unionized these mass production workers in the mid-1930s. Organization in these new industries opened union doors for the first time to hundreds of thousands of black workers, though some discrimination continued. A host of new union leaders came to the fore, including a few Communists. Many unions affiliated with the AFL also took advantage of the new organizing opportunities and greatly increased their memberships. Union membership, which had fallen to 2.7 million by 1933, rose to more than 8.5 million by the end of the 1930s—from less than 12 to almost 30 percent.

The surge in union growth continued during World War II, and by 1945 membership topped 14 million. Nearly 35 percent of all wage earners were union members. The tide of public opinion, however, began to shift away from unions during World War II. Strikes that threatened wartime production, as well as several large strikes just after World War II— most notably those led by John L. Lewis and the coal union, which had withdrawn from the CIO shortly before the United States entered the war—angered the general public. Employers, too, had regained some of the power and prestige they had lost during the depression, and they stepped up their activities against unions. Finally Congress enacted the Taft-Hartley Act of 1947 over President Harry S. Truman's veto. This law substantially amended the National Labor Relations Act by providing new limits on union activities as well as stricter controls and reporting systems for union finances. Revelations by congressional investigators about financial misconduct on the part of some union officials and indica-

tions of ties between union officials and gangsters led to further legislation. The Landrum-Griffin Act of 1959 was, for example, designed to regulate the government of unions, to guarantee members' rights, and to provide for extensive public financial reporting.

The AFL and CIO merge. A social and political environment in the 1950s that was less favorable to unions, the passing of leaders who had led the struggle between the AFL and CIO, and other factors led to the unification of the two federations in 1955. AFL President George Meany and Walter Reuther, president of both the CIO and the United Automobile Workers (UAW), took the initiative. The new organization, the AFL-CIO, accepted the principle that both craft and industrial unions could exist side by side, as all AFL and CIO affiliates were accepted into the new body intact. Membership of the united movement was about 15 million, with an additional 2 million outside the AFL-CIO in independent unions. Within a few years the International Brotherhood of Teamsters with about 2 million members and several smaller unions were suspended from the AFL-CIO on the grounds of corruption and ties to racketeers. The Teamsters union has remained independent.

The great economic growth in the decades following World War II helped the unions to add to their membership, though at a much slower pace than was true from 1933 to 1945. While membership grew, it did not expand as rapidly as did the total labor force. By 1980 labor organization membership was slightly more than 22 million but below 25 percent.

Generally, American unions had their greatest successes among blue-collar, or manual, workers, especially in the great goods-producing sectors of the economy. In recent decades there has been a shift away from goods to service production. Unions have not been as successful in organizing workers in the services, large numbers of whom are women, including many part-time employees.

Independent unions. A notable exception to the trend has been government unionism. Aided by more friendly government attitudes, labor organizations surged forward in organizing federal government employees and those in a large number of state and local governments. While most of the nearly 50 percent of full-time public employees who are organized belong to AFL-CIO unions, important gains in recognition for bargaining have also been registered by independent professional bodies. Labor organizations and such associations now report about 6 million members in public employment.

While union membership growth slowed somewhat in the 1950s and '60s, American unions made striking gains in collective bargaining. Systems of private pensions that are complementary to social security, health insurance, and extensive paid vacations and holidays are some of the benefits gained.

During the same decades, and especially after the merger of the AFL-CIO, labor unions played a more important role in American political life. While unions generally lent their support to Democratic party candidates, they studiously avoided allying themselves with any one party.

Changing conditions. For several decades the leading unions of the AFL-CIO in terms of membership and effective collective bargaining were the United Automobile Workers and the United Steelworkers, and to some extent the International Association of Machinists. Each has had about a million or more members, mostly among manual workers in what are basic manufacturing industries. Economic stagnation and the recession of the late 1970s and early '80s—as well as intensified foreign competition for such American products as steel, autos, and machinery—have brought about what appears to be a permanent loss in those industries and in their unions. While these unions continue to be large, unions such as the American Federation of State, County, and Municipal Workers of America—with 1.1 million members—and the United Food and Commercial Workers—with nearly 1.3 million members—are of growing importance in the AFL-CIO. The Teamsters and the National Education Association, each with more than 1.5 million members, are also particularly important. Future union growth will to a great extent depend on unions' ability to organize effectively in the growing service sector and the expanding high technology manufacturing industries.

The future relationship between the United States government and unions appeared uncertain in the early 1980s. In the '60s and '70s legislation brought extensive government regulation over union and management in such areas as the protection of employment and earnings rights of minorities and women (the Equal Pay Act of 1963 and the Equal Employment Opportunity Act of 1964), the control of pension programs (the Employment Retirement Income Security Act of 1974), and the protection of occupational safety and health (the Occupational Safety and Health Act of 1970). The administration of President Ronald Reagan, however, seemed to have reversed this regulatory trend.

Europe After World War II

The decades following World War II were a period of unparalleled expansion for most Western European labor movements. The great period of economic expansion that began in the late 1940s and extended well into the '70s laid the foundation for much higher living standards. The membership of European unions expanded even more rapidly than in the United States, and union membership as a percentage of the wage and salary force has been higher. European employers have generally not resisted the recognition

SOME NOTABLE LABOR FIGURES

Some prominent persons are not included below because they are covered in the main text of this article or in other articles in Compton's Encyclopedia (see Fact-Index).

Abel, I. W. (1908–79). American labor leader who helped organize and served as president of the first CIO local at Canton (Ohio) Timkin Roller Bearing in 1936. He became president of the AFL-CIO industrial union department in 1968.

Chavez, César (born 1927). American labor leader who formed the National Farm Workers Association in 1962. He organized a grape boycott in 1967 that eventually won contracts and a new minimum wage from California grape growers. He later supported the United Farm Workers' fight against lettuce growers, but the group had little success.

Dubinsky, David (1892–1982). American labor leader who served as president of the International Ladies' Garment Workers in 1932. In 1935 he became a vice-president of the AFL.

Green, William (1873–1952). American labor leader who served as United Mine Workers international secretary-treasurer from 1913 to 1924. From 1924 until his death he was president of the AFL. In 1936 he expelled CIO unions from the AFL.

Hill, Joe (1879–1915). American labor leader and writer of union-related articles and songs. He joined the IWW in 1910 and took part in the San Pedro, Calif., dockworkers strike in 1912 and was arrested. In 1914 he was indicted for murder and was later executed.

Hoffa, James R. (1913–75?). American labor leader who was vice-president and then president of the Teamsters from 1952 to 1971. He was charged with attempting to bribe a United States Senate committee investigator in 1957 and was convicted of mail fraud and of mishandling union funds in 1964. He later disappeared and was presumed murdered.

Meany, George (1894–1980). American labor leader who was elected president of the AFL-CIO after its formation in 1955.

Randolph, Asa Philip (1889–1979). American labor leader who organized the Brotherhood of Sleeping Car Porters in 1925 and was its president until 1968. He helped found the Negro American Labor Council in 1960 and was its president from 1960 to 1966.

Reuther, Walter (1907–70). American labor leader who became president of the UAW and a vice-president of the CIO in 1946. In 1952 he became president of the CIO and helped with the merger of the AFL and CIO in 1955.

Walesa, Lech (born 1943). Polish labor leader who organized the Solidarity trade union in Gdansk, Poland, in 1980. He was awarded the Nobel peace prize in 1983 for his "contribution . . . to ensure the workers' right to establish their own organizations."

Webb, Beatrice Potter (1858–1943). English writer on economics and sociology. With her husband, Sidney, she helped advise the British Labour Party beginning in 1914. In 1919 she proposed the nationalization, or government takeover, of coal mines. Sidney was a founder of the Fabian Society in 1885.

of unions to the extent that American employers have done so.

Contrasting ideologies. Although the bulk of union membership in Western European labor federations can be broadly identified as socialist in orientation and is allied with labor or socialist parties, there are important Christian and/or Catholic union federations in several countries, including West Germany, Belgium, The Netherlands, Luxembourg, and Switzerland. While Christian labor unions existed before World War II, the bulk of their growth has come since then. In Italy and France the leading labor federations have generally been under Communist leadership since the end of World War II, but in each of these countries there are rival federations of socialist, Christian, or more neutral philosophies.

Broad industrial organizations. Unlike the United States, where unions are predominantly craft (a trade such as electrician or carpenter regardless of where employed) or industrial (all the workers in an industry such as automobile, steel, petroleum, or rubber manufacturing), European unions tend to be more broadly industrial. In most European countries there are, for example, large metal unions that organize all metal workers in a variety of manufacturing industries and large chemical unions that include such diverse industries as rubber and petroleum. In addition, several European countries have large general workers' unions that include a variety of semi-skilled and unskilled workers in miscellaneous industries.

European unions have been aided during the postwar decades by the fact that socialist or labor parties, with whom many unions are loosely allied, have often been in power. The movements have won such things as extensive social security and health insurance systems, protection against plant closings and layoffs, and annual vacations of three, four, or five weeks for all workers. European unions also made wage gains in collective bargaining with employers, though collective bargaining as such is less important in Europe than in the United States. For a large part of Western Europe, even the settlement of day-to-day grievances depends more on national legislation establishing work councils or committees and labor courts. In several countries—West Germany is a notable example—legislation also assures workers' representatives the right to sit on the boards of directors of large companies. Such representation exists only in a few American companies and not through legislation.

Economic stagnation and recession in the late 1970s and early '80s have been difficult for European unions, but membership has been more stable than in the United States largely because of greater success in organizing white-collar employees. European unions, moreover, generally do not run into the same resistance from employers in new, high-technology and service industries.

Developing Countries

Asia and Africa. For the most part, continuous union organizations in Asia and Africa began after World War II, though significant beginnings existed earlier in such countries as India. Union movements were often part of the struggle for liberation from foreign domination. With the end of foreign domination, relations between unions and the newly independent governments and political parties underwent considerable change, and union power decreased.

Unions in the newly independent countries, however, did not encounter the deep hostility characterized by the early decades of unionism in the United States and Europe. Some large employers, including many multinational companies, carried their more sophisticated personnel policies with them to the new countries. These policies, plus the unsure political positions of the multinationals, frequently made them easy targets for unionism. The increased strength of the United Nations' International Labor Organization, as well as various international trade union organizations, also acted as something of a protective shield for many new-country union movements.

On the other hand, the great instability of political institutions in most new countries, as well as such destabilizing social forces as the traditions of tribalism or the existence of rigidly separate castes, led many new governments to extend their control over any potentially independent force.

Latin America. In Latin America, where political independence was achieved mostly in the 19th century and economic development therefore is more advanced, union organization is more varied. Among such larger countries as Argentina and Brazil, a special kind of corporatist labor development has occurred. The governments have virtually combined the union movements with government itself, giving them some limited bargaining functions and control over certain social security administration.

Communist Countries

Unions as independent associations of wage earners to advance their common interests really do not exist in the Soviet Union and other Communist-bloc countries. Here unions function as a kind of extension of the government. In recent years there have been some efforts to establish independent union movements in the Soviet Union and also in Poland, where the Solidarity union forces became significant. Such independent union movements, however, have been declared illegal by their governments, and some union leaders have been imprisoned.

BIBLIOGRAPHY FOR LABOR MOVEMENTS

Haskins, Jim. The Long Struggle: the Story of American Labor (Westminster, 1976).

Kassalow, E. M. Trade Unions and Industrial Relations: an International Comparison (Random, 1969).

Levy, Elizabeth. Struggle and Lose, Struggle and Win (Four Winds, 1977).

Meltzer, Milton. Bread—and Roses: the Struggle of American Labor, 1865–1915 (Knopf, 1967).

Paradis, Adrian. Labor in Action: the Story of the American Labor Movement (Messner, 1975).

Schwartz, Alvin. The Unions (Viking, 1972).

Terkel, Studs. Working (Pantheon, 1974).

Battle Harbor is a major fishing village of Labrador. Trading vessels bring supplies to such coastal villages during the summer.

Ewing Galloway

LABRADOR. The northeastern corner of the Canadian mainland is the peninsula of Labrador. This peninsula, which extends from Hudson Bay to the Atlantic Ocean and from the Gulf of Saint Lawrence to Hudson Strait, has an area of about 625,000 square miles (1,620,000 square kilometers). Labrador as a political entity refers only to the Atlantic coast of Labrador, which is a portion of the province of Newfoundland (*see* Newfoundland). The remainder of the peninsula is the northern Quebec portion. This part is known as Ungava.

The entire Labrador peninsula is a part of the rocky, glacier-scoured Laurentian Plateau, or Canadian Shield (*see* Laurentian Plateau). Over the southern part stretches a great spruce forest. The forest thins out toward the north, and the northern third of the peninsula is tundra, a treeless subarctic plain.

The peninsula is covered with numerous marshes, lakes, and streams. The Atlantic coastline, about 1,200 miles (1,930 kilometers) long, is fringed with islands and deep arms of the sea called fjords. The south coast is low. Toward the north, however, bold rocky cliffs rise 2,500 to 5,500 feet (760 to 1,860 meters) out of the sea.

The cold Labrador Current flows southward from the Arctic Ocean and makes the climate along the coast very severe. The climate inland is somewhat more mild, though winter temperatures reach −50° F (−46° C). Snow usually covers the ground from September to June, thus summers are short and cool.

Labrador has Canada's most important deposits of iron ore. A hydroelectric power plant is operating at Churchill Falls and one is proposed at Gull Island. Waterpower potential in the peninsula is enormous. Fishing and lumbering are also important.

Labrador in Newfoundland has 31,318 permanent residents (1981 census). Labrador in Quebec (Ungava) has a population of 157,021. The white people, of English and Scottish ancestry, are called *Livyeres* ("live heres"). Almost all of them live in tiny villages perched on the bleak rocks of the south coast. Labrador City is the largest town. In the north are Eskimos (Inuits). A few Indians of the Montagnais and Naskapi tribes live in the interior forests.

Labrador was visited by the Norse as early as 986 and by Leif Ericson in the year 1000. John Cabot rediscovered the peninsula in 1498. The people of Labrador lived in great poverty until an English doctor, Wilfred Grenfell, arrived in 1892 to help them. The International Grenfell Association, founded to carry on this work, maintains schools, hospitals, nursing stations, and industrial centers in Labrador.

Except for fishing villages on the coast, the peninsula was unbroken wilderness until 1941. Then Goose Bay, an air base, was built at the head of Hamilton Inlet. This airport is on the great circle air route between North America and Western Europe. Goose Bay is an important military and commercial base. (*See also* Canada.)

LA BRUYÈRE, Jean de (1645–96). One of the masterpieces of French literature, the satirical and somewhat bitter 'Les Caractères ou les moeurs de ce siècle' (Characters, or the Manners of This Age), was written by Jean de la Bruyère. In the book of portrait sketches, the author attempts to define the various characteristics of human nature and then gives examples in descriptions of real people—without giving any names. Implicit in the book is the notion that there is a standard of human behavior for all places and times; divergences from the standard, though common, are to be considered reprehensible.

La Bruyère was born in Paris in August 1645. After studying law in Orléans, he obtained a position as a tutor to the grandson of the Prince de Condé, one of France's greatest generals. He remained in the Condé household for most of his adult life. It was there he was able to observe the lives of the nobility, witness the power of money, and discover the tyranny of social custom among the aristocratic and idle rich, who pursued the fads and fashions of the day.

La Bruyère's work first appeared in 1688 as an addition to his translation of Theophrastus, a 4th-century BC Greek philosopher who had also written a volume of character sketches. The great and immediate popularity of the book led La Bruyère to expand it from its original 344 sketches to 420 in later editions. He died at Versailles in May 1696.

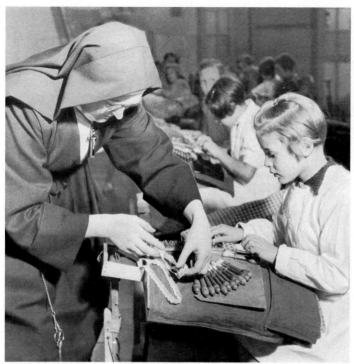
In the Belgian town of Bruges lacemaking by hand is still an important occupation. The community's girls are taught the art from an early age.

LACE

LACE. The most delicate of textile fabrics is lace. Wealthy women once wore dresses made entirely of lace. Now, however, it is used mostly as decoration.

Until the end of the 18th century lacemaking was an art, produced by hand. Today the fabric generally is made of cotton thread by machine. The modern lacemaking machine weighs about 17 tons and covers about 10 by 50 feet of floor space.

On one of these huge machines shining little flattened bobbins swing through threads which spin from reels. The bobbins dart swiftly over one thread and under the next. Sometimes they stop and vibrate rapidly a fraction of a second before they go on. This vibration twists the threads. Patterns are made by these twisted threads. Machine-made lace in many cases is so delicate that only an expert can tell it is not handmade. In one day a machine can produce a piece of lace which would have required six months' work by a skillful hand worker.

The Development of Lace Machines

The first machine-made lace was produced on a stocking machine. This turned out a lacy material which was really a knitted fabric. By about 1780 net machines were at work in France and England. Net produced by these devices was used as a background on which lace designs were worked by hand. In 1802 Robert Brown invented an excellent machine that produced nets of all sizes.

John Heathcoat in 1809 patented a bobbin net device, so-called because the threads were wound on bobbins. This was the forerunner of the lace machine that we know today. Joseph M. Jacquard meanwhile had perfected a pattern-weaving device in 1801. In 1813 John Leavers used the principles of the Heathcoat machine and of the Jacquard machine to invent a device which would produce a fancy pattern at the same time that the background of net was being made. Although laws forbade the export of lace machines, the Leavers models were taken apart and smuggled into France.

By 1837 French lacemakers had achieved the final goal. Using a punched-card system incorporated into the machine they reproduced the fine designs that had been possible only by handwork.

Machine-Made Lace

Washing, bleaching, dyeing, and finishing are now done by machine. Loose threads are clipped by machine, and scallops are also machine-cut.

The United States lace industry began early in the 20th century. It had a slow start. England forbade the export of lace machines to protect its industry. Many, however, were brought to the United States in parts. They were assembled by workers who had also been imported from England.

In 1909 England lifted the ban on lace-machine exports, and the United States Congress permitted them to be imported duty free for a period of 17 months. Many of the machines were brought into the country during this time. The American lace industry was then well under way.

For a time the industry grew steadily despite the fact that a three-year apprenticeship was required to learn the trade. In recent years, however, the demand for lace has declined sharply. The industry has suffered as a consequence. The main centers of machine-made laces today are Nottingham, England; Calais and Caudry, France; and several areas of the United States.

How Lace Is Made by Hand

Handmade lace is still produced all over the world. The manufacture of it in quantities is confined to China, France, Belgium, Ireland, Italy, England, and the Philippines. The infinite care and the great amount of time required to produce handmade lace will always make it expensive. There are many

On this huge lace-curtain loom many pieces of fabric can be made at one time. Cotton is most often used in machine-made lace. Silk, rayon, nylon, and wool threads are also used.

different grades of these laces. They vary in value according to the fineness and the design of the fabric and the time needed to make each piece.

There are two types of handmade lace—(1) needle point, or point, and (2) bobbin, or pillow. Needle point is made with a needle and a single thread. The pattern is drawn on parchment and then stitched to a piece of heavy linen in order to hold it straight. Threads are laid on the many lines of the pattern and are lightly fastened through to the linen. The entire figure is then worked. When it is completed the stitches holding it to the linen are cut, and the lace comes free.

In making bobbin lace the design is drawn on stiff parchment which is carefully stretched over a *pillow.* This is a round or oval board which is stuffed to form a cushion. The lacemaker places the pillow on her knees. The pattern is picked out along the outline of the drawing, and small pins are stuck in at close intervals. Around these pins threads wound on bobbins of varying size are twisted and crossed to form the various meshes and openings. The pattern, called a *gimp,* is formed by interweaving a much thicker thread. Needle point is the heavier of the two types of lace. Pillow lace is very supple and is prized for the way it can be draped.

History of Handmade Lace

The ancient Persians, Greeks, Chinese, and Egyptians made a kind of lace, but little is known about its appearance. The arts of drawn thread work and netting practiced by the ancient Egyptians were completely lost for centuries. They were rediscovered in the 15th century in Italy.

The earliest specimens of Italian lace were produced in convents. Nuns had the time, patience, and skill to produce these works of art. As a decoration lace has long been important to religion. Priceless altar cloths and vestments made of the delicate fabric are still stored in cathedrals. At the height of the Venetian lace industry, in the 16th century, the doge (chief magistrate) required that material be submitted to him before it was put on sale so that he could choose the best for religious use.

Lacemaking became a pastime for gentlewomen and a means of livelihood for the workers. The art spread to France, Flanders, Belgium, England, and Ireland. Countries and regions competed to create new patterns which were jealously guarded. Ambassadors acted as spies. They were required to report on developments in the lace industry of the countries to which they were sent.

Lace in France

In 1533 Catherine de' Medici came to France from Italy to marry the future King Henry II. She introduced the art of lacemaking at the French court. In an inventory of her household goods were 381 squares of unmounted lace in one chest and 538 in another. She kept her waiting women constantly at work making lace to decorate her bedchamber.

The French royal court became the center of new designs. Venice remained the source for the heavier needle lace. French workers made lighter types of new grace and delicacy. These were worn as cravats and ruffles by men and were used for fans, handkerchief borders, and gowns for women.

Until the last quarter of the 17th century French lace was similar to the Italian. Jean Baptiste Colbert, the finance minister under extravagant Louis XIV, used lacemaking to increase France's prosperity and was responsible for creating a distinct French type of lace. He imported workers from Venice. These artisans and others whom they taught spread the art throughout the country. Schools and workshops were set up in many French towns.

Lace in England

During the reign of Elizabeth I close relations between the courts of France and England encouraged the use of lace in England. Elizabeth's high ruff of lace is familiar to everyone who has seen her portraits.

Both the art and the fine materials for lacemaking were limited in England. In 1662 such huge sums of money were going out of the country for the material that Parliament prohibited its importation. This posed a problem for merchants who had to fill large orders for the court of Charles II. They began smuggling the choicest Brussels lace into England and selling it as "English point." Today Brussels lace is still called *point d'Angleterre.*

Belgian Lace

Belgium, with Flanders, was a leading lace center in the 16th century. Even at the height of production, in the 18th century, Belgian lace was very expensive. An artisan working 12 hours a day could turn out only one third of an inch a week. As many as 1,200 bobbins were sometimes used on one pillow. Today schools in Belgium teach children the art of making the fabric from an early age.

American Lace

When French officers came to the American Colonies to help fight the Revolution, they brought with them the fashion of wearing lace. Nearly all that was used in the colonies was imported. The manufacture of handmade lace was never an industry in the United States. Soon after lace became popular with Americans, it could be made by machine.

Modern Handmade Lace

Belgium produces some of the finest modern handmade lace. The flax which grows there is an important factor in this Belgian industry. In the town of Bruges almost every woman makes lace. Special ordinances require that only the handmade article can be so labeled. *Point d'Angleterre* is still made in Belgium, as are handmade fabrics of Italian, French, and English origin.

France produces *point d'Alençon,* which is still the high luxury lace. It is very expensive. It is used for the finest lingerie. The art of making it is taught at a school in Alençon. In convents at Argentan is taught the making of a light lace which is less expensive. It is used for household decoration rather than for clothing. Lace is also produced at Bayeux, Le Puy, and Lyons.

Alençon is a fine French needle-point lace. It is made in small segments, joined with invisible seams. Each part is done by a different workman. It dates from the 1600's.

Brussels lace (left) is the finest of all. It is made on the pillow with fine thread. In bridelace (right) the ground is made entirely of bars without a net foundation.

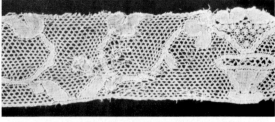

Valenciennes (left) is a durable pillow lace originally produced in France, now handmade in Belgium and machine-

made elsewhere. Antwerp (right) is a pillow lace. It is recognized by the vase of flowers which always appears in it.

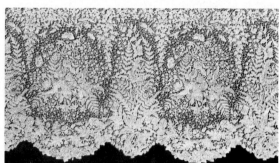

Cluny (left) is a coarse, strong lace with a leaf motif. It is principally used for interior decoration. Honiton (right) is

an English pillow variety still made in the county of Devonshire. A lacemaking school is conducted there.

In Italy the island of Burano, near Venice, is the center of lacemaking. When girls there are eight years old they go every afternoon to the Royal School of Lace to learn their art. Each girl specializes in some aspect of manufacture. The finished products of Burano are the work of many co-operating hands. Burano lace is used for larger articles such as tablecloths, curtains, and bridal gowns.

Types of Handmade Lace

There are many types of lace. With a few exceptions each bears the name of the town from which it originally came, and each one is different from all others. These are some of the most famous.

Alençon is a fine needle-point lace of linen thread. Its manufacture was established by Colbert, who brought Venetian lacemakers to his château near Alençon. They could not teach the French to make true Venetian stitches, so they invented a new kind of lace.

It is made with a fine needle on a parchment pattern. Small sections are joined together with invisible seams. About a dozen steps are required to complete this lace. It is now made in France and Italy. Patterns in the handmade variety are heavier than in the machine-made type.

Argentan is a needle-point lace which originated in Argentan, France. It is similar to Alençon, and like Alençon it was originally called *point de France*. Designs are still made in Argentan. They are larger and bolder than Alençon and less expensive. It is reproduced by machine.

Arras is a strong, firm, very white lace made in France. It has little variety in its patterns. Workers

have acquired great skill and speed in the production of Arras lace.

Binche is of the Brussels bobbin type. Floral or bowknot designs and sprigs made with bobbins are appliquéd to net. The earlier, finer type of this lace was popular in Paris in the middle of the 18th century. It is similar to Valenciennes in texture and pattern.

Brussels is the finest and filmiest of all lace. It is made on the pillow of an amazingly fine thread. Before the cost became prohibitive, this thread was hand-spun underground. Because of its fineness contact with the air made it break. Brussels has less "relief" than Alençon; that is, the motifs are not raised from the background.

Carrickmacross is the oldest Irish type. Lacemaking is still done near Carrickmacross, where the industry was established about 1820. A pattern is cut from fine cambric and applied to net with point stitches. The rose and the shamrock are the most popular patterns.

Chantilly is a bobbin lace made of silk. Its patterns usually consist of vases, baskets of flowers, and elaborate combinations of flowers, sprays, and leaves. Modern Chantilly is often even more beautiful than old laces. No handmade fabric is now produced in Chantilly, France. Machinery has taken over the making of this material.

Chinese lace was introduced to China by the Syrians. The technique is the same as that of the Venetian type, but the thread and the designs are inferior. When good thread and well-drawn patterns are used, the Chinese Venise lace is excellent.

Cluny is a coarse, strong fabric still made by hand

in France, Belgium, and China. Its name was taken from the Cluny Museum in Paris. It is also made by machine. Heavy linen thread is used, and the design is so open that the product is light and pleasing.

Duchesse is also called *point de Flandre*. It is widely regarded as the most beautiful of the pillow laces. It is pure white and has a graceful, rhythmic pattern. The designs consist of leaves, flowers, and scrolls. Bridal veils of the Flemish Duchesse lace are often heirloom treasures.

Honiton is a form of *point d'Angleterre*. It was the favorite of Queen Victoria, whose coronation gown was made of Honiton. It is a pillow lace, first produced about 1568 in Honiton, England. The pattern parts are worked on a pillow and then fastened to a net ground that is made separately.

Lille has a simple design. It was originally made at Lille, France. The plain net ground often has a heavy sprinkling of dots. The formal patterns are outlined with thick, flat thread.

Limerick was originally made in Ireland about 100 years ago. There are two types—tambour and run. Run is finer and lighter.

Macramé is a heavy fabric of the Venice type that was used in Spain and Italy during the 15th, 16th, and 17th centuries to decorate church vestments. It is one of the oldest laces and is still made in convents of the Riviera.

Maltese is a heavy, attractive pillow lace. The pattern is of geometrical forms, often a Maltese cross, joined by a purled background. It was originally made on the island of Malta. Now it is produced in England, France, and Ireland.

Mechlin is a valuable lace that looks like Lille. It is very fine, but added strength is given by extra stitches at every mesh of the grounding. It is made in one piece on the pillow. All Flanders laces up to 1665 were called Mechlin except Brussels.

Spanish includes many varieties of lace, the most famous called *point d'Espagne*. It is usually gold or silver, sometimes embroidered with colored silk.

Torchon is a coarse pillow lace made of a soft, loosely twisted thread. The patterns are simple, and this lace is used to trim muslin and heavy linen garments. It is manufactured in many places in Europe, especially in Saxony, where it is made by men.

Tulle is a silk net that is very fine. During the 17th and 18th centuries a type of pillow lace used for women's sleeves was made at Tulle and Aurillac, in France, and also in Germany.

Valenciennes is one of the best-known varieties. It is a durable pillow lace in which the pattern and ground are worked together. Great skill is required to do this. First made in Valenciennes, France, in the 18th century, many fine types of this lace are now made by machine.

Threads used in lacemaking may include nylon or wool as well as linen, cotton, and silk. Other types of lacemaking are crocheting, made with a hooked needle, and tatting, made by looping and knotting a single cotton thread.

LACHAISE, Gaston (1882–1935). Now generally considered the finest American sculptor of his day, Gaston Lachaise suffered negative criticism of his early creations. His thorough training in the techniques of the decorative arts, however, made it possible for him to earn a living as a craftsman during this beginning period.

Lachaise was born in Paris on March 19, 1882, the son of a cabinetmaker. At the age of 13 he entered a craft school and in 1898 the École des Beaux-Arts, but he found the current fashions in French art of no interest. For a time he designed art nouveau glass objects. The American woman who became his wife and his lifelong model and inspiration persuaded Lachaise to emigrate to Boston in 1906. He moved to New York City in 1912 and established his own studio, becoming an American citizen in 1917.

During the 1920s he did decorative garden sculptures and portrait sculptures of such people as John Marin, Marianne Moore, and e. e. cummings. From 1919 to 1925 *Dial* magazine often used pictures of his work, including the relief (a type of sculpture in which the forms rise from a flat supporting surface) 'Dusk' as its frontispiece. Lachaise became best known for his sculptures of female nudes, and by far the most famous is 'Standing Woman', cast in 1927. It typifies much of Lachaise's work in the 1920s—full matronly figures that are explicitly sensuous. In the 1930s Lachaise's nudes became more stylized and geometric. He died on Oct. 18, 1935, in New York City.

LACQUER *see* PAINT.

LACROSSE. The oldest organized sport played in North America is lacrosse. French and English colo-

English school children battle for the lacrosse ball in the National Schools Lacrosse Championships. Lacrosse, a native North American sport, has been exported across the Atlantic.

Times Newspapers Ltd., London

nists found the Indians playing a fast, rough contest called "baggataway." White men in Canada adopted the game about 1840. They revised the rules and called it *lacrosse* because the curved end of the playing stick resembled a bishop's staff, or *crosier*. In 1867 an act of Parliament made lacrosse the national game of Canada.

From Canada the game soon spread to the United States, particularly along the Atlantic seaboard. Today it is a popular summer sport of Eastern schools and athletic clubs.

Lacrosse is played with a rubber sponge ball $7\frac{3}{4}$ to 8 inches around and 5 to $5\frac{3}{4}$ ounces in weight. Each player carries a *crosse*, a 6-foot hickory stick shaped like a long-handled tennis racket. At the end of the crosse a 12-inch crook is bent at right angles to the main shaft. Within this crook a net of cord and rawhide lacings provides a pocket to catch and carry the ball.

Scoring a Goal

At each end of the playing field is a goal, 6 feet wide and 6 feet high. The goal posts support a pyramid-shaped cord netting which slopes back to the ground 7 feet from the mouth of the goal. Each team tries to advance the ball to a position where it can be thrown into the opponent's goal net. One point is scored for each goal.

There are 10 men on a team—the *goalkeeper* defends his team's goal. The *point* is the first defense man in front of the goal crease. The *cover point* plays ahead of the point. The *first defense* and the *second defense* protect their goal. The *center* represents his team on the *facing line* at the beginning of each quarter. The *first attack* and *second attack* carry the play into the opponent's territory. The *out home* and *in home* provide much of the scoring punch.

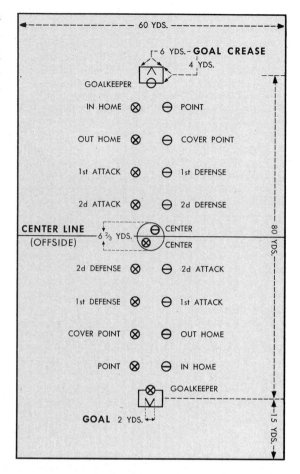

This diagram shows the layout of a lacrosse field. It also gives the general positions taken by the players at the start of a game. Each quarter starts with a face-off.

Play is started by facing the ball in a ten-foot circle. The referee places the ball between the reverse surfaces of two crosses. Only the two players (centers) who are facing the ball are allowed into the circle until the ball has cleared it.

Each player wears a padded helmet and a wire face mask to protect himself against an accidental blow from a crosse. Other equipment includes thick gloves, hip pads and shoulder pads worn under the uniform, and canvas shoes with cleats to assure the player of a firm grip on the ground.

Each quarter of play starts with a *face-off* in the center of the field. The referee places the ball between the two rival centers. At a signal from the official each of the centers tries to get the ball by scooping it up with his crosse.

The team with the ball then works it toward the opponent's goal. It may be passed from one man to another or carried on the crosse. Opponents may knock the ball out of a player's crosse or *check* a rival by running in front of him.

A goalkeeper may bat the ball away with his hand, but other players are not permitted to touch the ball or another player with the hand. A player who violates the rule may be suspended from the game for one to three minutes, or his opponents may be given the ball to put in play (*free throw*).

During play each team must have at least four men in their own half of the field and no less than three men across the center line in their opponent's territory. A lacrosse game is divided into four quarters of 15 minutes each.

Women's Rules

Since about 1910, in England, lacrosse has been played by women. Women's teams consist of 12 players, and a game is made up of two 25-minute periods. The face-off is called a *draw*. The goals are set from 90 to 110 yards apart.

LADOGA, LAKE. Some 70 rivers pour their icy waters into Lake Ladoga, Europe's largest fresh-water lake. The lake lies in the northern Soviet Union near the Finnish border. It has an area of 6,800 square miles (17,700 square kilometers). Its greatest depth is 754 feet (230 meters).

Ladoga is ice-free only about six months of the year. Severe storms and rocks and shoals make navigation dangerous. Canals have been built along the southern shore through which pass vessels carrying timber, iron, granite, and other products from Leningrad by way of the Neva River.

Through the broad Neva the lake's surplus waters flow into the Gulf of Finland. A system of waterways, including the Svir' River and Lake Onega, connects Ladoga with the White Sea to the north.

LADYBUG *see* INSECT.

LAËNNEC, René (1781–1826). Considered the father of chest medicine, René Théophile Hyacinthe Laënnec was a French physician who invented the stethoscope. Using his stethoscope—a foot-long, trumpet-shaped wooden cylinder that he placed on the chests of his patients—he was able to hear the various sounds made by the lungs and heart. Listening to sounds of organs, or auscultation, helps provide accurate diagnosis of disease.

Laënnec was born on Feb. 17, 1781, in Quimper, France. He was introduced to medicine by his physician uncle in Nantes. He continued his medical education in Paris, winning in 1803 the prize for surgery and sharing the prize for medicine awarded by the Grandes Écoles. Laënnec practiced at the Hôpital Necker from 1806 and became chief physician there in 1816. While associated with that hospital, Laënnec invented the stethoscope in 1819.

In 1819 Laënnec wrote 'Traité de l'auscultation médiate' (Tract on Indirect Auscultation), in which he described his methods and findings; it has become a classic in the field. Laënnec also made numerous other contributions to the literature of respiratory and heart disease. He was appointed to the chair of medicine and a lectureship at the Collège de France in 1822. After that honors came rapidly, including being made chevalier of the Legion of Honor. Laënnec died on Aug. 13, 1826, in Kerlouanec.

LAFAYETTE (1757–1834). Among the heroes of the American Revolution only the name of Washington ranks above that of Lafayette. He was a gallant Frenchman who generously placed his life and his fortune at the disposal of the American colonists.

By birth Marie-Joseph-Paul-Yves-Roch-Gilbert du Motier belonged to one of the old noble families of France. His father was killed in the battle of Minden, in 1759. The young man inherited from his father a castle and the title of marquis and from his mother a princely fortune. When he was 16 years old he married into one of the greatest families in France.

Three years later, when Lafayette was 19 and a captain in the French army, came the news that the American colonies had declared their independence of England, France's ancient foe. "At the first news of this quarrel," Lafayette afterward wrote, "my heart was enrolled in it." So he disobeyed the commands of his king and his angry father-in-law, purchased a ship, and after many difficulties sailed for America in 1777. He offered to serve without pay, and Congress gave him the rank of major general. Washington soon became a firm friend—almost a father—to the young Marquis de Lafayette.

Lafayette proved a good officer and a wise adviser. He was slightly wounded in his first battle, that of the Brandywine River, in September 1777. The next year he was commended for a masterly retreat from Barren Hill and played an honorable part in the battle of Monmouth Court House and in the Rhode Island expedition.

More important, however, was his influence in inducing the French government to sign a treaty of alliance with the colonies, in 1778. Without this treaty America could not have won the war. To aid this alliance he was back in France in 1779, but he returned to America in time to assist in the Virginia campaign and in the final movements that led to Cornwallis' surrender at Yorktown, in 1781.

Lafayette's love for liberty led him to join those French noblemen who favored the Revolution of 1789 in his own country. He was elected to the Estates-General and in that body presented a draft for a Declaration of Rights modeled on the American Declaration of Independence. On the day after the storming of the Bastille on July 14, 1789, he was made commander in chief of the new national guard, organized to safeguard the Revolution.

Lafayette rescued Queen Marie Antoinette from the mob that stormed the Palace of Versailles on Oct. 5, 1789, and issued orders to stop King Louis XVI when he sought to escape from France. Gradually Lafayette became dismayed at the growing excesses of the Revolution. As the head of an army raised to defend France against Austria, he planned to overthrow the Jacobins and to support a limited monarchy. The monarchy was overthrown on Aug. 10, 1792, and he was proclaimed a traitor. To escape arrest and the guillotine he fled to Belgium, where he was imprisoned by the Austrians. For five years, from 1792 to 1797, he remained in captivity. Then Napoleon obtained his release.

Lafayette disapproved of the rule of Napoleon and took no part in public affairs until after Napoleon's overthrow. Under the restored Bourbon monarchy, Lafayette generally was politically inactive until the people were again oppressed. Then he led the opposition, and in 1830 he took part in his third revolution. He commanded the Army of National Guards that drove Charles X from France and placed on the throne Louis Philippe, the "citizen king."

Twice after the close of the American Revolution Lafayette visited the United States—in 1784 and 1824. On the latter visit, Congress voted him $200,000 and a township of land. This was a welcome gift, for his own property had been taken during the French Revolution.

Lafayette's death, in Paris, saddened both the French and the American people. He was not a great general or a great statesman. He was, however, a lifelong lover of liberty who played a vital part in three important revolutions.

LAFITTE, Jean (1780?–1826?). The pirate Jean Lafitte was also a patriot. Little is known about his early life. No one knows who his parents were. A dozen French cities claim to be his birthplace. His exact birth date is also unknown.

Jean Lafitte appeared in New Orleans about 1806. He opened a blacksmith shop as a cover for his smuggling business. He sold goods captured by pirates from ships sailing the Caribbean Sea.

For two years Lafitte prospered. He was handsome, educated, and pleasant. When the United States outlawed the importing of slaves, in 1808, Lafitte began smuggling them in as a new source of profit. Lafitte became the leader of smugglers who had a base on Grand Terre Island, about 50 miles (80 kilometers) south of New Orleans. From here he controlled imports into New Orleans. He insisted that

The Bettmann Archive

Jean Lafitte

his captains operate as privateers, legally commissioned to capture ships and cargoes of enemy nations. At that time this meant British and French ships.

Because other business suffered from Lafitte's activities, he and his men were indicted as pirates. In 1814 his base on Grand Terre was destroyed by a United States Navy force. Lafitte escaped.

At this time an English captain offered Lafitte $30,000 and a commission to help the British attack New Orleans. Instead, Lafitte told Governor Claiborne of the planned attack and offered his help. During the battle Lafitte fought well. Later President James Madison pardoned him and his men for their acts of piracy.

Lafitte's successful days were over. Many of his men deserted him as he sailed for three years looking for a new base. In 1817 he settled on the island that is now Galveston, Tex. In 1821 Lieutenant Lawrence Kearney of the United States Navy ordered Galveston evacuated. After that, Lafitte located his base of operations on Mujeres Island off Yucatán, Mexico, but his forces were small. He died about 1826 at Teljas, on the Yucatán mainland.

LA FOLLETTE, Robert M. (1855–1925). A name that will forever be associated with the Progressive Era in American politics is that of Robert M. La Follette of Wisconsin. For the first 25 years of the 20th century, as governor and a Republican United States senator, he dominated the politics of his state and promoted ideas and policies that endure today.

La Follette was born in Primrose, Wis., on June 14, 1855. He graduated from the University of Wisconsin in 1879 and was admitted to the bar in 1880. His career in politics began as district attorney in the early 1880s. He served in the United States House of Representatives from 1885 until 1891. He was elected governor in 1900 and reelected in 1902 and 1904. In 1906 he resigned the governorship and was elected to the Senate. There, to combat conservatism, he organized the National Progressive League in 1911. The League became the Progressive party the next year. He remained in the Senate until his death in Washington, D.C., on June 18, 1925.

La Follette was one of the most eloquent voices of his day in speaking out in favor of popular democracy and in opposition to government by special interests. As governor, he developed the "Wisconsin Idea," the use of university professors to draft reform legislation and administer policy. He also succeeded in establishing direct primary elections, a state civil service, and regulation of the railroads.

His greatest national prominence came when he spoke out forcefully in opposition to the United States entry into World War I, believing it to be a war to protect overseas business investments. In 1924 he ran for the presidency on the Progressive party ticket but lost to Calvin Coolidge.

LA FONTAINE, Jean de (1621–95). One of the world's favorite storytellers was Jean de La Fontaine. He wrote the beloved 'Fables'. French children have for years learned these verse stories. They have been translated into many languages. Adults never tire of the wisdom in these tales. (*See also* Fable.)

Jean de La Fontaine was born at Château-Thierry, in the French province of Champagne. His father was a government official in charge of forests. Young Jean attended school at Reims. In 1641 he went to the Oratory of Saint Magloire in Paris, intending to become a priest. He never took his studies seriously, however, and soon returned home.

In 1647 La Fontaine took over his father's job. He was married in that same year. Before long, he gave up his job, separated from his wife, and went to live in Paris, where he spent his most productive years.

La Fontaine was a genius at making and keeping friends. Rich patrons took a liking to his wit, and they were happy to support him. A relative introduced the young man to Nicolas Fouquet, finance minister to Louis XIV. The minister gave La Fontaine a pension in return for four poems a year.

From 1672 to 1693 La Fontaine lived at the home of Madame de La Sablière, a wise and studious woman. In 1683 he was elected to the French Academy. In about 1685 he met Monsieur d'Hervart, his last patron. With him he spent the last two years of his life.

The first six books of 'Fables' appeared in 1668. They were followed by two more in 1678 and 1694. Today only scholars read his other books, but the 'Fables' are read everywhere.

The 'Fables' are both realistic and fantastic. In one story, a fool thinks it is wrong for big pumpkins to grow on small vines and little acorns on great oaks. He changes his mind when a falling acorn awakens him from a nap under an oak tree.

LAGERKVIST, Pär (1891–1974). The most internationally known Swedish writer in the first half of the 20th century was Pär Lagerkvist. He was born in Växjö, Sweden, on May 23, 1891. He attended the University of Uppsala, and lived for a time in Paris, where he became acquainted with avant-garde ideas on literature, politics, and art.

His first works, 'Ångest' (Anguish, published in 1916), and 'Kaos' (Chaos, 1919) were filled with pessimism that owed much to the tragedy of World War I. There was less pessimism in his writing of the 1920s: 'Det eviga leendet' (The Eternal Smile, 1920), 'Den lyckliges väg' (The Happy Man's Way, 1921), and 'Gäst hos verkligheten' (The Guest of Reality, 1925), an autobiographical novel. During the next two decades he became preoccupied with the rise of fascist movements in Europe. His novels from this period, 'Bödeln' (The Hangman, 1933), 'Dvärgen' (The Dwarf, 1944), and his most famous work, 'Barabbas' (1950), focused on evil and the abuse of power. His contempt for fascism was also evident in the play 'Mannen utan själ' (The Man Without a Soul, performed in 1936). In the same vein he wrote his most unusual play, 'Låt människan leva' (Let Man Live, 1949), about man's willingness to judge and destroy his fellows. Lagerkvist was awarded the Nobel prize for literature in 1951. He died on July 11, 1974.

LAGERLÖF, Selma (1858–1940). In 1909 Swedish novelist Selma Lagerlöf became the first woman to win the Nobel prize for literature. Her books are skillful portrayals of Swedish life, using as their subject matter folklore, magic, her family, and the countryside in which she grew up.

Selma Lagerlöf was born on Nov. 20, 1858, in Mårbacka, Sweden. At 22 she went to Stockholm to study at Sjoberg's Lyceum for a teaching career. After a year there she finished her education at the Royal Women's Superior Training College. Beginning in 1885 she taught at Landskrona in southern Sweden. Her first published work, 'Gösta Berlings saga' (Gösta Berling's Saga, published in 1891), is probably her best novel. Her next books are: 'Osynliga lankär' (Invisible Links, 1894); 'Antikrists mirakler' (The Miracles of Antichrist, 1897), a socialist novel set in Sicily; and 'Jerusalem' (1901–02). She had given up teaching in 1895 to travel and write.

Deeply disturbed by the crisis of World War I, Lagerlöf wrote very little during the conflict. But in the next two decades she published several works: 'Mårbacka' (1922), 'Ett barns memoarer' (Memories of My Childhood, 1930), and a trilogy, 'Löwensköldska ringen' (The Ring of the Löwenskölds, 1925). In 'Dagbok för Selma Lagerlöf (The Diary of Selma Lagerlöf, 1932) she recreated her childhood.

Lagerlöf was an ardent feminist and pacifist. She attended the Women's Congress at Washington, D.C., as a delegate in 1924. In the late 1930s she assisted refugees from Nazi Germany. She died at her family home in Mårbacka in the province of Värmland on March 16, 1940.

LAGOS, Nigeria. The largest city of the West African country of Nigeria, Lagos is located at the southwestern end of Nigeria's Atlantic coastline. The city's area comprises Lagos Island, in Lagos Lagoon, on the Bight of Benin in the Gulf of Guinea. Lagos is the country's industrial and commercial center and its principal seaport and international airport. The city controls a large part of the national economy, and its rate of annual population growth is five times that of Nigeria as a whole.

The city of Lagos is the second largest (after Kinshasa) in tropical Africa. It is afflicted with industrial pollution, slums, and traffic congestion, but it is a thriving economic center with a cosmopolitan cultural life. Industry includes automobile and radio assembly, food and beverage processing, metalworks, and the production of paints and soaps. Textile, cosmetic, and pharmaceutical manufacture is also important. The fishing industry has trawlers, laboratory facilities, and a research library.

The Lagos landscape is dominated by a system of islands, sandbars, and lagoons. It consists of a strip of the mainland on the western shore of the lagoon, several islands and marshes, and the western end of a sandbar. The four main islands are connected to each other and to the mainland by bridges and a railway. Bus service operates throughout the city, and it is well served by taxis. There are also many private automobiles, motorcycles, and bicycles. Constant traffic jams on the mainland and on the connecting bridges cause major communication problems. The city is the hub of the nation's road network.

The core area of Lagos city is on the northwestern tip of Lagos Island; it is a slum with narrow streets, poor housing, overcrowding, and a lack of sanitation facilities. City services such as electricity, water, and telephones have not kept up to the growing population's demand. The main business district occupies the island's western shore. Suburban developments are north and west of Lagos Island. The smaller islands at the western entrance to Lagos Lagoon are swampy and only sparsely inhabited. Lagos has a tropical climate with scattered palm trees and green vegetation on the mainland.

The city was under the domination of Benin from the late 16th century to the mid-19th century. Lagos was ceded to the United Kingdom in 1861 and thrived as a trade and administrative center. In 1874 it became part of the Gold Coast Colony, and in 1886 it achieved separate status under a British governor. In 1906 it became part of southern Nigeria. In 1960 it became the capital of independent Nigeria. Until 1975 Lagos was both the federal and state capital. In 1976 Abuja was designated as the Federal Capital Territory in order to relieve Lagos' rapid expansion and to provide for a more central location. The official seat of the Lagos State government was transferred to Ikeja, a suburb of Lagos city. In the 1980s, however, Lagos remained the unofficial seat of many government agencies. (*See also* Nigeria.) Population (1982 estimate), 1,404,000.

LAGRANGE, Joseph-Louis (1736–1813). By the time he was a teenager, the mathematical genius of Lagrange was already apparent. In his lifetime he became one of the preeminent mathematicians of his age, one who excelled in all areas of the subject, especially analysis, number theory, and analytical and celestial mechanics. His major work, 'Analytical Mechanics', published in 1788, is a classic in the field.

Joseph-Louis Lagrange was born in Turin, Italy, on Jan. 25, 1736, the son of a wealthy French family that later lost its fortune in bad speculations. In his late teens he was already teaching mathematics at the artillery school in Turin. By age 26 he was recognized as one of the outstanding mathematicians of his time. From 1776 until 1787 he was, at the invitation of Frederick the Great of Prussia, a teacher in Berlin. Upon Frederick's death he returned to Paris. During the French Revolution he helped reform the metric system. In 1795 he became a professor at the École Polytechnique (Technical School) in Paris. His published lectures provided the first textbooks on real analytical functions. Lagrange died on April 10, 1813.

LA GUARDIA, Fiorello (1882–1947). One of the most beloved and colorful United States politicians in 20th-century, La Guardia served as a United States congressman and three times as mayor of New York City. Always allied to progressive forces in politics, he fought and won many a battle for the poor and disadvantaged of his city and country.

Fiorello Henry La Guardia was born in New York City on Dec. 11, 1882. He attended high school in Prescott, Ariz., and held several jobs in the United States and abroad before graduating from the New York University Law School in 1910. By offering free legal aid to immigrants in New York he established a loyal following that helped get him elected to Congress in 1917. In the armed services during World War I, he returned home to serve for a short time as president of the city's board of aldermen. He was reelected to Congress in 1922 and remained there, a liberal Republican, until 1934 when he became mayor of New York City.

In Congress he had become well-known for his advocacy of laws favoring organized labor. He also fought for child labor laws and women's rights. As mayor he instituted a wide-ranging program of reform and city improvement, including low-cost housing and slum clearance. He did much to beautify the city and improve the operations of its departments, all the while battling political corruption and organized crime. He saw to the building of public clinics, recreational facilities, and the airport that today bears his name. Called affectionately "The Little Flower" (the meaning of Fiorello), he became even more popular when, during a newspaper strike, he read the Sunday comics to children over the radio.

After leaving office La Guardia served briefly as director of the United Nations Relief and Rehabilitation Administration. He died on Sept. 20, 1947, in New York City.

LA GUMA, Alex (born 1925). His own experiences as a victim of South Africa's policy of apartheid (racial segregation) served novelist Alex La Guma as a basis for his realistic writing. He was born in 1925 in Cape Town, South Africa, to a family that was active in the black liberation movement. His own activism caused the government to imprison him or place him under house arrest several times. Yet he persisted in working with the Coloured People's Congress and in writing against the government.

His stories for the newspaper *New Age*, along with his novels, prompted the South African authorities to ban his writing and speaking on racial issues. As a result, he and his family moved to England so he could continue his career.

The novels written while he still lived in South Africa were all directed against apartheid. 'A Walk in the Night', published in 1962, describes the moral disintegration of a black man unjustly fired from his job and depicts the struggles against oppression of a group of Cape Town residents. 'And a Threefold Cord' (1964) is the story of a ghetto family's degradation under the policy of segregation. 'The Stone-Country' (1965) is based on La Guma's prison experiences. 'In the Fog of the Seasons' End' (1972) is a portrayal of the underground resistance movement in South Africa. 'Time of the Butcherbird' (1979) is a tale that tells of murder and revenge that is set in the African grasslands.

LAHORE, Pakistan. The second largest city of Pakistan after Karachi, Lahore is located in a fertile region of the upper Indus plain. The city sits on the banks of the Ravi, a tributary of the Indus, on gently sloping land about 700 feet (200 meters) above sea level. Six miles (ten kilometers) east are the Shalimar Gardens (Abode of Joy). Laid out in 1641 by Shah Jahan, these gardens are among the most magnificent in the world. The Mela Chiraghan (Festival of Lamps) is held there to herald the advent of spring.

Known also for its historical monuments and for the gardens of the four Mughal emperors, Lahore has notable growths of greenery in the form of roadside ornamental trees. The city has a subtropical continental type of climate, with hot summers and cool winters. From July to September the weather in Lahore is oppressively hot and humid.

Lahore is diverse in its street patterns, landscape, and architectural features. There is an old walled city with many 15th- and 16th-century buildings and narrow, winding streets; although congested, it continues to expand vertically. There are also modern marketing districts and fashionable residential areas. Circling the inner city is an extensive and strictly planned area, still to be developed, of residential localities, industrial sites, educational institutions, and agricultural land.

Railways link Lahore with the important urban centers of Pakistan. Air traffic is increasing. Production of textiles is the major industry. Lahore is also an educational center, with two universities and numerous colleges and schools.

The city of Lahore was the capital of the Punjab for more than 900 years. In 1955 it was selected as the capital of West Pakistan. After West Pakistan was divided into four provinces in 1970, Lahore became the capital of a new province of the Punjab. Population (1981), 2,922,000.

Animaldrawn carts and wagons crowd a bustling marketing street in old Lahore. Modern marketing and residential centers are found elsewhere in the centuries-old city.

Robert Frerck

LAKE. Technically, a lake is an inland body of water surrounded by land. It is larger than a pool or pond. The name, however, is sometimes given to the widened parts of rivers and to bodies of water that are in direct connection with the sea. Coastal lakes, for example, are often formed where waves and shore currents build sandbars across bays or wide river mouths. A large river may build an arm of its delta outward in such a way as to enclose an area of water. Lake Pontchartrain in Louisiana had this origin. All such coastal lakes are shallow.

More of the world's lakes have been formed by glacier action than in any other way. During the Ice Age in the Northern Hemisphere, great sheets of glacial ice crept slowly southward across northern North America, Europe, and Asia, carrying masses of dirt and debris gouged from the rocky surface below. The glaciers dug thousands of basins in the weaker areas of rock. Other basins were formed where glaciers left behind some of their debris, and it dammed up former river valleys. Today the thousands of lakes in central Canada, Minnesota, Michigan, and Wisconsin and similar glaciated regions lie mainly in these types of basins, called drift basins.

Certain large lakes are the result of both massive erosion and great amounts of deposition by former glaciers. The Finger Lakes of western New York lie in old river valleys gouged deeper by ice and dammed by glacial deposits. The Great Lakes of North America lie in ancient river valleys or lowlands that were gouged deeper by the glaciers, while their rims were built up by glacial deposits, which are called moraines. The Great Lakes cover about 95,000 square miles (245,000 square kilometers) and form a great inland waterway and the largest expanse of fresh water in the world. Lake Superior is the largest of all freshwater lakes in surface area. Only the Caspian Sea, a saltwater lake, is larger.

Another way that lakes have been formed is through volcanic action. In many parts of the world the craters of extinct volcanoes hold small lakes. Many examples of these are found in the Auvergne district in southern France, the Eifel region of northern Germany, and an area around Rome in Italy. Some volcanoes have blown off their tops in great explosions, or their centers have collapsed, leaving great pits, or calderas, that hold lakes. Mount Katmai in Alaska exploded violently in 1912, forming a great pit 2½ miles (4 kilometers) in diameter and more than 3,000 feet (900 meters) deep. A mile-wide lake of warm water has existed in the bottom ever since. Another lake of outstanding beauty formed in this way is Crater Lake in southern Oregon. It is 1,932 feet (589 meters) deep and of deep-blue color.

In the past, parts of the sea bottom have been uplifted to form land areas. Shallow, irregular basins on such surfaces are left as lakes. They become freshwater lakes as rain replenishes their original salt water with fresh water. Some of the lakes in southern Florida and in the cold plains of Siberia have been formed in this way.

Saltwater and Freshwater Lakes

Not all lakes contain fresh water. The Dead Sea is a very salty lake that lies in a sunken rift in Israel and Jordan. With a surface 1,316 feet (401 meters) below sea level, it is the lowest lake in the world. The highest navigable lake in the world is Lake Titicaca in the Andean plateau of Peru at 12,500 feet (3,810 meters) above sea level. Another body of salt water, the Great Salt Lake in Utah, is what remains today of a once much larger freshwater body named Lake Bonneville. The freshwater lake shrank as the climate became drier, and the lake began to evaporate. All the dissolved salts brought in by its tributary rivers were slowly concentrated in less and less water, so each year the water became saltier. This process is still going on. A novel feature of these saltwater lakes is the buoyancy they offer to swimmers: it is much easier to float on the Dead Sea or the Great Salt Lake than on a freshwater lake.

By far the greatest amount of the Earth's fresh water—probably more than four fifths—is tied up in glaciers, polar ice sheets, and groundwater. Of the available fresh water in lakes, about 30,000 cubic miles (125,000 cubic kilometers), four fifths, occurs in a small number of lakes, perhaps no more than 40. Lake Baikal in central Asia is the deepest continental body of water on Earth, with a maximum depth of 5,315 feet (1,620 meters), and it contains about one fifth of the fresh water on the Earth's surface (*see* Baikal). The next largest lakes are Lake Tanganyika in Africa and Lake Superior in North America. All the Great Lakes together contain about 5,500 cubic miles (22,900 cubic kilometers) of water, about the same as Lake Baikal alone. (*See also* Great Lakes; Tanganyika, Lake.)

Lakes as Limited Resources

Modern industrial societies make enormous demands on some freshwater lakes. Water is channeled from lakes to population centers for drinking and bathing. It is used in a variety of manufacturing processes, for power generation, as a coolant in nuclear power plants, for irrigation, and for recreation. From many of these uses has arisen the serious problem of water pollution, caused primarily by the return of unclean used water to its lake source, as well as by the dumping of a large variety of harmful chemicals and other waste matter into lakes.

Thermal pollution—the heating of lake waters—is considered to be one of the major hazards facing lakes in the future. A major source of heated water is the modern power plant, which uses water to cool its parts and, in the process, heats the water. The power requirements of modern societies increase at the rate of about 7 percent a year, and there is great concern about the thermal heating of even the larger lakes.

Chemical and thermal pollution, in large amounts, may eventually kill a lake by destroying all the plant and animal life in it. Those who study lakes—limnologists—deal with the physical, chemical, and biological properties of lakes. One of their most pressing recent tasks has been the assessment of damage being done by the enormous amount of pollutants being disgorged into lakes every day. (For table of world lakes, see Fact-Index.)

An engraving of Jean-Baptiste Lamarck by W. H. Lizars

Courtesy of the Museum National D'Histoire Naturelle, Paris

LAMARCK, Jean-Baptiste (1744–1829). The man who coined the word *biologie* (biology) and one of the pioneers in that field was a French scientist named Lamarck. He is remembered most for his theory of evolution, that proposed that the characteristics an organism develops during its lifetime in response to its environment are inherited by, or passed on to, its offspring. Charles Darwin's theories, published 30 years after Lamarck's death, disagreed with Lamarck's conclusions, which were later discarded by most scientists as invalid.

Jean-Baptiste de Monet Lamarck was born on Aug. 1, 1744, in Picardy. After his schooling he served in the French army from 1761 to 1768, during which time he became interested in botany and the classification of plants. In 1778 he published a three-volume work on the plants of France. After the start of the French Revolution in 1789, Lamarck promoted and became one of the originators of the Museum of Natural History, founded in Paris in 1793. He was placed in charge of the invertebrate animals at the museum, and from his work was able to revise the classification of lower animals that had been unfinished by the Swedish biologist Carolus Linnaeus (see Invertebrate; Linnaeus). His continued study of invertebrates led to the publication of his major work, 'Histoire naturelle des animaux sans vertèbres' (The Natural History of Invertebrate Animals, published in 1815–22). Although Lamarck's theories on evolution were discarded after Darwin, he succeeded in establishing procedures of inquiry for the study of invertebrates that were useful long after his death.

Lamarck was a generalist in science at a time when specialization was emerging. He sought for the unities that underlie the natural world. This led to his increasing isolation from other scientists. He died lonely and in poverty in Paris on Dec. 18, 1829.

LAMARTINE, Alphonse de (1790–1869). Honored today as the first of the French Romantic poets and a man of great literary ability, Lamartine was also a political activist who headed the provisional government in Paris for a few months after the Revolution of 1848. His life may be divided into three fairly distinct periods. Up to 1830 he devoted himself mostly to writing poetry. From 1830 to 1848, a time when socialism was emerging as a popular political and economic theory, he championed the cause of the working class. From 1848 on he again devoted himself to writing, largely in an effort to ward off bankruptcy and pay his debts.

Alphonse de Lamartine, the son of an aristocrat, was born at Mâcon in east central France on Oct. 21, 1790. Through the period of the French Revolution and Napoleon I, his life was fairly idle. After Napoleon's defeat at Waterloo in 1815, Lamartine devoted himself to poetry. He married in 1820, the same year his first collection of poetry, 'Poetic Meditations', was published. While continuing to write, he served for ten years, from 1820 to 1830, as secretary to the French embassy in Naples, Italy. Other works that were published in that decade were 'New Poetic Meditations', 'The Death of Socrates', and 'Poetic and Religious Harmonies'.

Social and political interests consumed much of his time, particularly from 1839 on. After the short-lived Second Republic (February to June 1848), he abandoned politics. Over the next 20 years he did a great deal of writing—poetry, novels, and histories. In his later years he was gradually forgotten by his contemporaries, and he died in relative obscurity in Paris on Feb. 28, 1869.

LAMB, Charles (1775–1834). An essayist, critic, and poet, Lamb was also a brave and tender man. Despite a life full of tragedy, his writings were often filled with humor.

Charles Lamb was born on Feb. 10, 1775, in the heart of London in the Inner Temple, a great rambling old building filled with lawyers' offices and living quarters. His father was a lawyer's clerk and quite poor. At the age of seven Charles was sent to school at Christ's Hospital. Here he met another poor boy who became his lifelong friend—the poet Samuel Taylor Coleridge. These days are delightfully described in Lamb's essay 'Christ's Hospital Five-and-Thirty Years Ago'. At 17 Lamb became a clerk in the accountant's office in the East India House. There he remained until he retired on a pension 33 years later to Edmonton, where he died on Dec. 27, 1834.

When he was 21 his sister Mary went insane, killed her mother, and was confined in an asylum. She recovered temporarily and was released upon her brother's promise that he would care for her the rest of her life.

Thenceforth Charles Lamb sacrificed everything for his sister. When her illness returned, he would take her by the hand and walk mournfully with her to the asylum. In her healthy intervals that he called "between the acts," there was much that was cheerful and beautiful in their lives. They became famous for their evenings at home with the brightest wits of London gathered for talk and laughter and good cheer. Mary Lamb shared in many of her brother's literary labors. They wrote together the 'Tales from Shakespear', a retelling of Shakespeare's plays that has given pleasure to many children.

Charles Lamb's fame today rests chiefly on the essays written under the name of Elia. In these essays he has taken the most trivial subjects and put into them his own whimsical, pathetic, quaintly humorous personality. His 'A Chapter on Ears', 'Imperfect Sympathies', 'The Praise of Chimney-Sweepers', 'Old China', and 'Complaint on the Decay of Beggars' are all fine works. Probably no essay in the English language has aroused more laughter than his 'Dissertation on Roast Pig', and none is more full of pathos than his beautiful 'Dream Children'.

In addition to the 'Essays of Elia', Lamb's most important prose works include the critical notes in his 'Specimens of English Dramatic Poets who lived About the Time of Shakespear', 'The Adventures of Ulysses', a tragedy entitled 'John Woodvil', and his romance 'A Tale of Rosamund Gray'. His best-known poem is 'The Old Familiar Faces'.

L'AMOUR, Louis (born 1908?). When more than 130 million copies of his books were in print, Louis L'Amour became one of the best-selling authors of all time. His tales of the American West have enthralled millions of people worldwide, and several of his stories have been made into movies. While most of his books have been published in paperback, his 1983 novel 'The Lonesome Gods' was issued in hardback and immediately found a place on the best-seller lists.

L'Amour was born Louis Dearborn LaMoore in Jamestown, N.D., about 1908. Even as a schoolchild he loved to hear and retell stories of the Old West. He read all the books he could find about the American frontier. As an adolescent he dropped out of school and became a roving laborer, riding freight trains from place to place. For a time he worked as a merchant seaman and traveled the world. He returned and settled in Oklahoma City, Okla., in the late 1930s and began writing, but his career was soon interrupted by service in World War II.

After the war he bagan contributing short stories to Western magazines and other journals. He wrote his first novel, 'Hopalong Cassidy and the Rustlers of West Fork', using the pen name "Tex Burns," in 1951. His first great success, however, was 'Hondo', which was later made into a film starring John Wayne. By the early 1980s he had published more than 80 novels and several hundred short stories. Sixteen of his novels make up a series on the Sackett's, a family living in frontier days. Other novels include 'Shalako', published in 1962, 'Catlow' (1963), and 'Comstock Lode' (1981).

LAMP *see* LIGHTING.

LAMPREY. Fishers everywhere dread the eellike lamprey. It destroys millions of valuable food and game fishes every year. The lamprey has no jaws. The mouth is a cuplike sucker disk lined with sharp projections, and the tongue also has sharp files. With these the lamprey rasps a hole in its victim's body so it can suck the blood and other body juices.

Lampreys are distributed throughout the world. They thrive in fresh water as well as in the sea. Before World War II sea lampreys invaded the Great Lakes through the Saint Lawrence River canals. Lake trout were their favorite prey. They virtually destroyed the trout fisheries of Lakes Michigan and Huron and threatened to deplete Lake Superior.

In August 1958 scientists announced they had discovered a poison which kills the eel but is harmless to other fishes and wildlife. It is used against the larvae, a young stage, of the lamprey.

Sea lamprey

Like the salmon, lampreys migrate upstream to spawn. Soon thereafter they die. The eggs hatch as larvae. The larvae drift downstream until they reach mud flats. There they bury themselves with only the head protruding. They feed on minute organisms that float near their mouths. The larval life lasts four years. Then the larva develops into a mature lamprey, emerges from the mud, and drifts down to the lake or sea, where it lives for about a year. It grows, on the average, one to three feet (0.3 to 0.9 meters) long. In late spring the lamprey reenters the streams to spawn and die.

Besides the naturalized sea lampreys, there are several relatively harmless native varieties. The lamprey is primitive, with a skeleton of gristle. The sea lamprey's scientific name is *Petromyzon marinus*.

LAND, Edwin H. (born 1909). The inventor of many optical devices, including the Polaroid Land camera, was Edwin H. Land. His research on how color is seen challenged long-accepted views.

Edwin Herbert Land was born in Bridgeport, Conn., on May 7, 1909. He attended Norwich Academy and Harvard University. While still at Harvard, Land experimented with polarized light (*see* Light). This led to his invention of a light polarizer that proved to be a superior new camera filter.

Land was a government adviser on guided missile technology in World War II and developed optical instruments that helped the war effort. In 1947 he introduced the first Polaroid camera, which delivers a black-and-white picture in seconds. In the 1950s Land began experimenting with three-dimensional color photography. Dissatisfied with current knowledge about how the eye sees color, he performed experiments that produced a new concept of color perception. He concluded that the retina of the eye does not select each specific wavelength of various colors, but rather color perception by the retina depends on a broad interplay of long and short wavelengths over the entire scene. In 1963 Land introduced Polacolor film, which makes a colorphoto in less than a minute. In 1972 came completely automatic, pocket-size cameras and films. He headed the Polaroid Corporation until 1982. (*See also* Color; Photography.)

LANDAU, Lev Davidovich (1908–68). The man most responsible for introducing and developing theoretical physics in the Soviet Union was Lev Davidovich Landau, one of the 20th century's most brilliant scientists. For his research on the remarkable behavior of liquid gases, particularly helium, he was awarded the Nobel prize for physics in 1962.

Landau was born on Jan. 22, 1908, at Baku in Azerbaijan. A brilliant student, he attended the Baku Economical Technical School. In 1927 he graduated from Leningrad State University, at that time the center for Soviet physics. In 1929 he went to Copenhagen to study under the famed physicist Niels Bohr (*see* Bohr) at the Institute for Theoretical Physics, a place where most of the leading physicists of the period spent some time working.

From 1932 to 1937 Landau was director of the Theoretical Division of the Ukrainian Physico-Technical Institute at Kharkov. He turned it into the leading center for the study of physics in the Soviet Union. While there he began his work as coauthor of the nine- volume 'Course of Theoretical Physics'. In 1937 he moved to Moscow to become head of the Theory Division of the S. I. Vavilov Institute of Physical Problems. It was there that he developed his theory on liquid helium, a fluid that has less resistance to moving through a tube than any other liquid.

He worked without interruption, except for a brief imprisonment in 1938 during the Stalin purges, until an auto accident in January 1962 left him unconscious for several weeks. He never recovered his former capabilities, and he died on April 1, 1968.

LANDOWSKA, Wanda (1879–1959). Responsible for the 20th-century revival of the harpsichord, a keyboard instrument with one or more sets of strings that are plucked, Wanda Landowska was one of its greatest players. She also promoted a renewed interest in the performance of early keyboard music.

Wanda Louise Landowska was born in Warsaw, Poland, on July 5, 1879. Her father was a lawyer and amateur musician. She graduated from the Warsaw Conservatory when she was 14, studied composition in Berlin in 1896, and in 1900 moved to Paris. There she married the folklorist Henry Lew, who encouraged her to research old keyboard music.

Landowska commissioned the French piano firm Pleyel to build a modern harpsichord, and she played it in public for the first time in 1903. She taught at the Schola Cantorum and in 1925 founded the École de Musique Ancienne (School of Ancient Music) near Paris. The first modern works composed for harpsichord were commissioned by her—a concerto by Manuel de Falla in 1926 and 'Concert champêtre' by Francis Poulenc in 1929.

When the Germans invaded France in 1940, Landowska escaped to Switzerland and later made her home in Lakeville, Conn. She taught extensively and gave concerts in the United States. In addition she made a number of recordings, including Bach's 'Goldberg Variations' and 'The Well-Tempered Clavier' and Haydn's 'Concerto in D'. She died in Lakeville on Aug. 16, 1959.

LANDSTEINER, Karl (1868–1943). The Austrian immunologist and pathologist who discovered the major blood groups was Karl Landsteiner. Based upon these groups, he developed the ABO system of blood typing that has made blood transfusion a routine medical practice.

Landsteiner was born in Vienna on June 14, 1868. He studied medicine at the University of Vienna, graduating in 1891. For the next five years he studied chemistry at several European universities. As a research assistant at the Vienna Pathological Institute, Landsteiner found in 1900 basic differences in human blood that explained the danger encountered in transfusing blood from one person to another. A year later he showed that there are at least three major types of human blood. The types vary according to the kinds of antigens—types of molecules—attached to the plasma membrane, or outer envelope, of red blood cells. He labeled the types A, B, and O and a year later found a fourth type, AB, containing both antigens A and B. Landsteiner's classification system made blood transfusions safe because it became possible to classify blood by type and to transfuse a type compatible with a patient's own. Landsteiner received the 1930 Nobel prize for physiology or medicine for his discovery of the major blood groups and the development of the ABO typing system.

Landsteiner was professor of pathology at the University of Vienna from 1909 to 1919. At the Rockefeller Institute for Medical Research in New York City from 1922, he discovered the Rhesus (Rh) blood factor. It is the basis of a series of events that can occur in the blood of a pregnant woman and her unborn child and result in a disease causing a miscarriage or a dangerous illness in the newborn.

Landsteiner's book 'The Specificity of Serological Reactions', published in 1936, is a classic text that helped to establish the science of immunochemistry. Landsteiner died in New York City on June 26, 1943.

LAND USE

LAND USE. The surface of the Earth—apart from oceans, seas, lakes, and rivers—is land. Much of it might appear to be unused: mountain ranges, the great deserts, swamps, and vast tracts of forest and jungle. But even for many of these areas a kind of use has been found, normally as a tourist attraction. Ski resorts are located in the mountains. Parts of forests have been protected and set aside as national parks and nature areas, such as Yosemite National Park in California, the Black Forest in West Germany, and El Yunque rain forest in Puerto Rico. But such use does not involve anything being done with the land itself. The term land use usually refers to land that is owned and has something done on it, in it, or with it.

Many millions of people live on land in villages, towns, and cities. Because of the large number of such communities, it would appear that a great deal of land is used to accommodate human populations. In fact, the reverse is true. In the United States alone, less than 3 percent of the land is occupied by human settlements. The percentage is even smaller on a worldwide basis.

Farmland

A major form of land use is for agriculture. In most countries, as much of the tillable land as possible is set aside for farming in order to feed the country's people and, if possible, to raise products for export. In many nations, where the terrain is mountainous or hilly, every possible parcel of land may be carefully tilled for maximum benefit. In some places, especially the wine-producing areas of West Germany, even the hills are planted, with vines. Sometimes the hills are used to provide grazing land for farm animals, if no marketable crops can be grown on them.

These attempts to put every bit of arable land to its best use are necessary, because less than 12 percent of the world's land area is suitable for planting crops. Slightly less than one fourth of usable land is in permanent meadows or pastures.

As of the early 1980s, the total amount of farmable land in the world was about 3,588,037,000 acres. (One acre is equal to 0.405 hectares.) Of this, the greatest amount was in Asia (apart from the Soviet Union): 1,124,350,000 acres, of which only 244,638,000 acres were in China, the most populous nation. North and

Central America combined had a total of 669,668,000 acres; followed by the Soviet Union with 573,295,000; Africa with 447,269,000; Europe with 348,425,000; South America with 311,359,000; and Oceania with 113,671,000. The amount of arable land does not remain constant for a number of reasons including climatic changes, soil erosion, and the continual expansion of population settlements. (*See also* Agriculture.)

Forestland

Of the total world land area (excluding Antarctica), about 10,115,000,000 acres, 31 percent, is forestland. The Soviet Union, with 2,273,000,000 acres, has the greatest forest area of any nation. This figure represents 41 percent of its land area. In South America there are about 2,329,000,000 acres of forestland. Africa has about 1,720,000,000 acres; North and Central America, 1,688,000,000 acres; Asia (apart from the Soviet Union), 1,348,000,000 acres; Europe, 382,000,000 acres; and the Pacific region (with Australia), 374,000,000 acres.

Only a small amount of these enormous acreages is used every year. Timber industries, worldwide, harvest less than 1 percent of the standing volume of available timber each year, for a total of about 4 billion cubic yards (3 billion cubic meters). This percentage varies from region to region: In Europe about 2 percent of the growing stock is cut annually, while in North and South America and the Soviet Union the annual cut does not exceed 1 percent. The remoteness of markets from standing timber in much of North and South America, as well as in Siberia, is responsible for the smaller amount of timber harvesting. In Europe the markets are much closer to usable forests. In most of these forests, more wood is destroyed by fire, insect pests, and decay than is ever harvested for use by humans. (*See also* Forest and Forestry; Forest Products; Jungle; Wood.)

Mines and Quarries

Extensive use of land is also made by mining and quarrying. Whereas agricultural and timber lands may both be replanted after a harvest, and thereby reused in the same way on a periodic basis, mining and quarrying entail the removal of minerals (including petroleum) and stone from the earth. This means

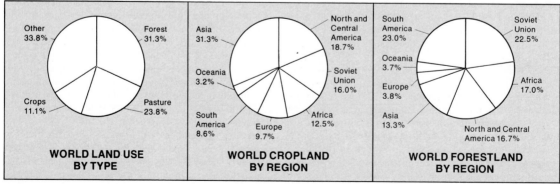

WORLD LAND USE BY TYPE
Other 33.8% | Forest 31.3% | Crops 11.1% | Pasture 23.8%

WORLD CROPLAND BY REGION
Asia 31.3% | Oceania 3.2% | South America 8.6% | Europe 9.7% | Africa 12.5% | Soviet Union 16.0% | North and Central America 18.7%

WORLD FORESTLAND BY REGION
South America 23.0% | Oceania 3.7% | Europe 3.8% | Asia 13.3% | North and Central America 16.7% | Africa 17.0% | Soviet Union 22.5%

Source: United Nations

an irreplaceable loss. Both mining and quarrying use either underground methods or surface, open-pit techniques. In spite of extensive mining and quarrying operations on all continents, the total area of land in use for mining and quarrying is negligible compared to that taken by agriculture and the timber industry. (*See also* Mines; Quarrying.)

LAND OWNERSHIP

The control and use of land within a given society ultimately rests with the government. In Russia, prior to the revolution of 1917, all of the land—in theory if not practice—belonged to the czars. They could give away particular plots as they pleased. On the other hand, in constitutional democracies the right of private ownership of land is guaranteed. Yet, even with such a guarantee, governments may seize land and put it to uses to benefit the nation as a whole. An instance of this in the United States has been the taking of land, normally with payment made, to build the interstate highway system. The purely arbitrary seizing of land, or other private property, is forbidden by the Constitution. Although most governments own land within their borders, democratic societies also generally respect the right of individuals and corporations to own, lease, rent, and sell land as private property.

For centuries, land in most societies has been owned and controlled by governments and by the very wealthy, but it has been worked by the very poor. Since the days of ancient Greece and Rome, land reform efforts have endeavored to redistribute agricultural lands among greater numbers of people. The purpose of this reform has normally been to enhance productivity by giving those who work the land the incentives of ownership and a larger return for their labor.

Land reform has not been a major issue in the United States, except for the period following the Civil War, when some of the Southern plantations were broken up and the land was given to former slaves. But in Asia, Eastern Europe, Africa, and Latin America there have been major efforts to restructure the land ownership system in the 20th century. In 1918 the Soviet Union abolished private ownership of land and established a policy of collectivization. Agricultural marketing became a monopoly of the state, and all farming was done by communities of people. Following World War II, the Communist countries of Eastern Europe generally followed Soviet policy. After the revolution of 1949, China also eliminated private ownership and organized farmers into village communes; but since the death of Mao Tse-tung in 1976, more private initiative and enterprise have been allowed in order to bolster production. Cuba, since its revolution in 1958, has introduced state farms on which the farmers became permanent wage workers. State farms have been subdivided, on the basis of crop specialization, into smaller operational units. Cuba does, however, still allow small private farms.

Land reform has also been carried out with varying success in non-Communist countries. The most comprehensive took place in Egypt, after the monarchy was overthrown in 1952. The Agrarian Reform Act of 1953, while not having great economic benefits, did a great deal to incorporate the farmers into the body politic and gain their support for the government. Japan, too, carried out wide-ranging reforms in the years after World War II. A law of 1946 set limits on individual holdings and provided for the expropriation and resale of excess tracts to individual farmers. Landlords were compensated for property taken from them. Farmers who preferred to remain tenants were protected by contracts, and their rents were limited to 25 percent of their produce. As a result of the law, tenancy declined by 80 percent in two years, while rent control and land redistribution helped to equalize incomes and bring farmers into more active political roles. Japan's reform policies were followed in Taiwan and in parts of Indochina, but in the latter area they were eventually abolished by successful Communist revolutions.

In Malaysia, Thailand, and Indonesia the reforms have emphasized getting landless people onto land that has never been settled. In Malaysia the program has been well organized to promote economic development through production of rubber and palm oil for export. A single project may result in the clearing of 5,000 acres of jungle, the construction of a village, and the division of cropland into parcels to be worked by teams of people until the trees have matured. Each farmer in the program receives a share of land with a lease title for 99 years. This land cannot be subdivided, subleased, or taken from the owner-leaseholder in any way.

The progress of land reform in Latin America, apart from Cuba, has been uneven; and its lack of success has spawned social and political unrest. Since the colonial era, most of the tillable land in Central and South America has been owned by very small, wealthy segments of the population. Much land is owned by foreigners and multinational corporations.

The power of concentrated wealth, in combination with government by authoritarian regimes, has served to block most efforts at redistribution of land in Central and South America. The one major exception has been Mexico, where reforms begun in 1915 and broadened in later decades, have attempted to restore land to the Indians and other farmers. This policy has been pointed to as a prime reason for Mexico's political stability as compared with other Latin American nations.

LANGE, Dorothea (1895–1965). The stark photographs of the victims of the Great Depression of the 1930s that were made by Dorothea Lange were a major influence on succeeding documentary and journalistic photographers. She has been called the greatest documentary photographer of the United States.

Dorothea Lange was born in Hoboken, N.J., on May 26, 1895. She first studied photography under

'Migrant Mother, Nipomo, California' by Dorothea Lange

Clarence White, a member of a well-known group of photographers called the Photo-Secession. At the age of 20 Lange decided to travel around the world, earning money as she went by selling her photographs. Her money ran out in San Francisco, where she settled and opened a portrait studio in 1916.

During the depression Lange photographed the homeless men who wandered the streets. Such pictures as "White Angel Breadline," shot in 1932, showed the hopelessness of these men and received immediate recognition from the renowned photographers of Group f.64. This led to Lange's being hired by the federal Resettlement Administration (later called the Farm Security Administration) to bring the conditions of the poor to public attention. Her photographs of California's migrant workers, captioned with the subjects' own words, were so effective that the state established camps for the migrants.

In 1939 Lange published a collection of her photographs called 'An American Exodus: a Record of Human Erosion'. Two years later she received a Guggenheim Fellowship, which she gave up in order to record with her camera the mass evacuation of Japanese-Americans in California to detention camps after the bombing of Pearl Harbor. Following World War II, Lange did a number of photo essays for *Life* magazine. On Oct. 11, 1965, she died in San Francisco after a long illness.

LANGLEY, Samuel P. (1834–1906). On May 6, 1896, a strange machine flew one half mile (800 meters) over the Potomac River near Washington, D.C. The odd craft was about 16 feet (4.8 meters) long and weighed some 26 pounds (12 kilograms). It flew about a minute and a half. This was the first time a power-driven, heavier-than-air machine stayed in the air for more than just a few seconds.

The builder of this airplane model was Samuel Pierpont Langley, secretary of the Smithsonian Institution. After many laboratory experiments, he had finally shown that extended mechanical flight was possible. Later he built a 56-foot (17-meter) machine for the War Department. Two attempts to launch it in 1903 failed. The Wright brothers, however, proved the worth of Langley's ideas in their successful man-carrying airplane (*see* Aerospace, subhead "Early Research"; Airplane, subhead "Experiments with Powered Flight").

Langley's interest in aeronautics began in Roxbury, Mass., where he was born on Aug. 22, 1834. He watched gulls wheel and soar, using their wings only to meet new wind currents. His father's telescope gave him knowledge of astronomy. He attended Boston Latin School but did not go to college.

After seven years with a Chicago engineering firm, Langley held positions with the astronomical observatories of Harvard University and the United States Naval Academy. In 1870 he became director of the Allegheny Observatory at Western University in Pittsburgh, Pa. He helped raise money for the observatory by selling the first standard time service to the Pennsylvania Railroad. Time signals were flashed to all stations on the road for engineers to set their watches. In 1878 he invented the bolometer, a sensitive electric thermometer for measuring the distribution of heat in the energy rays of the sun.

Langley was appointed secretary of the Smithsonian Institution in 1887. He made the exhibits interesting for people of ordinary education and ordered the institution's books to be written in simple language. He established the Children's Room. Langley put into it things that children like—stuffed birds with their nests and eggs, odd sea animals, bright shells, and coral formations. He collected animals for a zoo, and from this grew the National Zoological Park. Langley died on Feb. 27, 1906, in Aiken, S.C.

Samuel P. Langley

LANGUAGE

LANGUAGE. There is a sea of language around us. From that sea comes a constant flow of messages in Brooklynese and Basque, teenybop and Tibetan. And all those messages are wrapped in sounds and silences and signals.

Language Isn't: Animal Language

In a sense, animals talk to one another. But it is different from human talk. Every human language uses sounds. Not all animal languages do, though. The language of the bees, for instance, uses body movements.

Every person has to learn his language. A human baby raised by apes would learn only the language of apes and other animals. To learn a human language, he would have to hear it from humans. But much animal talk is not learned. It's inborn. A cat will purr and meow even if it never hears another cat.

With any human language, a person can talk about the future and the past. He can discuss ideas—kindness, truth, honesty, justice. He can make almost any number of sentences—including sentences he never heard before. No animal language is so rich in uses and possibilities.

Language Isn't: Written Language

Speech is what most writing starts out from. Writing is a secondhand way of trying to say what the sounds and the signals of language say. (*See also* Punctuation; Spelling.)

Written language is separate from spoken language. Children learn to speak without any special training. But reading and writing—written language—have to be specially taught.

Written language has a life of its own. Every written language was invented long after spoken language began. In fact, not all languages have a written form (*see* Writing).

Written language also has its own style. For one thing, written language doesn't change as fast as spoken language. For another thing, people do not commonly write the way they speak. Often writing is more formal. (*See also* Sentence.)

THE SOUNDS OF LANGUAGE

Sounds are what language comes wrapped in. But not all sounds made by people are language. A person can't say a sneeze, for instance. Or a burp. Burps and sneezes are sounds he can't usually help. The sounds of language are those a person wants to make—and that carry a message.

Bits of Sound

There are strings of sound called sentences, strings of sound called words, strings of sound called syllables. Syllables are strings of vowel and consonant sounds. And even vowels and consonants are strings of smaller sounds. But the smallest bits of sound people recognize are vowels and consonants.

Strictly speaking, no two language sounds are ever the same. But a person learns to ignore some differences between sounds, depending on his language. To a speaker of English, the sounds of *p* in *pot* and *spot* are alike. Actually, the first *p* is followed by a small puff of air. The second *p* isn't. But whether or not the *p* is puffed, the meanings of *pot* and *spot* do not change. So in English, no one pays attention to the difference. In other languages though—Northern Chinese, for instance—a puffed *p* may change meaning. So speakers of Northern Chinese learn to hear the difference.

English has one *p* sound. Northern Chinese has two—a puffed *p* and an unpuffed one. Such classes of sounds are called *phonemes*. A phoneme is the smallest bit of sound that may change meaning. Most often phonemes are vowels or consonants.

Below is a voiceprint, or *sound spectrogram*. It is a picture of the way one speaker is saying "the sea of language around us."

Other spectrograms of the same words—even by the same speaker—will be a little different.

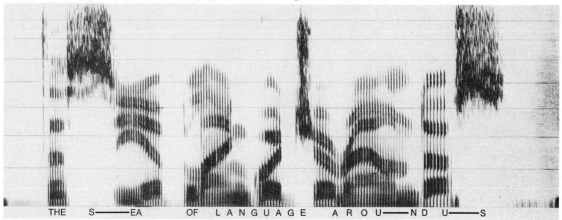

THE   S——EA   OF   LANGUAGE   A R O U——N D   U——S

Phonemes combine in patterns. And these patterns vary from language to language. In Spanish, for instance, the *sp* combination never begins a word. But many words in English begin with *sp*. So an English word like *Spanish* is difficult for a Spanish speaker to pronounce. Often he will say *Espanish*.

In English the sound *ng* comes only at the end of a syllable—*ring, ringer, ringworm*. But in some languages of Africa, *ng* may begin as well as end a syllable. The last name of Kenyan novelist James Ngugi is an example.

Strings of Sound

Most phonemes have no meaning. But they form strings of sound that do. The smallest string of sound with meaning is called a *morpheme*. A morpheme can be what we call a word, or it can be a piece of a word. Take *eater*, in English. *Eat* is a morpheme —it can't be broken down into anything smaller with meaning. The other morpheme is *-er*, meaning "someone who ——s." In *eaters*, there is still a third morpheme, *-s*, meaning "plural" or "more than one."

The Trouble with Words

If *eater* is a word, *eat* is a piece of that word. But in *anteater*, *eater* is only a piece of a word. Of course, *eater* can be used as a word in English. So can *eat* and *ant*. So on that basis they might be called words. This would set them apart from morphemes like *-er* and *-s*, which are commonly used only as pieces of words.

All languages have what might be called words. But the nature of a word varies from language to language. For instance take Chukchi, a language spoken in Siberia. In Chukchi, *the-big-reindeer-a-person-has-killed* is one unit, one word. It can't be broken up into smaller units the way it would be in English. There are many such words in Chukchi, Eskimo, and other languages. In Northern Chinese, on the other hand, many syllables—and even parts of syllables— are what might be called words in English.

Boundaries between words may shift or disappear in actual speech. In English, for instance, *found it* often comes out *foun dit; don't know* becomes *dunno*; and so on. This is one of the things that makes it hard for people learning a second language to understand speakers of that language.

Spoken Signals

The sounds of language include spoken signals. The voice rises and falls. It stresses some sounds. And it pauses between some sounds.

Such spoken signals may change meaning. In English, stress makes a difference between *con' tract* and *con tract'*. A pause makes a difference between *careless* and *care less*. And pitch—the rise and fall

of the voice—makes a difference between "Really?" and "Really."

In languages such as English, pitch is added in a sentence. And it belongs to a place in the sentence, not to a word. Compare "Really?"; "Truly?"; "Honest?" The rising pitch goes with a certain place in that type of sentence. It doesn't matter what the word is. In fact the same words will take different pitches in other sentences.

But in some languages, called *tone languages*, certain pitches belong to certain words. In Northern Chinese, for instance, *chyan* spoken in a level tone means "thousand." In a rising tone it means "money"; in a dipping tone, "shallow"; in a falling tone, "owe." In such languages, the same pitches and the same words always go together.

THE MECHANICS OF LANGUAGE

Language is in strings of sound. And it's in spoken signals. And these sounds and signals fit together in different ways.

Word Clumps and Word Order

Words and pieces of words clump together to form larger words. Prefixes and suffixes are added to a root. Or words are combined to form a compound

In English, intonation—the movement of the voice—sometimes makes a difference in the meanings of words.

How Intonation Changes Meaning

4		/
3		yeah
2	Oh	
1		

4		
3		
2	Oh	/
1		yeah

4		/
3		ye
2	Oh	ah
1		

4 = very high sound
3 = high sound
2 = middle sound
1 = low sound

This article was contributed by Harold B. Allen, formerly professor of English and Linguistics, University of Minnesota.

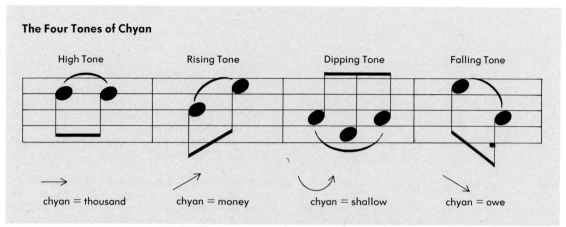

The Four Tones of Chyan

High Tone	Rising Tone	Dipping Tone	Falling Tone
chyan = thousand	chyan = money	chyan = shallow	chyan = owe

In Northern Chinese, the movement of the voice makes a difference in the meanings of most words. Northern Chinese has four tones. And the meaning of a word commonly depends on which tone it is spoken in.

word. How words combine with other words and pieces depends on the language. In English, for instance, nouns often add *-s* or *-es* to form the plural (book, books; box, boxes). (*See also* Noun.) Some languages, such as Japanese, usually add no endings for plural. Japanese *hon* means "book" or "books"; *hako* means "box" or "boxes." But Japanese verbs, like many English verbs, add an ending for past tense (*-mashita*). *Arukimasu* (walk) becomes *aruki-mashita* (walked).

Languages most often add prefixes and/or suffixes to a root. But sometimes changes are made inside a root instead. Thus, Arabic *bint* (girl) becomes *banāt* (girls), and English *mouse* becomes *mice*.

Words clump together in groups called phrases (*see* Sentence). Again, how they clump depends on the language. An Arabic speaker would say *the caliph rotten* instead of *the rotten caliph*. Instead of the phrase *in the kitchen*, a Swahili speaker would use the word *kitchen-in*.

Each language has its own special phrases. One type is what might be called a *usage clump*. These are words clumped together so often that they sound odd in any other order. *Stars and stripes* and *bread and butter* are examples in English. Another type of special phrase is the *idiom*. An *idiom* doesn't mean what its individual words mean. In Italian, "*In the mouth of the wolf*" is an idiom. It means "Good luck." And *kick the bucket* in English has nothing to do with buckets.

Words also clump together in clauses, but how the parts of a clause are arranged depends on the language. An example of one common type of arrangement is the English sentence *Bobby Joe* (subject) *ate* (verb) *my fortune cookie* (direct object). A Japanese speaker would use another common type of arrangement—*Bobby Joe* (subject) *my fortune cookie* (direct object) *ate* (verb). (*See also* Sentence.)

Parts of Speech

Chunks of speech are often grouped by types, such as nouns or verbs. These are sometimes called *parts* of speech (*see* Grammar). Parts of speech are not the same in every language. Nor is the way they act the same. Turkish, for instance, has postpositions instead of prepositions. Instead of *in your hat*, a Turkish speaker would say *hat-your-in*.

Parts of speech have jobs to do. Nouns in English, for instance, may act as subjects. And verbs may act as predicates (*see* Grammar).

The Shapes of Spoken Signals

The spoken signals of language form patterns in phrases and clauses. No two languages have exactly the same patterns. But in many languages a statement commonly has a special shape. Often it drops at the end and fades into silence. (I guess I'll get the papers and go home.) A question that can be answered *yes* or *no* often has a different shape. At the end it usually goes up and breaks off. (Did you see that?) (*See also* Sentence.)

THE MEANING OF LANGUAGE

Language is, above all, meaning. Meanings are attached to pieces of words, words, word groups. Meanings are attached to the spoken signals of language. Meanings are attached to the shifts and changes of grammar.

Meaning and No Meaning

The sounds of words have no meaning to begin with. It's people who attach meaning to them.

Every day someone thinks up a new word. Or he uses an old word in a new way. He might suddenly say, "Hey, that's *zonko*, you know? Boy, that's really *zonko*!" If no one pays much attention to him, that's the end of *zonko*. But maybe his friends and other people begin to use the word, too—"Wow! *Zonko!*" Then another word has been born.

Meaning More or Less

Some words have more of what might be called outside meaning than others. *Orange*, for instance, means "a reddish-yellow color, a fruit," etc. But it also means tigers and sunsets and excitement—meanings outside the dictionary definitions. Words like *the, and, to* have little outside meaning. They are sometimes called *function words* (*see* Grammar).

Much-repeated words may mean less after a while. *Clichés* are an example. A cliché is an expression that loses its punch through overuse. Used sparingly, "That's really great!" may get a listener's special attention. If it's used too often, however, it doesn't mean much.

Common expressions of courtesy often lose meaning. Chances are that a casual acquaintance who asks "How are you?" doesn't really want to know.

Same and Different Meaning

Few words have exactly the same meaning. Not only are the Burmese and Arabic words for "house" different, they mean different things to a Burmese villager and a desert Arab. *Return* and *take back* are much alike in English. But like all synonyms they do not always mean the same. There's a world of difference between "We *took* Ralphie *back* to the monkey house" and "We *returned* Ralphie to the monkey house." But in practice, speakers accept certain words as more or less the same. This helps them communicate more easily.

The same word often has different meanings, depending on how it's used with other words. In English, *go* can mean "leave" (Please don't *go*.); "work" (My watch won't *go*.); "reach" (It doesn't *go* far enough.); etc. Homonyms, or homophones, like *bear* and *bare* are more or less the same word to a listener. It's how they're used with other words that gives them different meanings.

Not only do the same words have different meanings; the same groups of words often do. "She drove into the bank this morning" is an example. Was it a drive-in bank? Or did she zig when she should have zagged? Or what? The surrounding sentences will give clues to the meaning.

A phrase or clause doesn't always mean the same as its words. Idioms are an example. Another example is the way the words are spoken. "Oh, sure I will!" in a sarcastic tone means something very different from what the words say.

Ways of Meaning

A word commonly has different ways of meaning. What a word refers to is only one way it means. Thus, the word *prunes* refers to a food. But much of the meaning of words has to do with the speaker's attitude. So the meaning of *prunes* depends also on how the speaker feels about them. The word has a pleasant meaning if he likes them, an unpleasant meaning if he doesn't.

The meaning a word refers to is its *denotation*. What a word suggests because of the speaker's or listener's attitude is its *connotation*.

Languages have different ways of separating meaning. Eskimo has separate words for falling snow, snow on the ground, etc. English has only one—*snow*. Shona, a language of Rhodesia, has three words for all the colors. One word means "red, purple, orange." Another means "white, yellow, green."

Social Meaning

People don't usually talk to themselves. They talk to other people. And their talk has social meaning.

Only part of the social meaning of a conversation is carried by the words. Take saying hello or talking about the weather. Often such talk has little dictionary meaning. It is a way of being friendly or polite.

Choice of language often has social meaning. An informal "Yeah" in the neighborhood carries a relaxed meaning. Often it is replaced by a formal "Yes" in a classroom or at a job interview. Spanish-speaking Americans often switch from Spanish at home to English in the classroom. Use of special work words may mean a speaker is an architect or plumber or foundry worker. In many countries, the words a speaker uses label him a member of the upper or lower classes.

Dirty words have social meaning. So do expressions using God's name in vain. The same goes for conversation about such things as going to the toilet. Usually these are no-no's, and they have that meaning attached to them.

Grammatical Meaning

Some meanings attach to words. These are dictionary meanings. And some meanings, called *grammatical meanings*, attach to the signals of grammar.

The form a word takes may have grammatical meaning. In English, *-s* or *-es* added to a noun means "plural" or "more than one." A *-mashita* ending on a Japanese verb means "past tense."

Word order may have grammatical meaning. Take the English sentence "Mary bit John." In English, the common order for statements is subject-verb-direct object. So *Mary* means "subject," and John means "direct object." It's Mary who does the biting, John who gets bitten.

Function words have grammatical meaning. In English, *the* or *a* means that a noun is coming up. *Quién* (who) at the beginning of a Spanish sentence means that the sentence is a question.

Spoken signals can have dictionary meaning. Pitch in the words of tone languages is an example. But spoken signals can also have grammatical meaning. In English, for example, stress on *sus-* in *suspect* signals that the word is a noun. Stress on *-spect*, on the other hand, means "verb." At the end of a clause, a drop in pitch with a fading into silence commonly means "statement."

The Trouble with Translation

The words of one language seldom mean the same as the words of another. Take the Russian "*Ja govorila*." It can be translated into English as "I said." But the meanings are not exactly the same. The verb *govorila* tells a Russian that "I" is a female.

It also tells a Russian she spoke more than once or that she hadn't finished speaking. Neither of these meanings is carried by the English words.

Even the same word may not have the same meanings. English borrowed *sputnik* from Russian. It means "artificial satellite." But in Russian, the word also means "fellow-traveler" and "guide." So *sputnik* the English word does not mean the same as *sputnik* the Russian word.

A translation is, at best, something like. It tries to transfer meanings from one language to another. But different words and different mechanics of language must be used. Take the Japanese "*Musukosan wa hebi wo tabemashita.*" Word by word it reads,

Japanese sentences are not built like English sentences. So in translating, parts of a sentence must be shifted around.

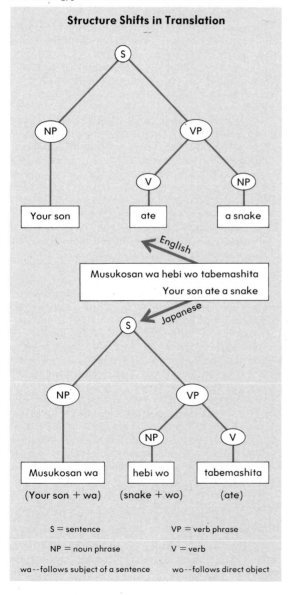

Structure Shifts in Translation

S = sentence	VP = verb phrase
NP = noun phrase	V = verb
wa--follows subject of a sentence	wo--follows direct object

"Your son+wa+snake+wo+ate." But that's not a translation. *Wa* and *wo* have no dictionary meaning, only grammatical meaning—*wa* comes after a subject, *wo* after a direct object. So *wa* and *wo* are dropped in translation. Thus, "Your son snake ate." But in English the direct object (snake) follows the verb (ate). So the words must be switched around to read "Your son ate snake." That's not comfortable English, though. Japanese has no word for *a*, so it must be added. The result is "Your son ate a snake." Still that doesn't carry over all the meanings. *Musukosan*, for instance, has a meaning of respect that is missing in *your son*. Just the same, it's a good translation. A Japanese speaker trying to translate "Your son ate a snake" into Japanese faces the same problems in reverse.

A translation doesn't usually take the same form as the original. Sometimes a noun can be translated by a noun, a phrase by a phrase. But it doesn't work that way very often. German "*Guten Tag*" means "Good day," but it's better translated as "Hello"—people don't usually say "Good day" in English. French *s'il vous plaît* (if it pleases you) is better translated in English as *please*.

The idea of one correct translation is false. For instance, Italian "*La casa è a Sua disposizione*" can be translated as "The house is at your disposal," "Make yourself at home," etc. It is partly a matter of choice. It is also partly a matter of style—whether the words were used in a formal or informal way.

When computers are used in translation, it is called *machine translation*. A computer can work much faster than a human—in looking up a word, say. But the machines have many problems. They have trouble identifying the same sounds made by different people. Sometimes different sounds are spelled with the same letters. (Compare the sounds of the *s* in *cats* and in *dogs*.) Computers have trouble with those. And computers have much trouble with meaning—words with different possible meanings, sentences with different possible meanings.

A computer is only as good as the information put into it. And that's the heart of the machine translation problem. No one has all the answers to how any language works.

BEYOND LANGUAGE

When people talk, they don't stop short at language. They use their voices in ways that go along with language. People also talk with their bodies. And they use substitutes for language.

Paralanguage

The voice carries more than the sounds of language. It carries sounds that go along with language.

A voice may tell whether the speaker is sick or healthy, sleepy or wide awake, drunk or sober. A voice can cry or laugh, moan, groan, or giggle—apart from the words. A voice can drawl. It can hiss or hesitate. It can even fall silent in a special way—the silence of shame, the silence of anger, the silence of bitter disappointment. None of these sounds is language. They are *paralanguage,* sounds that go along with language.

Body Talk

Body movements, too, go along with language. Sometimes they take the place of actual speech.

Some body signals probably can't be helped. Someone who says "Wha-a-at?" may show disbelief by actions as well as words. His eyes may widen, his mouth open a little wider perhaps. Eyebrows may draw together as angry words are spoken. A slight hunch of the shoulders may go along with a confession of fear.

Body signals that can't be helped sometimes contradict the messages of spoken language. A look may say *yes,* even if the words say *no.* The way a person stands may say "I don't like you," even if the words say "We're friends."

Some body signals are deliberate. Deliberate signals, called *gestures,* have to be learned. People in different places use different gestures and attach different meanings to them. In many places, an up-and-down nod means *yes.* But in the Middle East, an upward jerk of the head may mean *no.* Western Europeans often shake the head from side to side to say *no.* But in some Arab countries, that same gesture means *yes.* Most Chinese motion "Come here" with palm down instead of palm up. French people often substitute a shrug for "I don't know."

Even among the same group of people, a gesture can have many possible meanings. In the United States, for instance, a wink can mean "Hi, there." Or it might mean "This is our secret," or "You'll get a laugh out of this," and so on.

Language Substitutes

People have many ways of getting through to one another (*see* Communication). And some of these are substitutes for language.

Most written languages are substitutes for spoken language. Morse code and semaphore code, too, are language substitutes. (*See also* Signaling.) Their signals stand for letters of the alphabet, which in turn stand for spoken language. The same is true of braille, the reading alphabet for the blind (*see* Braille). Another substitute for language is the hand alphabet for deaf-mutes.

Another system of hand signals is Indian sign language. But it isn't a substitute for language, at least not in a direct way. Indian sign language is used by people speaking different languages. So the signs cannot stand for words. Instead the signs themselves have meaning. For instance, two spread fingers moving past the mouth mean "lie," or "forked tongue." Each person translates the meaning of the hand signals into the words of his own language.

Other language substitutes include whistle talk and drum talk. Whistle talk is used for communicating over long distances by people of the Canary Islands. Drums are used to send messages in many parts of Africa. The signals of these systems stand for the words of spoken language.

LANGUAGE CHANGE

A language is always changing. And it keeps changing as long as it is spoken.

Borrowing from Without

One way a language changes is by borrowing words from other languages. It's easier to borrow a word for a new thing than to make one up. English, for instance, borrowed *hula* from Hawaiian, *karate* from Japanese, *pizza* from Italian. Words are often borrowed from a language that has prestige. In the far East, Chinese culture was much admired from early times. As a result, many Chinese words were adopted into other languages of Asia. In Europe, Greek culture had great prestige. Today there are many Greek words in European languages.

Borrowed words are often changed somewhat. For one thing, they're not pronounced the same. *Sauerkraut,* for instance, begins with a *z* sound in the original German. For another thing, borrowed words often don't mean exactly the same. The word *dancing,* borrowed from English, means "nightclub" in French, for instance.

Not just words are borrowed. Sometimes a way of saying something is borrowed, though the actual words are not. For instance, German *Wolkenkratzer* (cloud-scratcher) is borrowed from English *skyscraper.* Sounds also are borrowed. A few languages of South Africa, for instance, have borrowed a kind of click sound from neighbor languages. Sometimes even a way of putting words together is borrowed. Take "The children want that they eat" instead of "The children want to eat." Balkan languages have borrowed such an arrangement from each other.

Borrowing from Within

Borrowing from other languages is a way a language changes from the outside. But some changes come from the inside.

Sometimes a language borrows from itself. New words are coined from the old, or old words take on new meanings. *Hamburger* dropped the *ham* to become *cheeseburger, chiliburger,* etc. The French *traire,* which meant "to pull," now means "to milk."

Sometimes old words take on new sounds, new forms, and even new ways of acting. English *brethren* became *brothers. Bug* stopped being just a noun (Eek! A *bug!*) to become a sometime verb (Don't *bug* me.).

Sometimes there is a sort of minus borrowing—words slowly fade out of use. Hardly anyone wears *breeches* anymore. People rarely say *verily* or "*Lo!*" And *lamplighters* and *organ grinders, iceboxes* and *3-D movies* are mostly things of the past.

Changing the Rules

Another way of changing from within has to do with the way a language works. A language changes its rules, so to speak.

In Old French a phrase like *my back* used to have *the* in front of it—*the my back*. French doesn't work that way any more. In English, *not* used to follow any verb. Now it can follow only a few. Thus, people still say "You had better not" or "I did not." But they would no longer say "I like it not" or "The mailman comes not."

Language sounds, too, work by what might be called rules. In Latin, a word of fewer than three syllables was stressed on the first syllable. Thus, *nav′ is* (ship), *pu′ er* (boy). But in French, one of the languages that grew out of Latin, stress no longer works that way. Thus, *che val′* (horse), *a mi′* (friend).

KINDS OF LANGUAGE

People speak many kinds of language. There is the language of different places, and there is the language of different groups.

Language and Dialect

A speaker of Arabic and a speaker of Malay have different speech habits and don't understand one another's speech. A speaker from the Tennessee hills and a speaker from Chicago have different speech habits too. But they can pretty much understand each other. Arabic and Malay are called languages.

The origin of a word—its etymology—often reveals borrowings from other languages. English is especially rich in borrowed words. For instance, many roots, prefixes, and suffixes in English were long ago borrowed from Greek.

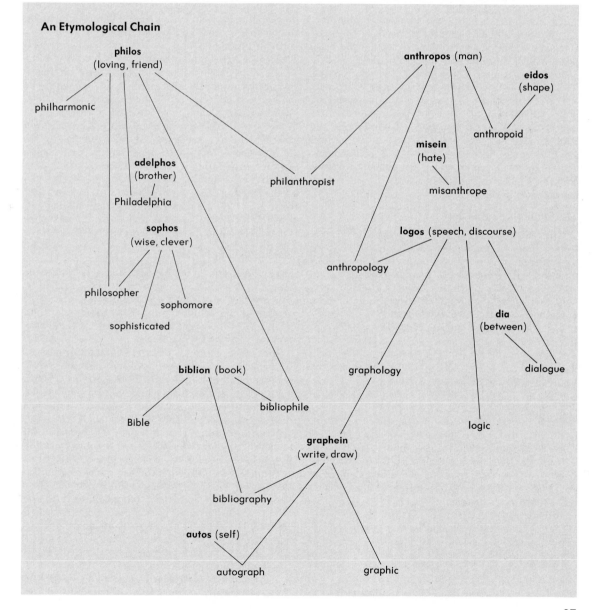

An Etymological Chain

Chicagoese and Tennessee mountainese are called *dialects*. A dialect is a variety of a language.

The line between languages and dialects is not always clear. Dialects are sometimes called languages, and languages are sometimes called dialects. Northern Italians and Sicilians commonly do not understand each other's speech. Yet both speak so-called dialects of Italian. Danish and Norwegian are called different languages. Yet Danes and Norwegians pretty well understand one another.

A country's boundaries can be marked on a map. But language boundaries can't—at least, not in the same way. A line between two languages would mean everyone on one side of the line spoke one language. It would also mean everyone on the other side of the line spoke another language. But language just doesn't work that way.

For one thing, some people use two or more languages. French and English are spoken by many Canadians. Many people of Paraguay are fluent in both Spanish and Guarani, an American Indian language. Quite a number of Israelis understand Hebrew, Yiddish, and a European language, such as Russian.

For another thing, languages have dialects. And often the dialects of one language merge into the dialects of a neighbor language. Take French and Italian. Anyone going from Paris to Naples can hear small language differences between each town and the next. At no point can a sharp line be drawn. Yet the French of Paris and the Italian of Naples are different languages.

The Difference in Dialect

Differences in speech habits are what make dialects. Speakers pronounce words differently. They use different words for the same thing. And they sometimes put words together in different ways.

A London cockney will say *'arry* for *Harry*, *'orrible* for *horrible*. *Hot dog, frankfurter, wiener,* and *red hot* are all words for the same thing in the United States. "Goin' git me some" and "I'm going to get some" are two ways of saying much the same thing. Each way of pronouncing words, of using words, is right for a particular dialect. No dialect is better or worse than another—only different.

All Kinds of Dialect

Strictly speaking, no two people have exactly the same dialect. Every speaker pronounces at least some words a little differently from everyone else. Probably no two persons know exactly the same set of words. Everyone puts his words together in his own ways. And to complicate matters, a person's dialect is always changing.

Just the same, there are patterns of dialect. People in certain neighborhoods, certain cities, certain regions speak a lot alike—even if there are some differences. Many New Yorkers have a way of speaking that sets them apart. The speech of most people from the South is distinctive. American English is distinct from Australian English, which is distinct from English English. Such dialects, spoken by people of different places, might be called *geographical dialects*.

Another type of dialect is the *social dialect*. Social dialects are spoken by people of different groups. In many countries, people in high society speak differently from working-class people. People who work together—astronauts, doctors, gangsters—often share special work words, a sort of shop talk. Men's talk is a little different from women's talk. The language of older people is not the same as that of the young.

In many places one dialect has more social standing than the others. Often it becomes the language of government and is taught in the schools. Such a dialect is called a *standard dialect*. Take the dialect of Paris. Originally it was one of many dialects spoken in what is now France. As Paris became more important, so did the Parisian dialect. Now it is the standard French dialect.

All people have more than one dialect. A person's dialects depend on where he lives, what groups he moves with, his education, and so on. For instance, a Tokyo engineer from Kyoto might use his own Kyoto dialect at home, the standard dialect of Tokyo at work. His speech would differ in some ways from that of his wife. And it would differ from that of his teen-age son. With other engineers he would use a kind of engineering shop talk. Such switching from one dialect to another is common.

People also have more than one way of using their dialects. There is a relaxed way—for talking with friends, for instance. And there is a formal way—for talking with a job interviewer, say.

Standard Languages

Language has no boundaries. Speakers of the same language may live in many countries. And every country has many languages. But often, one of the languages of a country is chosen as the standard language. And this is the language taught in the schools and used for official business.

In France, for instance, the standard language is French. But not all Frenchmen speak French. There are German speakers in Alsace-Lorraine, Breton speakers in Brittany, Basque speakers in the Pyrenees mountains. And in southern France the Provençal dialects are so different from standard French that they can be considered a separate language. The standard language is used for easier communication. It is also used to unite the people of a country.

Often a standard language does make communication easier. French is taught in all the schools of France. So most Frenchmen can get through to each other. A Basque speaker can use French to talk to a Breton speaker, for instance. A standard language can also help give speakers of different languages a feeling of oneness. An example is Modern Hebrew, the standard language of Israel.

The trouble is, a standard language doesn't always work the way it's supposed to. There are no first-class or second-class languages. But because a standard language is the official language, it often has a higher social standing. And nonstandard languages are often considered less important, even looked down on.

In such instances, a nonstandard speaker learns the standard language only if he has to. And even then he resents it. His resentment may take the form of not learning it well—just enough to get by with. Or he may simply refuse to learn it at all.

Some countries have more than one standard language. Belgium uses French and Flemish. Canada uses French and English. Yugoslavia uses Serbo-Croatian, Slovenian, and Macedonian. India has no less than 14 standard languages. But often even such countries have language problems.

Problems arise because one language is—or seems to be—more favored than another. In Belgium, Flemish speakers have protested the favored position of French. In India, many have protested the favored position of Hindi. Problems also arise because most people in most places use only one language. So unless all a country's languages are taught in the schools, which usually isn't practical, most people can't understand speakers of another language.

In some countries, an outside language is sometimes chosen as a standard language. Take Ghana. Its people speak perhaps 50 or more languages. So English was adopted as an official language. And it was used for teaching in the schools.

Second Languages

Most people speak only their first language—the language learned in the home. But many also learn a second language. There are several kinds of second languages. One kind is the language of the other speaker. When a Basque speaker uses French to talk to a French speaker, for instance, he is using the other speaker's language.

But sometimes speakers of different languages don't use the language of the other speaker. They use a third language. Such a language is sometimes called a *lingua franca*. A speaker of Telugu from southern India and a speaker of Hindi from northern India may talk to each other in English. Then English is being used as a *lingua franca*. A Ukrainian speaker and a Yakut speaker from Siberia may use Russian as their common language. In that case, Russian is their *lingua franca*.

Another kind of second language is a *pidgin language*. Pidgins are often used for brief contacts between people—between two traders, say. A pidgin is a sort of hybrid of both the speakers' languages. But the vocabulary is greatly reduced. And the way words fit together is greatly simplified. The first known Pidgin English was used by English speakers and American Indians. One justice of the peace wrote to an Indian policeman, "You, you big constable, quick you catch um Jeremiah Offscow, strong you hold um, safe you bring um afore me." Russonorsk was a pidgin of Russian and Norwegian. It was used by Russian and Norwegian fishermen for about a hundred years before World War I. A pidgin of Dutch and Malay, known as Bazaar Malay, was used in the Dutch East Indies. *Bahasa Indonesia*, the official language of Indonesia, is based on Bazaar Malay.

Sometimes a pidgin becomes the first language of a group of speakers. Then it is a *creole language*. In the Caribbean, African slaves from the same tribe were often separated. This was to reduce the danger of revolt. So the slaves on a plantation had no common language. They could only talk to each other in a pidgin of their owner's language—such as Pidgin French or Pidgin Spanish. In time the slaves married and had children. The children learned the pidgin as their only language. At that point, their language was a creole language.

Gullah is a creole language. It is spoken on and near the Sea Islands off Georgia. Louisiana Creole is a French-based language. Another French-based creole is Haitian Creole, the language of Haiti. Speakers of Louisiana Creole and Haitian Creole commonly understand each other. Jamaican Creole is an English-based language of Jamaica. So-called Hawaiian Pidgin English is actually a creole language. It is the speech of a large number of people brought up in the Hawaiian Islands.

Interlanguages

The Old Testament tells of a time when there was one world language. And how Nimrod ruined it all by building a tower to reach Heaven. And how the Lord made the workmen speak different languages. So the Tower of Babel was never finished.

The idea of a world language, or *interlanguage*, is very old. Hundreds have been invented. But few have received much attention. The first one to become well known was Volapük. It was introduced by a Bavarian clergyman, Johann Martin Schleyer, in 1879. Schleyer based his language mostly on German and English, with many words also from languages like Latin—French, Italian, Spanish, and so on. The name *Volapük* meant "world speech."

Volapük was popular in Europe for a while, but it didn't last. For one thing, some of its sounds were difficult for non-German speakers. The *ü* sound in Volapük is an example. For another thing, the way its words fit together was complicated. Volapük went out of use shortly after the invention of another—and simpler—interlanguage, Esperanto.

Esperanto is probably the best known interlanguage. It was introduced in 1887 by a Polish doctor, L. L. Zamenhof. The name *Esperanto* is based on a word for "hope." Zamenhof felt that language was at the root of problems between people. He believed a world language would bring peace and understanding.

Esperanto is based mostly on languages like French, Italian, and Spanish, with a number of words also from German and Greek. Both the sounds and the mechanics of the language are fairly simple—for most Europeans. Esperanto is used in many countries. Schools teach it, and books are published in Esperanto.

Major Living Languages of the Indo-European Family

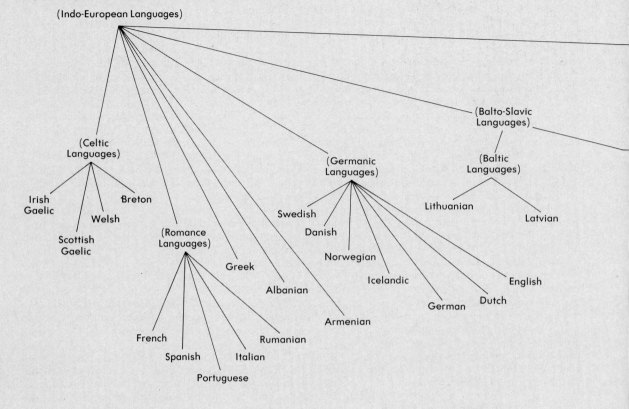

The trouble with world languages is that they're not. Mostly they are made for speakers of English, German, French, Spanish, Portuguese, Italian, and a number of related languages. A speaker of Northern Chinese, for instance, would have as much trouble with Esperanto as with French or German. The same is true of a speaker of Eskimo or a speaker of Tamil, a language of southern India. Esperanto ignores the sounds and mechanics and meanings of most of the world's languages.

Another problem with world languages has to do with language change. Suppose Esperanto, say, were adopted as a world language. It would soon be spoken in many different dialects. For one thing, people have different speech habits. For another thing, language is always changing. Dialects of people far apart would become more and more different. This would be especially true of people in remote places, people having little or no contact with speakers of other dialects. It would probably also be especially true of people who felt that Esperanto was not "their" language, that it represented the languages of other people. Given time enough, resistance or resentment enough, and separation enough, speakers of different dialects would no longer be able to understand one another. And a new interlanguage would have to be invented all over again.

Related Languages

Languages have dialects. And some of those dialects grow so far apart that they become languages. And the new languages separate into dialects. And some of those become languages. Such related languages are called a *language family*.

Indo-European. The family to which English belongs is the Indo-European family. It consists of many groups of languages.

The Germanic, or Teutonic, group includes the Scandinavian languages—Danish, Norwegian, Swedish, and Icelandic. German is commonly divided into High German and Low German. High German includes the dialects of southern Germany, the dialects of Austria, and the German dialects of Switzerland. Dutch, Flemish (spoken in Belgium), and the dialects of northern Germany make up Low German. Afrikaans, an offshoot of Dutch, is spoken in South Africa. English, which is also a Germanic language, is closely related to Dutch. But even closer to English is Frisian, spoken mostly in the northern Netherlands. Yiddish, a language of the Jewish people, is for the most part a High German of the Middle Ages.

The Romance group descended from Latin. After the Roman Empire fell apart, the Latin dialects of the different regions grew farther and farther apart.

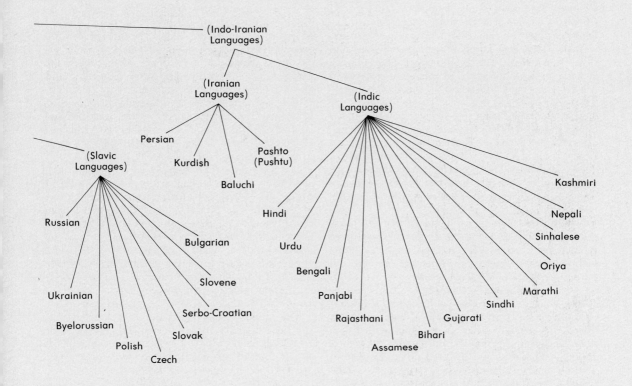

Best known of the Romance languages are French, Spanish, Portuguese, Italian, and Rumanian. Provençal, a name for the dialects of southern France, is sometimes considered a separate language. Catalan is spoken mostly in eastern Spain. Romansh is spoken in Switzerland. And Sardinian is spoken on the island of Sardinia.

The Balto-Slavic group consists of the Baltic languages and the Slavic languages. Lithuanian and Latvian (or Lettish) are Baltic languages. The Slavic languages include Russian, Ukrainian, and Byelorussian (or White Russian), all spoken in the Soviet Union. Czech and Slovak, spoken in Czechoslovakia, are very closely related. Indeed they might be called varieties of the same language. Serbo-Croatian is one language written in two alphabets—Croatian in Roman letters, Serbian in the Cyrillic alphabet. (*See also* Writing.) It is spoken chiefly in Yugoslavia, as is the Slovenian language. Other well-known Slavic languages include Polish and Bulgarian.

The Celtic group of languages, once spoken over a large territory, today are used only in the British Isles and northwestern France. And the number of speakers is small. Irish Gaelic and Scottish Gaelic are Celtic languages. Welsh, spoken in Wales, and Breton, a language of Brittany in northwestern France, form another branch of Celtic.

The Indo-Iranian group consists of Indic languages and Iranian languages. Persian is an Iranian language. So are Pashto (or Pushtu), spoken in Afghanistan and Pakistan; and Kurdish, spoken in Kurdistan. Baluchi, spoken mostly in Pakistan and Iran, also is an Iranian language. Sanskrit is an Indic language. It is the oldest living Indo-European language, now used chiefly as the sacred language of Hinduism. Hindi, the leading language of northern India, and Urdu, the national language of Pakistan, are also Indic languages. Both Hindi and Urdu are varieties of the same language. But Urdu has more Persian and Arabic words and is written with a different alphabet. Other Indic languages include Bengali, Panjabi, Gujarati, Marathi, Rajasthani, Bihari, Kashmiri, Oriya, Sindhi, Assamese, and Nepali. Sinhalese, spoken in Sri Lanka, is also an Indic language. And so is the language of the Gypsies, Romany.

Greek belongs in a separate group. The same is true of Armenian. And the same is true of Albanian. An Indo-European language called Tocharian was once spoken in what is now Sinkiang, China. The language of the Hittites, a people mentioned in the Bible, was also Indo-European.

Uralic. The Uralic family has two main groups: Finno-Ugric and Samoyed. Of the Finno-Ugric group, the best known Ugric language is Hungarian (or

41

Magyar). Finnish, Estonian, and Lapp are the best known Finnic languages. Lapp, the language of the Lapps, is spoken mostly in Norway, Sweden, and Finland. Two other Finnic languages, Mordvin and Cheremis, are spoken in the Soviet Union. The Samoyed group of languages are spoken in Siberia.

Altaic. The Altaic family is commonly divided into three main groups: Turkic, Mongolian, and Manchu-Tungus (or Manchurian). Turkish is the best-known Turkic language. Other Turkic languages include Azerbaijani, Uzbek, Kazakh, Tatar, Kirghiz, and Turkoman (or Turkmenian), all spoken mostly in the Soviet Union. Azerbaijani is also spoken in Iran. Another Turkic language, spoken mostly in Sinkiang, China, is Uighur. Yakut, spoken in Siberia, is also a Turkic language. The Mongolian group of languages are spoken in Mongolia and China. The Manchu-Tungus group of languages are spoken in Manchuria and Siberia.

Sino-Tibetan. The Sino-Tibetan family has many groups of languages. Of these, the best known is the group called Chinese. Chinese has about half a dozen main dialects, so-called. But they are, for practical purposes, separate languages. They are very different—in sounds and vocabulary mostly. And the speakers of one dialect cannot understand the speakers of another. Northern Chinese (or Mandarin) is considered the standard language of China. Other Chinese languages include Wu, Min (or Fukienese), Hakka, and Cantonese (or Yue). Most Chinese in Taiwan speak Min. Cantonese is used by most of the Chinese speakers in the United States.

Tibetan and Burmese also belong to the Sino-Tibetan family. Sometimes they are considered one group, sometimes two. Another group includes Thai and Lao. Thai is spoken in Thailand mostly, Lao mostly in Laos. The Miao-Yao languages are sometimes considered Sino-Tibetan. They are spoken by tribespeople in southwest China, northern Burma, and Indochina.

Austronesian. The Austronesian, or Malayo-Polynesian, family is spoken from Madagascar, off the coast of Africa, to Hawaii. One of its best-known languages is Malay. The standard languages of Malaysia and Indonesia are varieties of Malay. Tagalog, Visayan, and Ilocano, all spoken in the Philippines, also belong to this family. So does Malagasy, a language spoken on the island of Madagascar.

Maori, spoken in New Zealand, is an Austronesian language. And related languages are spoken in many of the South Sea Islands. These include Fiji in the Fiji Islands, Samoan in the Samoan Islands, Tahitian in the Society Islands, Hawaiian in the Hawaiian Islands, and Chamorro on Guam.

Congo-Kordofanian. The Congo-Kordofanian family has two main groups: the Niger-Congo and the Kordofanian. The Kordofanian languages are spoken in the Sudan. The Niger-Congo languages are spoken over a great part of central and southern Africa.

Well-known languages of the Niger-Congo group include Ibo, Yoruba, and Efik, spoken in Nigeria. Fulani (or Fula) is spoken mostly in Nigeria and Guinea; Mandingo mostly in Mali, Ivory Coast, and Guinea. Twi has many speakers in Ghana. Mossi, Wolof, Ewe, and Tiv also are Niger-Congo languages.

The Bantu languages are only one branch of one division of the Niger-Congo group. But they are very numerous. A few better-known Bantu languages are Swahili, Ruanda and Rundi, Sotho and Tswana, Ganda, Shona, Kongo, Kikuyu, Xhosa, Zulu, and Swazi.

Afroasiatic. The Afroasiatic family is divided into four main groups. The best known is Semitic. Arabic, with its many dialects, is the most widely used Semitic language. It is spoken in many countries of the Near East and North Africa. Modern Hebrew, the standard language of Israel, is also a Semitic language. So is Amharic, the standard language of Ethiopia.

The other groups of Afroasiatic are Berber, Cushitic, and Chad. The Berber languages are spoken in North Africa. The Cushitic languages are spoken over a wide area in East Africa. Somali is the best known Cushitic language. Hausa, the best known Chad language, is widely spoken in West Africa.

Other Families. The Dravidian family of languages are spoken mostly in southern India. They include Telugu, Tamil, Kanarese (or Kannada), and Malayalam. Tamil is also spoken in Sri Lanka. Brahui, a Dravidian language, is used in Pakistan and Iran.

The Munda family consists of a few languages in central India. The Mon-Khmer family is spoken in Southeast Asia. Its best-known language is Cambodian, or Khmer, spoken in Kampuchea. Most Mon speakers live in Burma and Thailand.

Among the better-known languages of the Nilo-Saharan family are Kanuri, Dinka, Luo, and Masai. Kanuri is spoken in Nigeria and Niger, Dinka and Luo in Kenya, Masai in Tanzania. The Khoisan family of languages are spoken mostly in South Africa. The best known of these languages are Bushman and Hottentot. Khoisan speakers use special click sounds. Some of these sounds have spread to nearby Bantu languages like Zulu, Sotho, and Xhosa.

Japanese seems to be the only member of a family. The same is true of Korean. And the same is true of Vietnamese. Basque is spoken mostly in the Pyrenees mountains region of France and Spain. It has no ties with any other language. Another language without ties is Burushaski. It is spoken in and around Hunza, in the Karakoram mountains of Kashmir. Andamanese, spoken by a handful of people in the Andaman Islands, has no known relatives. Neither has Ainu, once the language of a non-Japanese people of northern Japan. The Ainu people survive, but only a few words of their language are still used.

About 25 or so languages spoken in the Caucasus Mountains have no known relatives. Some of them seem to be related, but the language picture there as a whole is not clear. Sometimes they are divided into two groups, a northern group and a southern. Among the better known of these languages are Circassian and Georgian. How the languages of Australia are related also is not known. The same is true of most languages of New Guinea.

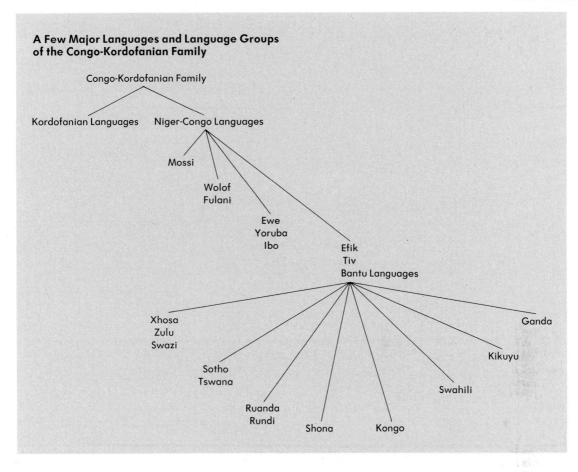

A Few Major Languages and Language Groups of the Congo-Kordofanian Family

Congo-Kordofanian Family

Kordofanian Languages — Niger-Congo Languages

Mossi

Wolof
Fulani

Ewe
Yoruba
Ibo

Efik
Tiv
Bantu Languages

Xhosa
Zulu
Swazi

Ganda

Kikuyu

Sotho
Tswana

Swahili

Ruanda
Rundi

Shona

Kongo

A few languages of Siberia do not belong to families elsewhere. These are sometimes called Paleosiberian languages. Some of these are related. But it is not certain that all are. Probably the most numerous group, the Chukchi group, includes Chukchi and Koryak. The American Indian languages in North and South America are sometimes called Amerindian languages. Like the Paleosiberian languages, they are not clearly understood. Some Amerindian languages are related—Eskimo and Aleut, for instance. And most seem to fit into families such as Iroquoian, Siouan, etc. But many do not.

LANGUAGE THROUGH LANGUAGE: GUIDELINES FOR A MODEL SECOND-LANGUAGE PROGRAM

No language is hard for a child. He picks up any language easily and naturally—by listening and talking. But that ability soon fades. And then he must learn a new language through the one he already has. And that's where the second-language teacher comes in. The following are some guidelines for a model second-language program.

1. Sounds are first. Students concentrate on listening and speaking, especially to begin with.

2. Students get lots of practice in listening—to the teacher, to records and tapes, and so on. Then they imitate. They try to hear groups of words, not just one word at a time.

3. Students get lots of practice in speaking, too. Everyone gets to do some talking every period, especially slow learners. And the students do most of the talking—the teacher already knows the language.

4. Learning a new language is hard. Students are told—slow learners especially—not to worry about making mistakes, that everybody makes them.

5. The teacher explains about the new language when necessary. But mostly students practice using the language. Practice helps them understand how the language works.

6. Students get drill. They need it to break old language habits and form new ones. But the teacher doesn't overdo drill and tries to make it interesting.

7. Students don't translate from the new language to English. That builds the wrong skill—making sentences in English. And they go easy on translating from English. Instead they concentrate on thinking in and using the new language.

8. Students are surrounded with second language. As much as possible, the teacher teaches in it.

9. Students practice in lifelike situations—asking directions, ordering a meal, shopping, and so on. That

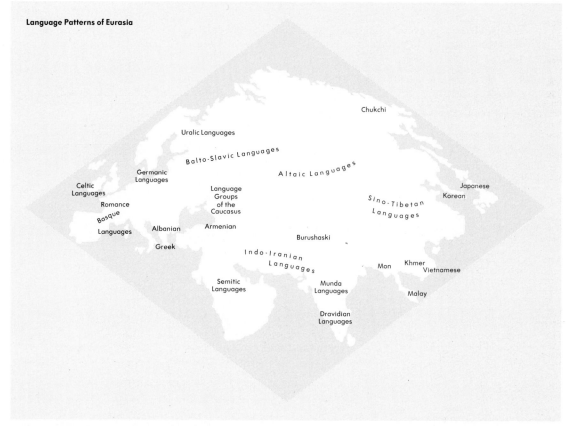

Language Patterns of Eurasia

Chukchi

Uralic Languages

Balto-Slavic Languages

Altaic Languages

Germanic
Languages

Celtic
Languages

Language
Groups
of the
Caucasus

Romance

Basque

Languages

Albanian

Armenian

Greek

Burushaski

Indo-Iranian
Languages

Sino-Tibetan
Languages

Japanese
Korean

Mon

Khmer
Vietnamese

Semitic
Languages

Munda
Languages

Malay

Dravidian
Languages

The above diagram is not a language map. It is meant only to give a rough idea of language patterns in Europe and Asia.

Languages shown are not the only languages spoken in a particular area. And they are not confined to that area.

way, they get to feel the new language is as alive as their own. And they get to understand about varieties of language.

10. Students learn the body talk that goes along with language. They watch live speakers. Or they see films and videotapes. Then they practice using language and body talk together.

11. Class time is used for live language interchange—between teacher and student, between student and student. Outside time is set aside for language lab work, for practice work of various kinds.

12. Many kinds of materials are used—no one kind works best with all students. Practice materials are available for use outside of class.

13. Students use the hardware of second-language learning—a language lab, tape recorders, records, and other aids. These are sometimes used at random. But they are also part of every student's program.

14. The teacher uses many approaches to language learning. He knows the best method is the one that works with a particular student at a particular time.

15. The teacher adjusts the program to each student's abilities, especially with slow learners.

16. Classes are small—small enough for everyone to have a chance to talk every day, small enough for the teacher to get around to everyone.

17. The teacher aims for interest and excitement in materials and in the daily work.

LINGUISTICS: THE THEORY OF THE LITTLE BLACK BOX

Linguistics is the study of language in a scientific way. But the linguist, or language scientist, has a problem. How can he study something he can't get at?

In the mind of every speaker is what might be called a mysterious little black box. And it powers the machinery of language. But the linguist can't open that box without destroying the mechanism inside. So he can't directly examine how language works. What he can do is observe the effects of that mechanism on the organs—such as the larynx and the tongue—that produce the sounds of language. And he can study those sounds—how they're made, how they fit together, what the difference sound patterns mean, and so on. That's what linguistics is mostly about.

Linguists also study how language influences people and affects society. That's called *sociolinguistics*. Another branch of linguistics is *psycholinguistics*. It deals with how language is learned and how it can be taught. *Computational linguistics* deals with computers and language. Machine translation is part of it.

BIBLIOGRAPHY FOR LANGUAGE

Books for Children

Connell, Donna. Integrated Total Language (Can-do, 1978).
Hofsinde, Robert. Indian Sign Language (Morrow, 1956).
Holmer, Keith. Student Guide to Language Skill (Educational Service, 1960).
Kohl, Herbert. A Book of Puzzlements (Schocken, 1982).
Ogg, Oscar. The 26 Letters, rev. ed. (Crowell, 1971).
Preiss, Byron. The First Crazy Word Book (Watts, 1982).
Schwartz, Alvin. The Cat's Elbow and Other Secret Languages (Farrar, 1982).
Scott, J. H. and Lenore. Hieroglyphs for Fun (Van Nostrand-Reinhold, 1974).
Showers, Paul. How You Talk (Harper, 1975).
Thomson, D. S. and others. Language (Time-Life, 1975).
Wolff, Diane. Chinese Writing (Holt, 1975).

Books for Young Adults and Teachers

Barnard, Ellsworth. English for Everybody (Dinosaur, 1979).
Bernstein, Theodore. The Careful Writer (Atheneum, 1965).
Bernstein, Theodore. Dos, Don'ts and Maybes of English Usage (Times, 1977).
Bernstein, Theodore. Miss Thistlebottom's Hobgoblins (Farrar, 1971).
Chicago Manual of Style, The (Univ. of Chicago Press, 1982).
Diamond, Harriet and Dutwin, Phyllis. Grammar in Plain English (Barron, 1983).
Follett, Wilson. Modern American Usage (Warner, 1974).
Fowler's Modern English Usage, 2nd rev. ed. (Oxford, 1965).
Gallant, Roy. Man Must Speak (Random, 1969).
Harper Dictionary of Contemporary Usage (Harper, 1975).
Hayakawa, S. I. Language in Thought and Action (Harcourt, 1972).
Helfman, E. S. Signs and Symbols Around the World (Lothrop, 1967).
Howard, Philip. Words Fail Me (Oxford, 1981).
Lenneberg, E. H., ed. New Directions in the Study of Language (MIT Press, 1964).
Newman, Edwin. A Civil Tongue (Warner, 1977).
Partridge, Eric. A Dictionary of Slang and Unconventional English, 7th ed. (Macmillan, 1970).
Pei, Mario. The Story of the English Language, rev. ed. (Simon & Schuster, 1968).
Pei, Mario. The Story of Latin and the Romance Languages (Harper, 1976).
Pei, Mario. Weasel Words (Harper, 1978).
Pei, Mario. The World's Chief Languages (Vanni, 1960).
Roth, Audrey and Camacho, Oliver. Words People Use (Little, 1972).
Russell, William. The Parents' Handbook of Grammar and Usage (Stein & Day, 1982).
Safire, William. On Language (Avon, 1981).
Safire, William. What's the Good Word? (Times, 1982).
Shaw, Harry. Dictionary of Problem Words and Expressions (McGraw, 1975).
Timmons, Christine and Gibney, Frank, eds. Britannica Book of English Usage (Doubleday, 1980).
(*See also* bibliographies for **Ciphers and Codes; Communication; Phonics; Reference Books; Spelling.**)

Learning Foreign Languages

Calyer, Penrose. I Can Read Spanish (Watts, 1976).
Cooper, Lee. Fun with German (Little, 1965).
De Francis, John. Beginning Chinese, 2nd rev. ed. (Yale Univ. Press, 1976).
Feelings, Muriel. Jambo Means Hello: Swahili Alphabet Book (Dial, 1974).
Hautzig, Esther. At Home: a Visit in Four Languages (Macmillan, 1968).
Joslin, Sesyle and Barry, Katharina. There Is a Bull on My Balcony (Harcourt, 1966).
Lemaitre, Joseph. French: How to Speak and Write It (Dover, 1962).
Maeda, Jun. Let's Study Japanese (Tuttle, 1965).
Magocsi, P. R. Let's Speak Rusyn (Transworld, 1976).
Pei, Mario. New Italian Self-Taught (Harper, 1982).

LANSING. The capital city of Michigan is Lansing. It was settled in the 1830s on densely wooded land along the Grand River. The first industry was lumbering. In 1847 the state capital was moved to Lansing from Detroit. The site at that time was still

mostly wilderness and included only a sawmill and a log cabin. At first called Michigan, in 1848 it assumed the name of Lansing Township in which it was located. Today the city lies within Ingham County. A plank road to Detroit was open in 1852, and the first rail line reached the town in the 1860s.

Forests were cleared from the countryside, and farms were started. The townspeople began making horse-drawn vehicles. In the 1900s, under the leadership of Ransom E. Olds, the manufacture of automobiles and trucks was begun. Lansing soon became an industrial center, with metalworking the leading industry. Today its Oldsmobile and Fisher Body divisions of General Motors and Motor Wheel Corporation are nationally known. Other factories in Lansing make automotive parts, farm tools, machinery, and refrigerating units. Lansing is also a trade and marketing center for the surrounding fertile farming area of south-central Michigan.

The city lies in a shallow, cuplike valley formed by the Grand and Red Cedar rivers. The business area and the ten-acre (four-hectare) capitol park are set in the city's center, atop a slight elevation bordered on three sides by the Grand. The Capitol, with its 276-foot (84-meter) dome, was completed in 1878. The building contains the state library and display cases on Michigan's military history. Located nearby the Capitol are the Lewis Cass and Stevens T. Mason state office buildings.

On the fringe of the downtown business district is the Civic Center, dedicated in 1955. In Lansing are the Michigan Historical Museum, Impression Five Science Museum, Kresge Art Center, Lansing Community College, a state school for the blind, and a state vocational school for boys. The city has about 35 parks, including Carl G. Fenner Arboretum Park, with flower gardens, Woldumar Nature Center, and Potter Park, which contains a zoo.

East Lansing, which is separately incorporated, adjoins the capital city. It is the home of Michigan State University, founded in 1855 as the first land-grant agricultural college in the United States. First called College Park, it was given the name East Lansing by the state legislature at the time of its incorporation in 1907. East Lansing has a noted planetarium and botanical garden.

Lansing was incorporated as a city in 1859 and chartered in 1907. It owns its water and electric supply systems and a sewage disposal plant. It has a mayor-council form of government. (*See also* Michigan.) Population (1980 census), 130,414.

Nicholas Wollaston—Camera Press

Villagers at Vientiane form a line and wade in the Mekong River, casting fishing nets. After a few minutes, the nets are pulled out of the water and the fishes are placed in floating baskets.

LAOS.

The Lao People's Democratic Republic, or Laos, is the only landlocked country of Southeast Asia. The Mekong River is its only natural outlet to the sea. The former kingdom lies entirely within the tropics and occupies a rugged central strip of the Indochinese peninsula, surrounded by Vietnam on the east, Kampuchea (formerly Cambodia) on the south, Thailand on the west, Burma on the northwest, and China on the north.

Land and Climate

The landscape of this country of 91,429 square miles (236,800 square kilometers) is dominated by inhospitable, forest-covered mountains, which in the north rise to 9,248 feet (2,819 meters) above sea level. The principal mountain range, the Annamite Chain, runs from northwest to southeast along the Laos-Vietnam border. Secondary ranges running perpendicular to the Annamite Chain are separated by narrow, deep river valleys. The slope of the land is generally downward from east to west, and most of the rivers drain into the Mekong, which forms the boundary with Burma and most of the boundary with Thailand. The only lowlands lie along the eastern bank of the Mekong, where more than half the population is concentrated. Most are engaged in wet

Facts About Laos

Official Name: Lao People's Democratic Republic.

Capital: Vientiane.

Area: 91,429 square miles (236,800 square kilometers).

Population (1982 estimate): 3,901,000; 43 persons per square mile (16 persons per square kilometer); (1975) 11 percent urban, 89 percent rural.

Major Language: Lao (official).

Major Religion: Buddhism.

Literacy: About 34 percent of the people over 15 years of age can read and write.

Mountain Range: Annamite Chain.

Highest Peak: Mount Bia, 9,248 feet (2,819 meters).

Major River: Mekong.

Form of Government: People's Republic.

Chief of State: President.

Head of Government: Prime Minister.

Legislature: National Congress.

Voting Qualifications: All citizens 18 years of age.

Political Divisions: 13 provinces subdivided into districts, towns, and villages.

Major Cities (1973 census): Vientiane (176,637), Savannakhet (50,690), Pakse (44,860), Luoangphrabang (44,244).

Chief Manufactured and Mined Products: Tobacco products, lumber, matches, rubber shoes, tin, gypsum, iron ore, lead, zinc, and coal.

Chief Agricultural Products: *Crops*—cassava, coffee, corn (maize), opium poppies, potatoes, rice, sugarcane, sweet potatoes and yams. *Livestock*—buffaloes, pigs, poultry.

Flag: *Colors*—blue, red, and white (*see* Flags of the World).

Monetary Unit: 1 kip = 100 at.

rice farming. The fertile floodplains of these lowlands are formed from soil carried by the river and its tributaries (*see* Mekong River). The only other important fertile area is the Bolovens Plateau, a region in the far southeast underlain by volcanic basalt. Its fertile, reddish soils are well suited for plantation crops such as rubber. The hills and mountainsides can be brought into temporary cultivation by primitive slash-and-burn agriculture, but they quickly lose their fertility and the cultivators must move to other areas and repeat the process. A vital area strategically and politically is the Plain of Jars, a plateau area in the north that often changed hands during the Vietnam War. Its name derives from large prehistoric stone jars discovered there.

The tropical monsoon climate in Laos varies with altitude and latitude. More than 80 percent of the rain falls from May to October, when the winds blow from the southwest and deposit an average rainfall of between 50 and 90 inches (1,300 and 2,300 millimeters). On the Bolovens Plateau precipitation reaches 160 inches (4,100 millimeters) per year. The dry season is from November to April. Temperatures average between 60° to 70° F (16° and 21° C) from December through February, and increase to more than 90° F (32° C) in March and April.

Laos has tropical rain forests of broadleaf evergreens in the north and monsoon forests of mixed evergreens and deciduous trees in the south. In the monsoon forest areas the ground is covered with tall, coarse grass called *tranh;* bamboo and scrub and wild banana trees are abundant.

The People

More than half of the people are the Lao-Lu, who speak virtually the same language as the Thai of Thailand and live mainly in the lowlands. The mountain peoples are known collectively as Kha, a derogatory term meaning slaves. They may be classed in three groups: Lao-Tai, or tribal Tai, who unlike most Laotians believe in spirits rather than in Buddhism; the Lao-Soung, including the Meo and Man, who have migrated from southwest China since the late 1800s; and the Lao-Theng, or Mon-Khmer, who are thought to be descendants of the earliest inhabitants of the region. There are also a few thousand Vietnamese and some Chinese town dwellers.

The typical lowland Lao village is strung along a road or a stream. Houses are raised on timber stilts. They have steep thatched roofs and verandas. Animals find shelter beneath the houses. Tropical fruit trees and vegetable gardens grow nearby. Rice fields surround the village.

The Lao and most of the other ethnic groups are Theravada (or Hinayana) Buddhists. Village life has long centered about the temple, with its guesthouse, monastery, and monastery school. Each Lao youth traditionally spends some time as a Buddhist monk, with shaven head, saffron robe, and begging bowl. Buddhism prevails, but there is widespread belief in spirits, called *phu.*

Two women in Laotian dress (left) shop in a market. The baby rides in a sling on his mother's back. The man, a member of the Lu tribe, carries produce in a basket hung from a yoke.

Physically the Lao resemble the Thai of Thailand. They are slight in stature and have light brown skin and black hair. Typical Lao clothing consists of a saronglike garment, worn by both men and women, and a blouse or jacket. Shoes are seldom worn.

The diet is barely adequate. It consists chiefly of rice combined with a pungent fish sauce. Little meat is eaten, largely because of Buddhist beliefs.

Only a few Laotians live in cities or large towns. There is little manufacturing to offer employment, and most trade is carried on by Chinese. Vientiane, the national capital, is the largest city. Pakse, Luoangphrabang (Luang Prabang), Thakhek, and Savannakhet are regional centers.

The Laotian Economy

Most Laotians depend upon agriculture for a livelihood, though less than 4 percent of the country is under permanent cultivation. Rice accounts for about 90 percent of the permanently tilled acreage. Also raised are melons, cassava, sweet potatoes, corn (maize), potatoes, tobacco, coffee, sugarcane, and plants yielding drugs, especially opium poppies.

Each village attempts to meet its own needs. Weaving, basketmaking, forest gathering, and fishing help supply village needs. Some lumbering is carried on, and tin is produced in southern Laos.

The Mekong River system is the chief transportation route, though it is only partly navigable. Between Vientiane and Savannakhet it can handle larger vessels. Navigation on other sections is hampered by shallows, rapids, and falls. In 1956 the Thai railroad system was extended to the Mekong, near Vientiane, providing northern Laos with access to the sea through Bangkok. Good roads are scarce.

History and Government

Laos began to develop in the 9th century as Tai-speaking peoples moved southward from China. The powerful kingdom of Lan Xang was founded in the 14th century. It split into the kingdoms of Vientiane and Luang Prabang in the 18th century. In 1828 Vientiane was destroyed by Thailand.

The French established a protectorate over the kingdom of Luang Prabang in 1893 and governed the rest of Laos as a colony. The Japanese occupied Indochina in World War II. The French recognized the king of Luang Prabang as king of all Laos before they returned in 1946. In 1953 Laos became independent and in 1955 was admitted to the United Nations. Although both Communist and Western nations recognized its neutrality, Laos became a divided state. Its two northernmost provinces were controlled by the Communist Pathet Lao. Military and technical aid came from North Vietnam and China.

In keeping with its policy of halting Communist expansion in Southeast Asia, the United States gave massive aid to the anti-Communist government. The Royal Laotian Army, however, was unable to stem the advances of the pro-Communist Pathet Lao forces, and by early 1961 the Communists controlled much of the country. In May a cease-fire was signed. A coalition government of neutralist, Communist, and pro-Western factions was formed in June 1962. In July, 14 nations signed a pact guaranteeing the neutrality of Laos. All foreign troops were ordered removed. United States forces withdrew, but the International Control Commission found no evidence that North Vietnamese troops had left.

Prince Souvanna Phouma, neutralist premier of the coalition government, failed to get cooperation among the contending factions. Political assassinations and military and political coups harassed the government. The Pathet Lao and its North Vietnamese allies fought to extend and strengthen their control over Laotian territory. Their grip on the strategic corridor paralleling the Vietnamese border enabled them to protect the Ho Chi Minh Trail, the network of jungle trails over which North Vietnam sent men and arms to South Vietnam.

Souvanna Phouma sanctioned the bombing of the trail by United States planes. The Royal Laotian Air Force bombed the trail and Pathet Lao positions. The neutralist premier's position became stronger when a rightist coup failed in 1965.

In 1968 the Pathet Lao dislodged royalist troops from their last position on South Vietnam's frontier. By 1968 about one tenth of the Laotian people were refugees from areas held by the Pathet Lao. In 1969 and 1970 government and Pathet Lao military activity increased. In 1971 a South Vietnamese invasion into southern Laos failed to cut North Vietnamese supply routes along the Ho Chi Minh Trail. In 1973 the Laotian government and the Pathet Lao signed a peace pact setting up a coalition government.

In late 1975, after Communist victories in Vietnam and Kampuchea, the Pathet Lao took full control. With the proclamation of the Lao People's Democratic Republic, both the coalition regime and the monarchy were ended. (*See also* Vietnam War.)

Lao-Tzu, right, was depicted in a Taoist temple fresco in southern Shansi, China, during the Yuan dynasty.

LAO-TZU. In all the literature of China, the most translated work is a small book entitled 'Lao-Tzu', also called 'Tao-te Ching'. The book is the earliest document in the history of Taoism ("the Way"), one of the major philosophical-religious traditions that, along with Confucianism, has shaped Chinese life and thought for more than 2,000 years. It is a viewpoint that emphasizes individuality, freedom, simplicity, mysticism, and naturalness.

Some believe that only one man wrote the book, and he, too, is called Lao-tzu. If it is true that one man wrote the book, knowledge of him is so lost in the mists of ancient history that only legends remain. His earliest biographer, who wrote in about 100 BC, relates that Lao-tzu lived in the district of Hu in present-day Honan Province during the Chou Dynasty. Presumably he worked in astrology and divination at the court of the emperor. The biographer tells of a meeting of Lao-tzu with the younger Confucius, which would mean Lao-tzu lived about 500 BC. Another story says that he left China during the decline of the Chou Dynasty, and on his way west wrote the 'Tao-te Ching', after which he disappeared.

Scholars today believe that the book cannot have been written by one man. Some of the sayings in it may date from the time of Confucius, while others are from a later period. It is possible that the name Lao-tzu represents a type of scholar and wise man, rather than one individual.

LA PAZ, Bolivia. The highest government seat in the world is La Paz, Bolivia. It lies 11,800 feet (3,600 meters) above sea level in a deep gorge cut in the Altiplano (a high plain) by the Río de La Paz. Snowclad peaks of the Cordillera Real (Royal Range) on the

east give it a magnificent setting. Mount Illimani is 21,201 feet (6,462 meters) and looms above the city.

La Paz is Bolivia's administrative capital. Sucre is the judicial capital where the Supreme Court meets. A crossroads between the interior and the sea, La Paz is Bolivia's largest city and the center of industry, commerce, and culture. It is connected by rail and highways with Argentina, Brazil, and Chile.

Most travelers reach La Paz through El Alto Airport on the plateau. The tableland stops abruptly, and a long narrow canyon opens out. Its walls slope almost straight down to a green-floored valley, 4,000 feet (1,220 meters) below, where the city lies.

The main street is Avenida 16 de Julio, popularly known as the Prado. Along the Prado are modern hotels, shops, restaurants, and theaters. Here the people stroll in the evenings and on holidays, while the military band plays in a plaza at one end and the municipal band plays in a plaza at the other end. Indians, the women wearing shawls and odd derby hats, and an occasional llama train add color to the scene.

The Prado is part of a series of avenues, actually the same street but with different names, linked by plazas. Near Plaza Roma is the University of San Andres, housed in a 16-story skyscraper. On Plaza Tamayo is the national library. Across the Río de La

The Government palace in La Paz, Bolivia, stands on the Plaza Murillo in the heart of the city.

E. P. A., Inc./EB Inc.

Paz from the Prado is Plaza Murillo. On this broad square are the huge cathedral, the Presidential Palace, and the Legislative Palace. A few blocks away is the covered Central Market. Important cultural buildings are the National Museum of Art and the National Museum of Archaeology.

Textile manufacture is the chief industry. There are flour mills, breweries, and a match factory. Jewelry and wood carvings are made in home workshops.

The Spanish conquerors founded La Paz in 1548. The name (*paz* is Spanish for "peace") reflects the desire at the time to encourage trade along the route between the old Inca capital at Cuzco and the Potosí silver mines. When railroads were constructed they also converged on La Paz. (*See also* Bolivia.) Population (1982 estimate), 881,400.

LAPLACE, Pierre-Simon (1749–1827). One of the most brilliant astronomers in the history of the field was Pierre-Simon Laplace. This Frenchman predicted many things with mathematics that were to be seen later with powerful telescopes.

Laplace was born on March 23, 1749, in Beaumonten-Auge, a village in Normandy. His father was poor, and the boy could expect little education. Wealthy neighbors took an interest in him, however, and sent him to the university at Caen. There he did very well in mathematics. At 18 he went to Paris with a letter of introduction to Jean le Rond d'Alembert, a leading mathematician. D'Alembert refused to see him, so Laplace sent him an outline of mathematical principles. This deeply impressed d'Alembert, and he helped the young man get a position as professor of mathematics at the École Militaire.

One of Laplace's first investigations was to disprove that the moon would eventually crash into the Earth. From this work grew one of his great principles—that variations in the movements of planets are regular and predictable.

With the mathematician Joseph-Louis Lagrange, Laplace reviewed the studies made since Sir Isaac Newton's time on gravitational forces in the universe. Then he wrote 'Mécanique céleste' (Celestial Mechanics), issued in five volumes from 1799 to 1825. A condensed version contained his nebular hypothesis, a theory of the origin of the solar system (*see* Planets). Laplace won many awards for his studies and was made a marquis, but he remained modest, saying, "What we know is little. What we know not is immense." He died in Paris on March 5, 1827.

LAPLAND. The region called Lapland (Finnish, *Lapi* or *Lappi*; Swedish, *Lappland*) stretches across Arctic Norway, Sweden, Finland, and includes the Kola Peninsula of the Soviet Union. It is bounded by the Atlantic Ocean on the west and the Arctic Ocean on the north and east. The western part of Lapland contains high mountains that are deeply eroded into fjords and headlands in Norway. Across the border in Sweden, Lapland contains that country's highest peaks. From these peaks the land slopes downward to the east where in Finland and the Soviet Union it becomes low-lying and marshy tundra. All of Lapland is windy and has virtually no trees, but sheltered swamplands and river valleys support natural meadowland. Game birds are abundant and waterways are well stocked with fishes.

Native Lapps are citizens of the country in which they maintain permanent villages. The origin of the Lapps is uncertain—they may be descendants of one of the original Finnic tribes in the Baltic region or they may be descendants of immigrant Siberian tribes. In either case they were present north of the Gulf of Finland long before any of the other present-day Baltic peoples. The Lapp language belongs to the Finno-Ugric group of languages and is related to that of the Finns and Hungarians. Lapp has several distinctly different dialects, so that when speakers of different Lapp groups meet, they generally converse in Finnish, Swedish, or Norwegian. The Lapps' own name for themselves is *sabme*. They are one of Europe's smallest people, averaging only 4½ to 5 feet (137 to 152 centimeters) tall. Most Lapps are stocky, strong and agile, and fair-skinned and blue-eyed.

Nomadic reindeer herding is the traditional way of life for most Lapps. Although the wild reindeer herds have been largely domesticated, the people go wherever the animals can find lichens (reindeer moss) to eat. Reindeer provide the people with milk, cheese, and meat for food, and skins for tents, blankets, moccasins, leggings, and harnesses. From the sinews they make thread, cord, and braided lassos. Bones and antlers are carved into tools and household utensils. To foreigners they sell sinew, for use as surgical thread, and reindeer hair, for stuffing life belts.

When they are following the grazing herds, the Lapps live in a tent of skins stretched over poles. There is a smoke hole about 4 feet (1.2 meters) in di-

A family stands outside its reindeer-skin tent in Finnish Lapland. The hole at the top allows smoke to escape.

ameter in the center of the top. Dried reindeer meat and fish hang from overhead poles. The smoke from cooking fires helps cure and preserve these meats. Reindeer-drawn sleds, called *pulkas*, provide transportation over frozen rivers, lakes, and plains. Some Lapps use outboard motorboats for summer travel.

Traditional dress is colorful. Lapps wear bright blue pull-over tunics, decorated with red and yellow trim, and wide leather belts. The women don fringed shawls and gay red and blue bonnets. The men wear blue breeches and large four-cornered blue caps with red pompons. They use no stockings inside the reindeer-hide moccasins but pack fresh hay around their bare feet. Changed every day, the hay provides excellent insulation and absorbs perspiration.

Most of the Lapps today are only partially nomadic. The coast people for instance are largely engaged in fishing, farming, and livestock-raising. However, because of the short growing season, agriculture is limited. The chief crops are potatoes, barley, and rye. Lapps also work in iron ore mines and lumber and pulp mills. In the winter seminomadic Lapps live in permanent villages in cabins of hand-hewn logs. A wooden church, usually Lutheran, and a school are found in every village. Town meetings are held in which such problems as grazing and fishing rights are settled with the authorities of the country in which they live. Important towns include Tornios, Kemi, and Lulea, all seaports on the Gulf of Bothnia.

In the Swedish part of Lapland, tourism has become increasingly important. There are such attractions as the Sareks, Stora Sjöfallets, Peljekaise, and Muddus national parks. Abisko, Björkliden, and Riksgränsen are well-known winter sports resorts.

The Lapps number about 50,000. Some 30,000 of them live in Norway, about 17,000 in Sweden, and 2,500 in Finland. A few remain in the Soviet Union.

LARK. The lark is primarily a bird of the Old World. Only one species, the horned lark, is native to North America. The meadowlark and the titlark, sometimes called pipit, are not true larks (*see* Meadowlark; Titlark).

All larks are mostly brown streaked with dark brown or black. The breast is buff, yellow, or white, with dark streaks. The outer tail feathers are white. The horned lark has two black tufts on the top of the head and black patches on head, cheeks, and throat. Throat and eyestreaks may be yellow.

Larks nest on the ground in open fields and prairies. They rarely perch on trees. As they move over fields in search of grain and insects, they walk instead of hop. The male usually sings as he flys.

The larks form the family Alaudidae. The skylark (*Alauda arvensis*) is widely distributed across Europe and Asia. The bird has been introduced into the United States but has never established itself there. On Vancouver Island, in British Columbia, however, it has become a resident.

The horned lark (*Eremophila alpestris*) is also widely distributed. It ranges from Alaska and the Arctic coast of Canada to northern Europe and Asia and south to Egypt and Africa in the Eastern Hemisphere and to South America in the Western Hemisphere. The horned lark migrates south in winter from the more northern parts of its range.

LA ROCHEFOUCAULD, François de (1613–80).
The literary reputation of La Rochefoucauld rests on one book: 'Refléxions ou sentences et maximes morales', published in 1665. Generally called the 'Maximes', these moral reflections and maxims are a collection of cynical epigrams, or short sayings, about human nature—a nature that the author felt is dominated by self-interest. Typical of his point of view are the following sayings: "We seldom find such sensible men as those who agree with us"; "Virtues are lost in self-interest as rivers are lost in the sea"; "The surest way to be deceived is to think oneself cleverer than the others"; and "We always like those who admire us; we do not always like those whom we admire."

François de La Rochefoucauld was born to one of the noble families of France on Sept. 15, 1613, in Paris. His notions of human faults and foibles grew out of a life immersed in the political crises of his time. The public life of his family was conditioned by the attitude of the monarchy toward the nobility—sometimes flattering, sometimes threatening. Having served in the army periodically from 1629 to 1646, La Rochefoucauld became one of the prominent leaders in the civil war from 1648 to 1653. Wounded in 1649 and again in 1652, he finally retired from the struggle with extensive face and throat wounds and with his health ruined.

After convalescing, he settled in Paris where he became involved with a circle of brilliant and cultivated people who debated intellectual subjects of all kinds. As an exercise, they attempted to express their thoughts with the greatest brevity. In so doing they made great use of the epigram, or maxim, which creates surprise through the devices of exaggeration and paradox. La Rochefoucauld soon gained mastery of this device. The first edition of his 'Maximes' contains, in fact, some longer selections along with the epigrams. Altogether he authorized five editions of the book in his lifetime, the last appearing in 1678. Two years later, on March 17, 1680, he died in Paris.

LARVA. The word larva is applied to the young of certain animals that must undergo great physical changes before they become adults. A young frog hatches from the egg as a water-living tadpole and gradually becomes transformed into the air-breathing adult. A tadpole is therefore a larva. More than one larva are called larvae.

Many insects go through a larval stage. This is one way of meeting the difficulty all insects have in growing. The outer covering, or exoskeleton, of an adult insect is made of a tough substance called chitin that cannot stretch or grow bigger. The larvae of many insects, such as grasshoppers, have this skin and must shed, or molt, it several times while they are growing. Other insect larvae remain soft-skinned during the growing period, usually with altogether different shapes and habits from those they will have later on. Before they are ready for adult life, insect larvae pass through another stage, called the pupal stage, in which they get their more adult, hard outer skin. Insects that go through the four stages of egg, larva, pupa, and adult are said to have complete metamorphosis (*see* Insect).

Many insect larvae have special names. The larvae of beetles are grubs; of flies, maggots; of butterflies and moths, caterpillars.

The white grub (right) is the larva of the June bug. The larva (below) of a large African butterfly rests on a leaf.

(Right) D. Dwight Davis; (below) E. S. Ross

LA SALLE, Sieur de

(1643–1687). The father of the great Louisiana Territory was the French explorer René Robert Cavelier, sieur de La Salle. He was the first to voyage down the Mississippi River to the Gulf of Mexico. As a result of this exploration France laid claim to the entire Mississippi Valley under the name of Louisiana.

René Cavelier was born Nov. 22, 1643, at Rouen, France. The son of a rich merchant, he was educated by the Jesuits. When he was only 23 years old he sailed for Montreal, Canada, to seek his fortune. He got a grant of land at Lachine, near Montreal, from the Seminary of St. Sulpice, where his older brother was a priest. He was more interested, however, in Montreal's greatest activity, the fur trade, than he was in farming. Every spring Indians in hundreds of canoes, led by French agents called *coureurs de bois* (wood runners), came to trade bales of furs for trinkets, cloth, firearms, and brandy. For ten days or two weeks Montreal hummed with business and riotous celebrations. Then the Indians vanished into the West until the following year.

La Salle's First Explorations

Soon La Salle learned the Iroquoian language and several other Indian dialects. From the Indians he heard that south of the Great Lakes a broad river ran southwest to "the Vermilion Sea." La Salle thought that this sea might be the Gulf of California. If so, "the great river" would be a splendid

On April 9, 1682, La Salle gave the name Louisiana to the entire Mississippi Valley and claimed the territory for France.

route to China, and by discovering the route La Salle could become rich.

La Salle sold his land to finance an expedition in 1669–70. He ascended the St. Lawrence River to Lake Ontario. His men paddled along the southern shore until they came to the west end of the lake. The records of his exploration from here on were lost. Historians today cannot say where he went next. He may have made his way to a branch of the Ohio River and descended the Ohio as far as the rapids at Louisville, Ky. Upon his return he found Count Louis de Frontenac in power (*see* Frontenac).

A Grand Plan for an Inland Empire

In 1673 Louis Joliet and Father Jacques Marquette had explored the Mississippi far enough to prove that the river emptied into the Gulf of Mexico. Frontenac and La Salle at once proposed to build a chain of forts and trading posts along the Great Lakes and the Mississippi to hold the region and its fur trade for France. This protection was needed because the Iroquois Indians were trying to force the fur trade through New York into the hands of their allies, the Dutch and English traders at Albany.

Frontenac had made a start on this plan by building Fort Frontenac (1673), where the St. Lawrence flows out of Lake Ontario near Kingston. La Salle was to be made governor of the West and given a monopoly of trade in the region. In return, he was to build and maintain the needed forts. La Salle made two trips to France, in 1674 and 1677, before he received the monopoly and was given his title of *sieur* ("sir," in English).

In the winter of 1678–79 an advance party built a fort at the Niagara River and started to build a 40-ton ship, the *Griffon*. On Aug. 7, 1679, La Salle with his lieutenant, Henri de Tonti, started for Green Bay on the first voyage ever made by a ship on the Great Lakes.

Tonti was an able, bold adventurer who served La Salle faithfully in the New World. The Indians called him the "man with the iron hand." He had a metal claw at the end of one arm to replace a hand blown off in battle.

La Salle and Tonti reached Green Bay in September and sent the ship back laden with furs. In December 1679 they established Fort Miami on the southeastern shore of Lake Michigan. Then La Salle followed the route to Lake Peoria, shown on the map on the facing page. Here, early in 1680, he built Fort Crèvecoeur ("heartbreak"). From this fort he sent Father Louis Hennepin with two companions to explore the upper Mississippi (*see* Hennepin).

Leaving Tonti in charge of the new fort, La Salle made a fast trip back to Fort Frontenac, where he found out that the *Griffon* never had been heard from. On his return westward, he learned the Iroquois had ravaged the country. Fort Crèvecoeur was in ashes. Tonti and his men had vanished. La Salle traced him northward to Mackinac. The veteran had fought his way out through the Green Bay region.

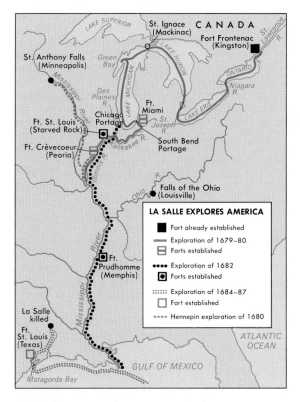

La Salle Explores America

- Fort already established
- ━━━ Exploration of 1679–80
- Forts established
- ●●●● Exploration of 1682
- Forts established
- ∷∷∷∷ Exploration of 1684–87
- Fort established
- ---- Hennepin exploration of 1680

Exploring the Mississippi in 1682

La Salle now spent a year organizing the Illinois Indians to resist the Iroquois. Early in 1682 the explorer followed the Illinois River and the Mississippi to the Gulf of Mexico. On April 9 he named the entire Mississippi Valley Louisiana and claimed it for France. Retracing his steps La Salle built Fort St. Louis at Starved Rock, Ill., as a rallying point for the Illinois Indians.

In 1683 he returned to civilization, to find that Frontenac had been recalled and his own rights canceled by the new governor. He went to France and persuaded Louis XIV to renew his rights and to help him procure four ships and about 400 men for a post at the mouth of the Mississippi.

The Final Disaster of 1684–87

This expedition by sea ruined La Salle. The naval commander, Beaujeu, who had charge of the ships, opposed him constantly. In the West Indies La Salle fell sick. Many men deserted. When the explorer set sail again with only about 180 men he lost his way. He had not known how to fix the longitude of the Mississippi's mouth at the time he had discovered it, in 1682. Now he could not choose the right opening from among the river's many bays and bayous. Finally he landed at Matagorda Bay, Tex., where Beaujeu left him with one small ship on March 12, 1685.

La Salle started to build a second Fort St. Louis (Texas) and scouted for the Mississippi. His ship was wrecked, and he lost all but 36 of his men. In January 1687 he took half the men on an overland trip to reach Tonti in Illinois. On March 19 in eastern Texas three of his men murdered him.

LAS CASAS, Bartolomé de (1474–1566). The first person to oppose the enslavement and oppression of the Indians by Spanish colonists in the Americas was Bartolomé de las Casas, a 16th-century missionary and theologian. As soon as they had settled in the West Indies, the Spaniards enslaved the Indians as laborers in the mines and on the plantations. Hard labor and brutal treatment, as well as disease, killed the Indians by the thousands.

Las Casas was born in August 1474, probably in Seville, Spain. By 1502 he was a lawyer, when his father, who had accompanied Columbus on his second voyage, sent him to Hispaniola (now the Dominican Republic) to manage a newly acquired estate. He soon began to teach the people Christianity, and in 1512 he became a priest—probably the first person ordained in the Americas. In 1515 he returned to Spain and presented to King Charles I a plan for the reformation of the Indies. Las Casas was appointed "protector of the Indians." In his zeal to aid the Indians, however, he advocated the use of black slaves from Africa—a decision he later much regretted.

Las Casas returned to Hispaniola in 1521. Disillusioned with the likelihood of reform, he joined the Dominican order and began to write his great work, 'The History of the Indies', which was published after his death. The last decades of his life were again taken up with enforcing better treatment for the Indians, an endeavor that met with opposition from the colonists. He retired to Spain in 1547 and died in Madrid on July 17, 1566.

Las Casas, an engraving by an unknown artist

Newberry Library

LASER AND MASER

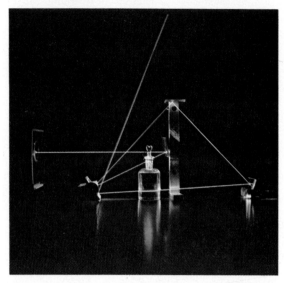

Orville Andrews

The thin beam of intense green light was produced by an argon laser. Smoke blown in the path of the light made it visible.

LASER AND MASER. The first men to land on the moon left a quartz reflector—the lunar laser reflector. Later, a beam of light was sent from earth all the way to the moon, where it bounced off the reflector and returned to earth. The instrument that produced this intense beam of light was a *laser* (from light amplification by stimulated emission of radiation).

Light emerges from a laser in a narrow beam that can be focused down to less than 0.001 inch in diameter. Such concentrated beams are so powerful that they are used to drill tiny holes in diamonds, taking minutes where old methods took days. Ultrathin wires are also made by pulling metal through these holes. Laser light can then be used to weld these tiny wires.

Laser beams are used in delicate eye surgery. A beam of light can be aimed through the pupil onto a detached retina, forming a tiny scar that "welds" the retina back in place. No incision is made in the eye.

Lasers mark a straight line with extreme accuracy. A laser beam guided the construction of the linear accelerator at Stanford University, in Stanford, Calif., and is still used to signal when parts of the two-mile-long accelerator move out of line.

Laser light has several features that are significantly different from white light. To begin with, light from most sources spreads out as it travels, so that much less light hits a given area as the distance from the light source increases (*see* Light). Laser light travels as a parallel beam and spreads very little.

Furthermore, laser light is *monochromatic* and *coherent*. White light is a jumble of colored light waves (*see* Light; Color). Each color has a different wavelength. If all the wavelengths but one are filtered out, the remaining light is monochromatic. If these waves are all parallel to one another, they are also *coherent:*

the waves travel in a definite phase relationship with one another. In the case of laser light, the wave crests coincide and the troughs coincide. The waves all reinforce one another. One special application of coherent light is the recording of three-dimensional images called holograms (*see* Color).

The laser uses a process called *stimulated emission* to amplify light waves. (One method of amplification of an electromagnetic beam is to produce additional waves that travel in step with that beam.) A substance normally gives off light by *spontaneous emission*. One of the electrons of an atom absorbs energy. While it possesses this energy, the atom is in an *excited state*. If the electron gives off this excess energy (in the form of electromagnetic radiation such as light) with no outside impetus, spontaneous emission has occurred.

If a wave emitted by one excited atom strikes another excited atom, it stimulates the second atom to emit energy in the form of a second wave that travels parallel to and in step with the first wave. This *stimulated emission* results in amplification of the first wave. If the two waves strike other excited atoms, a large coherent beam builds up. But if they strike unexcited atoms, they are absorbed, and the amplification is lost. In normal matter on earth,

The diagrams below show the structure and workings of a ruby laser. Light from the flash tube excites the chromium atoms in ruby. When an atom emits a light wave, it may hit a second excited atom, stimulating emission of a second wave. The beam grows stronger and bursts out of the cylinder.

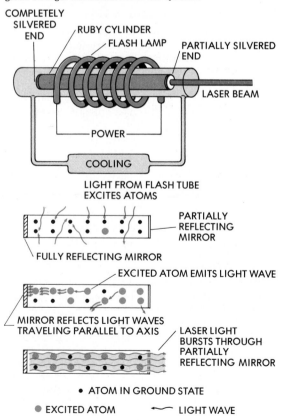

54

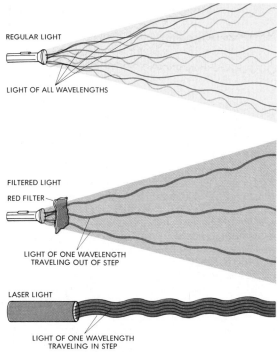

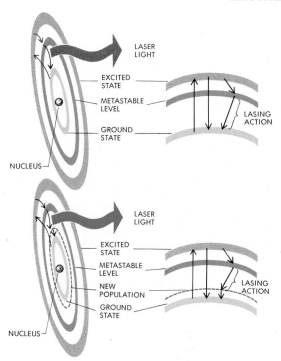

White light contains many wavelengths of light. A filter transmits light of one wavelength (monochromatic light) but weakens the original beam. Lasers produce light that is monochromatic and coherent (traveling in step).

When atoms in a ruby laser (top) emit light, they return to the ground state, where they can absorb light. In the helium-neon laser (bottom) atoms form a new population at a lower excited level that does not absorb the laser light.

the great majority of atoms are not excited. As more than the usual number of atoms become excited, the probability increases that stimulated emission rather than absorption will take place.

The first laser, constructed in 1960 by T. H. Maiman, contained a synthetic ruby shaped like a cylinder, with a completely reflecting silver layer on one end and a thin, partially reflecting silver layer on the other. Ruby is composed of aluminum oxide with chromium impurities. The chromium atoms absorb blue light and become excited; they then drop first to a metastable level and finally to the ground (unexcited) state, giving off red light.

Light from a flash lamp enters the ruby and excites most of the chromium atoms, many of which fall quickly to the metastable state. Some atoms then emit red light and return to the ground state. The light waves strike other excited chromium atoms, stimulating them to emit more red light. The beam bounces back and forth between the silvered ends until it gains enough energy to burst through the partially silvered end as laser light. When most of the chromium atoms are back in the ground state, they absorb light, and the lasing action stops. In continuous-wave lasers, such as the helium-neon laser, electrons emit light by jumping to a lower excited state, forming a new atomic population that does not absorb laser light, rather than to the ground state.

The principle of stimulated emission was first successfully applied in 1954 when Charles Townes constructed the *maser* (microwave amplification by stim-

ulated emission of radiation). Townes bombarded excited ammonia molecules with microwaves. The ammonia molecules were in a box that vibrated at the same wave frequency as the microwaves, so the waves bounced back and forth, causing the ammonia molecules to emit more microwaves, until an amplified microwave pulse was emitted. The stable and accurate ammonia maser amplifies microwave signals from radio stars and in satellite communications.

BIBLIOGRAPHY FOR LASER AND MASER

Burroughs, William. Lasers (Watts, 1982).
Goldman, Leon. Applications of the Laser (Krieger, 1982).
Klein, H. A. Masers and Lasers (Harper, 1963).
Maurer, Allan. Lasers: the Light Wand of the Future (Arco, 1982).
Orton, D. H. and others. The Solid State Maser (Pergamon, 1970).

LASSALLE, Ferdinand (1825–64). One of the chief 19th-century theorists of socialism and a founder of the German labor movement was Ferdinand Lassalle. In contrast to the revolutionary theories of Karl Marx, Lassalle believed in a legal and evolutionary approach to political change, particularly through the introduction of allowing all citizens to vote. (*See also* Marx; Socialism.)

Ferdinand Lassalle was born on April 11, 1825, in Breslau (now Wroclaw), Poland. He attended universities at Breslau, Berlin, and Paris. While in Paris he met the French socialist Pierre-Joseph Proudhon.

From 1848 to 1857 Lassalle lived in Düsseldorf, where he took part in the abortive revolution of 1848 to establish a constitutional monarchy that would

Ferdinand Lassalle in about 1860

foster civil rights. It was there that he first came in contact with Marx and Friedrich Engels, the leading proponents of Communism. One of the few radical leaders who did not leave the country to escape persecution during the revolution, Lassalle remained in Germany after the revolution's failure. Although he was repeatedly arrested, indicted, and imprisoned for his ideas, Lassalle counted his years in Düsseldorf—where he was active both as a writer and a labor organizer—among the happiest of his life.

In 1859 he settled in Berlin where, as a political journalist, he tried to persuade workers' associations to organize into a general federation to promote voting rights at all levels of society. He hoped, by integrating the working class into political and social life, to achieve a transition from a bourgeois state based on private property to a democratic constitutional state. When the General German Workers' Association was founded in 1863, he became its president.

Rejected because of his authoritarian leadership and disappointed by his political failures, Lassalle traveled to Switzerland in 1864. There he fell in love with a woman who was already engaged. On August 28 he was wounded in a duel with her fiancé, and three days later he died in Geneva.

LAS VEGAS, Nev. A year-round desert resort, Las Vegas is known primarily for its luxury hotels, gambling casinos, and nightclub entertainment. The main business of the city is tourism, which contributes more income to the state of Nevada than agriculture, manufacturing, and mining combined. The city, located in the southeastern part of the state, is also the hub of a commercial and mining area.

The chief tourist attraction is gambling, which is legal in Nevada. The major casinos are at the downtown Casino Center and on the Strip, a stretch of highway leading into the city. The casinos, many of which are within the luxury hotels, operate 24 hours a day. At night their brilliant, multicolored signs light up not only the streets, but also the desert sky.

With its focus on gambling and entertainment, Las Vegas has become a major convention center. In the city is the largest single-level convention hall in the United States. Las Vegas also now attracts major sporting events that range from golf and tennis to bowling and boxing. Nearby are popular tourist sites, including Hoover Dam and Lake Mead Recreational Area, Cedar Breaks National Monument, and Death Valley National Monument. Adjacent to the suburb of North Las Vegas is Nellis Air Force Base, and 60 miles (100 kilometers) to the northwest lies Indian Springs Gunnery Range. The city also has a branch of the University of Nevada.

Mormons from Utah were the region's first settlers, sent in 1855 by Brigham Young to build a fort. They were attracted by the artesian springs in the arid valley along the Old Spanish Trail. From the landscape came the name Las Vegas, meaning "the meadows." The Mormons abandoned the site in 1857, and the United States Army built Fort Baker there in 1864. With the coming of the San Pedro, Los Angeles, and Salt Lake Railroad in 1905, Las Vegas became a railroad town. In 1911 Las Vegas became a city and grew as an agricultural center. Its growth was further stimulated by legalized gambling, begun in 1931, and by construction in the 1930s of the Hoover Dam. After World War II large financial investments in the city rapidly increased its development. (*See also* Nevada.) Population (1980), 164,674.

LATIMER, Hugh (1485?–1555). One of the chief promoters of the Protestant Reformation in England during the 16th century was a priest named Hugh Latimer. He lived during the reigns of Henry VIII, when the Reformation began; Edward VI, when Protestantism gained a strong foothold; and Queen Mary Tudor, when Catholicism was reinstated in England. During Mary's reign, Latimer was burned at the stake for his anti-Catholic preaching.

Hugh Latimer was born about 1485 at Thurcaston. The son of a wealthy farmer, he attended Cambridge University and was ordained a priest around 1510. For about 20 years he remained at Cambridge, where he gained a reputation as a fine preacher. In the mid-1520s, contacts with a group of university clergy who had been influenced by Martin Luther's theological revolution in Germany converted him to Protestantism. His support for Henry VIII's efforts to gain an annulment of his marriage brought Latimer to the attention of the king and other powerful figures. In 1535 he was named bishop of Worcester, but a temporary reaction in favor of Catholic doctrine forced him to resign in 1539. For a time he was imprisoned in the Tower of London for his views.

When Edward VI came to the throne in 1547, Latimer was released from prison and regained his popular following through his preaching. When Mary Tudor became queen in 1553, Catholicism was restored as the state church and Latimer was arrested. He was burned at the stake in Oxford on Oct. 16, 1555. (*See also* Anglican Communion.)

Victor Englebert

On a high Ecuadorian plain, a cowboy herds cattle in view of the Andes Mountains, the major range of Latin America.

LATIN AMERICA

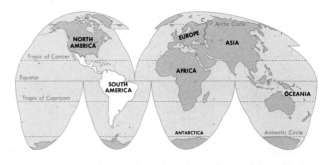

LATIN AMERICA. The region of Latin America is made up of South America, Mexico, Central America, and the West Indies. Within this region are 33 independent nations and several colonies, plus other political units that have special ties with the United States, Great Britain, France, or The Netherlands.

Spanish and Portuguese colonies in Central and South America became independent during the first half of the 19th century. Haiti, the first Latin American country to win independence, gained its freedom from France in 1804. In the West Indies the Spanish-American War in 1898 freed Cuba and Puerto Rico from Spanish rule. Since World War II, Great Brit-

This article was contributed by Oscar H. Horst, Professor and past Chairman, Department of Geography, Western Michigan University.

ain and The Netherlands have granted independence to a number of colonies.

Latin America, one of the world's three major developing regions, is making rapid economic progress. Foreign investments in mining and manufacturing have greatly stimulated development. The region is a major world supplier of tropical agricultural commodities, such as coffee, sugar, and bananas. Wheat, soybeans, wool, and meat come from its cooler temperate regions. Rich deposits of important minerals are found throughout Latin America. The United States depends heavily on Mexico and Venezuela for much of its supply of petroleum.

The people of Latin America reflect a degree of ethnic blending that is unmatched in any other region. Intermarriage among Indians, whites, and blacks has created large populations of mestizos and mulattos. Traditions inherited from Indians, black

57

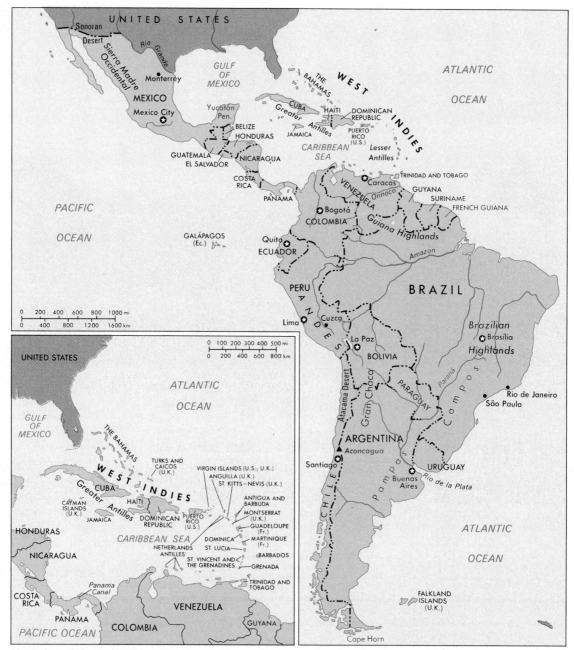

Physical map of Latin America

slaves, and white immigrants have contributed to a rich regional culture. Music, arts and crafts, foods, religion, architecture, and language all reflect the contributions of American, African, and European heritage. (*See also* Central America; South America; West Indies; and articles on the individual places and physical features of Latin America.)

The Land

Nearly 250 million years ago, giant plates of the Earth's crust broke apart from the ancient landmass of Gondwanaland. Those that drifted westward serve as platforms upon which the Latin American mainland rests today, and the landscape bears the imprint of that historic geologic event.

This breaking up and drifting produced physical results in South America different from those of the Caribbean Basin to the north. The continent of South America consists of three major landforms. The plateaus of Guiana and Brazil lie to the east. The Andes Mountains rise along the shoreline of the Pacific Ocean. Sandwiched between are the interior

plains of South America, which extend from the llanos, or tropical grasslands, of Venezuela and Colombia, across the upper basin of the Amazon River, and into the pampas, or grassy plains, of Argentina.

The highlands of Guiana and Brazil, separated by the Amazon Basin, rise abruptly from the Atlantic Ocean and crest a short distance inland. From the crest, these ancient geologic surfaces slope gradually westward and finally plunge beneath the sediments of the interior plains. This old upland surface is composed of broad rolling tablelands and stubs of old, greatly eroded mountain ranges. Many rivers plunge off the tablelands in majestic falls and, because drainage flows largely to the interior of the continent, streams tend to take indirect routes to the sea. The crystalline mass that composes these uplands is rich in mineral resources, except for hydrocarbons, such as coal, natural gas, and oil. With the exception of the Paraná Plateau in southern Brazil, the soils tend to be of limited value for crop raising.

The Andes are on the leading edge of the South American plate. This massive mountain system and a parallel offshore oceanic trench resulted from the collision between the westward-moving South American plate and the eastward-drifting Nazca plate. This geologic action produced the Earth's highest continuous mountain barrier. Throughout their 5,500-mile (8,900-kilometer) length, the Andes have many peaks more than 20,000 feet (6,000 meters) high. Travel across the Andes is difficult because there are few low passes. From Peru southward, the Andes are particularly rich in mineral resources. The range area within the tropics has long been important for settlement. However, earthquakes and volcanic eruptions occur throughout the mountains.

The interior plains of South America are highly isolated. They are separated from the Pacific on the west by the Andes, and from the Atlantic to the east by the broad, rough terrain of the Guiana and Brazilian plateaus. Seasonal rainfall converts the dry, sunbaked plains into seemingly endless swamps. The vast size of the upper tributaries of the Amazon makes it difficult to build bridges across them.

Major oil and natural gas fields lie beneath the interior plains of South America that border the Andes. Because of isolation, adverse climate, and drainage problems, these plains are sparsely populated. Only the more temperate and accessible southern areas of the Gran Chaco and Pampas have been settled significantly.

The Middle American portion of Latin America—Mexico, Central America, and the West Indies—has many landforms characteristic of intercontinental regions. It is fragmented into countless cays, rocks, islands, and peninsulas. During the 20th century,

Unusual sand formations of the Peruvian coastal desert mesh with irrigated fields (right, top). A stand of Paraná pines breaks the flat plain of Minas Gerais state in Brazil. A Peruvian villager unloads potatoes from llamas, a native animal of Latin America. Flood waters of the Amazon engulf a forest along the river's edge (right).

(Second from top) Chip & Rosa Maria Peterson; (others) Victor Englebert

tens of thousands of people have been killed in earthquakes and volcanic eruptions in the West Indies, Central America, and Mexico. Rugged terrain dominates this region of Latin America. There is little lowland except on the Yucatán Peninsula and that extending from the islands of the Greater Antilles.

Areas created by the upthrust of volcanoes in Mexico and Central America provide major regions for human settlement and economic activity. Sugar, produced on the volcanic slopes of the Lesser Antilles and on the limestone platforms of the Greater Antilles, has dominated the socioeconomic history of the West Indies since the middle of the 17th century.

Climate and Vegetation

Between the North and South poles, there is a series of wet and dry belts that ring the Earth parallel to the equator. They are separated by bands of the Earth that are seasonally wet or dry. This seasonal pattern is produced by the north-south shift of wind and pressure belts between the tropics of Cancer and Capricorn. Latin America extends about 6,000 miles (9,700 kilometers) from north to south, so it crosses a number of climates that, in turn, results in a variety of vegetation and soils.

The Amazon Basin of South America lies astride the equator. Heavy rainfall occurs here throughout the year, creating the selva, one of the world's great tropical rain forests. This region supports rich forest growth, but the soil has limited value for agriculture. The attempt of the Brazilian government to open the Amazon Basin for development has led to widespread controversy. Some scientists fear the effects of such action on the physical environment and on the Indian tribes of the region.

About 500 miles (800 kilometers) north and south of the equator, rainfall becomes seasonal. North of the equator, a rainy season during the period between May and October, dominates every area except northern Mexico. West Indian hurricanes occur frequently during this season.

South of the equator, a rainy season prevails from November to April across the highlands of central Brazil and into Bolivia. Because of the long periods without rainfall in these regions, tropical forests give way to tropical grasslands and low scrub forests. To the north, in Venezuela and Colombia, this feature is illustrated by the tropical grasslands known as the llanos. In central Brazil, extensive grasslands are called the campos. The *campo cerrado* and *caatinga* of northeastern Brazil are extensive grassland regions with scattered, open scrub and thorn forests. Palms may dominate locally in either savanna or scrub forests. Ranching and farming are carried on in these areas, but the uncertain rainfall is a constant threat. Periodic droughts in northeastern Brazil have resulted in great hardship on the people there.

The savannas and scrub forests of Latin America give way, in turn, to the Sonoran Desert of northern Mexico, the Atacama Desert of Chile, and the interior deserts of Bolivia and Argentina. The coastal desert of Peru extends unusually far north because of the influence of the cold Peru, or Humboldt, Current.

Along the Pacific shoreline south of the Atacama Desert, increasing rainfall results in scrub forests in central Chile and rain forests in southern Chile. The Mediterranean climate of central Chile has encouraged the production of grapes, citrus fruits, and olives since early colonial times.

High elevations in the Andes produce cooler weather than might be expected in the tropics. Temperatures average 77° F (25° C) at sea level along the equator, but Quito, Ecuador, which lies 9,200 feet (2,800 meters) above sea level, has an average temperature of 55° F (13° C). The cool temperatures enable farmers to produce grains, fruits, and vegetables that are normally grown in temperate climates.

Animal Life

The Indians who inhabited the New World when the Spanish and Portuguese first arrived had no knowledge of European domesticated animals, such as horses, mules, cattle, sheep, pigs, and chickens. There was no herding of animals, and except for the llama, in the central Andes, there were no animals to carry burdens or pull plows. Many European species of wild animals did not live in the New World. Instead, the Spaniards encountered anteaters and sloths, and monkeys that swung by their tails. There were opossums, vampire bats, and large rodents. The Europeans also came upon species of reptiles, fishes, and birds that they had never seen before, such as iguanas, electric eels, rattlesnakes, large-billed toucans, and giant Andean condors. Some mammals, including tapirs and jaguars, tended to be smaller than those of the Old World. Great herds of animals were unknown in Latin America, except for the bison.

Since the arrival of the Europeans, the rapid depletion of tropical forests and the deterioration of other natural habitats have reduced the range of many animals. Some are now classified as endangered species. National parks have been established to preserve native habitats, but the relentless population growth continues to threaten animal life.

The People

Origins. When Europeans first came to Latin America, no other region of its size was inhabited by people who resembled one another so widely. The native Indians appear to have been of Mongoloid origin, which strongly indicates that they crossed into the Americas from northeastern Asia by way of a land bridge across the Bering Strait. Small bands of Indians wandered south for thousands of years in search of food. Some of them reached Tierra del Fuego, a group of islands off the southern tip of South America, about 8,000 years ago.

In Latin America, the evolution of agriculture and the rise of advanced Indian civilizations started in two major areas. The Inca empire arose in the central Andean highlands, and the Chibcha empire developed in Colombia. Two other empires, those of the

(Top) Milt & Joan Mann; (above) Oscar H. Horst

Distinctive styles of housing and dress have developed in various parts of Latin America. Houses in an Andean village of Bolivia are insulated by thatched roofs (top). Gaily dressed women shop for vegetables at a Guatemalan market (above).

Aztec and Maya, evolved in the region of central Mexico and northern Central America. Ruins at Cuzco in Peru, Chichén-Itzá on the Yucatán Peninsula, and Tenochtitlán in central Mexico testify to the achievements of these civilizations.

Racial and language groups. Because of the relatively recent arrival of human beings in the New World, and the small area from which they came, racial distinctions between Indian groups are not as evident as might be expected. Nevertheless, a large number of native groups evolved that spoke a variety of languages and dialects. Today, most of the people of Latin America speak Spanish or Portuguese, and a smaller number speak English, French, or Dutch. Spanish is the official language of most Latin American nations, and Portuguese is the state tongue of Brazil, the largest country.

Between 20 and 25 million Indians in Latin America continue to speak in their native tongues. The main language groups remaining today include the Quechua and Aymara of Peru and Bolivia, the Chibcha of Colombia, the Mam and Quiché of Guatemala, the Nahuatl of central Mexico, and the Maya of the Yucatán. Increasing contacts with civilization and exposure to the modern world are causing a gradual decline in the use of Indian languages. In the areas occupied by Indians, children are encouraged to attend classes in the national language of their country to prepare them for elementary school.

Ethnic groups. At the time of the Europeans' arrival in the New World in 1492, from 60 to 75 million people lived in Latin America. Most of them inhabited the highlands of the central Andes and the region between northern Central America and central Mexico. These were areas under the control of the Inca, Maya, and Aztec. (*See also* Aztecs; Incas; Mayas.)

Within 50 years after the arrival of the Europeans, more than half the Indians had perished. Within a century, no more than a fourth remained. The disappearance of the native population has often been attributed to cruel treatment by the Spaniards. However, the introduction of such European diseases as smallpox and measles, against which the Indians had no natural immunity, had an equal effect.

To provide a supply of labor in places uninhabited by Indians, the Portuguese and, to a lesser degree, the Spaniards imported African slaves. After 1650, settlers from the colonizing nations of northern Europe transported slaves into the territories they had seized from the Spaniards in the West Indies. During the three centuries prior to 1850, as many as 14 million slaves may have been introduced into Latin America, compared with about 500,000 brought into the United States. In Latin America, most of the slaves were taken to northeastern Brazil and the islands of the Caribbean, where they worked on sugar plantations.

The slave trade ended during the early decades of the 19th century. Thereafter, the need for labor was satisfied by the immigration of about 8 million Europeans into southern Brazil and nearby Argentina and Uruguay. Europeans migrating to Latin America during the 100 years following 1850 exceeded by 15 times the number that arrived in the 300 years prior to that date. Beginning in the mid-1800s, the new arrivals became involved primarily in the production of coffee, grains, wool, and meat, all destined for the markets of northwestern Europe.

Today, Indian and mixed Indian and white populations tend to be concentrated in tropical highlands of South America, Central America, and Mexico. Large numbers of blacks and mulattos live in northeastern Brazil, the West Indies, and the tropical lowlands around the Caribbean Sea. The temperate lands of southern South America serve as the homeland of European peoples who are primarily of Portuguese, Spanish, or Italian origin.

Throughout Latin America, language, religion, architectural forms, education, and many other aspects of life reflect European culture. However, Indian and African traditions are strongly represented in regions where Indians and blacks prevail. Arts and crafts, behavior patterns, forms of music, types of food, methods of farming, and other ways of life represent elements of Indian and black heritage that add to the diversity of Latin American society.

Population characteristics. The population of Latin America increased slowly during the period be-

61

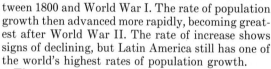

(Top left) Oscar H. Horst; (above and left) Victor Englebert

Latin America displays Indian and colonial heritages. Pyramids at Teotihuacán, Mexico, are remains of an ancient Indian culture (top left). Women in striking Indian costumes accompany a Christian religious procession in Lima, Peru (left). A Lima building reflects the style of the Spanish colonial period (above).

tween 1800 and World War I. The rate of population growth then advanced more rapidly, becoming greatest after World War II. The rate of increase shows signs of declining, but Latin America still has one of the world's highest rates of population growth.

The 1980 population of Latin America was estimated at about 368 million, of which about a third lives in Brazil. Another third lives in other parts of South America, and the remainder dwells in Mexico, Central America, and the West Indies.

Most Latin American population centers are near the sea. In 1960, in an effort to attract people into the thinly inhabited interior of Brazil, the government moved the capital from Rio de Janeiro to Brasília, 600 miles (960 kilometers) from the Atlantic coast.

The rapid population increase in Latin America has led to an unprecedented growth of cities and fewer opportunities for employment. Limited resources make it extremely difficult for governments to provide adequate housing and services for the new arrivals, many of whom live in the slums that ring most of the larger cities. Another result of the population explosion has been the large number of adolescents who have difficulty finding employment as they reach working age.

Religion

The European conquerors of Latin America were Roman Catholics, and Catholicism is the dominant religion throughout the region today. About 90 percent of all Latin Americans belong to the Catholic church. The Indians, though they are formally classified by the church as Catholics, have integrated many of their pagan tribal practices and traditional beliefs into the Catholic faith. This is also true of the blacks, who are considered Catholics although they may observe voodoo rituals of African origin. Protestantism is established wherever the British or Dutch have had long-standing control. Since the early 1960s, Protestant missionaries have attracted many converts, especially among middle- and lower-class Central Americans. In Guyana, Suriname, and Trinidad and Tobago, numerous mosques reflect the presence of Muslims from southeastern Asia.

Art and Literature

Since the time of European conquest in Latin America, the development of various forms of art and literature has shown the influence of Indian heritage and of African and European contributions. During the 20th century, Latin Americans have started to break away from foreign influences and to pioneer distinct types of art and literature.

The Indians were renowned for their work in gold and silver, the creation of artistic objects of clay, and weaving intricate designs in cotton textiles. The Spaniards marveled at the natives' accomplishments in architecture and the use of decorative motifs in elaborate Indian palaces and temples.

Throughout the colonial period, European artistic influences began to appear in Latin America. Gothic churches were decorated with Biblical paintings in

62

the Italian tradition. Public buildings and private homes were constructed in Spanish and Portuguese styles. Music of Iberian origin was performed on instruments brought from Europe. The foot loom and the wheel, introduced by the Spaniards, provided new techniques for weaving cloth and working clay and thus modernized native craft techniques.

The arrival of blacks in northeastern Brazil and the Caribbean brought new musical forms that were later expressed in such dances as the rumba, samba, and tango. Wood carvings produced by Haitian artists also originated in African tradition.

In the 20th century the Mexican Revolution gave birth to the *corrido,* a form of protest music. Mural art depicting historic events also arose. During the 1930s, the Mexican painter Diego Rivera was in great demand in the United States, where his murals may be seen in art museums. The mural art form was expanded to other mediums and is perhaps best represented in tile mosaics as part of an innovative architectural style incorporated in buildings of the National University in Mexico City. Original styles of architecture appear in buildings in Rio de Janeiro and Brasília designed by Oscar Niemeyer.

The famous poem 'Martín Fierro', by José Hernández of Argentina, was published in 1897. In this poem he describes the life of the gauchos, or cowboys, on the pampas of his country. Breaking with foreign influence, it set the stage for literature depicting Latin American scenes and moods. Euclides da Cunha's account of life in northeastern Brazil and the works of Mariano Azuela and Martín Luis Guzmán about the Mexican Revolution are recognized as classic pieces of literature. The poets Gabriela Mistral and Pablo Neruda of Chile and the Guatemalan novelist Miguel Asturias have been awarded Nobel prizes in literature. (*See also* Latin American Literature.)

In architecture, art, music, literature, and film, Latin American influence is increasing on the world scene. Indian arts and crafts have also gained recognition abroad and among the growing number of tourists who visit Latin America.

Education and Health

Latin America has relatively high literacy levels and health standards except in tropical highlands inhabited chiefly by Indians and tropical lowlands where blacks and mulattos make up a major part of the population. These physical regions are in such places as Haiti, Bolivia, Guatemala, and northeastern Brazil. People who live in industrial urbanized regions of southern South America or in central Mexico have higher literacy and health standards.

In the past, educational systems throughout Latin America were highly influenced by European traditions. For example, educators emphasized the training of young men for careers in law or medicine. Today there are increasing efforts to broaden the base of education. All Latin American nations claim to provide at least a sixth-grade education, but many children still do not go to school.

The growth of industry and cities has brought about the expansion of universities and has greatly increased enrollments. Many young people study abroad, especially in the United States, to gain expertise for solving problems at home.

The health of Latin Americans has improved significantly since World War II, particularly in the tropics. Death rates have declined dramatically, partly in response to assistance provided by foreign governments and private and international relief agencies. However, infants remain particularly vulnerable to a variety of diseases that have been largely controlled elsewhere in the world. Malnutrition and a lack of medical facilities also contribute to a rate of infant mortality that is two to four times that of the United States, United Kingdom, Japan, or the nations of continental Europe.

Dysentery and diarrhea are major causes of death in nearly all tropical nations. Widespread poverty in these areas and a lack of doctors, nurses, and medical facilities contribute to higher rates of mortality. On the other hand, deaths attributed to food shortages occur less frequently in Latin America than in other regions of the Third World.

Economics

Although Latin America is a developing region, it has advanced further economically than has either Africa or Asia. It is more highly urbanized and industrialized, and the well-being of its people, as measured by the per capita distribution of the gross national product, is far greater than that existing in other developing areas.

Most of the nations of Latin America depend highly on income earned from exports. Until about 1960, nearly all these countries relied on the export of only one or two products for most of their foreign income. For example, coffee was the product for Brazil, Colombia, El Salvador, and Guatemala; bananas for Panama and Honduras; sugar for Cuba, Jamaica, and the Dominican Republic; tin for Bolivia; and

School girls in Colombia play a circle game at recess. Free elementary education is available to most Latin Americans.

Chip & Rosa Maria Peterson

63

copper for Chile. Today, there is a far greater balance in the export trade of these nations. During the 1970s and early 1980s, Mexico and Brazil made the most rapid strides toward industrialization, especially in the diversification of their export trade. Manufactured products now make up more than a fourth of their sales abroad. Both nations have become exporters of automobiles, and Brazil now exports aluminum and iron and steel products to the United States.

Since 1973, sharp increases in the price of petroleum have slowed economic progress in Latin America, particularly among the oil-poor nations. In the early 1980s, the unstable price of petroleum, and a worldwide recession, created financial crises even in the oil-rich nations of Venezuela and Mexico.

Agriculture. Although agriculture is declining rapidly in relative importance as an economic activity in Latin America, it continues to be the leading source of employment. Exports consist primarily of farm products, except in Brazil, Mexico, and a few mineral-rich nations. However, inefficient agricultural production and the rapid population growth have made the import of foodstuffs increasingly necessary.

In many parts of Latin America, most farmers still use traditional agricultural systems of pre-Columbian and African origin. Corn, beans, and squash are primary staples in Central America and Mexico. In the Andes, these products, as well as potatoes and lesser-known grains and tubers, are the mainstays of the rural population. In the tropical lowlands, cassava, yams, and other root crops also play a significant role in the diet. More recently, plantains and rice have become important for people living in tropical areas. Peasant farmers grow some specialty crops for local urban markets, but these people produce very little food for export.

Throughout Latin America, governments have introduced programs to reform patterns of land ownership and increase agricultural production. Most of these plans have failed to ease the plight of the rural poor or to increase the supply of food required for rapidly growing populations.

Sugar was one of the early agricultural exports from Latin America. Sugar production became a major enterprise during the 17th century and strength-ened the role of slavery in Brazil and the West Indies. In the mid-1800s, native and European laborers were drawn into coffee production in Brazil, Colombia, and Central America. Expanding commercial output followed with a number of major export products, including meat, wool, and grains in Argentina; bananas in Central America; and cotton in Peru, Mexico, and Brazil. More recently, soybeans and sorghums became important in Brazil and Mexico.

Through the centuries, income from the export of a succession of agricultural products has supported the economic development of Latin American nations. However, governments have become increasingly aware of the need to diversify exports and, where possible, to convert raw commodities into finished products. Such products include meal and oil made from fish and soybeans, fabrics and finished clothing manufactured from raw wool and cotton, and instant and freeze-dried coffee produced from coffee beans.

The explosive growth of Latin American cities and improvements in the economic well-being of their inhabitants are changing the people's diets. In future years, these changes will probably be reflected by decreasing demands for the types of commodities traditionally produced and consumed by peasant farmers, and by increasing reliance on fruits, vegetables, meat, and dairy products. The dietary change is expected to lead to a transition from traditional peasant agriculture to the practice of modern farming methods and animal husbandry.

Forestry and fishing. About 80 percent of Latin America lies within the tropics, and the rain forests of this area serve as the major source of wood products. Brazil and Colombia produce about 70 percent of the lumber from the forests. Only a few high-value species, such as mahogany, are exported. The Paraná pine forests in southern Brazil provide about half of Latin America's coniferous lumber production.

The exploitation of forests for charcoal and firewood and the clearing of land for agriculture have destroyed the vegetative cover over large areas. This condition has led to extensive soil erosion, which has become a major concern in Latin America.

The richest fishing grounds of Latin America lie along the Pacific shoreline. Peru is a leading producer of fish and seafood products, and these items rank among the ten chief Latin American exports. Occasionally a warm current off the coast of Peru greatly reduces the fish catch. Large supplies of shrimp from the coastal waters of Mexico and Central America are shipped to the United States.

The desire of Latin American nations to guard their fishing rights led to the establishment of a 200-mile (320-kilometer) offshore limit within which they claim sole rights. This action has created considerable controversy, with Peru, Ecuador, and Mexico opposing the United States and other nations whose fishing fleets come to Latin American waters.

Mining. Mining is a minor source of employment in Latin America, but it has long been an important source of income for many nations. In colonial times,

Peruvian workers shovel fishes into baskets for loading onto refrigerated trucks. Fish is a major Latin American export.
Victor Englebert

Mining has been important to Latin American economies since colonial times. Miners in Bolivia work at different levels to extract tin (right), the most important mineral mined in that country. Densely grouped oil rigs protrude above the surface of Lake Maracaibo in Venezuela (far right). Petroleum products are the leading export of Latin America.

(Right) Victor Englebert; (far right) Milt & Joan Mann

gold and silver from Mexico, Bolivia, Brazil, and Peru were vitally important to Spain and Portugal.

Since independence, the export of other minerals has far exceeded the value of precious metal exported from Latin America. Copper from Chile; tin from Bolivia; and copper, zinc, and lead from Peru have made the southern Andes one of the world's richest sources of minerals. Mexico also produces these minerals, but the country is increasingly converting them into finished products.

The opening of Brazil's interior during the 1960s and 1970s led to large-scale mining of iron ore and of bauxite, from which aluminum is made. The Guianas, Venezuela, and Jamaica are also important world suppliers of bauxite.

Minerals occur largely in the eastern plateaus and in the Andes, and oil and natural gas tend to be found beneath the interior plains of South America. Every nation sharing the eastern flank of the Andes, between Venezuela and the southern tip of Chile, shares in this wealth of oil, but only Ecuador and Venezuela have significant exportable surpluses. Major deposits of oil have also been found in Mexico, which has become one of the world's leading exporters of petroleum products. Oil and natural gas are, by far, Latin America's leading source of export income, providing about a fourth of all revenue from abroad.

Manufacturing. Since about 1940, manufacturing has become one of the most rapidly growing economic activities in Latin America. However, not all nations have shared equally in this growth. Because of national aspirations and the desire to encourage internal development, Latin American governments are increasingly urging that raw materials not be exported but be converted into finished products for sale abroad. Tariffs have been established to protect domestic industries. As part of the attempt to encourage industrialization, common markets have been established to enlarge the market base of the nations involved. These organizations include the Latin American Free Trade Assocation (LAFTA), the Cen-

tral American Common Market (ODECA), and the Caribbean Community (Caricom).

In South America, the temperate southern areas, settled primarily by people of European origin, are the most highly industrialized. About half of all manufactured products that are exported from Latin America come from these areas. Major centers of industrial activity are concentrated in the São Paulo district of southeastern Brazil and the vicinity of Buenos Aires, Argentina. Those centers include basic industries for the processing of food products and the manufacture of consumer goods. Machinery and transportation equipment destined for both domestic and foreign markets originate there.

Brazil and Mexico are the only Latin American nations that earn more from manufacturing than from agriculture or mining. Mexico's industrial output, which ranks second only to Brazil's, greatly exceeds the combined total of neighboring Central America and the West Indies. Brazil and Mexico both rank high in the manufacture of automobiles and commercial vehicles. The city of São Paulo, Brazil, is that country's chief industrial center. Mexico's three largest cities—Mexico City, Guadalajara, and Monterrey—are also major hubs of industry.

Transportation and Communication

Before the arrival of the Europeans, communication in Latin America was handled by couriers, who carried messages from place to place. Goods were transported on small boats or by human bearers, but only within small areas.

The Europeans brought about a major change in the transportation of goods. They introduced horses, mules, burros, and wheeled vehicles, which enabled people to carry heavier loads over longer distances. Oceangoing sailing vessels carried cargoes between Latin America and Europe. An enlarged network of roads and trails was established to transport supplies and food into the growing cities. This system of transportation lasted well into the 19th century.

65

After 1850, financiers in Great Britain, the United States, and other countries invested heavily in rail transportation in Latin America. One of the first railroads was constructed across Panama to provide a route for people in the California gold rush. Railroads were also built in Chile, Peru, and Mexico to transport copper and other minerals. In Argentina they moved grain, meat, and wool; in Central America they carried coffee and bananas; and in Cuba they transported sugar. The primary purpose of these railroads was to move products to seaports for export. Railroad construction in Latin America ended during the 1930s except for minor lines in the 1960s.

Airlines were established early in Latin America to overcome rugged mountain terrain that impeded other travel. The first commercial airline in the Western Hemisphere was founded in Colombia in 1919.

Latin American highway construction has occurred only since about 1940. Its main purpose has been to provide an improved network of transportation and communication within countries and between nations. A primary system is the Pan-American Highway, which runs about 16,000 miles (26,000 kilometers) from Mexico through Argentina.

International Relations

The nations of Latin America share a common heritage that influences the nature of their relationships with other countries. For example, their policies toward European states tend to be the products of mutual long colonial associations with Spain and Portugal, and more recent commercial contacts with Great Britain, France, and West Germany. International relations within the Americas are influenced by the powerful presence of the United States. As early as 1821, the Monroe Doctrine established the self-proclaimed right of the United States to protect all Latin American nations from foreign intervention.

The southernmost nations of Chile, Argentina, and Uruguay remain primarily European in outlook. After independence, strong cultural ties with Europe were reinforced by the arrival in those countries of about 4 million European immigrants. Investments, especially from Great Britain, flowed into the region. Economic bonds, as well as cultural ties, particularly with Spain and Italy, have been powerful factors in fostering close relationships with Europe. However, the Falkland Islands conflict between Argentina and Great Britain in 1982 seriously strained relations between those two nations (*see* Falkland Islands).

The Spanish-American War of 1898, followed in 1905 by the Roosevelt Corollary to the Monroe Doctrine, imposed the right of the United States to intercede in Latin American affairs (*see* Monroe Doctrine). The United States enforced this policy in the acquisition of the Panama Canal Zone; military occupations of Nicaragua, Haiti, and the Dominican Republic; intervention in Cuba; and incursions into Mexico. The Good Neighbor Policy announced by President Franklin D. Roosevelt in 1933 improved inter-American relations. (*See also* Panama Canal.)

The Cuban revolution that brought Fidel Castro into power in 1959 renewed the concern of the United States for its Caribbean interests. Military intervention in the Dominican Republic, in 1965, and increased economic and military support of regimes friendly to the United States are outgrowths of an effort to limit Cuba's influence in the hemisphere.

Within Latin America, peace has frequently been hampered since World War II by internal conflicts. In 1969 the so-called soccer war broke out between El Salvador and Honduras when a soccer match between the two nations resulted in violence and, eventually, armed conflict. Since 1980, Argentina and Chile as well as Peru and Ecuador have approached war over boundary disputes. Bolivia continues to seek an outlet to the sea as the result of its war with Chile between 1879 and 1883. Venezuela and Guatemala persist in their attempts to reacquire territory from neighboring Guyana and Belize.

On the other hand, international and regional organizations have been established to promote political harmony and economic well-being in Latin America. The Organization of American States, founded in 1948 as an outgrowth of the Pan-American Union, has been an instrumental force in working for peace and economic cooperation. The United Nations has developed programs to promote peace, food production, monetary cooperation, education, child welfare, and human rights in Latin America. Since World War II, a number of common markets have been established in Latin America to advance joint economic aims. These include the Latin American Free Trade Association, the Central American Common Market, and the Caribbean Community.

History

Christopher Columbus' arrival in the New World in 1492 introduced a colonial era during which Spain and Portugal brought almost all of Latin America under their control. The West Indies, where Columbus landed on his first voyage to the New World, offered the Spaniards little in wealth or a reliable labor supply. However, the islands served as footholds for explorations of the mainland. In 1519 Hernando Cortez set sail from Cuba for the coast of Mexico. He marched inland from what is now the city of Vera Cruz, conquering Indian tribes and gaining allies on the way to Tenochtitlán (now Mexico City), the capital of the Aztecs. Cortez finally defeated the Aztecs in 1521. Diseases brought by the Spaniards and superstitions associated with the arrival of the whites contributed to the collapse of the Indian empire.

From Tenochtitlán Cortez sent expeditions north and south to complete the conquest of neighboring lands. Pedro de Alvarado marched to Central America in 1524, and Álvar Núñez Cabeza de Vaca explored northwestern Mexico through 1536. In 1540 Francisco Coronado led an expedition to northern Mexico in search of the legendary seven cities of Cíbola.

Throughout the region of New Spain, Spanish clergy under the leadership of Padre Bartolomé de Las

Casas attempted to protect the Indians and brought them into the Roman Catholic church. The priests were constantly opposed by landowners who needed laborers for their large estates.

In 1513 Vasco Núñez de Balboa opened the path to the riches of the Inca empire in South America by crossing the Isthmus of Panama and sighting the Pacific Ocean. In 1530, after several unsuccessful efforts between 1524 and 1528, Francisco Pizarro, with his brothers and Diego de Almagro, set forth from Panama to search for the reported treasures of Peru. He completed his quest in 1533 with the capture of Cuzco, the Inca stronghold in southern Peru. Pizarro's subordinates then fanned out to continue the conquest of the Incas. Sebastián de Belalcázar marched north to Ecuador and pushed into southern Colombia in 1536. Pedro de Valdivia went south across Bolivia and into central Chile in 1540. In 1542, during a journey to the east that gave rise to the legend of warlike Amazon women, Francisco de Orellana followed the Amazon River 2,000 miles (3,200 kilometers) to its mouth in the Atlantic Ocean.

Between 1516 and 1535, Spaniards ventured into the estuary of the Río de la Plata. In 1835 Pedro de Mendoza failed in his attempt to establish a city on the present-day site of Buenos Aires. The city of Asunción, located upstream, was founded later that year and served as a permanent center from which settlement expanded.

Portugal, preoccupied with trade in the Orient, moved slowly in its conquest of Brazil. The first permanent settlement did not take place until 1532. The exploitation of brazilwood for dye and the production of sugar and cotton were limited by the shortage of labor. In 1580, fewer than 75,000 Portuguese, blacks, and Indians were available to exploit the resources of this vast territory.

The American and French revolutions in the late 1700s helped ignite a revolt against European colonial powers. The first to achieve independence was Haiti in 1804. By 1810, revolts had flared throughout Latin America, and within 15 years freedom had been largely achieved. In Mexico the independence struggle was launched in 1810 by Padre Miguel Hidalgo y Costilla. The liberation of South America was achieved by the forces of Simón Bolívar in the north and José de San Martín in the south.

Since independence, most Latin American nations have suffered periods of instability and tyranny. Constitutions have often followed one another in rapid succession. Anarchy has alternated with tranquillity. Radical, conservative, and liberal governments have served their turns. Revolutions and wars have contributed to the political tumult.

Lengthy dictatorships have been common in Latin America, though less evident today than in earlier times. They include the dictatorships of Rafael Leónidas Trujillo Molina in the Dominican Republic from 1932 to 1961, the Somoza dynasty in Nicaragua from 1937 to 1979, Juan Perón in Argentina from 1945 to 1955, Adolfo Stroesner in Paraguay from 1954 to the present, and Fidel Castro in Cuba from 1959 to the present. Among the many earlier dictators were Porfirio Díaz of Mexico from 1876 to 1911 and Juan Vicente Gómez of Venezuela from 1908 to 1935.

During the 20th century, revolutions brought major social reforms in Mexico in 1910, Bolivia in 1952, Cuba in 1959, Chile in 1973, and Nicaragua in 1979. These uprisings appear to be occurring with increasing frequency. In the early 1980s dissident elements threatened the governments of Honduras and El Salvador. At the same time, the movements in such nations as Mexico, Costa Rica, Venezuela, and Colombia have been toward democratic governments with freely elected officials. Nevertheless, a number of autocratic governments led by military regimes with restrictive political policies also continue to hold power in Latin America.

BIBLIOGRAPHY FOR LATIN AMERICA

Books for Children

Archer, J. H. Planet Earth (Crowell, 1977).

Baum, Patricia. Dictators of Latin America (Putnam, 1972).

Bishop, C. H. Martin de Porres, Hero (Houghton, 1973).

Caldwell, J. C. Let's Visit Central America, rev. ed. (John Day, 1973).

Clayton, Robert. Mexico, Central America, and the West Indies (John Day, 1971).

Comins, Jeremy. Latin American Crafts and Their Cultural Backgrounds (Lothrop, 1974).

Hoey, Mary. Journey South: Discovering the Americas (Friend, 1980).

Summerlin, Sam. Latin America (Watts, 1972).

Villicana, Eugenio. Viva Morelia (Evans, 1972).

Books for Young Adults and Teachers

Arkena, Joseph and others. Regionalism and the Musical Heritage of Latin America (Univ. of Texas Press, 1980).

Bacarisse, Salvador. Contemporary Latin American Fiction (Columbia Univ. Press, 1980).

Bailey, H. M. and Nasatir, A. P. Latin America: the Development of Its Civilization, 3rd ed. (Prentice, 1973).

Crow, J. A. The Epic of Latin America, 3rd ed. (Univ. of Calif. Press, 1980).

James, P. E. Latin America, 4th ed. (Odyssey, 1969).

Janes, Regina. Gabriel García Márquez: Revolutions in Wonderland (Univ. of Mo. Press, 1981).

Knight, Thomas. Latin America Comes of Age (Scarecrow, 1979).

Lamb, R. S. Latin America (Ocelot, 1973).

Madariaga, Salvador de. Latin America Between the Eagle and the Bear (Greenwood, 1976).

Mayers, M. K. A Look at Latin American Life Styles (Summer Inst. of Ling., 1976).

Parker, F. D. The Central American Republics (Greenwood, 1981).

Robertson, W. S. Rise of the Spanish-American Republics As Told in the Lives of Their Liberators (Gordon, 1976).

Schmid, Peter. Beggars on Golden Stools (Greenwood, 1975).

South American Handbook (Rand, annual).

Szule, Tad. Latin America (Atheneum, n.d.).

Tannenbaum, Frank. Ten Keys to Latin America (Random House, 1966).

Van Hagen, V. W. The Ancient Sun Kingdoms of the Americas (Beekman, 1977).

Walton, R. J. The United States and Latin America (Seabury, 1972).

Wiarda, H. J. Politics and Social Change in Latin America (Univ. of Mass. Press, 1982).

Wilhelm, R. D. Two Ways to Look South (Friend, 1980).

Worcester, D. E. and Schaeffer, W. G. The Growth and Culture of Latin America, 2 vols., 2nd ed. (Oxford, 1970–71).

Wythe, George. Industry in Latin America (Greenwood, 1968).

(*See also* bibliographies for **Argentina; Brazil; Latin American Literature; Mexico; South America.**)

LATIN AMERICAN LITERATURE.

In 1539—less than 50 years after Christopher Columbus landed in the New World—the first printing press in the Americas was set up in Mexico City and the first Latin American book was published. Thus literature became deeply rooted in the history of the countries of Latin America.

There were several reasons for the early rise of this literature. In each country conquered by Spain, there was only one dominant language—Spanish. In Brazil, which was ruled by Portugal, a single language also dominated—Portuguese. The sharing of a common language encouraged literary expression.

This encouragement was strengthened in 1551 when two universities were founded: one in Mexico City and the other in Lima, Peru. But there was perhaps a more important factor. The turmoil of European conquest was subsiding. Among the colonists there was a growing leisure class with more time for intellectual pursuits.

Close ties with homelands across the ocean did much to influence literary trends in the colonial period, but there were fresh new ideas and voices, too. In his epic poem 'La Araucana' (The Araucanian), Alonso de Ercilla y Zúñiga (1533–94), a Spanish poet and soldier who had fought against the Araucanian Indians in Chile, saluted their indomitable courage and nobility of spirit. Published in 1569, this epic is often considered the first notable literary work produced in the Americas. Other writers were also gradually creating a new literary tradition that was uniquely of the New World.

The following works of explorers and others illustrate a gradual change from a literature by foreigners, using forms, languages, and loyalties brought from the Old World, to productions as characteristic of the New World as anything that was written by Benjamin Franklin:

'Diary', Christopher Columbus (1451–1506).
'History of the Indies', Bartolomé de Las Casas (1474–1566).
'Letters', Hernando Cortez (1485–1547).
'Shipwrecked', Alvar Núñez Cabeza de Vaca (1490–1557).
'The True History of the Conquest of New Spain', Bernal Díaz del Castillo (1492–1581?).
'The Chronicle of Perú', Pedro de Cieza de Léon (1518–60).
'Florida of the Inca','"El Inca," Garcilaso de la Vega (1540–1616). This author, the son of an Inca princess, tells a story sympathetic to his people.
'Arauco Subjugated', Pedro de Oña (1570–1645?).
'The Truth Suspected', Juan Ruiz de Alarcón y Mendoza (1580?–1639). Born in Mexico, the author went to Spain when quite young. He did all his writing there, but Mexico justly claims him.

The Struggle for Independence

Toward the end of the 18th century, as the power of Spain and Portugal waned, the Latin American colonies began to struggle for political freedom. This struggle was stimulated by the writings of the French Revolutionists and by the successful revolt of the North American colonies against Britain. In the fight for liberty, Latin American writers played an important role.

José Joaquín Fernández de Lizardi (1776–1827) is often called "The Mexican Thinker," the name of a revolutionary journal he founded in 1812. His picaresque novel, 'The Itching Parrot' (published in 1816), is considered the first Latin American novel.

Ecuador's José Joaquín de Olmedo (1780–1847) wrote passionately about the dreams and spirit of the revolution. His poem 'The Victory of Junín, Song to Bolívar' (1825) was inspired by the patriots' victory at Junín, one of the battles that secured independence for the South Americans.

Andrés Bello (1781–1865) was born in Venezuela but spent most of his life in England and Chile. A scholar and a poet, he left a lasting mark on Latin American literature. One of his most famous poems, 'Eulogy to the Agriculture of the Torrid Zone' (1826), exhorted his countrymen to turn from the sword to the plow. But perhaps his most enduring achievement was his 'Grammar of the Spanish Language', which did much to preserve the purity of the Spanish tongue in Latin America and is still considered an authority on its grammar.

Independence did not bring freedom from political tyranny to Latin America, and this was reflected in 19th-century Romanticist literature. Domingo Faustino Sarmiento (1811–88) of Argentina wrote a stirring denunciation of the dictator Juan Manuel de Rosas in 'Facundo' (1845). This book was also the first penetrating study of the great plains, or pampas, and of gaucho life. It was the forerunner of a uniquely Latin American genre, the gaucho novel. But it was the gaucho poem "Martín Fierro" (1872) by José Hernández (1834–86) that became the national epic of Argentina. A sequel, "The Return of Martín Fierro," was published by Hernández in 1879.

This search for cultural roots also influenced another uniquely Latin American genre—the *tradición*, or historical anecdote. The ironically humorous short stories presented in 'Peruvian Traditions' by Ricardo Palma (1833–1919) of Peru are delightful masterpieces of this genre.

After the mid-19th century, the novel took a commanding lead in Latin American literature. Jorge Isaacs (1837–95) of Colombia wrote the tragic 'María', which is perhaps the most widely read South American novel. José Martiniano de Alencar (1829–77) of Brazil began the vogue of the idealized Indian with 'The Guaraní Indian'. Two other Brazilian novelists wrote more realistically. Aluísio Azevedo (1857–1913) movingly dealt with the tragedies associated with racial prejudice in 'The Mulatto'. Joaquim Maria Machado de Assis (1839–1908) displayed his psychological probing, his wry humor, and his profound understanding of humanity in 'Epitaph of a Small Winner' and 'Dom Casmurro'.

New Literary Movements

A measure of political and economic security gave rise to a new literary movement—Modernism. This movement was characterized by the freedom of the writers to create their own worlds and also by their pessimism and melancholy, their use of exotic imagery, and their continual experimentation with old and new verse forms.

One of the first Modernists was Manuel Gutiérrez Nájera (1859–95) of Mexico, whose graceful poetry and rhythmical prose sketches and stories led the way from Romanticism. Some critics believe that José Martí (1853–95), the Cuban patriot and martyr to freedom, published the first Modernist work in 'Ismaelillo'. But there is no doubt that the literary giant of the Modernist movement was Rubén Darío (pen name of Félix Rubén García Sarmiento; 1867–1916) of Nicaragua. His 'Profane Hymns and Other Poems' and 'Songs of Life and Hope' show Modernism at its peak. His writings defined and stimulated Modernism in Spain, where he lived for several years, as well as America, and his influence was so profound that it has been said: "...of any poem written in Spanish it can be told with certainty whether it was written before or after him."

Many of Darío's fellow Modernists were also writers of stature. Among them was Amado Nervo (1870–1919), a Mexican poet. As a young man, he studied for the priesthood, and this experience was reflected in the mysticism in much of his poetry. His early works, such as 'Black Pearls' and 'Inner Gardens', place him in the center of Modernism. Later his poetry became more subjective, and his 'Serenity' expresses the asceticism that marked the poet's later life.

José Santos Chocano (1875–1934) was the leading Modernist in Peru. A poet and a revolutionary, his most famous work appeared in the collection 'The American Soul', in which he expressed his fear of United States domination in Latin America.

Ricardo Jaimes Freyre (1872–1933) of Bolivia used Scandinavian mythology to create 'Castalia bárbara'. The philosopher and essayist José Enrique Rodó (1872–1917) of Uruguay is considered to be the leading critic and the foremost prose writer of the Modernism movement. His most famous essay, 'Ariel', exerted wide-spreading influence on the Latin American intellectual community.

The horror and carnage of the Mexican Revolution that began in 1911 and endured until 1917 had repercussions in many other Latin American countries. Latin American intellectuals were shocked into the realization that their own homelands held oppressed peoples. The Spanish Civil War in the 1930s, World War II, and the political and economic turmoil that followed further galvanized the writers of Latin America into a fervor of self-examination, self-discovery, and creation.

The leaders of Modernism were turning from its tenets, but an amazing group of women poets remained loyal, and their lyrical love poems were widely popular. The star of this galaxy was Gabriela Mistral (Lucila Godoy Alcayaga) (1889–1957) of Chile. Her early poems, collected in 'Desolation', sang passionately of the tragedy of romantic love. Later her poetry expressed love and compassion for all humanity, with a special tenderness for children. In 1945 she was awarded the Nobel prize for literature.

Another Chilean poet who won the Nobel prize, in 1971, was Pablo Neruda (Neftalí Ricardo Reyes) (1904–73). In his early poems he also wrote in the Modernist manner. His later poetry revealed a deep self-questioning as Neruda began to see himself in relation to mankind. From the early 'Twenty Love Poems and a Song of Despair' to the often surrealistic 'Residence on Earth' to his later 'Extravagario', Neruda's poetry traces the development of a man as well as a poet—a poet who has been called the greatest Spanish American poet since Rubén Darío.

It was in prose, however, that 20th-century Latin American writers were creating a literature that expressed their deep awareness of social injustice. Mariano Azuela (1873–1952) was a Mexican novelist and physician who had served as an army doctor with the revolutionary Pancho Villa. In 'The Underdogs' he wrote the most powerful and penetrating novel of the Mexican Revolution. But this was only one of several major novels that revealed his abiding concern for justice. In 'Weeds', for example, he presented a scathing indictment of the Mexican landowning class.

In 'Rebellion in the Backlands' Euclydes da Cunha (1866–1909) wrote a book that has been considered a

Gabriel García Márquez of Colombia, who gained international renown with 'One Hundred Years of Solitude', won the Nobel prize for literature in 1982.

Rodrigo García Barcha

Newberry Library
OLMEDO

Pan American Union
BELLO

Pan American Union
SARMIENTO

Pan American Union
PALMA

classic of Brazilian literature. Partly a geographical and social treatise, it gave a brilliant description of the drought-plagued backlands and the misery of its impoverished people. But it was also a moving and swiftly paced novel. Altogether, it was the first protest on behalf of Brazil's forgotten people.

In this surge of social conscience, it was natural that the popular *indianista*, or Indian, novel took on a new dimension. The image of the Indian changed: he was now not a noble hero nor a romantic figure, but instead the victim of political and economic forces. One of the first and most outstanding of these novels was 'Birds Without a Nest' by Clorinda Matto de Turner (1852–1909) of Peru. In 'The Indian', Gregorio López y Fuentes (1897–1966) also espoused the cause of the Indians as he depicted the injustices inflicted upon them in his native Mexico.

The clash between old and new cultures, between the pastoral life of the pampas and the industrial urban centers, was recreated vividly in regional literature that also was often literature of protest. Jorge Amado (born 1912) expressed his sympathy for the powerless in 'The Violent Land' as he depicted the cacao boom and the havoc it caused in the frontier districts of his native state of Bahia, Brazil.

In his somber short stories, Javier de Viana (1868–1926) of Uruguay also wrote movingly of this culture clash. The early writings of Carlos Reyles (1868–1938), also of Uruguay, were psychological studies of rural life, as in 'The Native Country'. He wrote a realistic portrayal of gaucho life in 'The Elegant Gaucho'. But it was Ricardo Güiraldes (1886–1927) of Argentina who best captured the essense of gaucho life on the pampas in 'Shadows on the Pampas'. Based on the author's childhood experiences on the family ranch, this novel is both realistic and nostalgic as it compassionately salutes a vanishing way of life.

In their search for their own roots, Latin American writers were also rediscovering the *selva*, or jungle. José Eustasio Rivera (1889–1928), a Colombian poet and novelist, wrote perhaps the finest novel in this genre, 'The Vortex'. It describes the travels of the hero through the tropical forest that destroys the humans who tamper with its mysteries, and the book also presents an unforgettable picture of the workers who are exploited in a rubber boom in the selva.

One of the outstanding urban novelists was Manuel Gálvez (1882–1962) of Argentina. His novels, which probe into social ills, reveal his sympathy for people struggling in a web of circumstance they cannot break. His best known novels are 'The Schoolmistress' and 'Nacha Regules'.

Contemporary Latin American Literature

After the Cuban revolution in 1959, there was an amazing eruption of fresh, creative, and dazzling literature from the writers of Latin America. This phenomenon has been called "El Boom," and it marked the coming of age of Latin American literature. Characterized by a preoccupation with solitude and a search for identity, writers explored the past to confront the present and the future and drew upon all the colorful strands of Latin American culture: Spanish and Portuguese social mores, religion, and Indian and African mythology.

As they wove these strands together, writers also experimented with new forms and techniques to restructure the novel. The new movement was called "magical realism," where myth is so firmly believed that it becomes reality—and thus demonstrates how fantastic reality itself may be.

Nearly every contemporary Latin American writer used magical realism, but each used it in an individual way. Jorge Luis Borges (born 1899) of Argentina, a short-story writer, essayist, and poet, was in the vanguard. In his short-story collections 'Ficciones' and 'The Aleph and Other Stories', he invented new forms and structures and played with time and space (*see* Borges). Julio Cortázar (born 1914), also of Argentina, juggled time, space, and characters in a very different way in 'Hopscotch'. Miguel Ángel Asturias (1899–1974) of Guatemala, winner of the 1967 Nobel prize, wrote a terrifying surrealist novel in 'The President'. In 'The Obscene Bird of Night' José Donoso (born 1924) of Chile wrote what many consider a hallucinatory classic.

The grand master of magical realism was Gabriel García Márquez (born 1928) of Colombia, who was

Archives General, Buenos Aires
GÜIRALDES

Library of Congress
ANDRADE

Hispanic Society of America
MEDINA

Pan American Union
MARTÍ

awarded the Nobel prize for literature in 1982. In 'One Hundred Years of Solitude', a mesmerizing tale of a mythical town, he captured the imagination of readers around the world. He created another masterpiece in 'Chronicle of a Death Foretold', a dark and brooding story of destiny that pursues men and women and of the fateful tragedy that people themselves evoke by their codes of honor.

Two memorable books, both written by Mexicans, are 'The Death of Artemio Cruz' by Carlos Fuentes (born 1928) and 'The Labyrinth of Solitude' by Octavio Paz (born 1914). João Guimarães Rosa (1908–67) of Brazil wrote 'The Devil to Pay in the Backlands', a complex and provocative novel that is one of the masterpieces of Latin American literature. Mario Vargas Llosa (born 1936) of Peru wrote the lighthearted autobiographical novel 'Aunt Julia and the Scriptwriter'.

One of the most provocative women writers was Luisa Valenzuela (born 1938) of Argentina. In a short-story collection, 'Strange Things Happen Here', she wrote with bitter humor and shocking re-

alism of the terror and political chaos that swept Argentina in the decade after the death of its dictator Juan Perón in 1974.

While some contemporary Latin American authors, such as Valenzuela, may have rejected magical realism, the movement has made a lasting mark on writers outside the borders of Latin America. Its influence can be seen in the exuberance of 'Hotel New Hampshire' by John Irving and in the work of Robert Stone and Paul Theroux.

BIBLIOGRAPHY FOR LATIN AMERICAN LITERATURE

Anderson-Imbert, Enrique. Spanish-American Literature: a History, 2 vols., 2nd rev. ed. (Wayne State Univ. Press, 1969).
Fitts, Dudley, ed. Anthology of Contemporary Latin-American Poetry (Greenwood, 1976).
Foster, D. W. and V. R., eds. Modern Latin American Literature, 2 vols. (Ungar, 1975).
Franco, Jean. An Introduction to Spanish-American Literature (Cambridge Univ. Press, 1969).
Jones, W. K., ed. Spanish-American Literature in Translation, 2 vols. (Ungar).
Monegal, E. R., ed. The Borzoi Anthology of Latin American Literature, 2 vols. (Knopf, 1977).

Latin American Literary Figures by Country

ARGENTINA

The great names in the literature of Argentina are mainly those of the 19th and 20th centuries. After the ousting of the dictator Juan Manuel de Rosas in 1852, the republic was strongly united with centralized authority. Under a new constitution it encouraged a rapid advance in education, political stability, and art. Domingo Faustino Sarmiento, educator, politician, and writer, was one of the great creators of modern Argentina.

Argentina's chief contribution to Latin American literature was the gaucho theme, used in both poetry and prose fiction. Some of Argentina's finest writers are:

Andrade, Olegario Víctor (1841–82) — 'Song to the Future of the Latin Race in America'.

Borges, Jorge Luis (born 1899) — 'Ficciones'.

Cortázar, Julio (born 1914) — 'Hopscotch'.

Echeverría, Esteban (1805–51) — 'Rhymes'.

Gálvez, Manuel (1882–1962) — 'Nacha Regules'.

Güiraldes, Ricardo (1886–1927) — 'Shadows on the Pampas'.

Hernández, José (1834–86) — 'Martín Fierro'.

Larreta, Enrique (1875–1961) — 'The Glory of Don Ramiro'.

Lugones, Leopoldo (1874–1938) — 'Golden Mountains'.

Lynch, Benito (1885–1951) — 'The Englishman of the Bones'.

Mármol, José (1818–71) — 'Amalia'.

Obligado, Rafael (1851–1920) — 'Argentine Legends'.

Ocantos, Carlos María (1860–1949) — 'León Zaldívar'.

Payró, Roberto J. (1867–1928) — 'Upon These Ruins'.

Puig, Manuel (born 1932) — 'The Buenos Aires Affair'.

Rojas, Ricardo (1882–1957) — 'Ollantay'.

Sarmiento, Domingo Faustino (1811–88) — 'Facundo'.

Storni, Alfonsina (1892–1938) — 'The Rosebush's Restlessness'.

Valenzuela, Luisa (born 1938) — 'Strange Things Happen Here'.

LATIN AMERICAN LITERATURE

Hispanic Society of America
ZORILLA DE SAN MARTÍN

Hispanic Society of America
OLIVEIRA

Hispanic Society of America
SANÍN CANO

Pan American Union
DARÍO

BOLIVIA

Bolivia, in spite of its chronic economic difficulties, its large number of unassimilated Indians, many of whom do not speak Spanish, and its relative isolation from major cultural centers of the world, has produced some important literature.

The greatest of Bolivia's poets, Ricardo Jaimes Freyre, spent much of his life in Argentina. Some contemporary writers, especially Alcides Arguedas, are interested in presenting the problems of the lower economic classes. Some notable Bolivian writers are:

Arguedas, Alcides (1879–1946)—'The Bronze Race'.
Calvo, Daniel (1832–80)—'Rhymes'.
Cerruto, Oscar (born 1907)—'Rain of Fire'.
Chirveches, Armando (1883–1926)—'The Rojas Candidacy'.
Galindo, Nestor (1830–65)—'Tears'.
Jaimes Freyre, Ricardo (1870–1933)—'The Conquistadores'.
Lenz, Benjamín (1836–78)—'Poems'.

BRAZIL

Brazil holds a unique place among the countries of the New World—it is the only one in which Portuguese is the official language. The literature of Brazil, like that of Mexico, Peru, and Chile, started in colonial times. Although the primary inspiration for writing came from a well-developed motherland literature, the influence of French letters also was felt at the outset.

José de Anchieta, one of the earliest Brazilian writers, set the tone and spirit still to be found in the nation. His description of the beauties of the country and his recognition of the white man's responsibility for the Indian's welfare make him truly Brazilian though he was born in Europe.

Antônio José da Silva worked to keep the drama alive in the 18th century, while Tomás Antônio Gonzaga in his 'Chilean Letters' shows the influence of Rousseau. Literature soon became more realistic, and even pessimistic, with Brazil's greatest writer, Joaquim Maria Machado de Assis. Stories dealing with the socioeconomic problems continue to be of primary importance among Brazilians writing today. Brazil's best writers include:

Amado, Jorge (born 1912)—'Limitless Lands'.
Anchieta, José de (1534–97)—'Poems'.
Azevedo, Aluísio (1857–1913)—'The Mulatto'.
Castro Alves, Antônio de (1847–71)—'Poems'.
Da Cunha, Euclydes (1866–1909)—'Rebellion in the Backlands'.

Da Silva, Antônio José (1705–39)—'Life of the Great Don Quixote'.
Escragnolle Tounay, Alfredo de (1843–99)—'Innocence'.
Gonçalves Dias, Antônio (1823–64)—'American Poems'.
Gonzaga, Tomás Antônio (1744–1807?)—'Chilean Letters'.
Graça Aranha, José Pereira da (1868–1931)—'Canaan'.
Guimarães Rosa, João (1908–67)—'The Devil to Pay in the Backlands'.
Lima, Jorge de (1893–1953)—'Poems'.
Machado de Assis, Joaquim Maria (1839–1908)—'Posthumous Memoirs of Braz Cubas'.
Martiniano de Alencar, José (1829–77)—'The Guaraní Indian'.
Monteiro Lobato, José Bento (1883–1948)—'Light Tales'.
Oliveira, Antônio Mariano Alberto de (1859–1937)—'Sonnets and Poems'.
Veríssimo, Érico (1905–75)—'Night'.

CHILE

Chile's literature is most significant. It began in the colonial period with 'The Araucanian' by Alonso de Ercilla y Zúñiga. Two Chilean poets have received the Nobel prize for literature—Gabriela Mistral, in 1945, and Pablo Neruda, in 1971. Alberto Blest Gana, called the Balzac of Chile, wrote for nearly 70 years. A few of the outstanding writers are:

Alegría, Fernando (born 1918)—'Four White Feet'.
Barrios, Eduardo (1884–1963)—'The Men Within the Man'.
Blest Gana, Alberto (1831–1920)—'Martín Rivas'.
Bombal, María Luisa (1910–80)—'Islands and Other Stories'.
Donoso, José (born 1924)—'The Obscene Bird of Night'.
Ercilla y Zúñiga, Alonso de (1533–94)—'The Araucanian'.
Lillo, Baldomero (1867–1923)—'The Devil's Pit and Other Stories'.
Medina, José Toribio (1852–1930)—Bibliographical and historical works.
Mistral, Gabriela (Lucila Godoy Alcayaga) (1889–1957)—'Desolation'.
Neruda, Pablo (Neftalí Ricardo Reyes) (1904–73)—'Twenty Love Poems and a Song of Despair'.
Prado, Pedro (1886–1952)—'Alsino'.
Subercaseaux, Benjamín (born 1902)—'Jemmy Button'.
Vicuña Mackenna, Benjamín (1831–86)—Histories, biographies.

RODÓ

LARRETA

CHOCANO

VASCONCELOS

COLOMBIA

Colombians—especially in the three main cities of Bogotá, Cali, and Medellín—have always prided themselves on a tradition of culture. Colonial traditions and customs are strong in 'María', by Jorge Isaacs. 'The Vortex', by José Eustacio Rivera, pictures life in the dense tropical jungles. In José Asunción Silva is found a source of the Modernism of the great Nicaraguan Rubén Darío. Gabriel García Márquez received the Nobel prize for literature in 1982. Best known writers of Colombia include:

Álvarez Lleras, Antonio (1892–1956)—'The Claw'.

Arboleda, Julio (1817–61)—'Poems'.

Caro, José Eusebio (1817–53)—'Poems'.

Carrasquilla, Tomás (1858–1940)—'The Marquise of Yolombó'.

García Márquez, Gabriel (born 1928)—'One Hundred Years of Solitude'; 'Chronicle of a Death Foretold'.

Gutiérrez González, Gregorio (1826–72)—'Poems'.

Isaacs, Jorge (1837–95)—'María'.

Palacios, Eustaquio (1830–98)—'The Royal Ensign'.

Rivera, José Eustacio (1889–1928)—'The Vortex'.

Sanín Cano, Baldomero (1861–1957)—'Literary and Philological Disquisitions'.

Silva, José Asunción (1865–96)—'Poems'.

Tablanca, Luis (Enrique Pardo y Farelo) (born 1883)—'The Country Girl'.

Valencia, Guillermo (1873–1943)—'Poems'.

COSTA RICA

Costa Rica is one of the most progressive Central American countries. Several Costa Rican intellectuals have been leaders in the advancement of education—particularly Roberto Brenes Mesén and Joaquín García Monje. Some notable Costa Rican writers are:

Brenes Mesén, Roberto (1874–1947)—'The Gods Return'.

Echeverría, Aquileo (1866–1909)—'Rustic Rhymes'.

Fallas, Carlos Luis (born 1910)—'Mother United'.

Fernández Guardia, Ricardo (1867–1950)—'Tican Stories'.

García Monje, Joaquín (1881–1958)—'Daughters of the Soil'; editor, *Repertorio Americano*.

Lyra, Carmen (María Isabel Carvajal) (1888–1949)—'Stories of My Aunt Panchita'.

Pacheco Cooper, Emilio (1865–1906)—'Poetry'.

Sotela, Rogelio (1894–1943)—'Writers and Poets of Costa Rica'.

ECUADOR

Ecuador has contributed significantly to Latin American literature. The first poet to eulogize the independence of Latin America in epic style was José Joaquín de Olmedo. The high percentage of Indians in the population has helped make racial themes popular. Some of the writers are:

Carrera Andrade, Jorge (born 1903)—'Place of Origin'.

Gil Gilbert, Enrique (born 1912)—'Our Daily Bread'.

Icaza, Jorge (1906–78)—'Huasipungo'.

Mera, Juan León (1832–94)—'Cumandá or a Drama Among Savages'.

Montalvo, Juan (1832–89)—'Chapters Cervantes Forgot to Write'.

Olmedo, José Joaquín de (1780–1847)—'The Victory of Junín, Song to Bolívar'.

Zaldumbide, Gonzalo (1885–1965)—'Bitter Fruits'.

EL SALVADOR

The small, densely populated republic of El Salvador claims with Guatemala a pre-Columbian literary work. This is the 'Popol-Vuh', the history or mythology of the Quiche Indians. It is said to have been written in the 17th century in Latin characters, reproducing in part a pre-Columbian original in Mayan hieroglyphics. A few of El Salvador's writers are:

Ávila, Julio Enrique (born 1892)—'The World of My Garden'.

Cañas, Juan José (1826–1918)—'Departure of the Ship *Gold Hunter*'.

Lars, Claudia (Carmen Brannon de Samayoa) (born 1899)—'Stars in the Pool'.

Quijano Hernández, Manuel (born 1871)—'Stories of My Country'.

Salazar Arrué, Salvador (1899–1975)—'That and More'.

Ulloa, Juan (born 1898)—'Humble Lives'.

GUATEMALA

Guatemala has begun to lead the Central American republics in publishing. The educational system has been reorganized. Many people believe that a real literary renaissance has emerged. Miguel Ángel Asturias received the Nobel prize for literature in 1967. A few of the writers worthy of mention are:

Arévalo Martínez, Rafael (born 1884)—'Depths'.

Asturias, Miguel Ángel (1899–1974)—'The President'.

Batres y Montúfar, José de (1809–44)—'Traditions of Guatemala'.

Diéguez, Juan (1813–66)—'April Afternoons'.

Ralph B. Swain
GARCÍA MONJE

Neal Boenzi—*The New York Times*
FUENTES

Hispanic Society of America
MISTRAL

Hispanic Society of America
A. REYES

Irisarri, Antonio José de (1786–1868) — 'Satirical and Burlesque Poems'.

Jil, Salom (José Milla y Vidaurre) (1827–82) — 'Don Bonifacio'.

HONDURAS

The literature of Honduras had early beginnings, but the country's output was not large. Since the second half of the 19th century a real awakening has been noted. Some of the best known writers are:

Carcoma, Jacob (1914–59) — 'Pines of Honduras'.

Castro, Jesús (born 1906) — 'Fragrance of Spring'.

Díaz Lozano, Argentina (born 1909) — 'Pearls from My Rosary'.

Durón, Jorge Fidel (born 1902) — 'American Stories'.

Molina, Juan Ramón (1875–1908) — 'Song to the Río Grande'.

Reyes, José Trinidad (1797–1855) — 'Pastorals'.

Turcios, Froilán (1875–1943) — 'Almond Blossoms'.

MEXICO

Mexico, with the largest population of the Spanish-speaking countries of the New World, has one of the richest literatures of Latin America. From the earliest times, even during the days of the conquistadores, important writing was done. Cortez's 'Letters' and Bernal Díaz del Castillo's 'True History of the Conquest of New Spain' are two interesting works produced by the conquistadores.

The Spanish Golden Age was enriched by the Mexican-born dramatist Juan Ruiz de Alarcón y Mendoza. The 17th-century nun Juana Inés de la Cruz produced great love poems. The best picaresque novel of the New World, 'The Itching Parrot', was written by a Mexican, José Joaquín Fernández de Lizardi.

During the 19th century several Mexican poets contributed significantly to Modernism. It is probable, however, that in the novel of the Mexican Revolution Mexico developed a new type of fiction. Notable Mexican writers include:

Altamirano, Ignacio Manuel (1834–93) — 'Christmas in the Mountains'.

Azuela, Mariano (1873–1952) — 'The Underdogs'.

Delgado, Rafael (1853–1914) — 'La Calandria'.

Díaz Mirón, Salvador (1853–1928) — 'Poems'.

Fernández de Lizardi, José Joaquín (1776–1827) — 'The Itching Parrot'.

Fuentes, Carlos (born 1928) — 'The Death of Artemio Cruz'.

Gamboa, Federico (1864–1939) — 'The Highest Law'.

Gorostiza, Manuel Eduardo de (1789–1851) — 'The Clown's Daughter'.

Gutiérrez Nájera, Manuel (1859–95) — 'Poems'.

Guzmán, Martín Luis (born 1887) — 'The Eagle and the Serpent'.

Juana Inés de la Cruz (1651–95) — 'Poems'.

López y Fuentes, Gregorio (1897–1966) — 'The Indian'.

Nervo, Amado (1870–1919) — 'The Moment That You'll Love Me'.

Paz, Octavio (born 1914) — 'The Labyrinth of Solitude'.

Reyes, Alfonso (1889–1959) — 'Sea Gulls'.

Romero, José Rubén (1890–1952) — 'The Useless Life of Pito Pérez'.

Ruiz de Alarcón y Mendoza, Juan (1580?–1639) — 'The Truth Suspected'.

Rulfo, Juan (born 1918) — 'Pedro Páramo'.

Sierra, Justo (1814–61) — 'The Jew's Daughter'.

Torres Bodet, Jaime (1902–74) — 'Poems'.

Usigli, Rodolfo (born 1905) — 'The Apostle'.

Vasconcelos, José (1882–1959) — 'Ulises Criollo'.

NICARAGUA

Rubén Darío was the leader, if not the founder, of Modernism. Because of his international acceptance and reputation, he has overshadowed the other writers of this turbulent and interesting country.

The several invasions of Nicaragua have been the subject of hundreds of poems, essays, and works of fiction. The fear of Yankee imperialism was expressed by Rubén Darío in his famous poem 'To Roosevelt'. A few of the outstanding writers of Nicaragua are:

Aguilar Cortés, Jerónimo (born 1890) — 'The Necklace of False Pearls'.

Calero Orozco, Adolfo (born 1899) — 'Rustic Tales'.

Cuadra, Pablo Antonio (born 1912) — 'Nicaraguan Poems, 1930–1933'.

Darío, Rubén (1867–1916) — 'Azure'.

Robleto, Hernán (born 1895) — 'Blood in the Tropics'.

PANAMA

Panama has been an independent country only since 1903. As the youngest of the Spanish American republics, it is often given scant recognition by literary historians. Even before its independence, however, Panama's writers were showing characteristics distinct from those of authors in Colombia. A marked trend toward cosmopolitanism was noteworthy. A few outstanding writers are:

Fábrega, José Isaac (born 1900) — 'The Crucible'.

Geenzier, Enrique (1888–1943) — 'Dusk and Shadows'.

UPI
NERUDA

© Layle Silbert
PAZ

© Layle Silbert
VALENZUELA

Wide World
ASTURIAS

Méndez Pereira, Octavio (1887–1954) — 'The Treasure of the Dabaibe'.

Miró, Ricardo (1883–1940) — 'Silent Paths'.

Obaldía, María Olimpia de (born 1891) — 'Orchids'.

Sinán, Rogelio (Bernardo Domínguez Alba) (born 1904) — 'Holy Week in the Mist'.

PARAGUAY

Paraguay has passed through very difficult times. It has been engaged in an almost continuous series of wars since it became independent. Now it has emerged into a period of enlightenment.

Paraguay is virtually bilingual. The Guaraní Indian language has reached the status of a literary language. Writers of note include:

Alsina, Arturo (born 1897) — 'The Brand'.

Barrett, Rafael (1877–1910) — 'Short Stories'.

Casaccia, Gabriel (born 1907) — 'La Babosa'.

Pla, Josefina (born 1909) — 'Here Nothing Has Happened'.

Ramos Giménez, Leopoldo (born 1896) — 'Eros'.

Roa Bastos, Augusto Antonio (born 1918) — 'Nightingale of Dawn'.

PERU

Several evidences of pre-Columbian literature are found in Latin America. Perhaps the most interesting is an Inca drama, 'Ollantay', first set down by a Peruvian priest in the 18th century. Early literature in Spanish is represented by the historical writings of "El Inca" Garcilaso de la Vega and the poet Juan del Valle y Caviedes.

A famous Peruvian prose writer of the modern period was Ricardo Palma. His nine-volume 'Peruvian Traditions' is a mixture of history and fiction. The stories are amusing and delightfully written tales and anecdotes from Peruvian history. José Santos Chocano was second to Rubén Darío among the great Modernists. A few of the many Peruvian writers are:

Alegría, Ciro (1909–67) — 'Broad and Alien Is the World'.

Chocano, José Santos (1875–1934) — 'Song to the Future'.

García Calderón, Ventura (1886–1959) — 'Worth a Peru'.

Garcilaso de la Vega, "El Inca" (1540?–1616) — 'Florida of the Inca'.

González Prada, Manuel (1848–1918) — 'Peruvian Ballads'.

Matto de Turner, Clorinda (1852–1909) — 'Birds Without a Nest'.

Palma, Ricardo (1833–1919) — 'Peruvian Traditions'.

Valle y Caviedes, Juan del (1652–92) — 'Poems'.

Vargas Llosa, Mario (born 1936) — 'Aunt Julia and the Scriptwriter'.

URUGUAY

The small country of Uruguay is one of the most literate and progressive of the Latin American nations. It has a rich literature. Its best known poet is Juan Zorilla de San Martín. The novelist Carlos Reyles was both an escapist and a psychological analyst.

Many Uruguayan writers are claimed both by their home country and by Argentina. Florencio Sánchez and Horacio Quiroga were born in Uruguay and moved to Argentina. Quiroga wrote of the Argentine Chaco and Misiones. Sánchez became a newspaperman and a playwright in Buenos Aires. A few of Uruguay's notable writers are:

Acevedo Díaz, Eduardo (1851–1924) — 'Soledad'.

Agustini, Delmira (1886–1914) — 'Poems'.

Herrera y Reissig, Julio (1875–1910) — 'Lyrical Anthology'.

Ibarbourou, Juana de (honorary name: Juana de America) (born 1895) — 'The Hour'.

Quiroga, Horacio (1879–1937) — 'Stories of Love, Madness and Death'.

Reyles, Carlos (1868–1938) — 'The Spell of Seville'.

Rodó, José Enrique (1872–1917) — 'Ariel'.

Sánchez, Florencio (1875–1910) — 'My Son the Doctor'.

Viana, Javier de (1868–1926) — 'Yuyos'.

Zorilla de San Martín, Juan (1855–1931) — 'Tabaré: Novel in Verse'.

VENEZUELA

Venezuela was influential in the Latin American movement for intellectual and political emancipation from Spain. One of its leaders, Andrés Bello, was notable in the fields of journalism, poetry, law, history, philology, and literary criticism. Today fiction is more accepted than poetry and drama. A distinguished contemporary novelist, Rómulo Gallegos, was a former president of the republic. Rufino Blanco-Fombona was a poet, critic, and novelist. Among the best known writers are:

Bello, Andrés (1781–1865) — 'Eulogy to the Agriculture of the Torrid Zone'.

Blanco-Fombona, Rufino (1874–1944) — 'Man of Gold'.

Gallegos, Rómulo (1884–1969) — 'Doña Bárbara'.

Padrón, Julián (1910–54) — 'Spring Nights'.

Parra, Teresa de la (1895–1936) — 'Mama Blanca's Souvenirs'.

Picón-Febres, Gonzalo (1860–1918) — 'Sergeant Phillip'.

Rosales, Julio (born 1885) — 'Under the Golden Skies'.

Uslar Pietri, Arturo (born 1906) — 'Red Lances'.

LATIN LANGUAGE *see* ROMANCE LANGUAGES.

LATIN LITERATURE. The concept of inventing a universal language may sound visionary, but such a language existed for many centuries—from just before the dawn of the Christian Era almost to contemporary times. This world language was Latin. It was spread by the victorious Roman legions over Europe, Asia, and Africa. It finally became the speech of Western civilization. It was spoken in one form or another from the British Isles to the Persian Gulf.

In the Indo-European family of languages, Latin might be called a sister of Sanskrit and Greek (*see* Language). When Greek was already a major world language, Latin was still a tongue spoken only by a few tribes in Latium, a district that included Rome. It was not until the 3rd century BC that it was spoken throughout Italy. It superseded for the most part the other Italic dialects. It was not until the 1st century BC, however, that it had been developed into a superb literary language, a marvelous instrument for prose and poetry. The Latin of this so-called Golden Age had a stateliness and an artistic finish of style that have never been surpassed in any tongue. The masters of the language knew the limitations of their instrument. Latin did not lend itself to expressing fine shades of meaning. Therefore the great Roman writers strove rather for clearness and precision. The language did not have the variety of sound that Greek possessed through its more numerous vowels and diphthongs and its musical accent. The monotony of Latin was further increased by the great number of long syllables. But this very monotony could be utilized to give weight and dignity and a beautiful rhythmic cadence.

The Beginnings of Literature

Before the influx of Greek culture, about 270 BC, the Romans had already developed a type of literary form, called Saturnian verse. The meter of this verse was based upon accent. Its form was capable of adaptation to a variety of poetical purposes. The Greek measures that Latin afterward followed were based not on accent but on long and short syllables.

The first Roman book, however, apparently was a translation of the Greek 'Odyssey'. This was made in the latter half of the 3rd century BC by a Greek slave, Lucius Livius Andronicus, who also translated some Greek plays. The next known epic poet, Gnaeus Naevius (died about 200 BC), continued to translate or imitate Greek drama, often using subjects from Roman history and introducing allusions to contemporary politics. He also used the pattern given by Andronicus' 'Odyssey' to write an epic of the First Punic War. Thus, from its beginnings, Roman literature was based upon Greek models.

On this foundation Quintus Ennius (239–169 BC), the most important Roman writer before the age of Cicero, reared the stately edifice of his 'Annales'. This tremendous epic history of the Roman state is unfortunately known today from only a few fragments. In his poem Ennius remolded the still rude and clumsy Latin to fit the stately flow of the Greek hexameter verse form. Thus he influenced the whole later history of the language. A tireless and prolific worker, Ennius also produced an astonishing number of translations from the Greek tragedy and comedy, as well as many original dramas and other works. This massive output won for him the title "father of Roman poetry."

The first Latin writer whose works have survived in any considerable body is Titus Maccius Plautus (254?–184 BC), considered the greatest comic dramatist of Rome. Twenty of his farcical plays have been preserved more or less intact through the centuries, making him one of the world's chief dramatic influences. His plots—which he borrowed from the Greek comic poets—have in turn furnished a rich mine for later playwrights, including Shakespeare and Molière. Many of the stock characters of the present-day comic stage are adaptations of the types that he took from Greek comedy. (*See also* Drama.)

Though Plautus got the substance of his plots and characters from Greek sources, his manner and spirit were essentially Roman. His great successor Terence, who was born about the year Plautus died, deliberately avoided any impulse toward originality or the expression of national quality. Terence copied his Greek originals with slavish fidelity. There is nothing Roman about his work except the language. His merit is that he thus brought into Roman literature the Greek standards of elegance, artistic perfection, and moderation. His defect is that he "struck Latin literature at the root with the fatal disease of mediocrity." His six plays, which all survive, have served as models of classical perfection to every generation of playwrights since. Some of his exquisitely polished lines—such as *Homo sum: humani nihil a me alienum puto* ("I am a man; and I think nothing pertaining to mankind foreign to me")—have passed into the currency of common speech.

In addition to these poets, there was Cato the Censor (234–149 BC), the first writer of prose history in Rome to employ his native tongue. His published speeches were greatly admired by Cicero. Another poet was Lucilius (about 180–103 BC), whose satires were the first written in the modern sense of witty social criticism. These were the most important contributors to the early period of Latin literature.

The Golden Age

The Golden Age, that great period when Latin literature reached its fullest splendor, covers about a century (80 BC–AD 14). It started with the beginning of Cicero's rise as an orator and ended with the death of the Emperor Augustus, under whose patronage arts and letters flourished as never before in Italy. Cicero brought Latin prose as an instrument for oratorical, philosophical, literary, and epistolary expression to such a pitch of perfection that the adjective "Ciceronian" become a synonym for "classically perfect," "polished" (*see* Cicero). A leading modern critic of Latin literature, J. W. Mackail of Oxford University, once wrote: "Cicero's unique and imperishable glory is that he created a language which remained for 16 centuries the language of the civilized world, and used that language to create a style which 19 centuries have not replaced, and in some respects have hardly altered."

Different but in no way inferior to the stately sonorous periods of Cicero was the simple straightforward style of Caesar. Caesar's 'Gallic Wars', recording his campaign in Gaul, remains a model of prose narration (*see* Caesar).

The other chief writers of the Ciceronian period are Sallust, Lucretius, and Catullus. Sallust (86–34 BC) is placed in the front rank of Roman historians because of his accounts of the Catilinarian conspiracy and the Jugurthine War. The philosophical epic 'De rerum natura' (Concerning the Nature of Things) of Lucretius (96?–55 BC) is perhaps the most original and certainly, next to the 'Aeneid', the greatest poem in Latin. The love poems of Catullus (84–54 BC) present the joy and pain of the passing moment with the same vividness that is found in the sonnets of Shakespeare. These authors wrote during the period of the Roman Republic.

As the significant authors of the Ciceronian era had perfected Latin prose, so the poets of the Augustan age perfected Latin verse. First of these was Virgil, or Vergil (70–19 BC), the "Homer of Rome." His great national epic, the 'Aeneid', written in a deftly handled Latin hexameter, is one of the supreme masterpieces of the world, second only to the 'Iliad' and the 'Odyssey' (*see* Virgil).

In the field of lyric and satiric verse, the genial and accomplished Horace (Quintus Horatius Flaccus, 65–8 BC) triumphed as surpassingly as did Virgil with the epic. He embodied his philosophy of "idealized common sense" in phrases of such unforgettable charm that many of them have become as familiar as proverbs. In his mildly ironical 'Satires' and 'Epistles' he preserved what is still the most complete and vivid picture of life in the Augustan age.

The Elegiac Poets

There was nothing of Horatian self-restraint and even-souled calm in the brief erratic life of Sextus Propertius (50?–15 BC). He flashed on the Roman world when he was 20 with a volume of passionate colorful poems celebrating his love for the capricious "Cynthia." A gentler and more refined young poet was Tibullus (54?–19 BC), in whom grace and melodiousness took the place of Propertius' fire. These two

An introductory section of a Latin-language text graces a book in the Vatican Library collection.

CHRISTOPHORI LANDINI FLORETINI
AD ILL^MV FEDERICVM VRBINATVM
PRINCIPEM CHAMALDVLENSI
VM DISPVTATIONVM LIBER
PRIMVS CONTEMPLATIO AN AC
TIO PREFERENDA SIT FELICITER
I N C I P I T

Vatican Library, Rome

A portrait of the Italian author Petrarch appears on one page of his book 'De Remediis Utriusque Fortunae'.

poets both used the metrical form called the elegiac. Their brilliant contemporary Ovid (43 BC–AD 17?) polished this form to the same perfection to which Virgil had brought the hexameter and Horace various lyrical forms. Ovid was a facile and copious writer. He became the uncrowned laureate of the later Augustan age, whose glittering coldness and cynical worldliness he perfectly embodied in his licentious 'Art of Love'. His greatest work is the romantic 'Metamorphoses'. In this fascinating narrative poem he interwove a vast number of stories that were borrowed from ancient mythology.

The Augustan age was the Golden Age of Latin poetry, but it was also the time of the most famous Roman historian. Livy (59 BC–AD 17) is noted for his splendid rhetoric (*see* Livy). He preferred literary effectiveness to historical accuracy. Thus his narrative of Rome from its founding is more like a prose epic, a series of splendid pictures, than history.

The Silver Age

After Ovid and Livy the decline of Roman literature set in rapidly. All writing suffered from the custom of public readings. An author was tempted to write brilliant passages to win his listeners' praise, even though he might injure his work as a whole.

The satirist Juvenal (AD 60?–140) and the epigrammatist Martial (AD 40?–104) belong to this Silver Age of Latin literature. Juvenal's savage castigations of Roman life have been translated and imitated by many English poets (*see* Juvenal). These men are chiefly interesting now for the picture they give of life in the days of the empire.

The tragedies of Seneca were models for early English dramatists. Today they are read as curiosities, but Seneca's philosophical studies can still be enjoyed (*see* Seneca).

Tacitus (AD 55?–120?) in his terse and vivid style provides a number of illuminating historical pictures (*see* Tacitus). The 'Germania' is the only view of central Europe under the early Roman Empire. His

'Agricola' is a fine biography. What remains of his 'Annals' and 'Histories' is a chief source for the events of the first century of the Roman Empire. Suetonius (AD 75?–160) was a writer of much less distinction than Tacitus. He was one of Hadrian's private secretaries and therefore had access to documentary sources that he used to write his gossipy 'Lives of the Twelve Caesars'.

Perhaps the most interesting writings in the Silver Age are the letters of Pliny the Younger (AD 61?–113). The most famous one tells of the death of his uncle Pliny the Elder in the eruption of Vesuvius that buried Pompeii. As a whole these letters give a racy picture of the time that is also described by Juvenal and Tacitus. Pliny the Elder (AD 23–79) was the author of a 'Natural History', a priceless storehouse of information about the science of ancient times. Two other works of the Silver Age strike a more modern note—the literary criticism of Quintilian and the 'Satyricon', the prose novel of Petronius Arbiter.

The Middle Ages

The classical period of Latin literature came to a gradual end as the Roman Empire began breaking up under the onslaughts of barbarian invasions. But the use of Latin as a literary vehicle persisted in the West for more than a thousand years.

One of the chief reasons for the survival of Latin resulted from the empire's domination over much of Europe for about 500 years. Even when the empire was gone, the use of Latin remained because it had been for so long the language of the ruling classes. An even more significant reason was the presence of the Christian church—still headquartered at Rome—as the dominant social and religious force of the whole medieval period.

The language of the church in the West was Latin, and the bulk of classical and religious learning was preserved and transmitted by the monasteries and cathedral schools and, much later, in the early universities. Latin prose of the Middle Ages was used in official documents, laws, treaties, and diplomatic correspondence, as well as in theological and philosophical works, scientific treatises, devotional exercises, personal correspondence, textbooks, history, and biographies of the saints.

Christian writers in the West created a great body of Latin literature, beginning in the 4th and 5th centuries. Two outstanding authors of this early period were Saint Jerome (347?–420) and Saint Augustine (354–430). Jerome's translation of the Bible into Latin, called the Vulgate, had a profound influence on both religious and secular thought in the Middle Ages (see Bible). Among the works of Augustine that have become classics are 'The City of God', 'The Confessions', and 'On Christian Doctrine' (see Augustine of Hippo). An influential work of the 6th century was 'The Consolation of Philosophy' by Boethius (480?–524), a statesman, theologian, and scholar.

From the 6th to the 9th centuries there was little noteworthy in Latin literature. But early in the 9th century, under the rule of Charlemagne, a revival of learning took place during what has been called the Carolingian Renaissance. Scholars and poets from all over Europe flocked to the court of Charlemagne and created a number of notable works. Probably the most memorable was 'On the Division of Nature', a philosophical theory of the universe by Johannes Scotus Erigena (815?–77). (See also Charlemagne.)

Some of the most enduring medieval—and world— literature was produced during the 12th and 13th centuries. The Englishman Geoffrey of Monmouth (1100?–54) wrote 'History of the Kings of Britain'. The chief scientific writer of the era was Roger Bacon (1214?–94?), a philosopher whose ideas on experimental science led to his imprisonment (see Bacon, Roger). Among the major theologians of the period were Peter Abelard (1079–1142), author of 'Sic et Non' (Yes and No); the outstanding Saint Thomas Aquinas (1225?–74), author of many significant works that included 'Summa Theologica' (Summary of Theology); and Bernard of Clairvaux (1090–1153), whose many writings and sermons had a profound influence on the religious and political life of his time. (See also Abelard; Aquinas.)

The Renaissance

During the late Middle Ages the use of what are now the national languages of Europe began to find greater expression in writing, though works in Latin were still being published as late as the 18th century. Early Renaissance writers often used it as well as their vernacular languages. The use of Latin was perpetuated in the Renaissance because so much of the scholarship of the time was devoted to the revival of the classical culture of ancient Rome. This was particularly true of the Italian Renaissance. In the northern European countries, the Renaissance tended to emphasize a revival of early Christianity and its literature. (See also Renaissance.)

Notable among the early Renaissance writers were Albertino Mussato (1261–1329), an author of plays modeled on those of Seneca; Petrarch (1304–74), a poet whose many writings include the epic 'Africa'; and Giovanni Boccaccio (1313–75). Boccaccio is best remembered for his remarkable 'Decameron', in Italian, but he also wrote 'On the Genealogy of the Gods of the Gentiles', in Latin (see Boccaccio).

Perhaps the greatest of the later Renaissance authors in northern Europe was Erasmus of Rotterdam (1466?–1536), a classical scholar and the editor of the first Greek version of the New Testament. Of his Latin writings, the most enduring is 'The Praise of Folly'. Other major figures of the late Renaissance who used Latin were Thomas More (1478–1535), Francis Bacon (1561–1626), Hugo Grotius (1583–1645), René Descartes (1596–1650), Baruch Spinoza (1632–77), and Isaac Newton (1642–1727).

In the modern period, the major written documents of the Roman Catholic church, such as papal encyclicals, continue to be published in Latin. (See also Romance Languages.)

LATITUDE
AND LONGITUDE

LATITUDE AND LONGITUDE. A system of lines is used to find the location of any place on the surface of the earth. Commonly called a *grid system*, it is made up of two sets of lines that cross each other. One set—*lines of latitude*—runs in an east-west direction. The other set—*lines of longitude*—runs in a north-south direction. Although these are only imaginary lines encircling the earth, they can be drawn on globes and maps as if they actually existed.

Drawing the Earth Grid

To draw the lines of the grid system on a globe or map, it is necessary to have starting points, or points of reference. There are two such points of reference on the earth. These are the *North Pole* and the *South Pole*. The poles are the points at which the earth's *axis* meets the earth's surface.

Halfway between the poles is an east-west line called the *equator*. It encircles the earth and divides it into two equal parts, or hemispheres. The North Pole is in the hemisphere north of the equator—the *northern hemisphere*. The South Pole is in the hemisphere south of the equator—the *southern hemisphere*.

One set of lines in the earth's grid system is drawn around the globe parallel to the equator. These are east-west lines, or lines of latitude. In the basic grid there are 89 such equally spaced lines to the north of the equator, 89 to the south. Where the 90th east-west lines would be are two points—the North and South poles. Each east-west line is a circle. The farther it is from the equator the shorter its length. The 60th east-west line, for example, is only half as long as the equator.

East-west lines are numbered from 0 at the equator—the east-west base line—to 89 near the poles. The east-west lines between the equator and the North Pole are north of the equator; those between the equator and the South Pole, south of the equator. The city of New Orleans, La., is located on the 30th east-west line north of the equator. But many other places in the world are also situated on this line. That is why a second set of lines is needed to locate the exact position of New Orleans—or of any other place.

The second set of lines in the earth's grid system is drawn from pole to pole. These are north-south lines, or lines of longitude. One north-south line has been chosen by international agreement as the zero, or base, line. It passes through Greenwich, England, a borough of London. In the basic grid there are 180 such equally spaced lines to the east of the Greenwich base line, 180 to the west. Unlike east-west lines, all north-south lines have the same length.

FACTS ABOUT LINES OF LATITUDE

- Are known as *parallels*.
- Run in an east-west direction.
- Measure distance north or south from the equator.
- Are parallel to one another and never meet.
- Cross the prime meridian at right angles.
- Lie in planes that cross the earth's axis at right angles.
- Get shorter toward the poles, with only the equator, the longest, a great circle.

FACTS ABOUT LINES OF LONGITUDE

- Are known as *meridians*.
- Run in a north-south direction.
- Measure distance east or west of the prime meridian.
- Are farthest apart at the equator and meet at the poles.
- Cross the equator at right angles.
- Lie in planes that pass through the earth's axis.
- Are equal in length.
- Are halves of great circles.

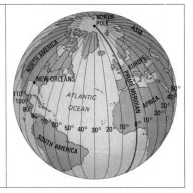

THE EARTH'S GRID SYSTEM

Only the city of New Orleans, La., is located at the crossing of the 30th east-west line north of the equator and the 90th north-south line west of the prime meridian.

- Lines of latitude cross lines of longitude at right angles.
- Although only a few lines of latitude and longitude are shown on globes and maps, their number is infinite.

LATITUDE AND LONGITUDE

North-south lines are numbered from 0 at the north-south base line both east and west to the 180th north-south line. The zero line and the 180th line together form a complete circle that, like the equator, cuts the earth into two hemispheres. The half west of the zero line can be called the *western hemisphere;* the half east of the zero line, the *eastern hemisphere.*

The north-south lines and the east-west lines together form the global grid system used to find the exact location of any place on earth. New Orleans, on the 30th east-west line north of the equator, is also on the 90th north-south line west of the north-south base line. Many places in the world—among them, Memphis, Tenn.; East St. Louis, Ill.; and the Galápagos Islands of Ecuador—are on or near the same north-south line as New Orleans. Many other places —for example, Port Arthur, Tex.; St. Augustine, Fla.; and Cairo, Egypt—are on or near the same east-west line as New Orleans. But only New Orleans is situated on both lines—exactly where they cross each other. Likewise, each place in the world—and only that place—is situated at the intersection of a given east-west line and a given north-south line.

Parallels and Meridians

All east-west lines are equidistant from the equator and from each other. This means that they are all parallel to the equator and to each other. Every point on a given east-west line, therefore, is the same distance from the equator, the same distance from the North Pole, and the same distance from the South Pole. For this reason east-west lines, or lines of latitude, are commonly referred to as parallels of latitude, or simply *parallels.*

The north-south lines, or lines of longitude, also have another name. They are commonly referred to as meridians of longitude, or simply *meridians.* The zero meridian, or base line for numbering the north-south lines, is called the *prime meridian.* Each meridian goes only halfway around the earth—from pole to pole. Each has a twin on the other side of the earth. Like the prime meridian and the 180th meridian, all such pairs of meridians form circles that cut the earth into hemispheres. These circles are known as *great circles.* Only one parallel, the equator, is a great circle.

Measurements of Angular Distance

A cutaway drawing of the earth demonstrates how latitude is determined. It makes clear that latitude is a measure of the angle between the plane of the equator and lines projected from the center of the earth. For example, the angle between a line drawn from New Orleans on the 30th line of latitude to the center of the earth and a line drawn on the plane of the equator is 30 *degrees* (30°). In each hemisphere the 30th line of latitude connects all points whose pro-

This article was contributed by Clyde Kohn, Professor of Geography, The University of Iowa.

jections to the center of the earth form a 30° angle with the plane of the equator.

The latitude of the equator is zero degrees (0°). Lines of latitude north and south of the equator are numbered to 90° because the angular distance from the equator to each pole is one fourth of a circle, or one fourth of 360°. There is no latitude higher than 90°. The North Pole is situated at 90° north latitude, or simply 90° N. The South Pole is at 90° south latitude, or 90° S.

The cutaway drawing of the earth also shows how longitude is determined. Longitude is seen to be a measure of the angle between the planes of two meridian circles, one of which is the prime meridian. For example, the plane of the 90th line of longitude, on which New Orleans is located, forms a 90° angle with the plane of the prime meridian. All places on the 90th line of longitude west of the prime meridian, therefore, are at 90° west longitude.

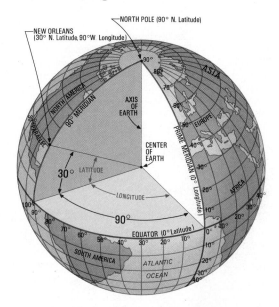

This cutaway drawing shows that the latitude and longitude of any place are based on the sizes of two angles that originate at the center of the earth. For New Orleans these angles are 30 degrees (north latitude) and 90 degrees (west longitude).

The prime meridian is designated zero degrees (0°) longitude. Lines of longitude are numbered east of the prime meridian from 0° to 180° east longitude and west from 0° to 180° west longitude. There is no longitude higher than 180°, and the 180th meridian east and the 180th meridian west are identical.

Degrees of latitude and longitude can be divided into sixtieths, or *minutes* ('). Any location on earth can be described as lying at a certain number of degrees and minutes of latitude either north or south of the equator and at a certain number of degrees and minutes of longitude either east or west of the prime meridian. For example, the United States Capitol in Washington, D. C., is at 38 degrees 53 minutes north latitude (38°53' N.) and 77 degrees 0 minutes west

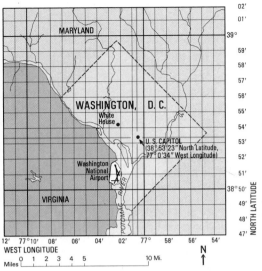

As shown on the small-scale globe perspective, Washington, D. C., is located at the crossing of the 39th east-west line north of the equator (39 degrees north latitude) and the 77th north-south line west of the prime meridian (77 degrees west longitude).

The large-scale map locates the city more precisely and pinpoints specific places of interest within it. The dome of the United States Capitol, for example, is at 38 degrees, 53 minutes, 23 seconds north latitude and 77 degrees, 0 minutes, 34 seconds west longitude (38°-53′23″N., 77°0′34″W.). To the nearest minute, what are the latitude and longitude of the White House? the National Airport?

longitude (77°0′ W.). Minutes of latitude and longitude can be divided into sixtieths, or *seconds* (″), when more precise information on the location of a place is needed, for example, by navigators, surveyors, or map makers.

A degree of latitude can easily be changed into miles. Since the circumference of the earth is roughly 25,000 miles, the length of each degree of latitude is about 69 miles (1/360 of 25,000 miles). Degrees of latitude vary a little in length—the variation between the shortest and the longest is less than a mile—because the earth is not a perfect sphere but is flattened slightly toward the poles and bulges slightly around the equator (*see* Earth). The length of a degree of longitude, however, varies from about 69 miles at the equator to zero at the poles, where the meridians come together.

Finding Latitude and Longitude

The navigator of a ship or an airplane can determine the latitude of his position by using an instrument called a *sextant*. With it he measures the *altitude* (angle above the horizon) of the sun as the sun *transits*, or crosses, his meridian (longitude).

HOW DEGREES OF LATITUDE AND LONGITUDE VARY IN LENGTH

Lat.	Length of 1° of Lat.	Length of 1° of Long.	Lat.	Length of 1° of Lat.	Length of 1° of Long.
0°	68.70 mi.	69.17 mi.	50°	69.12 mi.	44.55 mi.
5°	68.71	68.91	55°	69.18	39.77
10°	68.73	68.13	60°	69.23	34.67
15°	68.75	66.83	65°	69.28	29.32
20°	68.79	65.03	70°	69.32	23.73
25°	68.83	62.73	75°	69.36	17.96
30°	68.88	59.96	80°	69.39	12.05
35°	68.94	56.73	85°	69.40	6.05
40°	68.99	53.06	90°	69.41	0.00
45°	69.05	49.00			

He then calculates his latitude by combining the observed altitude with information from an *almanac*—a book of data about the movement of the sun and stars. In the evening, latitude may similarly be found by observing stars (*see* Navigation).

Longitude is more difficult to determine than latitude because the sextant and the almanac together do not yield enough information. To calculate his longitude, a navigator must also know the exact time at which he is making his observations. The time is needed because the sun and stars, as they appear to move across the sky, look the same at all places in a given latitude at some time during each day.

The invention of clocks during the Renaissance was the first step toward the reliable calculation of longitude. The clocks of that era, however, were too inaccurate for use in navigation. In 1714 the British Board of Longitude offered a large cash prize to anyone who could build a clock that would meet certain standards of accuracy throughout long ocean voyages. By 1735 John Harrison, a British clockmaker, had submitted the first of several clocks, the last of which won the prize for him. They were called chronometers (*see* Watches and Clocks). In 1766 Pierre Le Roy, a Frenchman, built a chronometer more accurate than Harrison's. From that time on, sailors have been able to determine longitude accurately by comparing local time with Greenwich mean time (GMT). (*See also* Time.)

Shipboard chronometers are set to show GMT. Because of the speed and direction of the earth's rotation, local time at a given place will be one hour behind GMT for every 15 degrees west of the prime meridian and one hour ahead of GMT for every 15 degrees east of the prime meridian. For example, if a ship's chronometer reads 0300 (3:00 A.M.) and the ship's local time is 0800 (8:00 A.M.), the ship is 75 degrees east of Greenwich, or at 75° E. Special radio time signals allow navigators to check the accuracy of their chronometers.

How the Prime Meridian Was Selected

Before a prime meridian was agreed upon, map makers usually began numbering the lines of longitude at whichever meridian passed through the site of their national observatory. In the United States, for example, this was the Naval Observatory at Washington, D. C.; in France, the Paris Observatory; and in Great Britain, the Royal Greenwich Observatory, at Greenwich. Since Britain was a world leader in exploration and map making, navigators of other nations often used British maps. As a result, in 1884 the meridian of Greenwich was adopted throughout most of the world as the prime meridian. In the 1950's the Royal Greenwich Observatory was moved about 60 miles southeast of Greenwich. The Greenwich meridian, however, remained the prime meridian.

There was still another reason for the selection of the Greenwich meridian as 0° longitude. Travelers must change time by an entire day when they cross the 180th meridian (*see* Time). If this meridian crossed a large country, timekeeping and the establishment of calendar dates would be difficult. But with the Greenwich meridian set at zero, the 180th meridian is near the middle of the Pacific Ocean. It crosses only a small land area in northeastern Asia and divides some island groups in the Pacific. To avoid differing dates in those areas, the nations of the world established a special line across which dates change. It swerves from the 180th meridian whenever convenient. This line is called the *international date line* (*see* International Date Line).

Special Lines of Latitude and Longitude

Several lines of latitude have special significance. One of these is the equator. Two other special lines of latitude are the 30th parallels. The area between them, straddling the equator, is commonly referred to as the *low latitudes*. The low latitudes are generally warm lands. The two 60th parallels are also special lines of latitude. The areas north and south of the 60th parallels, which center on the North and South poles, are commonly referred to as the *high latitudes*. The high latitudes are generally cold lands. The areas between the 30th and 60th parallels in both hemispheres are commonly referred to as the *middle latitudes*. Generally, middle-latitude lands have four seasons—fall, winter, spring, and summer (*see* Seasons).

The latitude of a place, accordingly, is a clue to its climate. The yearly average of insolation, or heat energy received from the sun, depends in large measure on the angle or slant of the sun's rays. This angle varies with distance from the equator (latitude). Regions in high latitudes, both north and south, get less insolation and are therefore usually colder than regions in low latitudes. (*See also* Climate.)

Four other special lines of latitude are the *Tropic of Cancer* (23½° N.), the *Tropic of Capricorn* (23½° S.), the *Arctic Circle* (66½° N.), and the *Antarctic Circle* (66½° S.). These lines relate to the tilt of the earth's axis as the earth revolves around the sun. The Tropics of Cancer and Capricorn mark the limits of the zone astride the equator in which the sun appears directly overhead at some time during the year. The Arctic and Antarctic circles mark the limits of the areas around each pole in which the sun at some time during the year does not rise or set for a period of 24 hours or more.

The only special line of longitude is the prime meridian. Time zone boundaries and the international date line are based on certain lines of longitude but do not follow them exactly. (*See also* Directions; Maps and Globes.)

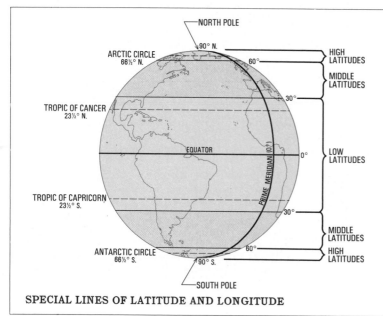

SPECIAL LINES OF LATITUDE AND LONGITUDE

Popperfoto—Pictorial Parade

Where the prime meridian passes through Greenwich, England, it is marked by a special plaque.

LATTER-DAY SAINTS *see* MORMONS.

LATVIAN SOVIET SOCIALIST REPUBLIC.

Latvia was one of the three Baltic states that established democratic governments after the Russian Revolution of 1917 but lost independence in 1940 when they were incorporated in the Soviet Union. (*See also* Estonian Soviet Socialist Republic; Lithuanian Soviet Socialist Republic.) Once mainly an agricultural country, the Latvian Soviet Socialist Republic has become industrialized under Soviet rule.

Yury Belinsky—TASS/Sovfoto

The Doma Cathedral, built about 1215, dominates an old section of Riga on the banks of the Western Dvina River.

The Land and Climate

Latvia is covered with glacial deposits, some of which have formed hills. In the west the Kurzeme Uplands reach about 600 feet (180 meters) in height. In the northeast the Vidzeme Uplands have summits of more than 1,000 feet (300 meters). In the southeast the lower Latgale Uplands contain many small lakes. The center of the country consists of the Zemgale Plain, while the Vidzeme Uplands are surrounded by the Latvian and East Latvian plains. These plains are marshy in places, with several small lakes, and are crossed by a number of rivers, the largest of which is the Daugava, or Western Dvina.

The climate is cloudy, cool, and humid. Winters are not very cold, and summers are not hot. The Gulf of Riga freezes for much of the winter, but the rest of the coast is ice-free.

The People

The Latvians, or Letts, speak a Baltic language allied to Lithuanian. They are predominantly Lutheran Protestants, though some are Roman Catholics. The republic's population of 2,521,000 (1979 census) includes about 1,344,000 Latvians. Because of a low birthrate their numbers have grown little in recent years. Many fled the country after World War II. There are about 821,500 Russians, and some Belorussians, Ukrainians, and Poles who have migrated to Latvia since 1940.

The advanced culture of Latvia includes not only many modern writers and artists, but also a rich folk heritage—especially songs and poetry. The Latvian national poet Rainis (Jan Plieksans) used legends and folk music as themes for his modern plays and poems. The main center of Latvian culture is the capital, Riga, which has museums, theaters, a university, and an Academy of Sciences.

Economy and Transportation

In spite of Soviet industrialization, agriculture is still essential in the economy. Because of poor soils and the cool climate, growing crops is less important than raising livestock—mainly dairy cattle and pigs. Some rye, barley, flax, potatoes, sugar beets, and fodder crops are grown. Fishing is important along the Baltic coast and also in the Atlantic. The fish is processed at the ports of Ventspils, Riga, and Liepaja.

Latvia has few industrial raw materials. The only fuel is peat, which is used in several large electric-power plants. There are a few small hydroelectric plants. Natural gas comes by pipeline from the Ukraine. There is a small steel plant at Liepaja. Manufacturing has developed rapidly in recent years, and electric motors, farm machinery, buses, railroad equipment, and ships are produced. Latvia also manufactures radios, television sets, and household equipment for the entire Soviet Union. Much of this industry is located in Riga, which has a large skilled work force. Timber from Latvia's forests is used in the manufacture of furniture.

Latvia has the densest rail network of all the Soviet republics. Riga is connected by rail with the other Latvian cities and with other regions of the Soviet Union. The ports of Riga, Ventspils, and Liepaja are important for Soviet overseas trade. Riga is linked by air with the major Soviet cities.

Government and History

Latvia is one of 15 Soviet Socialist Republics. It has its own Communist party and government, but they are controlled by the central government, located in Moscow.

In the Middle Ages Latvia was conquered and ruled by the Germans as the provinces of Courland and Livonia. In the 16th century the Poles seized the region, but in the 17th century the Swedes obtained control of northern Livonia. Russian attempts to control the Baltic coast finally succeeded when Peter the Great took northern Livonia from Sweden in 1721. By the end of the 18th century all of Latvia was controlled by Russia. Independent after the Russian Revolution, Latvia was annexed to the Soviet Union after the Red Army invaded it in 1940. During World War II the Germans occupied Latvia, but in 1944 the Soviets reclaimed it.

The public laundry area in Karachi, Pakistan, is on the Layari River and is known as Washermen's Laundry. Laundry is done here mostly by professional *dhobis*, or washermen.

LAUNDRY.

It has always been necessary to keep wearing apparel and linens clean by using some method of laundering or cleaning. When clothes are not washed frequently, the buildup of bacteria causes offensive odors. During earlier periods of Western civilization, perfumes and other masking agents were used to overcome such odors rather than washing the garment itself.

As civilizations matured and learned the importance of clean, sanitary linens and garments to health and well-being, the emphasis on cleanliness increased. People found that the use even of cold water without the help of soap or detergents was partially effective in removing soil and bacteria. With the use of hot water, detergents, and bleaches in washing machines, clothing and linens can now be kept clean and virtually free of bacteria. (*See also* Dry Cleaning.)

In the Home

Home laundering is most familiar, as it is a part of daily living in many parts of the world. Since World War II great strides have been made in the convenience of home washing. Earlier it was a laborious task at best, usually consuming an entire day of a housewife's week. The automatic washer and dryer revolutionized the chore of home laundering. Heating

This article was contributed by Kenneth W. Faig, Director of Education, International Fabricare Institute, and President, Walnut Hills Laundering Company.

water to fill the washer, using the washer and wringer, and hanging linen and clothing to dry have become obsolete with the home laundering equipment now available. By merely loading clothes in a washing machine and adding detergent, the modern home machine automatically puts the clothes through one suds cycle and one or two rinses. A person is freed to do other things while the wash is being done. Instead of hanging the clothes to dry, a person can now remove them from the washer and quickly dry them in a home dryer.

The chemical industry has supplied laundry products far superior to the tallow soaps of the past. Detergents that are not affected by minerals in the water supply have made possible cleaner and whiter clothes than formerly. The combination of detergents, bleaches, fabric softeners, and fluorescent brighteners enable the home washing process to produce clean, sparkling linens.

The textile industry has helped home washing by supplying fabrics of polyester and cotton blends that do not require ironing—often called "wash and wear." Sheets, pillowcases, tablecloths, and wearing apparel made with these fabrics can now be dried to a satisfactory appearance without ironing.

Laundromats

For those without home washing equipment, the neighborhood laundromat is available. A typical laundromat has coin-operated machines that may include 30 to 40 washers and 15 to 20 dryers. Ample table space for folding the laundry after drying is usually provided, as well as vending machines for laundry supplies and for snacks and electronic games for amusement. The customer must operate the equipment, but most laundromats have an attendant present to help with problems and to ensure that all machines are operating properly. Some laundromats also offer coin-operated dry-cleaning machines for customer use or have a professional dry-cleaning operation so that a customer can accomplish all garment and linen care in one location. Laundromats are a big business in the United States, with annual sales of more than 1.5 billion dollars in the early 1980s.

Commercial Industry

The commercial laundry is different from both home laundering and a laundromat in its procedures and its structure. It is usually a medium-sized company that serves customers through either walk-in stores or home delivery. Soiled garments and linen are sent to the laundry and returned clean and ready for use. Although there will always be people who by necessity or desire use the service of a commercial laundry, the advent of polyester and cotton fabrics and the improvement of home washing equipment have reduced retail customers to a small percentage of the work processed by commercial laundries. They now serve mostly hospitals, motels, restaurants, hotels, and businesses. The retail customer volume consists primarily of shirts and dry cleaning.

The laundering process in the commercial laundry is technical, involving much chemistry. There are precise chemical additions to each step. Instead of one suds bath, there are three or four. Each operation is carefully controlled to obtain maximum soil and stain removal. The sudsing operations are followed by four or five rinses that remove all of the chemicals used in the sudsing operations. Such control is needed to assure that everything is clean and free of bacteria when it is returned to the customer.

Laundries have often been called steam laundries from the great amount of steam used in their work. Laundries use large amounts of water, usually averaging 3 to 3½ gallons (11 to 13 liters) of water per pound (.5 kilogram) of clothes processed. Two of the three gallons of water are heated to 160° F (71° C). Of the steam produced by the boilers, two thirds is used to heat the hot water required. The other third heats machinery for finishing flatwork and wearing apparel. The fuel and electricity consumed make up a major expense in the operation of a laundry. The vast amount of water used is also costly, both in its supply and its disposal, as it often contains pollutants.

Modern laundries have become very automated. Procedures that once required many employees now are accomplished by very few or none at all. In many cases the soiled laundry is loaded into the washers by overhead slings, and the machines operate by means of programmed controls that automatically add water, dump waste water, and add supplies at the proper time. After the washing is complete, much of the water is removed from the laundry items by rapid spinning much as in the home washer. Other systems dump the wet clothes into containers in which compression devices squeeze the water out or remove it by spinning machines called centrifugal extractors.

All finishing in a commercial laundry begins by ironing materials while they are damp, approximately 40 percent moisture by weight. The moisture is driven off by heat under pressure, and the result is a finish not obtainable with a hand iron.

Finishing equipment is highly specialized. Flatwork is ironed by a large flatwork ironer with padded rolls that ride against steam-heated chests. As the linen travels between the roll and the chest, it dries and develops a smooth finish. It is not unusual for such machines to iron a thousand sheets per hour. Clothing, such as shirts and blouses, are finished on specialized presses that press the sleeves, the collar and cuff, and the entire body of the shirt. Two operators using such equipment can finish from 110 to 120 shirts per hour.

Items that require only drying, such as bath towels, are dried in large tumblers that resemble home dryers. Their capacities range from 20 to 400 pounds (10 to 80 kilograms).

There are approximately 3,000 commercial laundries in the United States. In the early 1980s the annual sales volume of the commercial laundry business totaled nearly 800 million dollars.

Specialized Laundries

Institutions such as hospitals, hotels, and motels often have their own laundry facilities, which can range in size from two pieces of equipment to large automated plants, depending on the size of the institution. Their work load is primarily flatwork such as sheets, pillowcases, and towels. Most institutions also process the uniforms worn by their employees. Considering the number of employees at a large hospital or hotel, uniforms can be a major factor in the size of an institutional plant.

The use of polyester and cotton blends for uniforms has greatly reduced the laborious job of pressing. It allows the laundry to wash and merely dry the uniforms. Some laundries process uniforms through a steam tunnel after laundering. The uniforms are hung on a conveyor and travel through a steam chamber. The steam relaxes the fibers of the fabric, and the garments are then dried by warm air. While the finish is not the same as that produced by pressing, satisfactory quality is obtained.

Hospitals and hotels. All of the technical procedures used by commercial laundries are found in the institutional laundry. Sanitary linen is of prime importance to hospitals. Finished linen is closely checked for bacteria count, and great efforts are made to prevent transmission of bacteria through the hospital by linens. The linen is virtually free of all bacteria when the washing and finishing are completed, but there is danger of picking up airborne bacteria before the linen is used. To help prevent and slow the growth of such airborne bacteria, a bacteriostatic chemical is used during the washing cycle. All baskets, carts, and transports for the linen are steam cleaned on a regular schedule to reduce further the possibility of bacteria transmission.

A typical patient in a hospital uses from 12 to 15 pounds (5.5 to 6.8 kilograms) of linen per day. The laundry for a 500-bed hospital, therefore, must process from 6,000 to 7,500 pounds (2,700 to 3,400 kilograms) of laundry per day. As a hospital operates seven days a week, its laundry might handle up to 52,500 pounds (23,800 kilograms) of linen per week. A typical hotel room generates from seven to nine pounds (three to four kilograms) of linen per day. The hotel laundry may also furnish laundry and dry-cleaning services for guests of the hotel.

Linen supply. Another specialized segment of the laundry industry is called linen supply. This business supplies linens—both flatwork and uniforms—to such customers as restaurants, hotels, motels, and manufacturing plants and increasingly to hospitals. It differs from other laundries in that the supplier owns the goods instead of the customer. The customer does not receive the same laundered item each day, week, or other prescribed period of time but is provided with like items—always clean—on a regular schedule. Linen supply has a great advantage over the commercial laundry because it does not need to identify individual pieces for each customer. Clean standardized items are provided in bulk.

In the United States the linen supply business totals more than one billion dollars in yearly sales volume. Approximately 21 percent of the billing is for the initial cost of the items, making inventory control an important element of the operation.

Industrial laundry. The industrial laundry supplies uniforms and dust control items for industry and business. In recent years an overlapping has occurred between the linen supply and the industrial laundry businesses. Most linen supply plants now also furnish uniforms and dust control items. Uniforms, shop towels, dust mops, dust rags, and mats are the principal items supplied by the industrial laundry. Most of these contain a great amount of soil, so the washing process is different from the typical laundry. Approximately 30 percent of the plants dry clean uniforms rather than wash them. A great amount of the soil is oily or greasy in nature, and it can be removed more easily and more effectively by dry cleaning. Many uniforms worn by factory employees, janitors, and automobile dealers and garages are supplied by industrial launderers. The mats or rugs at the entrances of many buildings are supplied by this type of service. Most floors of commercial establishments are maintained by treated mops supplied by an industrial laundry.

The industrial laundry had the largest growth rate of any segment of the laundry industry in the 1970s, reaching an annual total sales in the United States of more than one billion dollars. It is, however, vulnerable to periods of business recession. When factories lay off employees, the uniforms remain with the supplier. Fewer mops, mats, and shop towels are used when business is slack. Distribution and delivery in both linen supply and the industrial laundry require fleets of trucks.

Diaper service. Supplying clean diapers for babies is a very special part of the laundry business. It also requires a fleet of trucks and a staff of service drivers that must be separate, as the quantity and nature of the soil on diapers prohibits their being collected with other laundry. The service is offered in two forms: the customer may own the diapers and use the service for laundering or rent the diapers along with the service as in the linen supply business. Washing procedures must be meticulous, using cleaning agents that are able to remove the soil and yet not cause irritation of babies' tender skin. The decline in the birth rate and the use of disposable diapers have greatly reduced the diaper service business.

History

Centuries before the modern power laundry came into existence, ancient civilizations had their own unique methods of washing and ironing clothes. The first known record of laundering goes back almost 4,000 years to a tomb at Beni Hasan in Egypt. On the wall of the tomb is a representation of two slaves washing a cloth. One pours water over the material while the other rubs it. The water runs into a trough below. In some parts of the world clothes are still washed by similar crude methods.

Ancient Rome. The early Romans were proud of the garments they wore draped in graceful folds as they strolled in the Forum. Because the cloth was mainly wool, it needed skillful manipulation to retain its size and shape. Garments were ordinarily sent to a public laundry where the fuller, or laundryman, washed, whitened, redyed, and pressed the garments.

After they washed the clothes, the fullers placed them in a fuller's press. This consisted of two uprights, two planks, and a large screw top. Turned by cranks, it flattened the cloth between the planks. This press was probably the first step toward the development of calenders and manglers. These appeared in England many centuries later and were the forerunners of the present-day commercial laundry's flatwork ironer.

United States. In the United States the first patent on "washing cloaths" was issued to Nathaniel Briggs in 1797. In the next half century more than 200 patents were granted on washing machines alone. Until about 1850, models instead of drawings were filed with the patent office. As a result of this policy, no drawings or descriptions of these many washing machines have been recorded.

The first laundry is thought to have been started in 1837 by Independence Stark in Troy, N.Y. Stark had a collar factory and opened a plant for laundering his product. He called it the Troy Laundry. Many laundries are named Troy after the first one in the United States.

Soiled items are fed into tunnel washers (right) at an institutional laundry. They move on a conveyor to a "squeezebox" extractor (far right). Wet laundry is loaded into a dryer (below), and dried items are fed to a flatwork ironer (below right).

Larry Kai Ebert—American Laundry Digest

The first complete power laundry in the United States was probably born of the needs of the "forty-niners" during the gold rush days of California. Oakland was then a struggling settlement with a population made up almost entirely of men. There were no women to wash their clothes. A few Chinese operated individual laundries along creek banks. Some men sent their laundry all the way to Hawaii. They had to wait up to six months for delivery. In 1851 a man named D. Davis established the Contra Costa Laundry in Oakland. At first all the work was done by hand. Later a 12-shirt washing machine was built and operated by a ten-horsepower donkey engine.

The man who is credited with making power laundries commercially practical is Hamilton E. Smith of Philadelphia, Pa. In 1863 he patented the reciprocating mechanism to reverse the movement of the revolving drum in the washing machine. That same year he established a power laundry in the Saint Charles Hotel and the Monongahela House located in Pittsburgh, Pa.

Companies were soon formed for the manufacture of laundry machinery. As they worked to perfect their products, the laundry business grew rapidly. In 1898 the editor of the *National Laundry Journal* estimated that United States laundry owners collected 52 million dollars a year. In 1909 the United States census figures showed that earnings had increased to $104,680,000. In spite of this phenomenal growth, it remained chiefly a shirt-and-collar business until about 1915. Then, along with the development and successful marketing of electrically operated washing machines, came "wet-wash" laundries.

Changes. Laundries had priced what little family wash they had formerly done on a per-piece basis. With the introduction of the wet wash, they began to charge on a per-pound basis for all classes of work. Up until this time deliveries were made to customers on a bicycle or in horse-drawn wagons. It was not long, however, before the industry's pickup and delivery service became motorized.

Laundry machinery continued to develop and improve. The revolving cylinder was the first major development in washers. It failed to do the job at first because centrifugal force caused the wet clothes to cling to the sides of the cylinder. There was not enough action to remove the dirt. This problem was solved by the rotary washer with reversing action. It turned over the clothes inside the cylinders and splashed them in sudsy water. Centrifugal extraction became the normal method of removing water from wet fabrics and the heated tumbler dryer the standard machine for final drying.

Similar progress was made in apparel presses. Instead of imitating a traditional hand iron, with its sliding action, pressure was applied through a steam-heated chest, or buck, which closed over the garment or over which rollers traveled. The ultimate improvement, however, is probably the development of fabrics that require little or no ironing.

The mountain laurel shrub (above) produces clusters of beautifully colored flowers at the ends of its branches. Individual flowers (left) are saucer-shaped.

Photos, George Taloumis

LAUREL. One of the most spectacular of wild shrubs is the laurel. Its masses of pink, crimson, or white blossoms may blanket whole mountainsides and tinge great marshy areas with rich color. The laurels are hardy evergreen shrubs. The flowers grow in clusters. Each blossom is saucer-shaped with five lobes. There are five sepals and one pistil. Ten stamens curve outward and over from the center of the blossom, their tips (anthers) hidden in pouches below the rim of the flower (for illustration of these parts, *see* Flower). At the touch of an insect, the anthers spring out of their pouches and dust the visitor with pollen. Thus the insect fertilizes the plants as it travels from flower to flower. There are several kinds of laurels in North America, all members of the heath family, Ericaceae.

Mountain laurel (scientific name, *Kalmia latifolia*) grows in the mountains of eastern North America from New Brunswick to the Gulf coast. The shrubs may reach 20 feet (6 meters) in height. Thick clusters of pinkish-white flowers grow at the ends of the branches. The large leathery leaves are pointed at both ends, smooth-edged, and bright glossy green.

Sheep laurel, or lambkill (*Kalmia angustifolia*), is much smaller than mountain laurel. It grows in swamps and wet pastures from Labrador to Georgia and westward to the Pacific coast. Crimson flowers cluster around the stem, which is terminated by the new leaves. Its leaves and flowers are poisonous to young animals.

The bay, or sweet, laurel (*Laurus nobilis*) is a small tree found in the Mediterranean region of Europe, in Great Britain, and in southern Asia. It has yellowish-green flowers. It belongs to the laurel family, Lauraceae, not, like mountain laurel and sheep laurel, to the heath family. The laurel family includes sassafras, camphor, and spicebush, or wild allspice—trees and shrubs that are noted for their scents. From the berries and other parts of the sweet laurel is distilled an aromatic oil used in the manufacture of toilet waters. Dried bay leaves are used for flavoring in cooking and pickling.

The ancient Greeks used the entwined twigs of bay, or sweet, laurel to crown victors of the Pythian games. The tree was sacred to Apollo. The nymph Daphne, when pursued by Apollo, was, in answer to her prayers, changed into a laurel. The custom of placing a laurel crown on the brow of poets dates from the Middle Ages (*see* Poet Laureate).

LAURENTIAN PLATEAU, or CANADIAN SHIELD. About half of Canada's area consists of some of the oldest rock in the world. This Precambrian igneous rock is in a vast mass called the Laurentian Plateau, or Canadian Shield. It was dry land ages ago when the oceans still rolled over the sites of the Appalachian and the Rocky mountains. It was uplifted to form a plateau, and then carved by stream erosion. Finally glaciers scraped it almost level.

This combination of uplift and erosion gave eastern Canada its present-day appearance as a rocky tableland deeply carved by rivers. The Saguenay, a tributary of the Saint Lawrence, with great cliffs rising in some places to 1,500 and 1,700 feet (460 and 520 meters) has some of the most beautiful river scenery in the world. The whole plateau is covered with winding waterways and lakes; one can travel across it in almost any direction by canoe, with only occasional short distances of land travel.

Shaped like a great "V," with Hudson Bay in the center, the Laurentian Plateau comprises some 1,850,000 square miles (4,790,000 square kilometers). On the east it underlies most of Quebec and Labrador. On the south it extends through Ontario as far as Lake Superior and the Adirondack Mountains. Portions of its southern edge are exposed in northern Michigan and Wisconsin. Its western edge borders the interior plains and lowlands. It may be traced by the line of lakes running northwest from Lake Winnipeg to Great Slave and Great Bear lakes. The plateau is tilted from a clifflike edge in Quebec and Labrador to sea level around Hudson Bay. The average elevation is 600 to 1,200 feet (180 to 365 meters) above sea level. The highest point is Cirque Mountain, 5,160 feet (1,570 meters) in the Torngats.

The plateau is one of the world's leading sources of iron, nickel, and copper. Thick forests cover much of the region, but the soil is too shallow and rocky for farming. Great herds of caribou and musk oxen; fur-bearing animals; and ducks, geese, and other birds make the plateau their home.

Wilfrid Laurier

LAURIER, Wilfrid (1841–1919). The first French Canadian to become prime minister of Canada was Wilfrid Laurier. Although French was his native tongue, he became a master of English oratory. This and his picturesque personality made him popular throughout Canada, and he led the young country in a 15-year period of great development.

Wilfrid Laurier was born at Saint-Lin, Quebec, and studied law at McGill University. After three years in the Quebec legislature, he was elected to the Canadian House of Commons in 1874. There he rose rapidly to leadership. Although he was a French Canadian and a Roman Catholic, he was chosen leader of the Liberal party in 1887. Nine years later he became prime minister. He was knighted in 1897.

"Build up Canada" were the watchwords of Laurier's government. Laurier was loyal to Great Britain, sent Canadian volunteers to help in the Boer War, established a tariff favorable to British goods, and worked to strengthen the ties between the two countries. But he saw the British Empire as a worldwide alliance of free and equal nations, and he opposed every attempt to limit Canada's freedom.

Laurier's liberal immigration policy brought hundreds of thousands of settlers to the western provinces. He reduced postal rates, promoted the building of railroads needed for national expansion, and appointed a commission to regulate railroad rates. After 15 years in office his government was defeated, presumably on the issue of reciprocal trade with the United States. Laurier believed, however, that his political defeat was caused primarily by opponents in Ontario who considered him too partial to Roman Catholic interests in Quebec.

Prior to World War I, Laurier ardently supported the formation of a Canadian navy. His own Liberal party defeated this measure, however, and Canada

entered the war without a fleet of its own. During the early years of World War I, Laurier supported the war policy of Sir Robert Borden's Conservative government. In 1917 he refused to join a coalition government that was formed to uphold conscription. Laurier felt that he could not back a measure so unpopular in the province of Quebec. He died in Ottawa on Feb. 17, 1919. (*See also* Canada.)

LAVA AND MAGMA. Molten, or hot liquefied, rock located deep below the Earth's surface is called magma. When a volcano erupts or a deep crack occurs in the Earth, the magma rises and overflows. When it flows out of the volcano or crack, usually mixed with steam and gas, it is called lava. Fresh lava ranges from 1,300° to 2,200° F (700° to 1,200° C) in temperature and glows red hot to white hot as it flows. (*See also* Rock; Volcano.)

Enormous quantities of lava, enough to flood the whole countryside, may be produced by the eruption of a major volcano. During the eruption of the volcano Mauna Loa in Hawaii in 1887, about 2½ million tons (2.3 million metric tons) of lava per hour poured out for more than six days.

Some lavas are liquid enough to flow downhill at 35 miles (55 kilometers) per hour. Others move at the rate of only inches per day. The speed of the flow depends on the temperature and composition.

All lavas contain a high percentage of silica, a compound made up of the chemical elements silicon and oxygen. Lavas containing from 65 to 75 percent silica are called rhyolites; those with 50 to 65 percent silica are andesites; and those with less than 50 percent silica are basalts (*see* Basalt).

Rhyolites melt at lower temperatures and are lighter in weight and color than basalts. Rhyolitic lavas are quite viscous, or thick, and contain large quantities of gas. The gas often boils off with explosive force, expelling large amounts of glowing ash and

Pahoehoe lava in the crater of Kilauea in Hawaii presents a wrinkled appearance when hardened.

cinders. Sometimes, however, it is released more slowly or even trapped as bubbles when the lava hardens. When the bubbles are tiny and closely packed, a lightweight stone called pumice is formed. Any kind of lava may turn into pumice, but most of it develops in rhyolites. Pumice is used commercially for cleaning and polishing wood, metal, and other surfaces. More recently it has found use in precast masonry, poured concrete, insulation, acoustical tile, and plaster. Rhyolite pumices are white. Andesite pumices are usually yellow or brown. Basaltic pumices are black. Commercially useful pumices are found in the Canary Islands, Iceland, Italy, Hungary, Greece, New Zealand, and West Germany. In the United States it is mined in the Rocky Mountains, on the West Coast, and in Hawaii.

Andesites, which are named for the Andes Mountains, are a large family of rocks found in nearly all volcanic areas. They are of three basic types: quartz-bearing (called dacites); hornblende- and biotite-andesites, quite rich in feldspar; and pyroxene-andesites, the most common kind.

Basaltic eruptions can produce two different types of flow. Each type is designated by a Hawaiian name: the *aa* and the *pahoehoe*. Aa lava moves slowly and is covered with tough, cindery rock called clinker. The pahoehoe develops as a thick flow that contains more gas and is erupted at about 2,000° F (1,100° C). A flexible, glassy skin forms on the surface, insulating the lava that lies beneath and keeping it molten for weeks or even years.

Volcanoes and cracks may pour forth lava under the sea as well as on land. Many islands have been formed by successive lava flows building a volcanic island higher and higher, until it rises above sea level. The Hawaiian Islands were formed in this manner. In 1963 the island of Surtsey, near Iceland, was also formed in this way.

LAVAL, Pierre (1883–1945). A politician who was twice elected premier of France, Pierre Laval led the government established at Vichy to collaborate with Germany during World War II. He was ultimately executed as a traitor to his country.

Pierre Laval was born on June 28, 1883, in Châteldon, France. He joined the Socialist party at the age of 20, became a lawyer in Paris in 1909, and began defending trade unionists and others on the political left. He held various public offices, beginning in 1914, and first became premier in 1931. Defeated a year later, Laval was reelected in 1935, but his cabinet fell in 1936. In 1940 he became vice-premier under Marshal Henri Pétain. After Paris was occupied by German forces, Pétain had formed a fascist state at Vichy. Laval helped persuade Pétain that the Third Republic should be dissolved, but Pétain eventually opposed the close Franco-German collaboration advocated by Laval. Pétain dismissed him in December 1940.

Under pressure from Germany, Pétain restored Laval's power, and he became head of the Vichy government in April 1942. Laval agreed to provide French laborers for German industries and, in a notorious speech asking for volunteers in June 1942, he announced that he desired a German victory. His control of France deteriorated with the growth of the resistance movement against the German occupation. After the Vichy government collapsed in August 1944, Laval fled to Spain. He returned to France in July 1945 and was put on trial for treason. He was executed, after attempting to poison himself, on Oct. 15, 1945, in Paris.

LAVOISIER, Antoine Laurent (1743–94). One of the most honored men in the history of science is the Frenchman Antoine Laurent Lavoisier. For more than a century before his day, chemists had been hampered by a false theory about fire and the burning of matter. By revealing the truth about fire and burning, Lavoisier helped chemistry make its remarkable advance from that time on.

Lavoisier was born in Paris on Aug. 26, 1743, the son of a wealthy lawyer and landowner. His father bought a title of nobility and wanted an aristocratic career for the boy. Young Lavoisier preferred science, however, so his father sent him to many distinguished scholars. He studied mathematics at Mazarin College under Abbé Lecaille and botany under the renowned botanist Bernard de Jussieu. He was much influenced by a family friend, the geologist Jean-Étienne Guettard, and contributed to the latter's geologic and mineralogic atlas. In 1788 he presented his theory on geological stratification to the Academy of Sciences.

When Lavoisier was but 23 he won a prize from the Academy for an essay on the lighting of cities. In 1768 he was elected to the Academy, an unusual honor for so young a man. The same year he was appointed to the *ferme générale*—a body of men who held the right to "farm" (collect) taxes. In 1776 he began a career as director of the government arsenal.

The American Colonies issued their Declaration of Independence in the same year, and soon colonial troops were using his improved gunpowder. By 1783 Lavoisier had solved what was the most significant chemical problem of the day by proving the connection between oxygen and fire. By brilliant experiments and delicate measurements, Lavoisier proved that burning, the rusting of metals, and the breathing of animals all consisted of the union of oxygen with other chemicals. Since this union, called oxidation, is one of the most important chemical processes, his discovery started the development of modern chemistry. He published his conclusions in 1789 in a work called 'Traité élémentaire de chimie' (Elements of Chemistry).

Lavoisier had become commissioner of weights and measures, and in 1791 he was appointed a commissary of the treasury. In 1794, however, the French revolutionists accused him and other members of the *ferme générale* of plotting to cheat the government. Because of this he was executed in Paris by the revolutionary tribunal on May 8, 1794.

Actor John Houseman, as Professor Kingsfield, explains a point of law in the television series 'The Paper Chase'. The series and the motion picture from which it sprang portray the arduous efforts of law school students in their years at a prestigious law school.

Twentieth Century-Fox Television

LAW.

LAW. All the rules requiring or prohibiting certain actions are known as law. In the most general sense, there are two kinds of law—natural law and positive law. Natural law has been recognized since the ancient world to be a general body of rules of right conduct and justice common to all mankind. This concept grew from the observation of the operation of the laws of nature and their uniformity. Positive law, on the other hand, consists of regulations formulated by the heads of a country or society. In many cases, natural laws have been written into positive laws by governments. The prohibition against killing, for example, is common to virtually all of mankind, and most nations have enacted laws against it. This article is concerned primarily with the many aspects of positive law in Western society.

Development of Positive Law

When people first began to live in groups they had few rules or laws, but they soon realized that each individual had to pay attention to the needs and welfare of his neighbors in order to make life not only tolerable but pleasant for the greatest number of people. It was considered necessary, for instance, for each person to recognize everyone else's rights to life and the ownership of property. Without this mutual recognition, society could not function in peace.

With the emergence of written languages it was possible to put laws into written form. One of the best known of the early codes, or collections of written laws, is that of Hammurabi, king of Babylon, who lived about 1800 BC (*see* Babylonia and Assyria). Probably the most famous of the ancient codes, however, is that found in the first five books of the Bible, the laws of Moses. The heart of this code is the Ten Commandments presented by Moses to the people of Israel. These commandments are the basic summary of all moral law designed to regulate the behavior of individuals with regard to each other.

All other societies in the ancient world devised sets of laws. In the 7th century BC, a lawgiver named Draco drew up a very harsh code that punished offenses, no matter how trivial, with death. Not many years later, another Greek lawgiver, Solon, repealed all but the laws dealing with murder (*see* Solon). In the Greek city-state of Sparta, there was a legendary lawgiver named Lycurgus who, after giving the Spartans a code of law, left the city with the instruction that the laws were not to be changed until he returned. He never did return (*see* Lycurgus).

The most complete and complex system of laws in the ancient world was developed by the Romans. It was the product of many centuries of civilization, from the early years of the Republic until the end of the Empire. In the 6th century AD, the emperor Justinian (*see* Justinian) collected and organized the laws for use as the Roman Civil Law. Roman law has strongly influenced the general character of the laws in every nation of Western Europe except England.

After the fall of the Roman Empire in the West, AD 476, the Christian church, as the strongest institution in society, became a major lawmaking and law enforcement body. Called canon law (canons are regulations), a body of rules formulated by the church was designed to regulate human behavior, with respect to religious matters primarily. But it eventually came to apply to the actions of people on social, economic, and political levels as well.

To enforce its laws against those who disagreed with it, the church of the Middle Ages created the Inquisition (*see* Inquisition). Church courts in several countries examined those who were suspected of breaking church laws. Many people were cleared of wrongdoing, but others were not and were punished, frequently with death. One of the best known trials was that of the scientist Galileo. He agreed, under pressure, to deny his opinion that the planets orbit the sun in favor of the church doctrine that the sun circled the Earth (*see* Galileo).

The society of the Middle Ages was rigidly structured, with kings, princes, and nobles at the top and the common people—mostly peasants working the

Acquittal. The action taken by a jury when, upon trial, they find that the accused is not guilty and enter a verdict accordingly.

Administrator. A person appointed by probate court to manage and to distribute the estate of a person who has died without a will; distinguished from an executor.

Affidavit. A written statement which is sworn to before an officer who has authority to administer an oath.

Alias (ā′lĭ-ȧs). A description of the defendant that results from adding to his real name other names by which he is known.

Alibi (ăl′ĭ-bī). Proof offered by one accused of a crime that he was in a different place from that at which the crime was committed at the time it was committed.

Alien. A resident of a country who was born outside that country and who has not become a naturalized citizen.

Arraignment. The calling of a prisoner before a judge (sitting in his courtroom) to answer the accusations contained in an indictment.

Arson. Under common law, the malicious burning of the house owned by another person; under statutes, the house need not be one owned by another person.

Assault. Force unlawfully directed or applied to another under circumstances of personal violence.

Assignment. Transfer of a property right or title to some particular person under an agreement, usually in writing.

Attachment. Preliminary legal seizure of property to force compliance with a decision which may be obtained in a pending suit.

Bailment. Delivery of possession of, but not title to, tangible personal property by one person to another under an agreement that it will be held in trust for a special purpose and that it will be returned when the purpose has been accomplished.

Bankruptcy. The condition of being unable to pay one's debts as they become due.

Bench warrant. An order issued by a judge for the attachment or arrest of a person.

Bequest. A gift by will of personal property. A bequest is the same as a legacy.

Blue laws. A name applied to certain laws, originally in force in the New England states, which were extremely rigorous.

Brief. A written or printed argument furnished to the court by an attorney which sets forth the pertinent facts of the case being tried and the laws applicable to it.

Carte blanche (kärt blänsh′). Unlimited authority—granted by one person to another—to impose conditions which will be binding upon the person granting such authority.

Chattel. Personal property, movable or immovable, which is less than a freehold; for example, a book, a coat, a pencil, growing corn, a lease.

Codicil. A written instrument that adds to or qualifies a last will and testament.

Common law. The body of law which includes both the unwritten law of England and the statutes passed before the settlement of the United States.

Confiscation. Appropriation of private property for public use without compensation.

Contempt of court. Any willful disobedience to, or disregard of, a court order or any misconduct in the presence of a court; punishable by fine or imprisonment or both.

Contract. An agreement between two or more competent persons to do or not to do some lawful act for a consideration.

Copyright. The exclusive privilege of printing, publishing, and vending copies of writings or drawings.

Corespondent (kō-rē-spŏn′dĕnt). A term sometimes applied to a third person, who is accused of committing unlawful acts with the defendant, by the party seeking a divorce from the defendant.

Corporation. A fictitious legal person which has rights and duties independent of the rights and duties of real persons and which is legally authorized to act in its own name through duly appointed agents.

Decree. The judgment or sentence of a court of equity which corresponds to the judgment of a court of law.

Deed. A written document for the transfer of land or other real property from one person to another. A quitclaim deed conveys only such rights as the grantor has. A warranty deed conveys specifically described rights which together comprise good title.

De facto. A term used to denote a thing done in fact but without strict legal authority as contrasted with *de jure*, which denotes a thing done according to law.

De jure. *See* De facto in this table.

Dower. The provision which the law makes for the support of a widow during her lifetime out · of income produced by the real estate owned by her husband during the marriage. This provision for the support of a widow is usually favored over the claims of her deceased husband's creditors.

Easement. A right enjoyed by the owner of one parcel of land, by reason of this ownership, to use the land of another for a special purpose.

Endorsement (also **indorsement**). The act of transferring title to a written negotiable instrument by having the temporary owner write his name on the back of the document.

Equity. A system of law designed to furnish remedies for wrongs which were not legally recognized under the common law of England or for which no adequate remedy was provided by the common law.

Escrow. A written agreement between two parties providing that a third party hold money or property until the conditions of the agreement are met.

Estate. A term commonly used to denote the sum total of all types of property owned by a person at a particular time, usually upon his death.

Evidence. In law, all facts, testimony, and documents presented for the purpose of proving or disproving a question under inquiry.

Executor. In law, the person designated by a testator in his will to carry out the terms of that instrument.

Ex officio (ĕks ŏ-fĭsh′ĭ-ō). Term used to designate powers exercised by public officials by virtue or because of the office they hold.

Ex parte (ĕks pär′tē). Term used to designate action taken by one party in the absence of the opposite party, usually after giving notice.

Ex post facto. Term used to designate action taken to change the effect given to a set of circumstances. This action relates back to a prior time and places this new effect upon the same set of circumstances existing at that time.

Extradition. The surrender by one state to another of a person charged with a crime. This surrender is made in response to the demand of the latter state that the accused be returned to face the charge.

Felony. A serious crime, such as murder, larceny, or robbery, punishable by death or by imprisonment in a state or federal penitentiary.

Fine. Payment of money demanded of a person convicted of a crime or a misdemeanor; the fine is imposed by a court as punishment.

Fixture. An article which was once a chattel but which has now become a part of the real estate because the article is permanently attached to the soil or to something attached to the soil.

Foreclosure. The legal process by which the mortgagor's equitable or statutory right to redeem mortgaged property is terminated.

Forgery. The act of criminally making or altering a written instrument for the purpose of fraud or deceit; for example, signing another person's name to a check.

Freehold. An interest in land which permits the owner to enjoy possession of real estate during his life without interference from others.

Garnishment. The process by which a judgment creditor seizes money, which is owed to his judgment debtor, from a third party known as a garnishee.

Grand jury. At common law, a group of persons consisting of not less than twelve nor more than twenty-four who listen to evidence and determine whether or not they should charge the accused with the commission of a crime by returning an indictment. The number of members on a grand jury varies in different states.

Guarantee. In law, a contract under which one person agrees to pay a debt or perform a duty if the other person who is bound to pay the debt or perform the duty fails to do so.

Habeas corpus. An order signed by a judge directing a sheriff or other official, who has a person in his custody, to bring that person before the court to determine whether or not he should be released from custody.

Hearsay. That kind of evidence which is not entirely within the personal knowledge of the witness but is partly within the personal knowledge of another person.

Heir. At common law, this term was restricted to lawfully born children who could inherit land from an ancestor; under statutes, it includes all those who have the right to inherit from a deceased person.

Honorarium. Money or other valuable property given in gratitude for services rendered; for example, payments to ministers for presiding at weddings and funerals.

Indemnity. An agreement whereby one party agrees to secure another against an anticipated loss or damage.

Indictment. A formal written charge against a person which is presented by a grand jury to the court in which the jury has been sworn.

Indorsement. *See* Endorsement in this table.

Injunction. A court order which restrains one of the parties to a suit in equity from doing or permitting others who are under his control to do an act which is unjust to the other party.

Ipso facto. By the fact itself or by the very nature of the case.

Joint tenancy. A method by which one person mutually holds legal title to property with other persons in such a way that when one of the joint owners dies his share automatically passes to the surviving joint owners by operation of law.

Judgment. The declaration, by a court, of the rights and duties of the parties to a lawsuit which has been submitted to it for decision.

Larceny. Illegal taking and carrying away of personal property belonging to another with the purpose of depriving the owner of its possession.

Lease. An instrument conveying the possession of real property for a fixed period of time in consideration of the payment of rent.

Legacy. A gift of money or of personal property, title to which is passed under the terms of a will.

Libel. In law, a false defamation expressed in writing, printing, or picture which injures the character or reputation of the person defamed or which exposes him to public ridicule; distinguished from slander.

Lien. In law, the right to retain the lawful possession of the property of another until the owner fulfills a legal duty to the person holding the property, such as the payment of lawful charges for work done on the property.

Manslaughter. The unlawful killing of a human being without malice or premeditation; distinguished from murder, which requires malicious intent.

Misdemeanor. A crime—less serious than a felony—which is punishable by fine or imprisonment in a city or county jail rather than in a penitentiary.

Mortgage. The transfer of title to real estate which is made to secure the performance of some act such as payment of money by the person making the transfer. Upon the performance of the act, the grantee agrees to convey the property back to the person who has conveyed it to him.

Murder. *See* Manslaughter in this table.

Notary public. An official authorized by the state to attest or certify legal documents.

Option. A contract whereby one person purchased the right for a certain time, at his election, to purchase property at a stated price.

Patent. A grant made by the government to one or more individuals entitling them to exercise some privilege not granted to others during the period they are so authorized to exercise that privilege.

Per capita. Term used to designate a system of inheritance under which an individual descendant takes a share which is equal in size to the shares of each of the other descendants, regardless of whether that descendant is the child, grandchild, or great-grandchild of the decedent.

Perjury. The offense of willfully making a false statement when one is under oath to tell the truth.

Per se (*pĕr sē*). By or of itself; for example, slander *per se*, where the words spoken are obviously defamatory and the injured party is not required to prove damage to his character.

Per stirpes (*pĕr stĕr′pēz*). Term used to designate a system of inheritance under which children take among them the share which their parent would have taken had he survived the decedent. Thus the children are said to claim their shares by representing their parent.

Petit jury. The ordinary trial jury of twelve persons whose duty it is to find facts as opposed to the grand jury whose duty it is to return an indictment.

Power of attorney. An instrument by which one person authorizes another to act for him in a manner which is as legally binding upon the person giving such authority as if he personally were to do the acts.

Precedent. The body of judicial decisions in which were formulated the points of law arising in any case.

Prima-facie (*prī′ma-fā′shĭ-ē*) **evidence.** Evidence that is sufficient to raise a presumption of fact or to establish the fact in question unless rebutted.

Probate. In law, the process of proving before a probate court that a will has been properly executed according to the statutory requirements.

Pro rata (*prō rā′ta*). Term used to designate the system of distributing the assets of an estate in equal proportion among all the members of the same class of beneficiaries.

Referendum. A system of legislation whereby proposed laws are submitted to popular vote.

Replev′in. A proceeding employed by a party to regain possession of personal property which was illegally taken from him.

Riparian rights. Legal rights of owners of land bordering on a river or other body of water; also, law which pertains to use of the water for that land.

Sedition. Conduct which is directed against a government and which tends toward insurrection but does not amount to treason. Treasonous conduct consists of levying war against the United States or of adhering to its enemies, giving them aid and comfort.

Slander. In law, a false defamation (expressed in spoken words, signs, or gestures) which injures the character or reputation of the person defamed; distinguished from libel.

Statute. A law established by an act of the legislature.

Subpoena (*sŭb-pē′na*). An order directed to an individual commanding him to appear in court on a certain day to testify in a pending lawsuit.

Summons. The proceeding to commence an action in a court of law which consists of a notice to the defendant requiring him to serve an answer to the complaint.

Testator. One who has made a last will and testament.

Title. The sum total of legally recognized rights to the possession and ownership of property.

Tort. In law, a wrong or injury which does not grow out of a breach of contract and for which one is entitled to damages; for example, fraud, slander, or libel.

Treason. *See* Sedition in this table.

Trespass. In law, an unlawful intentional intrusion upon another's property or person.

Trust. An agreement under which one person transfers title to specific property to another who agrees to hold or manage it for the benefit of a third person.

Usury. An illegal profit received on a loan of money.

Venue (*vĕn′ū*). The county in which the facts are alleged to have occurred and in which the trial will be held.

Verdict. The unanimous decision made by a jury and reported to the court on matters lawfully submitted to them in the course of the trial of a case.

Warranty. A statement or agreement by a seller of property which is a part of the contract of sale. The truth of the statement is necessary to the validity of the contract.

Will. In general, any instrument, executed with the required formalities conferring no present rights but intended to take effect on the death of the maker, which contains his intention respecting the disposition of his property.

land—at the bottom. Within each kingdom the ruler issued the laws by which his people were to live. Such laws could not conflict with those of the church.

In England, each locality had its own laws based on custom and tradition. After the Norman Conquest, 1066, judges appointed by the king moved from one place to another to administer these local laws. As time passed, local laws gave way to judges' interpretations of a broader system of laws accepted in more than one area. Eventually the decisions of the judges, constantly modified by later decisions, were accepted as the body of English common law.

In France, under the guidance of Napoleon, a civil code was enacted in 1804. With revisions, it still remains in force and has been a major influence in the legal systems of most European countries and in Latin America. The Code Napoléon was made necessary by the diversity and confusion of laws that had developed in France and other parts of Europe during the Middle Ages and early modern period. The premise for the code was the idea that, for the first time in history, a law based purely on common sense should be created, free of all past prejudices and inequities. Under the code all citizens were recognized as equal, and all class privileges were done away with. The code was originally introduced in areas under French control in 1804: Belgium, Luxembourg, northwestern Italy, and parts of Germany. After the Napoleonic conquests it was introduced into conquered Italy, The Netherlands, and most of Germany. It was voluntarily adopted during the 19th century in a number of other places, including Haiti, the Dominican Republic, Chile, Bolivia, Ecuador, Colombia, and Argentina. In the United States, only Louisiana has a civil code closely connected with the Napoleonic code.

The influence of the Napoleonic code was somewhat diminished at the start of the 20th century by the introduction of the German Civil Code in 1900 and the Swiss Civil Code in 1912. Japan adopted the German code and Turkey the Swiss code.

Common Law and Statute Law

As noted above, the law in England developed over the centuries from the combined decisions of judges, the decisions based on rules already established. Known popularly as the common law, it was embodied in reports of decided cases that originated in the early Middle Ages. The broad acceptance of the common law in England was largely due to the dominant position of the royal courts, especially the King's Court established at Westminster (now part of London). The royal judges went out to the provincial towns and interpreted the law of Westminster in both civil and criminal cases. Hence common law came to apply everywhere in England. This early centralization of the court system removed the necessity of importing into England any foreign system, such as Roman law.

Statute law differs from common law in that it is legislation, or codes of law made by legislative bodies such as parliaments, congresses, and legislatures. In England, for example, statutes are passed by Parliament. In the United States laws are passed by the Congress in Washington, D.C. Each state in the United States has its own legislature that makes statute laws, and there are many local lawmaking bodies such as city councils and town councils as well. Statute law grew up because conditions arose to which common law did not apply.

The chief difference between common law and statute law is that common law is based on what has happened, on precedents, while statute law is passed to meet present circumstances and future possibilities. The complexity of modern society in every industrialized nation has bred an enormous amount of statute law that affects the private and public life of every individual—laws on compulsory education, taxation, regulation of businesses, protection of the environment, and many more.

In recent years, governments under the common-law system have increasingly adopted statute laws and regulations. In this situation, the difference between common law and statute law has become much less distinct than it once was.

The American System of Law

Law in the United States has become a complex blend of common and statute law. When the first English colonists came to America in the 17th century, they brought English customs with them, but there was little expertise in law. Colonial charters, or agreements with England, gave the colonists the Englishmen's traditional rights that had developed as part of the common law. An example is the right to trial before a jury of one's peers, or equals. But there were few men trained in the law, few judges, and no schools of law. Local jurisdictions passed their own statutes to meet specific situations.

By the early 18th century, there were lawyers practicing in the colonies. They used English lawbooks and followed English procedures and precedents. In 1701 the colony of Rhode Island accepted English law in full, subject to local legislation. The Carolinas soon followed suit, and eventually most of the colonies had their own mixture of English common law and local statute. Legal battles before the American Revolution were fought on common-law principles. After the revolution many Americans wanted to divorce themselves from English practices, but other European legal systems were too different and written in unfamiliar languages. The 'Commentaries' of William Blackstone had been printed in the colonies in 1771 and had come into wide use. Thus, despite the objections of many citizens, English common law remained the heart of the American legal system (*see* Blackstone).

The work of Blackstone was reinforced by judges in the United States. As chief justice of the Supreme Court, John Marshall had a powerful influence in shaping the development of constitutional law through his legal decisions (*see* Marshall, John). In the 1830s two important judges, James Kent of New

York and Joseph Story of Massachusetts, produced significant commentaries on common law, stressing the need for legal certainty (*see* Kent, James).

Along with the development of the common-law tradition in the United States, there has also arisen an enormous body of statute law on the federal, state, and local levels. This body of law has been made to work well with the common-law tradition by means of the American judiciary. In 1803, in one of the most famous decisions in the area of constitutional law— *Marbury versus Madison*—Chief Justice John Marshall ruled that federal courts are the final authority in determining the conformity of all laws with the federal Constitution. In addition, the Sixth Article of the Constitution makes the Constitution the supreme law of the land, "any thing in the constitution or laws of any state to the contrary notwithstanding." Later, in 1868, the 14th Amendment guaranteed to every citizen of the United States the equal protection of the laws. (*See also* Bill of Rights.)

The Main Branches of Positive Law

In modern legal systems there are two primary branches of law. These are criminal law and civil law. Criminal law defines offenses so harmful to society that violations are punished by fines, imprisonment, or even death. Such offenses include murder, armed robbery, theft, rape, kidnapping, assault, and embezzlement. In the late 20th century, many nations have added laws on airplane hijacking and terrorist activities to their books because both involve violence against people. There are also lesser offenses, such as driving through a stop sign or behaving badly in public, that may also bring fines. But even these so-called lesser offenses can become serious, if injury or death results from them.

Civil laws define the rights and liabilities of individuals in relation to each other and to society. Actions in civil law may enable one person to recover money from another, for example, but it does not require payment of money to the government in the form of a fine. If, for instance, one person hires another to do work for him, and they sign a contract, the individual must do the work or he is considered to have broken the contract. The one who breaks the contract may be sued in court. One of the most common types of civil actions is the divorce trial, in which a contract is at issue.

In a criminal action a governmental unit asks the court to try an individual who is alleged to have committed a specific offense. Normally the person has been indicted for the offense by a grand jury (*see* Jury System). In the United States the governmental unit may be the federal, state, or local jurisdiction, depending on the law that has been violated. Murder, robbery, and rape are state crimes. Traffic offenses are usually handled locally—by the town, city, or county; though they occasionally fall within the jurisdiction of a state. Robbery of banks insured by the Federal Deposit Insurance Corporation, an arm of the federal government, is a federal offense. In all cases, the person on trial—the defendant—is presumed innocent until found guilty beyond a reasonable doubt. In criminal trials the plaintiff—the party bringing the complaint—is the governmental unit through its attorneys. The prosecuting arm of the federal government is the Department of Justice and regionally based federal attorneys. In a local jurisdiction, it is the state's attorney or the attorney general of a state who brings the action.

In civil cases, generally one person—the plaintiff—asks the court to determine whether another person—the defendant—has violated the plaintiff's rights in some way and should, therefore, make up for it in some way. Usually the plaintiff asks the court to order the defendant to pay an amount owed, either because of a promise in the form of a contract or by way of damages because the defendant caused injury to the plaintiff. If the court agrees, it will issue an injunction, an order that a person take some action (such as deliver goods that were promised in a contract) or refrain from doing something (such as playing a radio so loud that it disturbs the neighbors). Violation of an injunction, however, changes the action from a civil one to a criminal one, because failing to carry out the instructions of the court is a criminal offense, that is, an offense against the state. An individual who violates an injunction is, therefore, subject to imprisonment or fine. Most civil cases do not involve injunctions, fines, or penalties if there is a settlement or judgment in the trial. Sometimes there is what is called an out-of-court settlement. If, for instance, one person is suing another over injuries received in an auto accident and wants a large sum of money, the two parties may settle on a lesser sum,

The diorite stela on which the Code of Hammurabi is inscribed is displayed at the Louvre museum in Paris. The code, the most complete collection of Babylonian laws, derives from the 18th century BC.

Art Resource

agreeable to both, outside of court. Such a settlement can take place even if a trial is already in process.

European Civil Law

Most of the laws of the legal systems of continental Europe are traditionally classified as civil law. This term is not to be confused with the civil law discussed above in relation to criminal law. It is, rather, derived from the ancient Roman term *jus civile*, meaning "civil law," which was used to distinguish the proper or ancient law of the city of Rome from the laws applying to the people of the Roman Empire.

During the Middle Ages, Roman law in western Europe fell into disuse and was replaced by canon law and by the customs of the several Germanic peoples that overran the empire. But in the late 11th century Roman law was rediscovered and studied by scholars in northern Italy, especially at the University of Bologna. With the increased demand for trained experts in law and administration, students flocked to Bologna from all over Europe, and soon the revival of Roman law had spread to other centers of learning. Hence, Roman law came to influence the developing legal systems of the newly emerging nations of Europe. The system that resulted was called everywhere the *jus civile*. In actual practice it varied from place to place, but it can be considered a unit that was held together by a common tradition and stock of learning.

In Europe civil law similarities that had been attained by the end of the Middle Ages were split by the Reformation and by the rise of strong nationalism in many countries. Individual nations organized and put down in writing all of their specific laws. In Denmark this occurred in 1683. Norway followed four years later. Sweden-Finland codified law in 1734, as did Prussia in 1791. France did the same with the Napoleonic code of 1804. Because of the different dates of codification and the different styles of legal learning in Europe, the civil law of the Continent is divided into the French and Germanic branches. The civil law system, in both of its branches, is still dominant in Europe and has found wide acceptance in other parts of the world except where the common-law tradition of England has taken hold.

The Soviet Legal System

Law, in the Soviet Union, is regarded as an instrument of state, or government, policy. Its purpose is to further the aims of Communist ideology. Its two major tasks were formulated to be the elimination of the political power of the middle classes and the education of citizens in the pattern of life believed necessary to achieve the perfect socialist society.

Lenin and the other leaders of the 1917 revolution lacked a precise pattern for a legal system, since Karl Marx and his associate, Friedrich Engels, had left no scheme for such a system. The revolutionaries therefore issued a few decrees designed to establish a framework for the new society. These decrees deprived individuals of the ownership of land, banks, insurance companies, shipping fleets, and large-scale industry; created restrictions on the employment of labor; and removed marriage and divorce from the sphere of church activities.

Finally, in 1922 and 1923, statutes and legal procedures to be used in the courts were set down in codes covering criminal, civil, family, land, and labor matters. In principle, the legislature was to be the only source of law, but in practice the executive (especially during the rule of Joseph Stalin) has often made laws (*see* Stalin). More often it has been the Presidium, a smaller body elected from the membership of the legislature, that has created day-to-day changes in the law. Ratification by the whole legislature was, according to the Soviet Constitution, deemed necessary, but, in actuality, altering Presidium action became impossible. The Presidium thus became the most important source of law.

Technically, the orders and decisions of the Communist party were not a source of law. But, in fact, the party provided the initiative for a good deal of legislative action, especially in economic planning. The wishes of the party were followed because the party's secretary was normally the real ruler of the nation. Stalin, for example, was party secretary for the whole time he governed the Soviet Union.

Soviet law reflects the strong presence of the state in the lives of the people. The law codes cover virtually every activity in which the state and its citizens are engaged. There are extensive regulations concerning the ownership and management of property. At the heart of these regulations is the provision that the state owns and operates all the means of production. Only small plots of land and certain nonproductive property were left in the hands of individuals. The state also oversees all economic planning, the management of all social insurance programs, artistic creation and invention, family relationships, and the many aspects of criminal and civil law.

In the area of criminal law, new definitions of crime emerged that reflected socialism. Along with the traditional crimes dealt with in other legal systems—crimes against persons and property—the Soviet Union added certain "economic crimes" and counterrevolutionary activities. Among the economic crimes was the private employment of labor for production purposes. Counterrevolutionary activities, now called state crimes, constituted a broad range of actions that were viewed as subversive of state authority. Criticism of the state itself, or of its socialist policies, has frequently brought heavy penalties. Undertaking religious activity also falls within the sphere of the criminal code.

The court system of the Soviet Union was established by the judiciary act of Oct. 31, 1922. At the local level there are people's courts with a full-time judge and two lay judges, who are selected for a few days of service from a panel of local citizens. Appeals from the people's courts go to provincial courts, which also have original jurisdiction in certain security, criminal, and civil cases. At the top of the legal system is the Supreme Court of the Soviet Union. It hears cases on appeal from the provincial courts, but it is also responsible for disciplining the lower courts, issuing rulings to interpret the legal codes, and trying cases of a significant nature to the state.

In the Soviet Union there is no separation of powers as there is in the United States, and the courts are therefore subject to the legislative authority. The United States Supreme Court can declare an act of Congress unconstitutional. No such possibility exists in the Soviet Union.

Lawyers

Because law is complex and because most people are involved in legal actions only rarely, there is a group of professionals—lawyers—who study law and spend most of their time handling legal matters for other people. They advise individuals and organizations on the requirements of law, draft legal documents, and plead cases in court.

Another name for lawyer is attorney. Strictly speaking, an attorney is one who acts for another, an appointed agent. Someone so appointed who is not a lawyer is sometimes called an attorney-in-fact, as distinguished from an attorney-at-law.

Some lawyers maintain a general practice to assist the public in all matters of ordinary law. But many lawyers, because of the complexity of the field, become specialists in such areas as tax law, administrative law, family law, labor law, corporation law, criminal law, contract law, or other branches.

A substantial number of lawyers practice in partnership with others. They form partnerships, or law firms, because by law they are not usually permitted to form corporations. The reason for this is that shareholders in a corporation have limited liability, or legal responsibility, for the actions of the corporation, but lawyers are supposed to be fully liable for their actions. They may be deprived of their licenses to practice law if they fail to represent their clients properly. In some states lawyers may now form special corporations to take advantage of federal income tax provisions, but in these corporations the lawyer-shareholders have unlimited liability, just as in a partnership. (*See also* Corporation.)

Because so much of American public and private life revolves around law and the court systems, there are far more lawyers per person in the United States than in any other country: three times as many as in Germany, ten times the number in Sweden, and about 20 times the number in Japan. Although no clear proof is available, American lawyers seem to have a higher economic and social status than lawyers elsewhere. In Communist countries, lawyers are few in number, and the courts are run, in part at least, by laymen. In the People's Republic of China, civil cases are often decided by groups of people drawn from the neighborhood.

Careers in Law

Legal education varies from country to country. In England, law can be studied in college and a bache-

Barristers, wearing the wigs of their profession, confer on a case outside the courthouse at Winchester, England.

Eric Carle—Shostal Associates

lor's degree is awarded, usually after four years. But additional training is required to become an experienced, practicing lawyer. The graduate is articled, or apprenticed, to one or more senior lawyers for at least a year before being licensed to practice as a solicitor. Solicitors may not represent clients in court; only barristers may do that. There are associations of barristers who control admission of candidates to argue cases in the courts. This situation of having the legal profession divided into solicitors and barristers is called a "split bar." Some European countries have a split bar similar to England. In France, for example, only a special group of lawyers, *avocats*, meaning "advocates," are licensed to argue in court.

In the United States, lawyers are required to be college graduates and to attend a law school for three years. Upon graduating from law school, the student receives the degree of *Juris Doctor*, doctor of law. In addition, the law school graduate must pass an examination before being admitted to the bar. (Lawyers are collectively called "the bar" because, when the profession was developing in England many centuries ago, there was a fence in courtrooms separating the judges' area from the rest of the room. This fence was called the bar, and it became customary to say that a lawyer was called to the bar, meaning he was called upon to practice his profession.)

Whereas in England, the practice of law is regulated by associations of barristers, in the United States it is governed by the courts. Bar associations in the United States may discipline a lawyer or recommend disbarment, but the courts have the final say in the disposition of the matter.

The field of law is so vast today that lawyers, in addition to going into private practice or joining law firms, find employment in other ways. Some work exclusively for corporations. Others work for governments at the federal, state, or local levels in the executive, legislative, and judicial branches. Every department of a government is likely to have a full-time legal staff.

A legal education is also useful in other occupations. About 10 percent of the chief executive officers of large corporations are lawyers. Many bankers, stockbrokers, and businessmen have had a legal education. And most politicians are lawyers.

LAWRENCE, D. H. (1885–1930). In the English literature of the 20th century, few writers have been as original or as controversial as Lawrence. He was a man almost at war with the conventions, moral constraints, and technology of modern civilization. Much of his life was spent in the search for an ideal community of people in which to live. It was a search that failed in spite of his pilgrimages to such places as Italy, Ceylon, Australia, and New Mexico. His quirks of personality, his wandering way of life, and the desire to explore the depths of human relationships brought originality to his novels and poems.

David Herbert Lawrence was born on Sept. 11, 1885, in the mining village of Eastwood, Nottinghamshire, England. With his mother's help he escaped the fate of becoming a miner, and went instead to Nottingham High School and later to the University College at Nottingham. For several years he taught school, but when his first novel, 'The White Peacock', was published in 1911, he left teaching to concentrate on writing. This novel was followed by 'The Trespasser' (1912) and the semiautobiographical 'Sons and Lovers' (1913), as well as a volume of short stories, 'The Prussian Officer and Other Stories' (1914). These works, well done, but of a rather conventional nature, did not sell well but gave him a good reputation with literary critics.

Lawrence's conflict with the literary world began with the publication of 'The Rainbow' (1915), which, with its sequel, 'Women in Love' (1921), comprise his best work. These novels, intense psychological probings into human relationships, were condemned as obscene and their publication halted. The same fate met his most famous novel, 'Lady Chatterly's Lover', when it was first issued privately in 1928. The full text was not released to the public until 1959. Some few critics hailed his books as brilliant, others condemned them as neurotic and indecent.

Lawrence seemed naturally restless, and was constantly looking for the right place to live. He and his wife, Frieda Richthofen Weekley, lived in Europe prior to World War I, spent the war in England, then traveled to Germany, Sicily, Sardinia, Ceylon, Australia, and eventually, New Mexico. He died of tuberculosis at Vence, France, on March 2, 1930.

His other published works include the novels 'The Lost Girl' (1920), 'Aaron's Rod' (1922), and 'The Plumed Serpent' (1926); travel books, 'Sea and Sardinia' (1921) and 'Mornings in Mexico' (1927); and 'Studies in Classic American Literature' (1923).

LAWRENCE, James (1781–1813). "Don't give up the ship!" cried Captain Lawrence, commander of the United States frigate *Chesapeake*, as he was carried below, mortally wounded. These words, never forgotten, are still uttered today in urging someone to keep trying in the face of great difficulty.

James Lawrence was born Oct. 1, 1781, in Burlington, N.J. He entered the Navy as a midshipman at the age of 17 and rose to the rank of lieutenant in 1802. During the war with the Tripoli pirates from 1804 to 1805, he was second in command to Stephen Decatur. At different times he commanded the *Argus*, *Vixen*, *Wasp*, and *Hornet*.

On June 1, 1813, commanding a poorly trained crew on the *Chesapeake*, he sailed out of Boston Harbor to meet the British frigate *Shannon*. The two ships were about equal in size and guns, but the crew of the *Shannon* was experienced and well-trained.

Soon the *Chesapeake* was disabled and Lawrence fell fatally wounded but unwilling to surrender. He died a few days later in Halifax, where his captured vessel was taken. His body was later returned to the United States and buried in the yard of Trinity Church in New York City.

T. E. Lawrence

Courtesy of Lowell Thomas
and Harry A. Chase

LAWRENCE, T. E. (1888–1935). One of the most remarkable careers of World War I was that of "Lawrence of Arabia." He became famous for his exploits as leader of the Arab revolt against the Turks from 1916 to 1918. This and his dislike of publicity made him an almost legendary figure.

Thomas Edward Lawrence was born on Aug. 15, 1888, in Portmadoc, Wales. After secondary school he enrolled in the University of Oxford in England. He rarely attended classes, but he read continually. Lawrence was interested in the Middle Ages, and after college this interest took him to the Near East to study the castles of the crusaders. He traveled throughout Palestine, Syria, and Mesopotamia.

When World War I began in 1914 Lawrence was rejected for active service because he was too short. He found a place in the War Office and was transferred to the intelligence service in Egypt. Soon he was sent to Arabia with the rank of colonel.

To weld the scattered Arab forces into a fighting unit, Lawrence almost became an Arab himself. He wore an Arab's flowing robes and a chieftain's headdress and rode on camels. Under his leadership attacks against supply trains and other surprise maneuvers routed the Turks from strong positions. In a series of battles his forces destroyed the Fourth Turkish army and captured Damascus.

When the war was over Lawrence looked after Arab interests at the peace conference and took part in the Middle Eastern Settlement of 1921. Then he retired to write 'Seven Pillars of Wisdom', his account of the revolt. An abridged edition, 'Revolt in the Desert', appeared later. Meanwhile he had enlisted in the armed services as a private. To escape attention he had changed his name, first to Ross, and then later to Shaw. He refused any reward or decorations for his military service. Lawrence died in Clouds Hill, Dorsetshire, England on May 19, 1935, following a motorcycle accident.

LEAD. Few metals have been used in more different ways than lead. Lead ornaments and coins have been in use since ancient times. The Romans used lead for water pipes and for solder (*see* Metalworking). In the Middle Ages strips of lead called cames were used to assemble the pieces in stained-glass windows.

In the United States about two thirds of all the lead produced today is used in electric storage batteries of the kind found in automobiles (*see* Battery and Fuel Cell). Large amounts of lead are used as protective coverings for electrical cables, and lead compounds are in paints and pigments. The use of lead in paints has been decreasing because lead is poisonous, and many children have been poisoned by eating flakes of dried paint containing lead. Lead bullets and shot made gunpowder effective in firearms, and lead is the main ingredient of solder, used for joining pieces of metal.

Lead is the heaviest and the softest of the common metals. Because it resists attack by air and water as well as by many strong chemicals, it can be used to make water pipes, to protect electrical cables, or to line large vessels in which chemical processes are carried out. Screens to protect people from X rays, gamma rays, and radioactive materials are made from lead because it absorbs radiation.

Safety plugs and engine bearings are only two of the many products made of alloys that contain lead (*see* Alloy). Some lead alloys melt so easily that they change to liquid when held in the hand.

Useful lead compounds include lead monoxide, or litharge. This substance makes up a large part of the brilliant, lustrous glass called flint, or crystal, that is shaped into vases, bowls, drinking glasses, and lenses (*see* Glass). Another oxide of lead called minium, or red lead, is used in paints that protect iron and steel from rusting. Basic lead carbonate (white) and lead chromate (yellow) are pigments in paints. Lead azide, easily exploded by an electrically heated wire, is used in blasting caps to set off other explosives.

Sources

The most abundant source of lead is the mineral galena, or lead sulfide. Its chemical formula is PbS. Other important ores, or sources, are cerussite (lead

PROPERTIES OF LEAD		
Symbol .... Pb	Density at 68° F (20° C)	
Atomic Number 82	...............11.35 grams per cc	
Atomic Weight.................. 207.2	Boiling point	
Group in Periodic	...............3,164° F (1,740° C)	
Table................................. IVa	Melting point	
Color...................... Bluish white	...............621.5° F (327.5° C)	

carbonate, $PbCO_3$) and anglesite (lead sulfate, $PbSO_4$). Most lead ores contain zinc, and many also contain gold, silver, or other metals.

The ore is first pulverized, and the metal-bearing material is separated from the rock by the flotation process; that is, it is mixed with water and certain oils and chemicals, and air is blown in from the bottom. The lead-bearing particles are wetted by the oil and float to the surface attached to air bubbles. The waste, called gangue, is wetted by water; it sinks to the bottom and is discarded.

The concentrated ore is roasted in air to change lead sulfide to lead oxide. In the process, sulfur escapes in the form of the gas sulfur dioxide, which can be recovered and made into sulfuric acid. The crude lead oxide is smelted in a blast furnace or open-hearth furnace with coke and a flux of silica or lime. The lead metal settles to the bottom, dissolving and carrying with it any gold or silver that was present in the original ore. Most of the other metals combine with the silica or lime to form a slag that floats to the top. The slag is skimmed off, and the metals in it are recovered by other treatments. The lead is purified, and the gold and silver are recovered by further processing.

About 3.5 million tons of lead are mined in the world every year. The United States ranks first with about 13 percent of the known total, mostly mined in the state of Missouri. Other major mining countries are the Soviet Union, Australia, Canada, and Peru.

About 5.3 million tons of refined lead are produced in the world every year. Worn-out lead products, especially storage batteries, are recycled—which accounts for the great difference between the amount of lead mined and the amount produced by refineries. The United States ranks first in the refining of lead with about 21 percent of the total. Other major refining countries are the Soviet Union and West Germany. The United States consumes about 22 percent of the world's production of refined lead.

Chemistry

Ordinary lead is a mixture of four stable isotopes, or forms, of lead that have the mass numbers 204, 206, 207, and 208. Seventeen other isotopes, with mass numbers between 194 and 214, are radioactive. They are formed in the course of the "decay" of elements such as uranium, thorium, and actinium. (*See also* Chemistry; Radioactivity.)

All lead compounds are poisonous. Even small doses will accumulate in the body and eventually cause colic, paralysis, anemia, and brain damage. If the amount of lead in the body becomes large enough, the poisoning will be fatal.

LEAF

LEAF. The green color of forest, field, and garden is caused by leaves. They are the dress of trees and other plants. They are far more important than mere dress, however. The foods by which the plant lives and grows are made in the leaves. All the food eaten by human beings and other animals can be traced back to plants and the green leaf. Even our bacon and eggs start with plants, for pigs and chickens live on plant food. Without green leaves there would be no animal life on earth.

Most leaves are broad and very thin, but they have many different shapes. The needles of the pine trees are leaves. The long ribbon streamers of the seaweeds, the fronds of ferns, the tiny hairs of mosses, the hollow traps in which the pitcher plant catches insects, and the climbing tendrils of the garden pea are also leaves. The leaves of water plants show many interesting differences from those of land plants (*see* Water Plants).

The Structure of a Leaf

The broad, thin part of the leaf is called the *blade*. It is attached to a stemlike *leafstalk*, or *petiole*. The leafstalk grows from the stem of the plant. The blade holds its shape because it has a framework of hollow tubes, called *veins*. They are the blood vessels of the leaf. Water and dissolved minerals are carried from the soil through the roots and stems of the plant into the leafstalk and finally through the veins into the leaf. The liquid food materials formed in the leaf are carried back into the plant through the veins. (*See also* Plants; Plants, Physiology of.)

There are two principal kinds of veining —parallel and net. The grasses and lilies have the veins running side by side (parallel) from the leafstalk to the tip of the blade. In net veining, some leaves have the veins branching from a large central midrib. From its featherlike appearance, this type is called *pinnate venation*. In other leaves large veins of equal size fan out from a common point. This is *palmate venation* (shaped like the fingers and palm of the hand).

If the leaf is a single blade it is called *simple*. If it has two or more distinct parts, called *leaflets*, the leaf is *compound*. Leaves are said to be *opposite* if two are attached at the same point on opposite sides of the stem. If three or more are attached at the same point they are *whorled*. Single leaves attached to the stem first on one side and then on the other are said to be *alternate*.

The leafstalk twists and bends to hold the blade in the best position relative to light. Leafstalks on the same plant vary in length so that the leaves do not overlap and cut off light from one another. A leafy vine growing on a brick wall turns all its leaves outward to face the sun, forming a *mosaic* pattern. Most leaves expose their largest surface area to the sun. In very hot, dry regions they would lose too much moisture in this position; so some plants turn their leaves edgewise to the midday sun, and

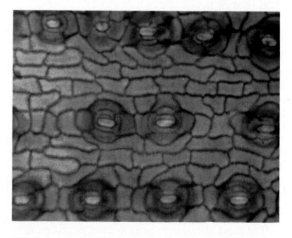

This is a magnified leaf surface. It shows breathing pores, called stomata (the light spots), surrounded by guard cells. Gases and water vapor enter and leave the leaf through stomata.

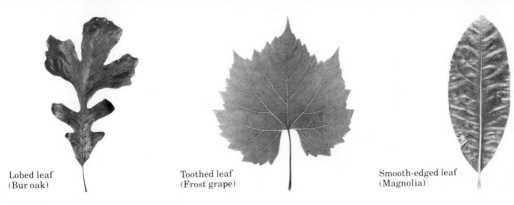

Lobed leaf
(Bur oak)

Toothed leaf
(Frost grape)

Smooth-edged leaf
(Magnolia)

CROSS SECTION OF A LEAF

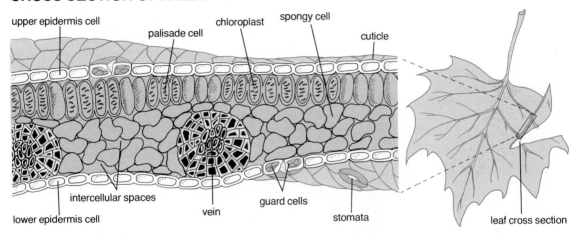

upper epidermis cell

palisade cell

chloroplast

spongy cell

cuticle

intercellular spaces

lower epidermis cell

vein

guard cells

stomata

leaf cross section

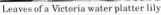

Leaves of a Victoria water platter lily

Spiny leaves of a
Mexican blade apple

Needle-like leaves of a bristle cone pine

Insect-catching leaves of a Venus's-flytrap

Photos. (bottom right) Virgil N. Argo. (all others) John H. Gerard

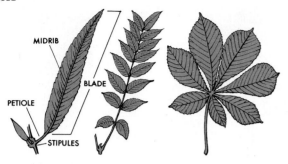

The willow is a simple leaf. Compound leaves have several leaflets. The walnut is pinnately compound, or feather-shaped. The horse chestnut is palmately compound, or hand-shaped.

the flat surface only to the morning and evening rays (see Compass Plants).

How the Leaf Makes Food

Between the veins of the leaf is a spongy mass of cells filled with green material which gives the leaf its color. The green cells are called *chloroplasts*. The coloring matter is *chlorophyll*. Food is made by action of the chlorophyll in the plant.

On the lower surface of the leaf, and sometimes on the upper surface, are many pores known as *stomata* (singular, *stoma*). Each stoma is a tiny opening between two bean-shaped guard cells. In most plants these pores are open all day and closed all night. There are great numbers of pores in a single leaf. An oak leaf may have 1,400 in one square millimeter of area. A square millimeter is no larger than the tip end of a lead pencil.

As sunlight shines on the leaf, carbon dioxide, in the form of gas from the air, enters the stomata. Inside the tissues of the leaf the carbon dioxide mixes with the water carried into the leaves from the roots. Then the green coloring matter, with the energy from sunlight, produces a wonderful chemical change. The carbon dioxide and the water are broken down into their separate parts (molecules), and the molecules are put together again in a new order to form sugars and starches (carbohydrates). These are the food materials of the plant. The chemical process, basic to all life, is called *photosynthesis*. The word comes from Greek words meaning "light" and "putting together." (*See also* Plants, Physiology of.)

The sugars and starches in liquid form pass back through the veins and leafstalk into the plant to nourish it. The hard woody material (cellulose) of the stem and branches is a carbohydrate (see Cellulose). Proteins are formed when the carbohydrates manufactured by the plant combine with dissolved minerals carried into the plant from the soil.

In the process of making food the plant uses only about 4 per cent of the water that it soaks up through its roots. The other 96 per cent evaporates into the air through the stomata. The process is called *transpiration*. Thus leaves keep the air which surrounds them fresh and moist. (*See* Trees; Water.)

In food making the plant also sends oxygen into the air through the stomata. Here again plants make life possible for animals and man. All animals use oxygen and must have a constant supply.

Why Leaves Change Color and Fall

In the autumn, leaves turn from green to brilliant shades of scarlet, gold, orange, and purple. Then they finally fall to the ground. It is not a season of dying. The tree or shrub is preparing for winter.

In late summer, as the growing period slows down, a corky layer of cells forms at the base of the leafstalk where it joins the stem. It is called the *separation layer*. It does not pass through the woody fibers which connect the leafstalk with the stem. These fibers hold the leaf in place until frost or wind tear it free. After the leaf has fallen the scar where it was attached to the stem is sealed and protected by the layer of cork.

As the separation layer forms, the manufacture of food materials slows down. The cells and veins in the leaf become clogged. No more chlorophyll is produced, and the green color disappears. Other colors were present in the leaf, but they were hidden by the stronger green. Now they appear in all their beauty.

All leaves contain yellow pigments called *carotene* and *xanthophyll*. The yellow pigments are formed in the protoplasm of the leaf cells. The reds and purples are due to pigments called *anthocyanins*. They are formed in cell sap which is rich in sugar. Sugar maples, oaks, and sumacs have the most brilliant scarlet and purple colors. To develop such high color they must be exposed to the sunlight. Sugar maples which are heavily shaded by larger trees do not become red but show only yellow coloring.

Jack Frost is usually given credit for autumn color. Actually frost has very little to do with it. A combination of favorable weather conditions is required. Red pigments are formed in the sunlight in leaves which have stored sugar. Cloudy, rainy weather or a very hot, dry summer prevents the pigments from developing. If warm days are followed by warm nights the sugars drain out of the leaves and into the woody portions of the plant. Ideal conditions are bright, sunny days followed by cool nights.

Frost is chiefly responsible for freeing the leaves from the twigs. On a cold, frosty night ice crystals

A collection of leaves may be made without the labor of pressing and mounting them. Leaf prints are made from fresh leaves. They are attractive and fun to make.

form in the separation layer and break the woody fibers that hold the leaf in place. Then when the ice melts in the morning sun, the leaves flutter in a gold and scarlet shower to the ground. In some oaks the separation layer does not develop fully, and the leaves remain on the tree all winter.

The wise gardener does not burn fallen leaves but adds them to the compost pile. Rotted leaves (leaf mold) are a valuable soil conditioner (*see* Compost).

How to Make a Leaf Collection

Late spring, when leaves are fresh and green, is the time to start a leaf collection. Keep the leaves fresh and uncrushed as you collect them. Spread them carefully between two or three layers of newspaper on a flat surface. Then place books on the top layer of paper and put something heavy on the books. Change the papers every day for the first four days, then leave the leaves pressed, undisturbed, for another week. Next, remove them and mount them carefully with clear tape on heavy paper.

Leaf *prints* are less work to prepare than a pressed and mounted collection. A collection of *spatter prints* is interesting and easy to make. A bottle of ink, an old toothbrush, a piece of wire screening, and sheets of white paper are needed. Place a fresh leaf on the paper and pin it down flat. Then dip the toothbrush into the ink bottle, letting the excess ink drain off. Hold the wire screen over the paper and rub the bristles over it, working from side to side and from top to bottom. Draw the bristles *toward* you so the ink will spatter *away* from you. When the ink is dry remove the leaf. The imprint will remain.

For leaf *blueprints* use blueprint paper, a piece of window glass, and a basin filled with clear water. Working in dim light, lay the leaf on the treated side of the blueprint paper and cover with the window glass. Expose it to sunlight until the paper turns dark blue. Remove the glass and the leaf and quickly wash the paper in the basin of water until the color "sets." Dry the paper on a smooth, flat surface so it will not curl. The impression of the leaf will be white or pale blue on a darker blue background.

A *printer's ink print* shows the veins as well as the outline of the leaf. Needed materials are a tube of printer's ink, a sheet of window glass, two rubber rollers, and several sheets of paper. Spread a thin film of ink over the glass with one of the rollers. Place a leaf, underside down, on the inked glass. Cover it with a sheet of paper. Run the second (clean) roller over the paper several times. Now the leaf is thoroughly inked on its underside. Discard the inky paper and place the leaf, inked side down, on clean paper. Cover with a sheet of clean paper, and again work the clean roller over the paper. Finally remove the top paper and the leaf. Let the finished print dry.

A *plaster cast* may be made by putting a leaf in a greased saucer and covering it with plaster of Paris. After the plaster has set, the leaf may be removed. Its imprint in the plaster may then be painted and trimmed to the outline of the leaf.

LEAGUE OF NATIONS. The first international organization set up to maintain world peace was the League of Nations. It was founded in 1920 as part of the settlement that ended World War I. Weakened from the start by the refusal of the United States to join, the organization proved ineffective in defusing the hostilities that led to World War II in 1939. After World War II the League was replaced by the United Nations (*see* United Nations).

The League of Nations was first suggested in the Fourteen Points presented on Jan. 8, 1918, by Woodrow Wilson, president of the United States, as a basis for armistice negotiations. After the peace negotiations opened, the work was continued by a commission headed by Wilson. A working plan, called The Covenant of the League of Nations, became Section I of the Treaty of Versailles. The League came officially into existence with the ratification of this treaty on Jan. 10, 1920. The first Assembly met in Geneva, Nov. 15, 1920, with 41 nations represented. More than 20 nations joined later, but there were numerous withdrawals. (*See also* Wilson.)

The organization, powers, and purposes of the League were stated in 26 articles of the Covenant. Its specific aims were to promote arbitration for settling international disputes; to bring about reduction of armaments; to study and remove the causes of war; and to promote world interests in all fields of human work. The organization consisted of the Secretariat, headed by a secretary-general; the Council, normally 14 members, five permanent and nine nonpermanent; and the Assembly. The Council early set up the Permanent Court of International Justice, or World Court, at The Hague, The Netherlands.

All the member nations agreed to submit to the League's procedure any international dispute that was likely to lead to armed conflict. If the Council made a unanimous report (the votes of the disputing states not counting), the League members were bound not to declare war on the disputant complying with the Council's report. The members agreed to use "sanctions" (economic blockades) against any member nation that went to war instead of submitting its dispute to the League. The Council had no international army to carry out its decisions, but it could recommend the use of force against an offending nation.

After World War I, the League helped stabilize finances and bring relief to the war victims. It aided in suppressing slavery and illicit narcotics trade, helped improve working conditions, established institutions for the study of disease, and found havens for political and religious refugees. It successfully arbitrated a number of international disputes until its later years, when it suffered a series of defeats. In defiance of the League, Japan invaded Manchuria and China; Germany absorbed Austria and Czechoslovakia; and Italy took Ethiopia and Albania. (*See also* Europe; World War I.)

LEAGUE OF WOMEN VOTERS *see* WOMEN AND WOMEN'S RIGHTS.

Louis Leakey handles fossils that represent his many important discoveries.

Wide World

LEAKEY FAMILY. Louis Leakey, his wife, and their son Richard rank among the most famous anthropologists. With his wife, Mary Nicol Leakey, Louis Leakey made fossil discoveries in East Africa that proved man was far older than had previously been believed. Their son Richard unearthed extensive fossil finds of human ancestral forms there.

Louis Seymour Bazett Leakey was born on Aug. 7, 1903, in Kabete, Kenya. The son of British missionaries, he spent his youth with the Kikuyu people of Kenya. He was educated at Cambridge University and began his archaeological research in East Africa in 1924. He was later aided by his archaeologist wife and his sons Jonathan, Richard, and Philip. He held various appointments at major British and American universities and was curator of the Coryndon Memorial Museum in Nairobi from 1945 to 1961.

In 1931 Leakey began his research at Olduvai Gorge in Tanzania, which became the site of the family's most famous discoveries. The first finds were animal fossils and crude stone tools, but in 1959 Mary Leakey uncovered a fossil hominid, or manlike creature. The scientific name of the specimen is *Zinjanthropus,* and it was believed to be 1,750,000 years old. The Leakeys' work indicated that human evolution was centered in Africa, rather than in Asia, as earlier discoveries had suggested.

Louis Leakey wrote several books about his discoveries and theories. The first was 'Adam's Ancestors', published in 1934 and revised in 1953. The last was 'Animals of East Africa' (1969). He died in London on Oct. 1, 1972.

Richard Erskine Frere Leakey was born on Dec. 19, 1944, in Nairobi, Kenya. He was originally reluctant to follow his parents' career and became a safari guide. When he found an extinct near-human jaw while exploring the Lake Natron region in northeast Tanzania in 1963, he decided to become an anthropologist after all. In London the younger Leakey completed a two-year secondary education program in six months, but, running out of funds and out of interest in classrooms, he returned to Kenya without a university education.

From 1967 to 1977 he and his fellow workers uncovered some 400 fossils, representing perhaps 230 individuals, at Koobi Fora along the shores of Lake Rudolf in Kenya. This site contained the richest and most varied assemblage of early human remains found to date. Of particular importance was an almost complete fossil skull, found in 1972, which Leakey believed to represent a species called *Homo habilis* and to date from about 2,000,000 years ago.

In 1968 Richard Leakey became director of the National Museums of Kenya. He later founded the Louis Leakey Memorial Institute for African Prehistory. (*See also* Anthropology.)

LEAR, Edward (1812–88). The English humorist Edward Lear made famous the limerick form of verse and illustrated his work with amusing pictures. The gentle, friendly man was always fond of children, and most of his writing was done for their pleasure.

Edward Lear was born May 12, 1812, in London. He was the youngest in a family of 21 children. His father, once a wealthy stockbroker, was imprisoned for debt; and Edward had to start earning his own living at 15.

Lear had always enjoyed drawing pictures of birds, animals, and plants, and he soon began to specialize in natural history and medical drawings. He was hired to make drawings of the brilliantly colored parrots in the Regent's Park Zoo in London, and in a year he had produced 42 lithographic plates. Precise in line and faithful in color, these won the acclaim of many scientists.

Seeing them, the 13th earl of Derby invited Lear to come to Knowsley Hall, his estate near Liverpool, and make drawings of his private collection of animals. Lear became the favorite of the earl's nieces, nephews, and grandchildren. He entertained the children with comic drawings and with limericks.

A limerick is a short, humorous verse form consisting of five lines. The first, second, and fifth lines rhyme, as do the third and fourth:

> There was an Old Man who supposed
> That the street door was partially closed;
> But some very large rats
> Ate his coats and his hats,
> While that futile Old Gentleman dozed.

These verses were published in 1846 as 'A Book of Nonsense', which was dedicated to the Knowsley Hall children. It was followed years later by 'Nonsense Songs, Stories, Botany, and Alphabets' (1871), 'More Nonsense Pictures, Rhymes, Botany, Etc.' (1872), and 'Laughable Lyrics' (1877). For a number of years Lear traveled in Europe and Asia, making sketches for landscape paintings and writing illustrated travel journals. He gave painting lessons to Queen Victoria, and she and the Prince of Wales maintained a constant interest in his work.

Lear never married. He depended upon his friends, among them the poet Alfred Tennyson and the painter Holman Hunt, for companionship. He died in 1888, in San Remo, Italy, where he had spent his last years.

Microprocessors are among the newest devices used to enhance learning in the classrooms.

Don & Pat Valenti

LEARNING. The lifelong process of acquiring skills, information, and knowledge is called learning. Many scientists now define learning, for animals and for people, as the organization of behavior based on experience. There are other definitions of learning because there are many theories about how animals and human beings learn. But all learning involves an interplay between an individual's brain, the rest of the nervous system, and the environment—the surrounding world. (*See also* Brain; Nerves.)

An 18th-century philosopher, David Hume, stated that all knowledge comes through observation and experience. Other thinkers disagree with him on this understanding of knowledge; but when his assertion is applied to learning, it certainly seems to be true. Observation and experience come to a person through perception—becoming aware of something by means of the senses of seeing, hearing, smelling, touching, and tasting. Without these senses people would be like inanimate objects, unable to learn.

Functions and Forms of Learning

Learning affects an individual's behavior in a number of ways. One of the most obvious ways is the acquiring of a skill. If a person learns to tie shoelaces, ride a bicycle, or swim, that skill will remain with him or her and will be improved by practice. Other skills—playing the violin or programming a computer—are more difficult to acquire and will be virtually lost if they are not practiced frequently. Skills like cooking or driving a car may be partially lost through disuse but may be regained fairly easily.

One form of learning is called conditioning. If a certain signal is linked with a condition, and is repeated a number of times, there will be an automatic learned response to the signal that is just the same as if the condition were present. For example, the sudden sound of a nearby car horn will make people automatically jump for safety without stopping to see if a car is actually present. Phobias are also examples of conditioning. A person may develop a fear of something quite harmless because it has become associated with a condition that is threatening. Conditioning is sometimes deliberately used in medical therapy as "behavior modification" to break harmful habits or form desirable new ones.

An important feature of learning is known as concept formation, the ability to form concepts, or ideas. An aspect of this type of learning is the ability to classify perceived objects by their similarities and differences. Consider, for instance, a boy walking down a street to the corner mailbox. He notices that the leaves on all the trees are virtually identical in shape. On his way back, he notices that the leaves on the other side of the street are all of a different shape. Based on these two sets of visual perceptions, he is able—even without knowing botany—to make a simple classification based on similarities and differences. Later he learns that all the trees on one side are oaks, while those on the other side are maples. He is thereby able to give a name to the classifications he has already made by himself.

This ability to conceptualize, to form ideas, is necessary for higher levels of learning. A girl who is studying geometry must learn to perceive the difference between a variety of shapes: circles, triangles, and squares and other rectangles, as well as the different shapes of the conic sections. The perceived differences will give her the idea, for instance, of a triangle. Triangles all share certain specific features that distinguish them from other shapes.

Ideas, as simple classifications and distinctions, are of limited value unless they are aided by training. An untrained ear may perceive three different pieces of dance music and only know that they are different. The trained musician will know that the first is a waltz, the second a samba, and the third a mazurka. It is by training and by naming that ideas get content whereby they can be shared. Animals other than human beings can perceive and remember differences in shapes, sounds, and smells. But they do not give names to the ideas they get; nor do they build upon

105

their ideas over the passage of time. For humans, being able to name things and share ideas makes possible complex language and complex teaching systems. These are the basis of the human ability to exercise collective judgment, solve complex problems, and build on past learning.

Theories of Learning

For more than 2,500 years there have been theories about how people and other animals learn. No one theory has ever proved satisfactory to everyone for the simple reason that not enough is known about the brain and nervous system. Observations of animals in natural societies and in laboratories have contributed much to an understanding of the learning processes. With animals, experiments can be conducted under controlled conditions over a long period of time, and one or a few behaviors at a time can be studied. In these studies, learning is defined as a specific kind of relatively permanent change in the animal's performance that accompanies experience and is not accounted for by other factors. Once learning is defined as a specific set of behaviors, these behaviors can be measured. New or improved performance can be assessed, and the experiments repeated, until a general consensus is reached that learning has or has not taken place.

Learning by association. One of the first modern theories of learning is learning by association. For example, a baby is uncomfortable and begins to cry. The mother picks the baby up to comfort it. The baby learns to associate crying with being picked up and will therefore cry whenever it wants to be picked up even if there is no discomfort. This is called learning by stimulus-response (S-R) association. The sight of the mother is called the stimulus, the crying is called the response, and the act of picking the child up is called the reward, or the reinforcement. It is the reward that makes the baby learn to use crying.

The phenomenon of conditioning is a form of learning by association. It was discovered by Russian physiologist Ivan Pávlov. He found that dogs formed saliva in their mouths in response to a bell that had previously been rung each time they got food. This is an example of S-R learning with positive reinforcement (the food). An example of negative reinforcement would be if a dog who is uncomfortably hot learned to press a button that could turn the heat off. In learning by punishment, the third type of S-R learning, the response decreases because it is followed by an unpleasant event. For example, if the mother got exasperated with the baby's demands to be picked up and scolded her every time she cried, the crying (response) would decrease because it is followed by an unpleasant event.

Cognitive learning. Some theorists insist that learning takes place by organizing one's perceptions in certain useful ways. In a famous demonstration of learning by insight, the German-American psychologist Wolfgang Kohler showed that chimpanzees fit several sticks together in a makeshift pole to obtain food that was otherwise out of reach. Their behavior suggested a sudden understanding of how to solve the problem rather than achieving their goal by trial and error. This is an example of the cognition theory of learning—that is, learning by perceiving and using insight or knowledge. (It is sometimes called the "a-ha" theory.)

For a long time there were two separate schools of learning, the associationist emphasis on S-R and trial and error, and the cognitive emphasis on reasoning and problem solving. Learning theorists today believe that both kinds of learning are used. It is not known how many species learn by cognition.

Memory and Motivation

One learns that a burning candle is hot by feeling the heat. The ability of the brain to register the notion of heat, remember it, and later recall it means that a specific piece of information has been learned. Memory, therefore, is essential to learning.

Learning is a selective process. Far more is perceived than remembered; otherwise the mind would be a storehouse of miscellaneous, unassorted data.

There appear to be three levels of memory: immediate, short-term, and long-term. Immediate memory lasts no more than a couple of seconds, the time it takes for a sensory impression to register. Short-term memory is a matter of seconds or minutes: One looks up a phone number in the directory and makes a call; by the time the call is completed, the number has normally been forgotten. Long-term memory can last a lifetime, but some experts believe that information may be lost through disuse or may become flawed through reinterpretation.

Information often is transferred from short-term to long-term memory. One way this is done is by repetition and rehearsal, much the way an actor might memorize his or her lines from a script. Novel or vivid experiences seem to be more readily shifted to long-term memory. Other means of transfer are by the association of an unfamiliar name or fact with something that is already known, or grouping things together so that fewer facts at a time need to be absorbed. Many strategies are taught for improving memory, and most people develop their own devices.

The question just where memory takes place and how it is stored cannot yet be answered. Some studies of brain-damaged people are giving a few clues to brain physiologists, and sophisticated new tools are becoming available, but a great deal more has to be learned about how the brain functions before this veil of deep mystery is lifted.

To what extent motives aid learning is undecided. Motives do contribute as incentives to performance of what has been learned. If an individual expects to be rewarded for doing well, performance (perhaps on a test) may improve. It also may worsen, if the fear and anxiety over not passing is great enough. Human motives in relation to learning are so varied and complex that controlled experiments to analyze them are virtually impossible.

Before the tanning process, the hides are cured in salty water and hung up to dry.

James M. Cribb

LEATHER.

Nearly everyone uses leather in some way each day. People all over the world wear shoes, coats, belts, and gloves and carry handbags or billfolds made out of leather. Cowboys wearing leather boots ride on leather saddles, and industrial workers wear special safety work shoes or boots made from leather to protect their feet. Industry depends on leather products. The furniture and automobile industries, for example, use leather for upholstery, and leather gaskets are found in some engine blocks.

Manufacturing

The hides and skins of domestic animals are the main source of leather. The skins of large animals such as cattle and horses are called hides. Those of smaller animals such as sheep, goats, and calves are referred to as skins. The United States is the largest producer of hides and skins with an annual supply of more than 1,100,000 tons (1,000,000 metric tons).

Hides and skins are removed from animals after they are slaughtered at modern slaughterhouses. Electric knives and hide pullers that are powered by compressed air are used. After the hide is pulled off, hooves, tails, ears, horns, and other parts unusable for leather are trimmed off and used in the preparation of gelatin and glue. The hide is fleshed with modern machinery that removes any remaining meat tissue or fat.

Fresh fleshed hides are shipped in refrigerated trucks to a tannery for immediate processing into leather. If this is not possible, the fleshed hides are cured, or preserved by immersion for at least 16 hours, in large pools called raceways filled with salty water, or brine. After being cured, the hides can be stored for several months without rotting and can be shipped to manufacturers throughout the world.

Cured hides arriving at a tannery are rehydrated, or resoaked, and washed in large, rotating wooden drums. Hair is removed by chemical digestion; that

This article was reviewed by the staff of the Pfister & Vogel Tanning Company, Milwaukee, Wis.

is, by soaking the hide or skin for 10 to 12 hours in drums containing a solution of lime and sodium sulfide and rotating the drums occasionally. After the hair is removed, hides are delimed, or neutralized, with acids and treated with enzymes to remove any deposits and to increase softness. The next operation is called pickling. The hides are soaked in a solution of water, salt, and hydrochloric or sulfuric acid.

Tanning is the final process in turning hides and skins into finished leather. Properly tanned leather can pass the test of being boiled in water for three minutes without shrinking. There are several methods of tanning, but the two most common are chrome and vegetable tanning. Chrome tanning is the most used. Most leather shoe uppers and garment, upholstery, and bag leathers are chrome-tanned. The process begins in rotating drums with a bath in a chemical containing trivalent chrome. It usually takes eight hours for the chrome to soak all the way into the hide or skin. Once it has penetrated, the chrome is "fixed" by adding to the tanning bath an alkaline chemical such as sodium carbonate or bicarbonate. After this treatment the hide is considered tanned.

Vegetable tanning is used for such various products as shoe soles, luggage, saddlery, and belt leathers. The process is slower than chrome tanning and involves the chemical substance tannin, or tannic acid, which is extracted from the barks of trees. This process is performed in rotating drums, and it takes from two to four days.

Wringing, splitting, and shaving follow tanning. Wringing lowers the moisture content of the hides in preparation for splitting. Depending on the end use of the leather product, hides are split into sheets of the required thickness and processed further through a shaving machine for added quality. All three operations require specialized machinery run by highly skilled operators.

After shaving, chrome-tanned hides are again placed in rotating drums with water, dyes, and synthetic tanning materials at temperatures from 120° to 140° F (49° to 60° C) to obtain the desired color. They are then lubricated with natural fat, synthetic

The leather, sorted by type, is shaved by machine (left) to exact thickness. Coloring is usually done in large rotating drums (below left). A wringer (below) removes excess moisture from the leather.

fatty type chemicals, or a combination of both to obtain the softness required by the final product.

Finishing consists of placing a series of coatings on the surface of the leather. These coatings are designed to protect the leather and produce surface effects pleasing to look at and to touch. Finishing today reflects the latest technology in the use of coating materials. Some finishing processes apply plastics such as acrylic and urethane resins. Others coat with vinyls, waxes, nitrocellulose, dyes, and many other materials. Various mechanical operations are necessary to obtain the desired finish. Hydraulic presses, printing machines, automatic spray applications, and vacuum dryers are a few of the machines used in the finishing process.

The end use of the leather product determines the type of finish process to be applied. Each type requires different physical properties in the finish. Film flexibility and resistance to water and wear are a few of the required properties in the finish. Much research and development continues in the quest of improved surface coatings.

The Leather "Zoo"

Cowhide, the most useful leather, comes from cattle and is tough and long wearing. It is used in shoe soles and some shoe uppers as well as in machine beltings and harnesses. Split hides are made into luggage, gloves, clothing, and many other articles.

Calfskin has a fine grain. It is good for shoes because it withstands scuffing and hard wear. It is also used for handbags, gloves, fine bookbindings, luggage, and garments.

Goatskin and kidskin are used in women's fine shoes and gloves. Goatskin is also used in garments. Kid is one of the sturdiest leathers and also one of the softest and most pliable. It is an excellent material for suede, or leather with a napped surface.

Sheepskin and lambskin are good for shoe uppers and linings, gloves, garments, handbags, chamois, parchments, textile-mill rollers, hat sweatbands, and piano parts. Lambskins with the wool left on them are used for coats and boots.

Pigskin comes mainly from the peccary, a wild hog found in North and South America, and domestic

LEADING PRODUCERS OF HIDES AND SKINS, 1981

	Tons	Metric Tons
Cattle and Domestic Buffalo Hides		
United States	1,092,000	991,000
India	889,000	806,000
Soviet Union	791,000	718,000
Argentina	499,000	453,000
Brazil	318,000	288,000
Sheepskins		
Australia	179,000	162,000
Soviet Union	117,000	106,000
New Zealand	113,000	103,000
China	83,000	76,000
Turkey	64,000	58,000
Goatskins		
India	80,000	73,000
China	60,000	54,000
Pakistan	43,000	39,000
Nigeria	22,000	20,000
Bangladesh	16,000	14,000

Source: Food and Agricultural Organization of the United Nations

pigs. When the bristles are removed, pores are left that give it an unusual texture. Pigskin is used for gloves, saddles, wallets, sport shoes, fine bookbindings, upholstery, and razorstrops.

Buckskin is made from deer. Almost all buckskin sold in the United States is imported from Latin America and Canada. It is used for garments, gloves, and the uppers of high-quality shoes.

Alligator skins, though the animals are carefully protected, are legally available through controlled hunting and farming from Latin America, Florida, and Louisiana. The beautifully textured skins are made into luxurious shoes, handbags, luggage, belts, and billfolds. These accessories are also made from the skins of other reptiles, including water snakes, lizards, pythons, and cobras.

Kangaroo hide from Australia makes strong, flexible leather for shoe uppers.

Ostrich skin comes from the only bird that provides leather. Its pinkish skin is used for fine handbags and wallets. Many unusual leathers come from seals, sharks, and whales.

Synthetics have been used as substitutes for leather in a wide variety of products. These synthetics are mostly materials called polyvinyl plastics.

World Production

Total annual leather production throughout the world is about 7,275,000 tons (6,600,000 metric tons) of bovine, or cattle and domestic buffalo, hides; 1,200,000 tons (1,100,000 metric tons) of sheepskins; and 419,000 tons (380,000 metric tons) of goatskins. World trade in bovine leather is largely concentrated in industrialized countries. Argentina, Italy, West Germany, the United States, and Japan are the largest exporters. West Germany, Italy, France, South Korea, and the United States are the largest importers. Footwear, clothing, and accessories make up the largest groups of finished leather products with Italy and South Korea the leading exporters.

History

The story of leather is long and colorful. Many years before recorded history people probably wrapped themselves in dried animal pelts. The fact that the skins turned stiff and rotted were a problem, but ways of softening and preserving them were discovered. This was the beginning of leather processing. At first skins were probably dried in air and sunlight. Later they may have been soaked in water

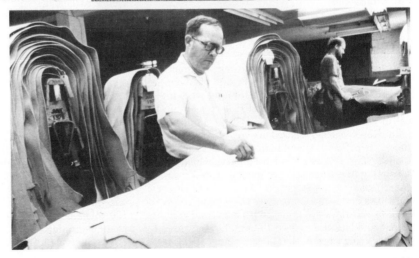

After the skins are dried, they are placed on a device called a truck, or horse (above). The plating operation (above right) adds a thermal plastic finish. After buffing, the leather goes through a quality check (right).

Photos, courtesy of Pfister & Vogel Tanning Co.

Special equipment (above left) produces a slick surface. A computerized measuring machine (above) makes a last, exact measurement check before the leather is piled on skids (left) for shipping.

Photos, courtesy of Pfister & Vogel Tanning Co.

and dried over a fire. Still later it was discovered that certain twigs, barks, and leaves soaked with the hides in water helped to preserve them.

Sumeria and Egypt. Evidence exists for the use of leather by the ancient Sumerians as far back as 6000 BC. Preserved specimens of leather dating to 5000 BC have been found. Egyptian stone carvings of about the same date show leather workers. Egyptian leather sandals more than 3,300 years old and an Egyptian queen's funeral tent of gazelle hides made in 1100 BC are in museums.

The Israelites learned to make leather from the Egyptians. A passage in the Old Testament reads, "Unto Adam and also unto his wife did the Lord God make clothes of skins and clothe them." By New Testament times tanning had become common.

Greece and Rome. The Greeks and Romans left evidence that their methods of tanning were highly developed. Both Herodotus and Homer mention the use of leather.

In Rome leather served as money, and leather shoes of different types indicated the rank of the wearer. The English word pecuniary, which means consisting of or measured in money, comes from the Latin *pecus,* meaning "cattle." Pliny the Elder, writing in the first century AD, gives the Roman recipe for tanning: "Hides were tanned with bark, and gallnuts, sumac and lotus were used." Gallnuts are caused by insects laying eggs on the leaves or buds of oak trees.

These eggs produce a growth that yields a high percentage of tannic acid. Gallnuts are still used in one type of tanning.

America. When the first settlers arrived in America, they found that the Indians' tanning method was much like the ancient shamoying, a method used by the Arabs and mentioned by Homer. The Indians taught the pioneers how to make buckskin.

The colonists brought oak-bark tanning methods from England. The first leathermaker, named Experience Miller, arrived in Plymouth in 1623. In 1629 two shoemakers arrived. By 1650 there were 51 tanners in Massachusetts.

The early leathermakers simply dug holes in the ground and walled them with planking. In these holes hides were covered with oak bark and left for at least six months. This method was no more advanced than that used by the ancient Hebrews.

In 1805 Sir Humphry Davy discovered that materials from other trees—hemlock, mimosa, chestnut, and ash—could be used in tanning. These trees were plentiful in the United States and helped make it the center of the leather trade.

Samuel Parker invented a machine in 1809 that could split hides to any thickness. Until then it took one worker an entire day to divide four hides. Now 100 could be split in the same length of time. From these beginnings grew the scientific process of modern leather manufacture.

A donkey driver hurries his animals along a momentarily traffic-free modern highway that runs through a densely crowded area of shops and apartments in Tripoli. The city is the second largest in Lebanon and an important port.

H. Gritscher—Peter Arnold Inc.

LEBANON.

LEBANON. The republic of Lebanon is an Arab state in western Asia. It occupies a long, narrow strip of land on the eastern shore of the Mediterranean Sea. The Lebanese coast is about 135 miles (215 kilometers) long, and the country has an average width of 30 miles (48 kilometers). Lebanon is bordered on the north and east by Syria, and on the south by Israel. It covers an area of about 3,950 square miles (10,230 square kilometers).

The Land and Climate

Lebanon is a rugged land with two mountain ranges that are almost parallel. The Lebanon Mountains extend the length of the country close to the narrow Mediterranean coastal plain. In the east, the Anti-Lebanon Mountains rise along the Syrian border. Between the two mountain ranges lies a high, fertile valley called the Bekaa. The Bekaa receives water from Lebanon's chief river, the Litani. The Litani flows south, then abruptly turns west, runs through a deep gorge in the Lebanon Mountains, and empties into the Mediterranean.

Lebanon's Mediterranean coast has warm, dry summers and mild, rainy winters. Summers in the Bekaa are hot and dry, and winters are cool. During winter, high winds and heavy rains and snows lash the mountains, particularly the western slopes.

Plant life in Lebanon varies with altitude and climate. Large groves of orange and olive trees thrive in the rich coastal soil, and farmers also grow bananas, figs, grapes, and other fruits there. Apples and potatoes are raised in the foothills. The Bekaa is an equally rich farming region, producing tobacco, vegeta-

bles, cotton, grains, and mulberries. In the mountains, much of the soil is barren. Erosion has destroyed almost all the natural vegetation, leaving only scattered bush and scrub. The cedars, for which Lebanon is famous, remain only in protected groves.

The People

Lebanon is rather densely populated, but the people are unevenly distributed. In 1982 the nation had a

---

This article was contributed by Ludwig W. Adamec, Professor, Near Eastern and Islamic Studies, and Director, Near Eastern Center, University of Arizona.

Facts About Lebanon

Official Name: Republic of Lebanon.

Capital: Beirut.

Area: 3,950 square miles (10,230 square kilometers).

Population (1982 estimate): 3,316,000; 839 persons per square mile (324 persons per square kilometer); 60 percent urban, 40 percent rural.

Major Language: Arabic (official).

Major Religions: Maronite Catholic, Sunnite and Shi'ite Muslim, Greek Orthodox, Druze, Jewish.

Literacy: 88 percent.

Highest Peak: Qurnat as Sawda'.

Major River: Litani.

Form of Government: Republic.

Chief of State and Head of Government: President.

Legislature: National Assembly.

Voting Qualifications: Citizens who are 25 years old may vote.

Political Divisions: Six governorates (*muhafazat*).

Major Cities (1978 estimate): Beirut 702,000, Tripoli 175,000, Zahlah 46,800, Sidon 24,740.

Chief Manufactured and Mined Products: Petroleum products, cement, food, textiles, iron ore, asphalt, coal, phosphate, sand and stone.

Chief Agricultural Products: *Crops*—oranges, potatoes, grapes, apples, tomatoes, lemons, wheat, bananas, olives. *Livestock*—poultry, goats, sheep, cattle.

Flag: *Colors*—red, white, and green (*see* Flags of the World).

Monetary Unit: 1 Lebanese pound = 100 piastres.

population of about 3,316,000, plus about 600,000 Palestinian refugees, who were not citizens. Most Lebanese are Arabs, but there are many racial and cultural groups. Arabic is the official language, but English and French are also spoken.

Until recently, Lebanon had a government in which religious communities operated like political parties. Muslims make up more than half of the population, and Christians comprise most of the rest. The chief Muslim sects include the Sunnites and the Shi'ites, who form the nation's largest religious community. The Druzes, whose religion is an offshoot of Islam, compose an independent sect. The Maronite Catholics are the largest Christian sect. Other Christian groups include the Greek Orthodox, Greek Catholic, Armenian Orthodox, and Armenian Catholic.

Lebanon also has small communities of Muslim Kurds, Arab Protestants, Jews, and followers of other religions. There are about 17 recognized religious communities. The majority are Arabic and all speak Arabic, but some minorities also use their communal languages at home or in religious services.

About 88 percent of the people can read and write. Lebanon has, relative to its size, the largest number of skilled medical and professional personnel among the Arab nations of the Middle East. The Christian communities, especially the Maronites, have a larger proportion of educated people than the other Lebanese groups, and the Shi'ites and Kurds have the highest levels of illiteracy. The major centers of learning include Saint Joseph University, the American University, the Lebanese University, and the Arab University, all in Beirut, the capital and largest city. Only about 47 percent of Lebanon's students attend public elementary and high schools, and the rest go to parochial and missionary schools. This educational division tends to keep the communities

apart, because from early childhood the people regard themselves as belonging to their community rather than being citizens of the Lebanese nation.

Economy

The Lebanese economy has traditionally been based on trade and on Beirut's position as the banking center of the Middle East, in addition to being a major port (see Beirut). Other principal cities include Tripoli, Zahlah, and Sidon. Oil tankers load offshore from pipeline terminals at Tripoli and near Sidon. A railroad system links Lebanon with other Arab countries and, through Turkey, with Europe.

Lebanese industries include oil refining, food processing, and textile manufacturing. Service industries, the manufacture of cement and chemicals, metal fabricating, and tourism also are important. Among Lebanon's major exports are foods, textiles, tobacco, manufactured goods, and precious metals, stones, jewelry, and coins. Civil war and foreign occupation in the 1970s and 1980s disrupted the economy.

Government

When the French created Lebanon in 1920, they set up a country with a small Christian majority, separating it from Muslim Syria. Lebanon became independent in 1943, and a government had to be established that would enable the various communities to live in harmony. To that end a government was set up in which the president must be a Maronite Christian, the prime minister a Sunnite Muslim, and the speaker of parliament a Shi'ite. Many defense ministers have been Druzes.

Members of the republic's one-house parliament, the National Assembly, are elected to four-year terms. They represent religious, rather than political, groups. The president is chosen by parliament for a six-year term, and he appoints the prime minister. By law, parliament includes six Christians for every five Muslims, and each group is represented according to its numerical strength.

History

The region that includes Lebanon had many rulers in ancient times, including the Phoenicians, Greeks, Romans, and Byzantines. Christianity was established in the region during the 5th century, followed by Islam two centuries later.

For many centuries, the mountainous terrain prevented conquerors from completely subjugating the people, and the region became a refuge for persecuted minorities. The Maronites established themselves in the north, and the Druzes found shelter in the south. Little friction occurred between the two communities until the 19th century. Peasant revolts against landowners then turned into wars between the Druzes and Maronites, and by 1860 thousands had been killed. The Turkish sultans of the Ottoman Empire, who conquered the region in the 16th century, assisted the Druzes and Muslims, and the Maronites looked to France and the West for support.

Following Turkey's defeat in World War I, France received a mandate from the League of Nations to prepare the region for eventual independence. Lebanon was carved out of Greater Syria and became the only state in the Middle East with a Christian majority. After Germany defeated France in World War II, the Free French government agreed to end the mandate. Elections were held in 1943, and Lebanon gained independence that same year.

Lebanon then experienced a brief period of prosperity and relative freedom that was unique in the Middle East. However, the birth of Israel in 1948, the emergence of an Arab nationalist movement and the unequal distribution of new prosperity among Lebanese factions contributed to widespread unrest.

In 1958 discontented religious groups, particularly the Muslims, revolted against the government because the Maronite president, Camille Chamoun, wanted to change the constitution to succeed himself for another term. The government appealed to the United States for help, and about 10,000 American troops landed in Beirut. Parliament chose Gen. Fuad Chehab, a Maronite who was acceptable to the major factions, to succeed Chamoun. Order was restored and the Americans withdrew.

In 1967, when war erupted between the Arab states and Israel, Lebanon declared a state of emergency, but it took no military action and lost no territory. The war increased the number of Palestinian refugees, and many thousands more arrived in 1970 after being expelled from Jordan. Palestinian guerrillas launched attacks on Israel that led to Israeli reprisals, causing death and destruction in Lebanon.

The violent situation, together with Muslim demands for more power in the government, led to civil war between Muslims and Christians in 1975. About 60,000 Lebanese were killed, and much of Beirut was destroyed. Syrian troops helped restore order, and a cease-fire was established in 1976. Lebanon began to rebuild, but the civil strife went on, as did Palestinian guerrilla attacks on Israel and Israeli reprisals.

The instability continued into the 1980s, leading to an Israeli invasion of Lebanon in 1982. About 14,600 troops of the Palestine Liberation Organization (PLO) withdrew from Beirut, and hundreds of Palestinian civilians then became victims of reprisal killings. The United Nations sent a peacekeeping force of largely French and Italian troops to Lebanon, and the United States ordered a Marine unit there.

In May Lebanon and Israel signed an agreement calling for the withdrawal of Israeli and Syrian troops from the country. However, Syria rejected the plan. By midsummer of 1983 Lebanon was in chaos, with battles going on between various factions. Druze and Muslim forces battled the Christian militia and all three struggled against the Lebanese army. Skirmishes continued between Israelis and Syrians and conflict broke out between loyal and rebel Palestinian forces. In September Israel redeployed its troops into southern Lebanon. The Syrian-backed Druzes then launched an offensive into the areas which had been vacated by the Israelis. The Lebanese army, with United States Marine and Navy support, resisted, and the United States sent additional troops to the area. In late September the factions finally agreed to a cease-fire and efforts to form an acceptable government continued.

LE CARRÉ, John (born 1931). One of the most adept and popular authors of spy fiction writes under the name John le Carré. The realism of his novels derives in great part from the knowledge of international espionage he gained while a member of the British foreign service from 1961 to 1964.

Le Carré was born David John Moore Cornwell in England at Poole, in Dorsetshire, on Oct. 19, 1931. He graduated from Oxford University in 1956 and worked as a tutor at Eton College for two years. His third novel, 'The Spy Who Came In from the Cold', published in 1963, was an enormous success, and from that time he devoted himself to a writing career. Other popular le Carré books were 'The Looking-Glass War' (1965), 'A Small Town in Germany' (1968), and 'The Little Drummer Girl' (1983), his first novel with a woman as the main character.

Of the spy-heroes le Carré has created, none has become more popular than the intrepid, brilliant, and sometimes plodding George Smiley, an agent for the British Secret Intelligence Service, MI-6 (*see* Intelligence Agencies). He is the main character in le Carré's first two novels and in the three later novels 'Tinker, Tailor, Soldier, Spy' (1974), 'The Honourable Schoolboy' (1977), and 'Smiley's People' (1980). Unlike most spy-heroes, Smiley is an aging, lonely man with an unfaithful wife. He works his way painstakingly through the maze of international intrigue in pursuit of his elusive goals. Much of the success of these novels derives from the insight they give into the workings of the intelligence community.

'The Spy Who Came In from the Cold' was made into a motion picture in 1965. 'Tinker, Tailor, Soldier, Spy' and 'Smiley's People' were adapted for television in 1979 and 1982, respectively.

LE CORBUSIER (1887–1965). A revolutionary influence in modern architecture and urban planning, Le Corbusier was also a painter, sculptor, and writer. His was a classic definition of architecture: "the conscious, correct, and magnificent interplay of volumes assembled under light."

Le Corbusier was born on Oct. 6, 1887, in La Chaux-de-Fonds, Switzerland, as Charles Édouard Jeanneret-Gris. His father engraved and enameled watch faces, and his mother taught piano. When he was 13, the boy left school to learn his father's trade. At the art school he was encouraged to become an architect, and he was given local projects for practice.

Le Corbusier's knowledge of architecture was largely self-taught. He learned much through his travels from 1907 to 1911 through central Europe and the Mediterranean area. He worked in Paris with Auguste Perret, an expert in the use of reinforced

LE CORBUSIER

One of Le Corbusier's most striking designs was for the Palace of the Assembly in Chandigarh, India.

concrete construction, and in Berlin with Peter Behrens, a pioneer of industrial design.

In 1917 Le Corbusier settled in Paris. Modern painting interested him, and he formed a close association with the artist Amédée Ozenfant. When he began to write, he used the pen name Le Corbusier on his articles for *The New Spirit*, an avant-garde magazine that he helped to found in 1920.

When Le Corbusier's book 'Towards a New Architecture' was published in 1923, it had considerable influence on the architectural world. In 1925 at the International Exhibition of Decorative Arts in Paris, Le Corbusier exhibited a two-story apartment unit that was a forerunner of his later residential blocks. He was already well known in the United States when he visited there in 1935. Through the years many of Le Corbusier's plans were rejected as too extreme. He proposed vertical environments that later were adopted internationally—for example, office skyscrapers set among parks and gardens and with apartment houses beyond.

In 1930, the year in which he became a French citizen, Le Corbusier married Yvonne Gallis, a former model who inspired many of his paintings. With the outbreak of war, Le Corbusier moved to southern France. His studies there centered on his "Modulor" concept, a scale of measures that set architectural elements in proportion to human stature.

In 1945 Le Corbusier had the chance he had waited for to build a large housing complex that represented his ideas of a social environment. It was the Marseilles project, a vertical community of 18 floors and 1,800 inhabitants. In 1953 Le Corbusier began to build the capital city of Chandigarh in the Punjab, India. He executed the overall plan and designed major government buildings.

Among Le Corbusier's other notable works are the Swiss dormitory at the Cité Universitaire, Paris; the chapel of Notre-Dame-du-Haut at Ronchamp,

France; the convent of Sainte-Marie de la Tourette at Eveux-sur-L'Arbresle, France; the National Museum of Western Art in Tokyo; and the Carpenter Visual Arts Center at Harvard University. His books include 'The City of Tomorrow', published in 1929, The Radiant City' (1935), and 'The Modulor' (1948). (*See also* Architecture.)

LEE, Light-Horse Harry (1756–1818). One of the most brilliant and daring officers in the American Revolution was Henry "Light-Horse Harry" Lee. He is also noted for his famous eulogy of George Washington in 1799: "First in war, first in peace, and first in the hearts of his countrymen." During the Civil War, his son Robert E. Lee became the Confederacy's most outstanding general (*see* Lee, Robert E.).

Henry Lee was born on his family's estate in Prince William County, Va., on Jan. 29, 1756. He graduated from the College of New Jersey (now Princeton University) in 1773 and intended to make a career at law. This course was interrupted by the outbreak of the Revolution in 1775. He became a captain in the cavalry, later rising to the rank of major and then lieutenant colonel. His troops fought in both the Northern and Southern theaters of the war and took part in the final victory at Yorktown, Va.

After the war Lee served in the Virginia legislature and the Continental Congress and was governor of his state from 1792 to 1795. In 1794 he commanded the troops that put down the "Whiskey Rebellion" in western Pennsylvania. He retired from politics after one term in the United States House of Representatives. In the next several years he was ruined financially by bad investments and was put into debtors' prison for a few years. After 1812 his health deteriorated. He spent a few years in the West Indies, hoping to recover, but died at Cumberland Island, Ga., on March 25, 1818, while on his way home.

LEE, Richard Henry (1732–94). On June 7, 1776, Richard Henry Lee offered the resolution in Congress "that these colonies are, and of right ought to be, free and independent states." Lee's fame rests on this history-making resolution, but he served his country in many other ways.

Richard Henry Lee was born on Jan. 20, 1732, in Virginia. At 25 he took a seat in the Virginia House of Burgesses. He was among the first to suggest that the colonists organize committees to achieve unified action against the British. Lee was a signer of the Declaration of Independence and president of the Continental Congress from 1784 to 1786.

Lee was opposed to the idea of a constitution. He and Patrick Henry were its most violent critics. They feared that it would deprive the states of their rights and might become an instrument of tyranny. In 1789 he accepted appointment as senator from Virginia. In the Senate Lee became one of the strongest advocates of the first ten amendments, the Bill of Rights. Ill health forced him to retire in 1792. He died on June 19, 1794, in Westmoreland County, Va.

LEE, Robert E. (1807–70). The Confederacy's greatest soldier, Robert E. Lee, was descended from an old and honored family. Several of Lee's forebears had played distinguished roles in Virginia's history. His father was the Revolutionary War hero Light-Horse Harry Lee, a friend of George Washington. The family was living at Stratford, Va., the ancestral home in Westmoreland County, when Robert was born on Jan. 19, 1807. He was the fourth of five children. Shortly after his birth, the family moved to Alexandria, near the nation's capital, where the tradition of George Washington lived on. Washington was young Lee's hero.

Partly because of the military tradition in his family and partly because an army career was attractive to him, young Lee decided to become a soldier. He entered West Point and was graduated in 1829, standing second in his class. He specialized in military engineering, and for several years he supervised various construction projects for the army. On July 5, 1831, he married Mary Custis, great-granddaughter of Washington's wife and heiress of the estate of Arlington, across the Potomac from Washington. The Lees had seven children.

Lee's application to his work won him promotion to the rank of captain. His first experience in actual battle came in the Mexican War. He was one of a group of young engineer officers on the staff of General Winfield Scott, the general in chief of the army. Lee was the ablest of the engineer officers and served with distinction in all the operations of Scott's victorious campaign.

After the Mexican War, Lee's next big assignment was as superintendent of West Point. From there, he went to Texas in 1855 as lieutenant colonel of the Second Cavalry Regiment. Here he served several years, policing the border areas against Indians. In 1859 he was home on leave when the abolitionist John Brown tried to start a slave uprising at Harpers Ferry in Virginia. From Washington, Lee led a party of Marines that captured Brown and his band. He returned to Texas for a short tour of duty but was recalled to Washington early in 1861. The secession movement had started. Some Southern states had left the Union, others were about to go. Lee's own Virginia was considering secession.

Lee's Fateful Decision

As much as he cared for the Union, he was first of all a Virginian and loved the Old Dominion. He could not bear to think of a national army invading Virginia to coerce it back into the Union or of himself as possibly leading that army. After days of deliberation, he decided his right course was to resign his commission, return home, and offer his services to his home state of Virginia.

Virginia had seceded from the Union but had not yet formally joined the Confederacy when Lee reached Richmond. The state appointed him commander of the Virginia military forces then being gathered. After Virginia joined the Confederacy, the

Robert E. Lee

capital of the new Southern nation was established in Richmond. The Confederate government took over the direction of all military forces in Virginia, including Lee's state troops. Although Lee was made a full general, he was a general without an army. Finally the president of the Confederacy, Jefferson Davis, sent him to repel the Federal forces that were invading western Virginia, the region that would be the future West Virginia. Lee failed to halt the Federal advance. He was then ordered to South Carolina and Georgia to build coastal fortifications.

Lee was recalled to Richmond early in 1862 and appointed by Davis to be general in chief of all Confederate armies under authority of the president. His title was important, but his position was not. Davis kept the direction of the war largely in his own hands and entrusted only minor matters to Lee.

Soon after Lee took office, a large Federal army approached Richmond and penetrated to the gates of the city. In the fighting before the capital, the commander of the Confederate army was seriously wounded. President Davis appointed Lee commander of the organization that was known as the Army of Northern Virginia.

Command in the Field

Lee assumed command in June 1862. The Union army, under the command of General McClellan, was a few miles from Richmond and astride the Chickahominy River before the city. Lee decided to mass his army and attack the smaller part of the enemy army on the north side of the river. He hoped to destroy this fraction and then smash the rest on the south side. He took the planned risk that McClellan would not discover there was only a small defending Confederate force directly in front of Richmond. Lee was partly successful in the battle of the Seven Days that followed. He drove the Union army back about 25 miles but was not able to destroy it.

At Arlington, Va., stands the Lee Mansion, where the Lees lived from 1831 to 1861. Restored as a museum and national memorial, it was opened to the public in 1925.

Richmond Cook

The Union government then withdrew McClellan's army to northern Virginia to regroup it with the smaller force of General Pope. Lee hurried northward to hit Pope before McClellan could arrive. In August he fought Pope, who had received some of McClellan's troops, at the second battle of Manassas. Again making a daring plan, he divided his army and sent part of it around to Pope's rear. Following with the rest of his troops, he defeated the confused Pope and drove him back into Washington. Lee next decided to invade Maryland, a state that had not seceded. His object was to get the armies out of Virginia during the harvest season and possibly win a victory in a Union state. McClellan, in command of the Union forces again, moved to meet him. The two met in September at the battle of Antietam, where McClellan attacked Lee but failed to break his lines. Lee, realizing that he was in a dangerous position and far from his supplies, retreated and took up a defensive position behind the Rappahannock River in northern Virginia. Here General Ambrose E. Burnside, who succeeded McClellan, attacked Lee in December at the battle of Fredericksburg and met a bloody repulse. As the year 1862 closed, Lee had given the Confederacy its greatest victories and had become the idol of the Southern people.

In the spring of 1863, General Hooker, the new Federal commander, crossed the Rappahannock above Fredericksburg to attack Lee's left flank. When Lee confronted him, Hooker drew back. In Lee's most daring move of the war, he sent Stonewall Jackson to turn the Federal right while he attacked from the front. His objective was to cut the Federal army in two and destroy it. In this engagement, the battle of Chancellorsville, Lee hit the Federals hard, but they managed to withdraw across the river.

After Chancellorsville, Lee started an offensive movement he hoped would win the war—an invasion of Pennsylvania. In the southern part of that state, he met the defending Federal army at Gettysburg in a three-day battle, from July 1 to 3, the greatest ever fought in North America. On the second and third days Lee threw strong attacks against the Union lines and was repulsed with heavy losses. He has been criticized for attacking a larger army in a strong position. (He had about 75,000 men to the 88,000 Federals.) It must be remembered, however, that he had great faith in his men and that even the best Civil War generals did not understand that the firepower of the new rifles was making frontal attacks dangerous to attempt. (*See also* Gettysburg, Battle of.)

After Gettysburg, Lee fell back into northern Virginia. For the rest of the war, with an army ever getting smaller, he had to employ a defensive strategy. In the spring of 1864, General Grant assumed direction of the Federal army in Virginia. His objective was to bring Lee to battle in northern Virginia and to destroy the Confederate army. Lee showed great skill in this campaign. He evaded attempts to trap him into decisive battle and inflicted heavy losses on Grant at the battles of the Wilderness, Spotsylvania, and Cold Harbor. Finally Grant swung south of Richmond to Petersburg, hoping to reach the railroads that carried supplies to Lee's army and make Lee fight there. Lee got to Petersburg first. Grant then decided the only way he could get at Lee was by the slow method of running siege trench lines around to the railroads in Lee's rear. Grant started his siege in the summer of 1864. Not until the spring of 1865 did he seize the railroads. Lee then abandoned Petersburg and Richmond. He retreated to the west, but Grant was right on his heels. With only 25,000 men left, Lee realized that his cause was hopeless. To continue fighting meant the needless loss of lives. Early in April he met Grant at Appomattox and surrendered the Army of Northern Virginia.

In the years after the war, Lee was the hero of the South. With dignity and without bitterness, he accepted defeat and preached to his people the necessity of peace and national unity. Offered many jobs, he accepted the presidency of Washington College at Lexington, Va. Later it became Washington and Lee University. It was his duty, he thought, to guide the youth of the South in the postwar years. He died on Oct. 12, 1870. His body rests in a mausoleum in the chapel of the university.

LEECH *see* WORM.

LEEDS, England. For centuries England has been noted for the quality of its woolen cloth. The manufacture of the fabric centers in Leeds, West Yorkshire Metropolitan County.

Leeds owes its importance to two principal factors: its extensive transport facilities and its situation on the edge of the great Yorkshire coal fields. The River Aire connects it with the east coast of England. The Leeds and Liverpool Canal provides cheap transportation to the west coast. Iron manufactures are nearly as important to the city as woolens. Leeds also manufactures boots and shoes, felt, ready-made clothing, artificial silk, glass, and pottery. The city houses markets and stock and corn exchanges. Leeds is also noted for the music festival that is held there every three years and for the University of Leeds. Other educational institutions include a technical college; colleges of art, commerce, housecraft, and physical training; Wesley Theological College; two teacher-training colleges; and a boys' grammar school, founded in 1552.

The Town Hall contains the law courts and a large concert hall, which was opened in 1858; nearby is the Civil Hall (1933). The city has a Civic Theater, a City Museum, a City Art Gallery, and a central public library. There is a nationally famous cricket ground at Headingley, an association football (soccer) ground, and many golf courses, including the Moortown championship course.

A suggestion of Leed's history, which goes back for 13 centuries, is found in the ruins of Kirkstall Abbey, a Cistercian monastery of the 12th century. In 1207 the local lord of the manor granted a limited charter to the inhabitants.

Leeds lies in the softwater area of the Pennines, and this facilitated the introduction of the woolen industry by Flemish weavers in the 14th century. In 1626 the first royal charter of incorporation created the municipal borough to regulate and protect the woolen trade. A 1661 charter remained the basis of the municipal constitution until its reform in 1835. With the Industrial Revolution, the woolen industry yielded to engineering, and in the 18th century the principal manufactures of the city became industrial and agricultural equipment. During the second half of the 19th century engineering was displaced by the wholesale clothing industry, which was introduced in 1855. Wholesale clothing remains the largest single industry in the city.

During the second half of the 18th century Leeds was also famed for its pottery, but the industry declined and the potteries closed down in 1878. The linen trade, introduced in 1788, enjoyed a similar brief period of prosperity. Other leading industries include engineering and electrical trades, paper and printing, textiles, and metal goods. Leeds became a city in 1893. Population (1981 census), 448,528.

Leeuwenhoek in a portrait by Jan Verkolje

LEEUWENHOEK, Anthony van (1632–1723). By means of his extraordinary ability to grind lenses, Anthony van Leeuwenhoek greatly improved the microscope as a scientific tool. This led to his doing a vast amount of innovative research on bacteria, protozoa, and other small life-forms that he called "animalcules" (tiny animals).

Leeuwenhoek was born at Delft, Holland, on Oct. 24, 1632. He probably did not have much scientific education, for his family could not afford it. He first became a haberdasher and draper and, in 1660, chamberlain to the sheriffs at Delft. His hobby was lens grinding; and in his lifetime he ground about 400 lenses, most of which were quite small, with a magnifying power of from 50 to 300 times.

It was not only his lenses that made him world famous but also his work with the microscope. His keen powers of observation led to discoveries of major significance. For example, he observed and calculated the sizes of bacteria and protozoa and gave the first accurate description of red blood cells.

Although Leeuwenhoek lived in Delft, he maintained a regular correspondence with the Royal Society of England, to which he was elected in 1680. Most of his discoveries were published in the society's 'Philosophical Transactions'. He continued his work throughout most of his 90 years. He died at Delft on Aug. 26, 1723.

LÉGER, Fernand (1881–1955). A French painter, Fernand Léger was deeply influenced in his work by modern industrial technology. He is known as the developer of machine art, a style characterized by enormous mechanistic forms in bold colors composed in a disciplined manner.

Fernand Léger was born on Feb. 4, 1881, in Argentan, France, a small town in Normandy. After completing his education in local secondary schools, Léger served a two-year apprenticeship in an architect's

117

office. In 1900 he went to work in Paris, first as an architectural draftsman and later as a retoucher in a photographer's studio. In 1903 he enrolled in the Paris École des Arts Décoratifs, becoming involved with the school of painting known as Cubism. Within this environment and influenced by the machine age, he began to develop his style. In 1909 he produced 'The Seamstress', in which he reduced his colors to a combination of blue-gray and buff and the human body to a construction of slabs and cylinders that resembles a robot. Beginning in the years before World War I, his style became vigorous, combining bright, posterlike zones of color. His favorite subject matter included acrobats, cyclists, and construction workers.

Léger served as a soldier in World War I. Gassed at Verdun, he was hospitalized for a long period. In 1919, inspired by the wartime artillery he had seen, he was in what has been called his mechanical period, marked by a fascination for motors, gears, bearings, furnaces, railway crossings, and factory interiors.

Léger took an interest in many arts besides painting. He designed sets for ballets and motion pictures. He also worked in ceramics and was a teacher and a designer of stained-glass windows and mosaics. He died on Aug. 17, 1955, at Gif-sur-Yvette, in the suburbs of Paris. At Biot, in southern France, there is a museum devoted to his work.

LEGUME. The more than 18,000 kinds of plants belonging to the pea family (Leguminosae) are known as legumes. The Leguminosae is the third largest family of flowering plants, being exceeded in numbers of species only by the Compositae (sunflower family) and Orchidaceae (orchid family). The word legume means seed pod and refers to the case that encloses the seeds. The pods come in a variety of shapes, sizes, and textures and are sometimes used to distinguish between similar but different legumes.

Except for the grasses, legumes are the most important plants in the world from an economic standpoint. They are an important food source for humans (peas, beans, and peanuts) and livestock (alfalfa and clover). Legumes provide timber (black locust, rosewood), oils (soybeans), and dyes (indigo). Some are economic nuisances to farmers and ranchers. Kudzu, the oriental vine legume introduced into the southern United States for erosion control, grows rapidly over adjacent vegetation in the spring and summer and can kill native trees or shrubs by reducing the amount of light they receive. Locoweeds of the western United States are poisonous to cattle. Many ornamental plants, such as redbud trees, sweet peas, and wisteria, are legumes.

The overwhelming majority of legume species occur in tropical and warm subtropical areas, but the

This article was contributed by J. Whitfield Gibbons, Associate Director and Associate Research Ecologist, Savannah River Ecology Laboratory, Aiken, S.C., and Professor, University of Georgia.

family is found worldwide. Although most representatives occur naturally in warm parts of the world, most of the economically significant species are grown in temperate areas.

Scientific Classification and Characteristics

The legumes are flowering plants (class Angiospermae) that belong to the family Leguminosae in the order Rosales. There are three major subfamilies: Mimosoideae (acacia subfamily), Caesalpinoideae (bird-of-paradise subfamily), and Papilionoideae (bean subfamily). A fourth subfamily, Krameriodeae, with a single genus is also recognized by plant taxonomists.

A wide variety of growth forms exists among the legumes, from small herbaceous species to large, woody trees. Most species have soft, green stems. Some form woody or herbaceous vines. Many legumes are shrubs or small trees.

Most legumes have flowers with five petals and are bisexual, having male and female parts on the same flower. The pod, or legume, develops from the plants' flowers. It surrounds a double row of seeds in most species, and it has a double seam so that it splits open on both sides.

The Mimosoideae, with about 2,800 species, have small flowers that are mostly radially symmetrical and grouped together in a cluster. Included in this subfamily are the acacia and mimosa trees, mesquites, and cat claws. The Caesalpinoideae, also with approximately 2,800 species, have flowers that are usually single, larger than those in the Mimosoideae, and bilaterally symmetrical. The subfamily includes trees found on savannas and in forests of South America, Asia, and Africa, as well as redbud, honey locust, and palos verdes trees. The Papilionoideae, which are represented by more than 12,000 mainly herbaceous species, have flowers with a distinct bilateral symmetry, with five petals that have a butterfly-like appearance. The larger central petal is called the banner, the middle pair are called wings, and the lower pair form the keel. The sweet pea has a flower characteristic of this subfamily that has members worldwide including the beans, peas, clovers, peanuts, and vetches.

Nitrogen Fixation

One of the unusual features of legumes is nitrogen fixation, a process characteristic of most legumes and found in few other plants. Nitrogen fixation is the obtaining of nitrogen, an essential nutrient for growth, from the atmosphere. Nearly all other green plants depend on nitrogen compounds in the soil to provide them with nitrogen. The nutrient is taken up directly by their roots.

For nitrogen fixation to occur, special soil bacteria (genus *Rhizobium*) must enter the root system of the legume through the tiny root hairs on each root. The bacteria then release enzymes that cause the root cells to divide so that a nodule is formed on the root. Obtaining energy from the legume, the bacteria living in these nodules take atmospheric nitrogen from

These illustrations represent a selection of some legume species and are not intended to be inclusive.

Acacia
(Acacia greggii)

Black Locust
(Robinia pseudoacacia)

Honey Locust
(Gleditsia triacanthos)

Mesquite
(Prosopis juliflora)

Mimosa Tree
(Mimosa pudica)

Redbud
(Cercis canadensis)

the air in the soil and produce ammonia, a nitrogen compound. The ammonia is available to both bacteria and legume, which convert it into amino acids and other proteins essential for growth. Such an association between two organisms, in which both benefit from the relationship in a manner that neither could alone, is known as mutualism.

The importance of nitrogen fixation to agriculture has been recognized since early Roman times, though the process was not understood until the 19th century. Once the edible parts of a legume crop such as beans or peas have been harvested, the remainder can be plowed into the soil. There, as it deteriorates, it releases into the soil the non-atmospheric nitrogen it made from the nitrogen in the air.

Major Legumes

Certain species of legumes are of regional or worldwide importance because of their commercial use as food for either humans or farm animals. However, despite the high number of legume species in the world, fewer than 20 have been extensively used commercially. Beans, peas, peanuts, soybeans, alfalfa, and clover are the major legumes used in world agriculture. Other species of importance include lentils, chick-peas, and mung beans. Some species deserve special mention.

Soybeans (*Glycine max*). One of the outstanding features of soybeans as a food source for humans or livestock is their high protein content. Protein comprises more than a third of a soybean, which is about twice as high as the protein content of meat.

The United States is the world's largest producer of soybeans. They are cultivated primarily in the midwestern and southern states with Iowa, Illinois, Indiana, and Minnesota producing more than half of the country's crop. Today the other major soybean production regions are in cool temperate zones such as eastern China and southern Brazil. The United States has averaged more than 1.5 billion bushels of soybeans per year since 1970. Corn and wheat are the only crops produced in greater quantity, on average, than soybeans in the United States. In certain years, more soybeans than wheat are harvested.

Soybeans are ordinarily planted in the spring and the seeds harvested in the fall. After the hull is removed, various processes are used to produce soybean oil and soybean meal, which is the crushed beans with the oil extracted. Soybean meal can be used directly as human food but most of it produced in the United States is used for livestock feed. Soybean oil is used in making a large number of commercial products both edible and inedible, including ice cream, salad dressing, soap, and explosives.

Peanuts (*Arachis hypogaea*). Peanuts are grown in warm temperate or subtropical areas throughout the world, and the major world crops are grown in Africa, Asia, and Indonesia. India, with 6.6 million tons (6

119

million metric tons) in 1981, and China with 3.9 million tons (3.5 million metric tons) are the largest producers of peanuts. The United States harvests more than 1.4 million tons (1.3 million metric tons) each year, but this is less than 10 percent of the world's supply. The largest peanut crops in the United States come from the South, particularly Georgia and Alabama. The annual production of peanuts in the United States is often greater than that of beans and peas combined. Some African countries (Sudan, Nigeria, and Senegal), as well as Indonesia, produce approximately 660,000 to 1 million tons (0.6 to 0.9 million metric tons) per year.

Peanuts are high in protein (about one fourth of their volume) and fatty oils (about one half). They

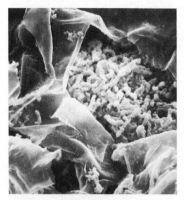

The spherical growths on soybean roots (below) are nodules containing *Rhizobium japonicum* bacteria, which use nitrogen from the atmosphere to make nitrogenous plant nutrients. A mass of the bacteria are revealed (left) through the microscope in a nodule that has been opened.

Photos, Winston J. Brill

are also high in calories. In contrast to soybeans, which are used primarily as feed for animals, peanuts are consumed directly as food by humans in the form of the nuts themselves or as peanut butter. Peanut oil is a highly versatile product, being used in a variety of food and industrial products.

A peanut plant has yellow flowers that appear on the stem. But after the flowers are fertilized, the developing pods and seeds they produce are pushed into the soil by an attachment called a "peg" that connects to the main stem. The seeds are the edible portion of the plant. From two to four seeds are encased in a pod, which develops underground for four or five months before they are harvested.

Beans (genus *Phaseolus*) **and peas** (*Pisum sativum*). These two members of the subfamily Papilionoidea are a staple in the diet of many humans because of their high nutritional value. Beans and peas are high protein, vitamin-rich foods that are easily prepared. Although both beans and peas come in a variety of shapes and colors, the different kinds are usually the result of a single species of bean or pea that has been developed experimentally.

The United States averages a harvest of about 1.1 million tons (1 million metric tons) of dry beans each year but less than 220,460 tons (200,000 metric tons) of dry peas. Both are cool temperate crops, and the highest production is in the northern states. Michigan is the highest producer of beans; Wisconsin and Washington grow the most peas.

Clover. Red clover (*Trifolium pratense*) and white clover (*Trifolium repens*) are two of the most common legumes used to add nitrogen to the soil for other crops. When used for this purpose they are simply grown for their nitrogen fixing ability then plowed into the ground as fertilizer. This is commonly called green manuring. Both these clovers are also commonly used as grazing crops and hay. Species in other genera, such as sweet clover in the genus *Melilotus*, are also referred to as clovers. The greatest production in the United States and Europe is red clover.

Alfalfa (*Medicago sativa*). The oldest known plant used for livestock feed is alfalfa, a legume that is known to have been grown as a crop earlier than 1000 BC in the Middle East. Today alfalfa, which is also called lucerne, is grown widely in the Western Hemisphere, Europe, and Australia. The United States is the world's largest producer of alfalfa as a feed crop, with the major supplies coming from the midwestern states and California.

Although alfalfa is sometimes used for cattle grazing, it is grown primarily for harvesting as hay or silage. Alfalfa hay, a major feed source for cattle and sheep, is obtained after the plants have been cut and dried in the fields. Silage, made from freshly cut alfalfa plants, is a higher nutrient source for livestock than hay. Silage is not dried and must be stored in silos, whereas baled hay can be stored more readily in any sheltered area and does not require immediate attention. Alfalfa can be ground into meal and be used for poultry as well as livestock.

Tropical Legumes

Legumes are remarkable plants in having protein contents that range from 20 percent to more than 50 percent and are characteristically two or three times richer in protein than are grain cereals. Thus, the exploitation of legume crops in the developing countries of the world, most of which are located in tropical or subtropical areas, can contribute considerably to the supply of protein that is usually deficient in the food of most of the human population.

Although most research on legumes of the world has been carried out on soybeans and peanuts, recent research has identified a variety of underexploited tropical legumes that could be utilized as food or other products. Once the many aspects of crop com-mercialization—such as disease control; determination of most favorable growing conditions; and storage, transportation, and marketing considerations—are adequately addressed, production of legumes may eventually become a major industry in the tropics as well as in the temperate regions.

Root crops. Many tropical legumes produce an underground root, known as a tuber, that is similar in appearance to a potato. In tropical America tubers called yam beans (genus *Pachyrhizus*) have been used for food for many centuries. Yet large-scale commercial production has never been successfully carried out. In experimental farming plots, yam beans have given extremely high yields (18 to 22 tons per acre, or 40 to 50 metric tons per hectare). Individual yam-bean tubers are large, up to 6½ pounds (3 kilograms),

Alfalfa
(Medicago sativa)

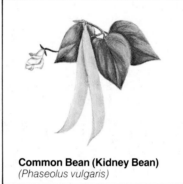

Common Bean (Kidney Bean)
(Phaseolus vulgaris)

Kudzu
(Pueraria thunbergiana)

Licorice
(Glycyrrhiza glabra)

Locoweed
(Astragalus mollissimus)

Pea
(Pisum sativum)

Peanut
(Arachis hypogaea)

Soybean
(Glycine max)

White Clover
(Trifolium repens)

These illustrations represent a selection of some legume species and are not intended to be inclusive.

have a potato-like texture, and a sweet taste. With sufficient research and development, yam beans and other leguminous tubers could become important root crops of tropical areas of the world.

Pulses. The edible seeds of beans or peas are referred to as pulses, and many species are native to the tropics. Most are only distantly related to the common beans and peas that are produced commercially in temperate regions. A major deterrent to development of certain varieties is the lack of research to establish proper growing conditions and factors affecting production. For example, the Bambara groundnut (genus *Voandzeia*) of Africa is considered to be a hardier, more disease-resistant species than the peanut but has been neglected as a food crop. Most tropical regions have similar examples of unexploited pulses that could provide a high source of protein and vitamins.

Trees. A variety of tropical leguminous tree has been identified that could be developed as pulpwood, lumber, or decorative wood sources. One example is rosewood (genus *Dalbergia*), which occurs in tropical regions of every continent. Rosewood trees have been exploited in natural areas to the point that few stands are left in the world. Despite the commercial value, few attempts have been made to cultivate rosewood trees or even to conduct the research necessary to make a start at it. Similar opportunities exist with other, less well-known species of tropical legumes that have commercial potential.

LE HAVRE, France. In French, *le havre* means "the harbor," or "the port," and the city of Le Havre is the second largest French port. Located in northern France, it is on the English Channel coast and on the right bank of the Seine River estuary. The city is 134 miles (216 kilometers) west-northwest of Paris.

The harbor maintains an important transatlantic trade, mainly with North America. Regular train- or car-ferry services run to England and Ireland. Le Havre's main imports are fuel oil and such tropical goods as coffee and cotton. Industries include oil refining, the processing of timber, and the manufacture of machinery and rope.

Air raids during World War II caused enormous damage, but about three fourths of the historic buildings have since been restored. A museum, built in 1961, houses a collection saved from the old museum that was destroyed in 1944. The spacious Place de l'Hôtel de Ville, in the center of the city, is typical of present-day architecture.

Le Havre was only a fishing village until 1517, when a harbor was built. Under various French rulers, the harbor continued to expand and adapt to accommodate larger vessels. It was also rebuilt after World War II, and development has continued. Population (1975 census), 216,917.

LEIBNIZ, Gottfried Wilhelm (1646–1716). Apart from his not being an artist, Leibniz was in many ways comparable to Leonardo da Vinci. He was recognized as the universal genius of his time, a philosopher and scientist who worked in the fields of mathematics, geology, theology, mechanics, history, jurisprudence, and linguistics.

Gottfried Wilhelm Leibniz was born in Leipzig, Germany, on July 1, 1646. He was educated at the University of Leipzig and received a doctorate in law at the University of Nuremberg. Because he was forced to earn a living, he spent his entire adult life in the service of nobility and royalty, particularly for the House of Brunswick-Lüneberg in Germany. His last employer was Duke George Louis of Hanover, who became King George I of England in 1714. This employment enabled Leibniz to travel a great deal throughout Europe and meet the leading scholars of his day. His many duties did not interfere with his extensive intellectual pursuits.

During his lifetime Leibniz perfected the calculating machine invented by Blaise Pascal (*see* Pascal); laid the ground for integral and differential calculus; founded dynamics, an area of mechanics; worked on mechanical devices such as clocks, hydraulic presses, lamps, submarines, and windmills; perfected the binary system of numeration used today in computer operations; devised the theory that all reasoning can be reduced to an ordered combination of elements such as numbers, words, sounds, or colors (the theoretical basis of modern computers); laid the foundation for general topology, a branch of mathematics; strove to formulate a basis for the unification of the churches; pursued the goal of writing a universal history; and also continued to perfect his philosophical-theological system.

Leibniz published his philosophy-theology in several works. 'Reflections on Knowledge, Truth, and Ideas' defined his theory of knowledge. In 'On the Ultimate Origin of Things' he tried to prove that only God could be the source of all things. 'Theodicy', his only major work published in his lifetime, explained his ideas on divine justice. 'Monadology', written two years before his death, spelled out his theory of monads, which he conceived of as simple, unextended, spiritual substances that formed the basis for all composite forms of reality. His theory of monads—a term derived from the Greek word meaning "that which is one" or "unity"—is elaborated in 'Monadology' and in 'Principles of Nature and Grace Founded in Reason'. The theory attempts to describe a harmonious universe made up of an infinite number of monads, or units, arranged in a hierarchy and originating in the Supreme Monad, which is God. Monadology had its roots in the philosophy of ancient Greece, especially in Pythagoras and Plato, and was carried on after Leibniz by such eminent thinkers as Immanuel Kant, Edmund Husserl, and Alfred North Whitehead. The hierarchy of monadology was, according to Leibniz, the "best of all possible worlds." The philosopher died in Hanover on Nov. 14, 1716.

LEIPZIG, East Germany. A major European intellectual and cultural center, Leipzig grew up around a castle in Saxony named Libzi, in the 11th century. It lies at the junction of the Weisse Elster, Parthe, and Pleisse rivers in the middle of a broad plain at the cross-

ing of two ancient trade routes. Its location made it a natural trade center, and Leipzig established a great medieval fair. Today the annual Leipzig Trade Fair, the major forum for international East-West trade, attracts visitors including scientists and business people from all over the world. The city's international fur auction is also well attended.

Leipzig is the capital of Saxony and the economic and cultural center of the German Midlands. Its industries include heavy constructional engineering and electrical, textile, clothing, chemical, and machine tool enterprises. Leipzig is the focus of railway lines and major roads, and there are two small airports, Leipzig-Mockau and Leipzig-Schkeuditz.

The city also became the heart of the great German book trade. As a music center it won world fame. It was the birthplace of Wagner and the home of Schumann and Bach. Bach was organist at the 13th-century Church of Saint Thomas. Other restored historic places include the Old Town Hall, the Old Exchange, Auerbach's Cellar, and residential and market squares.

The University of Leipzig, founded in 1409, became a great center of German education. In 1519, in the "Leipzig Disputation," Martin Luther and John Eck held a public debate on Christian doctrine.

Leipzig's history is stormy. It suffered six sieges in the Thirty Years' War. Napoleon met defeat here in 1813. After the devastation of World War II, the restoration and reconstruction of the city and its political and social institutions were carried out under the Communist policies of the German Democratic Republic. (*See also* Germany, East.) Population (1981 preliminary census), 560,012.

Leipzig's Neues Rathaus (New Town Hall) was built from 1899 to 1905 on the site of the old Pleissenburg citadel.

Karl Droste—Bavaria Verlag

LEISURE. What is leisure? Must it always be used wisely and well? Different people in different times have defined leisure in different ways. The Greek philosophers regarded leisure as labor of the mind, putting to use all one had learned—languages, mathematics, science, music, the arts—in order to expand an individual's intellectual horizons and become a better citizen. As the pursuit of leisure was limited to those who did not engage in trade and commerce or do the menial activities of society, it was necessarily a somewhat elite undertaking confined to those responsible for running the state. The Romans had a distinctive caste system with slaves to do the work, but to Romans leisure meant primarily rest from work. The Puritans, who settled in America in order to enjoy freedom of worship, thought that leisure was evil. Their work ethic required that they work from dawn until dusk six days a week and rest only on Sunday, a day they devoted to worship or recreation and spiritual contemplation.

Today leisure is often regarded as a block of time, a residual, or surplus, of time left over after caring for existence needs (eating, sleeping, brushing teeth) and subsistence (work or education). This leftover time is to be used as each individual chooses. Studies suggest that the average adult spends 80 to 85 hours weekly for existence and 35 to 40 hours for subsistence, leaving about 40 to 50 hours of leisure time.

Some see leisure simply as recreation. Others see it as an attitude or frame of mind, to be at leisure. It is considered the main objective of life, and work is merely a means to that end. Recent writers have defined leisure as a state of being free, an attitude of mind and condition of soul that aids in experiencing the reality of the world.

Still another definition is a function of the social class. Through history there has always been a leisure class—kings, rulers, and priests who did not work but lived a life totally supported by slaves, subjects, and followers.

No matter how it is defined, leisure time has increased for most people in most cultures. In the United States, for example, the workweek has gradually decreased from six days of 12 hours each to an average of about 34 hours when vacations, holidays, and sick leaves are included. Flexible working hours, four-day workweeks, personal leaves, and longer vacations have all allowed more time away from jobs and therefore more time for leisure.

In the early 1980s Americans of all ages spent more than $300 billion annually on leisure pursuits—from electronic video games to exotic trips to South America. Americans are becoming a leisured society as the earlier work ethic is being eroded. The need to use leisure wisely, therefore, is increasingly important.

This article was contributed by Arlin F. Epperson, author of 'Private and Commercial Recreation' (Wiley, 1977) and formerly Professor of Recreation, University of Missouri, and Director, Missouri State Parks.

Photography ranks high among the many possible creative leisure activities of young people and adults.

Dick Batchelor

Values

In his book 'Philosophy of Recreation and Leisure', J. B. Nash organized the concept of leisure by placing different kinds of leisure pursuits into a hierarchy based on their potential value to the individual in society. The higher up the ladder one goes, the more benefit leisure is, both to the individual and to the community. Time spent in creative activities such as music, art, hobbies, education, and community service are more beneficial than such amusements as television, radio, spectator sports, or other activities lower on the scale.

The benefits of leisure are generally considered to include such things as happiness, fun, creative expression, the opportunity for self-development and self-fulfillment, accomplishment, the challenge of experiment, adventure, and pure satisfaction. It should always be remembered, however, that leisure brings different rewards to different people.

Research has shown that preferences for leisure activities are related closely to types of personality. Some people enjoy stamp collecting, others reading. One of the first steps in learning how to use leisure wisely is to understand that each person's choice is individual. The old cliché "different strokes for different folks" is certainly appropriate.

Children

Children need guidance in their leisure as much as they do in schoolwork or in developing good personal habits. They need a variety of leisure opportunities in order to help them find the kinds of things that are of interest to them. These opportunities may develop into lifelong interests or lifetime activities. Creativity, patience, and ingenuity are required of parents, teachers, and club leaders to locate and present opportunities and resources that are challenging, stimulating, and of benefit to children. After initial exposure, they need opportunities to participate in their newly discovered interests, skills, or talents.

Youth

Young people have more leisure than their parents, and leisure for them in most cases is provided away from home by outside organizations. They desire change and experimentation, entertainment and variety. They enjoy activities with immediate satisfaction that have diversity and contrast. They desire novelty, mobility, and an opportunity to explore life and their own feelings. They need to develop close relationships outside the family and often to alter existing family relationships. They especially require acceptance by their friends and classmates.

Adults

Adults find leisure a time of changing interests, often from physical activities to less strenuous ones. Their interests change with those of their friends, relatives, and acquaintances in social organizations. They take up again those hobbies and interests learned in their youth, and they tend not to learn many new skills. Boredom results in passive activities such as watching television. In many cases they are so busy with their jobs that there is little leisure time available. They may desire to escape from their work environments or other responsibilities on vacations or trips in search of satisfaction. Those who make the effort to participate in more active or creative kinds of leisure activities are likely to find greater enjoyment and satisfaction.

Retirement

There are elements of society that have what is sometimes called enforced leisure. Such groups include those confined to institutions because of illness, handicaps, old age, or criminal punishment; the unemployed; and an increasing number officially retired. They have more leisure time than they really want or are able to use.

Retired people who have learned to use leisure well in their childhood, youth, and active adult years can turn to familiar activities for much enjoyment. Those who have not done so are likely to engage in aimless or meaningless activities. Most often retirees enjoy activities that involve people, especially people they know. They may enjoy many of the activities of their earlier years, but some must be adapted. In softball, for instance, bases are placed closer together so that players do not have as far to run.

If in the past they have developed a variety of interests, hobbies, and activities—both passive and active as well as creative—they will be able to continue them in retirement. If not, retirement can become for them a curse rather than a blessing.

BIBLIOGRAPHY FOR LEISURE

Brightbill, Charles. Educating for Leisure Centered Living (Wiley, 1976).
Brightbill, Charles. Man and Leisure: a Philosophy of Recreation (Greenwood, 1973).
De Grazia, Sebastian. Of Time, Work and Leisure (Kraus, 1973).
Godbey, Geoffrey and Parker, Stanley. Leisure Studies and Services (Saunders, 1976).
Ibrahim, Hilmi and Martin, Fred. Leisure: an Introduction (Hwong, 1978).
Kando, Thomas. Leisure and Popular Culture in Transition (Mosby, 1980).
Pieper, Josef. Leisure, the Basis of Culture (New American, 1964).

LEMUR. Lemurs resemble monkeys and are the size of cats and squirrels. They have big eyes, foxlike faces, and doglike nostrils. The name lemur comes from the Latin word *lemures*, meaning "ghosts." It was given to these animals because of the silent, ghostlike way they move about, mainly at night.

The lemurs are classified as primates, the group that also includes monkeys, apes, and humans. Most of them have tails, but they cannot hang from trees by them as some monkeys can.

With their many relatives, lemurs form the family Lemuroidea. Of the 90 or so species of lemuroids, 50 or more live in Madagascar. All of them are found only in the southern regions of the Old World—Africa, India, Sri Lanka and the Philippines. The true lemurs, however, are found only on the island of Madagascar and the nearby Comoros.

Among the lemuroids are the ring-tailed lemur, whose tail is marked with alternate rings of black and

Tierbilder Okapia, Frankfurt am Main

The ring-tailed lemur, whose scientific name is *Lemur catta*, is native to Madagascar.

white; the large indri, or babakoto ("little old man"), of Madagascar; the dark iron-gray lemur, which lives in the bamboo jungles; and the aye-aye of Madagascar, so named from its cry. Lemuroids eat leaves, fruits, insects, small reptiles, birds, and birds' eggs.

LENA RIVER. The Lena River is one of the longest rivers in the world. It flows generally northward for 2,730 miles (4,400 kilometers) from its headwaters near Lake Baikal to its delta in the Laptev Sea, an arm of the Arctic Ocean. In water volume it is the second largest river in the Soviet Union. The river basin covers about 961,000 square miles (2,490,000 square kilometers) in eastern Siberia.

Melting snow and rain contribute more than 95 percent of the Lena's water. High floods, especially flash floods, are typical of the Lena Basin in summer. In winter there is very little flow. Breakup of ice in the spring causes significant damage to the shores of the river. The ice floes grind the rocks, uproot trees, and carry away sections of the river's banks.

The people living in the Lena Basin are Russians, Yakuts, and Yukaghirs. There are many industrial and cultural centers, collective farms, and state farms in the area. The name Lena means "big river" in the Yakut language.

The Lena Basin is rich in fossil fuels, such as coal and natural gas, and in gold and diamonds. Near Olyokminsk are found salt beds, and to the south of Yakutsk are iron ore and coking coal.

The first exploration of the Lena was conducted by Russians at the beginning of the 17th century. In 1631 a fortress and a settlement was founded at Ust-Kut. The first scientific research was conducted from 1733 to 1743, but the first maps were not made until 1910. In 1912 the delta was surveyed and mapped from ice-breaking ships.

LENIN (1870–1924). The revolution that brought the Communist party to power in Russia in 1917 has been called the most important political event of the 20th century. Its leader was Lenin, a Marxian socialist. Lenin spent years studying the technique of revolution and building up a following. At the right moment he carried out his plan with great skill.

Lenin's real name was Vladimir Ilich Ulyanov. He was born on April 22, 1870, in Russia at Simbirsk (now Ul'yanovsk), a town on the Volga River. His father, a teacher, rose to be a provincial director of schools. Vladimir was 16 when his father died. The next year his older brother, Alexander, was executed for taking part in a plot to assassinate Czar Alexander III. Lenin's hatred of the ruling and propertied classes began at this time.

A few months after his brother's execution Lenin was expelled from school for taking part in a political demonstration. For several years he lived with relatives, studying law, languages, and the writings of Karl Marx (*see* Marx). In 1891 he passed his law examinations. He soon gave up his law practice to spend full time in the revolutionary underground movement in Saint Petersburg, then the Russian capital. The city is now called Leningrad in his honor.

Lenin was arrested in 1895, sent to jail, and later exiled to Siberia. There he married Nadezhda Krupskaya (exiled in 1898), whom he had known in the St. Petersburg underground. She later wrote: "As a whole the years of exile were not bad. These were years of serious study." It was in Siberia that he first used the pen name N. Lenin. It has been assumed that the "N" stood for Nikolai, but he is not known ever to have signed the full name. Today the initials of his given names are usually attached to his pen name and he is called V. I. Lenin.

When his jail term ended in 1900 Lenin went abroad. The next year his wife joined him. Most of

Lenin and his wife moved to Gorky near Moscow, where the photograph was taken, after his second stroke.

Sovfoto

the time until 1917 the couple lived as exiles, traveling from country to country, often with forged passports. With other Russian Marxists they published a newspaper, *Iskra* (The Spark), that was smuggled into Russia. Lenin soon built up a following in Russia and among the younger Russian exiles in Europe.

In 1903 some 60 Russian revolutionaries opened a congress in Brussels. The Belgian police ordered them to leave, and the congress was continued in London. Lenin's fanaticism made him unpopular with the more moderate old guard socialists; he advocated a small, secret party, or vanguard, of full-time revolutionaries who would lead ordinary workers to revolution. His ideas split the Russian Social Democratic party in two: Lenin's radical group, the Bolsheviks (Majority), and the more moderate group, the Mensheviks (Minority).

The party also split in Russia. The Bolsheviks, which were actually the smaller group, followed Lenin's instructions implicitly. He told them how to raise funds by breaking into banks, how to obtain and use bombs, how to set fires, and how to stop trucks with tacks. The party organized cells in trade unions, among transportation workers, and in the army and navy. (*See also* Communism.)

The Lenins were in Switzerland during World War I. Most socialists supported their governments in the war. Lenin called on the workers of all countries to revolt and end the war. This interested the German government, which wanted peace with Russia.

Russia's losses in the war were appalling. Revolution broke out in March 1917. The czar was dethroned by the new provisional government, but the war went on. The German government, hoping to change the course of the revolution, agreed to allow the Lenins and 30 other revolutionaries to return to Russia. The group arrived at Finland Station, in the Russian capital, on April 16. The next day Leon Trotsky arrived from New York City. Lenin and Trotsky made a formidable team. (*See also* Trotsky.)

In July the Bolsheviks took part in an unsuccessful uprising. The provisional government accused Lenin of being a German agent, and he fled to Finland. On October 22 he returned secretly. After instructing the Bolsheviks, he again went into hiding.

On November 6 Lenin reappeared to direct the revolution. Before daybreak on November 7 (October 25 in the old Russian calendar) the Bolsheviks seized the railway station, state bank, power stations, and telephone exchange. In the evening they arrested cabinet members meeting in the Winter Palace. On November 9 Lenin formed the world's first Communist government.

Lenin suffered two strokes in 1922. A third, in 1923, resulted in loss of speech. After a fatal stroke, on Jan. 21, 1924, Joseph Stalin succeeded him (*see* Stalin).

The Russians regard Lenin as their greatest national hero. His writings—particularly his directives for the Communist party—rank with the works of Karl Marx. His tomb, on Red Square in Moscow, is a national shrine.

The elaborate Grand Cascade of the Samson Fountain lies in front of the Great Palace of Peter the Great. Built from 1714 to 1728, the palace is located in the community of Petrodvorets.

LENINGRAD, U.S.S.R.

The second largest city and largest seaport of the Soviet Union, Leningrad lies on the Gulf of Finland. Capital of czarist Russia for more than 200 years, Leningrad is a showcase of 18th-century palaces and churches. It also remains a center of modern Russian culture, learning, and industry in the late 20th century.

Leningrad lies in the delta of the Neva River. Spreading over mainland and more than 40 islands, it is cut by more than 80 river branches and canals, and linked by more than 300 bridges. The city is subject to flooding from waves on the Gulf of Finland backing into the river.

Although Leningrad is among the northernmost of the world's large cities, the moderating effect of the warm Baltic waters gives it a comparatively mild climate. Temperatures average 64° F (18° C) in July and 18° F (−8° C) in January. The Neva River is frozen from about November through March. High humidity, fog, and heavy rainfall are common. A special feature of Leningrad summers is the period of white nights in late June, when—because the city is so close to the Arctic Circle—only a brief period of twilight intervenes between sunset and sunrise.

The Old City

Leningrad's ornate buildings and squares, erected by Peter the Great and his successors in the 18th century, have been carefully preserved. Palaces and other public buildings are grouped around squares or along distinctive avenues. The hub of the city is the Admiralty, one of the original sections of the city, on the south bank of the Neva. The broad avenues of downtown Leningrad converge there. Just upriver, the Winter Palace, former residence of the czars, houses the Hermitage Museum. Directly across the main channel of the Neva from the Admiralty is Vasilyevski Island, the largest of the city's islands. Just upriver, on Zayachy (Hare) Island is the Peter and Paul Fortress, which was begun in 1703. Today it is used as a historical museum. Within the fortress complex is the Saint Peter and Saint Paul Cathedral, burial place of the czars.

Everyday Life

Many of the people of Leningrad live in large-scale housing developments, built since 1920 on the outskirts of the city. Numerous five-story and nine-story apartment buildings are the result of a massive construction project begun in 1963.

Electric trains carry commuters from the suburbs into the central city. Within the downtown area, people travel on streetcars and subways (opened in 1955). A favorite shopping boulevard is the Nevsky Prospekt, famed for its large department stores.

The area is served by five newspapers, including the daily papers *Smena* and *Leningradskaya Pravda*. The 945-foot (288-meter) tower of Leningrad Television is the city's highest structure.

Leningrad's many parks are favorite places of recreation for the populace. Lenin Park, bordering the Peter and Paul Fortress, features the Leningrad Zoo, a planetarium, and several theaters and movie houses. Summer jazz concerts take place in the gar-

127

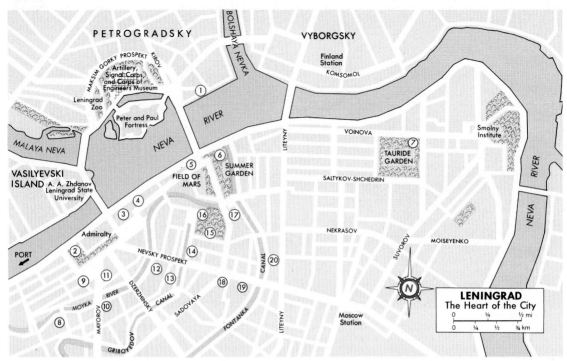

PETROGRADSKY

VYBORGSKY

BOLSHAYA NEVKA

MAKSIM GORKY PROSPEKT KIROV
Artillery,
Signal Corps,
and Carps of
Engineers Museum

Leningrad
Zoo

Peter and Paul
Fortress

Finland
Station

KOMSOMOL

VOINOVA

Smolny
Institute

RIVER

NEVA

LITEYNY

⑦
TAURIDE
GARDEN

MALAYA NEVA

⑤ ⑥
SUMMER
GARDEN

FIELD OF
MARS

SALTYKOV-SHCHEDRIN

NEVA RIVER

VASILYEVSKI
ISLAND A. A. Zhdanov
Leningrad State
University

NEKRASOV

MOISEYENKO

④
③

⑯ ⑰
⑮

Admiralty

PORT

②

NEVSKY PROSPEKT

⑭

CANAL

⑳

SUVOROV

N

LENINGRAD
The Heart of the City
0   ¼   ½ mi
0   ¼   ½   ¾ km

⑨ ⑪

⑫
⑬

⑱ ⑲

MOYKA

RIVER

DZERZHINSKY CANAL

⑩

SADOVAYA

FONTANKA

LITEYNY

Moscow
Station

⑧

GRIBOYEDOV

GUIDE TO PLACES OF INTEREST

1. Peter the Great's Cottage
2. Equestrian Statue of Peter the Great
3. Winter Palace
4. Hermitage Museum
5. Marble Palace (Lenin's Museum)
6. Peter the Great's Summer Palace

7. Tauride Palace
8. Yusupov Palace
9. St. Isaac's Cathedral
10. Mariinsky Palace
11. Hotel Astoria
12. Stroganov Palace
13. Kazan Cathedral

14. St. Catherine's Church
15. State Russian Museum (Michael's Palace)
16. Resurrection Church
17. Engineers' Castle
18. Saltykov-Shchedrin Public Library
19. Pioneers' Palace (Anichkov Palace)
20. Sheremetev's Palace

den of Pioneers' Palace, while inside are a planetarium, a puppet theater, and a dance hall. Visitors enjoy the Summer Garden surrounding Peter the Great's Summer Palace. The white nights of midsummer are the occasion for a week-long citywide festival of music and the arts. Another attraction is the Leningrad Circus, which has performed since 1876.

Kirov Stadium, on Krestovsky Island, seats 80,000 people. Nearby are smaller sports facilities, boathouses, and a seaside park with several swimming pools. International athletic meets are held at the Winter Stadium off Sadovaya Street. The Yubileiny (Jubilee) Sports Palace was opened in 1967, and a new multipurpose sports hall, seating 25,000 spectators, was built for the 1980 Olympic Games.

The Arts and Education

Leningrad is one of the great cultural centers of Europe. Traditions of leadership in music and the arts were established while Leningrad (then called Saint Petersburg) was the capital of czarist Russia. Peter Tchaikovsky and Dimitri Shostakovich are two of many famous composers who spent their lives in the city and studied at the Conservatory on Theater Square. A statue of Nikolai Rimski-Korsakov, who taught at the Conservatory, stands near the entrance. The Leningrad Symphony Orchestra per-

forms at the Philharmonia Concert Hall on the Square of the Arts. The largest concert hall in the city, the October Great Concert Hall, seats 4,000.

Ballet and theater are active in Leningrad. The dancers Anna Pavlova, Vaslav Nijinsky, and Galina Ulanova all studied ballet at the Ballet School on Rossi Street. On the west side of Theater Square the Kirov Opera and Ballet Theater was the starting place for the careers of Ulanova, Rudolf Nureyev, and Mikhail Baryshnikov. The Pushkin Theater performs classical and modern drama. Experimental productions are featured at the Gorki Drama Theater, founded by Maksim Gorki in 1919.

The outstanding art museum of the Soviet Union is the Hermitage, on Palace Square. Founded in 1764, it has a huge collection of Russian, Oriental, and Western European art. The State Russian Museum on the Square of the Arts houses a collection of Russian paintings. The Academy of Arts on Vasilyevski Island includes two museums as well as a school of painting, sculpture, and architecture.

In literature, too, Leningrad carries on traditions of eminence established when St. Petersburg was the capital of czarist Russia. A statue of Aleksander Pushkin in the Square of the Arts commemorates one of St. Petersburg's most important authors. Others include Fedor Dostoevski, Nikolai Gogol, Maksim

Gorki, and Ivan Turgenev. Leningrad has more than 30 publishing houses and some 2,500 libraries. The Saltykov-Shchedrin Public Library has one of the country's largest collections from czarist times.

The Leningrad M. I. Kalinin Polytechnical Institute and the Lensovet Leningrad Technological Institute are among the city's more than 40 colleges. A. A. Zhdanov Leningrad State University succeeded the University of St. Petersburg, founded in 1819. Its old main campus is on Vasilyevski Island, but much of the university moved to a new suburban campus in Petrodvorets. Some 30 institutes of the Academy of Sciences of the U.S.S.R. are in Leningrad.

Industrial Production

Heavy industry, in combination with scientific research conducted at the many institutes, makes Leningrad a leader in the production of modern heavy machinery and equipment. Turbines, turbogenerators, and nuclear-powered equipment supply power plants throughout the Soviet Union. Leningrad's shipyards produce large-capacity tankers, fish-processing ships, and nuclear-propelled icebreakers. Other products include tractors and subway cars, sophisticated laboratory instruments, and clothing.

Industrial districts of Leningrad are in many parts of the city, notably the center of Vasilyevski Island, the Nevsky District, the Prospekt Obukhovskoy Oborony, and a section near the Narva Gates.

Industrial products may be shipped by water either inland or out to the Baltic Sea. Always an important seaport, Leningrad is linked by water routes from the Baltic Sea, through the Volga Basin to the Caspian and the Black and Azov seas. Substantial new port construction on the Gulf of Finland began in the 1980s. Passenger ships dock at Vasilyevski Island. Passengers are also served by Pulkovo Airport, 11 miles (19 kilometers) south of the city center.

Government and History

Greater Leningrad is divided into 21 administrative districts, including eight suburbs. The City Soviet, the center of government, is in the former Mariinsky Palace on Saint Isaac Square. The Smolny, seat of the first Soviet government in 1917, serves as local headquarters for the Communist party.

St. Petersburg was founded at the beginning of the 18th century by Peter the Great, who wanted to "open a window to Europe." Thus it is younger than most other European cities. Peter began construction of the Peter and Paul Fortress in 1703 and moved his imperial court there in 1712.

The early 19th century was marked by crises. In November 1824 the Neva rose above its usual level and flooded half the city. A year later a group of noblemen, the Decembrists, rose in an unsuccessful revolt against the czars.

The first railroad in Russia linked St. Petersburg with Tsarkoye Selo (now Pushkin) in 1837. Industrial growth followed. By 1862 there were some 300 factories in the city. Worker unrest laid the groundwork

The Ascension Church, built from 1883 to 1907, is on the banks of the Griboyedov, one of Leningrad's many canals.

for revolution. On Bloody Sunday in 1905, workers demonstrating outside the Winter Palace were shot and killed by czarist soldiers. In 1914, at the beginning of World War I, the city's name was changed to the more Russian-sounding Petrograd.

Cold, hungry, and worn by war, revolutionaries of Petrograd deposed the czar in March 1917. They established a provisional government, which in turn was replaced by a Communist regime that took power through Nikolai Lenin's leadership in the October Revolution of 1917. At Lenin's death in 1924, the new name Leningrad was adopted.

World War II brought extreme hardship to the people of Leningrad. From 1941 until 1943, the city was besieged by German and Finnish soldiers. During that period electric power and transportation were wiped out and water had to be carried from the river. Some 17,000 citizens fell to bombs, while 640,000 more died of starvation. After the war, extensive housing construction was undertaken. (*See also* Union of Soviet Socialist Republics.) Population (1982 estimate), 4,719,000.

BIBLIOGRAPHY FOR LENINGRAD

Berezina, A. M. Leningrad: a Short Guide (Lenizdat, 1980).
Fodor, Eugene and others, eds. Fodor's Soviet Union (McKay, 1981).
Kann, Pavel. Leningrad in Three Days (Progress Publishers, 1980).

LENS *see* EYE; TELESCOPE.

LENTIL *see* LEGUMES.

In an illustration from a manuscript of the 11th century, Leo IX, left, blesses Abbot Warinus in Metz.

Courtesy of the Burgerbibliothek, Bern, Switzerland

LEO, Popes. In the history of the Roman Catholic church there have been 13 popes named Leo. Of these, five have been canonized, or declared saints: Leo I, Leo II, Leo III, Leo IV, and Leo IX. But of the popes who have borne this name, the ones who had the greatest impact on their times were Leo I, Leo III, Leo IX, Leo X, and Leo XIII.

Leo I (died 461). Only three popes have been awarded the title "the Great," Nicholas I, Gregory I, and Leo I. Leo's greatness has frequently been depicted by artists, writers, and historians in his memorable confrontation with Attila and the Huns in which the pope was able to persuade these barbarians not to attack Rome (*see* Attila; Huns). But his primary accomplishments were far more substantial.

Of the early life of Leo I very little is known, including his name. It is traditionally assumed that he was born and grew up in the Tuscan region of Italy. It is known that at the time of his consecration as pope on Sept. 29, 440, he was regarded as a well-educated, conscientious, and highly competent churchman. It was his misfortune to live during a time when the Roman Empire in the West was fast disintegrating and barbarian hordes were overrunning much of Europe. His success in dealing with the Huns was, in fact, not to be repeated when Genseric and his Vandals arrived in Italy and looted Rome for two weeks in 455.

It was as a staunch advocate of orthodoxy, or correct teaching, and as a theorist concerning the nature of the papacy itself that Leo made his greatest contributions to the church. In the conflict over Monophysitism, a doctrine that claimed Christ had only a divine nature, Leo won a great victory when the Council of Chalcedon (451) accepted his statement on the two natures of Christ and condemned the heresy.

In the matter of the papacy, Leo attempted to establish that the powers of Saint Peter as bishop of Rome and the first pope automatically passed on to his successors. Were this true, the pope could not be judged in his actions by any outside authority: He was infallible. Although the dogma of papal infallibil-

ity was not proclaimed officially for many centuries, Leo did much groundbreaking on the matter.

After the Vandal attack on Rome, Leo spent his remaining years overseeing the charitable work of the church in trying to mend the damage. He died on Nov. 10, 461.

Leo III (died 816). Neither an outstanding churchman nor an astute politician, Leo III is remembered basically for one thing: On Christmas Day in the year 800 he crowned Charles of the Franks, now called Charlemagne, emperor during worship services in the original St. Peter's Basilica at Rome. Thus was inaugurated the 1,000-year Holy Roman Empire, a political entity that endured until the 19th century. (*See also* Charlemagne; Holy Roman Empire.)

Little is known of the early life of Leo III except that because he was not born a nobleman he had the reputation in some circles for being an unsavory, perhaps immoral character. In any case, he was adept enough to be elected pope on Dec. 26, 795. Four years later, while taking part in a procession, he was attacked by followers of his predecessor Adrian I. He escaped them and fled the city to seek the protection of Charlemagne in Germany. What negotiations were conducted is not known, but the following year Charlemagne received the crown. In crowning Charlemagne, Leo established the principle that the pope had the right to crown the emperor. This act caused strife with the Eastern (Byzantine) Empire and aligned the papacy with the rulers in the West. The precedent was set for meddling in church affairs by emperors and kings when Charlemagne took over church reform within his domains. For his part, Leo spent the rest of his reign at Rome, building and beautifying the city. He died on June 12, 816.

Leo IX (1002–54). The reign of Leo IX is memorable for two reasons: the extensive reforms he implemented within the church and his forceful support of papal supremacy, which led to a formal break with the Eastern Orthodox church in 1054.

Born Bruno of Egisheim on June 21, 1002, in the Alsace region of France, he was educated for the clergy at Toul, France. At 25 he was consecrated bishop and soon made a reputation for himself by his reforming policies. At age 46 he was appointed pope by the emperor Henry III, but delayed taking the throne in order to get the vote of the people and clergy of Rome. He assumed office on Feb. 12, 1049.

He continued his bent for reform by inviting some of the ablest leaders in the church to Rome to formulate and carry out policy. One of these leaders was a monk named Hildebrand who later became the great pope, Gregory VII. Leo and his assistants succeeded in making the church the center of European religious life and in transforming the Holy See at Rome into an international political power. Leo IX, like his 20th-century successor John Paul II, was a traveling pope. He attended and conducted councils in Italy, France, Germany, and Sicily.

The low point of his papacy came in a conflict with the Norman rulers of Sicily. Leo made an alliance with Henry III to attack Sicily but the alliance broke down and, while leading the papal army, Leo was captured by the Normans in 1053. He was held prisoner for nine months.

The following year came the break with the Eastern church. The split had been a long time in the making but was finally brought about by Leo's uncompromising assertion of papal authority over all bishops—including the leader of the Orthodox church. In a conclave at Constantinople, the pope's delegates and the patriarch of the Eastern church excommunicated each other, thus causing a schism that has lasted until the present. Meanwhile Leo IX himself had died suddenly in Rome on April 19, 1054.

Leo X (1475–1521). One of the most colorful of the Renaissance popes and a member of the great Medici family in Florence, Leo X spent all the money he could gather to build Rome into a great city. He made the unfortunate mistake of regarding the German monk Martin Luther as a minor nuisance and thereby helped bring on the Protestant Reformation.

Born Giovanni de' Medici in Florence, Italy, on Dec. 11, 1475, Leo X was the second son of the city's ruler, Lorenzo the Magnificent. He was educated for the church. At 13 he was named a cardinal-deacon, and from 1489 to 1491 he studied at the University of Pisa. Ill will toward Pope Alexander VI kept him away from Rome from 1492 until 1503, and for most of the next 10 years he governed his native city. When the warrior-pope Julius II died in 1513, Giovanni was elected his successor (*see* Julius II).

Four issues dominated the reign of Leo X: the unsuccessful efforts of the Fifth Lateran Council to reform the church, his building programs for Rome, political ambitions to dominate Italy, and the Lutheran Reformation. The failure of the Lateran Council did not bother him, for he was little inclined to major reforms, nor did there seem any urgency about making changes. The council adjourned on March 16, 1517, 7½ months before Luther nailed his 95 Theses on the church door in Wittenberg, Germany (*see* Luther).

His determination to be the leading political ruler in Italy brought Leo X into conflict with both France and Spain and their respective leaders, Francis I and Charles I (Charles V of the Holy Roman Empire). Leo lost out on both counts. He was defeated by Francis I in 1515 and forced to sign a concordat that gave French kings virtual control of the church in their realm. Leo opposed the nomination of Charles I of Spain to be Holy Roman Emperor and supported Frederick the Wise of Saxony. Charles won, and Leo was forced to support him in his war with France.

Only in his lavish building programs in Rome did Leo X make a positive contribution during his years in office. Unfortunately one of the ways the church raised money was the sale of indulgences—the forgiving of sins for an amount of money. It was this practice that brought Luther into conflict with the church. Leo was convinced that Luther, like other advocates of reform, would soon lose popular support

Leo XIII in 1878

The Bettmann Archive

and become irrelevant. He condemned the reformer for heresy and finally excommunicated him in January 1521. Leo X died on Dec. 1, 1521, leaving all of Europe in a state of religious turmoil from which it was not to recover until the 17th century.

Leo XIII (1810–1903). When Leo XIII became pope on Feb. 20, 1878, at the age of 67, his reign was expected to be a brief, transitional one. In fact, he lived to govern the church for 25 years. As pope, Leo XIII found himself head of a highly centralized and authoritarian organization. The time was one of great scientific and technological advancement, as well as social, political, and economic upheaval. Western society was becoming more democratic. More people were getting the right to vote, and a sizeable working class—the result of industrialization—was seeking more rights for itself. The radical theories of socialism, communism, and anarchism were being propounded. It was to Leo's credit that he sought a rational accommodation with the new social forces, and in so doing, laid the foundation for many changes in the church's attitude toward the modern world.

Leo XIII was born Vincenzo Gioacchino Pecci on March 2, 1810 in Carpineto Romano, Italy. After education at Viterbo and Rome he was ordained a priest in 1837. For the next several years he worked in the diplomatic service of the Papal States. In 1846 he was named bishop of Perugia and remained in that post for 32 years. In 1853 Pius IX named him a cardinal. After the death of Pius IX in 1878, the College of Cardinals elected him pope.

Like his predecessor, Leo XIII was constitutionally opposed to many of the liberal and secularizing tendencies of the age. But he felt the need to show that the church was open to progress both in science and politics. He wanted the church to live in peace with modern democratic states. In a major encyclical, 'Rerum Novarum' (Of New Things), he recognized the problems of the working class. He also tried to renew contacts with other churches, particularly the Anglican Communion and Eastern Orthodoxy. Leo died at age 93 on July 20, 1903.

Alinari/Art Resource

Leonardo da Vinci, a self-portrait

LEONARDO DA VINCI (1452–1519).

The term "Renaissance man" was coined to describe the genius of Leonardo da Vinci. He was a man of so many accomplishments in so many areas of human endeavor that his like has rarely been seen in human history. Casual patrons of the arts know him as the painter of 'La Gioconda', more commonly called the 'Mona Lisa', and of the exquisite 'Last Supper', painted on the wall of the dining hall in the monastery of Santa Maria delle Grazie in Milan, Italy. These paintings alone would have assured him enduring fame as an artist, but they should not obscure the fact that he was also a sculptor, an architect, and a man of science who did serious investigations into the natural and physical sciences, mathematics, mechanics, and engineering. More than 300 years before flying machines were perfected, Leonardo devised plans for prototypes of an airplane and a helicopter. His extensive studies of human anatomy were portrayed in anatomical drawings, which were among the most significant achievements of Renaissance science. His remarkable illustrations of the human body elevated drawing into a means of scientific investigation and exposition and provided the basic principles for modern scientific illustration.

Life of Leonardo

The life of Leonardo da Vinci can be divided into five distinct periods: his childhood and youth in Florence, Italy; his first stay in Milan from 1482 to 1499; the second Florentine period from 1500 to 1506; his second stay in Milan from 1506 to 1513; and his last six years from 1513 to 1519, which were divided equally between Rome and Amboise, France, where he worked for King Francis I.

Leonardo was born in 1452 on his father's family estate at Vinci, near Florence. He grew up and was educated on the estate. When he was 15 his father apprenticed him to the artist Andrea del Verrocchio in Florence. Under Verrocchio he studied painting, sculpture, and the mechanical arts. In the nearby workshop of the artist Antonio Pollaiuolo he began his interest in anatomy. Leonardo was accepted into the painters' guild at Florence in 1472 and remained in the city for the next ten years.

Even in this early period, Leonardo's mastery of his art was evident, especially in two unfinished paintings: 'St. Jerome' and 'The Adoration of the Magi'. There were also a number of pen and pencil drawings that gave evidence of his great skill in sketching. Many of these drawings were of a technical nature—pumps, military weaponry, and other mechanical apparatus.

First service in Milan. In 1482 Leonardo was hired by the duke of Milan, Ludovico Sforza, to be artist and engineer in residence. In this capacity he was constantly kept busy as a painter and sculptor, though many of his paintings and all of his sculptures remained unfinished. He was also consulted in the fields of architecture, fortifications, and weaponry; and he served as a hydraulic and mechanical engineer. It was while he was in Milan that the full versatility of his genius began to unfold, and the full range of his interests in the world of mankind and nature in general became evident. Through his remarkable ability to understand what he saw, he determined to compose a unified theory of the world and to illustrate it in a series of voluminous noteboooks. Unfortunately his relentless pursuit of scientific knowledge forced him to leave unfinished many of his planned artistic creations. Today they are known primarily from drawings in the notebooks.

In his 17 years in Milan, Leonardo completed only six paintings: two portraits, the 'Last Supper', two versions of 'The Virgin of the Rocks', and a decorative ceiling painting in the Castello Sforzesco. Other commissioned paintings either were not done or have disappeared.

Return to Florence. Ludovico Sforza was driven from power by a French army in 1499. At the end of the year, or early in 1500, Leonardo returned to his home city after visits to Mantua and Venice. After his long absence, he was received as an honored and renowned artist.

In Florence, as in Milan, he was commissioned to do a number of paintings, but other interests and tasks kept him from finishing them. The most notable work to survive from this period was the 'Mona Lisa', which is now in the Louvre in Paris. His largest commission, a huge mural entitled 'Battle of Anghiari' for the Palazzo Vecchio, Florence's city hall, remained unfinished. (For a photograph of the 'Mona Lisa', *see* Painting).

Other technical matters took him away from his art. For ten months during 1502, Leonardo served as military adviser and engineer under Cesare Borgia in the latter's campaign to subdue the Papal States. He traveled through Borgia's territories, surveyed them, and made sketches of city plans and topographical maps that laid the groundwork for the field of modern cartography.

Back in Florence in 1503, Leonardo worked on the complicated engineering project of diverting the Arno River around Pisa in order to deprive that city of its access to the sea. The plan did not work, but it became the basis of a later project (never realized) to build a canal from Florence to the sea. He also busied himself with dissections of corpses at the hospital of Santa Maria Nuova, made observations on the flight of birds, and continued studies of the properties of water and its currents.

Second stay in Milan. In May 1506 Charles d'Amboise, governor of Milan for the king of France, invited Leonardo to return to that city. His work in painting and sculpture over the next seven years remained mostly in the planning stage—in sketches that he drew but that never became paintings or statues—but his scientific work flourished. He continued his notebooks with observations and drawings of human anatomy, optics, mechanics, and botanical studies.

Last years. During the years 1513 to 1516, Leonardo was in Rome at the invitation of Cardinal Giuliano de' Medici, brother of Pope Leo X. Some of the greatest artists of the time were at work in Rome for the church. Donato Bramante was building Saint Peter's Basilica; Michelangelo was working on the tomb of Pope Julius; and Raphael was painting the rooms of the pope's apartments.

Leonardo, on the other hand, was not kept busy. He executed a map of the Pontine Marshes near Rome, suggesting that perhaps he was involved in a planned reclamation project. He also did some sketches for a Medici residence in Florence that was never built. Otherwise he was lonely and unoccupied. Thus in 1516, at the age of 65, he accepted an invitation from Francis I, king of France, to leave Italy and work for him.

Leonardo spent the last three years of his life in the palace of Cloux, near the king's residence at Amboise, near Tours. He was given the title of "first painter, architect, and mechanic of the King" and given freedom of action in what he wanted to do. His duties were few. He virtually abandoned painting to concentrate on his scientific studies. He finished the final drafts of his treatise on painting and worked on the study of anatomy. He also did a variety of sketches, including 'Visions of the End of the World', that testified to his undiminished ability as an artist.

For the king he drew plans for a palace and garden at Romorantin and made sketches for court festivals. Otherwise the king left him alone and treated him as an honored guest. On May 2, 1519, Leonardo died at Cloux and was buried in the palace church. During the French Revolution the church, along with many other national monuments, was devastated and eventually was torn down. The whereabouts of Leonardo's remains is no longer known.

Leonardo's second 'The Virgin of the Rocks'

Leonardo's Legacy

Paintings and sculptures. Only 17 of the paintings that have survived can definitely be attributed to Leonardo, and not all of them are finished. Yet he is deservedly considered one of the greatest painters of all time. He excelled in inventiveness, technique, drawing ability, use of light, shadow, and color.

No sculpture survives that can be definitely attributed to Leonardo, but from the numerous sketches for unfinished projects it is known that he brought to sculpture the same ingenuity and inventiveness that he gave to painting. Two of his unfinished works were statues of men on horses—one a monumental figure in bronze to be erected in honor of Francesco Sforza, founder of the Sforza dynasty. He spent 12 years planning this statue, only to have the metal used for making cannon instead. But many sketches remain, and they give adequate evidence of Leonardo's concept of sculpture. The anatomical exactness of the horse, the proportions, and the feeling of movement in the sketches profoundly influenced the design of equestrian statues in the 17th century.

Architecture and engineering. Although concerned with architectural and engineering matters all of his adult life, Leonardo's role was primarily that of

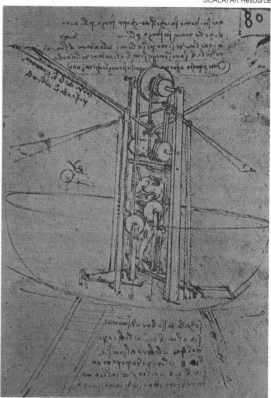

Leonardo's sketch of a cannon being assembled

Leonardo's sketch of a flying machine

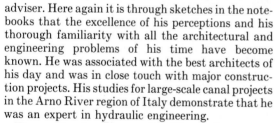

adviser. Here again it is through sketches in the notebooks that the excellence of his perceptions and his thorough familiarity with all the architectural and engineering problems of his time have become known. He was associated with the best architects of his day and was in close touch with major construction projects. His studies for large-scale canal projects in the Arno River region of Italy demonstrate that he was an expert in hydraulic engineering.

The notebooks. The greatest literary legacy any painter has ever bequeathed to the world is contained in the voluminous notebooks of Leonardo. His writing program began during the first stay in Milan, specifically between 1490 and 1495, when his strong inclination toward scientific studies showed itself.

The notebooks were to occupy him for the rest of his life. In them he envisaged treating four major themes: a treatise on the science of painting, a treatise on architecture, a book on the elements of mechanics, and a general work on human anatomy. To these themes were eventually added notes on his studies of botany, geology, aerology, and hydrology. Leonardo's intent was to synthesize all of his investigations with a unified world view based on his perceptions. He believed that true knowledge derived from what he called "knowing how to see," not from philosophical speculations.

Leonardo's notebooks are distinctive for two reasons: the relation of illustration to text and his use of "mirror writing." In the normal illustrated book, pictures amplify and clarify the text, but it is the text that contains the basic information. With him it was the reverse. Although his language was clear and expressive, Leonardo always gave precedence to illustration over the written word. The drawings, therefore, do not illustrate the text, but the text serves to explain the pictures.

Mirror writing, as the term implies, means putting words down on paper in such a way that they can be read normally only when the page is held up to a mirror. Leonardo was quite adept at this, probably partly because he was left-handed. The reason for using mirror writing is uncertain because he did not intend to keep his notebooks a secret.

Exactly how many notebooks Leonardo composed is not known. In all, 31 have been preserved. In addition to these, there are other bundles of documents, or codexes, by Leonardo that have found their way into various European museums. One of the most exciting finds of the 20th century was the discovery early in 1967 of 700 lost pages of manuscripts and drawings in the Spanish National Library in Madrid. These pages of Leonardo's work, bound in two volumes, had been missing for about 200 years. They contain, among other things, sketches of the large equestrian statue for the tomb of Francesco Sforza and drawings of complex gears, hydraulic machines, and other devices.

Tony Romano—Lyric Opera of Chicago Production

Ruggero Leoncavallo's opera 'Pagliacci' is performed in 1982 by the Lyric Opera of Chicago. It tells of a jealous clown who murders his wife and her lover.

LEONCAVALLO, Ruggero (1857–1919). The fame of the Italian composer Leoncavallo rests on his opera 'Pagliacci' (Players). First produced in 1892 in Milan, Italy, it has remained popular.

Ruggero Leoncavallo was born in Naples, Italy, on April 23, 1857. He studied music at the conservatory there and in 1876 graduated and began work on an opera. He gave the completed score—and all his money—to a producer who promised to arrange for the production of the opera. Instead the man disappeared, leaving the young composer penniless. Then began a long period in which Leoncavallo made his living by teaching singing and piano and by giving cafe concerts. His travels as a cafe pianist took him all over Europe and even to Egypt. He returned to Italy, having completed the first of three proposed operas concerning the Italian Renaissance.

New difficulties with producers postponed the performance of this work. In the meantime Leoncavallo wrote 'Pagliacci'. When it was produced, it made the composer's name famous throughout Italy. The opera, whose story is based on an actual murder, is an example of the realistic school of Italian opera called *verismo* (*see* Opera).

'I Medici', the first opera of a planned trilogy, was then performed, but it was a failure. Some of his later works were more favorably received. Of his 12 operas, 'Zazà' is probably the best after 'Pagliacci'.

Leoncavallo wrote the librettos, or stories and dialogues, not only for his own operas but occasionally for those of other composers. As a librettist he showed great dramatic ability and skill in using theatrical effects. He also composed operettas, songs, piano pieces, choral works, and a ballet. Leoncavallo died at Montecatini, Italy, on Aug. 9, 1919.

LEOPARD. This spotted animal of the cat family lives in Africa, Asia Minor, Central Asia, and the Far East. It is a large cat, closely related to the lion and tiger. Leopards vary greatly in size and markings. They average from 110 to 200 pounds (50 to 90 kilograms) and are about 84 inches (210 centimeters) long, excluding the 36-inch (90-centimeter) tail. Some leopards, however, can grow much larger.

The leopard, like its cousin the jaguar, is normally a buff or tawny color with dark spots. The undersurface of the body is usually lighter in color. The leopard lives in bush and forest areas. It is agile, can climb trees, and is a remarkable jumper. Normally active at night, it attacks antelope, young cattle, pigs, and occasionally humans.

The leopard that has completely black coloring is widely known as the black panther. This animal is more commonly found in the Far East than in the other areas where the leopard ranges. Some types of leopards are listed as endangered: the Barbary, Anatolian, Amur, and Sinai leopards.

The cheetah, or hunting leopard, of India is a slim animal that is tamed and trained to aid in hunting. This leopard, the first cat to which the name leopard was applied, was once thought to be a cross between the lion and the pard, or panther. In running over short distances the cheetah is the fastest land animal in the world.

The ocelot is another leopardlike cat, with striped and spotted fur, found in tropical America and the extreme southwestern United States. A full-grown ocelot weighs 25 to 35 pounds (11 to 15 kilograms).

The scientific name of the common leopard, or panther, is *Leo pardus;* of the cheetah, *Acinonyx jubatus;* and of the ocelot, *Felis pardalis.* (*See also* Cat.)

135

LEOPOLD, Kings of Belgium. Three kings of Belgium have borne the name Leopold.

LEOPOLD I (born 1790, ruled 1831–65) was the first king of an independent Belgium. The son of a German prince, Leopold married the heiress to the British throne, Princess Charlotte, but she died a year later. He was 40 when a Belgian national congress elected him the nation's king.

Leopold had a successful reign. Through wise administration, he helped the nation survive its early stresses and contributed to its economic growth. Although revolutions broke out in many European countries in 1848, his throne remained secure. Leopold also strengthened Belgium's position through skillful diplomacy. In 1832 he married Princess Louise, daughter of the French king Louis Philippe. Their oldest son became Leopold II.

LEOPOLD II (born 1835, ruled 1865–1909) was interested in acquiring colonial possessions in Africa. In 1876 he founded the International African Association to encourage exploration of the continent. In 1877 the explorer Henry M. Stanley returned from a long expedition to tell of the vast Congo region. Leopold eagerly commissioned Stanley to survey the area and sign treaties with the tribes. The king then claimed the territory and made himself sovereign of it. The abuses of the natives that developed under his administration were eventually brought to public attention. As a result the area was annexed by the government and made a Belgian colony in 1908.

Leopold's exploitation of the Congo made him unpopular. His only son died at an early age, and Leopold was succeeded by his nephew, Albert I.

LEOPOLD III (born 1901, ruled 1934–40 and July 22–Aug. 11, 1950) was the son of Albert I. He married Princess Astrid of Sweden, who died in an automobile accident in 1935.

In 1940, when the Germans invaded Belgium, Leopold ordered his army to surrender and refused to flee with officials to form a government-in-exile in England. His actions were widely resented in Belgium, and he aroused further criticism by his marriage in 1941 to a commoner, who was said to be pro-Nazi. Leopold was held prisoner by the Germans until the end of the war, when he went to Switzerland. In 1950 a plebiscite showed a small majority of the Belgians were in favor of his return. Protests arose as soon as he resumed office, however, and he delegated his powers to his son Baudouin on Aug. 11, 1950. On July 16, 1951, he abdicated. (*See also* Baudouin I.)

LEPROSY. Throughout the ages leprosy has been one of the most dreaded diseases and its victims the most shunned. Almost all cultures have believed that persons who contracted leprosy were spiritually unclean. In modern times the disease has still retained some of its mythical character, and many people do not realize that leprosy is a disease that is only mildly contagious and not fatal. In the early 1980s the World Health Organization estimated that more than 11 million people had leprosy.

Cause and symptoms. Leprosy is caused by a rod-shaped bacterium, *Mycobacterium leprae*, a relative of the tuberculosis bacillus. The organism was identified in 1874 by Armauer Hansen, a Norwegian physician, and an alternative name for leprosy is Hansen's disease. The infection is very slow to develop, ranging from six months to ten years, and children are much more susceptible than adults.

There are two main types of reaction to *M. Leprae* in the body. In the milder form of the disease, tuberculoid leprosy, the body's cells crowd around the invading organisms in the deep skin layers, which are the first areas of infection. This response sometimes seals off the infection from the rest of the body or at least limits its spread. The reaction, however, destroys hair follicles, sweat glands, and nerve endings at the site of infection. The skin above the site becomes dry and discolored and loses its sense of touch. Fingers and toes that have no feeling are easily injured, and, if the patient has not been trained to take protective measures, they may in time become mutilated and fall off.

In the second and more contagious form of the disease, lepromatous leprosy, the body is not able to mount a resistance, and the *M. leprae* multiply freely in the skin. Large, soft bumps, or nodules, appear over the body and face. Mucous membranes of the eyes, nose, and throat may be invaded. In extreme cases the voice may change drastically, blindness may occur, or the nose may be destroyed.

Treatment. Until sulfa drugs were developed in the 1940s and were found to be helpful, there was no satisfactory treatment. Patients were merely isolated in an attempt to protect the larger community, and many victims hid. To avoid the undesirable side effects of sulfa drugs, a group of related drugs known as sulfones was developed. Many patients improve with these drugs, especially those with the tuberculoid form of the disease. In most cases treatment must continue for years.

Research was long hampered by scientists' inability to induce leprosy in animals in order to study the disease. In 1960 it was found that *M. leprae* could be grown on the footpads of mice, but the yield was low. A search began for an animal with a body temperature similar to that of the mouse footpad and the cooler parts of the human body on which the bacteria thrive. In 1971 it was discovered that leprosy could be established in the armadillo. In 1976 it was found that armadillos frequently get leprosy in the wild.

LERMONTOV, Mikhail (1814–41). By the time of his death at only 27, Lermontov had established an unshakable reputation as a brilliant poet, novelist, and playwright. He is remembered today mostly for his realistic novel 'Geroy nashego vremeni' (A Hero of Our Time, published in 1840). It is the story of an alienated army officer and aristocrat of unusual intelligence and sensitivity.

Mikhail Yuryevich Lermontov was born in Moscow on Oct. 15, 1814. After his mother's death when he was 3, he was brought up by his grandmother on her estate and, from 1827 on, in Moscow. In his youth he was much affected by the Russia of his day: the beginnings of revolutionary ferment, the iron-fisted rule of the czars, and the miserable economic conditions of the serfs. His early poems reflected the notions of freedom and idealism that he shared with other students who deplored the centuries-old despotism and the slavery of the peasants.

In 1834 Lermontov graduated from the cadet school at Saint Petersburg and became an army officer, a career that he pursued faithfully but did not allow to interrupt his literary ambitions. Twice during his military service, in 1837 and in 1840, he was arrested because of his ideas and sent into exile in the Caucasus region of Russia. There, still in the army, he used his time to study the local culture and languages and to continue his writing. From 1838 to 1840 he was back in St. Petersburg, where his poetry began to appear in print. His poems, along with his drama 'Maskarad' (Masquerade, 1835), made him well known and popular in literary circles. On his way back to join his regiment during his second exile, he became involved in a duel with another officer and was killed on July 27, 1841.

LESOTHO.

LESOTHO. The small African kingdom of Lesotho is an enclave in that it is completely surrounded by another country, South Africa. On its southeastern border is Transkei, a tiny republic recognized only by South Africa. A constitutional monarchy, Lesotho is led by a prime minister and a hereditary king. Before independence in 1966 the country was a British colony called Basutoland.

Land and Climate

The Maloti and Drakensberg mountain ranges, which rise over 11,000 feet (3,350 meters) cover about two-thirds of the country's total area of 11,720 square miles (30,355 square kilometers). Communications and transportation are difficult for the people who live in the mountains—about one fourth of the population. The majority of the people live on the relatively flat plateau along Lesotho's western side. The plateau climate is temperate with cool winters and warm summers. Most of the 26-inch (660-centimeter) average rainfall occurs from October to April. Frost is common in winter.

People

Most of Lesotho's citizens are of the Basotho ethnic group and speak Sesotho, the official national language. Lesotho also has small minorities of people of Indian and European descent and of mixed race. English is used in high schools and is the second language of most of the people.

The mountain and rural people live in family com-

A typical home in Lesotho, a thatched-roof hut, is backgrounded by highlands, which cover much of the country.

pounds made up of one family extending over several generations. The villages are clusters of circular or rectangular huts made of earth and stone with thatched or corrugated iron roofs. Some of the people residing in the capital, Maseru, or in one of the other larger towns in the lowlands live in modern style houses or apartment buildings. Many low income families live in simple one-room apartments without electricity and other conveniences. Most of the people are Christians.

Education is important to the Basotho, who have one of the highest literacy rates in Africa. About 60 percent of the adult population can read and write. All primary education is free, and most schools are run by Christian churches. The Basotho may attend the National University of Lesotho in Maseru, which also attracts many international students.

Economy

Subsistence farming is the basis of Lesotho's economy. In order to make a better living, however, as many as 40 percent of the adult males cross the border to work in the mines and industries of South Africa. Most send some of their pay home to help support their families. South Africa does not allow the workers' families to come with them, and they may be separated for six to nine months a year.

Of those who remain in Lesotho about 85 percent work in agriculture even though only 13 percent of the land is suitable for crop-growing because of the mountainous terrain. All land belongs to the Basotho nation and cannot be bought or sold. Corn, wheat, beans, and vegetables are raised. About two thirds of the land is used as meadows and pastures for herds of cattle, sheep, and goats. The intensity of this farming contributes to overgrazing and soil erosion problems. Agricultural goods exported include mohair, wool, and hides, but Lesotho must import most of the products that are used in the country.

Industry comprises a small part of the economic activity. Small factories have been established, which manufacture candles, handicrafts, mohair yarn, and furniture. However, natural resources are very limited, with small deposits of industrial diamonds mined. Diamonds are the major export.

The lack of resources in Lesotho causes it to remain one of the world's poorest countries. The country relies on aid from many nations and international organizations. Lesotho is heavily dependent on South Africa for food and most consumer goods.

History and Government

The Basotho nation was formed in the early 1800s under King Moshoeshoe I when several African groups, who were displaced by the Zulu nation, sought refuge in the Maloti mountains. Later, due to conflicts with Boers, or Dutch-speaking white settlers, Moshoeshoe sought the protection of the British crown, which was granted in 1868.

Local chiefs maintained much power under British rule. The British left the traditional court and land allocation systems at the village level. In 1960 the first elections were held to form the Basutoland Council. In 1965 Chief Leabua Jonathan was chosen prime minister by the victorious Basutoland National Party (BNP), and in 1966 the country gained independence, with King Moshoeshoe II as the new nation's head of state.

The BNP headed by Jonathan continued to maintain power into the 1980s. Much of the traditional power of the chiefs has been supported by the government, while the national administration has been developed along British parliamentary lines. (*See also* Africa). Population (1982 estimate), 1,407,000.

LESSEPS, Ferdinand de (1805–94). Trained in his youth for government service, Ferdinand de Lesseps spent 24 years as a French diplomat; but it was his success in building the Suez Canal that earned him worldwide fame. His attempt to duplicate this feat by building a canal in Panama, however, ended in failure and scandal (*see* Panama Canal; Suez Canal).

Lesseps was born at Versailles, France, on Nov. 19, 1805, into a family that had a tradition of government service. Beginning in 1825, when he was appointed assistant vice-consul in Lisbon, he served in diplomatic posts at Tunis, Alexandria, Cairo, Rotterdam, Malaga, Barcelona, and Madrid. When the Italian republic was proclaimed in 1849, he was sent to Rome to try to work out a reconciliation between Pope Pius IX and the new Italian government. (The unification of Italy meant the end of the Papal States.) He failed in his arbitration, and a new French government recalled him. French troops then restored Rome to the pope, and Lesseps was censured and his diplomatic career ended.

His tenure in Egypt had inspired Lesseps with the idea of building a canal between the Red Sea and the Mediterranean. In 1854 the viceroy of Egypt, Sa'id Pasha, revived this ambition and authorized Lesseps to begin working on the project. The work started on April 25, 1859, and the canal was finished in 1869.

In 1879 the International Congress of Geographical Sciences voted in favor of constructing a canal in Panama, and Lesseps was put in charge of the project. He seriously underestimated the difficulties of the task. The climate, tropical diseases, and complicated engineering problems led to failure. The canal was later finished by the United States. His canal company was forced out of business, and the French government prosecuted its administrators for malfeasance. Lesseps and his son were convicted and sentenced to prison in 1893. The son served a partial sentence before an appeals court reversed the ruling. Lesseps died on Dec. 7, 1894, in Le Chenaie, France.

LESSING, Gotthold Ephraim (1729–81). The first major German dramatist and the founder of German classical comedy was Gotthold Ephraim Lessing. He was poor all of his life, forced to earn a living as a free-lance writer. In so doing he wrote some of the most incisive social, artistic, literary, and religious criticism of his day.

Gotthold Ephraim Lessing was born in Kamenz, Saxony, on Jan. 22, 1729, the son of a Lutheran parish pastor. In his youth he received an excellent classical education, and in 1746 went to the University of Leipzig. He lived alternately in Leipzig, Berlin, Wittenberg, Hamburg, and Breslau before settling at Wolfenbüttel as librarian for the last ten years of his life. During his first years in Leipzig, Lessing wrote a number of comedies, including 'Der junge Gelehrte' (The Young Scholar), 'Die alte Jungfer' (The Old Maid), 'Die Juden' (The Jews), and 'Der Freigeist' (The Free Thinker). The first major drama from his Berlin period was 'Miss Sara Sampson', a domestic tragedy. While at Breslau he studied aesthetics and philosophy, and in 1766 he published his masterful treatise, 'Laokoon: oder über di Grenzen der Malerei und Poesie' (Laocoon: or, On the Limits of Painting and Poetry). Another result of his stay in Breslau was the play 'Minna von Barnhelm', published in 1767. This play marked the beginning of classical comedy in Germany and was part of Lessing's attempt to formulate a German national drama at a time when Germany still consisted of many separate states. To further this goal he spent from 1765 to 1770 in Hamburg in an unsuccessful attempt to establish a national theater.

During his ten years as librarian at Wolfenbüttel, Lessing published a great number of critical pieces on drama and poetry; he also engaged in religious polemics with various theologians. In addition he published two major dramas: 'Emilia Galotti' (1772), a tragedy set in the court of an Italian prince, and 'Nathan der Weise' (Nathan the Wise, 1779), which urges acceptance of the equality of the major religions of Judaism, Christianity, and Islam, based on their ethical teachings. His last work, 'Die Erziehung des Menschengeschlechts' (The Education of the Human Race, 1780), stated his belief in the ability of human beings to achieve moral perfection. Lessing died in Braunschweig on Feb. 15, 1781.

LETTER WRITING. A direct, written message that is usually sent some distance from one person to another, or even to a group of persons or an organization, is called a letter. An old term for letter is "epistle," from the Greek word *epistolē*, meaning "message." In the course of history, letter writing has also developed into a popular literary prose form, a type of biographical or autobiographical literature, intended in some cases for reading by the general public (*see* Autobiography; Biography).

Letter writing began in the ancient world as soon as rulers of nations, separated by some distance, found the need to communicate with each other. It is known, for instance, from a remarkable collection of documents found in 1887 at El Amarna, Egypt, that many rulers in the ancient Middle East kept up a lively correspondence with the pharaohs. Among the ancients the Roman consul Cicero was a prolific writer of letters, especially to his friend Atticus. In the Bible most of the books in the New Testament are epistles, letters from Saint Paul and other Christian leaders to various congregations and individuals. Throughout history many well-known persons have written letters that, although originally intended as private correspondence, have been collected and published. Such collections are far too numerous to list, but in the modern period the letters of such famous persons as William Cowper, Charles Lamb, Robert Louis Stevenson, William Dean Howells, Ernest Hemingway, Groucho Marx, Sigmund Freud, Woodrow Wilson, George Eliot, Henry James, Katherine Mansfield, and D. H. Lawrence have proved rich sources of information on the persons themselves and on the world as they saw it. In the matter of published letters, it should be noted that a letter as a document becomes the property of the recipient; but the contents remain the property of the sender, who must consent to any publication.

In the late 20th century the practice of letter writing has diminished considerably, probably resulting from the influence of mass communication technology such as telephones and computers. Many people also use the occasional greeting card to replace letters, especially at Christmastime. Nevertheless, some types of personal correspondence remain in use: formal invitations and replies, business letters, thank-you notes and letters, and letters of application. Of these kinds of correspondence, only the thank-you note and letter are generally written at the warm, personal level. The others are more formal, even austere. Invitations, for example, hardly seem to be letters at all, since they often are engraved on high-quality paper and are very formal. One kind of correspondence that is more public than personal is the "letter to the editor," an individual expression of opinion on some issue of current interest written to be published in newspapers and magazines.

Kinds of Letter Writing

There are three basic kinds of letters: personal, social, and business. All letters contain four elements: the date, a salutation, the body of the letter, and the signature. In more formal letters, particularly business correspondence, a number of other features are added to this basic structure.

Personal letters are the most informal, written in the manner of one person speaking to another. Apart from containing the main elements mentioned above, such letters have no strict rules of style—not even grammatical rules. Personal letters may be handwritten or typed, but they are always signed by hand.

Social letters, which are more formal, include invitations and replies, letters of congratulation, thank-you notes, and letters of condolence. (Greeting cards are now made to serve all of these functions.) As with personal correspondence, social letters may be handwritten or typed. If desired, the name and address of the sender may be placed above the date, in the upper right-hand corner, or below the signature, on the lower right-hand part of the page. But if the sender is a relative or close friend of the recipient, the name (other than the closing signature) and address are normally omitted. They would, in any case, appear on the upper left-hand corner or flap of the envelope as a return address.

Depending on the relationship of sender and recipient, social letters may have much of the informality of personal correspondence. In the case of invitations, however, they must be precise: they must tell what the occasion is; give the exact date, time, and location; and tell the name of the host or hostess. They may also include the letters R.S.V.P. on the lower left-hand part of the page. This abbreviation for the French *Répondez, s'il vous plaît* ("Reply, if you please") means the recipient should let the host know whether he or she will be able to attend the function. Sometimes, instead of the R.S.V.P., the sender puts "Regrets only" at the end of the letter. This means that the recipient is to respond to the invitation only if he or she is not planning to attend.

Social letters, regardless of the level of formality, differ from personal correspondence in that they are usually shorter because they are intended for specific purposes. Once the purposes have been accomplished, these letters should be ended. The exception to this rule may be the thank-you note: it may become a longer, personal letter, depending on the relationship of the sender to the recipient. Thank-you notes, such as those that are sent for wedding gifts, are generally short and more formal.

Business letters are probably the most common type. The uses of a business letter are many: to give one's opinions to a public official, to place an order with a store, to apply for a job, to seek admission to a college. Regardless of the purpose, all business letters are considered formal and have a standard format.

The principal parts that make up the business letter are: the heading, date line, inside address, salutation, body, complimentary closing, and signature line. In addition to these basic components, there are several other elements that may be added to the letter, depending upon its content: an attention line, a subject line, identification initials, an enclosure notation, and a carbon copy notation.

The attention line follows the inside address and gets the letter to the specific person or department desired. A subject line, announcing the purpose of the letter, precedes the salutation. The identification initials, which are often not included, follow the signature line, with the initials of the writer preceding those of the typist. Any material enclosed with the letter is indicated by typing "Enclosure(s)," followed by the number of such enclosures in parentheses. This line immediately follows the line of identification initials. The carbon copy notation, telling to whom additional copies of the letter have been sent, is typed below the enclosure line. There may also be a special notation such as "CONFIDENTIAL" (always capitalized) on the envelope.

A great deal of business correspondence consists of letters from people in one company to those in another. In these cases, letterhead stationery, which identifies the company of the writer, is used; therefore no heading apart from the date is necessary. The rest of the format, however, remains the same.

A standard general format for the business letter is called the full block style. In this form all the principal parts of the letter, as well as any miscellaneous lines, appear flush with the left margin. Paragraphs are typed without indentation on the first line and are separated by a double space.

BIBLIOGRAPHY FOR LETTER WRITING

Avett, E. M. Today's Business Letter Writing (Prentice, 1977).

Fruehling, R. T. and Bouchard, Sharon. The Art of Writing Effective Letters (McGraw, 1972).

Gilbert, M. B. Communicating by Letter (Wiley, 1973).

Howard, Godfrey. Getting Through: How to Make Words Work for You (Davis and Charles, 1980).

Liles, Parker and others. Typing Mailable Letters, 3rd ed. (McGraw, 1978).

Saville, Jenny and Tim. The Business Letter Writer (Beekman, 1980).

Timmons, Christine and Gibney, Frank, eds. Britannica Book of English Usage (Doubleday, 1980).

LETTUCE. The world's most popular salad green is lettuce. It originated in western Asia and was popular with the ancient Persians, Greeks, and Romans.

Lettuce is a hardy plant that grows best in temperate climates with an ample water supply. It grows quickly and must be cut for table use before it produces the long slender stalk upon which its small yellow flowers grow and produce seeds.

There are five types of lettuce—crisphead, butterhead, cos, leaf, and stem. Stem, or asparagus, lettuce is grown primarily in China for its tall, thick, edible stems. In Europe the cos and butterhead, or cabbage, types are more common.

In the United States, lettuce is grown commercially in 13 states. By far the largest producer is California. The most important lettuce commercially is

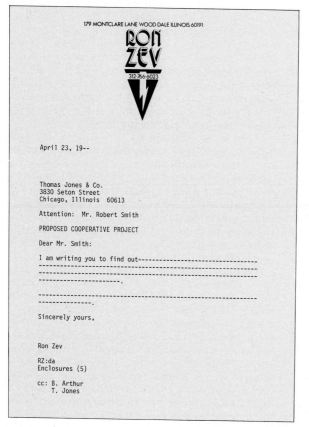

replaces heading

date line

inside address

attention line

subject line

salutation

body of
letter

complimentary
closing line

signature line

identification initials

enclosure notation

carbon copy
notation

Horace J. McFarland

Crisphead lettuce (top left) has a firm head with crisp leaves. Butterhead lettuce (top right) has a soft head and tender leaves. Cos, or romaine, (above left) and black-seeded Simpson (above right) are both leaf types of lettuce.

crisphead. The chief varieties are New York (popularly called iceberg), Imperial, and Great Lakes. Butterheads include Big Boston and the small, tender bibb. Most popular of the cos, or romaine, type is Paris white. Leaf lettuce is the easiest type to grow in the home garden. It includes Grand Rapids and the white-seeded and black-seeded Simpsons.

Lettuce belongs to the family Compositae. Its scientific name is *Lactuca sativa*.

LÉVI-STRAUSS, Claude (born 1908). In the field of social anthropology, Claude Lévi-Strauss became a leading exponent of structuralism. In this approach to the analysis of human cultures, the assumption is that all human societies develop and order themselves in similar ways. Elements that are common to all cultures are identified and studied. These structural similarities are explored through analysis of elements in various societies including myths, rituals, kinship, and languages.

Claude Lévi-Strauss was born in Brussels, Belgium, on Nov. 28, 1908. He studied law and philosophy at the University of Paris from 1927 to 1932 and taught in a secondary school before teaching at the University of São Paulo, Brazil, as professor of sociology in the late 1930s. While at São Paulo he did field research on the Indians of Brazil. From 1941 to 1945 he was a visiting professor at the New School for Social Research in New York City. After World War II

he returned to France to become associate director of the Musée de l'Homme (Anthropological Museum), and in 1950 he became director of studies at the École Pratique des Hautes Études (Practical School of Advanced Studies) at the University of Paris. In 1959 he was appointed to the chair of social anthropology at the Collège de France.

Lévi-Strauss' first major work was 'Les Structures élémentaires de la parenté' (The Elementary Structures of Kinship, published in 1949); but he first attained popular recognition with his intellectual autobiography, 'Tristes tropiques' (A World on the Wane, 1955), in which he describes the origins of his views on structuralism. Among his other publications are 'Anthropologie structurale' (Structural Anthropology, 1958), 'La Pensée Sauvage' (The Savage Mind, 1962), 'Le Totémisme aujourd'hui' (Totemism, 1962), and his massive, four-volume 'Mythologiques' (The Mythological), begun in 1964 and completed in 1971. In this large work, Lévi-Strauss attempts, through an analysis of the cultures of New World Indians, to demonstrate the common structural elements of their societies.

LEWIS, C. S. (1898–1963). The death of C. S. Lewis on Nov. 22, 1963, was not much noticed at the time, because it occurred on the same day as the assassination of United States President John F. Kennedy. Yet for three decades Lewis had been one of the most widely read authors on Christian teaching in the Western world.

Clive Staples Lewis was born in Belfast, Ireland, on Nov. 29, 1898. He was educated by private tutor and then at Malvern College in England for a year before attending University College, Oxford, in 1916. His education was interrupted by service in World War I. In 1918 he returned to Oxford where he did outstanding work as a classical scholar. He taught at Magdalen College, Oxford, from 1925 to 1954, and from 1954 until his death in Oxford he was professor of medieval and Renaissance English at Cambridge University in Cambridge. He was highly respected in his field of study, both as a teacher and writer. His book 'The Allegory of Love: a Study in Medieval Tradition', published in 1936, is considered by many to be his best work.

It was as an apologist for Christianity that Lewis gained his greatest audience. In his attempt to formulate a core of Christian understanding, Lewis wrote a number of highly readable books—intelligent, imaginative, and often witty. Among these were: 'The Pilgrim's Regress', published in 1933, 'The Problem of Pain' (1940), 'Miracles' (1947), and 'The Screwtape Letters' (1942), probably his most popular work. He also wrote a trilogy of religious science fiction novels: 'Out of the Silent Planet' (1938), 'Perelandra' (1943), and 'That Hideous Strength' (1945). For children he wrote a series of seven allegorical tales, beginning with 'The Lion, the Witch, and the Wardrobe' in 1950. His autobiography, 'Surprised by Joy', was published in 1955.

UPI

At a Congressional hearing, labor leader John L. Lewis expresses, with typical passion, his disagreement with members of a House of Representatives committee.

LEWIS, John L. (1880–1969). From 1920 to 1960 John L. Lewis was president of the United Mine Workers of America (UMWA). He also worked for unionization of the steel, automobile, and other mass-production industries and organized the Congress of Industrial Organizations (CIO), a labor organization. Demanding and unyielding, he aroused passions with his thunderous oratory and kept industry in turmoil throughout his long and dynamic career.

John Llewellyn Lewis was born in Lucas, Iowa, on Feb. 12, 1880. His father, a coal miner from Wales, was active in the Knights of Labor. Lewis quit school at 12, and at 17 he became a coal miner. He educated himself with the help of a schoolteacher, marrying her in 1907. He also directed a debating club and took part in amateur theatricals.

At 26 years old, Lewis was a delegate to a UMWA convention. In 1920 he was elected president of the organization. The membership was then about 700,000, the largest union in the American Federation of Labor (AFL).

Under Lewis' leadership, eight unions in the AFL promoted organizing drives on an industry-wide basis. When the AFL convention of 1935 rejected the plan, Lewis formed a Committee for Industrial Organization, which later became the Congress of Industrial Organizations. The group was regarded as a rival organization and in 1936 was expelled by the AFL. Lewis served as president of the new CIO until 1940. He then pulled the UMWA out of the CIO with much criticism, but he retained the miners' support. When Lewis retired in 1960, there were only 200,000 UMWA members, but their wages were high, and they were excellently insured. Lewis died in Washington, D.C., on June 11, 1969. (*See also* Coal; Labor Movements.)

LEWIS, Meriwether (1774–1809). The name of Meriwether Lewis is closely linked with that of another American explorer, William Clark. Together they led the expedition named for them (*see* Clark, William; Lewis and Clark Expedition).

Meriwether Lewis was born Aug. 18, 1774, on a plantation near Charlottesville, Va. Thomas Jefferson, a neighbor, was a friend of the family. Meriwether studied with private tutors, hunted, and learned nature lore. In 1794 he served in the militia during the Whiskey Rebellion. The next year he fought against Indians in the Northwest Territory. Between campaigns he lived in the wilderness and learned Indian languages and customs.

Soon after Jefferson became president, Lewis moved into the White House as his private secretary. They often discussed the exploration of a land route to the Pacific Ocean. Lewis was eager to lead the expedition. Congress, at Jefferson's request, appropriated $2,500, the sum Lewis estimated was needed. Jefferson asked the Lewis to choose a companion officer, and Lewis selected William Clark of Louisville. The success of the expedition was due to the combined abilities of the two leaders.

In 1807 Jefferson appointed Lewis governor of the Louisiana Territory, with headquarters at Saint Louis. Lewis was an excellent administrator, but his service in his new position was brief. In 1809 he started on a trip to Washington, D.C. On the night of October 11 he was found shot to death at an inn in Tennessee. He was probably murdered, though no proof of it was ever uncovered.

LEWIS, Sinclair (1885–1951). The novels that Sinclair Lewis wrote in the 1920s assure him a lasting place in American literature. Nothing he wrote before or after matches his work in 'Main Street', published in 1920, 'Babbitt' (1922), 'Arrowsmith' (1925), 'Elmer Gantry' (1927), and 'Dodsworth' (1929). In 1930 he won the Nobel prize in literature for the body of his writings. Lewis was the first American to receive the award.

Harry Sinclair Lewis was born on Feb. 7, 1885, in Sauk Centre, Minn. As a boy he read everything

Sinclair Lewis

The Granger Collection

obtainable. He graduated from Yale University in 1907 and was for a time a reporter and also worked as an editor for several publishers. His first novel, 'Our Mr. Wrenn' (1914), was treated favorably by the critics but had few readers. At the same time he was writing with increasing success for such popular magazines as *The Saturday Evening Post* and *Cosmopolitan*. However, he never lost sight of his ambition to become a serious novelist. The publication of 'Main Street' made his literary reputation. The power of the book derives from Lewis' careful rendering of local speech, customs, social amenities, and his double-edged satire. 'Main Street' became not just a novel but the textbook on provincial America.

'Babbitt', a study of the complacent American whose individuality has been taken away by Rotary clubs, business ideals, and general conformity is thought by many critics to be Lewis' best novel. This was followed by 'Arrowsmith', a satire on the medical profession. Next was 'Elmer Gantry', an attack on ignorant and predatory Protestant church leaders. 'Dodsworth' was Lewis' chance to contrast United States and European values.

Lewis wrote steadily, averaging a book every two years for over 30 years and writing short stories as well. In his final years he lived much of his time abroad. After 1930 his reputation declined considerably; critics said his work was shallow and overly sentimental. Lewis died near Rome, Italy, on Jan. 10, 1951. His biography, 'Sinclair Lewis: an American Life' (1961), was written by Mark Schorer.

LEWIS AND CLARK EXPEDITION.

Little was known about western America when the Lewis and Clark Expedition set out in 1804. Twelve years earlier Captain Robert Gray, an American navigator, had sailed up the mouth of the great river he named the Columbia. Traders and trappers reported that the source of the Missouri River was in the mountains in the Far West. No one, however, had yet blazed an overland trail.

President Thomas Jefferson was interested in knowing more about the country west of the Mississippi. In 1803, two years after he became president, he asked Congress for $2,500 for an expedition.

To head the expedition, Jefferson chose his young secretary, Captain Meriwether Lewis. Lewis invited his friend Lieutenant William Clark to share the leadership. Both were familiar with the frontier and with Indians through their service in the army. (*See also* Lewis, Meriwether; Clark, William.)

Before Lewis and Clark set out, word came that Napoleon had sold an immense tract of land to the United States (*see* Louisiana Purchase). The expedition would therefore be exploring American territory.

Plans for the expedition were carefully laid. The party was to ascend the Missouri to its source, cross the Continental Divide, and descend the Columbia River to its mouth. In preparation for the historic journey, Lewis studied map making and learned how to fix latitude and longitude.

In the winter of 1803–4 the expedition was assembled in Illinois, near Saint Louis. The party consisted of the two leaders, Lewis and Clark; 14 soldiers; nine frontiersmen from Kentucky; two French boatmen; and Clark's servant, York.

On May 14, 1804, the explorers started up the Missouri in a 55-foot (17-meter) covered keelboat and two small craft. On July 30 they held their first powwow, or meeting, with Indians at a place the explorers named Council Bluff. (Council Bluffs, Iowa, across the river from the site, perpetuates the name with the slight change.) On October 26 they reached the camps of the Mandan Indians.

On a site close to present-day Stanton, N.D., the explorers built Fort Mandan and spent the winter. It was here that they hired Toussaint Charbonneau, a French interpreter, and his Indian wife, Sacagawea, the sister of a Shoshone chief. While at Fort Mandan, Sacagawea gave birth to a baby boy. This did not stop her from participating in the group. She carried the child on her back for the rest of the trip. As an Indian interpreter she proved invaluable.

In the spring of 1805 the keelboat was sent back to St. Louis with dispatches for President Jefferson and with natural history specimens. Meanwhile, canoes had been built. On April 7 the party continued on up the Missouri. On April 26 it passed the mouth of the Yellowstone, and on June 13 reached the Great Falls of the Missouri. Carrying the laden canoes 16 miles

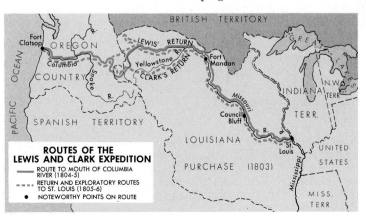

Lewis and Clark brought back from their expedition a mine of information in maps and diaries to help dispel ignorance about the vast territories west of the Mississippi. They also showed that there was no easy watercrossing of the continent.

143

Adapted from 'The American Heritage Pictorial Atlas of United States History'; copyright © 1966 by American Heritage Publishing Co., Inc.

(25 kilometers) around the falls caused a month's delay. On July 13 the canoes were launched again above the falls. On the 25th the expedition reached Three Forks, where three rivers join to form the Missouri. They named the rivers the Madison, the Jefferson, and the Gallatin.

For some time the explorers had been within sight of the Rocky Mountains. Crossing them was to be the hardest part of the journey. They decided to follow the largest of the three forks, the Jefferson.

They were now in the country of the Shoshone, Sacagawea's people. Sacagawea eagerly watched for her tribe, but it was Lewis who found them. The chief turned out to be Sacagawea's brother. He provided the party with guides and horses for the difficult crossing of the lofty Bitterroot Range.

After crossing the divide late in September, they reached a point on the Clearwater River. From here they were able to proceed by water.

On Nov. 7, 1805, Clark wrote in his journal, "Great joy in camp," for after a journey of over 18 months, the Pacific Ocean was within view. On the Pacific shore, near the mouth of the Columbia, they built a stockade, Fort Clatsop. There they spent the winter.

On March 23, 1806, the entire party started back. On June 24, with 66 horses, they began to cross the mountains. In the Bitterroot Valley the two leaders separated to learn more about the country.

Clark headed for the Yellowstone River and followed it to the Missouri. Lewis, with nine men, struck off toward the northeast to explore a branch of the Missouri that he named the Marias. On this trip he had a skirmish with Indians, the only one of the entire journey. Later, while out hunting, he was accidentally shot by one of his own men. He recovered after the party was reunited and had stopped at Fort Mandan. There they left Sacagawea and her family.

The party reached St. Louis on Sept. 23, 1806. Their arrival caused great rejoicing, for they had been believed dead. They had been gone two years, four months, and nine days, and had traveled about 6,000 miles (9,650 kilometers).

Lewis and Clark brought back much new material for map makers and specimens of previously unknown wildlife. American settlers and traders soon began to travel over the route they had blazed. The expedition also provided useful support for the United States claim to the Oregon country.

LEXINGTON AND CONCORD, BATTLE OF.

The American Revolution began on April 19, 1775, with the battle of Lexington and Concord. Some time before, General Thomas Gage, the military governor of Massachusetts, had received orders from England to arrest Samuel Adams and John Hancock, accused of stirring up rebellion in the colony. On the night of April 18 Gage sent a detachment of 800 troops to Lexington, where the "traitors" were staying. The troops were to arrest the two men, then push on to Concord to destroy military supplies stored there by the colonists. News of the expedition leaked out, and two

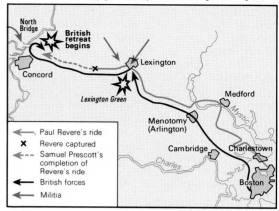

Some of what took place around Lexington and Concord on April 18 and 19 in 1775.

minutemen (as the colonial militia were called), William Dawes and Paul Revere, rode through the country warning people that the British regulars were coming. Revere was captured as he rode and his ride was finished by Samuel Prescott. (*See also* Adams, Samuel; Hancock, John; Revere, Paul.)

When the troops reached Lexington they found about 50 minutemen on the common, an open square in the center of the town. John Pitcairn, the British commander, ordered the rebels to disperse. Both sides milled about in confusion, and shooting broke out. Eight Americans were killed and ten were wounded. The others scattered, and the British went on toward Concord. Hancock and Adams, warned of their coming, had already fled.

The soldiers arrived at Concord at 7:00 AM. During the night the colonists had hidden most of their stores and ammunition. What they had not been able to hide, the British set about destroying. Then they met the minutemen at the Old North Bridge over the Concord River and fired upon them. The Americans fired back, and the war had begun. In this skirmish the British numbered about 200; the Americans, 400. The Americans poured over the bridge. The British began a retreat to Boston at about noon.

Meanwhile, the farmers, from behind rocks, fences, and buildings, picked off the brightly clad soldiers along the road. At Lexington the fleeing redcoats met another detachment of 1,500 soldiers sent out by General Gage. Thus strengthened, the British returned to Boston, having suffered 274 killed and wounded and 25 missing. The American loss was 88 killed and wounded.

At Lexington, 12 miles (19 kilometers) northwest of Boston, visitors may still see Munroe Tavern, which the British used as their headquarters; Buckman Tavern, which was the rendezvous of the minutemen; and the Hancock-Clarke house, where Adams and Hancock lodged the night before the battle. The Minute Man National Historical Park, established in 1959, preserves these structures and such memorials as Daniel Chester French's statue of 'The Minute Man' in Concord.

The Potala Palace stands on a hill at the main entrance to Lhasa. It was once the fortress of the Dalai Lamas.

Ewing Galloway

LEXINGTON-FAYETTE, Ky. The focus of the Bluegrass region and a major center for horse breeding, the city of Lexington was named in 1775 for the Battle of Lexington, Mass. The name Lexington-Fayette is derived from the 1974 merger of Lexington city and Fayette county to form an urban county government. However, the city is still commonly called simply Lexington. It ranks second in size only to Louisville among Kentucky's cities.

Located in north central Kentucky, 120 miles (190 kilometers) south of Louisville, the city is surrounded by rich farmland. It is an important market for beef cattle, sheep, spring lambs, bluegrass seed, and loose-leaf tobacco. Bourbon whiskey, paper products, and electronic equipment are also manufactured.

The American Thoroughbred Breeders Association has its headquarters in the city, and devotion to fine horses and racing is a strong local interest. The University of Kentucky and Lexington Theological Seminary were founded in Lexington in 1865. There are also two business colleges in the city, along with the Lexington-Blue Grass Army Depot Headquarters and the United States Government Hospital for Narcotics Addicts.

Lexington was chartered by the Virginia legislature in 1782 and was the meeting place for the first session of the Kentucky legislature in 1792. During the early 1880s Lexington called itself the Athens of the West, a reference to its cultural development, which included Transylvania College, a public subscription library, a theater, and a musical society. In 1817 the first Beethoven symphony heard in the United States was presented in Lexington.

John C. Breckinridge, United States vice president from 1857 to 1861; John Hunt Morgan, a Confederate general; the Todd family; and United States Senator Henry Clay are buried in Lexington Cemetery. The Morgan, Mary Todd Lincoln, and Clay homes are all on public display. A statue of Man O'War, the famous race horse, stands in Kentucky Horse Park in Lexington. (*See also* Kentucky.) Population (1980) city, 204,165; metropolitan area, 317,629.

LHASA, Tibet. Long isolated from the outside world and perched high in the Tibet Himalayas, Lhasa is the capital of the Tibet Autonomous Region of the People's Republic of China. It formerly served as the national religious center of Tibet. The city has undergone enormous change since its occupation by the Chinese in 1959. Although its physical facilities have improved under Chinese administration, much of the Tibetan population has fled in the face of cultural and political change. The majority of Lhasa's inhabitants are Chinese.

Lhasa stands on a level valley plain at an altitude of 11,830 feet (3,606 meters) and is surrounded by dark and barren hills. It is screened from view from the west by a lofty and narrow ridge with two high summits between which is the main entrance to the city. The ridge to the north is crowned by the majestic former winter palace of the Dalai Lama, spiritual head of Tibetan Buddhism. The city is filled with beautiful trees, including weeping willows, poplars, junipers, elms, and thorn trees. There are also fruit trees and colorful flowers of every variety.

Since the 1960s new roads have been built, and an airport has been constructed nearby. A highway system now connects Lhasa with the major cities in neighboring provinces. Automobiles have been introduced. During the 1960s, however, the mountain passes leading to India and neighboring Himalayan countries were sealed by the Chinese administration, and travel was restricted within Tibet and between Tibet and China. The Chinese administration has also changed trade routes, improved public utilities, updated health facilities, and taken over the educational system.

Lhasa has been the capital of Tibet since the 9th century. It continued to gain in religious importance despite internal power struggles. Since 1642 it has been the seat of the central Tibetan government. Although Lhasa and Tibet came under Chinese occupation in 1951, they remained under the Tibetan government until 1959. (*See also* China; Tibet.) Population (1982 estimate), 386,200.

145

LIAONING. The southernmost of the three Chinese provinces that form the region known as Manchuria, Liaoning is bounded by Jilin province on the northeast, North Korea on the east, the Yellow Sea on  the south, Hebei province on the southwest, and the Inner Mongolian Autonomous Region on the northwest. The provincial capital is Shenyang (Mukden).

Most of the Liaoning population is Han Chinese. Significant minorities are Manchu, mainly in the Liao Valley and around Shenyang, and Mongol, near the frontier of Inner Mongolia.

Liaoning is rich in mineral resources, especially iron ore and coal. Petroleum is produced from oil shale. There are also rich reserves of manganese and magnesium ore and substantial deposits of copper, lead, zinc, bauxite, and gold. Sea salt is produced for use in food and in the chemical industry.

The province ranks first in China in heavy industrial production, producing steel, cement, crude oil, and approximately one fifth of the nation's electrical power. Other industries in Liaoning include nonferrous-metal processing, machinery manufacture, textiles, foodstuffs, paper, and cement. Crops include corn (maize), *gaoliang* (grain sorghum), vegetables, and soybeans.

The area was known as Sheng-ching in Manchu times (1644–1911). In 1928 the boundaries were altered, and it was named Liaoning. From 1932 to 1945 the region was part of the Japanese-dominated, "independent" state of Manchoukuo. In 1948 Mukden fell to the Chinese Communists. In 1954 it was established as a single province and achieved its present form in 1956. (*See also* China.) Population (1982 census), 35,721,693.

LIBERALISM. Based on the Latin word *liber*, meaning "free," liberalism is a political point of view opposed to any system that threatens the freedom of the individual and prevents him from realizing his full human potential. Liberalism has flourished in Western society since the 18th century, but its history may be divided into two markedly distinct periods—the classical and the modern.

Classical liberalism had its roots in the revolt of the growing middle classes against government control of the economy. In the late Middle Ages and early modern period, governments played a decisive role in expanding and controlling commerce and industry. This practice, commonly called mercantilism, was felt by many to inhibit rather than enhance economic growth. The opposition to mercantilism found its greatest expression in philosopher and economist Adam Smith's 'The Wealth of Nations'. This book promoted the ideal of a free market economy that would operate without government interference.

Formulations of liberal theory thus had as their basis Thomas Jefferson's notion that the government is best that governs least. The goal of liberals was to find ways to control excessive government power and to limit government to its primary purposes of providing for the common defense, preserving domestic tranquility, and guaranteeing the rights of private property and the obligations of contract.

During the late 18th and the 19th centuries, liberals did succeed, through various means, in limiting the powers of government. (The separation of powers, as delineated in the United States Constitution, is a clear example of the operation of classical liberalism.) What liberals did not foresee was that while governments became incapable of controlling economies, they were thereby also unable to prevent great economic power from concentrating in the hands of a few people who could be as despotic in their own way as any authoritarian government. The situation soon became an unhappy reversal: formerly, governments had exercised control over the economy; but by the late 19th century, economic power was beginning to exercise control over governments.

Slowly, in the late 19th century and the early decades of the 20th, the liberal theories that had been formulated by Adam Smith and other social theorists, such as John Locke, Jeremy Bentham, and John Stuart Mill, began to yield to the view that government should use its power to intervene in the economy for the general welfare of all citizens. (*See also* Bentham; Locke, John; Mill.)

The goals of modern liberalism have, therefore, shifted dramatically from those of classical liberalism. They may be summed up in the notion that the powers of government are to be used to achieve a redistribution of political and economic power in society. In the United States, such liberal goals were first spelled out in detail in the Progressive party platform of 1912; and many of them were incorporated into the New Deal programs of President Franklin D. Roosevelt during the 1930s. These programs involved a variety of social and labor legislation designed to benefit nearly all segments of the population. Such programs have become a part of most Western countries and Japan; and since World War II many of the nations emerging from colonialism have imitated them. The regimes of the Soviet Union and Eastern European nations have adopted a broad range of social welfare programs in the name of socialism. (*See also* Labor and Industrial Law; Social Security.)

LIBERIA. A small country on the west coast of Africa, Liberia has been influenced by the United States in several ways. This influence has its origins in the efforts of the American Colonization Society to settle freed American slaves in Africa, beginning in 1822. The government, a republic, was modeled on that of the United States. Monrovia, the capital and principal port, was named after United States President James Monroe. To black Americans this country has special significance. As Africa's oldest repub-

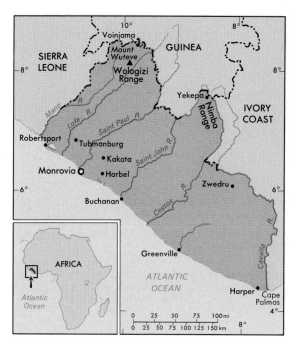

estimated that 44 percent of the people practice traditional African religions. About 35 percent of the population are converts to Christianity, which was introduced by the settlers. About 21 percent of the people follow Islam, which was brought to the country by migrants from the fringes of the Sahara.

Economy

Farming is the most important economic activity for nearly 80 percent of the people. They grow rice, cassava, palm trees (for palm oil), vegetables, and fruits for their own needs. But Liberia's economy is highly dependent on the export of raw materials. This dependence began when rubber became the first major export crop. The first Liberian rubber plantation was established by the British in 1906. It was acquired from the British in 1924 by an American company, the Firestone Tire and Rubber Company. Firestone improved and expanded its rubber plantations, but in 1983 they cut off operations. The Liberian government then sought another foreign buyer. Rubber farms and plantations owned by Liberians account for one third of the total rubber produced.

Liberia also exports minerals. Rich deposits of iron ore in the mountains along the Liberian-Guinea border provide the chief export in terms of earnings. Most of it is sent to the United States. Timber and other tree products form a third major export.

Since the 1950s the network of roads in Liberia has been greatly expanded by the government as a way of opening up the country's hinterlands. Most of the existing roads were constructed to meet the needs of the plantations rather than the needs of small rural farmers. The only railroad is owned and operated by foreign iron-ore mining concessions. A telephone and radio-communication system, one of the first in Africa, was introduced in Liberia in 1910. As early as 1826 the first public schools had been established.

lic, established by former black American slaves, Liberia played an important role as a model for African colonies seeking independence.

Land and People

Liberia has a land area of 43,000 square miles (111,400 square kilometers). Except for a strip of coastal savanna and mangrove swamps, the land is covered by tropical rain forest. Although warm throughout the year, Liberia has two seasons. The dry season lasts from November to April, and the wet season from May through October. Annual rainfall averages 200 inches (5,080 millimeters) along the coast and diminishes to about 70 inches (1,778 millimeters) farther inland. The physical environment is ideal for tree crops, such as rubber, cocoa, coffee, palm oil, bananas, and kola. These are produced on large plantations and timber is cut from the forests.

The country is rich in wildlife. About 130 species of mammals have so far been identified. There are fifteen species belonging to the cat family, among which the largest and most beautiful is the leopard. The number of leopards has been decreasing rapidly, however, along with the elephant and the bush cow. Monkeys, the chimpanzee, the antelope, and various rodents also abound. Two rare mammals found here are the manatee and the pygmy hippopotomus. In addition to mammals there are some 140 species of birds including eagles, kites, and hawks. Fishes, reptiles, and insects are numerous.

Liberians of black American ancestry, known as Americo-Liberians, live along the coast and make up about 5 percent of the nation's almost two million population. The bulk of the population belongs to three of the five major West African language groups known as Kru, Atlantic, and Mende. In 1980 it was

Government and History

On July 26, 1847, Liberia adopted a constitution that made it a republic headed by a president, a vice president, and a cabinet. It established a Senate and House of Representatives as the chief legislative bodies. The constitution and its provisions at first applied only to Americo-Liberians and not to the African tribespeople. William S. Tubman, who was president from 1944 until his death in 1971, made a serious effort to encourage participation of African tribespeople in the political life of the country. After his death Tubman was succeeded by William R. Tolbert, who had been vice president. President Tolbert was assassinated in 1980 in Liberia's first military coup, led by army sergeant Samuel Kanyon Doe.

The new leader became head of state with the title of General. Under Doe the country is administered by the People's Redemption Council. Doe pledged to return his country to civilian rule by the year 1985. In April 1981, the first anniversary of the military government, Doe named a commission to prepare a new constitution. Population (1982 estimate), 1,990,000.

Photo Trends

© Peter B. Kaplan

The Statue of Liberty stands on its star-shaped base (left) on Liberty Island in New York Harbor. A crack near an eye and the nose and rust at the base of the crown (above) are to be repaired in an overall restoration program.

LIBERTY, STATUE OF. The giant statue 'Liberty Enlightening the World' has become a symbol of freedom to oppressed people everywhere. It stands on Liberty Island in New York Harbor. The statue was a gift from the people of France to the people of the United States commemorating the alliance of the two nations during the Revolutionary War.

Édouard de Laboulaye, a French historian, proposed in 1865 that his country present a suitable memorial to the United States on the 100th anniversary of the signing of the Declaration of Independence. The Franco-Prussian War intervened, but in 1874 a young Alsatian sculptor, Frédéric-Auguste Bartholdi, was sent to New York City to confer with American authorities. As he sailed into the harbor, Bartholdi envisioned a colossal goddess of liberty at the gateway to the New World.

The Franco-American Union was formed to collect the funds. The total cost of about one million francs was contributed in France by popular subscription. Americans subscribed $250,000 for the pedestal. The statue was dedicated on Oct. 28, 1886.

In her uplifted right hand the goddess holds a torch lighted by mercury-vapor lamps. In her left hand is the tablet of law bearing in roman numerals the date July 4, 1776. A broken shackle lies at her feet. The star-shaped wall around the base of the statue is the wall of old Fort Wood, which was built from 1808 to 1811. The statue was made a national monument in 1924 and is maintained by the National Park Service. The American Museum of Immigration in the base of the statue was opened in 1972.

On the pedestal appears the following sonnet by Emma Lazarus, entitled 'The New Colossus':

> Not like the brazen giant of Greek fame,
> With conquering limbs astride from land to land,
> Here at our sea-washed, sunset gates shall stand
> A mighty woman with a torch, whose flame
> Is the imprisoned lightning, and her name
> Mother of Exiles. From her beacon-hand
> Glows world-wide welcome; her mild eyes command
> The air-bridged harbor that twin cities frame.
> "Keep ancient lands, your storied pomp!" cries she
> With silent lips. "Give me your tired, your poor,
> Your huddled masses yearning to breathe free,
> The wretched refuse of your teeming shore.
> Send these, the homeless, tempest-tost to me,
> I lift my lamp beside the golden door!"

The figure is composed of more than 300 copper shells $\frac{3}{32}$ of an inch (2.4 millimeters) thick. It is supported by an iron framework designed by Gustave Eiffel, builder of the Eiffel Tower in Paris. Bartholdi first built a 9-foot (3-meter) model. This was enlarged to a figure 36 feet (11 meters) tall, which was divided into sections. Each section was further enlarged to full size, and patterns were made over which the copper was hammered by hand. In the assembled statue each section of the shell was bolted to the central framework. The figure is nearly 152 feet (46 meters) tall and weighs 225 tons (204 metric tons). It stands on a 150-foot (46-meter) pedestal.

Tourists climb the crowded stairs inside the statue to its crown. Air pollution, age, and wear and tear have taken their toll. In 1982 a private commission was created to raise 39 million dollars to repair and clean the statue and to expand the island's museum.

City Museums, Edinburgh, Scotland

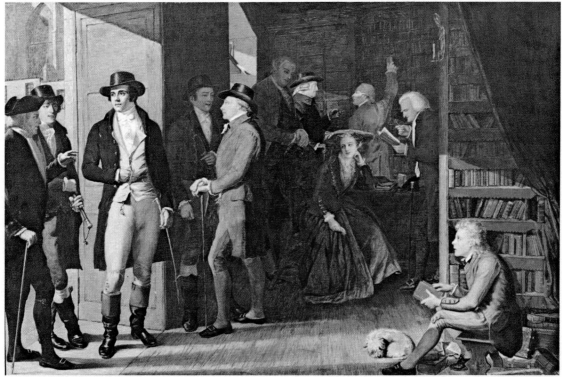

The poet Robert Burns stands at the door of James Sibbald's Circulating Library in Edinburgh, Scotland. The novelist Sir Walter Scott, at the right, has been portrayed in his youth.

LIBRARY

LIBRARY. Walls cannot embrace a library. It is more than a place, more than books and films and records, more even than the people who make it work. Basically a library is a gathering of ideas, of information—put in order and shared. And the sharing is the whole point of a library.

Reading Martin Luther King, Jr.'s "I have a dream" speech touches the mind and heart. But hearing it on tape or record sets the blood rushing and the ears tingling. Seeing the speech delivered on film or videotape adds a further visual dimension. The many ways of understanding come through books, records, tapes, films. That's why librarians today stock a great variety of materials.

THE LIBRARY: AN INTRODUCTION

Different groups of people use libraries—teachers and learners, youngsters and oldsters, police and plumbers and politicians. Each group, each person has different library needs. Because no one library can handle all needs, there are different kinds of libraries, and there is sharing among libraries.

A Difference in Libraries

No two libraries are exactly alike. But some have more in common than others.

Because the money to run a *public library* comes from taxes, it is a free library for the public—every-

one who lives in a certain neighborhood, city, county, or province. Such a library serves all ages and groups as an information center, as a reading-and-viewing-and-listening-for-pleasure library. There were early types of public libraries in ancient Greece and Rome. However, they did not lend materials freely as do the world's public libraries today.

Throughout the school day, students and teachers in elementary and secondary school need *school libraries* to work in. The modern school library in many countries is a learning center designed for both group and independent study. Besides books, the library may contain magazines, newspapers, maps, posters, charts, models, teaching machines, films and filmstrips and slides to look at, records and tapes to listen to, and the equipment to use these. There may be special study and listening areas, conference rooms, and even a recording or TV studio. Such a library is called a *materials center* or *media center*. A large secondary school library may have separate *resource centers* for science, social studies, and other subjects.

An *academic library* is found in a college or university. Like a school library, this library is a workshop for the students and teachers, but it often has anywhere from 50,000 to millions of books and other materials covering many special subjects. That's why scholars from outside the college or university frequently use such a library for research. A university may include 50 or more libraries in its many schools —a Far Eastern studies library, a fine arts library, an engineering library, and so on. There may be separate libraries for undergraduates and for rare books and manuscripts. Because of the vast amount of materials they handle, some academic libraries use computers to keep track of the collections.

The medical library of a hospital is a *special library*. So are the libraries of a law office, a weather bureau, a labor union, or a museum. A special library is part of a hospital, business, or other organization, and it offers practical information to the workers or members. Such a library is not generally open to the public. Usually it concentrates on a particular subject or subjects—medicine, law, climate and weather, labor, art. A special library may have few books, relying heavily instead on such materials as magazines, reports, and computer printouts. These enable the library to keep up in fast-moving fields such as aerospace.

Public, school, academic, and special libraries are the four main kinds the world over, but there are libraries that don't fit neatly into one of these groups. *Research libraries* are an example. Because scholars use them for study, they're much like academic libraries. Research libraries are not always attached to

Harrison Forman

Throughout the world, people who wish to enrich their lives with knowledge seek the services of a library to fill their needs.

Young Buddhist monks, for example, read American magazines in a school library in Thailand.

This article was contributed and critically reviewed by the following: Eleanor E. Ahlers, Professor, School of Librarianship, University of Washington, Seattle; John F. Anderson, Director, Public Library, Tucson, Ariz., Lester Asheim, Professor, Graduate Library School, University of Chicago; Augusta Baker, Coordinator of Children's Services, New York Public Library; Rebecca T. Bingham, Director, Library Media Services, Louisville Public Schools, Louisville, Ky.; Lillian M. Bradshaw, Director, Dallas Public Library, Dallas, Tex.; Henry C. Campbell, Chief Librarian, Toronto Public Libraries, Toronto, Ont.; David H. Clift, former Executive Director, American Library Association; Emma Cohn, Assistant Coordinator, Young Adult Services, New York Public Library; Robert L. Collison, Head, Reference Department, University Research Library, University of California at Los Angeles; Compton's Encyclopedia Canadian Advisory Board; Richard M. Dougherty, University Librarian, University of California at Berkeley; Sara I. Fenwick, Professor, Graduate Library School, University of Chicago; Emerson Greenaway, former Director, Enoch Pratt Free Library, Baltimore, Md.; Dean Wright Halliwell, University Librarian, University of Victoria, Victoria, B.C.; John G. Lorenz, Deputy Librarian, Library of Congress; Jean E. Lowrie, Director, School Department of Librarianship, Western Michigan University, Kalamazoo; Alice B. McGuire, former Associate Professor, Graduate School of Library Science, University of Texas at Austin.

Libraries reach beyond their walls to interest their communities in books and learning. This librarian from the Free Public Library in New Haven, Conn., tells stories to a front stoop audience of neighborhood children.

a college or university, however. Also, a research library often concentrates on a special subject or subjects, much like a special library. The Folger Shakespeare Library in Washington, D.C., for instance, deals with William Shakespeare and his times.

Then there are *government libraries* of many kinds. Some, like those of a weather bureau or other government department, are special libraries, offering information and materials that government people need in their work. Others, like state or provincial libraries, are many things. They're public because they serve all the people of a particular region. But they also include research facilities and special libraries such as law libraries for officials.

National libraries are government libraries, too. These are the superlibraries of the world, with upwards of 80 million books and other materials in the largest. Because a national library serves the government of a country, it's a special library. It's also a research library for scholars. In addition, many national libraries are public in that they are for the people of an entire country.

Other libraries that don't fit neatly into one group include those for prisoners in jail, for visitors in such places as YMCA's, for members of the congregation in churches, shipboard libraries for sailors, and army post libraries for soldiers. These are sometimes considered special libraries. But like public libraries,

151

they include much reading material for pleasure as well as for information.

Whatever type it is, every library serves a kind of community—a city, a school, a college or university, a hospital or engineering firm or labor union. Every library, also, shapes itself towards the people of its community—an aerospace library with its complicated computer printouts, an elementary school library with its bright decorations and children's furniture.

A Sharing Among Libraries

No library, no matter how large, has every book or the answer to every question. So libraries share with each other as well as with the people who use them.

or *catalogs* are published by libraries. These list the materials a library has, thereby making them easier to find and share.

Libraries also form groups, called *systems* or *networks*, for sharing. A public library system in a city, for example, generally consists of a main library and its branches. The city system might be part of a larger system such as a county system. The county system, in turn, might be part of a state system. And that system might be part of a national system. Libraries within a system share books and other materials. In addition, they share services such as storage of little-used books, preparation of materials for library use, and on-the-job training of librarians.

Brooklyn Public Library, New York City

A library is a way of sharing ... with city people ...

If someone wants a book or magazine the library doesn't have, the library can borrow it from another library. This is called *interlibrary loan*. Should the book or magazine be needed where it is, a photographic copy, or *photocopy*, can be made of the pages wanted, and the photocopy can be sent instead. Some modern libraries use the Teletype to speed up requests for materials. Also, where equipment is available, photos of materials requested are sent back by electronic signals over telephone wire or via satellite. This is called *facsimile transmission*.

It's not just materials that are shared; it's information too. Larger libraries, for instance, often answer questions smaller libraries can't. Also, *union lists*

Libraries in different regions sometimes form networks. Tied in to each other by Teletype or TV or computer, they can exchange information faster and more easily. All the sharing among libraries are steps toward a giant memory cell, with all the world's libraries plugged in.

The Why of a Library

People are what a library is all about. A library serves all who use it and reaches out to all who don't or can't. That's what the materials in a library, and the people who work there, are for.

It is common for a public library to have story hours for children, including preschoolers. There are also

country people ...

people who don't know ...

people who don't see ...

people who don't get out ...

picture books for them to page through, filmstrips and films to watch, and records to listen to. Children can see an exhibit of dolls or mobiles, watch a puppet show, or take part in an art contest. Some public libraries even have educational toys to play with and to take home. Tables, chairs, and shelves in a children's department are built to smaller and more convenient scale. Children's librarians introduce children's books to parents and help children choose books that are right for them. Sometimes storytellers are sent out into a community, and children in some places can call on the telephone to have a story read to them.

For those attending school, there is the school as well as the public library. Books and—where these are available—records, even cassettes and cassette players, can be taken home. Study booths and tables allow youngsters to work alone or in groups. Screening rooms in some libraries are for viewing of films, filmstrips, and videotapes. For sound tapes and records there are usually special listening areas. Both school and public librarians teach students how to use a library.

From secondary school on, young people are served by many kinds of libraries. Public libraries may have young adult sections with books and other materials of interest to young people. Young adult librarians plan film programs, pottery or karate or origami workshops, and discussions on topics that concern the

153

young in that particular community. In a few school and academic libraries, a student can dial to get a foreign language lesson or hear a lecture that has been stored in an *information retrieval bank*. Research libraries, when not part of a university, usually do not loan their materials. But all types of materials can be checked out of many other libraries. What can't be checked out can often be borrowed through interlibrary loan or photocopied—many libraries have photocopy machines, or *copiers*, for people to use. There may also be machines called *microfilm, Microcard*, and *microfiche readers*. With these, a person can read books, magazines, and newspapers that have been photographed and much reduced in size.

union halls, and housing projects. In special libraries, librarians not only find information for company workers but often summarize it for them.

For people of all ages, there are librarians specially trained to answer questions or help people get materials. There are also reference books such as encyclopedias to use in finding information without help. Finding out is easier for people interested in special subjects because library collections are arranged by subject. Library interiors are designed to be inviting and comfortable for reading, listening, viewing, and studying. Special devices such as wheelchair ramps are installed for the physically handicapped. Many public libraries are community centers, with local

Brooklyn Public Library, New York City

grown people ...

Adults, too, are served by many kinds of libraries. Film programs and discussion groups, concerts and plays held in library auditoriums, and art exhibitions often are planned. In many places women's groups, business management groups, labor groups, and others can request materials and conference rooms for meetings. Librarians provide materials and guidance on recreation, income tax, travel, health, and retirement. Adults who don't speak the language of the country well or who have little schooling can attend special programs at public libraries. Public librarians also reach out with books and services to such places as schools, nursing homes for the elderly, jails, factories,

artists showing their work, or community leaders giving talks. A public library in the city reaches into the neighborhoods with branch libraries and bookmobiles. For people in the country, there are books by mail, bookmobiles, book sleds, book boats, book trains, and even book planes. "Talking books" and the record players to use them are sent to the blind. So are magazines and books in braille, as well as books with large type for people with poor eyesight. Libraries reach out to help deaf, sick, poor, and forgotten people. A library in ancient Egypt was called "The Healing Place of the Soul." That goes a long way towards explaining the why of a library.

Alaska State Library

Eastfoto

teen people...

kid people...

IBM Corp.

working people...

...and more

The How of a Library

A library is not just to learn about; it's to use. And using it begins with knowing how that particular library is arranged.

To make books easier to find, those of the same type are commonly kept together. Stories are kept in one section, science books in another, and so on. There are often separate sections for magazines and newspapers, and for films, records, tapes, and such.

The Secret of Library Codes. Books are marked, or coded, in different ways. On the spine of a storybook or novel there may be such marks as a PB for picture

book, an E for easy, a J for juvenile, or an F for fiction. No matter how they are marked though, such storybooks and novels are put in alphabetical order by author's last name. So Paula Fox's books come before those of Astrid Lindgren. Books by the same author are in alphabetical order by title. Lindgren's 'Seacrow Island' comes after her 'Pippi Longstocking'.

The story of someone's life may be marked with a B for biography. Such biographies are put in alphabetical order by last name of the person the book is about. Thus, Howard Fast's 'Haym Salomon' comes before Earl Conrad's 'Harriet Tubman'. Biographies about many people—collective biographies—are grouped

155

separately. Such books are in alphabetical order by the last name of the person who wrote the book.

Of the many codes for marking books, two systems are used more often than the others in many parts of the world. One is called the Dewey decimal classification. It was designed by a librarian named Melvil Dewey, and school and public libraries use it most.

In the Dewey system, there are ten main subjects. Each subject has a three-figure number. The number 400, for instance, stands for language; 500 for science. In each Dewey number, the first figure is the key to the main subject. All books that begin with 5 are about science, and all books that begin with 4 are about language.

**Dewey Decimal Classification
Main Subjects (Simplified)**

000–099 many subjects (general works)
100–199 man's ideas (philosophy)
200–299 religion
300–399 people in groups (social sciences)
400–499 language
500–599 science
600–699 uses of science (technology)
700–799 the arts
800–899 literature
900–999 history, geography, biography

Author, subject, and title cards in the card catalog offer quick access to a library's information resources.

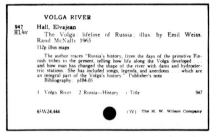

AUTHOR CARD

SUBJECT CARD

TITLE CARD

Each main subject is divided into ten parts. Literature (800) is divided into American literature (810), English literature (820), German literature (830), French literature (840), and so on. Each part of a subject can be divided into ten smaller parts. They, in turn, can be divided into ten still smaller parts. And that's what the decimal in the Dewey decimal classification is all about. Take 973. It includes all books on United States history. But that takes in books on the exploration of North America (973.1), the American Revolution (973.3), the Civil War (973.7), and so on. The smaller the part of a main subject, the more numbers after the decimal. Number 629.134354 stands for books about rocket engineering.

It isn't necessary to memorize the Dewey system. What is important, though, is to understand how it works. The same is true of the other much-used code, the Library of Congress (LC) classification. It was designed by librarians working in the Library of Congress, the national library of the United States. Academic and government libraries use it most.

In the LC system, there are twenty one main subjects instead of ten. The keys to subjects are capital letters, not numbers. For most main subjects, there is one key letter. But for the many books on North and South American history, two key letters are needed, so all books on that subject are coded with a beginning E or F.

The LC and Dewey systems also divide subjects differently. Dewey includes book lists and books about libraries in 000 (general works). LC separates them. Philosophy (100) and religion (200) are separated in Dewey, but in LC they are grouped together.

In the LC system, one capital letter stands for a main subject. Two capital letters together stand for part of that subject. World History (D), for instance, is divided into Great Britain (DA), Russia (DK), Asia (DS), Africa (DT), and so on. Each two-letter division can be further divided into 9,999 parts. For these, numbers are used. For smaller and smaller parts beyond that, a decimal point is used, followed by letters and numbers again. All books on the grow-

ing of carnations begin with LC number SB 413.C3.

A Dewey or LC number may be only part of a book's code number. In many libraries, there is another part, a bottom line. Dewey number 580, for instance, is for books on flowers. But there are many books on that subject, so they are set apart from one another by adding a second code. John Kieran's 'Introduction to Wild Flowers' $(\frac{580}{K54})$, Clarence J. Hylander's 'Flowers of Field and Forest' $(\frac{580}{H99})$, and Illa Podendorf's 'True Book of Weeds and Wild Flowers' $(\frac{580}{P75})$ are examples.

The bottom line is a code for the first few letters of the author's last name—K54 (or Kie) for Kieran, H99 (or Hyl) for Hylander, and P75 (or Pod) for

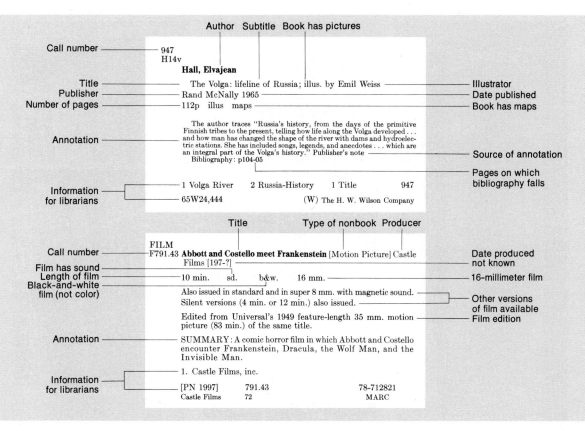

Library of Congress Classification
Main Subjects (Simplified)

A	general works	M	music
B	philosophy, religion	N	the arts
C	subjects closely related to history	P	language, literature
D	world history (except American)	Q	science
E–F	North and South American history	R	medicine
G	geography, anthropology	S	agriculture
H	social sciences	T	technology
J	politics	U	armies
K	law	V	navies
L	education	Z	book lists, libraries

Podendorf. A small letter after the numbers is used for books by the same author on the same subject. Author C. Clarke's 'Man and Space' ($^{629.25}_{C55m}$) and his 'Interplanetary Flight' ($^{629.25}_{C55i}$) are examples. The small letter stands for the first word in the title.

The top and bottom lines together are the book's *call number*. That's what people use to find the book on the shelves or ask for it at the call desk.

Catalog: House of Cards. A library is for browsing. But when information is wanted, finding the right books by browsing may take too long. That's when a catalog comes in handy.

Some catalogs are in book form. But most school and public libraries have card catalogs—stacks of slide-out drawers with printed cards inside, all in alpha-

betical order. The cards list and describe every book the library has. Other kinds of material are also listed, sometimes in the same catalog, sometimes in separate catalogs. On the outside of each drawer is a label: A–AK or AL–AM, for example. These are guides to the part of the alphabet covered by the cards inside. There are inside guides, too, cards which stand a little above the rest. In the A–AK drawer, for instance, inside guide cards might read: ADAMS, ADVENTURE, AFRICA, AGRICULTURE, AIRPLANES.

Different types of cards are found in a catalog. An *author card* has the name of a book's author on the top line. On a *title card*, the top line is the title of the book. The subject of the book is the top line of a *subject card*. Books are usually listed on more than

Libraries use labels to help patrons find books quickly. The label on the edge of a bookstack indicates the range of call numbers on its shelves. Labels above the shelves indicate the main subject or part of a main subject found below.

one type of card so that they will be easier to find. On all these types of cards, the call number will be in the upper left-hand corner.

Author, title, and subject cards also give other information. The author's birth and death dates are often given. If the book has drawings or photos, the card will say *illus.* or *illus. with photographs. Rev.* or *Rev. ed.* means that the book is a revised edition of the original. The card shows the date of publication. It tells the publisher's name and sometimes the place of publication. Number of pages is given. If the book is one of a series—Great Illustrated Classics, for example—the name of the series will appear in parentheses. Sometimes there is a short paragraph, called an *annotation*, that describes what the book is about. *Bibliography: p171–2* may appear on the card, meaning a list of books and other materials on the same subject can be found on those pages. Near the bottom of the card is information meant for librarians—other subjects the book will be listed under, and Dewey and LC numbers.

"See also" cards, found at the end of all cards on a subject, direct a person to additional related subjects. The "see also" card for *Fish* might read:

> Fish
> see also
> Aquariums
> Fisheries
> Marine Animals

Cards for magazines and newspapers are listed by title only—*Sports Illustrated* and the *New York Times*. Cards for materials such as films, records, and tapes are sometimes kept in a separate catalog. Such cards may have the word *Film, Filmstrip,* or *Tape* above the call number. They may also be blue, red, or some other color to tell them apart from book cards.

The Dewey decimal call numbers on these books show that they are about philosophy and religion. Libraries can add extra symbols to call numbers. The library holding these books used the letters "y" and "s" to indicate reading level.

A catalog also has *cross reference* cards. These are of two types. "See" cards direct a person to a different subject or name. Someone looking for books by Mark Twain, might find cards that read:

> Twain, Mark
> see
> Clemens, Samuel L.

The How of Finding a Book. Here are some ABC's of bookfinding with the help of a catalog.

1. Unless you can memorize everything at a glance, bring pen or pencil and paper with you.
2. Save time with the outside and inside guides.
3. Keep these things in mind:
   a. Abbreviations are filed as if spelled out, as *Saint* for *St.* and *Mister* for *Mr.*
   b. The same is true of numbers. For '100 Famous Stories', read 'One Hundred Famous Stories'.
   c. Names beginning with *Mc* are filed as if spelled *Mac*. The Mac names may begin the M section, before *Maas* and *Mabinogion*.

d. Authors are listed last name first. But people with three names may be listed under the second one—some Spanish names, Von names, and De names. Some names may be filed under what looks like the first name—Kim Yong Ik under Kim, for example. Just because you can't find a non-English name right away doesn't necessarily mean it isn't there.

e. Titles are listed alphabetically by first word of title. But *a, an,* and *the* are not counted as first words, so look for 'The Coming of the Space Age' under C.

f. Just because you can't find a subject right away doesn't mean it isn't in the catalog.

5. Write down call numbers, titles, and authors.

6. Now go to the bookcases, or *stacks,* and use the *case labels.* In many libraries, labels on the side of each stack give the Dewey or LC numbers it holds: *202–238, 239–276.*

7. Use the *shelf labels* if the library has them. Shelf labels give code number and subject of books in that section—*Language 400, Poetry 808.1.*

8. Just because you can't find a book doesn't mean you should quit. Sometimes it's in the wrong place. Sometimes there's another copy around, maybe in another library. Sometimes another book will do just as well for you. Ask a librarian for help—that's what librarians are for.

Frank Verticchio

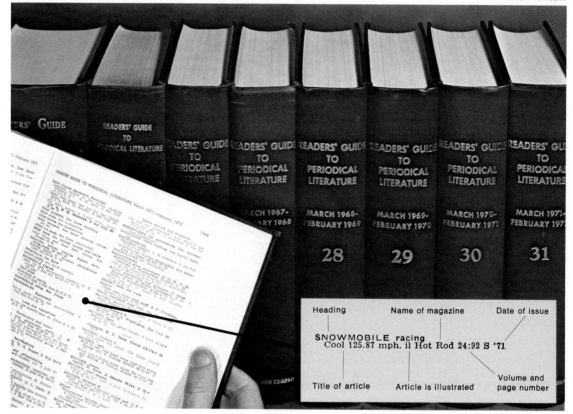

Heading   Name of magazine   Date of issue

SNOWMOBILE racing
Cool 125.87 mph. il Hot Rod 24:92 S '71

Title of article   Article is illustrated   Volume and page number

Try a similar subject—*petroleum* instead of *oil.* Or try a larger subject—*Civil War* instead of *Battle of Gettysburg.* Also try inverting the subject to bring out the key word —*Gettysburg, Battle of.*

g. Alphabetical order may be word by word, with *house fly* coming before *housebreaking.* Or the order may be letter by letter. Then *house fly* is considered as one word, and it comes after *housebreaking.* Find out which order you're using.

4. Cards are to read—make sure you're getting the books you want. Also follow up the "see" and "see also" cards.

The How of Choosing a Book. Finding books is not enough. Some may be too difficult, some too brief. The idea is to choose the most suitable ones.

1. Check out the author's special knowledge of the subject. Look at the *title page*—the one with

KAPLAN, Allan
  Poem: I don't know whether I am light or heavy. Poetry 115:227 Ja '70
KAPLAN, Johanna
  Babysitting; story. Commentary 50:60-6 D '70
  Dragon lady; story. il Harper 241:78-83 Jl '70
  Sudden luck; story. Redbook 136:84-5 D '70

In addition to subject entries, the 'Readers' Guide' lists authors, followed by an alphabetical inventory of their works.

title, author, and publisher. It may tell something about the author and other books he or she has written. If the book is a paperback or has a paper jacket, the cover may provide such information. If neither of these yields any clues, try the preface or introduction.

2. Check to see how recent the information is. On the back of the title page is the *copyright page*. A copyright date—© 1971—tells you that the information is new as of roughly that year. The title page may give a different year—1974, say—but that only means the book was reprinted in 1974 after all the 1971 copies were sold.
3. Find out more about what the book is trying to cover, what kind of readers it's for. The preface or introduction will tell you. So will the *table of contents*, which gives an outline of the book. Skimming through parts of the *text*, or main body of the book, will tell you whether it's hard or easy to read. If you want to know whether a certain subject is discussed, check the *index* in the back. It lists all subjects alphabetically and tells what pages they're on.
4. Check for special features that may be useful. A list of illustrations often comes right after the table of contents. It includes the maps, charts, diagrams, or pictures in the book and tells where they can be found. Between the text and the index may be a glossary or bibliography. The *glossary* explains foreign or uncommon words. A *bibliography* may suggest materials for further reading. It may list the materials the author used in writing his book. Bibliographies are sometimes found at the end of chapters.

Reference Power. Some books are not to read through but to refer to for pieces of information. These are *reference books*. Because so many people use them, reference books usually have to stay in the library, though some may be taken home for a short time.

There are different types of reference books, differently arranged. Each answers different kinds of questions.

Frank Verticchio

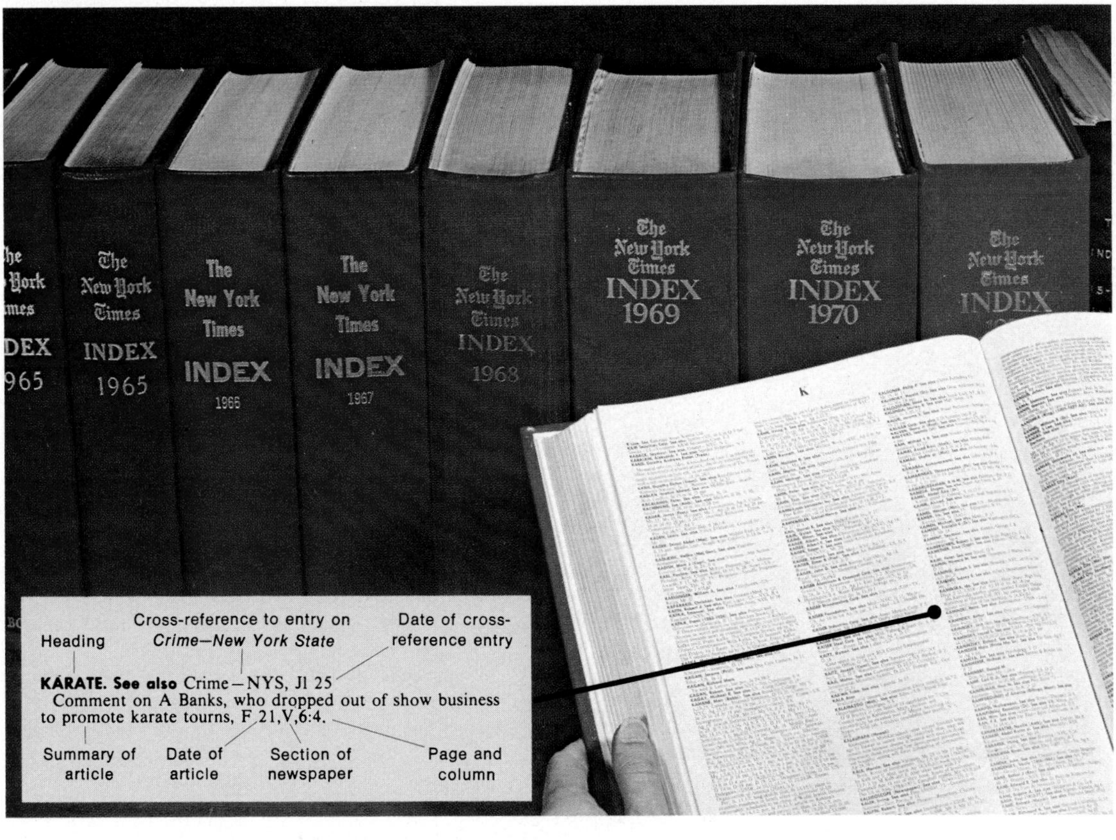

The New York Times INDEX 1965
The New York Times INDEX 1966
The New York Times INDEX 1967
The New York Times INDEX 1968
The New York Times INDEX 1969
The New York Times INDEX 1970
Heading
Cross-reference to entry on *Crime—New York State*
Date of cross-reference entry
KARATE. See also Crime—NYS, Jl 25
Comment on A Banks, who dropped out of show business to promote karate tours, F 21,V,6:4.
Summary of article
Date of article
Section of newspaper
Page and column

A **dictionary** answers questions about words. It gives meanings and spellings of a word, tells how it may be pronounced, breaks it up into syllables, shows where it came from, even lists synonyms and antonyms. At the tops of pages, *guide words* show first and last words on a page. They help in finding words faster. In the back may be special sections—facts about famous people, facts about places. In the front, how to use the dictionary is usually explained.

A **general encyclopedia,** usually a set of books, covers just about every subject. It has information about people, places, and things. Like a dictionary, an encyclopedia is alphabetically arranged. Every year parts of it are brought up to date, and a year-

book that goes along with it is put out. To help find information, an encyclopedia has *outside guides* (letters on each book, showing what part of the alphabet it covers), *inside guides* (guide words on top of each page), headings and subheadings to break up larger subjects, and an index. Some encyclopedias cover only one subject, such as religion or art. These are called *subject encyclopedias*.

An **atlas** is a book of maps. It also contains charts, tables, and other geographical facts. There are *political maps* to locate countries and cities, rivers and mountains; *physical maps* to show the highs and lows of the land; *economic maps* to show farming and business and industry; *historical maps* to show im-

Newspaper clippings, maps, photos, and sheet music are among the many items that are stored in a library's vertical files.

portant places and events in history. To read a map, a person needs to know the map symbols. These are explained in the front part of an atlas. The index in back helps locate places on a map.

A **gazetteer** is a geographical dictionary. Names of places, rivers, mountains, and so on are listed in alphabetical order. From a gazetteer a person can find out such facts as where a place is, how many people live in it, the height of a mountain, the length of a river. 'Webster's Geographical Dictionary' is a gazetteer.

Yearbooks, almanacs, and handbooks are sometimes hard to tell apart. A **yearbook** mostly reviews the important happenings or facts of a particular year. Ex-

amples include encyclopedia yearbooks. An **almanac,** too, comes out every year. But it concentrates more on giving up-to-date facts about hundreds of subjects—sports, births and deaths, foreign countries, famous people, radio and TV, dams and rivers. One of the best known is 'The World Almanac and Book of Facts'. It is one of the very few reference books in English with the index in front. A **handbook** is a guide to a particular subject—'Crowell's Handbook of Classical Mythology', 'Guinness Book of World Records', and 'Chilton's Auto Repair Manual'.

A **biographical dictionary** is a book of important people's names, with facts about their lives. Order is alphabetical by last name. Some biographical dictionaries list only living people ('Who's Who'), others only dead people ('Who Was Who'). Some list people from many countries, others from only one. Before using a biographical dictionary, it's important to know whether a person is still alive and what country that person comes from. Who is and isn't included is explained in the front part of the book.

A **book of quotations** is used to find out who said something worth quoting and exactly what the words were. It's a collection of phrases and sentences, usually from the works of many authors. But some such collections are from one author (Walt Whitman) or work (the Bible). Quotations may be arranged alphabetically by subject or by author—either alphabetically or by date, from ancient to modern times. Each such book has a large index that includes not only the subjects of quotations but also the key words.

An **index** can be a book by itself. It tells where to find information and items in other books or materials. 'Index to Plays in Collections', for instance, tells in which book or books a particular play can be found. To read an index, a person has to understand the many abbreviations explained in front of the book. A person may also have to ask the librarian for help in getting materials mentioned in the index. Generally not all of them are in the library.

A **bibliography,** too, can be a book by itself. Some bibliographies not only list books and other materials but tell something about them. Often a bibliography is on a particular subject.

A **directory** gives information about people, organizations, or institutions. Names and addresses are listed. A telephone book is a directory.

Of all the types of reference books, dictionaries and encyclopedias are probably the most used. They are also the first works to consult, as a rule. It's difficult to look up a subject that isn't spelled right or to find out about things that aren't clearly understood. Those are the problems a dictionary can help solve. An encyclopedia, too, can make things clearer. In trying to find out about a subject, the person who checks the encyclopedia first—even before the catalog—can get a fast focus on the big picture.

Even an encyclopedia is just the beginning. In each subject there are hundreds of special reference works such as handbooks, indexes, and bibliographies. Someone who wants to dig has to find out what the reference works in a particular subject have to offer. It's also important to check more than one reference work to compare different ways of looking at the same facts. (*See also* Reference Books.)

Nonbooks: Magazines and Newspapers. Because it takes time to put out a book, even a brand-new one is yesterday's facts. For many kinds of information—the height of a mountain, the spelling of a word—newness isn't too important. Such things aren't likely to change or change much for a long time. But for what's happening now, special kinds of materials are needed. These include magazines and newspapers.

A magazine comes out periodically—weekly, twice a month, monthly. So magazines are sometimes called

card for a magazine, won't help find articles on a certain subject. To locate such newspaper articles, 'The New York Times Index' is very useful. It's a key to other newspapers, too, because most of them have pretty much the same news on the same day. Like the 'Readers' Guide', 'The New York Times Index' comes in many volumes, each covering one year. To save space, many libraries keep back volumes of the *New York Times* and other newspapers on microfilm.

'Readers' Guide': a Guide. Anyone who can use the card catalog can learn to use 'Readers' Guide'. It is one of the easiest indexes to work with.

Authors and subjects of articles are listed in heavy type—**SPIRO, Howard M.; SPONGES; SPORTS;**

Large amounts of printed material can be photographically reduced for storage on microfilm. Microfilm is commonly seen as long strips of film wound on reels, with each frame of the film containing the image of at least one page of the material.

periodicals. Every six months or so, a library puts the back issues of some magazines together and has them bound in book covers. This is called a *volume*.

A card in the catalog tells the name of a magazine, which volumes are in the library, and so on. But if someone wants articles on a certain subject, the card won't help. For that kind of information, there are special indexes. Of these, probably the best known is the 'Readers' Guide to Periodical Literature', which indexes articles of about 150 magazines. Like those magazines, 'Readers' Guide' itself is a periodical. So it comes in volumes, each volume covering one or two years, with the dates printed on the spine.

The catalog card for a newspaper, like the catalog

SPRAGUE, Marshall. Under each author heading are listed articles by that author; under each subject heading, articles on that subject. Titles are in alphabetical order by first word. Some subjects are broken up into smaller and smaller subjects. **Manned flights** is a division of the subject **SPACE flight to the moon.** And *Apollo 17 flight* is a subdivision of **Manned flights.**

Sometimes a person is both a subject of articles and an author of other articles. Then articles by that person are listed first. And a subheading **about** is followed by articles about that person.

To use 'Readers' Guide', there are many abbreviations to figure out. The names of most magazines are abbreviated—*Pop Mech* for *Popular Mechanics*,

Bsns W for *Business Week*, and so forth. These are explained in front of each 'Guide'. So are the other abbreviations used. To understand a 'Readers' Guide' entry, a person has to learn its parts and the order of those parts. For instance, an entry on Mark Spitz, the Olympic swimmer, reads:

SPITZ, Mark
  All out to be number 1; with report by
    B. Bruns. il pors Life 63:47–8+ S15 '67
That translates into title of article ("All Out to Be Number One"), author (B. Bruns), illustrated article (il), with portrait photos (pors), name of magazine (*Life*), volume number (63), page numbers (47–48), continued on later pages (+), and date of issue

volumes or for John Dillinger in 1970's volumes. **Three** is to use the front of the *Guide* to clear up reading problems. **Four** is to copy entries that seem to do the job. That means title of article, author (if any), name of magazine, volume and page numbers, and date of issue. **Five,** of course, is to get hold of the actual magazines.

More Nonbooks: Vertical File. Every library has a place for clippings. Such things as newspaper articles on local people and places are worth cutting out and keeping. The same is true of special articles and pictures from magazines. Clippings are usually put in folders, alphabetically arranged by subject. The folders are kept in a deep-drawer cabinet called a

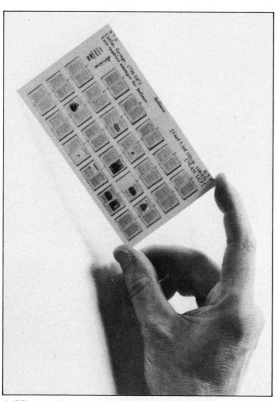

A Microcard is a positive print of reduced images produced from a microfilm negative. Because this reduction process uses opaque stock rather than transparent film, an array of images can be stored on both sides of the Microcard.

(September 15, 1967). It's important to keep in mind that the number before the colon is the volume number. Numbers after the colon are page numbers.

Some poems and stories are also indexed in 'Readers' Guide'. Poems are listed only under author, stories under author and title. Poems and stories in magazines can also be found with the help of such aids as 'Granger's Index to Poetry' and 'Short Story Index'.

There's a routine to 'Readers' Guide' that can save a lot of stumbling around. **One** is to find out what magazines are in the library. It's best to know beforehand which articles may take a while to get. **Two** is to get the right volumes of the *Guide*. There's not much point in looking for Elvis Presley in 1930's

vertical file. There are no catalog cards for individual clippings, but many catalogs have cross reference cards to the subjects in the file.

The vertical file has *pamphlets*, too. These are paperbound booklets, each often dealing with one subject. Like newspapers and magazines, many pamphlets give fast, up-to-date facts—on jobs, for instance—too new to be in books. Information that's hard to get elsewhere often comes in pamphlet form. Some libraries have special shelves or boxes for pamphlets, where they are arranged by subject. There are indexes for pamphlets as well as for magazines. *The Vertical File Index* is widely known. Also helpful is the *Monthly Catalog of United States Government Publications.*

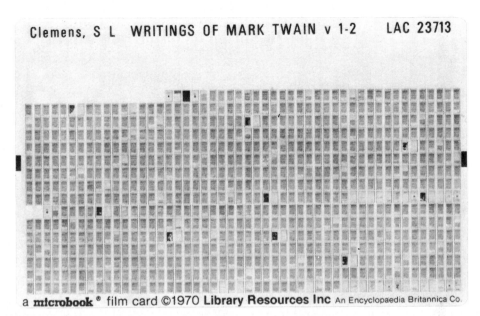

Clemens, S L   WRITINGS OF MARK TWAIN v 1-2   LAC 23713

a **microbook** ® film card ©1970 **Library Resources Inc** An Encyclopaedia Britannica Co.

Hebrew University of Jerusalem

A microfiche is a small sheet of microfilm containing from a few to many hundreds of negative or positive photographic images arranged in rows and columns. An entire book or even several books can be reproduced on a single microfiche.

A vertical file may also include maps, charts, graphs, posters, postcards, photos, and even sheet music. Some such items may be kept in a separate place—in a picture file or map file, for example.

Nonbooks: Talking and Otherwise. The what of a library is books, including paperbacks; magazines and newspapers; clippings and pamphlets and other vertical file material; and more, much more. Anything that's to learn with—and to dream with—is the stuff of libraries. There are records and sound tapes of music, poetry, language lessons; videotapes of neighborhood people and places, of amateur plays. For would-be artists and art lovers, color slides of buildings and paintings and sculpture are available. Films and

filmstrips show the growth of a plant, the pollution of a stream, the agony of a violin lesson. Not even the best map shows relationships between places as well as a globe, so libraries have globes and other models. Specimens are sometimes arranged to show how a piece of tree becomes a pencil, or how crude oil is changed into gasoline.

Then there are mini-nonbooks: microfilm, Microcard, microfiche. These hold greatly reduced pictures of newspaper, magazine, and book pages that must be read with machines. The way records, films, and other nonbook materials are arranged varies from one library to another. Such materials may be listed in the main catalog or in separate catalogs near where they are kept.

165

A versatile and well-stocked library can offer its patrons many nonbook items, including motion picture films, filmstrips, photographs, color slides, phonograph records, and tape recordings.

Public Library of Cincinnati and Hamilton County, Ohio

LIBRARY PEOPLE

Without people a library would be a mere place, a warehouse. Above all it is people using a library who make it come alive, but people are also needed to make a library work. Even the computerized memory cells of the future could not function without library people—the professionals called *librarians* and the many who help them.

The Who of Library Service: Nonlibrarians

Most libraries are not run by librarians alone. If it were not for other library workers, in many places a person could not get a library card, find a clipping in the vertical file, use a microfilm reader, or take out a book.

On any given day, one person may return half a dozen books, a magazine or two, and several records to the library. Multiply that by several hundred or several thousand, and the result is a mountain of materials that must be sorted and put back in the right place. This is usually the work of a library *page*. Sorting and shelving are also done by temporary student employees, or *student assistants*. Pages have to be accurate—a book or magazine or record misplaced is as good as lost for days, weeks, or months.

Library clerks work out in front or behind the scenes. A clerk who deals with the public may help a youngster register for a library card, check materials in and out, collect overdue fines, help renew or reserve materials, or show someone how to operate a copying machine. A copying machine or charge-out machine can be mastered in a matter of minutes. What can't be mastered as easily is a pleasant attitude toward all people, springing from a desire to help them. Such an attitude is a must for all library people dealing with the public.

A clerk who prefers to work behind the scenes may file and keep records, check in new materials and get them ready for use, type overdue notices in libraries where this isn't done by computer, operate a teletype, feed a computer the information needed to order a book or record or film. Both out-front and behind-the-scenes clerks need a high school diploma usually, or the ability to pass a civil service exam. All clerks work under the supervision of a librarian or library aide, and student assistants often do clerical work.

Library aides assist with many of the librarian's jobs. A library aide dealing with the public may help people find materials, answer easier reference questions, explain the library's services. Behind-the-scenes aides may operate audiovisual equipment, arrange displays, keep up the vertical file, look up prices and other information the librarian needs to order materials, supervise pages and clerks. For supervising others, aides must be tactful, firm, and able to follow the librarian's instructions as well as translate those instructions to others. A job as library aide requires at least a high school diploma, and many who do such work are *library technicians*, with two years of college. Aides who are college graduates are sometimes called *library associates*. Often they and library technicians do the more skilled types of library work.

Other library workers include audiovisual technicians to inspect and repair the audiovisual hardware of a library, book repairers to mend and rebind books and other materials, artists and photographers to prepare displays and public relations materials, and maintenance workers to keep library buildings in good condition. People with advanced training in related fields such as computer science and accounting also work in libraries.

The Who of Library Service: Librarians

A librarian in a modern school may be called a *media specialist*. In a computerized business library, the librarian may be called an *information scientist*, or *documentalist*. There are children's librarians and young adult librarians in public libraries, institutional librarians in hospital and prison libraries, university librarians in university libraries. All librarians, whatever their work, have this in common: they are members of a profession in the service of mankind—like teachers, like doctors. Librarians also share knowledge and skills learned in college, in library school after college, and on the job.

The Three Faces of Librarianship. A librarian does three main kinds of work: selecting materials for the library, organizing them so that they'll be easy to find and use, and helping people get materials or information they need. To select materials, a librarian finds out what the library's users and potential users need. Rarely, if ever, can a library afford to buy all materials needed. So the librarian must be an expert not only on what materials are available but on which are more dependable, more useful to the library than others. To make room for new materials, the librarian regularly reviews the library collection, removing materials no longer useful. A good collection offers many points of view on any given subject. An important part of the librarian's job is to resist pressure from special groups who want to get rid of—or add—material because of the point of view.

If it weren't arranged, if it didn't have a catalog, a library would be a trackless jungle of information. That's where the organizer of materials comes in. This librarian examines every new book, record, film, or other item to determine what it's about. After the librarian decides what the subject is and how the item is related to other materials in the library, the item is *cataloged*, or described. Most libraries use card catalogs, but some modern libraries use a book catalog made and printed by computer.

Helping people get materials or information they need is circulation and reference work. The librarian in charge of circulation supervises the use of all materials. In many libraries, this librarian works behind the scenes. Clerks usually issue library cards, lend and receive materials, keep records of materials borrowed, even help people find materials they want. The way in which each such job is done is determined by the librarian in charge. Much circulation work is automated in libraries today—there are computerized systems to keep a record of materials lent and returned, for instance.

Nobody knows all the answers. The librarian in reference pursues a deeper wisdom—to understand all the questions. To learn what exactly the questioner is trying to find out, a reference librarian must be an expert interviewer. The whole point of reference work is personal assistance, either finding the answer or guiding a person to it. The same question may call for different types of help—for people of different ages and backgrounds, for example. Much reference work is done by phone.

The Librarian as Specialist. The three main kinds of library work are part of every librarian's education.

But, as in other professions, many librarians become specialists. An *acquisitions librarian* specializes in locating and ordering materials, a *cataloger* in organizing materials, a *reference librarian* in helping people get information. In many school and public libraries there are *media specialists* and *readers' advisers*. A media specialist is an expert on the use of all materials, both print and nonprint. A readers' adviser helps choose materials or prepares a special reading list for a particular person. Readers' advisers in hospital and prison libraries practice *bibliotherapy*, helping treat the sick, the disturbed, the downhearted with books and other materials.

Public librarians may specialize by age group of user. A children's librarian must know about such things as child behavior, what children study in school, nonprint materials and their uses, the teaching of reading, children's literature, and how to tell a story. Guiding children in their reading is an important part of the work. So are selecting materials, holding story hours, working with parents and Parent-Teacher Associations, visiting nearby classrooms, teaching the use of the library, and planning such special projects as Book Week.

A young adult librarian works with roughly the teenage group. Such a librarian must know what young adults are like, what they study in school, what they read and listen to and look at in their free time. It is especially important for a librarian working with this age group to be outgoing, unflappable, imaginative, and socially aware. The young adult librarian selects materials, keeping up with ever-changing teenage interests; acts as a readers' adviser; visits schools to talk about books and other materials; and explains how to use a library. An important part of work with young adults is planning programs for them.

The DIALOG information retrieval system of Lockheed Missiles and Space Company has thousands of references from material in the firm's technical library stored on computer tapes.

Lockheed Missiles and Space Co.

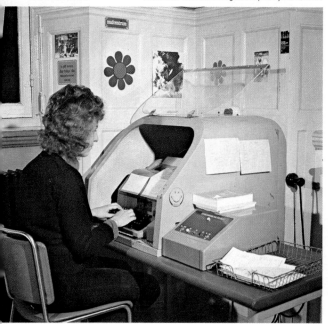

Librarians use Telex machines to receive and answer requests from other libraries for loans of library materials.

A public librarian may also specialize in the hard-to-reach, neglected, and unserved. These include school dropouts, the elderly, the uneducated, ghetto dwellers, the rural poor, and minorities. Many in such groups have reading problems and are reluctant or unable to come to a library. If there is one ingredient a librarian in such work needs above all, it is heart. To bring hope to the hopeless and a feeling of belonging to the outcast, professionalism is not enough. Also needed are initiative and imagination to draw such people to the library as well as to take the library to the people. A contagious enthusiasm for books is a must. So is a strong background in nonprint materials because they draw many people in such groups. The librarian should also know about the teaching of reading and the use of easy-to-read materials for adults.

Many academic and research librarians are subject or language specialists. Such librarians usually have special training in music, or African materials, or Spanish and Portuguese literature, or the sciences, or whatever. Subject specialists are found also in government libraries—*archivists* specializing in historical papers, librarians specializing in law.

There are many subject specialists in special libraries. The special librarian makes searches for information—helping an engineer gather materials for a report, preparing a reading list on water pollution for a steel company executive. Because engineers, doctors, and other specialists don't have time to read everything published in their field, the special librarian may review and summarize new articles and reports. Such summaries, or *abstracts*, keep busy people up to date and help them decide what to read

for more information. Another part of special library work is having important articles and reports translated. Information searches are made more and more with the help of computers. Some translation, too, is done by machine, but there are serious problems involved (*see* Language, section "The Trouble with Translation"). Because special librarians often make much use of other libraries, they must know not only their own but other library collections in their subjects. Special librarians often have advanced training in the field of concentration of their library. They should also have a background in library technology, automation being common in special libraries.

Many librarians do not specialize. They are *generalists*, working with a variety of groups and subjects. Included among generalists are most school librarians. School librarians work closely with teachers in helping students get the reading habit, learn study skills, and understand how to use a library. Besides an understanding of children or young adults, school librarians need a background in print and nonprint materials. In many places also, a school librarian must be qualified as a teacher. This is especially important as the school library becomes more and more a learning lab, an extension of the classroom.

The Librarian as Information Scientist. A librarian is a mover of ideas, of information from one mind to another. So it is not enough to know library science. A librarian must understand the bigger picture called *information science*, of which library science is only a part. To teach the use of a library, a librarian must understand how people think when they attack look-it-up problems. That's part of information science. To index a vertical file a librarian must understand how language works. That, too, is part of information science. A librarian often has to know something about computers to work with them. In addition he or she may need some math to use computer language. Both mathematics and computer technology are part of information science. To run a library, the librarian must learn techniques for analyzing and improving a system. Information science includes systems management, too.

Many librarians who work in automated libraries are called *information scientists*. But the term is not used by all such librarians. Basically every librarian must be an information scientist.

The Librarian as a Person. A librarian is not an old lady with a built-in "Shhh. . . ." The libraries of the world have room enough—and work enough—for many types of people. There are reference jobs for the I-want-to-work-with-people type; jobs with the underprivileged for the I-want-to-improve-the-world type; jobs as catalogers and bibliographers for the I-want-to-do-research type. There are jobs for close-to-home and away-from-home types, for small-library and large-library types, for specialists and generalists, book addicts and nonbook addicts, teacher types, leader types. While librarians do not run to one type, though, they do have some things in common.

• **A librarian serves the people of a community**—a college, a school, a plastics company—either directly or indirectly.

• **A librarian is a matchmaker,** bringing people and knowledge together.

• **A librarian is sometimes the uninvited.** Not everyone who needs help asks for it, and being a "come-to" librarian isn't always enough.

• **A librarian is a bookeater.** Ideas come in many kinds of packages, most of them books, and a librarian has to know what's between the covers.

• **A librarian is curious.** He or she has not only an itch to know but an open mind that doesn't fear new ideas.

• **A librarian has a sense of order.** Everybody in a library has to know where things are and how to find them, quickly.

And that isn't all . . .

Tips for Tomorrow's Librarian. A library is not a place to get away from people, nor a sanctuary from the disagreements of the outside world. Even librarians behind the scenes must work with others. As for controversy, the librarian is where the action is, dealing with a continual flow of new ideas in the books and nonbooks that come to the library.

Anyone who wants to be a librarian must decide what type of work most interests him or her. As with any profession, it is necessary to plan ahead. A good general education is essential to someone who is going to guide and teach others. So are a good reading background and a knowledge of nonprint materials and automation. For specialist library work, training in that specialty is often required. An advanced degree is needed to teach in a library school or to run a large library. All librarians must have at least a college degree and library school beyond that.

Pamphlet material on library jobs and on scholarships is available in most libraries. Library school catalogs, found in large public and college libraries, tell what various schools have to offer. The schools listed on the following page meet certain requirements of the American Library Association. Many excellent schools in Canada, the United States, and elsewhere are not included in the list.

Library Power: The Togetherness of Associations. Librarians the world over work together in many associations to improve library service. Of these, the oldest and largest is the American Library Association, or ALA, founded in 1876 with the help of Melvil Dewey. Among the divisions of the ALA are associations for public librarians, school librarians, academic and research librarians. Most special librarians have their own associations—for medical librarians, law librarians, and so on.

The work of associations and other organizations friendly to libraries crosses national boundaries. The ALA has helped found library schools in several countries. It also works to improve library service in many parts of the world. So do agencies of various nations and of the United Nations (UNESCO, UNICEF). Private groups such as the Asia Foundation and Ford Foundation are also library builders, especially in Asia, Africa, and Latin America.

Just as libraries share with one another, so do the associations. The ALA and the Canadian Library Association (CLA), for instance, have worked closely together since the founding of the CLA in 1946. The International Federation of Library Associations, representing more than 50 countries, works at international library cooperation. So do international associations in particular fields—school library, medical library, and music library associations for instance.

The Library in the Eye of Time

Libraries were born as collections of records—on animal bones and tortoise shells, clay tablets, papyrus and silk scrolls, or animal skins. Such collections go back some 4,500 to 6,000 years in Asia and Africa. Elsewhere, libraries developed much later.

Library science students learn to use the card catalog at the library of Makerere University in Kampala, Uganda. Trained librarians are instrumental in the efforts to decrease illiteracy in developing nations.

UNESCO

A World of Libraries: Yesterday

All libraries have their roots in ancient times. To understand the library of today, it is necessary to know something about the history of libraries.

Bone Libraries and Others: Ancient Times. The earliest known libraries were connected with palaces and temples. In China, records of the Shang dynasty (1767?–1123? B.C.) were written on animal bones and tortoise shells. An early library called "The Healing Place of the Soul," in the palace of Egypt's King Ramses II (1304?–1237 B.C.) at Thebes, consisted of thousands of papyrus scrolls. Among the most important libraries in the ancient Near East was the palace library of Ashurbanipal (668?–627? B.C.) at Nineveh in Assyria. This early type of national library, collected "for the sake of distant days," consisted of over 30,000 clay tablets. Early librarians were usually priests, teachers, or scholars. The first known Chinese librarian was the philosopher Lao Tse, who was appointed keeper of the royal historical records for the Chou rulers about 550 B.C.

Early types of public and academic libraries were founded in ancient Greece. Public libraries were opened in Athens perhaps as early as the sixth century B.C., but they weren't lending libraries. People who could read generally studied or copied scrolls in the library. A well-known Athenian library was that of the Lyceum, a kind of college founded by the philosopher Aristotle in 335 B.C. The most famous library built by the Greeks was attached to a kind of university called the Museum in Alexandria, Egypt. Scholars were encouraged to use and even borrow scrolls from the Museum Library, which had a vast collection.

A library located at Pergamum (near present-day Smyrna, Turkey) began using parchment instead of papyrus for its scrolls around 200 B.C. Parchment is made from thin layers of animal skin. Another animal-skin library was an important part of a Hebrew religious community founded at Qumran, Palestine, probably early in the first century B.C. This library contained the "Dead Sea Scrolls." In China, paper was invented about A.D. 100 and soon began to replace other book materials such as silk and bamboo.

Roman libraries were much like those of Greece. The most famous public library in the city of Rome was the Ulpian Library, founded in A.D. 114. It had separate sections for its Latin and Greek papyrus scrolls. The Romans were great builders of public libraries, establishing them throughout the empire. The Imperial Library, founded at Constantinople in the Eastern Roman Empire in about A.D. 330, attracted scholars from all over the world to its great collection. In early Roman libraries, scrolls were kept in pigeonholes or on shelves in the walls. Gradually papyrus scrolls were replaced by parchment sheets, folded and sewn in book form. These were kept in book chests.

None of the great libraries of ancient times survived. Some were destroyed in fires, some by volcanoes, others in wars and invasions. Many libraries simply died of neglect.

Libraries for Saints and Scholars. In ancient India, great libraries were built in the Buddhist monastery centers. Among the most famous was that of the Buddhist University of Nalanda, founded about A.D. 414 in what is today Bihar. Temple and pagoda libraries were common also in Buddhist monasteries in Asia.

Papyrus rolls lined the shelves of ancient Greek and Roman libraries. The Romans called the roll a *volumen*, from which the English word *volume* is derived. The great Museum Library at Alexandria, Egypt, held many thousands of these early books.

The Bettmann Archive

Keystone

This earthenware statuette represents an oxcart used in China more than a thousand years ago to transport books. Imperial libraries, which originated as royal archives, were maintained by the emperors, many of whom were patrons of literature.

Christian monasteries were founded in Egypt, Palestine, and nearby areas during the second and third centuries A.D. But it was not until after the fall of the Roman Empire in A.D. 476 that monastery libraries became vitally important in the West. A famous monastery library was founded in about 550 by Flavius Cassiodorus, a Roman politician, on his family estate in Calabria, Italy. In Cassiodorus' Vivarium monastery was a *scriptorium*, where books were carefully copied by hand. Copying of books was also part of the routine in the Italian monastery at Monte Cassino, which was founded in 529 by St. Benedict. The scriptorium idea took hold in monastery libraries from Greece to Iceland, helping preserve the knowledge of the past in Europe throughout the Dark Ages. Other notable monastery libraries included those at St. Gallen in Switzerland, Corbie in France, and Fulda in Germany. The typical monastery library contained a small number of books kept in one or two book chests in or near the scriptorium. Most books were of parchment. There was some interlibrary loan, books being lent for copying as well as reading.

The cathedrals of Europe were also religious schools. Because their libraries were meant for educational reading, they commonly contained more books of a nonreligious nature than did the monastic libraries. Also, books were generally more plentiful in cathedral libraries. Reading desks with shelves replaced book chests in later cathedral libraries, with reference-type books often chained to the desks. To make information easier to find, libraries had devices such as bookwheels, which rotated so that the reader could refer to as many as a dozen books without changing position. Better known cathedral libraries were at Canterbury and York in England, Notre Dame and Rouen in France, Bamberg and Hildesheim in Germany, Toledo and Barcelona in Spain.

The early Moslems and Byzantines built many university and public-type libraries. Shortly after he became Caliph of Baghdad in 813, al-Mamun founded the "House of Wisdom," a great university. Its library was open to scholars from all over the Moslem world. A famous library was that of the University of Constantinople, opened by the Byzantines in about 850. One of the best academic libraries in Africa today is that of al-Azhar University, founded in Cairo, Egypt, in about 970. University and public-type libraries were scattered throughout the Moslem world—from North Africa to Central Asia, as well as in Moslem Sicily and Spain.

Books in Moslem libraries covered all subjects. Sometimes books on different subjects were located in different rooms, with a subject specialist in charge of each room. Students and scholars were generally encouraged to use and borrow books. In many public libraries, there were not only rooms for reading but for meetings and debates. Most of the early Moslem libraries were eventually destroyed through natural disasters, war, and neglect.

China, too, had early academic libraries. From Sung dynasty times (960–1279) on, libraries of the Imperial Academy and provincial colleges were open to all students. However, in Europe the earliest universities had no libraries at first.

Great Libraries Take Shape. From the 1200's on, some of today's great academic libraries began to take shape in Europe. France's University of Paris had a library by about 1250, when Robert de Sorbon gave them a collection of books. In England libraries were established at Pembroke College, Cambridge University in 1347 and at Merton College, Oxford University in 1377. The University of Prague (now Charles University) started a library in 1348, which eventually became the core of the national library of Czechoslovakia. In 1365 the University of Vienna began its library. The oldest library in Poland, that of the University of Cracow, dates from before 1400, as does the University of Coimbra library in Portugal. Other early universities that had some

sort of library by the 1400's included those at Bologna and Florence in Italy, Salamanca in Spain, Heidelberg and Cologne in Germany, Basel in Switzerland, and Copenhagen in Denmark.

Some of the world's outstanding research libraries started in the 1400's. The private family library begun by Cosimo de'Medici (1389–1464) and expanded by his grandson Lorenzo later became the Laurentian Library in Florence, Italy. A former librarian to Cosimo de'Medici, Pope Nicholas V began to build up the Vatican Library in Vatican City about 1450. It is a world-famous research library today. In Istanbul, Turkey, the Topkapi Museum library contains Islamic manuscripts collected by sultans, generals, and officials of the Turkish empire since 1452.

Many of today's national libraries began in the 1400's and 1500's. The Marcian national library in Venice, one of Italy's many national libraries, originated with the gift of a book collection to that city in 1468 by Johannes Cardinal Bessarion. The history of France's National Library in Paris dates back largely to the late 1400's, when it was the royal library of Louis XI, a continuation of an even earlier royal library founded by Charles V. Another royal library of the late 1400's, that of England's Henry VII, developed into the British Museum in London, one of the world's largest libraries. The origins of the Austrian national library in Vienna lie well before 1526, when it was the royal library of the Hapsburgs. Sweden's

Arabs founded great libraries throughout the Islamic world—such as those at Baghdad (now in Iraq), at Cairo, Egypt, and at Córdoba, Spain. This drawing from a 13th-century miniature depicts an Arab library in about A.D. 1000.

The Bettmann Archive

national library, the Royal Swedish Library in Stockholm, began as a collection of books brought together by the first Protestant king, Gustavus Vasa (1523–60).

After 1500 there were more and larger university libraries in Europe. Printing had come to Europe by about 1450, making large numbers of cheaper books available. In addition, as monasteries were closed in many places, the books and manuscripts often ended up in university libraries. One of Spain's great libraries, at the University of Madrid, began in the 1500's. So did those at the universities of Wittenberg and Leipzig in Germany, Graz in Austria, Wroclaw in Poland, Vilna in Lithuania, and Ljubljana in what is today Yugoslavia. In the 1500's also, academic libraries began to appear in Latin America. A library was established at the University of Santo Domingo in the Dominican Republic in 1538. Among the famous libraries of Latin America are those at the University of San Marcos in Lima, Peru, and the National Autonomous University of Mexico in Mexico City, both founded in the late 1500's. The University of Mexico library later became the National Library.

The year 1558 marks the beginning of one of Germany's great libraries—the Bavarian State Library in Munich. One of the great history libraries of Spain, the Escorial Library near Madrid, dates back to 1575. The University of Leiden in the Netherlands, with a small library, was founded in 1575. The Bodleian Library at Oxford University originated in about 1598 when Sir Thomas Bodley began to rebuild an Oxford library that had been largely destroyed. In Dublin, Ireland, the library of Trinity College began as a gift of books by the English army that defeated the Irish in the Battle of Kinsale (1601).

One of the many great libraries of Italy, the Ambrosian Library in Milan, was founded in 1609. Libraries were established at Córdoba National University in Argentina (about 1614) and at the University of Uppsala in Sweden (1620). Hungary's largest academic library, that of Eötvös Loránd University in Budapest, dates back to 1635. The first academic libraries in North America were those of the Jesuit College of Quebec (1635) and Harvard University in Massachusetts (1638). The Harvard library started with books and money donated by John Harvard, a Massachusetts clergyman. In gratitude the university was named after him, and the name of the city was changed from Newtowne to Cambridge because he had graduated from Cambridge University in England. Finland's national library, at Helsinki University, had its beginnings in Åbo (now Turku) in 1640. After a fire destroyed much of it, the library was moved to Helsinki and rebuilt there along with the new university. In Paris, France, a cardinals' college library was founded by Jules Cardinal Mazarin in 1643—the Mazarin Library. One of its librarians, Gabriel Naudé, worked out a system of running a library that is still used today.

Three important national libraries were formed in the late 1600's. Frederick III, who ruled Denmark from 1648 to 1670, acquired the collection that was to

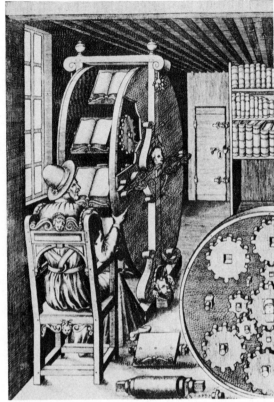

Newberry Library, Chicago

The book-wheel, a device somewhat resembling a waterwheel, was used to make several books readily available at one time. A reader turning the book-wheel could consult several volumes arranged on its shelves without ever having to leave his seat. Book-wheels began to be used in European cathedral and monastic libraries during the late Middle Ages.

Newberry Library, Chicago

During the Middle Ages, monasteries and cathedrals were the guardians of classical learning, and many had large libraries.

Monastic scribes copied ancient manuscripts in a room called a "scriptorium" (above).

The Laurentian Library (below) in Florence, Italy, was founded by the Medici family during the Renaissance. The most fre-

quently used books and the valuable illuminated manuscripts were often chained to the shelves for safekeeping.

The traveling library of Sir Thomas Egerton, lord chancellor of England under King James I, was composed of miniature books on history, theology, and poetry. The Egerton family collection was one of the great private libraries of Europe.

become the Danish Royal Library in Copenhagen. The German State Library of East Berlin dates from 1661, where it began as the private library of Frederick William, ruler of Brandenburg. Later it was known as the Prussian State Library. When Germany was divided after World War II, part of the collection remained in East Berlin and part was moved to West Berlin and the University of Marburg. In Edinburgh the Advocates' Library was formed in 1682 as the private library of Scottish lawyers. It became the National Library in 1925.

The Idea of a Public Library: Early Types. The idea of a public library goes at least as far back as ancient Greece and Rome. There citizens able to read could study or copy the books in the library. Such libraries were also common throughout the Muslim world from about the 1200's. In Europe early types of public libraries began to appear from the 1400's on, as more and more people learned to read.

Community or town libraries were opened in such places as London, England (1423); Lyons, France (about 1530); Edinburgh, Scotland (1580); Antwerp, Belgium (about 1609); Boston, Massachusetts (about 1656); and Frankfurt-am-Main, Germany (1668). Generally such libraries did not *circulate*, or lend, books, and they were open for a few hours only.

Collections were often poorly arranged, and books were so scholarly or dull that few people used them. Frequently the person in charge was a "bookkeeper," neither experienced nor interested in library work.

Parochial or parish libraries for public use began to appear in the late 1600's. Many of them were founded by an Englishman, Reverend Thomas Bray of the Society for the Propagation of the Gospel in Foreign Parts. Collections of books—mostly of a religious nature—were put into parish churches. A Bray library was opened as early as 1698 in New York City. Churches in various places soon followed the example of the Bray libraries.

Rental and subscription libraries charged fees for the use of books. *Rental libraries*—in bookshops or peddlers' packs, on boats or carts or wagons—were known in many parts of the world. For small fees, people could read books they couldn't afford to buy— everything from religious books to joke books.

Subscription libraries were formed by groups of readers, usually well-to-do. These people paid dues that were used to buy books, rent a reading room, and perhaps hire a keeper of the books. In return for dues paid, members could use the reading room and borrow books from the collection. Perhaps the earliest subscription library was the Library Company of Phila-

The Bodleian Library at Oxford University in England was dedicated in 1602 by Sir Thomas Bodley to replace a library destroyed by royal purges during the Reformation.

The Evanston (Ill.) Public Library was an early user of book wagons. As public libraries improved around the turn of the 20th century, many urban libraries extended services to outlying areas.

delphia, Pa., founded by Benjamin Franklin in 1731. Canada's first such library, established in Quebec in 1780 by Governor Frederick Haldemand, stocked books in both French and English. The National Library of Singapore began as a subscription library. Subscription libraries went by many names—atheneums, lyceums, and others. The *social libraries* of the 1700's were a type of subscription library.

Mercantile libraries and mechanics' institutes, for office and shop workers, also charged small fees. They began as self-improvement libraries. One of the first mechanics' institutes was the Birmingham Artisans' Library in England (1795). Early mechanics' institutes were opened in the United States at Bristol, Conn. (1818), and in Canada at St. John's, Newfoundland (1827). A mechanics' institute in Toronto, Ont., later became the Toronto Public Library, and the Auckland Public Library in New Zealand owes its origin to an early mechanics' institute founded there. An early mercantile library was the Mercantile library in Philadelphia (1821).

Early **school district libraries,** in spite of the name, were a type of public library. The collections, usually kept in schools, were meant largely for adults. Libraries of this type were established in such places as France, Canada, and the United States from about the 1830's on. Later, school district libraries were planned more for students.

YMCA libraries began to appear in Canada and the United States in 1851, when the Young Men's Christian Association was founded. Open to the public even on Sunday's, YMCA reading rooms contained newspapers, magazines, and books. But the religious nature

of such libraries tended to limit the number of users.

In the late 1800's **railroad libraries** appeared. They included popular books for the use of railroad employees as well as passengers. Beginning in 1881, employees of the Baltimore and Ohio Railroad could borrow books from its library in Baltimore, Md. The Atchison, Topeka and Sante Fe Railway had a passenger library on every long-distance train.

Great Libraries Multiply. Most of today's national libraries trace their beginnings to the 1700's and 1800's. But great libraries of other types developed during that time also.

Yale University in New Haven, Conn., was started by 11 ministers, each of whom brought a few books for a library. At the urging of Father Pedro Robinet of the Society of Jesus, King Philip V opened the Royal Library in Madrid in 1712. It is Spain's National Library today. One of the Soviet Union's great science libraries, that of the Academy of Science in Leningrad, was founded in 1714. At the University of Göttingen in Germany (1737), librarian Christian Heine began to build a great collection.

What is now the Princeton University library began at the College of New Jersey about 1750, as did the library of the University of Pennsylvania (then an academy) in Philadelphia. The Soviet Union's oldest university library, at the Moscow State University, was founded in 1755. At about the same time King's College (now Columbia University) opened its library in New York City. Dartmouth College in New Hampshire was chartered as a college in 1769, but its library began several years earlier as a collection of books gathered together by the school founder, Eleazar Weelock.

The children's story hour and cinema show has always been a popular activity at the Baroda Central Library in Baroda, India. The establishment of this library in the early 1900's spearheaded a public library movement throughout India.

Kenya National Library Services

A librarian at the Kenya Children's Library in Nairobi, Kenya, helps young patrons check out their favorite books.

The collection of the library of Seoul National University in Korea dates back to 1776, when it was the Chang-Duk Palace Library. In 1778 the Museum Library in Djakarta began its collection of Indonesian culture. Sicily's National Library in Palermo was opened as the Royal Library by Ferdinand I, King of the Two Sicilies, in 1782. In 1786 Italy's National Braidense Library in Milan opened. A library was begun at Central University in Quito, Ecuador, in 1787. Portugal's National Library in Lisbon was founded in 1796; that of the Netherlands—the Royal Library in The Hague—in 1798.

One of the world's largest libraries, the Library of Congress in the United States, started in 1800 when the government moved to the new city of Washington, D.C. Hungary's National Széchenyi Library in Budapest goes back to 1802, when Count Ferenc Széchenyi gave about 10,000 books to the nation for public use. National libraries were founded in Buenos Aires, Argentina (1810); Rio de Janeiro, Brazil (1810); and Santiago, Chile (1813). The University of Oslo library, established in 1811, now serves as Norway's national library. In 1815 the Library of Parliament in Ottawa, Ont., began to serve the legislatures of Upper and Lower Canada. Peru's National Library in Lima dates from 1821. In 1828 newly independent Greece opened a national library at Aegina, the capital. Both capital and library were later transferred to Athens. When McGill University in Montreal, Que., opened in 1829, a library had been established.

The National Library of Medicine in Bethesda, Md.—one of the great medical libraries of the world— began in 1836 as the library of the Surgeon General's Office. Belgium's national library in Brussels, the Albert I Royal Library, was created in 1837. One of the world's great technology libraries, the Technological Institute in Delft, Netherlands, started in 1842.

The National Library of Singapore uses a bookmobile to provide service to children in rural areas. About half the library's holdings are in English—but the collection also includes works in the Chinese, Malay, and Tamil languages.

Singapore Ministry of Culture

The National Museum Library in Colombo, Sri Lanka, was organized in 1845 as a branch of the library of the Royal Asiatic Society. Later it was combined with the Government Oriental Library. In 1856 the General Assembly Library in Wellington, New Zealand, was founded.

From the late 1800's important libraries began to appear more often in Asia and Africa. Libraries were founded at the universities of Bombay, Calcutta, and Madras, all in India, in 1857. In Africa the University of Liberia started a library in Monrovia in 1862. The Egyptian National Library in Cairo began as the Khedival Library in 1870. In 1872 the Emperor of Japan opened the Imperial Library in Tokyo. It was to become the National Diet Library, somewhat like the Library of Congress or Canada's Library of Parliament. A library was begun in 1880 at the University of Algiers, Algeria. The National Library in Saigon, South Vietnam, was founded in 1882, as was the library of the University of the Punjab in Lahore, Pakistan.

In 1887 the Newberry Library in Chicago, Ill., opened its doors to scholars. It is one of the great private research libraries. That same year marks the beginning of the State Library in Pretoria, South Africa, and the library of the University of Tokyo in Japan. The following year the National Library for the Blind opened in London, England. In Illinois the University of Chicago began with a considerable library in 1892. Jewish National and University Library in Jerusalem owes its origin to that city's B'nai B'rith Lodge library, started in 1892. Kyoto University in Japan founded a library in 1899.

The Time of the Public Library. The time of the modern public library, of the free lending library open to all, varied from place to place. There were few such libraries until the late 1800's. But before that, the idea of opening free libraries to the public—even if they didn't lend books—was spreading.

Antonio Magliabechi was a librarian and book lover who worked, ate, and slept among his books. In 1714 he died in Florence, leaving his collection to the people of the city. The Magliabechiana Library, opened in 1747, later became the National Central Library. In 1748 the Zaluski Library opened in Warsaw. It was given to the public by two bishops, Joseph and his brother Andrew Zaluski. It is today the National Library of Poland. From the mid-1700's, reference libraries were open to the public in many places in Japan. In China in 1783, Emperor Ch'ien-lung ordered six copies made of every important work in the imperial Four Treasures Library. Three of these duplicate libraries were opened for public study in other cities.

In St. Petersburg (now Leningrad), the Imperial Russian library opened in 1811. Later renamed for Russian writer Mikhail Evgrafovich Saltykov (Shchedrin), the Saltykov-Shchedrin Library is one of the U.S.S.R.'s largest. In what is today Czechoslovakia, a public reference library opened in Zlonice, Bohemia, in 1817. The South African Public Library opened—but not to black people—in 1818. It is today one of South Africa's national libraries, the State Library in Pretoria being the other.

In Grossenhain, Germany, a library began lending books to the general public in 1828. It was one of the first. A public library was established in Bucharest, Rumania, in 1831. In 1833 one of the first public libraries in the United States opened at Peterborough, N.H. India's National Library in Calcutta began life as the Calcutta Public Library in 1836. The Red River Library was formed in Manitoba in 1847.

Harrison Forman

Future attorneys examine reams of court decisions at a law library in India.

At the university library in Samarkand, U.S.S.R., Uzbek students cram for examinations.

Harrison Forman

Rich oriental carpets provide a magical setting for fairy tales at the Children's House of Books in Tashkent, U.S.S.R. Spe- cial children's libraries are a feature of the modern Soviet public library system.

In 1852 the Manchester Free Library began to lend books in England. Its first librarian, Edward Edwards, was a founding father of public libraries in his country. Dickson Public Library in Göteborg, Sweden, opened its doors in 1861.

At his death, Russian Count N. P. Rumyantsev left his collection of books in St. Petersburg for public use. Transferred to Moscow, it opened as the Moscow Public and Rumyantsev Museum Library in 1862.

Today it is the Lenin library, one of the largest in the Soviet Union. The people of Mexico City got their first public library in 1869. Many public libraries were established in Argentina after 1870, when President Domingo F. Sarmiento pushed through a law to found them throughout the country. In 1872 the Imperial Library was set up for the public in Tokyo, Japan. Some of the reading clubs started in Bulgaria about 1860 grew into public libraries after indepen-

The Oblast Library in Mogilev, U.S.S.R., provides music enthusiasts with a listening room and a fine literature-of-music collection. Many people attend evenings of music organized at the library.

dence from the Turks in 1878. Puerto Rico's Municipal Library in San Juan opened in 1880. The following year an American millionaire, Andrew Carnegie, offered a public library to Allegheny City (now part of Pittsburgh), Pa., where many of his steelworkers lived. It was the first of more than 2,500 public libraries he was to build in the United States and Canada.

In 1883 the Public Library in Tunis was founded. It is the Tunisian National Library today. Vienna, Austria, had its first free public library in 1887. That same year a free city library was established in Frederiksberg, Denmark. Alexandria Municipal Library opened in Egypt in 1892. In 1898 the Deichmann Library in Oslo, Norway, turned public. It had first been organized as a privately financed free library in 1780. In what is today the Netherlands, a public library opened in Dordrecht in 1899.

In many places free lending libraries open to all were not available until the twentieth century. Not until 1905 did China have such a library, the first one being in Hunan province. Malaysia's first public library, a Carnegie library, opened at Kota Bharu, Malaya, in 1938. Thailand had no public library until 1950. Black people in such places as the Congo (now Zaire) and the United States could not use all public libraries until the 1950's and 1960's. Despite blank spots and blemishes, the public library really came of age in the 1900's. Modern libraries were formed in more places, and library services were extended to all people wherever they were located.

National and University Libraries: the 1900's. Many national libraries formed in the 1900's were in Asia and Africa. The Philippines acquired a national library in Manila in 1901. Four years later King Chulalongkorn of Thailand formed the Vajiranana National Library out of three older collections in Bangkok. The National Library of Peking, by far the largest in Asia, opened in 1909. Another national library of China, the National Central Library, was later founded in Nanking. Part of it was taken by the Nationalist Chinese to Taipei, where it became Taiwan's national library. In 1923 national libraries were established in Phnom Penh, Cambodia, and Seoul, Korea. Korea's National Central Library was later augmented by the National Assembly Library, also located in Seoul. Liaquat Memorial Library in Karachi (1951) later became Pakistan's national library. The National Library of Burma (1952) was built upon the holdings of Rangoon's Bernard Free Library. National libraries were also begun by Iraq (Baghdad, 1963) and Malaysia (Kuala Lumpur, 1971).

In Africa national libraries opened in Rabat, Morocco (1920), and Addis Ababa, Ethiopia (1944). The French Institute of Black Africa libraries, begun by the French in 1946, later became national libraries in Yaoundé, Cameroon, and Lomé, Togo. Nigeria, the Malagasy Republic, and Ivory Coast set up national libraries in the 1960's in Lagos, Tananarive, and Abidjan respectively.

In Australia the National Library grew out of the Commonwealth Parliament Library, founded in Can-

A researcher gleans information from the newspaper collection at the library of the University of Warsaw in Poland.

This youth at a library in São Paulo, Brazil, is fascinated by a coin-operated record player.

Youngsters enjoy browsing among displays of new books at the International Youth Library in Munich, West Germany.

181

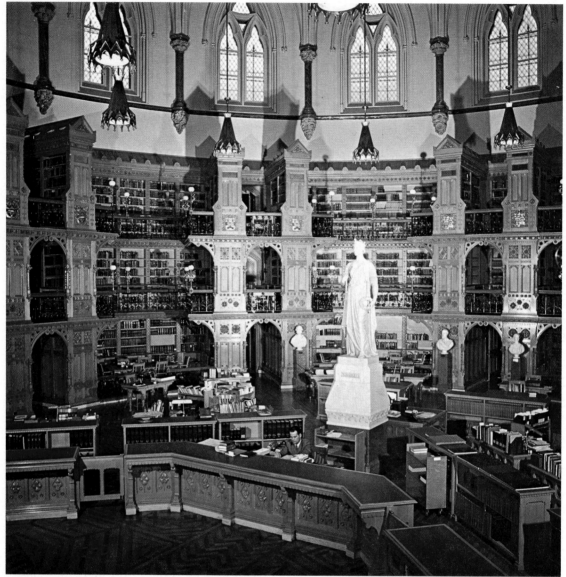

A magnificent interior graces the Library of Parliament in Ottawa, Canada. The library, founded in 1815, is open to scholars as well as lawmakers. Most of its books were destroyed in a fire in 1855, but the collection was replaced.

berra in 1902. The world's greatest collection of Welsh materials started as the National Library of Wales in Aberystwyth in the 1900's. A country of many great libraries, Canada did not formally open a national library until 1953 in Ottawa, Ont. New Zealand's National Library, established in 1966 in Wellington, includes its General Assembly Library and the Alexander Turnbull Library, a great research library dating back to 1918.

In many places the greatest growth in university libraries occurred in the 1900's. Not only did already established libraries grow larger, but many new libraries were built, especially after World War II. Thailand's most outstanding academic library is that of Chulalongkorn University in Bangkok (1917). The approximately 40 libraries of National Taiwan University in Taipei date back to 1928, when the university was founded as Taihoku Imperial University by the Japanese. In Korea the great library of Seoul National University opened in 1946. Nanyang University in Singapore was founded in 1953, the University of Singapore in 1959. Each began with a library.

Notable northern African university libraries opened in the 1900's include those of Alexandria University in Egypt (1942) and the University of Khartoum in Sudan (1945). Among the largest and best libraries in central Africa are those of the University of Ghana in Legon (1948), the University of

Ibadan in Nigeria (1948), the University of Dakar in Senegal (1952), and National University in Kinshasa, Zaire, founded in 1954 as Lovanium University. A library at Ethiopia's Haile Selassie I University dates from 1950. The University of East Africa (1961) in 1970 became three independent universities, each with its own library—National University in Nairobi, Kenya; the University of Dar es Salaam in Tanzania; and Makerere University in Kampala, Uganda.

Even in countries rich in academic libraries, the 1900's were a period of great growth—especially the post-World War II period. Canada's University of Alberta and University of British Columbia libraries were formed in the early 1900's. So were the libraries of the University of Hawaii and the University of Alaska. When Czechoslovakia became independent in 1919, Comenius University in Bratislava and Purkyne University in Brno were founded, both with libraries. In the Soviet Union, Lenin established university libraries as early as 1920, including those at Tashkent State University and Urals State University in Sverdlovsk. Many eastern European university libraries such as those of the University of Lodz in Poland and the University of Sarajevo in Yugoslavia date from the 1940's. By World War I, many older university libraries were so large that they began to break up into separate libraries. There was a reverse trend after World War II toward combining the separate collections. From the 1950's on, numerous new university libraries were formed in many parts of the world.

The Time of the Special Library. There have been special libraries since earliest times. Shang dynasty historical records, or *archives*, made up a special library. So did medical collections of ancient Egyptian medical schools; business documents of Babylonian and Assyrian trading houses; sacred writings of early temples, pagodas, churches, and mosques. But it was not until the 1800's and especially the 1900's that the great growth in special library services took place. The Special Library Association in the United States was founded in 1909; the Association of Special Libraries and Information Bureaus (ASLIB) in England, in 1924.

Some modern special libraries date back to before 1900. The Lincoln's Inn library in London, England, for instance, was founded in 1497. It is one of the world's most famous law libraries. The Gazi Husrev Beg Library in Sarajevo, Yugoslavia, was begun under Turkish rule in 1537. It concentrates on the history and culture of the Balkans and Near East. In Antwerp, Belgium, the Plantin-Moretus Museum library specializes in, among other things, the early history of printing. It was established in 1640. Czechoslovakia's State Technical Library in Prague grew out of an engineering school library started in 1707. France's Arsenel Library in Paris, a great French literature library, was formed in the 1700's. So were the Royal Horticultural Library in Copenhagen, Denmark; the Library of the Academy of History in Madrid, Spain; the Library of the Society for the Literature of the Netherlands in Leiden; and the Li-

Toronto, Canada, Public Library

Avid listeners enjoy a storytelling festival at the Toronto Public Library, the largest of Canada's public libraries.

brary of the Royal Academy of Sciences in Stockholm, Sweden.

An important technical library, the Polish Society of Friends of Science Library in Warsaw, was opened in 1802. The Boston Athenaeum Library, a history collection, began as a subscription library in 1807. In the early 1800's, special libraries started to appear in public institutions—prisons, reformatories, mental hospitals. Early prison libraries were established in the State Penitentiary at Philadelphia, Pa., in 1829; at Sing Sing Prison in Ossining, N.Y., about 1840. The New York State Lunatic Asylum in Utica had a library in 1875. In London special library service took a leap forward with the founding of the National Library for the Blind in 1888.

Players contemplate their opening moves during a chess tournament at a branch of the Chicago Public Library, Chicago, Ill.
Art Shay—Chicago Public Library

Teachers often look to libraries in search of audiovisual materials for use in their classrooms. Two young teachers, above, listen to recordings in front of a background mural depicting the families of musical instruments. Another teacher, below, selects slides with the aid of a modern viewer.

Important special libraries formed in the first part of the 19th century include the Royal Conservatory of Music library in Brussels, Belgium (1832); the Royal Portuguese Reading Room in Rio de Janeiro, Brazil, which specializes in the history and literature of Brazil and Portugal (1837); and Advocates Library in Montreal, Que., a law library. The National Agricultural Library in Washington, D.C., one of the largest of its kind in the world, started as the library of the Department of Agriculture in 1862. In 1888 two outstanding Latin American libraries were founded—the Library of the National Academy of History in Caracas, Venezuela, concentrating on the history of Latin America, and the Pedagogic Museum and Library in Montevideo, Uruguay, for the use of teachers. The John Rylands Library, a great private research library in history and literature, opened in Manchester, England, in 1899. That same year, King Chulalongkorn founded the Siriraj Medical Library in Bangkok. It is one of Thailand's finest.

Important private research libraries opened in the first half of the 20th century include the Mitchell Library in Sydney, Australia (1910); the Alexander Turnbull Library in Wellington, N.Z., now part of the National Library of New Zealand (1918); the Henry E. Huntington Library in San Marino, Calif., with collections chiefly in English and American literature and history (1919); the Gennadius Library in Athens, Greece, devoted to materials on Greece and the Greeks (1926); and the Folger Shakespeare Library in Washington, D.C., which concentrates on Shakespeare and his times (1932). From the 1920's, the Soviet Union developed strong special libraries of many types. Trade union libraries, for instance, which served both as technical libraries on trade union history and popular reading collections for workers, were built under the direction of the Gorki Reference Library of the All-Union Central Council of Trade Unions in Moscow.

Beginning in the 1920s, library services for children were expanded in many places. Boys and Girls House in Toronto, Ont. (1922), was the first library building in North America specifically for young people. An outstanding example of services to youth in Latin America was the Children's Library in São Paulo, Brazil, founded in 1935. The International Youth Library in Munich, West Germany, opened in 1949, offers services to the young and encourages the publication of juvenile literature all over the world.

An important industrial library formed in the 1920's was that of the Rubber Research Institute in Kuala Lumpur, Malaysia. It is one of the world's most comprehensive sources of information on the growing of rubber. The National Science Library in Ottawa, Ont., founded in 1927, is the heart of Canada's national scientific and technical information network.

A great number of special libraries have been formed especially since the 1940's. Business libraries, such as those of banking and insurance companies, came into widespread use. Industries of all kinds found company libraries essential, as did magazines, professional societies, educational associations, and labor organizations. Hospital, prison, and other institutional libraries came into their own. The demands of industrial and scientific research led to the establishment of research and documentation centers, often with highly automated ways of storing, retrieving, and duplicating information. India set up its Indian National Scientific Documentation Center in 1952. It supplies photocopies of scientific material from India and abroad, has a translation service, and makes up bibliographies. Special library services are offered by the Brazilian Institute of Bibliography and Documentation, set up in Rio de Janeiro in 1954. Foremost among special libraries in the Arab world is the

National Information and Documentation Center in Cairo, Egypt, opened in 1955. Similar special library service was begun by the Pakistan National Scientific and Technical Documentation Center in 1955, the Japan Information Center of Science and Technology in 1957, the Korean Scientific and Technical Information Center in 1962, and the Iranian Documentation Center in 1968.

The Libraries of Canada and the United States

Canada and the United States provide among the best library services in the world. School and public libraries are within the reach of most people. For those living in remote areas, there are bookmobiles,

These high school students are using a library of lessons recorded on computer tapes. Each student can study at his own
Ampex Corp.

speed, playing and replaying his selections. Students can also record their own comments, questions, and answers.

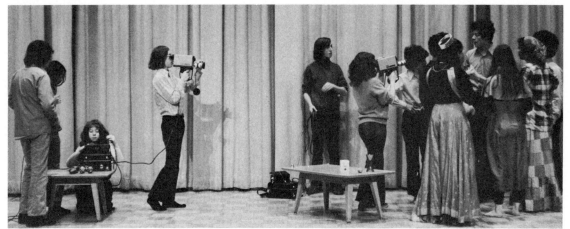

Teenage drama students learn the technical aspects of their craft as they videotape their dress rehearsal at a New York Public Library sound stage. This facility is an example of the varied services offered by today's library system.

©*Film Library Quarterly*

books by mail, and other types of extension services. State and provincial libraries also provide services for all the people living in a particular region. They plan statewide or province-wide library programs, serve as interlibrary loan headquarters, supply public and school libraries with expensive and little-used materials, and set up regional centers to more easily reach all with materials and services.

State and provincial libraries also act as special libraries, serving the government as well as the public. Not only is such a library a general information center for officials; it also includes special libraries— a law library for judges and lawmakers, a medical library for health officials, a technology library for highway and mining officials.

Every department of the two governments has its own library. Some of these also provide national and international services. The Library of Parliament in Ottawa, Ont., serves the needs of scholars as well as Canadian lawmakers. The National Science Library and the National Archives are also in Ottawa. Canada's National Library in Ottawa publishes a National Union Catalog, which lists materials in more than 300 Canadian libraries. In the United States, the National Union Catalog is published by the Library of Congress and lists materials in more than 700 United States and Canadian libraries. The Library of Congress also serves other government departments and agencies, libraries, scholars, and the general public. Other national libraries of the United States include the National Agricultural Library, the National Library of Medicine, and the National Archives.

There are important academic libraries in every province or state of Canada and the United States, many of them with outstanding library schools. The largest university libraries in Canada are those of the University of Toronto, the University of British Columbia, the University of Alberta, and Montreal's McGill University. Harvard University at Cambridge, Mass., has the world's largest academic library, with about 90 separate collections. Both Canada and the United States are rich also in special libraries such as industrial, technical, business, medical, and private research libraries.

The Brave New World of Libraries

Every year a deluge of more and more information pours from the world's presses or appears on records, films, and tapes. How does the librarian keep track of the flood of materials, store them, and retrieve the information they contain? With a little help from some mechanical friends.

The photocopy has revolutionized the library. It

Modern advances in electronics have revolutionized information storage. Here, computer consoles display taped material.

Lockheed Missiles and Space Co.

is a fast, cheap, and easy way of getting parts of books, magazines, and other materials for everyone who wants them. Libraries can also enlarge their collections with photocopies of out-of-print books.

The library has also been revolutionized by the microform—the microfilm, the Microcard, the microfiche. These make it possible to store information in less space. One microfiche card, for example, can hold up to 1,000 pages of a book.

The magnetic tape, too, has revolutionized the library. Magnetic tapes called *data bases* provide a variety of information. To get information on magnetic tapes, it is necessary to use a computer. That, too, has contributed to the technological revolution in libraries. Computers are used by librarians to store and to find information, to order books or to keep records, and to produce book or card catalogs. The library has also been revolutionized by facsimile transmission machines, with which libraries can quickly send and receive a picture of a page.

In the past, libraries were largely for the learned and cultured. Even in highly literate countries, libraries existed to serve perhaps one third of the population. Many of today's librarians feel that the goal of the right book for the right library user is no longer enough. Today's libraries also reach out to nonusers, who generally include the uneducated, the poor, the minorities. Books are used, yes, but also films and records and tapes, easy-to-read materials, minority literature, job and health information. Storefront libraries and mobile libraries of various types carry the library to the people, serving their urgent needs. Often librarians go out of their way to help nonusers with practical problems, not only gathering information but putting it into easily understood form. Ignorance, poverty, and apathy are being attacked in many parts of the world, and libraries are in the forefront of that attack.

Reaching out to new users sometimes involves gathering nontraditional materials, materials they can relate to and understand—minority literature, for example. A library exists to serve its community. Unless it reflects the thinking of the entire community, it is serving only a portion of that community. One of the librarian's most important jobs is to preserve freedom of access to all kinds of ideas.

BIBLIOGRAPHY FOR LIBRARIES

Various Aspects of Libraries

Aldrich, Ella V. Using Books and Libraries (Prentice, 1967).
Baker, Robert K. Doing Library Research (Westview, 1981).
Becker, Carol A. A Community Information Service (Univ. of Md. Library Service, 1974).
Benge, Ronald. Cultural Crisis and Libraries in the Third World (Shoe String, 1979).
Bloomfield, Masse. How to Use a Library (Mojave Books, 1970).
Brown, Eleanore F. Cutting Library Costs (Scarecrow, 1979).
Carnovsky, Leon, ed. Library Networks—Promise and Performance (Univ. of Chicago Press, 1969).
Corcoran, Eileen. Gaining Skills in Using the Library (Richards Pub., 1980).
Currie, Dorothy H. How to Organize a Children's Library (Oceana, 1965).

Golden, Charlotte. How to Find What You Want in the Library (Barron, 1979).
Harvard-Williams, P. Learning and Communication: Libraries in Developing Countries (Lexington, 1982).
Jones, Frances M. Censorship in Libraries (Oryx Press, 1983).
Lee, Sul H. Emerging Trends in Library Organization (Pierian, 1978).
Lyman, Helen H. Literacy and the Nation's Libraries (ALA, 1977)
McClellan, A. W. The Reader, the Library, and the Book (Shoe String, 1973).
Marshall, Margaret R. Libraries and Literature for Teenagers (Lexington, 1975).
Orr, J. M. Libraries as Communications Systems (Greenwood, 1977).
Penland, P. R. and Mathai, A. The Future Library as a Learning Service (Dekker, 1978).
Ray, Sheila. Children's Librarianship (Shoe String, 1979).
Smith, Ruth S. Setting Up a Library (CSLA, 1979).
Steele, Colin. Major Libraries of the World (Bowker, 1976).
Turow, Joseph G. Getting Books to Children (ALA, 1979).
Von Marion, Beaujean, ed. Metropolitan Libraries on Their Way Into the 80's (Shoe String, 1982).

History of Libraries

Armour, Richard. The Happy Bookers: A Playful History of Librarians and Their World from the Stone Age to the Distant Future (McGraw, 1976).
DuMont, Rosemary R. Reform and Reaction: The Big City Public Library in American Life (Greenwood, 1977).
Johnson, Elmer D. and Harris, Michael H. History of Libraries in the Western World (Scarecrow, 1976).
Pater, Alan F. and Pater, Jason R., eds. The Great Libraries of America (Monitor, 1983).
Reichmann, Felix. The Sources of Western Literacy (Greenwood, 1980).
Rider, A. D. A Story of Books and Libraries (Scarecrow, 1976).

Automation in Libraries

Boss, Richard W. Automating Library Acquisitions (Knowledge Indus., 1982).
Corbon, John. Developing Computer-Based Library Systems (Oryx Press, 1981).
Gore, Daniel and others. Requiem for the Card Catalog (Greenwood, 1979).
Kimber, Richard T. and Boyd, A. Automation in Libraries (Pergamon, 1974).
Sigel, Efrem and others. Books, Libraries, and Electronics (Knowledge Indus., 1982).

Books for Young People

Baker, Donna J. I Want to Be a Librarian (Children's, 1978).
Charles, Donald. Calico Cat Meets Bookworm (Children's, 1978).
Mathews, Virginia H. Libraries for Today and Tomorrow (Octagon, 1976).
Shapiro, Lillian L. Teaching Yourself in Libraries (Wilson, 1978).

Children's Libraries

Broderick, D. M. Library Work With Children (Wilson, 1977).
Fleet, Anne. Children's Libraries (Lexington, 1973).
Long, H. G. Public Library Service to Children (Scarecrow, 1969).
Sayers, W. C. A Manual of Children Libraries (Gordon, 1980).

Libraries and Student Readers

Benge, Ronald. Libraries and Cultural Change (Shoe String, 1970).
Bundy, M. L. Metropolitan Public Library Users (Univ. of Md. Library Service, 1968).
Corcoran, Eileen. Gaining Skills in using the Library (Richards, 1980).
Kirkendall, C. A., ed. Teaching Library Use Competence (Pierian, 1982).
Sutherland, Zena, ed. Children in Libraries (Univ. of Chicago Press, 1981).
Vosper, R. G. and Koops, W. R., eds. Libraries for All (Shoe String, 1980).
Wyandt, C. R. A Librarian's Hints for Students (Exposition, 1979).

Andre La Terza

Derna, in eastern Libya on the Mediterranean coast, was founded in the 15th century on the site of an ancient Greek colony. Today it is a minor port and a small winter resort area.

LIBYA. The petroleum-rich country of Libya lies in northern Africa along the southern coast of the Mediterranean Sea. Libya blends its role as one of the world's most important producers of petroleum with a traditional Arab society based on the Islamic religion. In Tripoli, the capital and the largest city, nomadic herders mingle with construction engineers and bearded imams, or Islamic religious teachers. In rural areas herds of sheep, goats, and camels graze alongside modern highways.

Libya's official name is the Socialist People's Libyan Arab Jamahiriya. Jamahiriya is an Arabic word meaning "socialism" or "brotherhood." Libya extends south from the Mediterranean coast into the vast Sahara and ranks fourth in size among the countries of Africa. It covers about 675,000 square miles (1,749,000 square kilometers), an area one sixth larger than that of Alaska. Libya is bordered by Tunisia and Algeria on the west, Niger and Chad on the south, and Sudan and Egypt on the east.

Land, Climate, and Natural Resources

Libya is a combination of contrasting land forms. Its three main regions are Cyrenaica on its eastern Mediterranean coast, Tripolitania on its western coast, and Fezzan, a series of oases in the southwestern desert. In Cyrenaica and Tripolitania, the coastline rises sharply out of the sea. The elevation and coastal rainfall create excellent conditions for growing grains, olives, dates, and tropical fruits. Away from the coast and directly south of the Gulf of Sidra, the land is arid and suitable mainly for herding livestock. Farther south and east lies the Libyan Desert, one of the largest in the world. Less than 6 percent of Libya's land is economically useful.

This article was contributed by James McCann, Assistant to the Director of the African Studies Center, Michigan State University.

Libya has *wadis,* or riverbeds, rather than continually flowing rivers. The wadis are dry most of the year, and more than 90 percent of the land receives less than 4 inches (100 millimeters) of rain annually.

In the desert, groundwater rises from beneath the surface and forms oases that provide relief for travelers and water for agriculture. To obtain water where there is none on the surface, Libyans dig artesian wells. Such a well is often shared by an entire village.

Facts About Libya

Official Name: Socialist People's Libyan Arab Jamahiriya.

Capital: Tripoli.

Area: 675,000 square miles (1,749,000 square kilometers).

Population (1982 estimate): 3,425,000; 5 persons per square mile (2 persons per square kilometer); 60 percent urban, 40 percent rural.

Major Language: Arabic (official).

Major Religion: Islam (official).

Literacy: 49 percent.

Highest Peak: Bette.

Major Rivers: There are no permanently flowing rivers.

Form of Government: Republic.

Chief of State: Chairman of the Revolution Command Council.

Head of Government: Secretary General of the General People's Committee (premier).

Legislature: General People's Congress.

Voting Qualifications: Citizens who are 19 may vote.

Political Divisions: Ten governorates (*muhafazat*).

Major Cities (1981 estimate): Tripoli (858,000), Banghazi (450,000).

Chief Manufactured and Mined Products: Cement, chemicals, fertilizer, food products, petroleum products, tobacco products, crude petroleum, natural gas.

Chief Agricultural Products: *Crops*—barley, citrus fruits, corn (maize), dates, grapes, olives, potatoes, tomatoes, wheat. *Livestock*—camels, cattle, goats, poultry, sheep.

Flag: *Color*—green (*see* Flags of the World).

Monetary Unit: 1 Libyan dinar = 1,000 dirhams.

Libya's most important natural resource is its oil, which was first discovered in Fezzan in 1956. The first major discovery came in Cyrenaica in 1959. The country also has supplies of natural gas and a huge iron ore deposit in Fezzan.

The People

Libya had a population of about 3,425,000 in 1982, the smallest among the five countries of North Africa. Most of the people live in the temperate climate of the Mediterranean coast, and about 60 percent make their homes in towns with populations above 5,000. About two thirds of Libya's people live in Tripolitania, one third in Cyrenaica, and a small fraction in Fezzan. Away from the towns and agricultural areas of the Mediterranean coast, most Libyans live in small, widely separated nomadic groups.

The vast majority of the people speak Arabic, the national language. Pastoral groups in the south, such as the nomadic Tuareg, use dialects of the Berber language. Many Libyans also speak Italian, English, or French as a second language.

An important part of Libya's population consists of the large number of foreign-born people who work as technicians and laborers in the nation's oil industry. They include Europeans and Americans as well as people from other Arab countries.

Religion, Art, and Music

Most Libyans are Muslims who belong to the Sunnah branch of Islam. Islam is practiced by all the language groups, including the Berber-speaking people who maintain much of their traditional culture. In Cyrenaica and Fezzan, an important sect of Libyan Muslims called the Sanusiyah practices a distinctive type of militant Islam.

Libya's art and music are a part of its heritage from the Roman Empire and the Islamic world. Ruins from the Roman period include beautiful mosaics that decorated temples and the houses of wealthy merchants. Large, richly ornamented mosques reflect the importance of art as a decoration in Islam. In local markets and small shops, Libyan craftsmen and craftswomen make carpets, baskets, leather goods, and elaborately designed jewelry.

Economy

Libya's economy is based overwhelmingly on oil production, though agriculture and livestock herding are still important to many rural families. Receipts from oil exports account for nearly all income from foreign trade.

Libya has invested much of its oil profits in the development of other parts of its economy, including agriculture, industry, and mining. Agriculture is expanding south from the coast to newly irrigated areas of desert. Most of the large farms, which are owned by the government, have begun to produce foods that were formerly imported, including corn (maize), wheat, and citrus fruits, as well as cattle, sheep, and poultry. Libya hopes to be able to feed itself in the

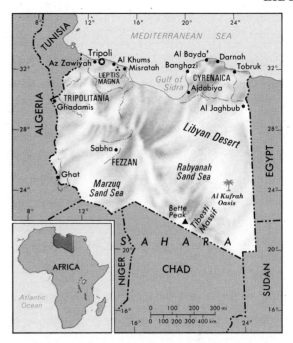

near future without importing food. Industry is dominated by oil production, but forms of local industry include traditional handicrafts, food processing, textiles, and construction. The government is working to develop medium and heavy industry to help reduce Libya's dependence on imports.

Transportation, Communication, and Education

Libya's transportation network is based on the Tripoli-Banghazi highway, which stretches about 1,000 miles (1,600 kilometers) along the coast. Small rural roads connect the highway system to rural villages, oil-producing areas, and government farms. Libya has its own international airline. Telecommunications were very poor in the past, but the government has given top priority to their development.

Education in Libya is free, and all young people must attend school through the high school level. In the past, only cities and towns had schools. Today, schools in rural villages enable the children of farmers and nomads to acquire an education. Libya also has literacy schools for adults. Illiteracy has been greatly reduced since 1973, when almost half the population could not read. In the past, girls and women were not encouraged to learn to read or to go to school, but they now have an opportunity to do so.

History and Government

From about 1000 BC, Libyans had contacts with Africans south of the Sahara. A people called Garamantes, who probably were the ancestors of the present-day Tuareg, captured the important oases along routes leading south to the Niger River. They controlled the gold and slave trade between sub-Saharan Africa and the Mediterranean. During the 7th century BC, Greek colonists settled in the area of Cyrenaica

189

and founded the city of Cyrene, which flourished as a center of Greek art and science. In the 6th century BC, Tripolitania was absorbed as the eastern province of the Phoenician city-state of Carthage.

Later, Libya became an important part of the Roman Empire. It produced much grain and was influential because of its location across the Mediterranean from Italy. Libya's prosperity during this period is reflected by the extensive Roman ruins in the three cities of Leptis Magna, Sabrata, and Oea. Libya's capital, Tripoli (which means "three cities"), is named for the cities represented by these ruins.

In AD 395, the Roman Empire split and Libya fell under the control of the eastern half, which was governed from Constantinople. The empire's rule in Libya ended in 439, when Gothic Vandals from Spain conquered Tripolitania and Cyrenaica. A century later, an army from Constantinople drove the Vandals out of Libya.

In 642 Arab armies moved into Tripolitania and Cyrenaica. They arrived in Fezzan the next year. The simple, direct beliefs of Islam appealed to Libyans of both the city and countryside. Islam brought with it the Arabic language, a system of writing, and beliefs compatible with urban and nomadic ways of life. The Arabic language and culture spread quickly in the cities and along the coast. Farther inland, Berber peoples formed their own version of Islam and resisted the political control of Arab dynasties based in Damascus and Baghdad.

In the mid-11th century, groups of migrants called the Beni Salim and Beni Hilal settled in the area of present-day Libya and started to dominate the local Berbers. Under their influence, the Arabic language and culture spread from the cities into the countryside. Some Berber groups adopted Islam despite maintaining their language and culture, but they resisted Arab political control and moved farther into the drier, more isolated areas to the south.

Since its conversion to Islam, Libya has had many invaders. The Spaniards came in 1510, and the Ottoman Turks in 1551. In 1804 Libya fought a brief war with the United States over control of the sea lanes in the southern Mediterranean.

Italy took control of Libya in 1911 after invading the country and fighting the Turks, who had occupied the area since the 16th century. After World War I Italy's leader, Benito Mussolini, declared his intention of forming a second Roman Empire. Italy, which had quickly occupied the main cities and coastal areas, began a policy of bringing Italians to settle in the best agricultural zones. They constructed roads to improve communications for their military forces, developed irrigation schemes for immigrant Italians, and built a large naval base at Tobruk.

The Libyan people never accepted Italian rule. Between 1911 and 1932, Libyans in Tripolitania, Fezzan, and Cyrenaica fought the Italian colonial government. The Italians, who had superior military power, finally subdued northern Tripolitania in 1923. However, resisting groups of Arabs, Berbers, and Sanusi continued to fight in Cyrenaica under the religious leader Omar Mukhtar, a modern Libyan folk hero. Under him, the people of southern Cyrenaica held off the Italians until 1931, when he was captured and hanged. Italy made Libya a colony in 1939.

During World War II, Libya was a major battleground for the combined forces of Germany and Italy fighting the Allied powers. A British military government ruled Libya after the Allies defeated the Italians and Germans. Later, a French military government took control of Fezzan and shared the rule of the country with Britain.

After the war, Libya became the first country to gain independence through the United Nations. The independent kingdom of Libya was created in December 1951. Libya joined the Arab League in 1953 and the United Nations in 1955. The three zones of the country were merged into one national unit in 1963. For the first time since the Roman period, Tripolitania, Fezzan, and Cyrenaica were joined. That same year, Libya was one of the 30 founding members of the Organization of the African Unity (OAU).

In September 1969, a group of young army officers calling themselves the Revolutionary Command Council (RCC) overthrew the government and abolished the monarchy. The leader of the group was Muammar Al Qadhafi, a 27-year-old colonel. In 1972 Qadhafi was named head of state, commander in chief of the armed forces, and chairman of the RCC. On March 2, 1977, the government changed the name of the country from the Libyan Arab Republic to the Socialist People's Libyan Arab Jamahiriya. Since 1973 the political decision-making body of Libya has been the General People's Congress. The Congress appoints a General People's Committee with executive powers, but Qadhafi remained head of state.

The policies of the Libyan government are now based on jamahiriya, which has been defined as Islamic socialism. The foundations of these policies are set forth in the 'Green Book', a collection of essays by Qadhafi. Under jamahiriya, the government has used oil profits to undertake a major program of building housing, roads, communications networks, and a modern educational system. Libyan music, dance, and other arts have been promoted to strengthen national pride. Large sums have also been spent on armaments, making Libya an important military power on North Africa.

In 1981 Libya's oil production fell to less than a third of the amount considered necessary to finance the programs aimed at developing various parts of its economy. The production slump continued in 1982 and, though the nation maintained development programs already underway, new ones were severely hampered. Early in 1983, Libya promised military support for what it called "revolutionary forces" in Arab countries. Qadhafi had long denounced Egypt and the United States for their policies toward Israel, and the General People's Congress called for armed bands of Libyans to attack Arab land held by the Israelis. (*See also* Egypt; Israel.)

LICHEN. On places like tree trunks, rocks, old boards, and also on the ground grow strange splotches of various-colored plant life called lichens. They are of great scientific interest because they are not single plants; instead, each lichen is formed of a fungus and an alga living together so intimately as to seem a single plant. The lichens are one of the best illustrations of symbiosis, the intimate living together of two different kinds of organisms. The fungus makes the bulk of the body with its interwoven threads, and in the meshes of the threads live the algae. The special fungi that take part in this arrangement are almost never found growing separately, but the algae are found growing free.

There are about 15,000 different kinds of lichens distributed worldwide. They are especially suited for growth in harsh regions, where few plants can survive. They grow farther north and south than most plants, as well as higher on mountains. One unusual type grows completely submerged in the cold coastal waters of Antarctica. Some lichens inhabit the Earth's driest deserts, where they grow almost entirely underground and obtain light and moisture through small openings in the ground. Few grow near cities because most cannot survive in industrial air pollution. There are notable exceptions, however: in England, for example, *Lecanora conizaeoides* is actually confined to areas of high pollution.

The body of the lichen, the thallus, has three basic growth forms. These forms are crustose, foliose, and fruticose. Each form is adapted to live under different moisture conditions. The crustose lichens resemble a crust that has become attached to a surface and are well suited to dry areas. Foliose, or leafy, lichens need much greater amounts of water. Some of them even grow on rocks in streams. Fruticose lichens thrive in humid regions, where they are able to absorb water from the air. In desolate areas, when growth conditions are at their best and there is little competition, lichens will expand over vast areas. Lichens have a peculiar and effective method of repro-

ducing. Upon the surface of the body there are often minute granules that give it a dusty appearance. Each of these granules, called soredia, consists of a few cells of the alga surrounded by threads of the fungus. When these soredia are blown off they start new lichen bodies.

Many scientists think that the fungus and the alga are mutually helpful in their intimate relationship. Such a relationship is called mutualism. The claim is that the fungus, which is unable to make food for itself, uses food made by the alga, while on the other hand the alga is protected from drying out by living on the spongelike network of the fungous threads. Other scientists believe that the alga is not benefited by the presence of the fungus, but is held in slavery by it. Such a relationship is called helotism.

In any event the combination produces a structure that is able to exist where neither one could live alone. The result is lichens' ability to grow in the most unfavorable and desolate places. In such exposed situations the fungus could not live because it depends upon other organisms, and the alga could not live because it would dry out quickly. But the two can live together.

Certain kinds of lichens, such as the ones called Iceland moss and reindeer moss, are used as food by reindeer and even by humans. Other kinds are used to produce dyes, drugs, and other products. (*See also* Algae; Fungus.)

A species of *Pseudocyphellaria* (below) is a foliose lichen. *Alectoria sarmentosa* (below right) is a foliose lichen sensitive to warm temperatures. *Omphalina* and the *Coriscium* (right) are fruticose lichens.

Photos, (right) Heli Heikkila; (below left and right) Vernon Ahmadjian

A 1964 acrylic painting by Roy Lichtenstein exemplifies the United States pop art movement.

LICHTENSTEIN, Roy (born 1923). A painter who was a pioneer in the so-called pop art movement, Roy Lichtenstein took his subject matter from the phenomena of mass culture. The first one-man show of his cartoon paintings in New York City in 1962 was considered to be a sensation.

Roy Lichtenstein was born in New York City on Oct. 27, 1923. He received a master of fine arts degree from Ohio State University, where he taught from 1946 to 1951. He also taught at New York State University College, in Oswego, and at Douglass College of Rutgers University, in New Brunswick, N.J.

In 1951, at the beginning of his career, Lichtenstein painted cowboys and Indians in modern art styles. His interest in the comic-strip cartoon as an art theme probably began in 1960 with a painting he made for his children of the Walt Disney character Mickey Mouse. As his technique developed, the comic-strip characters were greatly enlarged, including the tiny, barely noticeable dots that make up the image in most pictures printed in newspapers and comic books. Lichtenstein simulated and enlarged these dots by using a metal screen as a stencil. Bright colors and black outlines added to this technique, which resulted in paintings that were a combination of abstract and commercial art.

Lichtenstein also drew subjects from romance magazines, with their words in typical comic-strip balloons, and created landscapes using the comic-strip technique. His sculptures of the late 1960s derived from the glass-and-chrome styles of the 1930s era.

LICORICE. The drops, sticks, and slender "whips" that are flavored with licorice owe their taste to the licorice plant's juice. The juice comes from the long pliant roots that extend straight down into the ground for more than a yard. The plant is cultivated chiefly in Mediterranean countries, including Spain, Italy, Greece, Turkey, and Syria, and in Iraq. The United States imports most of its supply. Some is grown in Louisiana and California. It takes three or four years before the crop of a new licorice plantation may be harvested.

Stick licorice is made by boiling the crushed roots and straining and concentrating the solution. For making cough drops, sirups, and candy, the solution is mixed with sugar. It is used also to cover the disagreeable taste of some medicines. Licorice paste, prepared from the first extract of the roots, is an ingredient in the manufacture of tobacco.

There are a dozen or more varieties of licorice plants. *Glycyrrhiza glabra* is the most important species. They are perennial herbs, 3 to 4 feet (.9 to 1.2 meters) tall, with fernlike leaves and with flowers that are usually pale violet.

LIEBIG, Justus von (1803–73). Before Justus Liebig's time, chemistry was mainly theoretical and of interest only to scientists. Liebig helped to make chemistry useful in people's daily lives. His work with carbon compounds laid the foundations for modern organic chemistry.

Justus Liebig was born in Darmstadt, Germany, on May 12, 1803. He was the son of a paint dealer. Liebig began to learn chemistry as a boy when he first watched, then helped, his father improve paints. While serving as an apothecary's apprentice at 15, he read all the chemistry books he could find. Later he went to the University of Bonn, then transferred to the University of Erlangen. There he received a doctor's degree in 1822.

At 21 Liebig was invited to read his research report on fulminic acid to the French Academy of Sciences. The paper won praise and attention, and he gained the friendship of several important scientists. In 1824 Liebig was appointed to the University of Giessen, where he set up the first experimental laboratory for college students. He was made a baron in 1845. Liebig taught at Giessen until 1852, when he became a professor at the University of Munich. There he devoted himself to more literary activities, stressing broad applications of chemistry to human life. He died in Munich on April 18, 1873.

Liebig discovered chloral and chloroform, important contributions to medicine, and aldehyde, a chemical widely employed in industry. He improved methods for producing potassium cyanide, used in electroplating and in making ferrocyanides. Liebig's studies of meat juices resulted in meat extracts and special baby foods. With Friedrich Wöhler he did research on the benzol compounds and uric acid.

Liebig showed that the mineral and organic worlds are composed of the same elements. He showed that plants use elements from the soil for growth and pass them on to animals that eat the plants. His studies of soil led to the use of chemical fertilizers to replace minerals withdrawn by crops and to supply minerals lacking in some soils.

Photo Research International

The Meuse River flows through Liège, noted for its commerce, industry, and the charming architecture of its older buildings.

LIECHTENSTEIN. One of the smallest independent states of Europe is Liechtenstein, 62 square miles (160 square kilometers). It is situated between Switzerland and Austria. The Rhine forms the boundary with Switzerland. From the Rhine's narrow valley the land rises eastward to rugged uplands.

The highest peak is Grauspitz, 8,527 feet (2,599 meters), on the southern border.

About half of the land is devoted to crops and pasture. Farm products include such items as beef and milk cattle, corn, cereals, grapes, and potatoes. Since World War II the country's industry has developed rapidly. Small-scale plants in Liechtenstein produce calculating machines, precision instruments, boilers for central heating, furniture and upholstery, chemical and pharmaceutical goods, toys, oil tanks, ceramics, and canned foods.

Tax rates are low and business regulations are somewhat liberal. To take advantage of this, thousands of foreign companies have established headquarters there. The moderate fees paid by these companies provide much of the country's revenue. The tourist trade and the sale of postage stamps are other important sources of income.

Most of the people are German-speaking Roman Catholics. They are descendants of old German tribes and are ruled by a prince. Liechtenstein was made a principality in 1719 by the Holy Roman emperor Charles VI. In 1866 it became independent. It adopted the Swiss franc in 1821 and became a member of the Swiss customs union in 1824. After World War II the country underwent rapid industrialization. The capital is Vaduz. Population (1982 estimate), 26,200.

Gutenberg Castle, a superbly preserved medieval fortress, stands atop a forested hill in southern Liechtenstein.

E.P.A., Inc./EB Inc.

LIÈGE, Belgium. Situated on the Meuse River near the rich coalfields of the Meuse Valley, the city of Liège is one of the chief manufacturing centers in Belgium. Steel is the city's foremost finished product. Liège has long been noted for its armaments industry. Even during the Middle Ages it was one of the arsenals of Europe, supplying lances and armor. Today it is a trade center for steel and related metal industries, rubber, glass, chemicals (particularly petrochemicals), and electronic equipment.

Completion of the Albert Canal in 1939 gave Liège a shipping route to the sea. The city is also a rail center, and a heliport was installed in 1955 (see Belgium).

The history of Liège (in German, *Lüttich*) goes back to Saint Lambert, bishop of Maastricht, who is credited with the city's founding in the 7th century. He was murdered in the city in 705. The chapel built in his honor by Saint Hubert was the start of the present city. From its beginnings until 1795, the city was ruled by bishops. For many centuries the "Prince-Bishops of Liège" sat in the diets (parliaments) of the Holy Roman Empire. The city was famous as a center of religion and learning long before its mineral wealth was discovered. Several times in the 1460s, when Belgium was under Burgundian rule, Charles the Bold ordered the destruction of the city as punishment for rebellions (see Charles the Bold).

Because of its strategic location on the Meuse Valley route through Belgium into France, Liège was the scene of fighting in both world wars. In the first major battle of World War I, the city fell after a heroic defense. It was seized again by the Germans in 1940 during World War II and suffered extensive damage from both German and Allied bombs.

Many old and stately buildings still stand amid the modern factories of Liège. The university, founded in 1817, is noted for its schools of science, including those of astrophysics and nuclear physics. Population (1981 estimate), 216,604.

LIFE *see* LIVING THINGS.

LIGHT

Life on earth depends on light from the sun. Green plants provide food for the world by changing light energy into food energy. The plants are eaten by animals that may, in turn, be eaten by other animals or by humans.

LIGHT. One of the most familiar and important forms of energy is light. Light is what makes it possible to see things. Nothing is visible when light is totally absent. But light is even more important for other reasons. Many scientists believe that millions of years ago light from the sun triggered the chemical reactions that led to the development of life on earth. Without light the living things now on earth would be unable to survive. Light from the sun provides energy for the inhabitants of the earth. Plants change the energy of sunlight into food energy. When light rays strike a green plant, some of their energy is changed to chemical energy, which the plant uses up as it makes food out of air and minerals. This process is called *photosynthesis*. Very nearly all living organisms on earth depend directly or indirectly on photosynthesis for their food energy. (*See also* Plants, Physiology of.)

Some of the energy of sunlight is absorbed by the earth's atmosphere or by the earth itself. Much of this energy is then changed to heat energy, which helps warm the earth, keeping it in the temperature range that living things have adapted to.

LIGHT AND ELECTROMAGNETIC RADIATION

Different kinds of light are visible to different species. Humans see light in what is called the visible range. It includes all the colors beginning with red and continuing through orange, yellow, green,

blue, and violet (*see* Color). Some people can see farther into the violet region or the red region than other people. Some animals have a different "visible range." Pit vipers, for example, have sense organs (pits) that "see" rays that humans feel as heat. These rays are called *infrared radiation*. Bees, on the other hand, not only see some of the colors that humans see but are also sensitive to *ultraviolet radiation*, which is beyond the range visible to humans. So, though human eyes cannot detect them, infrared rays and ultraviolet rays are related to visible light. Instruments have been built that can detect and photograph objects by means of infrared rays or ultraviolet rays. *X rays*, which can be used to photograph objects, are also known to be related to light.

Scientists have learned that all these forms of energy—visible light, infrared rays, ultraviolet rays, X rays—and many other kinds of energy, such as radio waves, microwaves, and gamma rays, have the same structure. They all consist of electrical and magnetic fields that move together and are all called *electromagnetic radiation*. (*See also* Radiation; X Rays.)

SOURCES OF LIGHT

Unlike many animals, humans depend primarily on sight to learn about the world around them. During the day primitive man could see by the light that came from the sun; but night brought darkness and danger. One of the most important steps man has taken to control his environment occurred when he learned to conquer the dark by controlling fire—a source of light.

Torches, candles, and oil lamps are all sources of light. They depend on a chemical reaction—burning—to release the energy we see as light. Plants and animals that glow in the dark—glowworms, fireflies,

This article was reviewed by Dr. John H. Pomeroy, Assistant Director, Lunar Sample Program, National Aeronautics and Space Administration, and by Dr. A. A. Strassenburg, Director, Office of Education and Manpower, American Institute of Physics.

and some mushrooms—change the chemical energy stored in their tissues to light energy. Such creatures are called *bioluminescent*. Electric-light bulbs and neon lights change electrical energy, which may be produced by chemical, mechanical, or atomic energy, into light energy.

Light sources are necessary for vision. An object can be seen only if light travels from the object to an eye that can sense it. When the object is itself a light source, it is called *luminous*. Electric lights are luminous. The sun is a luminous object because it is a source of light. An object that is not itself a source of light must be *illuminated* by a luminous object before it can be seen. The moon is illuminated by the sun. It is visible only where the sun's rays hit it and bounce off toward earth—or to an observer in a spacecraft.

In a completely dark room, nothing is visible. When a flashlight is turned on, its bulb and objects in its beam become visible. If a bright overhead bulb is switched on, its light can bounce off the walls, ceiling, floor, and furniture, making them and other objects in its path visible.

Heating some things causes them to give off visible light rays as well as invisible heat rays. This is the case for electric-light filaments, red-hot burners on electric stoves, and glowing coals. The light of such objects is *incandescent*. Other light sources emit light energy but no heat energy. They are known as *luminescent*, or *cold light*, sources. Neon and fluorescent lights are luminescent.

MEASURING LIGHT

The clarity with which an object can be seen depends in part on the amount of light that falls on it, on how well it is illuminated. The amount of light that a light source gives off (called its *intensity*) is one factor in determining how well a surface will be illuminated by it. Other factors are the slant of the illuminated surface in relation to the light source and the distance between the surface and the source. As a light beam travels outward from most light sources—the exceptions include lasers and searchlights—the beam spreads to cover a larger area. Distance greatly weakens illumination from such sources. The same amount of light will cover a larger area if the surface it reaches is moved farther away. This results in weaker illumination, following the inverse-square law. If the distance from the source is doubled, the amount of light falling on a given area is reduced to one fourth—the inverse of two squared. If the distance is tripled, the area receives only one ninth of the original illumination—the inverse of three squared.

One way of varying the amount of illumination on a surface is to vary the intensity of the light source. Intensity is measured in *candles* (or *candelas* in the international system). A candle used to be the amount of light given off by a carefully constructed wax candle. It is now more precisely defined as one sixtieth of the light intensity of one square centimeter of a perfectly black object at the freezing point of platinum (2,046° K, or 3,223.4° F). *Photometers* are devices that are used to measure the intensity of light sources.

People are often more interested in measuring the illumination of a surface—a desk top or the floor and walls of a room—than in measuring the light that leaves the light fixture. When distance is measured in feet, the illumination of a surface is measured in *footcandles*. At a distance of one foot the illumination provided by a light source of 100 candles is 100 footcandles. Under the inverse-square law, the same source gives one fourth as much illumination, or 25 footcandles, at a distance of two feet.

Another measurement that scientists find useful is the total amount of light energy that a source gives off over a certain period of time. This amount of light

The inverse-square law describes the light received from most sources. If the distance between an object and the light source is doubled, a given area receives only one fourth as much light; if the distance is tripled, only one ninth.

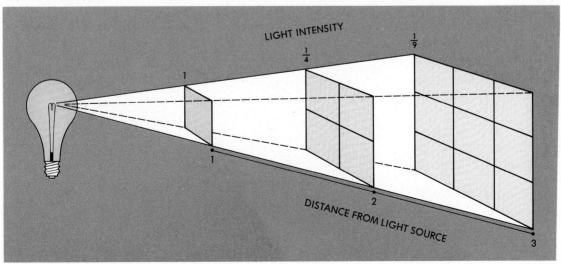

LIGHT INTENSITY

DISTANCE FROM LIGHT SOURCE

energy is called the *luminous flux* of a source and is measured in *lumens*. An ideal one-candle source gives off 4 π lumens. One footcandle is equal to one lumen per square foot.

LIGHT AND MATTER

The way substances look depends greatly on what happens when light hits them. It is possible to see through *transparent* substances more or less clearly because light can pass through them without being scattered or stopped. Light that bounces off the objects behind a transparent substance can pass right through it almost as if it were not in the way. Clear window glass, clean water, clear plastic, and air are all transparent, at least for short distances.

Only the surfaces of *opaque* substances are visible. Light cannot pass through them, and it is not possible to see through them. Opaque substances either absorb or reflect light. The light energy they absorb usually turns into heat and raises their temperature. Mercury, steel, and wood are examples of opaque substances.

Translucent substances permit some light to pass through them, but the light is scattered, and the images of objects behind them are not retained. Usually, if translucent substances are made thinner they become transparent; if they are made thicker they become opaque. Frosted light bulbs, waxed paper, and some kinds of curtain materials are translucent.

Reflection

Reflection occurs when a light ray hits a surface and bounces off. The angle at which the ray hits the surface is equal to the angle at which it bounces off. If the surface is made very flat and smooth by polishing, all the light rays bounce off in the same direction.

In the reflection of light, the angle of incidence is equal to the angle of reflection, measured from the normal (the line perpendicular to the point of impact). When the surface is smooth,

This type of reflection is called regular, specular, or mirror reflection.

A mirror surface forms an image of things that reflect light onto it. This occurs because the light rays maintain the same pattern, except reversed from left to right, that they possessed before being reflected. Mirrors are usually made of smooth glass with a thin layer of a shiny metal such as silver bonded to the rear side (*see* Mirrors).

When an opaque surface is rough, even on the microscopic level, the light rays that hit it are scattered, causing the surface itself to become visible. This is diffuse, or irregular, reflection. If a piece of raw steel with a rough opaque surface is polished smooth and flat, it reflects light rays regularly and takes on the qualities of a mirror.

Refraction and Dispersion

Light travels in a straight line as it passes through a transparent substance. But when it moves from one transparent material to another of different density— for example, from air to water or from glass to air— it bends at the interface (where the two surfaces meet). This bending is called *refraction*. The amount, or degree, of refraction is related to the difference between the speeds of light in the two materials of different densities—the greater the difference in densities, the more the speed changes, and the greater the bend. A slanting object partly out of water displays refraction. The object appears to bend at the interface of the air and water.

Lenses refract light. Those that have concave, or hollowed-out, surfaces spread light rays apart. Those that have convex, or bulging, surfaces bring light rays closer together.

so that all the normals are parallel, the rays maintain their spatial pattern. When the surface is rough, so that the normals are not parallel, the rays are scattered.

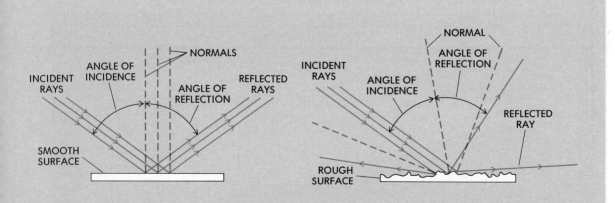

For centuries before the 1600's, scientists had known that when a ray of white light shines on a prism, a broad band containing several colors emerges. Some thought that the colors were caused by variations in lightness and darkness. But in 1672 Isaac Newton published the results of his experiments with light. He showed that a second prism placed in the path of a beam of one color could not add more color to the beam. It did, however, spread the beam farther apart. Newton concluded that the first prism broke white light down into its separate parts by spreading them apart, and he was able to establish that white light is not a pure color but a combination of all the colors in the spectrum. (*See also* Color.)

A prism spreads white light into the spectrum because each color has a slightly different speed within the prism, so each color bends (refracts) a slightly different amount as it enters and again as it leaves the prism. Violet light slows up the most, so it is bent the most; red light slows up the least, so it is bent the least. This spreading apart of white light into a spectrum is called *dispersion*.

Physicists often define dispersion as the fact that different colors move at different speeds within a substance, not necessarily causing a spectrum. For example, when white light enters a glass block that has parallel faces, the colors all have different speeds and bend different amounts as they travel through the glass. This, according to a physicist, is also dispersion. But the colors all bend back to form white light as they leave the second parallel face, so separate colors are not observed.

Opaque materials absorb all the colors of white light except their own, which they reflect. A piece of pure red material absorbs orange, yellow, green, blue, and violet but reflects red. Transparent colored materials absorb all colors except their own, which they both transmit and reflect. A piece of pure blue cellophane absorbs red, orange, yellow, green, and violet but transmits blue (it looks blue on the side opposite the light source) and reflects blue (it looks blue on the same side as the light source).

MEASURING THE SPEED OF LIGHT

Light can travel through a vacuum. Stars are easily visible on clear nights, though their light must travel for years through empty space before it reaches earth. A laboratory experiment demonstrates that light can travel through a vacuum. When air is pumped out of a glass vacuum chamber that contains a ringing bell, the bell remains visible while the sound fades away. The vacuum cannot transmit sound waves, but the light rays continue to pass through it.

It is much easier to describe the interaction of light with matter than to explain what light is. One reason for this is that light cannot be seen until it interacts with matter—a beam of light is invisible unless it strikes an eye or unless there are particles that reflect parts of the beam to an eye. Also, light travels very fast—so fast that for centuries men disputed whether it required any time for light to move from one point to another. Many scientists thought that the movement of light was instantaneous.

Galileo suggested one of the first experiments to measure the speed of light, and Italian scientists carried out his idea. Two men were stationed on two hilltops. Each had a shaded lantern. The first man was to uncover his lantern. As soon as the second man saw the light, he was to uncover his lantern. The scientists tried to measure the time that elapsed

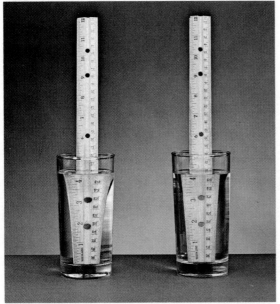

Light rays bouncing off the ruler on the left, in mineral oil, are bent (refracted) more than light rays from the ruler on the right, which is in water.

This alligator appears to be cut in half at the water line. Light reflected from the alligator underwater is refracted compared with the light reflected from above the water.

between the moment the first lantern was uncovered and the moment a return beam was detected. The speed of light was much too fast to be measured in this way, and the scientists therefore concluded that light might well travel instantaneously.

Olaus Roemer, a Danish astronomer, was dealing with an entirely different problem when he came across the first workable method for measuring the speed of light. He was timing the eclipses of Jupiter's moons and noticed that the time between eclipses varied by several minutes, depending on the position of the earth in its orbit. As the earth approached Jupiter, the time between eclipses grew shorter. As the earth receded from Jupiter, the time between eclipses grew longer. In 1676 Roemer proposed that these discrepancies be used to calculate the time required for light to travel the diameter of the earth's orbit. Since the exact size of the earth's orbit was not yet known, and since Jupiter's irregular surface caused errors in timing the eclipses, he did not arrive at an accurate value for the speed of light. But he had demonstrated that light took time to travel and that its speed was too quick to measure on earth with the instruments then available.

In 1849 Armand Fizeau, a French physicist, devised a way to measure the speed of light on earth instead of relying on uncertain astronomical measurements. His experimental apparatus included a beam of light that was sent through a notch in a rotating disk, was reflected from a mirror, and returned to the disk. The disk had 720 notches cut into it. When the returning light passed through a notch, an observer could detect it; if it hit between notches, the light was eclipsed. The distance light would travel (from the open notch to the mirror and back to the point where a tooth

could eclipse the light) was measured. Fizeau timed the eclipses and observed the rotational speed of the disk at the time of the eclipses. With this information he calculated that the speed of light in air was 194,000 miles per second. Later investigators refined this method. Jean Foucault, for example, replaced the disk with rotating mirrors and arrived at a value of 186,000 miles per second.

One of the most surprising and confusing facts about light was discovered by Albert Michelson and his co-worker, Edward Morley. They measured the speed of light very accurately as it traveled both in the same direction as the earth's movement and in the direction opposite to the earth's movement. They expected to get slightly different values, believing that the speed of the earth would be added to or subtracted from the speed of light. The situation, as they saw it, was similar to that of a person looking out the window of a car traveling at 60 miles per hour. If another car going 80 miles per hour overtakes it, the second car then seems to be moving at a speed of 20 miles per hour, or its own speed *minus* the speed of the car it has passed. If a car going 80 miles per hour approaches a car going 60 miles per hour, it seems to be traveling at 140 miles per hour, or its own speed *plus* the speed of the car that it is approaching. Light, the two men discovered, does not behave that way. Its speed appears to be the same, no matter what the speed or direction of movement of the observer making the measurement. Albert Einstein developed his theory of relativity to help explain this phenomenon (*see* Relativity).

The accepted value for the speed of light in a vacuum is 2.997924562×10^8 meters per second (about 186,282 miles per second), a fundamental

The distance between Jupiter and the earth differs at different times of the year. Olaus Roemer noted that the time between eclipses of Jupiter's moons decreased as the earth approached Jupiter and increased as the earth receded from Jupiter. He suggested that the discrepancies were caused by the time that light took to cross the diameter of the earth's orbit.

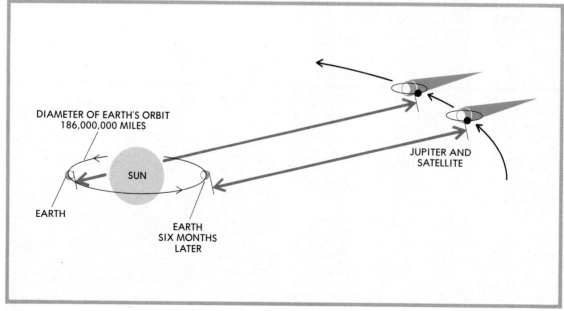

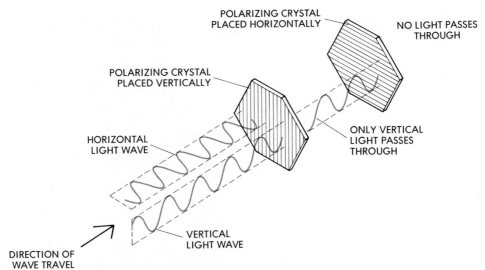

POLARIZING CRYSTAL
PLACED HORIZONTALLY

NO LIGHT PASSES
THROUGH

POLARIZING CRYSTAL
PLACED VERTICALLY

HORIZONTAL
LIGHT WAVE

ONLY VERTICAL
LIGHT PASSES
THROUGH

DIRECTION OF
WAVE TRAVEL

VERTICAL
LIGHT WAVE

The polarization of light can be explained by the theory that light acts like transverse waves. Light vibrating parallel to some part of the polarizing crystal can pass through it. But light vibrating at a different angle is stopped by the crystal.

constant of the universe. According to the theory of relativity, time and distance may change as the speed of an object approaches the speed of light (its length shrinks and any changes it regularly undergoes take longer to occur, *relative* to a stationary observer), but the measured value for the speed of light always remains the same.

LIGHT—WAVE OR PARTICLE?

The question remains, what is light? By the 17th century enough was known about the behavior of light for two conflicting theories of its structure to emerge. One theory held that a light ray was made up of a stream of tiny particles. The opposing theory regarded light as a wave. Both of these views have been incorporated into the modern theory of light.

Newton thought that light was composed of tiny particles given off by light sources. He believed that the different colors into which white light could be broken up were formed by particles of different sizes. He thought refraction resulted from the stronger attraction of the denser of two substances for the particles of light. Since the attraction was greater, the speed of light in denser mediums should also be greater, according to his theory. A basic piece of evidence supporting the particle view of light is that light travels in straight lines. This can be seen when a small, steady light source shines on a relatively large object. The shadow of the object has sharp borders. Newton felt that if light were a wave, it would curve slightly around obstacles, giving fuzzy-edged shadows. He pointed out that water waves curve as they pass an obstacle (for example, dock pilings) and that sound waves curve over hills and around the corners of buildings. Newton realized, however, that simple variations in the size of particles did not explain all light phenomena. When he tried to understand the shimmering coloration of soap bubbles, he had to introduce the idea that the particles vibrated.

Newton's contemporary Christiaan Huygens, a Dutch physicist, proposed that light was a wave. He postulated that a substance called the *ether* (not to be confused with the class of chemicals called ethers) filled the universe. Waves were generated in this pervasive substance when light traveled through it. Huygens assumed that light waves were like sound waves—the movement of alternately compressed and rarefied ether. Such waves are called longitudinal waves because the vibration of the wave is parallel to the direction in which it is traveling.

Polarized Light

One aspect of the behavior of light posed a problem for both the particle and wave theories. Neither could really explain the polarization of light by certain transparent crystals. Both Newton and Huygens knew that when light was directed through certain crystals, it would emerge much dimmer. If a second crystal of this class were placed at a certain angle in the path of the dimmed light, the light could pass through it. Then, as either of the two crystals was slowly turned, the light emerging from the second crystal grew dimmer until it was completely blocked. Evidently, something in the structure of the first crystal allowed only part of the light to pass. When the second crystal was lined up properly with the first, it allowed the same amount of light to pass; when it was at the wrong angle to the first crystal, it screened out the light from the first crystal.

Newton speculated that polarization occurred because light particles had various shapes on their sides, some of which were rejected by the crystal structure. This was not a very satisfactory explanation. However, Huygens had to make even more complicated assumptions to explain how crystals could polarize longitudinal waves. Neither the wave theory nor the particle theory was sufficiently developed to account for all the observed light phenomena, but the weight

199

Fritz Goro, Life© Time Inc.

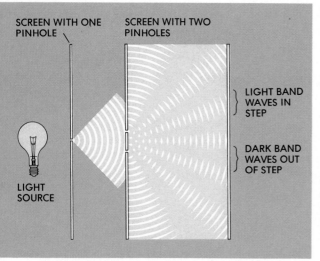

In Young's interference experiment, light that passes through the pinholes in the second screen sets up an interference pattern on the back wall. Such patterns are caused by waves.

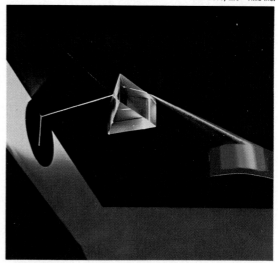

White light is a mixture of all the colors of the rainbow. A prism breaks up white light into its component colors by bending each color a different amount.

of Newton's reputation caused the particle theory to be accepted by most scientists.

Light Bends Around Corners

In the early 19th century Thomas Young, a British physician, took the next step in developing the wave theory. He demonstrated that light waves were so short that the amount they curved as they passed an object was too small to be visible. He showed that, though shadows from point sources of light appear to have sharp edges, there are thin light-and-dark bands along their borders that are caused by the bending of some light rays into the shadow. This scattering of light, called *diffraction*, can be observed under certain conditions. A thin tubular source, such as a fluores-

Matter cannot travel faster than the speed of light in a vacuum. In a transparent substance, however, particles can travel faster than light travels in that substance. When that happens, they give off visible light, called Cherenkov radiation. The photograph shows the core of an atomic reactor submerged in water. The blue glow is Cherenkov radiation. It is caused by charged particles whose movement through the water is faster than that of light in water.

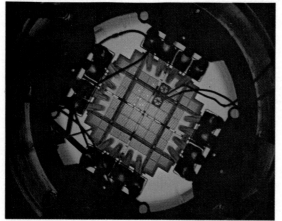

Argonne National Laboratory

cent light, is good. A very thin slit in an opaque material, or even two fingers squeezed loosely together so that light may pass between them, may cause diffraction. The slit is held a foot or two in front of one eye, parallel to the light source; the other eye is closed. Light shines through the slit, and a pattern of colored bands, or a colored glow, can be seen outlining the slit. The outline is colored because diffraction disperses white light into its separate colors in much the same way that a prism does. Young observed diffraction and concluded that it occurred because light was a wave.

Three important measurements describe a wave—speed, frequency, and wavelength. Frequency is a measure of the number of waves that pass a given point in a specified amount of time. Wavelength is the distance from one crest (the highest point) to the next crest, or from one trough (the lowest point) to the next. If all the waves have the same speed, a great many short waves will pass a point in the same time that only a few long waves pass it. Speed equals the wavelength times the frequency.

Young set up an experiment to measure the wavelength of light; using the principle of *interference*. When two sets of waves meet, they interfere with each other in a predictable way. Water waves, such as those made by the wakes of two boats, illustrate this. When two wakes meet, the water becomes choppy. Parts of the waves are very high and parts are very low; the individual waves can reinforce each other or cancel each other. Where two crests meet, the wave becomes higher. Where two troughs meet, the wave becomes deeper. And if a crest and a trough meet, they cancel each other and the water is level.

In his interference experiment Young used a single light source, a pinhole that admitted a single beam of sunlight. This beam fell on a screen that had two pinholes close together. As light passed through each

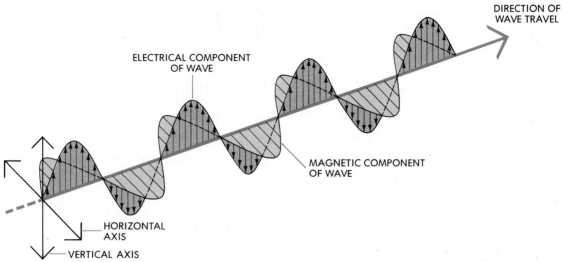

DIRECTION OF
WAVE TRAVEL

ELECTRICAL COMPONENT
OF WAVE

MAGNETIC COMPONENT
OF WAVE

HORIZONTAL
AXIS

VERTICAL AXIS

The movement of a light wave, or of any electromagnetic wave, through space is described as the growth and collapse of elec- trical and magnetic fields. The fields are at right angles to each other and to the direction of travel.

pinhole, it curved and spread out (diffracted). Because the pinholes were close enough together, the two light beams met and interfered with each other. Their interference pattern was seen on a screen behind the pinholes. With this pattern and knowing the distance between the screens, Young was able to calculate that the wavelength of visible light was about one millionth of a meter.

Subsequent measurements show that the wavelengths of visible light range from 7.60×10^{-5} cm. to 3.85×10^{-5} cm. (2.99×10^{-5} in. to 1.51×10^{-5} in.). Each color is associated with a range of wavelengths. Red has the longest lengths. The wavelengths decrease from orange through yellow, green, and blue. Violet has the shortest wavelengths visible to the human eye.

Transverse Waves Explain Polarization

Young and Augustin Jean Fresnel, a French physicist, cooperated in developing the idea that light waves are transverse, that they resemble the waves made when a rope stretched from a post is jerked up and down rather than longitudinal sound waves. The rope itself moves only up and down, at right angles to the forward travel of the wave. Young and Fresnel suggested the wave motion of light might also be at right angles to the direction in which the wave was traveling. The motion could be in any direction between sideways and up-and-down just so long as it was at right angles to the direction of travel. Wave motion of this kind could explain polarization. If a polarizing crystal admitted only those waves that were vibrating in a certain direction, then a second crystal would block those waves if it were turned at an angle to the first. The second one would be oriented to accept only waves vibrating in a different direction, and the first cyrstal would have already blocked all those waves. Fresnel made calculations that accounted for all the light behavior he knew of by assuming that light was made up of transverse waves.

Measurements of the speed of light in substances other than air presented additional difficulties for Newton's particle theory of light. The theory had assumed that light travels faster in dense substances than in rarefied substances. Fizeau and Foucault measured the speed of light in various transparent substances and discovered that it was slower in denser materials than in air.

"Invisible Light"

Around 1800—while Young was developing his wave theory—three scientists discovered that the color spectrum was bordered by invisible rays. Sir William Herschel, a British astronomer, was measuring the temperature of the colors dispersed by a prism. As he moved the thermometer down the spectrum from violet to red, he observed a rise in temperature. As he moved the thermometer beyond the red beam, the temperature grew even higher. Herschel had discovered a hot, invisible radiation that appeared to be a continuation of the spectrum. This radiation is called infrared radiation because it occurs just below red in the spectrum, where there is no visible light.

Ultraviolet rays were discovered by Johann Wilhelm Ritter and by William Hyde Wollaston, who were independently studying the effects of light on silver chloride. Silver chloride placed in violet light grew dark. When the chemical was placed in the area beyond the violet of the spectrum, it darkened even more rapidly. They concluded that a chemically powerful kind of invisible radiation lay beyond the violet end of the spectrum. (*See also* Ultraviolet Radiation.)

In 1864 James Clerk Maxwell, a Scottish physicist, published a theory of electricity and magnetism. He had developed equations that predicted the existence of electromagnetic waves caused by electrical disturbances. He calculated the speed of such waves and

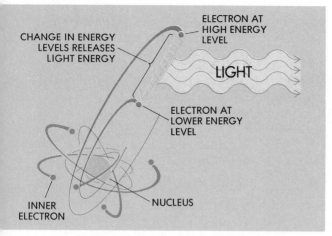

CHANGE IN ENERGY
LEVELS RELEASES
LIGHT ENERGY

ELECTRON AT
HIGH ENERGY
LEVEL

LIGHT

ELECTRON AT
LOWER ENERGY
LEVEL

INNER
ELECTRON

NUCLEUS

Modern theory explains the emission of light by matter in terms of electronic energy levels, diagramed above. An electron of relatively high energy may jump to a condition of lower energy, giving off the energy difference as electromagnetic radiation.

found it to be the same as the speed of light. Maxwell concluded that light was an electromagnetic wave. As a single light wave travels through space, its movement consists of the growth and collapse of electrical and magnetic fields. The electrical fields are at right angles to the magnetic fields, and both are at right angles to the direction in which the wave is moving.

Maxwell's theory implied that other electromagnetic radiations with wavelengths longer than infrared or shorter than ultraviolet might be found. In 1887 Heinrich Hertz produced radio waves, which have longer wavelengths than infrared rays, thus confirming Maxwell's theory. (*See also* Radiation.)

LIGHT: WAVE AND PARTICLE

In 1900 the German physicist Max Planck advanced a theory to account for the behavior of *blackbodies*. A blackbody is an ideal substance with a perfectly black surface that absorbs all the radiation that falls on it and emits radiation in specific ways dependent on temperature. While such an ideal material does not actually exist, some materials resemble it closely enough to provide experimental tests of blackbody theory. The observed behavior is that blackbodies do not emit all wavelengths in equal amounts.

Instead, certain wavelengths are emitted more often than others. As the temperature increases, the wavelengths that are emitted preferentially decrease in length. In other words, the wavelength of maximum emission varies inversely with temperature. Planck explained this behavior by suggesting that matter can handle energy only in specific amounts, called *quanta*, and that amounts of energy between these quanta cannot be absorbed or emitted. The amounts must be exactly right.

In 1905 Einstein expanded this idea in his explanation of the *photoelectric effect*. If light falls on certain metals, electrons in those metals are freed and can form an electric current. Einstein was trying to account for the observation that the energy of the electrons is independent of the amount of radiation falling on the metal. The maximum energy of the electrons was observed to depend on the wavelength of the radiation. Einstein suggested that not only does matter handle energy in precise amounts (quanta), but the photoelectric effect could also be accounted for by assuming that electromagnetic energy, including light, always occurs in these bundles. This reintroduced the particle theory. The results of many subsequent experiments supported the idea that light energy travels in quanta. An individual light "particle" possesses one quantum of energy and is called a *photon*.

The way matter becomes a light source can be explained in terms of quantum theory. When certain elements are heated, they give off light of a specific color. This light can be separated into a spectrum that is made up of many distinct bright lines (*see* Spectrum and Spectroscope). Each element has its unique spectrum, which can be accurately measured. Since a spectrum positively identifies each element, the chemical composition of astronomical bodies is determined by an analysis of their spectra.

Scientists wondered why the atoms of each element, when provided with a wide range of energies by the heating process, give off only the specific energies in their spectra. The modern theory of atomic structure makes this phenomenon understandable. An atom is made up of a heavy, positively charged nucleus which is surrounded by light, negatively charged electrons.

The electromagnetic spectrum ranges from very energetic gamma rays, which have high frequencies and short wavelengths, to radio waves, which have low frequencies and long wavelengths. The visible light region is a very small part of the entire spectrum.

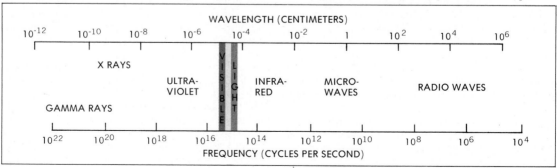

WAVELENGTH (CENTIMETERS)

10^{-12} 10^{-10} 10^{-8} 10^{-6} 10^{-4} 10^{-2} 1 10^2 10^4 10^6

X RAYS

ULTRA-VIOLET

VISIBLE LIGHT

INFRA-RED

MICRO-WAVES

RADIO WAVES

GAMMA RAYS

10^{22} 10^{20} 10^{18} 10^{16} 10^{14} 10^{12} 10^{10} 10^8 10^6 10^4

FREQUENCY (CYCLES PER SECOND)

Modern theory states that the electrons of an atom can assume certain fixed energy relationships, called *energy levels*, to one another and to the nucleus. These energy levels are the same for all the atoms of a single element. An electron must occupy one of the energy levels; it cannot possess any energy between levels.

When an atom is heated, enough energy may be given to one of the electrons to raise it to a higher energy level. But it usually jumps back to a lower level, giving off an electromagnetic wave—the energy difference of the two levels. When this energy is in the visible light range, it shows up as one of the lines in the element's visible spectrum. Each element has a different spectrum because each element has a different number of electrons and different energy levels available to these electrons.

Atomic theory had not yet explained why both a wave theory and a particle theory were needed to describe light. Physicists used both, depending on which was more useful in a given situation. The paradox was finally resolved in 1924 by Louis de Broglie. He postulated that matter, which had always been treated as a collection of particles, had a wave aspect as well. This wave nature has been demonstrated in experiments with electrically charged moving particles, such as electrons. (*See also* Matter; Energy.)

BIBLIOGRAPHY FOR LIGHT

Adler, Irving. Story of Light (Harvey, 1971).
Anderson, L. W. Light and Color (Raintree, 1978).
Beeler, N. F. and Branley, F. M. Experiments with Light (Harper, 1957).
Branley, F. M. Light and Darkness (Harper, 1975).
Freeman, Mae and Ira. Fun with Light (Sportshelf, 1971).
Heuer, Kenneth. Rainbows, Halos, and Other Wonders: Light and Color in the Atmosphere (Dodd, 1978).
Levin, Edith. The Penetrating Beam, Reflections on Light (Rosen, 1979).
Lorbeer, F. I. Philosophy of Light (Sun, 1981).
Marcuse, Dietrich. Light Transmission Optics, 2nd ed. (Van Nostrand-Reinhold, 1982).
Rainwater, Clarence. Light and Color (Golden Press, 1971).
Waldman, Gary. Introduction to Light (Prentice, 1983).
(*See also* bibliographies for **Color; Laser and Maser.**)

The candle and the fireworks convert chemical energy to light. The incandescent light bulb, the fluorescent lights, and the neon lights convert electrical energy to light. The steel slabs have been heated until they give off light.

(All but center) E. F. Hoppe—Alfa Studio, (center left) Bob Glaze—Artstreet, (center right) H. Armstrong Roberts

LIGHTHOUSE

LIGHTHOUSE. To help those on ships determine location and to warn of potential hazards, lighthouses have been built for centuries in areas where naval or commercial vessels sail. The history of lighthouses is filled with tales of lighthouse keepers, the men who once lived in or near the lighthouse whose light it was their responsibility to keep burning. Most modern lighthouses, however, have automatic lights that need little tending.

Some few lighthouses have become quite famous. The one built on the island of Pharos, near Alexandria, Egypt, about 280 BC was regarded as one of the seven wonders of the ancient world. Along the Hudson River in New York City, under the George Washington Bridge, stands a small lighthouse about which a children's book was written—'The Little Red Lighthouse and the Great Grey Bridge' by H. H. Swift and Lynd Ward. But the best known of all is the Eddystone Lighthouse on a reef 14 miles (22.5 kilometers) off the shore of Plymouth, England. Celebrated in ballad and folklore, it has had a long and sometimes tragic history. Four successive lighthouses have stood at this location. The first, opened in 1699, was swept out to sea only four years later. Its replacement was destroyed by fire in 1755. The third was replaced by the present tower in 1882.

Locations

In the ancient world lighthouses were constructed by the Phoenicians, Greeks, Romans, and other maritime powers throughout the Mediterranean region—from the Black Sea to the British Isles. For most of the Middle Ages, until about AD 1100 when commerce and trade revived, lighthouse construction halted. Italy and France took the lead in construction of new lighthouses, and by 1500 lighthouses were a standard feature of navigational charts.

Lighthouses are located along most of the commercial shipping lanes of the world. Most are on the heavily traveled parts of oceans and seas, but they are also quite frequently found on inland lakes and rivers where commercial ships are common. Many are located on the Great Lakes in the United States.

Lighthouses are built on shore, on offshore reefs, or are moored in the seabed. Since the construction of the third Eddystone Lighthouse, masonry and brick have continued to be used, especially for shore-based structures. But steel and concrete are now the most favored building materials.

Lighthouses built in the open sea are moored on submerged caissons, concrete-filled cylinders, or sand-filled concrete bases. Some open-sea lighthouses are similar to offshore oil platforms. These have large upper decks that contain all necessary machinery, the light tower, and a helicopter landing pad. They are built on tubular steel piles driven about 150 feet (45 meters) into the seabed.

Illumination

The means used to illuminate lighthouses have varied considerably over the centuries. Wood and

Photos (left) courtesy of the trustees of the British Library; photo, John R. Freeman & Co., (right) U.S. Coast Guard

The original Eddystone Lighthouse (left) of 1699 contrasts with the light tower (right) of 1961 at Buzzards Bay, Mass.

coal fires were gradually superseded by oil lamps. Vaporized kerosene came into use shortly after 1900, but the use of acetylene gas, pioneered in Sweden by Gustaf Dalén between 1900 and 1910, revolutionized lighthouse technology. Because the fuel is contained in storage cylinders, it made possible the establishment of automated lighthouses in remote locations. They needed only an annual visit to replenish the gas and to check the operation of the mechanism.

The use of arc lamps began in England in 1862, but these devices proved expensive and difficult to control. Electric-filament lamps came into general use in the 1920s and are standard today. They may be augmented by modern, more efficient arc lamps. In some lighthouses the xenon flash tube is used. It is similar to the flashing light mounted on some skyscrapers to ward off aircraft and birds.

To increase light intensity and focus it into a beam, mirrors and other reflectors came into use in the 18th century. Modern lighthouses have reflectors, as well as lenses and prisms, to carry the light farther. So that the light can be seen from all directions, the lantern rotates at a controlled speed. Depending on the candlepower of the light, a beam can be seen from as far away as 28 miles (45 kilometers), although normal range is closer to 20 miles (32 kilometers).

In bad weather, such as dense fog, even a modern light with 10 billion candlepower is barely visible from half a mile. To offset the problem of poor visibility, lighthouses also produce sound to give position and warning information. For centuries bells and explosive charges have helped guide mariners, but today the most common device is the foghorn, the sound of which is familiar to anyone who has lived near an area of water navigation. The largest of these, the diaphone, makes its sounds by a rapid release of compressed air. The noise may be heard up to a distance of eight miles (12 kilometers).

Because sound waves are subject to the vagaries of weather—humidity, wind direction and speed, and temperature—radio and radar beacons, called racons, have become a standard means of guiding ships. These are detected with special equipment.

Lightships and Buoys

Other aids to navigation, similar in function to lighthouses, are lightships and buoys. Lightships came into use in the 17th century in places where a lighthouse was impracticable. A modern lightship is a steel vessel about 120 feet (35 meters) long. Usually manned by a crew of about seven, it carries all the equipment standard to a lighthouse. Some lightships are unmanned floats with automatic acetylene lights. These are adequate for sheltered waters where high-powered illumination is not necessary.

Buoys are floating steel devices used to delineate channels in rivers, harbors, and estuaries. They also mark single, isolated dangers such as wrecks or rocks. They vary in size from five to ten feet (1.5 to three meters) in diameter and weigh from one to nine tons (910 to 8,160 kilograms). They are moored to heavy concrete or cast-iron sinkers by a length of chain. The color, shape, and markings of a buoy convey information to navigators. The standards for buoys, known as the Lateral and Cardinal systems, were drawn up by the League of Nations in 1936 and are still in use. Most buoys are in the shape of cones, spheres, or cylinders; and they are painted red or black, alternating with white or plain markings. They may also be lighted. The light may come from burning acetylene or propane, or from electricity. Large buoys that rise about 14 feet (4 meters) above water have recently come into use in treacherous open-sea conditions. They carry lights and sound devices.

Because lighthouses, lightships, and buoys are often located in remote, hard-to-reach places, the power used to operate them is usually derived from diesel generators located at the site or, in the case of buoys, from replaceable electric batteries.

Administration

In most maritime nations, lighthouses are administered by the central government. In the United States, their operation is overseen by the Coast Guard; in West Germany, by the Ministry of Marine; in Sweden, by the National Administration of Shipping and Navigation; in Norway, by the Directorate of Lighthouse Services; in Japan, by the Maritime Safety Agency; and in Canada, by the Aids of Navigation Division of the Department of Transport. An exception is Great Britain: lighthouses in England and Wales are governed by the Corporation of Trinity House, a public corporation independent of the government. Trinity House is financed by dues levied on shipping, based on tonnage, at ports in the United Kingdom. Similar corporations operate the lighthouses in Scotland and Ireland. (*See also* Navigation.)

LIGHTING. Since earliest times people have needed devices to help them see after sundown and to illuminate places of shelter. Light from the sun and the moon is free, but it is undependable, difficult to control, and impossible to move. The development of artificial lighting has been marked by the invention of light sources with ever-increasing efficiency, output, and convenience.

Origins and Early Types

One of the oldest lighting devices is the torch, a portable light made from a long stick with burning resin or with oil- or wax-soaked rags at one end. Evidence of torches has been found at some of the earliest archaeological sites.

The lamp was invented in the Stone Age, no later than 70,000 BC. Early lamps consisted of a vessel containing a wick soaked in some burnable material such as oil. At different times lamps were made from seashells, alabaster, bronze, and clay. In the 18th century a lamp was introduced with a wick that emerged from a closed fuel container through a metal tube and that could be raised and lowered to control flame size. It was also discovered that the flame could be made brighter by adding controlled amounts of air and a glass chimney.

Candles, slow-burning lights made of tallow or wax and usually cylindrical with a fiber wick at the center, were used from 3000 BC. Candles are still popular for decorative and emergency use.

The use of paraffin wax and kerosene, both derived from petroleum, produced different results in the 19th century. Paraffin replaced tallow as a candle-making material and is still employed today. Kerosene, which was safe and inexpensive, fueled the improved lamps then available.

Coal and natural gas, distributed under pressure, lit lamps in cities from 1820. The mantle, a thumb-sized, loosely woven network of cotton impregnated with chemical salts, was fitted to the lamp burner above the flame. Raised to white heat, the mantle gives off a strong light.

Electric Lighting

The first electric lighting devices were arc lamps, which had an arc, or band of light, struck between two carbon electrodes. Used to illuminate city streets, these huge, cumbersome lamps were reliable, efficient, and capable of producing a quality of light approaching that of natural sunlight.

The incandescent lamp radiates light from a thread or filament heated by passing an electric current through it until it glows. The filament is enclosed in a vacuum or an inert gas to keep it from burning itself out. Commonly called the light bulb, this modern lighting device was introduced in 1879 by the United States inventor Thomas Edison. Although Sir Joseph Wilson Swan in England had fabricated an incandescent lamp one year earlier, Edison developed a complete lighting system and thus receives major credit for the invention. Improvements

LIGHTING

Lighting Through the Ages

Oil lamp (pre-Christian)

Carbon-arc lamp (1809)

Kerosene lamp (1859)

Carbon-filament lamp (1879)

Gas-mantle lamp (1885)

Mercury-vapor lamp (1892)

206

include replacing the original carbon filaments with metal for longer life, tungsten filaments and coiling them for improved efficiency, and frosting the interior of the glass bulb to soften its light. The spiral groove arrangement on the metal lamp base for screwing the device into a fixture was invented by Edison and is called the Edison screw in his honor.

Vapor-tube lamps make up a large class of lighting devices that produce light by striking an arc between electrodes in a tube containing neon gas, gaseous sodium, or mercury. The French physicist Georges Claude discovered that a vapor tube filled with neon gas under low pressure produces intense orange-red light. Claude found that by adding small amounts of other substances to the neon tube additional colors could be produced. He recognized the value of his invention for advertising. Neon signs became popular in the 1920s and are used worldwide today.

Fluorescent lamps came into use during the 1930s. These long tubes contain mercury vapor, an inert gas such as argon, and on the inner wall a phosphor that fluoresces, or glows, when subjected to the radiation of the mercury discharge. The color of light produced—usually white or near white—depends upon the phosphors in the coating. Fluorescent lamps, which are far more efficient and longer-lived than incandescent lamps, were the first vapor-tube lamps to be used indoors. An electric transformer, or ballast, on fluorescent fixtures provides the high voltage needed to start the arc and then limits the current to just enough to maintain it.

High-intensity discharge (HID) lamps are vapor-tube lamps with a much shorter arc than fluorescents, and they contain the vapor at higher pressure. The HID lamp is valued for its great energy efficiency. There are three main types—mercury, metal halide, and high-pressure sodium—which vary in the metallic vapor used, internal construction, efficiency, cost, and life. Like fluorescents, HID lamps require ballasts for starting and current limiting. Unlike other vapor-tube lamps, an HID lamp glows dimly when it is first turned on and does not reach full power until it has warmed for one to ten minutes. Its light is extinguished at once when turned off, however, and the lamp must go through a warm-up period again if reactivated. HID lamps were originally used only outdoors because they showed color badly. Better phosphor coatings have largely eliminated the problem, leading to indoor use.

Lighting devices can fulfill special requirements. Immense fixtures find use as searchlights, at lighthouses, and on airport runways. Lamps with unique qualities are employed in photography, television production, and to help plants grow. Tiny flexible fibers that transmit light by internal reflection from a lamp at one end to a target at the other have aided the field of medicine. Some lamps radiate light from only one portion of the spectrum. The familiar ultraviolet sunlamp, for example, darkens the skin, and infrared lamps can produce heat or help people to see in the dark. (*See also* Light.)

Courtesy of (left and top right) Richard E. Orville; (above right) William S. Bickel, University of Arizona, Tucson

A flash of lightning strikes a tree (left) from 200 feet (60 meters) away. A discharge of "triggered" lightning (top right) is set off by a tall tower atop Mount San Salvatore near Lugano, Switzerland. Heat lightning (above right) gives off many colors of the visible spectrum.

LIGHTNING. A violent thunderstorm, with its loud claps of thunder and bright flashes of lightning, is an awesome thing. Everyone has seen, and probably been frightened by, these sudden jagged streams of electricity. It is estimated that, at any given moment, about 3,500 thunderstorms are occurring around the world. These storms produce more than 100 bright strokes of lightning every second. The strokes act as electrical conductors joining the Earth to its atmosphere. Thunderstorms and lightning are nature's ways of balancing the electrical forces that exist between the Earth and the upper atmosphere.

In ancient times men believed that lightning bolts were thrown from the heavens by angry gods. No scientific explanation of the cause of lightning appeared until the 1700s. In 1745 the invention of the Leyden jar (the first electrical condenser) proved that electricity could be collected and stored for indefinite periods. Benjamin Franklin applied this information in a series of experiments he performed in 1752. He proved that lightning was an electrical discharge by demonstrating that its actions were in agreement with the principles of electricity known at that time. During the 20th century, research scientists, electric-utility companies, and weather bureaus have joined forces to study the causes and occurrences of lightning. Many useful facts have been learned. However, it is a complicated subject, and much more work must be done before lightning is fully understood.

The Buildup and Discharge of Lightning

Great electrical changes occur in the atmosphere when a large cloud forms above the Earth. Inside the cloud, rapid heating and cooling of air masses produce violent activity. Rain falls, air currents rise, and water droplets freeze. Some drops of water in the cloud become charged with positive electricity. These are carried to the upper part of the cloud by air currents and form a positive-charge center. Ice crystals that are formed have a negative charge. Due to their weight, they move down and produce a negative-charge center at the base of the cloud. To balance this negative charge, positive charges on the ground are concentrated just below the cloud.

As cloud formation continues, the two opposite charges increase in strength. Since unlike charges attract, there is a powerful tendency for the charges to join and neutralize each other. Each charge exerts a strong electrical potential, or pressure, in an effort to bridge the air gap from cloud to ground. Air, a poor electrical conductor, resists the passage of the charges. At some critical point, however, the resistance of the air is overcome. A small discharge, called a pilot streamer, moves toward the Earth carrying negative charge. A stronger current, called a stepped leader, follows and ionizes the air in its path (*see* Electricity). The stepped leader moves in a series of jagged spurts, each about 150 feet (45 meters) long. When the pilot streamer touches the Earth, a high-current return streamer leaps from the ground toward the cloud. It travels along the path of ionized air created by the stepped leader. This is the part of the stroke that produces the brilliant flash we see.

As charge in one cloud center is dissipated, negative charge from an adjacent charge center moves in to replace it. A dart leader from the second charge

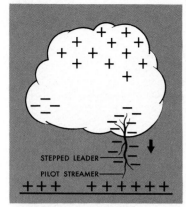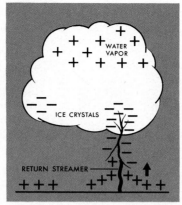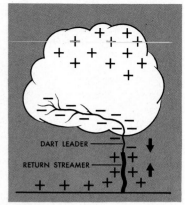

A lightning stroke begins when a pilot streamer moves down from a negative-charge center in a cloud (left). The stepped leader, a more powerful current, follows the pilot streamer. A return streamer, a current of high density (center) leaps from the Earth and travels along the path of ionized air created by the stepped leader. Discharge of a second negative-charge center in the cloud occurs when the dart leader (right) moves to the ground and is met by another return streamer.

center moves to the ground along the original current channel. This produces another return streamer that also travels up to the cloud. Discharging continues until all negative charges in the cloud have been drained off, restoring electrical balance between Earth and atmosphere. Lightning strokes also travel between two clouds, and, in the case of heat lightning, between charge centers in the same cloud.

Thunder follows a lightning flash. During the electrical discharge, the flow of electricity along the discharge path ionizes the gases of the air and produces great heat. The gases expand violently, causing compression waves that travel outward at the speed of sound. These compression waves produce thunder.

The Effects of Lightning

The thousands of thunderstorms on Earth each day produce more than 8 million flashes of lightning, most of which occur in tropical and subtropical areas, from 30° north to 30° south. Most of these flashes are harmless, but a number of them strike airplanes, buildings, ships, and people. A direct strike to a plane, building, or ship can cause fire or other damage. A direct strike to a person normally causes death. With people now spending more and more time outdoors, the number of lightning deaths is expected to increase. Lightning may even strike inside a structure by working its way through the electrical or telephone wiring in a house, or even along metal piping.

On the credit side, lightning produces significant chemical changes in the atmosphere. As a stroke moves through the air, it generates tremendous heat that unites nitrogen and oxygen to form nitrates and other compounds. These compounds fall to the Earth with the rain. In this way, the atmosphere is able continually to help replenish the supply of nutrients that soil needs to produce plants.

Protection Against Lightning Damage

The attraction of tall structures for lightning has been known for centuries. This is easily explained by modern electrical theory. Lightning is an electrical current that tries to bridge the air gap between the ground and a cloud. It follows the path of least resistance—the route that crosses the shortest air gap. Thus the positive ground charge will concentrate at the highest point on the ground, and the stroke will usually be between that point and the cloud. For this reason, a lightning rod, or shield, is placed higher than all other objects near it. A shield may be a single pole set in the ground or a group of masts supported in a framework that completely surrounds a building. The shield provides a good target for a lightning stroke and thus protects other nearby structures.

Lightning normally strikes the tallest object in its range. A person standing in the middle of a field is the tallest object and therefore the main target. A tall tree attracts lightning and is a poor conductor of electricity. It offers so much resistance to the passage of current that a part of the current may flash out at the sides and strike any neighboring object. That is the reason that it is dangerous to stand under a tree during a storm. Steel buildings, trains, automobiles, and aircraft provide good paths to ground for electricity and are well insulated.

LILIUOKALANI (1838–1917). The last reigning monarch of Hawaii before the islands were annexed by the United States in 1898 was Queen Liliuokalani. A woman of some musical ability, she is probably more remembered for writing the song 'Aloha Oe' than for her role as queen.

Liliuokalani was born in Honolulu on Sept. 2, 1838. Her mother, an adviser to King Kamehameha III, had her educated at one of the missionary schools on the island of Oahu. In 1862 she married John Owen Dominis, whom she outlived by many years. When her younger brother, the prince regent W. P. Leleiohoku, died in 1877, she was named heir presumptive to the throne. When David Kalakaua, the king and her older brother, died in 1891, she succeeded him, becoming Hawaii's first reigning queen.

Her reign of but four years was an unhappy one. In trying to strengthen the monarchy and break ties with the United States, she alienated a large community of foreign businessmen in Hawaii. Led by Sanford Dole, they established a Provisional Government and called for her abdication. She stepped down for a short time, but was restored by order of President Grover Cleveland. The businessmen ignored Cleveland and, in 1895, suppressed an insurrection by her supporters. She was finally forced to abdicate on Jan. 24, 1895. After trying, with only partial success, to regain some of her crown lands and gain a subsidy from the United States, she withdrew from public life. She died in Honolulu on Nov. 11, 1917.

LILY. The white lily stands for purity. Artists for centuries have pictured the angel Gabriel coming to the Virgin Mary with a spray of lilies in his hand, to announce that she is to be the mother of the Christ child. The lily is also the sign of the Resurrection. The lovely white Madonna lily of southern Europe was used for years as the Easter lily. It often failed to bloom in time for Easter, however, and so Bermuda lilies were substituted.

Some familiar colored lilies are the dark-red tiger lily, of Japan; the Siberian coral lily; the gold-banded, or Japan, lily, with yellow-banded purple-spotted white flowers; and the Japanese showy lily, with red-dotted pink flowers. Wild lilies of North America are the Turk's-cap, Canada, and wood lilies.

The bulb of a true lily is made up of loose scales that easily peel off. The bulbs never become completely dormant and must be kept moist in peat moss until they are planted. Professional breeders of lilies pull the bulbs apart and plant the scales. Each scale grows into a small bulb that in two or three years produces flowers. New varieties are created by shaking the pollen of one kind onto the stigma of another and planting the resulting seed.

True lilies belong to the genus *Lilium* of the family Liliaceae. Several hundred species and thousands of varieties are known. They have six-part flowers (three petals and three sepals colored alike) and usually six stamens.

The family includes many food plants—asparagus, onion, leek, garlic, and chives. Some of the flowers are the lily of the valley, mariposa, sego lily, tulip, hyacinth, and yucca, all members of different genera. The popular day lilies belong to the genus *Hemerocallis*. The plantain lily, or funkia, comprises the genus *Hosta*. Calla lilies belong to the unrelated Araceae family, of which Jack-in-the-pulpit is a member. (For picture in color, *see* Flowers, Wild.)

The sentinel lily is a true member of the lily family. This species can be grown in gardens, but more delicate types of lilies must be raised carefully in hothouses.

A–Z Collection

LIMA, Peru. Francisco Pizarro, the Spanish conqueror of Peru, founded the city of Lima in January 1535. He named it the City of Kings in honor of the Three Kings of the Bible. The name was changed to Rimac, the name of the river on which the city stands. Eventually Rimac became mispronounced Lima. For centuries Lima was the capital of Spain's realm in South America.

Lima is a blend of colonial styles and modern architecture. The ancient building materials of adobe, bamboo thatch, and wood have been replaced with steel, cement, and bricks. Structural innovations have been introduced to avoid earthquake disasters.

The heart of the old city is the broad Plaza de Armas, laid out by Pizarro himself. On one side rises the colonial era Cathedral. There Pizarro's shriveled body lies exposed to view in a glass coffin. The modern government palace also flanks the Plaza.

In the narrow crowded streets nearby are many ancient churches and colonial mansions. Among the finest colonial buildings are San Augustín Church, famous for its magnificent façade; and the Palace of the Tagle Tower, now the foreign office and also one of the most beautiful examples in the Western World of a Spanish-Moorish palace.

Lima is the seat of the oldest university in South America, the National University of San Marcos. It received its charter from Emperor Charles V in 1551. In the Archaeological Museum are rich remains of Inca and pre-Inca Indian civilizations.

Lima is the largest city of Peru and the center of its political, social, cultural, commercial, and economic life. The city's factories produce cotton and woolen textiles as well as many products for local use. Food-processing and beverage-making industries are numerous. The port of Callao, six miles (10 kilometers) distant on the Pacific Ocean, handles most of Peru's foreign trade.

The cold Peru, or Humboldt, Current provides the local Pacific waters with quantities of tiny plants and animals called plankton. The plankton provide food for other abundant marine life, including anchovies, flounders, shrimps, and lobsters.

A well-developed highway network radiates from the old city. Lima is connected through the Pan-American highway (Carretera Panamericana) to Trujillo in the north, to Arequipa in the south, and to Cuzco in the southeast; it is connected through the Central Highway with Pucallapa in the northeast.

The Jorge Chávez international airport is located at Callao. The Central Railway of Peru, the highest standard-gage railway in the world, climbs the Andes from Callao northeast to La Oroya and west to Huancayo. The railway line from the city to Callao was built in 1850 and is the oldest in South America.

Recreational facilities include a racetrack, a bullfight plaza, and soccer stadiums. There are three principal theaters and many experimental university theaters, drama centers, and dramatic schools.

Lima lies at an altitude of 500 feet (152 meters) above sea level, near the center of the arid Peruvian coastal plain. The Rimac River supplies water for irrigation. Though the city is only 12 degrees south of the equator, the Peru Current cools the air. The annual mean temperature is 65° F (18° C). Rain seldom falls and averages less than one inch (25 millimeters) per year, but fogs are common in winter. Numerous earthquakes have shaken the region. The cloud cover, the excessive humidity, and the lack of both winds and direct sunlight combine to produce a high degree of air pollution. This condition is further complicated by exhaust fumes from vehicles. The traffic in Lima is extremely congested. Metropolitan Lima contains about 30 percent of the country's total population. (*See also* Peru.) Population (1981 metropolitan area census), 4,600,900.

LIMA BEAN *see* LEGUMES.

LIME. Quicklime, or lime, as it is more commonly called, is calcium oxide (CaO). It is a white alkaline substance having considerable power to corrode, or "eat," animal tissues. Quicklime is usually obtained by roasting limestone in a kiln or furnace at about 1,800° F (980° C). This changes the calcium carbonate of limestone to calcium oxide. Since lime is alkaline and chemically active, it is useful in many processes. These include removing hair from hides and reducing acidity in soils and various liquids—for example, sugarcane juice. Other common uses are in making mortar and plaster and in the manufacture of glass, paper, and steel.

To make mortar, lime is slaked, or broken down, by adding water. This changes the substance to calcium hydroxide (CaOH). Coarse sand, cinders, or pulverized stone is mixed in, and the mixture is used to bind or cover bricks or stones. As the mixture dries, it absorbs carbon dioxide from the air to form calcium carbonate and also combines with the silica of the sand to form calcium silicate. These substances bind the bricks or stones together. Lime exposed to air is ruined for mortar making because it absorbs carbon dioxide from the air (air-slaking). Lime plaster is made by mixing hair with waterslaked lime.

Pure calcium oxide is formed by melting limestone, chalk, or oyster shells in an electric furnace. Under intense heat pure lime gives a strong white light. Limelights, also called calcium or Drummond lights, were formerly used for stage lighting.

A solution of calcium hydroxide in water is called limewater. This is used in medicine to correct acidity, to prevent milk from curdling in large lumps, and with certain oils as a liniment for burns. Limewater is also an antidote for poisoning by mineral or oxalic acids. (*See also* Limestone.)

LIMESTONE. Without help from chemistry and a microscope it would be hard to accept that the rock called limestone comes from sea shells and corals. But chemistry proves that shells and corals owe their stiffness to calcium carbonate ($CaCO_3$), often called "carbonate of lime." Limestone also is mainly calcium carbonate; and the microscope reveals the remains of animals that formed it.

Limestone is sedimentary rock, formed from shells and other "limey" material in the oceans that in past ages covered the limestone regions. Outstanding regions of this sort in the United States are the present site of the Rocky Mountains, the valleys of the Mississippi, Ohio, and Saint Lawrence rivers, and a large part of Texas.

Limestone has many important uses. It is the chief source of lime. It is used in making portland cement (*see* Cement) and in smelting iron and lead (*see* Iron and Steel Industry); and it is an important building material. It wears better than sandstone, is more easily shaped than granite, and weathers from nearly white to a beautiful gray. Oolitic limestone, quarried in Lawrence, Monroe, and Owen counties in Indiana, is particularly fine building stone. Its texture resembles fish eggs, hence its name, from the Greek *oion*, meaning "egg." Bedford, Ind., is an important limestone quarrying center. (*See also* Quarrying.)

Crushed limestone is used on macadam roads. Farmers use ground limestone to neutralize soil acids that attack calcium and other salts needed by plants. Such protection occurs naturally when soils have a limestone foundation.

Travertine limestone and calcareous tufa consist of calcium carbonate deposited from hard water. Stalactites and stalagmites in caves are formed in the same way. Limestone rock is often riddled with caves because water and carbon dioxide dissolve the limestone. Chalk is a soft white limestone containing the shells of foraminifera (*see* Chalk). Marble is a metamorphic, or transformed, limestone crystallized by pressure and perhaps heat (*see* Marble).

ABRAHAM LINCOLN—
16th President of
the United States

LINCOLN, Abraham (1809–1865; president, 1861–1865). Every boy and girl who knew Abraham Lincoln loved him as a friend. All the children around his home in Springfield, Ill., and around the White House in Washington felt that "Mr. Lincoln" understood them and truly liked them. Men and women who knew him admired him and called him "honest Abe." People throughout the world said he was one of the greatest men of all time.

He was an unusual man in many ways. One minute he would wrestle with his sons or tell a joke and slap his bony knees in laughter. The next minute he might be deep in thought and not notice anything around him. He was gentle and patient, but no one was more determined. He was tall—nearly six feet four inches—very thin, and stooped. He spent less than a year in school, but he never stopped studying. All his life he was a "learner." Born in a log cabin on the frontier, he made his own way in life and became the president who kept the United States united.

His Family Came from England

The first of the Lincoln family to come to America was Samuel Lincoln. He had been a weaver's apprentice at Hingham, England. He settled in Hingham, Mass., in 1637. From there the family spread southward to Virginia, where Abraham's father, Thomas Lincoln, was born in 1778.

When Thomas was four years old the family moved to Kentucky. There his father, who was a farmer, was killed by Indians. Thomas grew up in Kentucky. He never went to school, but he learned to be a carpenter. He was a strong, heavy-built man, who sometimes spoke sharply and at other times entertained his friends with jokes and stories.

Some historians have called him shiftless. True, he moved many times in his life, but he worked hard enough at carpentry to buy farms. He did not, however, make much of a living, because most of the land he cleared was too poor for good crops.

Marries Nancy Hanks, Mother of Abraham

In 1806 Thomas married Nancy Hanks. She had been born in Virginia, but little else is known of the Hanks family. Nancy was only a baby when her mother Lucy brought her to Kentucky. When Nancy married Thomas Lincoln she was 22 years old, tall, and slender. Some historians say she could neither read nor write, which was not unusual for pioneer women. Others say that she read the Bible daily.

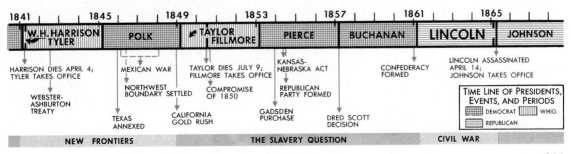

Thomas and Nancy settled in Elizabethtown in Hardin County, Ky. Their first child, Sarah, was born there. In 1808 Thomas bought a half-cleared farm at Sinking Spring on the Nolin River near Hodgenville. He hopefully moved his family to this first farm—a rolling stretch of thin, poor land on a lonely river.

Abraham Born in a Log Cabin

About sunrise on Feb. 12, 1809, the son of Thomas and Nancy Lincoln was born. They named him Abraham after his grandfather Lincoln. Abraham's birthplace was a one-room log cabin, 16 feet long and 18 feet wide. The logs were chinked with clay and light came dimly through the single window. The floor was earth, packed down hard, and the bed was made of poles and cornhusks. A roaring fire on the hearth and rough bearskin blankets kept Nancy and her son Abraham warm on that cold winter morning.

In the spring of 1811 Thomas Lincoln moved his family to a farm he had bought on Knob Creek, about ten miles northeast. In later years Abraham Lincoln said that the Knob Creek farm was the first home he remembered and he loved it. Like all farm boys in those busy days young Abe learned to plant, hoe, husk corn, build hearth fires, carry water, and chop wood.

When he was six years old, Sarah and he tramped "up the road a piece," some two miles each way, to a log schoolhouse. Here he learned to read, write, and "do sums" (arithmetic). He liked writing best of all. Later he said that he practiced writing "anywhere and everywhere that lines could be drawn." He wrote with charcoal on the back of a wooden shovel and even in dust and snow.

Between chores young Abe climbed the rocky cliffs at Knob Creek, roamed among the dark cool pines and cedar trees in the valley, or waded in the pebbly creek. Sometimes he stood in the hot, dusty clay to watch the covered wagons carrying settlers along the nearby Cumberland Trail. His buckskin breeches were pulled high on his spindly legs and his thin arms stuck out from his rough linen shirt.

There were no close neighbors. Abe got used to being alone. He did not mind because he loved the hills and the quiet hollows and the trees—especially the trees. He learned so well to tell the many kinds that many years later, on his walks around Washington, he would point out their differences. He smilingly told visitors, "I know all about trees in light of being a backwoodsman."

Lincolns Move to Indiana

In December 1816 Thomas took his family across the Ohio River to the backwoods of Indiana. For the last few miles Thomas, probably helped by Abe, had to cut a trail out of the wilderness of trees and tangle of wild grapevines. That winter was so cold that people remembered it as the year of "eighteen hundred and froze to death." The Lincolns settled on Little Pigeon Creek in Spencer County, about 16 miles from the Ohio River.

Young Abe and Sarah helped their father build a "half-faced camp." This was a shed of poles and bark, with one side left open toward a roaring log fire. They had to keep the fire burning day and night. They needed it for warmth, cooking, and drying their snow-soaked clothes and moccasins.

Abraham's father, Thomas Lincoln, built this one-room cabin near Hodgenville, Ky. Today it is preserved in a granite and marble building on the old Lincoln farm.

While the family huddled in their lean-to through the freezing winter, Thomas and Abe worked every day building a log cabin. Abe was only eight years old, but very large for his age, and he quickly learned to swing an ax. They cut and hewed logs for a cabin 18 feet by 20, then chinked the logs with clay and grass. Once in a while the boy shot a wild turkey, for the family lived mostly on wild game, with a little corn. He never became much of a hunter, however, as he did not like to shoot to kill. With Sarah he picked berries, nuts, and wild fruits for the family and trudged a mile to a spring for water. All around them was the unbroken wilderness.

Abraham's Fine Stepmother—Sarah

In the autumn of 1818 Nancy Hanks Lincoln died of the dread frontier disease called "milk sickness." Sarah, only 11 years old, took over the cooking and cabin chores while Thomas and young Abe cut timber to clear farm land. After a year the little family was in sorry shape. They needed a woman's help. Thomas rode back to Elizabethtown, Ky., and married a widow, Sarah Bush Johnston, whom he had known since boyhood. He brought her and her three children to the shabby little log cabin in Indiana.

Abe and his sister Sarah quickly learned to love their second mother. She was a big-boned woman, with clear skin, friendly eyes, and a quiet way of getting things done. She cleaned up the untidy cabin. She had Thomas make a wood floor and chairs and build a bed for the feather mattress she had brought from Kentucky. Young Abe and Sarah had never lived in a cabin so homelike. Thomas did better on the farm, too, and the children began to eat and dress better. Sarah Lincoln did all this without any criticism or impatient words. She knew well that the family needed her.

Best of all, she encouraged Abe to study. She was not educated, but she saw how eager he was to learn. In later years he said of her: "She was the best friend I ever had. . . . All that I am, I owe to my angel mother." Sarah Lincoln told people: "He was the best boy I ever saw. I never gave him a cross word in my life. His mind and mine, what little I had, seemed to run together."

Abe Grows Up with Books

Sarah made Thomas send the gangling 11-year-old to school. There was no regular teacher. When some man came along who knew a little about the three R's, he might teach the boys and girls for a few weeks— usually in the winter when farm work was slack. Whenever "school kept" at Pigeon Creek, Abe hiked four miles each way, his cowhide boots sloshing in the snow. He did not mind. He was learning.

In all his life his schooling did not add up to a year, but he made up for it by reading. A cousin, Dennis Hanks, who came to live with the Lincolns, said: "I never seen Abe after he was 12 that he didn't have a book somewheres around." By the time Abe was 14 he would often read at night by the light of the log fire. His first books were the Bible, 'Aesop's Fables', and 'Robinson Crusoe'.

When he was 15 years old he was so tall and strong that he often worked as a hired hand on other farms. Usually, while he plowed or split fence rails, he kept a borrowed book tucked in his shirt to read while he lunched or rested. He could turn in a good day's work when he had to. Many neighbors, however, called him lazy, saying he was "always readin' and thinkin'."

Once Abe grinned and told his farm boss, "My father taught me to work, but he never taught me to love it."

A farmer loaned him 'The Life of George Washington', by Parson Weems, and Abe left it in the rain. To make up for his carelessness, Abe shucked corn for him for three days. All his life Abraham Lincoln made every effort to do the fair thing.

He could never get enough to read. He said: "The things I want to know are in books. My best friend is the man who'll get me a book I ain't read." Once he tramped nearly 20 miles to Rockport to borrow one.

Storyteller, Ferryman, and Law "Listener"

After supper Abe often walked down the road to Gentryville to join the "boys" at Gentry's store. His humorous stories, sometimes told in dialect, were popular with the young men lounging against the log counter.

A replica of Lincoln's birthplace stands in the Chicago Historical Society Museum. Here we see the kinds of tools and furniture the Lincolns used.

He loved to imitate travelers and local characters and would throw back his head with a booming laugh. In his own speech he pronounced words as he had learned them on the Kentucky frontier, such as "cheer" for "chair" and "git" for "get." That was the way all Southern woodsmen talked.

Between farm chores he helped to run a ferry across the Ohio River to Kentucky. When he was 18 he built his own scow and rowed passengers over the shallows to steamers out in the river.

Always he kept teaching himself new things. He became interested in law. Borrowing a book on the laws of Indiana, he studied it long into the night. Whenever he could, he strode miles to the nearest courthouse to hear lawyers try their cases. He even crossed into Kentucky to listen in court. Every visit taught him more about the ways of lawyers and furnished him with new stories. Throughout his later life as a lawyer, politician, and statesman he shrewdly drew on this rich fund of stories to make a legal point or to win audiences.

Down the Mississippi to New Orleans

When Abe was 19 he got his first chance to see something of the "outside world." James Gentry, the owner of the country store, hired him to take a flatboat of cargo to New Orleans, then a wealthy city of some 40,000 people. With Gentry's son, Allen, Abe cut timber, hewed great planks, and built a flatboat called a "broadhorn."

New Orleans was 1,000 miles down the twisting Mississippi River. From sunup to sundown the two brawny young men pulled the long oars—about 40 feet long at bow and stern. Often they hurriedly hauled back on the side sweeps to swing the boat from snags, clumsy flatboats, or trim steamers caught in the shifting currents. They lived on board, cooking and sleeping in a rickety lean-to on deck. At night they tied up to a tree or stump on the muddy bank.

In New Orleans Abe saw his first auction of slaves. At that time slavery was lawful in all the United States south of the Ohio River. The tall, thoughtful young man winced at the sight of slave gangs in chains being marched off to plantations. Later he said, "Slavery is a continual torment to me."

To Illinois and Splitting Rails

Back from New Orleans, Abe clerked part time at Gentry's country store and helped his father get ready to move to Illinois. The Indiana farm had not

In a painting by Harold von Schmidt, young Lincoln wrestles Jack Armstrong in New Salem, Ill. Although thin as a rail, Lincoln was a mighty wrestler. Jack, the champion of the "Clary's Grove Boys," found him to be the first man he could not throw. The two became good friends.

Brown Brothers

The New Salem State Park in Illinois has restored the village buildings as they were in Lincoln's day. The Lincoln-Berry general store is stocked with goods like those Lincoln sold.

been a success. Through the winter the men built wagons and chests and made yokes and harness. In March 1830 they started their 200-mile trek.

Fording rivers and creeks, the heavy wagons often broke through the ice. Lincoln later said: "Once my little dog jumped out of the wagon . . . broke through, and was struggling for life. I could not bear to lose my dog, and I jumped out of the wagon and waded waist deep in ice and water, and got hold of him."

The family settled on the Sangamon River, some ten miles southwest of Decatur, Ill. Once more Abe helped to clear a farm. With a cousin, John Hanks, he then split 3,000 rails to fence some neighbors' land. He was truly "right handy with an ax." His feats with an ax on the Illinois prairie led his political supporters to call him, later in life, the "rail splitter." Even in his last years, as president, he could hold an ax straight out at arm's length—something very few young men could do.

Starts His Own Life at New Salem

After a winter of cold and illness Thomas Lincoln again moved, about 100 miles southeast into Coles County. This time Abe did not go. He was 21 years old and ready to live his own life. Loving the river, he again took a flatboat to New Orleans, loaded with pork, corn, and live hogs.

On his return he hired out as a clerk in the village store at New Salem, Ill. The tiny settlement stood on a bluff above the Sangamon, about 20 miles northwest of Springfield. Here he lived for six years (1831–37). For $15 a month and a sleeping room in the back, he tended store and a gristmill.

Tales sprang up fast about Lincoln in the New Salem days. People spoke about his strict honesty and his giant strength. Some told how he once walked six miles to give back a few pennies to a woman who had overpaid for dry goods. Whenever a settler bought furs, or an oxen yoke, gun, tea, or salt he knew he

would get his money's worth from "honest Abe." He would also enjoy a laugh at one of Abe's stories.

Lincoln's employer boasted of Abe's strength and wrestling ability so much that a gang of toughs in nearby Clary's Grove challenged him. Men trooped in from the neighboring villages to see the match. The Clary's Grove champion was Jack Armstrong, a thickset, powerful man. He had always thrown all comers. He rushed at Lincoln, trying to hurl him off his feet. Lincoln held Armstrong off in his long arms, then grappled and threw him to the grass where they rolled over and over.

After a panting, grunting tussle Lincoln let go of Armstrong and, according to some stories, said: "Jack, let's quit. I can't throw you. You can't throw me." Armstrong shook Lincoln's hand, saying he was the "best feller that ever broke into this settlement." They became good friends. In matches with other powerful wrestlers Lincoln often simply tossed them over his head. With his great long legs he was the fastest foot racer, and when he had to fight with his fists he did. No one challenged him a second time.

Captain in Black Hawk War

When the Black Hawk War broke out in April 1832 Lincoln and the Clary's Grove men enlisted. The war was a series of border raids by Sauk and Fox Indians led by Chief Black Hawk. They crossed from Iowa into Illinois and attacked and scalped settlers. (*See also* Indians, American, section "Centuries of Struggle between Indians and Whites.")

The Clary's Grove men elected Lincoln captain of their rifle company. The honor pleased him, but he knew nothing about military life. Once he could not think of the order he should give to march his company through a gate in formation. Scratching his head, he finally commanded: "Halt! This company will break ranks for two minutes and form again on the other side of the gate."

When Lincoln's term of enlistment ended in 30 days he re-enlisted as a private. In all, he served three months. He never fought in a battle, but he twice saw the horror of bodies scalped by the Indians. His army experience, learned on long marches and in rough camps, taught him sympathy for soldiers' hardships in the field. In later life, when he was commander in chief in the Civil War, he treated soldiers' failings with great understanding.

Loses in Politics; Opens a Store

Just before the outbreak of the Black Hawk War, Lincoln had decided to run for the Illinois legislature. After his war service he again started his campaign. He was 23 years old, lanky and so tall that his cheap linen pants never reached his ankles. His coarse black hair was always mussed and his dark-skinned face was already deeply lined.

In a circular he sent out to voters, he wrote: "I was born and have remained in the most humble walks of life." While he was speaking at one political rally a fight broke out. Lincoln strode up to the man who had started the brawl, seized him by the neck and seat of the pants, and hurled him out of the crowd.

Lincoln then calmly went back to his speech, saying: "My politics are short and sweet, like the old lady's dance." In just two or three sentences he told what he would vote for and ended by saying: "If elected I shall be thankful; if not, it will be all the same." He did not carry the district, but his local popularity gave him nearly every vote in New Salem.

Meanwhile the New Salem store failed. Lincoln was out of work. He thought of learning to be a blacksmith, but another New Salem store was put up for sale. Lincoln, with William Berry as partner, bought it on credit. Neither one, however, was much interested in tending to business. Lincoln preferred to visit with the few customers or to lean against the door and read. After several months Berry died, leaving Lincoln more than $1,000 in debt. Eventually he paid back every cent, but it took him years.

Becomes Postmaster and Surveyor

Failing as a storekeeper, Lincoln again was "hard up." In May 1833 his friends got him appointed the postmaster of New Salem. The job paid only about $50 a year, but it took little of his time and gave him the chance to read all the incoming newspapers free. He read every issue and was particularly interested in the political news. To earn his board and lodging, he also split rails and worked as a mill hand and hired man. In every spare moment he read or made political talks.

In the autumn of 1833 Lincoln gladly took an appointment as deputy county surveyor. To learn the work, he plunged into books on surveying and mathematics. By studying all day, and sometimes all night, he learned surveying in six weeks. As he rode about

An unknown artist did this oil painting about 1858, probably after Lincoln won fame in the Lincoln-Douglas debates. It shows Lincoln swinging a heavy maul as in New Salem days.

the county, laying out roads and towns, he lived with different families and made new friends.

The wife of Jack Armstrong, the Clary's Grove "champion," said: "Abe would drink milk, eat mush, corn bread and butter, and rock the cradle. . . . He would tell stories, joke people at parties . . . do anything to accommodate anybody."

Elected to Legislature and Becomes Lawyer

In 1834 Lincoln's old friends in New Salem and his new friends throughout Sangamon County elected him to the Illinois General Assembly. They re-elected him in 1836, 1838, and 1840. Before his first term began in November 1834 he borrowed $200 to pay the most pressing of his debts and to buy a suit for his new work.

Vandalia was then the capital of Illinois. Lincoln soon became popular in the legislature. One representative said that Lincoln was "raw-boned . . . ungraceful . . . almost uncouth . . . and yet there was a magnetism about the man that made him a universal favorite." By the time he started his second term he was a skilled politician and a leader of the Whig party in Illinois. A fellow Whig declared: "We followed his lead; but he followed nobody's lead. . . . He was poverty itself, but independent."

216

This first photograph of Lincoln was taken in Springfield, Ill., when he was 37 years old. Notice the strong, lined features. He did not grow his beard until February of 1861.

Encouraged by friends in the legislature, he determined to become a lawyer. Between terms he borrowed law books and took them back to New Salem to study. Often he walked 20 miles to Springfield and back to return one law book and get another. He was doing what he advised a young law student to do years later: "Get the books . . . and study them till you understand them in their principal features. . . . Your own resolution to succeed is more important than any other one thing." He took some time from studying to serve as New Salem's postmaster and, as he said, "mixed in the surveying to pay board and clothing bills." On Sept. 9, 1836, he received his law license.

Moves to Springfield, the New Capital

In 1837 Lincoln took the lead in getting the capital transferred from Vandalia to Springfield. The legislature did not meet there until 1839, but in April 1837 Lincoln left New Salem to make his home in Springfield. Putting his few belongings into saddlebags, he rode a borrowed horse to the thriving little town on the prairie (*see* Springfield, Ill.).

He was 28 years old and so poor he did not have $17 to buy furnishings for a bed. Joshua Speed, the storekeeper, recalled that when Lincoln said he could not afford it, "The tone of his voice was so melan-

choly that I felt for him." Speed immediately invited Lincoln to share his own lodgings. This kindness started a lifelong friendship.

Anne Rutledge, Mary Owens, Mary Todd

When Lincoln had lived in New Salem he had boarded various times at the log inn kept by James Rutledge, a founder of the village. Rutledge's daughter Anne was tall, slim, and blue-eyed, with auburn hair. Legend says that she was Lincoln's sweetheart and that when she died in 1835, at the age of 19, he nearly lost his mind in grief. The legend grew from a lecture by William Herndon, Lincoln's last law partner, a year after Lincoln's death.

Historians today, however, are not convinced that Anne Rutledge promised to marry Lincoln. At the time of her death, from "brain fever," she was engaged to one of Lincoln's friends, John McNamar.

Two years before Anne's death Lincoln had met in New Salem a visitor from Kentucky. She was Mary Owens, daughter of a wealthy farmer. Nearly a year older than Lincoln, she was well educated. He squired her to quiltings, huskings, and other "sociables," sometimes forgetting to help her cross creeks or climb steep hills. Apparently his absent-mindedness did not suit Mary Owens. When, in the summer of 1837, he proposed to her in a rather indecisive way, she "respectfully declined" to marry him.

By 1839 Lincoln was established as a lawyer in Springfield and was taking part in the busy social life of the city. One of the society belles was Mary Todd. She had come from her home in Lexington, Ky., to live with her sister and brother-in-law, son of the governor of Illinois. Mary was 21 years old— small, plump, pretty, gay, unusually well educated, and temperamental. Lincoln first met her in the winter of 1839 at a dance. He was immediately attracted to her and said, "Miss Todd, I want to dance with you in the worst way." Later, she laughingly told friends, "And he certainly did!"

Courtship and Marriage

Soon Lincoln was spending every free moment with Mary Todd. They both loved literature and poetry, especially Shakespeare and Robert Burns. Lincoln delighted in reciting passages from memory. He had always been, as he said, a "slow learner," but he never forgot what he learned. He was pleased too that Mary took an intelligent interest in politics.

Mary was also being courted by Stephen A. Douglas, a prominent lawyer, with whom Lincoln was later to debate dramatically. Her wealthy, aristocratic family were opposed to Lincoln—they thought him "uncouth, full of rough edges." Mary, as always, knew what she wanted. By spring she was devoted to him and told friends, "His heart is as big as his arms are long." She was also so sure of his remarkable abilities that she predicted he would some day be president of the United States. (*See also* White House, section "Hostesses of the White House.")

After a series of temperamental clashes between

This photograph was made during Lincoln's "stay-at-home" presidential campaign in 1860. He bought the house in 1843 in Springfield, Ill., for $1,500, then added the second story.

them, Mary Todd, the Kentucky belle, and Abraham Lincoln, son of the frontier, were married on Nov. 4, 1842. They were living in one room at the Globe Tavern in Springfield when their first child, Robert Todd, was born in 1843. The next year Lincoln bought a light tan frame house on the edge of town. There Edward, William, and Thomas (Tad) were born in 1846, 1850, and 1853. (*See also* White House, section "Children in the White House.")

The Lincolns' home life was often stormy. Both Mary and Lincoln were at fault. An extremely sensitive, high-strung woman, afflicted with migraine headaches, Mary frequently gave way to rages of uncontrollable temper. Sometimes they may have been justified, for Lincoln had trying habits. Most arose from his enormous power of concentration. When he became interested in a book or a problem, he forgot everything else. Once when he was pulling his baby sons in a little wagon and reading a book as he walked, one of the boys fell out. Lincoln did not notice his frightened howls until Mary rushed to pick him up, then gave the surprised father "what for."

Lincoln went to bed at all hours and got up at all hours. Often he came home two or three hours late to dinner, then was startled to find Mary upset over his tardiness. When he took off his stovepipe hat, his notes and legal papers spilled over the neat parlor floor. With a chuckle, he often said, "My hat is my walking office." If the parlor stove went out when he was lost in thought, he never noticed it. For no apparent reason he sank into black, silent moods for hours, and sometimes days, at a time.

When he thought of it, however, he would do anything to please her. Patiently, and a little humorously,

he let her teach him the "social graces." He was extremely careless about his dress and knew it bothered Mary, who wanted to be proud of him as a rising young lawyer. Every morning before walking slowly to his untidy law office, he stood in the doorway to let her inspect him. His shirt, which she made, must be fresh, his boots polished, his suit and stovepipe hat brushed. In wet weather she made him carry his baggy umbrella; on cold days, his gray shawl.

He knew she was in terror of thunder. No matter how busy he was, he would hurry from his office at the first warning of a storm. Rushing home, he would stay at her side till it ended.

Like Mary, he enjoyed entertaining. He neither drank nor smoked but loved music and people. Although he cared nothing for food and had to be prodded to eat, he liked to have friends in for supper. As he prospered in his law practice, Mary and he gave large dinner parties and became noted as generous and gracious hosts.

Both Devoted to Their Sons

Mary and Lincoln were blindly devoted to their sons. They thought the boys could do no wrong. The lads were hopelessly spoiled and neighborhood terrors. Sundays, while Mary was at church, Lincoln took the youngsters to his law office. While he worked unheedingly on his papers, they raced, wrestled, spilled ink, and overturned furniture until Lincoln's law partner, Herndon, told friends, "I'd like to wring their necks!" He never complained to Lincoln.

Brown Brothers

Lincoln's home in Springfield is a national historic site. All the rooms are open to the public. Many pieces of Lincoln's own furniture and china are in the attractive home.

room weep or slap their sides with laughter. Even more important to his success was his reputation for honesty. Honest Abe would not take a case unless he believed in his client's innocence or rights. He became an outstanding lawyer.

During this period he successfully handled important cases for the Rock Island Railroad and the Illinois Central Railroad. His most famous case, perhaps, was his victorious defense of "Duff" Armstrong, who was accused of murder. Duff was the son of Jack Armstrong, Lincoln's old wrestling foe. The accusing witness said he had seen Duff bludgeon and kill a man with a "slung shot" one night in the "bright moonlight." Lincoln opened an almanac and showed it recorded that the moon on that night had set long before the scuffle.

Returns to Politics

The threat of slavery being extended brought Lincoln back into politics in 1854. He did not suggest interfering with slavery in states where it was already lawful. The Kansas-Nebraska Act of 1854, however, enabled the people of each new territory to vote on whether the territory would be slave or free, thus threatening to extend slavery (see Kansas-Nebraska Act). Lincoln began a series of speeches protesting the act.

In 1856 he helped to organize the Illinois branch of the new Republican party, a political party formed by people who wanted to stop the spread of slavery (see Political Parties). He became the leading Republican in Illinois. When the Republicans nominated John C. Frémont for the presidency of the United States, Lincoln received 110 votes for nomination as vice-president (see Frémont). This brought Lincoln to the attention of the nation.

"House Divided Against Itself Cannot Stand"

The Republicans lost, but in 1858 Lincoln won the Republican nomination for senator from Illinois. Addressing the state convention at Springfield, he gave the first of his memorable speeches.

His huge hands tensely gripping the speaker's stand, he declared slowly and firmly: "A house divided against itself cannot stand. I believe this government cannot endure permanently, half slave and half free. I do not expect the Union to be dissolved—I do not expect the house to fall—but I do expect it will cease to be divided. It will become all one thing, or all the other."

Lincoln-Douglas Debates and Nomination

Lincoln's opponent in the senatorial election was Stephen A. Douglas, a Democrat and Lincoln's old-

At home Lincoln gave them boisterous "romps," or read aloud to them while they climbed over him, thumping him enthusiastically. In the yard they chased around him while he curried the horse or milked the cow. When he went to market to help Mary, grocery basket in hand, they trailed along swinging from his long arms or riding his shoulders. Often the noisy procession stopped while he and the boys and neighbor children held hopping contests. Springing with his great long legs, Lincoln "in three hops could get 40 feet on a dead level."

Elected to Congress, Retires to Resume Law

In 1847 Lincoln went to Washington, D. C., as a representative from Illinois. The Mexican War was on (see Mexican War). Lincoln opposed it. His antiwar speeches displeased his political supporters. He knew they would not re-elect him.

At the end of his term in 1849 he returned to Springfield. He sought an appointment as commissioner in the General Land Office in Washington, but failed to get it. Later that year he was offered the governorship of the Oregon Territory. He refused, convinced that he was now a failure in politics.

Returning to the law, he again rode the circuit, pleading cases in one county seat after another. The circuit kept him away from home nearly six months of each year. He missed his family but loved the easy comradeship of fellow lawyers staying in country inns and delighted in the sharp give-and-take in court. Wherever he went he could make the jury and court-

219

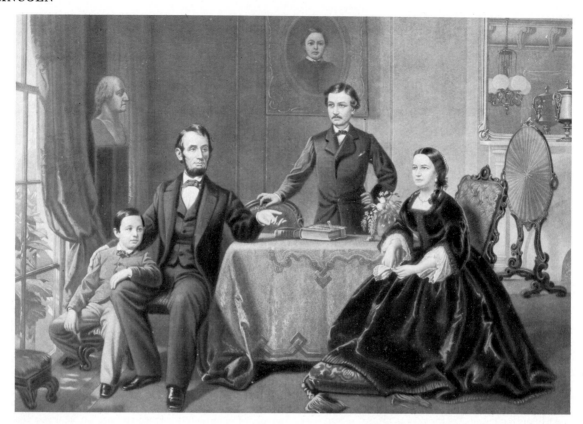

This painting shows the Lincoln family in the White House in 1862, after the death of Willie. Tad sits at Lincoln's knee. Robert, the eldest son, stands between his father and mother.

time acquaintance in Springfield. Douglas was running for re-election and had supported the Kansas-Nebraska Act. Lincoln challenged him to a series of debates on the slavery issue (*see* Lincoln-Douglas Debates). Although he overwhelmed Douglas in the debates, Lincoln lost the election. The debates, however, enlarged the public interest in Lincoln.

Realizing his country-wide fame, Lincoln's friends sought the Republican nomination for president for him in 1860. He himself worked tirelessly to win support. He now knew what he wanted—to be president of the United States in its time of crisis. He was determined to preserve the Union.

At the Republican national convention in Chicago in 1860 he was nominated on the third ballot. When the news was telegraphed to Springfield, Lincoln was sitting in a newspaper office. As jubilant friends congratulated him, he unfolded his thin legs, stood, and said, "Well, gentlemen, there is a little woman at our house who is probably more interested in this dispatch than I. If you'll excuse me, I'll take it up and let her see it."

Stay-Home Campaign and Election

The Democratic party was split, with the North nominating Stephen A. Douglas, and Southern Democrats naming John C. Breckinridge. Throughout the furious campaign Lincoln stayed quietly in Springfield, directing party leaders from a makeshift little office in the Capitol. He even carried his own mail back and forth from the post office. To avoid stirring up controversy and perhaps splitting the Republicans, he did not make a single political speech.

His strategy won. Lincoln was elected 16th president of the United States. He had 1,865,593 votes, Douglas had 1,382,713, and Breckinridge, 848,356. "Honest Abe, the rail splitter" was the first Republican to become president.

Alarm spread through the Southern states. They thought a Republican president would not respect their rights or property. They felt that secession was their only hope. Secession began Dec. 20, 1860, when South Carolina withdrew from the Union (*see* Confederate States of America).

As the time of Lincoln's inauguration approached, threats to kill him increased. They failed to frighten him, but no man was more aware of the danger of his position in a time of crisis. Saying farewell to friends at the Springfield railway station, he said prophetically: "I now leave, not knowing when, or whether ever, I may return, with a task before me greater than that which rested on Washington." The authorities were so fearful of a rumored assassination plot in Baltimore that they persuaded Lincoln to leave his special train at Philadelphia. He rode into Washington in a heavily guarded sleeping car. (For picture, *see* Civil War, American.)

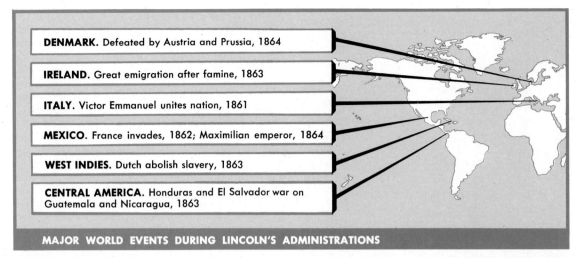

DENMARK. Defeated by Austria and Prussia, 1864	
IRELAND. Great emigration after famine, 1863	
ITALY. Victor Emmanuel unites nation, 1861	
MEXICO. France invades, 1862; Maximilian emperor, 1864	
WEST INDIES. Dutch abolish slavery, 1863	
CENTRAL AMERICA. Honduras and El Salvador war on Guatemala and Nicaragua, 1863	

MAJOR WORLD EVENTS DURING LINCOLN'S ADMINISTRATIONS

Inauguration and Outbreak of Civil War

In his inaugural address Lincoln assured the South that he would respect its rights, that there was no need of war. He said: "I have no purpose . . . to interfere with the institution of slavery in states where it exists. . . . In *your* hands, my dissatisfied fellow countrymen, and not in *mine*, is the momentous issue of civil war. . . . We must not be enemies."

Less than six weeks later, on April 12, 1861, the Civil War began (*see* Civil War, American). Abraham Lincoln shouldered the giant task of bringing the rebel states back into the national family and preserving the Union. He wrote: "My paramount object in this struggle is to save the Union, and it is not either to save or to destroy slavery. If I could save the Union without freeing *any* slave, I would do it;

On Oct. 2, 1862, shortly after the Union victory at Antietam, Lincoln went to field headquarters. He faces Gen. George B. McClellan. Lincoln made many such visits during the war.

and if I could save it by freeing *all* the slaves I would do it. . . . I have here stated my purpose according to my view of *official* duty; and I intend no modification of my oft-expressed *personal* wish that all men everywhere could be free."

Patient, Determined President

Lincoln was a strong president. At first his deliberate thinking and extraordinary patience deceived his Cabinet into thinking him uncertain. Several Cabinet members had strong political ambitions and feuded with each other. However, they all could serve the nation well, and so Lincoln patiently smoothed their differences and held them together with his great tact. He wanted their help, not their praise.

Profiting by his experience as a lawyer, he looked at every side of a question before deciding on an answer. "His mind acts slowly," said a friend, "but when it moves, it moves *forward*." When Lincoln reached a decision, he pressed his lips together firmly; then no one could change his mind. His Cabinet soon discovered this. Once every Cabinet member opposed Lincoln's plan. He smiled, said "Aye" for his own vote, and calmly announced, "The aye has it."

For months he had trouble finding capable generals to lead the Union forces. As with his Cabinet, he gave Gen. George B. McClellan and others every chance to prove themselves (*see* McClellan). When McClellan continued to delay attacking the Confederate forces, Lincoln said wryly, "He's got the slows." He kept urging McClellan to advance. Instead, McClellan childishly ignored Lincoln, his commander in chief. When Lincoln's secretary protested against McClellan's attitude, Lincoln answered quietly, "I'd hold his horse for him if only he would bring us success."

Soon Lincoln felt that he himself must take action. He read all he could on military science and made frequent inspection trips of forces in the field. Sometimes he took Mary Lincoln and his youngest son, Tad, with him to help boost the morale of the troops. Until he found competent generals, he directed much of the strategy for the Army and the Navy. He made

Four score and seven years ago our fathers brought forth on this continent, a new nation, conceived in liberty, and dedicated to the proposition that all men are created equal.

Now we are engaged in a great civil war testing whether that nation or any nation so conceived and so dedicated, can long endure. We are met on a great battle-field of that war. We have come to dedicate a portion of that field, as a final resting place for those who here gave their lives that that nation might live. It is altogether fitting and proper that we should do this.

But, in a larger sense, we can not dedicate —we can not consecrate—we can not hallow— this ground. The brave men, living and dead, who struggled here, have consecrated it, far above our poor power to add or detract. The world will little note, nor long remember what we say here, but it can never forget what they did here. It is for us the living, rather, to be dedicated here to the unfinished work which they who fought here have thus far so nobly advanced. It is rather for us to be here dedicated to the great task remaining before us— that from these honored dead we take increased devotion to that cause for which they gave the last full measure of devotion—that we here highly resolve that these dead shall not have died in vain—that this nation, under God, shall have a new birth of freedom—and that government of the people, by the people, for the people, shall not perish from the earth.

With this great speech Lincoln dedicated a national cemetery for soldiers at Gettysburg, Pa. One newspaper editor told readers, "Read it over, it will repay study as a model speech."

blunders but, on the whole, he was a successful commander in chief. When he found a capable general, such as Ulysses S. Grant, he supported him steadfastly despite great criticism (see Grant). For the greater part of the war most of the newspapers and people bitterly criticized Lincoln's policies. He never took the time to defend himself, convinced that he was doing what was right for the Union.

The bitter, tragic war surrounded Lincoln even in his home, the White House. Rifle companies patrolled the grounds and set up barracks in even the stately East Room. Every day secretaries brought him dispatches from the field, and his lonely mind tried to find solutions to the problems. Often he was at his desk before seven o'clock in the morning, working till Tad awakened. The lad then came down to Lincoln's office and they read the Bible together—Tad sitting in his father's lap.

A Harassed, Gentle President

Day after day office seekers crowded up to Lincoln's desk. He was trying to win a war, trying to save the Union, yet had to spend hours making or refusing appointments to political office. The greatest strain was reading and hearing petitions for clemency for soldiers sentenced to death for desertion or failing their duty. One time, near exhaustion, he said sadly, "I've had more cases of life and death to settle in four years than all the other men who sat in this chair put together. No man knows the distress of my mind." When a mother, wife, or sister stood before him pleading a soldier's case, Lincoln felt the pain himself. His deep-set gray eyes darkened and "sorrow seemed to flow from him." Whenever he could find the slightest excuse, he ordered a pardon for the soldier.

No one felt the tragedy of the war more than he. When Harriet Beecher Stowe, author of 'Uncle Tom's Cabin', met him, he said tiredly, "Whichever way the conflict ends, I have the impression that I shan't last long after it's over."

What little relaxation he got came from his sense of humor, occasional walks and horseback rides, and his companionship with Tad. Frequently he startled his Cabinet with humorous stories, explaining, "I have to get away from myself and this tiredness in me." His beloved Tad, the impish youngster with a lisp, could always make his father smile. Nearly every night he stayed in his father's office until he fell asleep. Lincoln then carried him up to bed.

Emancipation Proclamation

During 1862 Lincoln struggled with the problem of freeing the slaves. He knew that the slavery question must be settled if the United States, founded on the principles of liberty and equal rights for all, were to survive as a nation. He realized that the Union must be preserved, as a *free* nation—if democratic government was to succeed in the world.

With all the foresight he could muster, he worked out a plan to free the slaves. His Cabinet approved issuing the proclamation after the next Union victory. The summer passed with no victory. Then on Sept. 17, 1862, the Union forces stopped the advancing Confederate armies at Antietam.

On Sept. 22, 1862, President Lincoln issued the Emancipation Proclamation, one of the most important messages in the history of the world (see Emancipation Proclamation). He signed it Jan. 1, 1863.

Gettysburg Address

In July 1863 the Union armies threw back the Confederate forces at Gettysburg. This was the only battle on Northern soil (see Gettysburg, Battle of).

On Nov. 19, 1863, the great, shattered battlefield was dedicated as a national cemetery. The chief speaker was Edward Everett, a noted orator. As an afterthought, President Lincoln was invited "to make a few appropriate remarks." He worked and reworked his speech, seeking—as with all his formal documents —to make it as perfect as possible.

Lincoln's second inaugural, on March 4, 1865, occurred at a time when the Civil War had almost been won. Looking ahead to peace, Lincoln pleaded, "With malice toward none, with charity for all."

The crowd listened for two hours to Everett's extravagant oratory. Lincoln then rose slowly, put on his glasses, glanced at a slip of paper, then spoke gravely in his clear, high-pitched voice. In a little less than three minutes he finished his Gettysburg Address. He thought it a failure, as did most of the newspapers. Only a few recognized it as one of the noblest speeches ever made by any man. Everett wrote to him: "I should be glad if I could flatter myself that I came as near the central idea of the occasion in two hours as you did in two minutes."

Fears Defeat but Is Re-elected

By November 1864 Lincoln was nearly exhausted by the burden of the war and grief at the death of his son Willie in the White House. Wherever he turned he read or heard criticism of himself and his generals. He prepared a memorandum for his Cabinet, forecasting his defeat in the coming election. The people, however, at last rallied to him and re-elected him.

When he gave his inaugural address March 4, 1865, the end of the war was in sight. He looked forward to welcoming the Southern states back into the Union and to making their readjustment as easy as possible. He expressed that thought in these words: "With malice toward none, with charity for all, with firmness in the right as God gives us to see the right, let us strive on to finish the work we are in; to bind up the nation's wounds, to care for him who shall have borne the battle and for his widow and orphan, to do all which may achieve and cherish a just and lasting peace among ourselves and with all nations."

Victory and Death

Little more than a month later, on April 9, 1865, Gen. Robert E. Lee surrendered his Confederate army to Gen. U. S. Grant. On April 11 the Stars and Stripes of the United States were raised over Fort Sumter, where the war had begun.

223

The Lincoln Memorial, built of white Colorado marble, pink Tennessee marble, and Indiana limestone, stands in West Potomac Park in Washington, D.C. The outside columns are Doric; the inside, Ionic. A skylight lights the interior. The cornerstone was laid in 1915. Henry Bacon was the architect.

To celebrate with one of his favorite relaxations—the theater—Lincoln took Mary and two guests to Ford's Theatre on the night of April 14. During the third act of the play, 'Our American Cousin', John Wilkes Booth, a young actor who was proslavery, crept into the presidential box and shot Lincoln in the head. Booth then swung down onto the stage. Brandishing a dagger, he escaped. He presumably

The 'Seated Lincoln' is a strong and compelling statue in the main chamber of the magnificent Lincoln Memorial in Washington, D.C. The sculptor was Daniel Chester French.

died on April 26 in a Virginia tobacco barn hideout that had been set afire.

Soldiers carried the unconscious president across the street to the nearest residence, a boardinghouse. There, stretched diagonally on a bed too small for his long body, he died without speaking at 7:22 in the morning. It was April 15, 1865—28 years to the day since he had left the hamlet of New Salem. As the Great Emancipator died, Secretary of War Stanton said softly in the stricken room, "Now he belongs to the ages." A funeral train carried the first assassinated president back home to Springfield, Ill., where he lies buried in Oak Ridge cemetery.

Only after his death did the world begin to realize Lincoln's greatness. He was a superb statesman, a firm idealist who would not be swayed from the right, a man of kindly and brave patience, and, above all, a believer in what he called the "family of man."

BIBLIOGRAPHY FOR ABRAHAM LINCOLN

Angle, Paul M., ed. The Lincoln Reader (Greenwood, 1981).
Aulaire, Ingri and E. P. d'. Abraham Lincoln (Doubleday, 1957).
Balsiger, D. W. and Sellier, C. E., Jr. The Lincoln Conspiracy (Schick, 1977).
Bishop, J. A. The Day Lincoln Was Shot (Harper, 1964).
Coolidge, Olivia. The Apprenticeship of Abraham Lincoln (Scribner, 1974).
Coolidge, Olivia. The Statesmanship of Abraham Lincoln (Scribner, 1976).
Handlin, Oscar and Lillian. Abraham Lincoln and the Union (Little, 1980).
Horgan, Paul. Citizen of New Salem (Farrar, 1962).
Oates, S. B. With Malice Toward None (Harper, 1977).
Sandburg, Carl. Abraham Lincoln: the Prairie Years and the War Years (Harcourt, 1954).
Stone, Irving. Love Is Eternal (NAL, 1972).
Thomas, B. P. Abraham Lincoln (Knopf, 1952).

LINCOLN, Neb.

LINCOLN, Neb. The city of Lincoln is the capital of the Cornhusker State, Nebraska. Lincoln is located in the southeastern part of the state, about 60 miles (100 kilometers) southwest of Omaha. It lies in a shallow basin about 1,160 feet (355 meters) above sea level. Salt Creek and its tributaries thread through the basin. Lincoln serves as a center for educational, cultural, and religious institutions. The city also developed as the trade center for a wide agricultural area.

In the city are the buildings that house the various departments of the city, county, and state governments, the state mental and orthopedic hospitals, and the state penitentiary. Also located in Lincoln are a veterans' hospital and the regional headquarters of the Veterans Administration and the United States Department of Agriculture.

The University of Nebraska opened in Lincoln in 1871. The city is also the home of Nebraska Wesleyan University and Union College.

The State Capitol, designed by the architect Bertram Grosvenor Goodhue and completed in 1932, has a central tower that rises 400 feet (120 meters) from a massive two-story base and is considered a showpiece of American government architecture. 'The Sower', a statue symbolizing Nebraska's farms, stands atop the tower. Museums include those of the State Historical Society, the University of Nebraska, and the Sheldon Memorial Art Gallery. Pioneers Park includes a zoo. The Nebraska State Fair takes place in Lincoln each September. Other cultural groups include a symphony orchestra, the Lincoln Community Playhouse, and the National Art Association.

Lincoln got its first rail connection in 1870 and by the late 1800s had 19 different rail routes. Railroads gave Lincoln its most important industry—railroad-car repair. Among the city's manufactures are dairy and meat products, telephone equipment, agricultural machinery, cement, bricks, and drugs. There are also a number of printing and publishing plants, and the city is the headquarters for more than 30 insurance companies.

Lincoln arose from a settlement established in 1856 to work salt deposits. In 1859 it was named Lancaster, the seat of Lancaster County. When Nebraska became a state in 1867, the town was renamed for President Abraham Lincoln and became a compromise choice for the state capital over Omaha and a site south of Salt Creek. William Jennings Bryan, long a leader in American politics, lived in Lincoln from 1887 to 1921. His home, Fairview, has been restored with original furnishings and memorabilia.

Between the years 1926 and 1930 Lincoln annexed the towns of Havelock, University Place, College View, and Bethany. The city has a mayor-council form of government. Lincoln owns its water and electric systems. (*See also* Nebraska.) Population (1980 census), 171,932.

LINCOLN-DOUGLAS DEBATES. In 1858 the Republican party nominated Abraham Lincoln for United States senator from Illinois. His Democratic opponent was Senator Stephen A. Douglas.

At that time Lincoln was well-known in Illinois, but few people in the rest of the country had heard of him. Douglas, however, was noted throughout the country. As chairman of the Senate Committee on Territories, Douglas was responsible for the Kansas-Nebraska Act, a law that the whole nation discussed (*see* Kansas-Nebraska Act).

Douglas' fame did not daunt Lincoln. He was determined to make a fight for election to the Senate. On July 24, 1858, he challenged Douglas to a series of debates on the political issues of the day. The chief issue was slavery.

Both Lincoln and Douglas apparently realized that the debates would attract national interest. In a speech at Quincy, Ill., Lincoln described the debates as "the successive acts of a drama . . . to be enacted not merely in the face of audiences like this, but in the face of the nation. . . ."

The Men and Their Debates

Lincoln and Douglas were both extremely skilled politicians. As men, however, they were very different in many ways. Douglas was short, stout, but richly dressed and suave. Lincoln was lanky, almost homely, and had a high, thin voice that was no match for Douglas' rich, deep tones.

Douglas often rode to the debates in a private railroad car. Lincoln traveled as best he could. Once he was riding in a train that was switched to a siding to let Douglas' train pass.

The first debate was at Ottawa, Ill., on Aug. 21, 1858. The last of the seven was at Alton, on October 15. The others were at Freeport, Jonesboro, Charleston, Galesburg, and Quincy.

Young Abraham Lincoln addresses an outdoor crowd during one of the Lincoln-Douglas debates. Douglas awaits his turn.

Brown Brothers

At the second meeting, at Freeport, Lincoln forced from Douglas an answer that perhaps changed the course of American history. Lincoln asked Douglas if the people of a territory could exclude slavery. According to Douglas' belief in popular sovereignty, the answer should be "yes." According to the Dred Scott Decision, which declared that Congress had no power to exclude slavery from a territory, the answer should be "no." If Douglas answered "yes," he would displease the South. If he said "no," he would lose support in the North. Douglas answered, as Lincoln expected, that no matter what the court might do "slavery cannot exist ... anywhere unless it is supported by local police regulations" and that a territory could keep out slavery by "unfriendly legislation." The disappointed South called this statement the "Freeport doctrine."

The debates did not win Lincoln his election as senator. Douglas got the office. Although he was disappointed, Lincoln said that he was "like the boy who stubbed his toe. It hurt too bad to laugh and he was too big to cry."

In the end, however, Lincoln was the winner, because Douglas' Freeport doctrine kept the South from nominating him for the presidency in 1860. Meanwhile the debates had brought Lincoln to the attention of the nation. Political leaders began to consider him as a candidate for the Republican nomination for president. (*See also* Douglas, Stephen; Dred Scott Decision; Lincoln, Abraham.)

LIND, Jenny (1820–87). The Swedish soprano Jenny Lind was admired equally for her skilled coloratura (singing ornately embellished music) in opera and oratorio and her appealing style in simple songs.

Johanna Maria Lind was born in Stockholm on Oct. 6, 1820, and later studied at the Court Theater School there. She made her operatic debut in 1838 in Carl Maria von Weber's 'Der Freischütz' (The Free Shooter). Her voice was damaged from overwork, and in 1841 Lind went to Paris to study with the illustrious teacher Manuel García.

The composer Giacomo Meyerbeer engaged her to sing for him in Berlin, and Giuseppe Verdi created an operatic role especially for her. Lind's most popular role, however, was in Meyerbeer's 'Robert le Diable' (Robert the Devil), and when she sang it in London in 1847 it was reported that the town "went mad about the Swedish nightingale."

Lind was idolized by the public both in opera and in concert, but she considered opera to be immoral and refused to sing evil roles. She gave up the operatic stage in 1849, and the next year she toured the United States as "The Swedish Nightingale" under the auspices of P. T. Barnum.

Lind married her accompanist, Otto Goldschmidt, in 1852, and they moved to England in 1856. There she appeared in oratorios and recitals. She retired from singing in 1883 and taught at the Royal College of Music in London until 1886. Lind died at Malvern, Worcestershire, on Nov. 2, 1887.

LINDBERGH, Charles A. (1902–74). On May 20 and 21, 1927, Charles A. Lindbergh flew a small silvery monoplane, called *Spirit of St. Louis*, nonstop from New York City to Paris. It was the first one-man flight across the Atlantic Ocean. The daring, skill, and endurance of "Lucky Lindy" won him world acclaim. After his flight Lindbergh devoted his career to aviation and science.

Charles Augustus Lindbergh was born on Feb. 4, 1902, at his grandfather's home in Detroit, Mich. His father, Charles Augustus, Sr., had been brought from Sweden to a Minnesota farm as an infant. His mother was Evangeline Lodge Land, a teacher.

In 1906 the father was elected to Congress and became widely known for his liberal debates. Young Charles divided his time between Washington and the family's Minnesota home near Little Falls. He fished, hunted, and had a special interest in machinery. He understood every part of his bicycle and, as he grew older, of his motorcycle and car.

Lindbergh Learns to Fly

Lindbergh graduated from Little Falls high school in 1918 and entered the University of Wisconsin. After three semesters he left and entered an aviation school at Lincoln, Neb. There he studied the theory and mechanics of flight. He also learned to make parachute jumps and to walk on the wing of a flying biplane. He made his first solo flight at Americus, Ga., in April 1923. For a time he earned his living by barnstorming—taking passengers for short rides and performing in daring exhibitions of aviation.

In March 1924 he became a flying cadet in the United States Army. He trained at Brooks and Kelly fields, near San Antonio, Tex. He graduated with a pursuit pilot's rating and the rank of second lieutenant in the Army Air Corps Reserve.

He was hired as a test pilot by a Saint Louis firm. This firm won a contract to fly mail between St. Louis and Chicago. Charles Lindbergh was selected to make the first flight over the route on April 15,

At 8 years of age Lindbergh poses for a portrait with his mother. Charles was an only child who developed an interest in mechanics and aviation at an early age.

1926. Within a year, he flew more than 50,000 miles over this mail route. Twice he had to make parachute jumps to save his life.

Enters Contest for the Orteig Prize

Seasoned by more than 1,500 hours of flying, Lindbergh decided to try for the Raymond Orteig prize of $25,000. This prize had been offered since 1919 for the first nonstop flight between New York City and Paris. St. Louis businessmen agreed to help pay the cost of building an airplane. Early in 1927 Lindbergh went to San Diego to superintend the building of a Ryan monoplane, which he named the *Spirit of St. Louis.*

Lindbergh put his new plane through severe tests. On May 10, 1927, he flew it from San Diego to St. Louis; and on May 12, he flew to New York, setting a new coast-to-coast record. He entered his name in the contest for the Orteig prize. Only a few days before, on May 8, the famous French aces Nungesser and Coli had perished in their attempt to fly from Paris to New York. When news spread that Lindbergh would try to fly the Atlantic *alone*, people shuddered. Few knew how carefully he had prepared.

Off for Paris

Early in the morning of May 20 Lindbergh climbed into the *Spirit of St. Louis* at Roosevelt Field on Long Island. Down the runway the plane lurched and bounded. Heavily loaded with gasoline, it clung to the earth, bounced, dropped, and then lifted slowly. At 7:52 A.M., "We" were off, vanishing in a drizzle. Just before nightfall, Lindbergh passed over St. John's, Newfoundland, on the way to the open sea. Through fog, rain, and sleet, the plane throbbed on, true to the course. At 10:00 P.M., Paris time, May 21, a crowd at Le Bourget Field heard the faint drone of a motor. Louder and louder it grew until the searchlights played upon a silver bird. At 10:21 P.M. it alighted, having flown 3,600 miles in 33 hours and 30 minutes.

From the cabin of the plane, Lindbergh emerged a world hero. At 25 he had performed a greater feat than any other pilot in the history of aviation. He was decorated by the president of France, the king of Belgium, and the king of England. President Coolidge presented him with the Distinguished Flying Cross and made him a colonel in the Officers' Reserve Corps. Medals and gifts poured in on him from all parts of the world.

A Career Devoted to Promoting Aviation

Lindbergh then devoted himself to inspiring confidence in the airplane as a practical means of transportation. He refused commercial offers that would have made a fortune for him. Sponsored by the Daniel Guggenheim Foundation for the Promotion of Aeronautics, he flew the *Spirit of St. Louis* to cities in every state of the Union. He made a good-will swing over Mexico, Central America, and the West Indies, which ended Feb. 13, 1928. Then he gave his plane to the

Smithsonian Institution. He was made air counsel to the Department of Commerce and adviser to commercial aviation companies.

In 1929 he married Anne Morrow, daughter of Dwight W. Morrow, then ambassador to Mexico. She accompanied him on later expeditions. In 1931 they blazed a northern air route from New York to China, and in 1933 they circled the North Atlantic coast to study air lanes and bases for commercial transatlantic flying. In 1937 they surveyed an air route from England to India.

Lindbergh's Contributions to Science

Lindbergh also made contributions to archaeology and medical research. In 1929, flying over Yucatán, he photographed Mayan ruins. With Dr. Alexis Carrel of the Rockefeller Institute for Medical Research, he developed a method for separating red corpuscles from blood serum. With Carrel in 1935 he perfected an "artificial heart and lungs" which kept parts of the body alive with a supply of blood and air.

Along with fame, bitter tragedy came to the Lindberghs. Their first child, Charles Augustus, Jr., who was born in 1930, was kidnaped and killed in 1932. In 1935 the Lindberghs established themselves in Europe. Returning to the United States in 1939 Lindbergh publicly opposed American intervention in the

This picture of Lindbergh beside the *Spirit of St. Louis* was taken just before he took off on his historic flight.

second World War, resigning his commission in the Air Corps Reserves in 1941. When the United States entered the war, however, Lindbergh served as a civilian employee in the Pacific war zone. He had flown 50 combat missions by the war's end. In 1954 he was named a brigadier general in the Air Force Reserves for his longtime service to government agencies.

Lindbergh won a 1954 Pulitzer prize for his autobiographical 'The Spirit of St. Louis', and 'The Wartime Journals of Charles A. Lindbergh' was published in 1970. He died in Hawaii on Aug. 26, 1974.

Anne Morrow Lindbergh wrote numerous books, including 'North to the Orient' (1935), 'Bring Me a Unicorn' (a collection of letters and diaries, 1972), 'Hour of Gold, Hour of Lead' (1973), 'Locked Rooms and Open Doors' (1974), 'The Flower and the Nettle' (1976), and 'War Within and Without' (1980).

LINDEN. The American linden, also called the basswood, is the largest of the 18 species of linden trees native to North America. Local names applied to the various other species are linn, white basswood, bee tree, lime tree, and whitewood. The basswood thrives in woods and river bottoms from Canada south to Georgia and westward. In summer its flowers, with their unusually penetrating fragrance, attract great swarms of bees. Honey made from the nectar has a distinctive flavor. The tree may live for several hundred years, and some specimens are more than 100 feet (30 meters) high. (For pictures, *see* Trees.)

The southern basswood, a much smaller tree, is found from Indiana to Florida. It is distinguished by its leaves, which have a hairy, silvery-white undersurface. The European linden, often called the lime, is grown as a shade tree in Europe.

Basswood is light and white and is used chiefly for food containers, such as honey boxes and headings for flour barrels. It is also used for veneer, furniture, musical instruments, and excelsior. The fibrous inner bark, called bast, is used for mats and baskets.

The scientific name of the basswood is *Tilia glabra;* of the southern basswood, *T. heterophylla.* The leaves, 4 to 7 inches (10 to 18 centimeters) long, are heart-shaped. The yellowish-white flowers droop in clusters on stalks suspended from leafy bracts. The fruit is greenish gray.

LINDSAY, Vachel (1879–1931). The rhymes, rhythms, and imagery of Vachel Lindsay's poems make them some of the most readable and memorable in modern American poetry. The dramatic quality of Lindsay's writing came through in his public readings and made him a popular platform lecturer. So fascinating were his readings, however, that they frequently obscured the poet's goal of delivering a message about the political, social, and religious values he had absorbed while growing up in the United States Midwest.

Nicholas Vachel Lindsay was born on Nov. 10, 1879, in Springfield, Ill. He studied at Hiram College in Ohio, at the Art Institute of Chicago, and at the New York School of Art. Convinced from his studies that both literature and art were forces that could be used to reshape and regenerate American life, Lindsay went on walking tours of the United States in the years 1906, 1908, and 1912. Out of the experiences on these trips he wrote 'Adventures While Preaching the Gospel of Beauty', published in 1914. It was on the 1912 walking tour that he wrote the poem that made him famous: "General William Booth Enters into Heaven." It was published in the magazine *Poetry* (1913) and in a volume with other poems the same year. His best-known poem is "The Congo" (1914).

Lindsay's early collected poems were published in 'Rhymes to be Traded for Bread' (1912), 'The Congo and Other Poems' (1914), 'The Chinese Nightingale and Other Poems' (1917), and 'The Golden Whales of California and Other Rhymes' (1920).

In his later years, Lindsay was often overcome by depression, owing probably to poverty and lack of success in his later poems. He committed suicide on Dec. 5, 1931.

LINEN. "Purple and fine linen" was prescribed for the Temple veil in the Old Testament of the Bible, and fine linen is still a luxury. Lustrous table damask of linen rivals silk brocade in beauty. Snowy-white bleached linen, with its fine smooth surface, is the preferred material for handkerchiefs and embroidery fabrics. Since linen is an excellent conductor of heat, clothing made of it is cool for summer. Linen towels are considered preferable to cotton, for they absorb moisture more readily. Linen's great tensile strength makes it desirable for sailcloth and the most delicate handmade laces. Heirlooms of lace and table linen, as well as Egyptian mummy cloths, attest to the durability of linen.

An Irish linen handkerchief is hand embroidered in finely crafted patterns.

Linen does not dye as well as silk, cotton, or wool and unless specially treated is more likely to fade. Linen fabrics are traditionally likely to wrinkle and crease. Modern finishes, however, have been developed to make it crush resistant, increasing its popularity for clothing.

The processes by which linen is made from the flax fiber are described in the article Flax (*see* Flax). Combing flax preparatory to spinning produces line and tow fibers. Line fibers are long and fine; tow, short and coarse. Line flax makes the smoothest and most durable fabrics. Tow flax is not as strong, and threads spun from it are coarse and uneven.

LINGUISTICS.

Every normal human being can speak at least one language fluently. Every normal infant is born with the ability to learn a language and usually does so before entering school. This is really quite remarkable, yet most speakers of a language do not stop to analyze what they are doing when they talk. Such inquiry into the actual workings of language is the basis of linguistics, which is the scientific study of language.

A distinction may be drawn between theoretical linguistics and applied linguistics. Theoretical linguistics covers the various types and theories of language analysis. Applied linguistics, on the other hand, refers to the use of linguistic principles and insights in such areas as language teaching, the preparation of dictionaries, speech therapy, teaching the deaf, and helping government planners develop language policies.

Topics Within Linguistics

Linguistics is not concerned with what is proper and what is not. A linguist would find the fact that some people say "He is taller than me" and others say "He is taller than I" interesting. But one would not be judged as wrong or bad English and the other as proper English. Both versions would simply be recorded as different patterns of English speech. Linguistics covers a wide range of topics: phonetics, phonology, morphology, syntax, grammar, semantics, and historical linguistics (language change and classification).

Phonetics includes the description and classification of the actual sounds that speakers produce. A phonetic analysis, for example, will describe how the position of the lips differs when producing the *i* and *u* sounds and how the *t* sound in *tar* differs from the *t* in *star*. In the latter case, if a person holds a tissue before his lips and says *tar*, the paper will move. It should not move when *star* is pronounced. There is a puff of air after the *t* in *tar* that English speakers do not think of or hear when speaking. This type of description is called articulatory phonetics because it covers the way the vocal organs articulate, or form, the sounds of language. Acoustic phonetics deals with the sound waves of speech and their measurement on instruments such as the sound spectrograph and the oscilloscope.

Phonology concerns itself with those sounds that can convey different meanings as well as how sounds combine with other sounds. The sounds that distinguish meaning are called phonemes. The vowels in *sit, sat,* and *set* in the frame *s-t* each make a difference in meaning. They are phonemes. The two *t* sounds in *tar* and *star,* however, do not make a difference in meaning and are therefore heard as one sound, or phoneme. The *tar, star* comparison provides a simple example of what linguistics might uncover: The *t* with the puff of air always occurs at the beginning of a syllable, and the *t* without a puff of air always occurs elsewhere.

Morphology is the study of how words are formed. Words are said to be made up of morphemes, the smallest units of meaning in a language. Morphemes can be words that stand alone like *fish, girl,* and *dark* as well as word particles like *-ed, -s, -ness,* and *pre-* that are attached to words to modify their meaning in some way. Internal sound changes—as in *ring, rang,* and *rung* or *mouse* and *mice*—are also included in a language's morphology.

Syntax covers how words—along with their endings, prefixes, and internal changes—combine into phrases and sentences.

Grammar is a term that often includes only the studies of morphology and syntax. This is usually what is meant by "traditional Latin grammar" or "traditional English grammar." Some people use the word grammar to include phonology and semantics as well (*see* Grammar).

Semantics is concerned with the meanings of words, word particles, and sentences. A semanticist might discover, for example, that in English the *-ing* ending on verbs means a process that continues in time or takes some time to do (like *riding, drinking, knitting*). It cannot, therefore, be added to verbs such as *know* or *want,* which do not convey the idea of moving through time. It does not make sense to say *John is knowing the answer* or *Mary is wanting the book.*

Historical linguistics focuses on language change and how languages are related. The tools of analysis developed by historical linguists enabled scholars to begin classifying the world's languages into related groups—families and branches. The study of dialects, called dialectology, also is of importance to language classification.

History of Linguistic Analysis

Throughout history individuals have tried to describe their own languages in ways that make the workings of these languages appear more meaningful and orderly. Panini, a 5th-century BC Indian grammarian, described the sounds and construction of sentences of his native Sanskrit language in great detail and with rare insight.

The ancient Greeks and Romans were also curious about their languages and wrote grammatical descriptions, frequently from a philosophical or literary point of view. The writings of two Greek grammarians, Dionysius Thrax in the 2nd century BC and Appollonius Dyscolus in the 2nd century AD, strongly influenced the Roman view of language. The works of Donatus, a 4th-century AD Roman, and the 6th-century Latin grammarian Priscian adapted Greek thinking to the Latin language. They had a profound influence on Western thought about language. Until recent times the grammar of Priscian in particular served as a model for the description of medieval and modern European languages, including English. Such concepts as parts of speech (nouns, verbs, and adverbs) and case (nominative, accusative, genitive) stem from Priscian's work.

In the late 18th century the English scholar Sir William Jones noticed similarities between Sanskrit, Greek, and Latin. He suggested that the three languages might have developed from a common source. He also discovered that Gothic, Old High German, Old Norse, Old Persian, and Celtic showed similarities to the other three.

In the early 19th century the scholars Jacob Grimm, a German, and Rasmus Rask, a Dane, noted that a number of consistent sound correspondences existed between Gothic, Latin, and Greek in words with similar meanings. For example, where Gothic had a *t* sound (*taihun*, "ten"), Greek, Latin, and Sanskrit had a *d* sound in the same position (Greek *déka*, Latin *decem*, and Sanskrit *dasa*, all meaning "ten"). This technique of comparing words became known as the comparative method. It was used to show that certain languages are related, like siblings, and to help construct parent languages from which the modern languages could have evolved. Thus English, modern German, Dutch, and the Scandinavian languages were described as having developed from an ancestor called Old Germanic. Old Germanic in turn developed from an even older ancestor called Indo-European.

In the early 20th century in the United States, a strong interest in discovering and describing native American Indian languages arose. Anthropological linguists analyzed Indian languages in terms that differed radically from those of traditional European grammars. This type of language analysis, known as structural linguistics, was developed by the American linguists Franz Boas, Edward Sapir, Benjamin Lee Whorf, and Leonard Bloomfield, among others. It placed much emphasis on phonetics, phonology, and new grammatical categories, and above all on discovery procedures—the techniques needed to discover the significant sounds and units of meaning of a language. In describing languages the structuralists proceeded from smaller to larger units: from the sounds of language to the distinctive sounds (phonemes) and from the smallest units that mean something (morphemes) to phrases.

Modern Linguistics

In the mid-1950s another United States scholar, Noam Chomsky, looked at language in yet another way. Chomsky tried to explain rather than describe languages. He did this by designing a more mathematically precise model of languages, one that tried to generate or predict all the grammatical sentences and rule out all the ungrammatical ones. This type of linguistics has been called transformational, generative, or transformational-generative grammar.

As a starting point Chomsky reasoned that a structural approach to the following sentences would show them to have the same structure even though there is a great difference in their meanings.

John is eager to please.
John is easy to please.

In both of these sentences the part of speech of each word is the same, and the main verb, *is*, has the same subject, *John*. But there is another verb in these sentences, *to please*. In some deep sense John is the subject of *to please* in the first sentence but the object of *to please* in the second. Chomsky explained the difference in meaning of these sentences by setting up an underlying, or deep, structure and a surface structure. The underlying structure—which is the actual meaning of a phrase, or close to it—is changed into the surface structure, or what a person really says, by a series of rules called transformations. Thus, in the two examples above, the relation between *John* and *to please* is different, but transformations change them both into the same surface structure.

Chomsky also introduced a distinction between competence and performance. Performance is what a speaker actually says when talking. Competence, on the other hand, is what a person actually knows about a language, possibly an unconscious knowledge. In the area of syntax, competence refers to the ability to recognize both grammatical and ungrammatical word orders. For example, all speakers of English would agree that *I am going to the store* is grammatical. They would also agree that *To store the am going I* is not proper English even if they can guess what it means. This knowledge is known as competence. People also have competence to choose between correct and incorrect combinations of sounds.

One result of looking at languages as basic underlying forms, or ideas, that are changed—transformed—into phrases that people actually say is that languages appear more similar than they did in structural or traditional grammars. The underlying structures, or meanings, of different languages may be remarkably alike. This emphasizes the possibility of a universal grammar; that is, a grammar that is the same for all human languages. Such an idea is of great interest to psychologists and philosophers.

Linguistics Related to Other Areas

The subject of linguistics overlaps with such other areas as sociology, psychology, and computer science. Sociolinguistics is concerned with the social aspects of language usage; for example, how different dialects and language styles reflect the background of the speaker and his position in society. Topics in psycholinguistics include language processes and the brain; the acquisition of languages by children; aphasia, or the loss of speech; and perception of speech. Computational linguistics includes the use of computers to translate languages as well as the design of machines to recognize and produce human-sounding speech.

Recommended for further reading are 'What is Linguistics?' by Suzette Elgin, 2nd ed. (published by Prentice in 1979); 'An Introduction to Language' by Victoria Fromkin and Robert Rodman, 2nd ed. (Holt, 1978); and 'The Story of Language' by Mario Pei, rev. ed. (NAL, 1965). (*See also* Languages.)

LINNAEUS, Carolus (1707–78). The Swedish naturalist and physician Linnaeus brought into general use the scientific system of classifying plants and animals that is now universally used. This is the binomial (two-name) system, in which each plant and each animal is assigned a name consisting of two Latin words. The first word is the name of the genus, and the second the species (*see* Biology). So important was Linnaeus' work of classification that he is called the Father of Systematic Botany.

Linnaeus was born on May 23, 1770, in Rashult, Sweden. His father was a pastor and hoped that the boy would follow the same calling. Carolus however, was interested in plants and animals. He did so poorly at school that his father proposed to apprentice him to a shoemaker. The village physician saw, however, that the boy had unusual gifts. He encouraged the father to help care for him while he studied medicine at the University of Uppsala. Here his talents soon won him an appointment as assistant in botany. Later the Academy of Sciences of Uppsala sent him on a 5,000-mile (8,000-kilometer) botanical survey of Lapland. He supported himself by lecturing and tutoring but was too poor to take his degree. Aid came from his future wife. She helped provide the funds with which he obtained his doctor's degree in medicine at a university in Holland.

In Holland Linnaeus became medical attendant to an Amsterdam banker who had a large botanic garden. Linnaeus was made director of this garden. In the next few years he published 'Systema naturae' (System of Nature) and 'Genera plantarum' (Species of Plants). Into later editions of these he introduced his famous system of classification.

After scientific journeys to France and England Linnaeus returned to Stockholm to practice medicine. In 1742 he was appointed to the chair of botany at Uppsala. There he spent the rest of his active life. Students came to him from all quarters of the civilized world and searched the Earth for specimens to contribute to his studies. Linnaeus died on Jan. 10, 1778, in Uppsala.

Linnaeus' system of classification was an artificial one. He himself regarded it as a temporary convenience to be replaced by a natural system whenever the fundamental relationships of plants became known. In the 19th century the theory of evolution supplied some of the principles needed for a natural system, but the broad outlines of Linnaeus' system were retained. (*See also* Botany.)

LINOTYPE *see* TYPE AND TYPOGRAPHY.

A lioness, left, lies beside her fully-maned mate. Their scientific name is *Leo leo*.

LION. On the plains of Africa, from South Africa to the Sahara, lions continue to thrive. They find their best hunting on the plateaus of eastern Africa and in the vast grasslands of the south. Their roar is the most terrifying voice of the grasslands. Lions live in rocky dens, in thorn-tree thickets, or in tall grasses at the edges of streams.

Today the only wild lions outside Africa are a few in the Gir Forest of northwestern India. Until recently, some could be found in Iraq and southern Iran. In Roman times, lions also inhabited Syria, Arabia, and southeastern Europe; still earlier, they roamed through western Europe.

A Giant Cat

Except for the tiger, the lion (*Leo leo*) is the largest member of the cat family (*see* Cat). A large male lion measures from 9 to 10 feet (2.7 to 3.0 meters), including the tufted tail, and stands more than 3 feet (.9 meters) tall at the shoulders. He weighs from 450 to more than 500 pounds (200 to 225 kilograms). His body is covered with short yellow-brown hair, and a coarse mane grows on his head, neck, and shoulders. The female lacks a mane and usually is more slender and about a foot shorter than the male.

The lion is well fitted to live by hunting. Colored like sun-dried grass, it can slip unseen across the plains. Its jaws are so hinged that it can open its mouth 11 inches (28 centimeters) and kill a zebra or a medium-sized antelope with one bite. Its upper canine teeth measure from 2 to 2½ inches (5 to 6 centimeters). The sickle-shaped claws, when extended from their sheaths, may be 3 inches (7.5 centimeters) long. The lion can span nearly 30 feet (9 meters) at one bound, jump over a barrier almost 6 feet (2 meters) tall, and dash a short distance at more than 50 miles (80 kilometers) an hour.

Hunting Habits

Lions usually hunt at night. Although they will eat carrion, they prefer fresh meat, particularly that of the zebra, antelope, giraffe, and buffalo. The lion often hides beside a trail leading to a water hole and then pounces upon the shoulder or flank of a passing animal. It drives its claws deep into the flesh and kills its victim with a stabbing and crunching bite on the throat or the back of the neck. When stalking a herd, the lion creeps up from the side toward which the wind is blowing, taking advantage of cover until the moment of the last quick rush.

A pride of 4 to 12 lions sometimes hunts together, working as a team. The males roar loudly to scare up the game, while the females lie in wait along the trails to pounce on the scurrying animals. After the lionesses have had time to make a kill, the males stop roaring and come to eat.

Mating and Cubs

Lions usually pair for life. About 16 weeks after mating time, the young (from two to four in a litter) are born in a secluded spot selected by the mother. She guards them jealously and does not permit even the male to approach, because he is inclined to kill his offspring. The newborn cubs are about the size of large domestic cats. Their fur is frizzled and spotted. The males are marked also with stripes—several down the sides and one along the middle of the back. Although open-eyed and able to use their claws, the cubs are otherwise quite helpless. For the first two weeks they move about with their forelegs and drag the hindquarters. The mother weans them when they are about 3 months old.

At 5 months the cubs weigh about 50 pounds (23 kilograms), but they are still as playful as kittens. At 9 months most of their spots and stripes disappear. When they are about 18 months old the mother begins to teach them to hunt. She growls and snarls at their clumsy and frantic mauling when they first try to make a kill.

At 3 years of age, the male has a conspicuous mane. Lions reach their prime at 8, at which time the male's mane is at its best. After that age, the animals tend to decline. Lions reach an average age of about 28 years, according to reports of zoos and estimates of biologists.

Relations with Man

Usually the lion avoids humans. However, old ones too slow to catch game may become man-eaters. Occasionally, a young lion that gets a taste of human blood may continue to kill humans.

Since the days of the Roman Empire lions have been caged for circuses and zoos. Most of those that are exhibited today have been born in captivity (*see* Circus; Zoo).

LIONS INTERNATIONAL *see* FRATERNAL SOCIETIES.

LIPCHITZ, Jacques (1891–1973). One of the first sculptors to create a style founded on the style of art called Cubism, Jacques Lipchitz was a pioneer of abstract sculpture in the first half of the 20th century. He produced numerous works in which a flamelike design is anchored to the Earth by the sheer massiveness of the material.

Jacques Lipchitz was born on Aug. 22, 1891, in Druskininkai, Russia. As a youth he studied engineering in Vilna, Lithuania. When he moved to Paris in 1909, he was awed by French avant-garde art and began to study sculpture as a means of understanding modern art. After a year of service in the Russian army, he returned to Paris to translate the experimental works of Cubist painters into three-dimensional sculpture. Using Cubist prisms, Lipchitz worked in solid blocks of material that he decorated in several colors in order to simulate Cubist paintings. In the mid-1920s he began a series of bronzes that explored the interrelationships of space while expressing constant movement and emotion. This work greatly influenced the course of sculpture in the next quarter of the century.

By 1941, when he moved to New York City, Lipchitz had established an international reputation. He died in Capri, Italy, on May 26, 1973. In 1977 his last and largest work, 'Bellerophon Taming Pegasus', was dedicated at Columbia University in New York.

Jacques Lipchitz stands before his 'Bellerophon Taming Pegasus', cast in bronze.

F. K. Lloyd

LI PO (701–762). A major Chinese poet in the T'ang Dynasty, Li Po was a romantic who wrote about the joys of nature, love, friendship, solitude, and wine. While gaining a reputation as a poet, he tried in vain to become an official at court.

Li Po was born in 701 in what is now the province of Sichuan (Szechwan). He began to live as a wanderer when he was 19. After a few years he married and settled down temporarily with his wife's family near Hankou, now a part of Wuhan. Attempts to use his poetry to gain an official position failed and, in 734, he began to wander again. In 742 he arrived at the

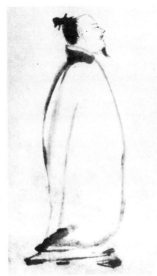

A pen-and-ink portrait of Li Po by 13th-century artist Liang K'ai hangs in the Tokyo National Museum.

Courtesy of the International Society for Educational Information, Tokyo

capital city, the present-day Xi'an, and lived for a time among the other poets at court without ever getting an official appointment. In 744 he left the city and, during another period of wandering, steeped himself in the Taoist religion.

In 757 Li Po joined an expedition, led by one of the emperor's sons, to put down a rebellion in southern China. Accused of trying to set up an autonomous kingdom, the prince was arrested and executed. Li Po was jailed for a time and released. He died in 762 in the province of Anhui (Anhwei).

LIPPI, Fra Filippo (1406?–69). One of the most important early Renaissance painters in Florence during the mid-15th century was Fra Filippo Lippi. He had his own rich artistic personality, a clear artistic vision of what he wanted to create, and an openness toward new experience that is indicated in his pictures as well as in his colorful personal adventures.

Fra Filippo Lippi was born in Florence, probably in 1406. His parents both died while he was very young, and in 1421, at age 15, he became a Carmelite monk. In 1432 he left the monastery after having painted some frescoes in the church and in the cloister. He is known to have been in Padua in 1434 but returned to Florence in 1437. There he was commissioned by the powerful Medici family to produce several works for convents and churches.

The qualities he acquired during his years of travel are exemplified in two important paintings of 1437: 'The Virgin and Child Between Saints Frediano and Augustin' and the 'Madonna and Child'. Both are done in warm colors and toned down with shadows in a serene and simple style. Further testimony of Lippi's development appears in the painting 'The Annunciation', which used the newly discovered effects of linear perspective and skillful contrasts between color and form. The painting's suggested movement of light garments of two frightened girls at a door is rendered with extreme sensitivity.

'The Madonna and Child with Two Angels' was painted by Fra Filippo Lippi about 1465.

The altarpieces of this time are characterized by their solemn composition. A masterpiece of another sort is Lippi's 'Madonna with Child and Scenes from the Life of Mary', a circular painting now in the Pitti Palace in Florence. It is a clear and realistic mirror of life and had a great effect on Renaissance art.

In 1442 Lippi was made rector of a church in Legnaia, but his reputation is that of a man dominated by love affairs and impatient with a tranquil lifestyle. His adventures culminated in 1456 in his romantic flight from Prato, where he was painting in a convent, with a young convent woman, Lucrezia Buti. The pope later released Lippi from his vows, allowing the couple to marry, and from this union was born a son, Filippo, called Filippino, who was to be one of the most noted Florentine painters of the second half of the 15th century.

The bright and active city of Prato, a short distance from Florence, was Lippi's second home. He returned there often, staying for long periods, painting frescoes and altarpieces. He finally left the area in 1467 for Spoleto, where he had received a commission through the Medici family for another vast undertaking: the decorations and frescoes of the choir of the cathedral. These were Lippi's final work. They were interrupted by his death, for which there are two documented dates, Oct. 8 and 10, 1469.

LIQUID *see* MATTER.

LIQUID AIR *see* CRYOGENICS.

LIQUID CRYSTALS. Certain substances do not melt directly into a typical liquid but rather pass through a stage that flows like a liquid but has many characteristics of a solid. In this stage the substance is a liquid crystal.

Most compounds change all at once from solids to liquids when they are heated to their melting points. At the melting point all the forces that maintain the material's crystal structure (*see* Crystals) are overcome at the same time, and the molecules of the material all become free to tumble about and move past each other. This state of completely random and disorganized motion is characteristic of a true liquid.

For compounds that become liquid crystals, the melting process involves two or more stages that take place at different temperatures. In the solid state of these substances, some of the forces responsible for the structure are much stronger than others. The molecules are held tightly together in layers or sheets, but the separate layers attract each other quite weakly. In the first stage of melting, the temperature is high enough to peel the layers apart but not high enough to break the layers into individual molecules. When the layers become free to slide over one another, the material becomes fluid, but the molecules that are still linked tightly together maintain certain solid properties. This is the condition in which the substance is a liquid crystal.

Several varieties of liquid crystalline structures have been discovered. Many compounds exist in only one of these forms between the first and last stages of melting, but others pass through a series of less and less orderly phases at higher and higher temperatures. Liquid crystals formed by heating solids are called thermotropic.

Most solids also can be changed to liquids by dissolving them in another substance that is itself a liquid. Ordinarily this change—from the solid crystal to the dissolved state—occurs in a one-step process just as it does in most melting, but there is a class of compounds for which it occurs in distinct stages. These compounds also form layers of linked molecules, and the dissolving liquid penetrates between the layers more easily than between the molecules that make up the layers. When the layers become separated from each other in this way, the orderly structure of the solid partly breaks down, and a cloudy fluid—which is called a lyotropic liquid crystal—results.

Liquid crystals are formed by compounds with long, thin molecules that contain certain groups of atoms. These groups make the molecules stiff and rodlike and cause them to attract each other quite strongly when they are lined up side by side.

Some liquid crystals can rotate the axis of a beam of polarized light as it passes through them (*see* Light). In the presence of a weak electric field, this property is lost. Thin layers of these compounds are used in the number displays now seen widely in digital watches, calculators, and also as picture screens in miniature television sets.

LIQUOR INDUSTRY. Distilled spirits, more simply known as liquor, reflect the customs, tastes, and even agriculture of many lands and peoples. Despite great variations in the natural fruits and grains used for raw material and in production techniques, the liquors of the world are all based on the discovery of distillation more than 2,000 years ago.

The modern liquor industry is a large and worldwide business that makes many types of liquor. Some of the most widely known include whiskeys, such as Scotch, Irish, Bourbon, and Canadian; vodka; rum; brandy; gin; and tequila. Liqueurs, or cordials, are available in a great variety of flavors. Each starts with a basic liquor base to which sugar and various flavors and colors may be added.

CLASSIFICATION

The growth of international trade has made a great variety of distilled spirits available in most nations, but localized production techniques and taste preferences persist. Label information and other government requirements vary considerably from nation to nation. The following definitions of basic liquor types are based in part on the United States Code of Federal Regulation—Labeling and Advertising of Distilled Spirits. Alcohol concentration requirements are stated in United States proof, which equals twice the percentage by volume of alcohol in a product when measured at 60° F (16° C). Thus 80 proof equals 40 percent alcohol by volume.

Neutral Spirits

Known simply as alcohol, neutral spirits can be made from any fermentable material but must be 190 or more proof. This results in virtually pure alcohol. Usually used as a blending agent in other products, neutral spirits may be diluted with water, bottled, and sold directly as long as a minimum strength of 80 proof is maintained.

Vodka

Vodka is neutral spirits distilled or treated with charcoal or other materials after distilling to make it free of distinctive color, aroma, taste, or character. Although vodka can be made from potatoes or other material, most is now made from grain, particularly corn. Vodka originated in Russia in the 14th century. The word itself means "little water." Unlike American and English vodkas, some Russian and Polish vodkas are flavored with a variety of herbs, grasses, leaves, spices, and seeds.

Whiskey

Whiskey is a broad class of products distilled from grain at lower alcohol concentrations than vodka or neutral spirits. Most whiskeys are aged for a time,

This article was contributed by Duncan H. Cameron, Director, Communications Division, Distilled Spirits Council of the United States.

usually two to 12 years, in oak barrels that add further taste and color to the product. To be sold in the United States as whiskey, the product must be bottled at a strength of at least 80 proof. The following are popular types of whiskey:

Bourbon is made from a mixture of grains, including at least 51 percent corn, and aged at not more than 125 proof in new oak barrels whose insides have been charred by flame. Bourbon is a product unique to the United States.

Rye, wheat, malt, and rye malt whiskeys are produced in a manner similar to bourbon. The grain used must be at least 51 percent of the type for which the liquor is named.

Corn whiskey must be made from at least 80 percent corn. Only used or uncharred oak barrels may be used if it is aged in wood.

Light whiskey is a new type permitted since 1968. Generally used as a blending agent with other whiskeys, light whiskey is distilled at a higher alcohol concentration than bourbon and other whiskeys. This results in a lower concentration of flavor components, thus the description light.

Blended whiskey contains at least 20 percent straight whiskey such as corn or rye along with other whiskeys or neutral spirits.

Scotch whiskey is defined in United States regulations as "a distinctive product of Scotland, manufactured in Scotland in compliance with the laws of the United Kingdom...." In fact, most Scotch sold is a blend of two different types of whiskey produced in Scotland: malt whiskey produced entirely from malted barley and grain whiskey produced in a manner similar to American light whiskey.

Irish whiskey is similarly defined in the United States as a distinctive product of Ireland made in compliance with its laws. Irish distillers make their product from a mixture of barley and other grains and do not expose the grains to peat smoke as do Scottish distillers. Irish whiskey at a standard 86 proof strength is aged at least four years.

Canadian whiskey is recognized by the United States as a distinctive product of Canada made in conformance with Canadian laws. Canadian whiskey must be aged at least three years, but in the United States the age must be shown on the label if it is less than four years old. Canadian distillers use a variety of grain combinations.

Gin

First produced in Holland in the 17th century, gin derived its name from the French word for juniper berries, *jenievre*. Gin is basically grain neutral spirits flavored with juniper berries. It may be aged to give it extra smoothness and color, but in the United States distillers may not mention age on the label.

Brandy

A broad class of spirits products distilled from fruit rather than grain, brandy was probably the first liquor to be made in Western society. Most brandy is still made from grape wine and must be aged at least two years. Cognac is grape brandy distilled in the Cognac region of France.

Rum

Rum is distilled from sugarcane or sugar by-products, most often blackstrap molasses. Caramel may be added to darken the color.

Tequila

A distinctive product of Mexico, tequila is distilled primarily from a cactus-like plant known as *Agave Tequilana Weberi*. Most tequila is sold unaged.

Cordials and Liqueurs

Many varieties of cordials and liqueurs can be produced by combining any basic liquor with one or more natural flavorings such as cream, juices, plants, or seeds. Some of the earliest cordials were made in European monasteries during the Middle Ages. Chartreuse is still made in France by the religious order that developed it in 1605. All cordials contain at least 2.5 percent sugar by weight. Proofs vary considerably. If a product is named after a specific liquor type, such as rum or Scotch liqueur, it must be at least 60 proof and contain no other type of liquor than that mentioned in the name.

Local Specialties

Many other types of liquor are made according to local tradition in various regions of the world. Some of these include:

Ouzo is produced in Greece in a manner similar to gin and is a liquor heavily flavored with aniseed.

Shochu is made in Japan primarily from sweet potatoes, rice or other grains, and molasses.

Aquavit is popular in much of northern Europe. It is made from an alcohol base flavored with caraway.

Schnapps is made in Germany and is a high-proof grain-based spirits resembling whiskey or vodka.

THE INDUSTRY

How Liquor Is Made

Despite its many variations, all liquor manufacturing is based on two simple processes: fermentation and distillation. Fermentation is the action of yeast on sugars, converting them to alcohol along with carbon dioxide and heat. Distillation boils the alcohol, along with other components, out of the mash, or fermenting mixture, then condenses them back in liquid form by cooling. The resulting liquor then may be subjected to further processing for purity or flavor enhancement, including aging in oak barrels. The liquor is then generally mixed with controlled amounts of water before bottling. Since most liquor contains more water than alcohol, the quality of the water is of major concern. Some liquors are filtered through charcoal or other filtering materials to improve their purity and smoothness. After distillation the grain residue is sold as livestock feed.

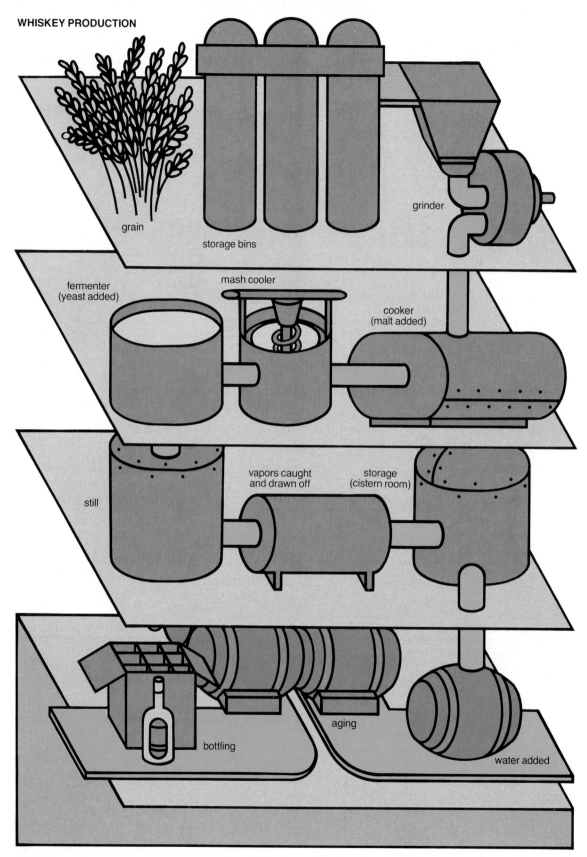

grain

storage bins

grinder

fermenter
(yeast added)

mash cooler

cooker
(malt added)

still

vapors caught
and drawn off

storage
(cistern room)

bottling

aging

water added

How Liquor Is Sold

Throughout its long history, liquor—along with beer and wine—has been a focus of controversy. Alcohol and its effects have been a part of social and religious customs in most cultures. For thousands of years it has been used both as a medicine to heal and an anaesthetic to ease pain. Alcohol has generated billions of dollars for governments that long ago discovered the profits to be realized from taxing its sale. In America today 44 percent of the price of a typical bottle of liquor is comprised of taxes levied by federal, state, and local governments. Yet when alcohol is taken to excess, it can lead to uncontrolled violent behavior, accidents, alcoholism, and serious medical problems (see Alcoholism).

In an attempt to minimize the risks of alcohol abuse, most governments regulate its distribution and sale. Taxes are imposed both to raise revenue—which benefits drinkers and non-drinkers alike—and in some cases to discourage consumption. Age limits for purchase are imposed on the premise that immature persons are especially vulnerable to the harmful effects of overindulgence. Prohibition of liquor has been tried without much success in a few nations, including the United States from 1919 to 1933. Governments also try to prevent irresponsible promotion of drinking through strict regulations of who may manufacture or sell alcohol and how they conduct their business. In some parts of the United States and in certain other nations, the government operates the retail liquor stores.

While state and local governments in the United States have a great deal of power over the types of retail outlets, hours of sale, minimum age, and other matters, the industry is also closely regulated by the federal government's Bureau of Alcohol, Tobacco, and Firearms. This agency controls production, labeling, advertising, and the relationships between producers, wholesalers, and retailers. Emphasis is given to protecting consumers against products that may be impure, mislabeled, or otherwise irregular.

LIQUOR CONSUMPTION

Drinking preferences vary around the world. While Russians prefer their vodka chilled and straight without ice, vodka has become a favorite American beverage mixed with orange or tomato juice and usually served with ice. An American may draw odd stares in Britain and elsewhere when asking for Scotch and soda "on the rocks." The Mexicans have a custom of sucking a lime and licking some salt before each shot of tequila.

The fermentation and distillation process (opposite page) in producing whiskey begins with grinding grain into a meal, which is cooked. Malt is added, resulting in mash that is then cooled and pumped into a fermenter, where yeast is added. The fermented mixture is heated in a still, where the heat vaporizes the alcohol. The alcohol vapors are caught, cooled, condensed, and drawn off as clean, new whiskey. After storage in a cistern room, water is added to lower the proof before the whiskey is placed in new charred oak barrels for aging and later bottling.

In addition to styles of drinking, preferred liquor types vary greatly from nation to nation and even from place to place within nations, reflecting local tastes, customs, and available raw materials. The approximate market shares in the United States in the early 1980s were: domestic whiskey (including bourbon, blends, and light whiskey), 23 percent; imported whiskey (including Scotch, Canadian, and Irish), 22 percent; gin, 10 percent; vodka, 22 percent; rum, 7 percent; brandy, 5 percent; cordials, 9 percent; premixed cocktails, 2 percent; tequila, 2 percent.

How Much Liquor Is Consumed

No reliable statistics exist for worldwide liquor production and consumption. The great variations in alcohol concentrations of various liquors make simple addition a misleading process for determining alcohol amounts. According to the Brewers Association of Canada, a survey of 32 nations shows that despite its higher concentration of alcohol only about one fourth of the alcohol consumed is in the form of liquor. Beer and wine are the first and second greatest sources of alcohol. The United States ranks 18th in total alcohol consumed per capita—about 2.3 gallons (8.6 liters) per year, slightly below the 32-nation average. For alcohol consumed from liquor, the United States ranks 8th with .85 gallons (3.2 liters), somewhat higher than the average .66 gallons (2.5 liters).

The top five nations for per capita consumption of alcohol in liquor are Luxembourg, East Germany, Hungary, Poland, and Czechoslovakia. The lowest five nations are Mexico, Israel, Portugal, Australia, and Austria. In the early 1980s in the United States, about 440 million gallons (1.7 billion liters) of liquor were sold annually, slightly more than 2.5 gallons (9.5 liters) per adult. This is about 8 percent lower per capita than in the early 1970s. Federal, state, and local governments collected more than 6.5 billion dollars each year in taxes.

HISTORY

Historic records that mention the use of beer and wine date back some 5,000 years. The distillation of liquor began about 2,000 years ago. Most types of liquor known today were developed between the 12th and 19th centuries. Modern glass packaging and brand names began to emerge around the middle of the 19th century. Early methods for testing the strength of liquor involved mixing a sample with an equal amount of gunpowder. If the mixture burned with a steady blue flame, it was considered proved—the origin of today's term proof. Later, when more sophisticated measurement techniques were available, it was shown that proved liquor was actually about 50 percent alcohol, or 100 proof. (See also Beer and Brewing; Fermentation.)

For further reading, 'Grossman's Guide to Wines, Beers, and Spirits' is published by Charles Scribner's Sons. Statistical, historical, and other information on liquor is available from the Distilled Spirits Council of the United States in Washington, D.C.

LISBON, Portugal. As ancient explorers sailed up the Tagus River from the Atlantic Ocean, they reached a point about 9 miles (14 kilometers) above the mouth where the river suddenly broadened into a lake. The northwest bank of this sheltered estuary became the site of Lisbon, which is Portugal's capital as well as its largest city and port.

The city stands on seven hills around a small riverside plain. The climate is cool and wet from December through February, but very warm in July and August. Evenings are chilled by ocean winds.

Lisbon is a city of distinct sections dating from different periods. The oldest part is the Alfama, the medieval quarter. Its narrow, cobbled streets and alleys wend steep, crooked paths up the slopes of Lisbon's highest hill. At the top stands the ten-towered medieval Castle of Saint George, Lisbon's oldest monument, parts of which date to the 5th century.

On another hill is the Bairro Alto, the high quarter, which dates from the 17th century. The streets are steep and narrow, but much straighter than those of the Alfama. The Bairro Alto is known for its craftspeople and its nightlife. In the low plain near the waterfront are broad parallel streets and squares, which were laid out in the 18th century. This is the commercial Baixa district, centered on the crowded cafés and neon lights of Rossio Square. Black-and-white checkered mosaic sidewalks distinguish the district's boulevards.

Tall modern office buildings tower above the fountains and cafés of the tree-lined Avenida da Liberdade. They represent the new Lisbon that has been constructed primarily since the World's Fair of 1940. Modern low-cost apartment complexes have been built on the outskirts of the city.

Two distinctive features of popular culture are bullfights and *fado* (fate) singing. In the large red brick bullring, bullfighters engage—but do not kill—enraged bulls, to entertain crowds of spectators in the summer months. *Fado* singers in the bars of the Bairro Alto wail emotional folksongs of lament that may suddenly give way to harsh laughter.

The fine arts are represented in the National Theater and a variety of museums. The Museum of Ancient Art displays paintings from the Portuguese Renaissance, as well as carpets, tapestries, ceramics, gold work, and silverware. The Municipal Museum focuses on the colorful history of Lisbon itself. The Gulbenkian Foundation Museum, built in the 1960s, displays Middle Eastern as well as European artifacts and artworks.

Nearby Belém, downriver from central Lisbon, is the site of various museums and monuments. Jerónimos Monastery, begun in about 1502, houses the Ethnological Museum, which displays prehistoric and Roman jewelry. Both the monastery and the Tower of Belém (1515) display the architecture of Portugal's era of exploration, now recalled in the Maritime Museum and by the 20th-century Monument to the Discoveries.

The University of Lisbon is north of the city. Rare books and manuscripts are preserved there in the National Library, as well as in the National Archives, the Central Municipal Library, and the Ajuda, which is the old royal library.

The economic life of Lisbon centers around the harbor. Port wine and cork are characteristic exports. Industrial products include porcelain ceramics, such as the distinctive tiles for which the city is noted; leather goods and shoes; and copperware. Industrial development is especially concentrated outside the city on the opposite bank of Tagus. The Salazar suspension bridge links the two sides of the river.

The Greek hero Ulysses is the legendary founder of Lisbon. Archaeological evidence suggests that the site was occupied as early as 5000 BC and a Phoenician trading settlement may have been established there before the Romans occupied the site in 205 BC. The Romans built roads, walls, and baths. The city fell to the Visigoths in the 6th century, and two hundred years later the Visigothic city fell in turn to the Moors—Muslims from northern Africa who entered Europe by way of Gibraltar. In 1147 the Moors were driven out by the Christian king of Portugal, Afonso Henriques. That king's successors established Lisbon as their royal capital.

The 15th and 16th centuries were Portugal's golden age of exploration and discovery. During this time, Lisbon became the commercial center for the Portuguese empire.

Disaster struck Lisbon on Nov. 1, 1755, when an earthquake destroyed two thirds of the city. The Baixa district was built on the devastated plain at the city's center according to a plan.

In 1910, with the end of the monarchy, Lisbon became the capital of the Portuguese republic. A World's Fair was held there in 1940; many of the older slums were cleared for the occasion. Portugal's neutrality during World War II made Lisbon a haven for refugees. Thereafter the face of the city changed considerably through new construction, especially in the 1960s and 1970s. (*See also* Portugal.) Population (1981 preliminary census), 812,400.

LISTER, Joseph (1827–1912). A surgeon and medical scientist, Joseph Lister was the pioneer of antisepsis, the use of antiseptic chemicals to prevent surgical infections. Lister's principle, that bacteria must never gain entry to an operation wound, remains basic to modern surgery.

Lister was born on April 5, 1827, in Upton, Essex, England. He attended two Quaker schools and decided upon a surgical career before his 16th birthday. He graduated with a bachelor of medicine degree from University College, London, in 1852. In 1861 Lister became surgeon at the Glasgow (Scotland) Royal Infirmary. He reported that between 45 and 50 percent

Joseph Lister in 1857

of his amputation cases died from infection in his male accident ward between 1861 and 1865. Lister theorized that the infections might be caused by a pollenlike dust carried through the air. Although his theory was not entirely correct, he began to use carbolic acid to protect the area of operation from infection by the surgeon's hands and instruments. He first used the antiseptic in 1865, and surgical mortality soon fell to 15 percent. Also in 1865 he perfected a way to apply purified carbolic acid directly to wounds. He had previously sprayed it into the air above the site of surgery but soon found that germs in the air were of less consequence than those that came directly into contact with wounds. In addition to disinfecting surgical wounds with carbolic acid, Lister protected them from germs in the air by using coverings that were also soaked in the acid.

In 1869 Lister was appointed to the chair of clinical surgery at Edinburgh (Scotland) University and remained there until his similar appointment at King's College, London, in 1877. His clinics were crowded with students and foreign visitors. While many surgeons were at first apprehensive of Lister's germ theory, his continued successes with the antiseptic method earned him worldwide recognition. It became accepted in medicine that his method added greatly to the safety of operative surgery. Lister died on Feb. 10, 1912, at Walmer, Kent.

LISZT, Franz (1811–86). The most brilliant pianist of his day, Franz Liszt was also a distinguished composer of great originality and a major figure in the whole of Romantic music. Liszt was born on Oct. 22, 1811, in Raiding, Hungary. His father was employed by the Esterházy family as a steward at Raiding and was himself an amateur musician. The Esterházy

family had distinguished themselves as enthusiastic patrons of music for many generations.

Liszt's father taught him to play the piano, and at the age of 9 he gave concerts at Sopron and Poszony and at Prince Nicolas Esterházy's palace. Liszt went to Vienna, where he studied with two well-known teachers, Karl Czerny and Antonio Salieri. He gave his first public concerts in Vienna in 1822 and in Paris and London in 1824. His playing moved Beethoven to kiss him. In England King George IV received him at Windsor. In Paris, where he lived for 12 years, he was sensationally successful.

In 1835 Liszt was joined in Geneva by the Countess Marie d'Agoult, though they never married. Their daughter Cosima became the wife of the conductor Hans von Bülow and then of the composer Richard Wagner. Triumphant concert tours dominated Liszt's life until September 1847, when he made his last appearance as a virtuoso.

From 1848 to 1859 he was conductor at the court and theater at Weimar. There he championed Wagner's music and produced his music dramas. Liszt also introduced and revived the works of other contemporary composers. It was his most productive period, during which he composed 12 of his symphonic poems, the 'Faust' and 'Dante' symphonies, the piano sonata, two piano concertos, and 'Totentanz' for piano and orchestra. It was also during this period that he revised versions of the 'Paganini Etudes' and the 'Transcendental Etudes' for piano.

At 50 he retired to Rome. He received minor orders in the Roman Catholic church in 1865. In Rome he was occupied with religious music, composing two oratorios and a number of smaller works. In 1869 he again began visiting Weimar regularly. The Hungarian government named him president of the Academy of Music at Budapest in 1870. Thereafter he divided his time among Rome, Weimar, and Budapest. His last works were harmonically very advanced, anticipating musical forms of the 20th century. These works were, however, long neglected. After a highly spectacular jubilee tour to Paris, London, and other cities in 1886, he died at Bayreuth, Bavaria (now West Germany), of pneumonia on July 31.

LITERACY AND ILLITERACY. The ability to read and write is called literacy; its opposite is illiteracy. There are no degrees of illiteracy—one either can or cannot read and write—but there are several degrees of literacy. In some societies a person who can read the letters of the alphabet or read and write his or her own name is considered literate. In general, however, literacy means the ability to read and understand a wide range of material, as well as the ability to write clearly and coherently.

By the 1980s, according to international but admittedly inconsistent definitions of literacy, about seven out of ten adults in the world were considered literate. The populations with the highest levels of literacy were in the most economically advanced nations: Japan, the Soviet Union, the United States,

Canada, Western Europe, Australia, New Zealand, and Iceland. The poorer nations had the highest rates of illiteracy, ranging from more than 95 percent in Mali to more than 70 percent in Nigeria, Bangladesh, Haiti, Morocco, Liberia, Burundi, Afghanistan, Nepal, Ethiopia, and Pakistan.

The increase in literacy from ancient times to the present has not been a story of unbroken progress. The ability of people within a given society to read and write has been influenced by a number of factors, including economic well-being, the availability of material to read, the amount of education available, and the basic matter of the usefulness of reading.

Of these factors, usefulness has probably been the most decisive. In ancient societies, as people settled into stable patterns of agriculture and trade, it became useful for some of them to read and write in order to keep records, to transact business, and to measure amounts of land, animals, goods, materials, and produce. Since all economic aspects of a society were closely tied to the operations of government, literacy became useful and even necessary for the keeping of records by officials. Those who did not make their living in agriculture, trade, or government, however, found literacy to be generally of little value and did not bother with it. The responsibilities of citizenship led to a fairly high level of literacy in ancient Greece and Rome, but in addition to that, there also grew an appreciation of good literature—poetry, drama, history, and philosophy.

During the early Middle Ages, with the general breakdown of society in Europe and the decrease of commerce, literacy became largely confined to the church. But in the late Middle Ages, in the period of the Renaissance, the great expansion of commerce and banking led to a revival in literacy for the same reason that had caused it to increase in the ancient world—usefulness.

With the invention of the printing press and inexpensive paper late in the 15th century there was for the first time a great availability of reading material for a much greater number of people. Religious reformers were among the first to utilize the situation, quickly getting translations of the Bible and educational tracts and booklets into the hands of many people. (*See also* Reformation.)

The broadened religious enlightenment that resulted was followed in later centuries by a political one. Political theorists who favored doctrines promoting the natural rights of man called for an attack upon illiteracy. Political revolutions, particularly in the United States and France, helped inaugurate an era in which all classes were called upon to become informed on public policy for their own welfare. Against this political background there emerged the movement for universal popular education (*see* Education). Literacy came to be understood as a means whereby the individual could benefit and advance, and gradually whole societies began to acknowledge that universal literacy among their citizens was an avenue to greater economic well-being.

LITERARY AWARDS. Hundreds of literary awards are given each year throughout the world. These prizes often honor established literary figures, but they may also help relatively unknown writers and illustrators to achieve greater recognition.

Literary awards usually consist of cash prizes, medals, or citations. The sponsors include individuals, organizations, and publishing firms.

Major Children's Book Awards

Of the many annual awards for children's literature, the most prestigious are the John Newbery and the Caldecott medals, presented by the American Library Association (ALA). They were established by Frederic G. Melcher, an American publisher.

The first John Newbery Medal—for the most distinguished contribution to literature for children published in the United States—was awarded in 1922. It was named for an 18th-century London bookseller and publisher who pioneered in children's literature. The first Caldecott Medal—for the most distinguished picture book for children published in the United States—was awarded in 1938. The medal was named in honor of Randolph Caldecott, who was a 19th-century English illustrator of children's books (*see* Caldecott; Newbery).

Library organizations also administer many of the other awards for children's books. The Laura Ingalls Wilder Award, established in 1954, honors a popular American author. From 1960 to 1980 a medal was awarded every five years by the ALA to an author or illustrator for substantial and lasting contributions to children's literature. The medal is now awarded every three years.

The ALA also administers the Mildred L. Batchelder Award, established in 1966. Named for a leader in the development of library services for children, the annual citation goes to a book originally published in a foreign language in another country and subsequently published by an American publisher in the United States. The Catholic Library Association has awarded the Regina Medal since 1959 to individuals who have made distinguished contributions to literature for children.

Monetary prizes include the Boston Globe-Horn Book and the American (formerly National) Book awards for children's literature. Regional, state, and religious awards honor specialized achievements.

Awards in Other Countries

Many other countries and organizations award prizes in the field. British awards include two medals given by the Library Association. The Carnegie Medal—established in honor of the industrialist Andrew Carnegie—has been awarded annually since 1937 for an outstanding book for children (*see* Carnegie). The annual Kate Greenaway Medal—honoring the 19th-century English illustrator—was established in 1956 for distinguished illustration.

The Canadian Library Association (CLA) has presented the Book of the Year for Children Award since

The face of the Newbery Medal (above left) depicts John Newbery with children. René Chambellan designed the medal, which is awarded annually.

Both sides of the Caldecott Medal, also designed by Chambellan, have reproductions of Randolph Caldecott's illustrations.

1947. From 1954 to 1974 individual awards were made for books in French as well as in English. Since 1971, the CLA has also awarded the Amelia Frances Howard-Gibbon Medal for outstanding illustration. The award is named for a 19th-century Canadian illustrator of children's books.

The New Zealand Library Association has presented an annual award for children's literature since 1945 and for illustration since 1978. In 1964 the Children's Book Council of Australia was formed; it makes annual awards for the best children's book and the best picture book.

The Hans Christian Andersen International Children's Book Medals, established in 1956, are administered by the International Board on Books for Young People (IBBY). Honoring the 19th-century Danish author of fairy tales, the awards have been given biennially to an author and, since 1966, to an illustrator for the body of their work.

Nobel, Pulitzer, and Other Prizes

The Nobel prize for literature is the highest international literary honor. First awarded in 1901, it is one of the prizes established by Alfred Bernhard Nobel, a 19th-century Swedish industrialist (see Nobel; Nobel Prizes). The Swedish Academy in Stockholm determines the award, which includes a gold medal and prize money that has ranged from $40,000 to $190,000. Nine Americans—Sinclair Lewis, Pearl Buck, Eugene O'Neill, William Faulkner, Ernest Hemingway, John Steinbeck, Saul Bellow, Isaac Bashevis Singer, and Czeslaw Milosz—have been winners of the prize.

Among the most important literary awards in the United States are the Pulitzer Prizes in Letters. They were established in 1917 by the will of Joseph Pulitzer, an American journalist who was the editor of the *St. Louis Post-Dispatch* and the *New York World* (see Pulitzer). Prizes of $1,000 each are given annually in six fields—fiction, drama, history, biography or autobiography, poetry, and general nonfiction. The trustees of Columbia University award the prizes. Columbia University trustees also award the annual Bancroft Prizes, first given in 1948 under the will of Frederic Bancroft, an American historian. Prizes of $4,000 may be given to works in American history or diplomacy, or both.

The National Book Awards were established in 1950 by the American Book Publishers' Council—now the Association of American Publishers (AAP), the American Booksellers Association, and the Book Manufacturers Institute. Until 1980 prizes of $1,000 each were given annually in six categories.

The AAP, which had been administering the National Book Awards, created the American Book Awards (TABA) as their successor. TABA was established to give recognition to a greater number of United States authors and publishers. Two monetary awards—one to a hardcover book and one to a paperback—were given in each of 13 categories, and seven additional prizes were given in special categories, including design. After the controversial TABA was boycotted by some authors and publishers, the number of categories was reduced and the name was amended to ABA, beginning in 1981.

One of the most prestigious American awards is the National Medal for Literature, established in 1964. Since 1977, an annual prize of $15,000 has been given by the AAP for a writer's overall contribution.

Among the national, regional, and special literary awards, two of the best known are the Bollingen Prize in Poetry and the O. Henry Awards. The Bollingen Prize was established in 1950 under the sponsorship of Yale University. The O. Henry Awards for short stories were first given in 1919. (*See also* Literary Awards tables in Fact-Index.)

Fellowship Awards

Fellowships are grants of money given to authors to support them while they do research and write. The John Simon Guggenheim Memorial Fellowships, established in 1925, are the most prestigious of these awards in the United States. The amounts of the grants vary. More than 8,000 Guggenheim Fellowships have been awarded, several hundred of them to poets, playwrights, novelists, and other writers. The American Academy of Arts and Letters and the American Academy in Rome collaborate to provide fellowships for study in Rome.

Grants of the National Endowment for the Arts, established in 1965, have included awards of up to $10,000 to writers for support of their work. Special programs have provided grants in varying amounts for young writers.

LITERATURE

LITERATURE. There is no precise definition of the term literature. Derived from the Latin words *litteratus,* or "literate," and *littera,* meaning a letter of the alphabet, it refers to written works that are intended for reading. But not everything intended for reading is classed as literature. Such things as cookbooks, diet books, travel books, or advertisements in newspapers and magazines are all meant to be read but are not included in what is called literature. Literature is an art form, much like music, painting, and sculpture. As art, it is a skillful combination of expression and construction, of content and form.

What is expressed in literature is some facet of the whole range of human experience, past and present. The excellence of construction depends on the craft of the writer. An author is a craftsman just as much as a silversmith or furniture maker is. He must take his materials—words—and put them together in the way most suited to what he wants to say and to the form he wants to use.

The Forms of Literature

One is likely to think of poetry, drama, novels, short stories, and essays, when literature is mentioned. But literary excellence has never been confined to these types of writing. Nor are all examples of these kinds of writing necessarily literature. There are long fiction works which, through lack of literary merit and worthwhile content, are not novels in the same sense that the works of such great writers as Tolstoi, Melville, Twain, Dostoevski, Dickens, or Austen are novels. The same may be said of poetry or any other form of literature.

Conversely, there are many published works of types other than those mentioned that have been classed as good literature because of the quality of their writing. Examples can be drawn from almost every field of writing. In history, a few are the 'Peloponnesian War' by Thucydides, 'The Decline and Fall of the Roman Empire' by Edward Gibbon, and Bruce Catton's histories of the American Civil War. There are famous literary biographies, of which the best known are probably Plutarch's 'Lives of the Noble Grecians and Romans' and James Boswell's 'Life of Samuel Johnson'. Philosophy and science also have their masterpieces. The dialogues of Plato are written with great narrative skill and beauty. In the 20th century, the Spanish philosopher George Santayana's 'Life of Reason' is read for the quality and clarity of its style as much as for its ideas. The founder of psychoanalysis, Sigmund Freud, produced several books and essays that merit reading not only for the ideas he expresses in them, but also for the passion and conviction with which he expresses them. Two other scientists of literary excellence were Charles Darwin ('Origin of Species') and Jules-Henri Poincaré ('Science and Hypothesis' and 'Science and Method'). Statesmen and political theorists have also produced works of distinction. Such writers include Niccolò Machiavelli ('The Prince'), Thomas Hobbes ('Leviathan'), and others whose writings are too numerous to mention, such as Cicero, Alexander Hamilton, James Madison, John Adams, Thomas Jefferson, Abraham Lincoln, and Winston Churchill.

Clearly, then, literature has a broad range. It cannot be defined by either a specific form or content, but it represents a fusing of the two in such a way that the result has a particular excellence. The average travel guide is not literature, but when a book on travel is written by Alexis de Tocqueville ('Democracy in America') or by Charles Dickens ('American Notes'), it can become a classic.

The Origins of Literature

Written language came into existence thousands of years ago, at a time when some humans were able to settle in relatively permanent communities (*see* Ancient Civilization). Much that was written was in the form of reports and records used by the few members of society who could read and write (*see* Literacy and Illiteracy). But very early after the dawn of civilization, there developed an oral literature, a spoken tradition, as people attempted to formulate ideas about the world, the gods, their history, and themselves as human beings. These ancient traditions, myths, and legends were normally expressed in poetry. Poetry is easier to remember than extended prose passages, because of its rhythms and cadences.

In ancient times there was not the great profusion of written, recorded, and filmed material that is available today. Traditions were passed from one generation to another in spoken or sung form. These orally expressed traditions evoked the common experience of a people in language, symbols, plots, allegories, and situations that all could understand.

The themes for this oral literature had a great deal of variety: songs about the origin of the world and in praise of the gods, love stories, tragedies, epic tales of

Fact Finder for Literature

Literature is a vast subject. Additional information appears in the articles listed here. (See also related references in the Fact-Index.)

African Literature
American Literature
Autobiography
Bibliography
Biography
Books and Bookmaking
Canadian Literature
Diary
English Literature
Essay
Fable
Folklore
French Literature
German Literature
Hebrew Literature
Indian Literature
Irish Literature
Islamic Literature
Italian Literature
Japanese Literature
Korean Literature
Latin American Literature
Latin Literature
Literary Awards
Literature for Children
Novel
Poetry
Reading
Russian Literature
Short Story
Spanish Literature
Storytelling

heroism and adventure, ballads of intrigue and murder, folktales, fables, proverbs, and riddles.

Long after these oral traditions developed, the spoken and sung were put into written form. The main reason for doing so was that they not be lost or altered, thereby losing or misrepresenting the whole past of a people. In written form, these traditions have provided the world with some of its greatest literary classics: the 'Epic of Gilgamesh' (*see* Babylonia and Assyria), the 'Iliad' of Homer, and much of the Old Testament portion of the Bible. The Old Testament, in fact, contains as great a variety of ancient oral traditions in written form as can be found in one book. It has creation legends, stories of epic heroism and adventure, love tales, intrigue and murder stories, lyric poetry, songs of praise, proverbs, riddles, and more (*see* Bible).

The Diversification of Literature

Poetry and song were the earliest means used to preserve and convey literary traditions, and they have persisted to the present as forms of literature. Other forms—drama and narrative prose—appeared later and received their greatest impetus from the ancient Greeks. The dramatic tragedies of Aeschylus, Sophocles, and Euripides, as well as the comedies of Aristophanes, were all written in poetic form, but they were a new way of executing poetry in contrast to earlier lyric poetry or the epic. Poetry as drama, brilliantly developed by the Greeks, continued to be used with great effect by a number of other authors. These include Shakespeare during the Renaissance and T. S. Eliot in the 20th century, to name only two. (*See also* Poetry.)

Most literature published today is in the form of prose, a term that covers the essay, novel, philosophical treatises, histories, and modern journalism. From ancient Greece and Rome and the Middle East there have survived a large number of remarkable and readable prose works, including the writings of the physician Hippocrates; the mathematical treatises of Euclid, Archimedes, and Apollonius of Perga; the philosophical books of Plato, Aristotle, Lucretius, Philo, and Marcus Aurelius; the historical writings of Herodotus, Polybius, Suetonius, Livy, and Tacitus; and the essays of Seneca and Plutarch.

Narrative fiction—the novel and short story—was the latest literary form to develop and belongs mostly to the modern period. Prose fiction did, however, have some few antecedents in the ancient world. The Greeks wrote romances and adventure stories comparable in length to a long short story. The first really extended piece of fiction that deserved to be called a novel was the 'Satyricon' by the Roman Petronius Arbiter who died about AD 66. Although existing today only in fragments, it is believed to have been a delightful novel, filled with roguish characters and their mischievous exploits.

After the long period known as the Dark Ages, from the end of the Roman Empire in the West to the dawning of the Renaissance, prose fiction resurfaced

Marlon Brando and Jean Simmons starred in the movie version of Damon Runyon's short story "Guys and Dolls."

in the form of medieval romances—heroic tales of romantic chivalry and tragic love. The most famous was Sir Thomas Malory's 'Morte d'Arthur' (The Death of Arthur), a retelling of the legends of King Arthur and the Round Table (*see* Arthurian Legend).

The modern novel appeared at the end of the Middle Ages and the beginning of the modern era with the publication of 'Don Quixote' by Miguel de Cervantes early in the 16th century. This masterpiece of comic satire is considered by many critics to be the greatest piece of prose fiction ever written (*see* Cervantes). Other early examples of the novel were 'The Princess of Cleves', published in 1678, by Madame de Lafayette; 'Les Liaisons Dangereuses' (Dangerous Acquaintances, 1782) by Pierre Choderlos; Henry Fielding's 'Tom Jones' (1749); and 'Tristram Shandy' (1759–67) by Laurence Sterne. While not precisely a novel, 'Gulliver's Travels' (1726) by Jonathan Swift is one of the great prose satires of all time.

The 19th century was the golden age of the novel, though in the case of some few authors such as Henry James, Edith Wharton, Thomas Hardy, and Joseph Conrad, the golden age lasted into the early years of the 20th. Properly within the framework of the 19th century were such great writers as Jane Austen, Charlotte and Emily Brontë, Charles Dickens, Victor Hugo, Leo Tolstoi, Fedor Dostoevski, Herman Melville, Mark Twain, William Makepeace Thackeray, James Fenimore Cooper, Nathaniel Hawthorne, George Sand, Stendahl, Honoré de Balzac, Gustave Flaubert, and Émile Zola.

This classic age of prose fiction ended abruptly with the publication of James Joyce's 'Ulysses' in 1922. A new era began, for 'Ulysses' represented a total transformation of the novel. It moved away from the social themes that had preoccupied previous writers and into a reinterpretation of mythology within the framework of everyday 20th-century life. The rest of the 20th century has witnessed a great diversification of prose fiction writing in forms that frequently have their roots in earlier centuries: gothic novels, romances, detective fiction, western (cowboy) stories, horror fiction, historical novels, war stories, spy fiction (thrillers), and science fiction, to name a few. (*See also* Novel.)

The short story as a fiction type has its origins in the oral traditions and legends of the ancient Middle East, India, and Egypt. Most of the early tales were used as teaching devices and to inspire moral behavior. Aesop's fables provide a good example of this (*see* Aesop). The Romans also used the short-story form; the classic example is Ovid's 'Metamorphoses', a collection of more than 100 popular short tales, woven into a thematic pattern. During the Middle Ages there was a great proliferation of short narrative tales on a large variety of subjects. Many of them were in verse form. Of the well-known collections from the Middle Ages are 'The Seven Sages of Rome', 'The Arabian Nights', Chaucer's 'Canterbury Tales', and Boccaccio's 'Decameron'.

The short story went into a temporary decline during the 17th and 18th centuries, owing primarily to the emergence of the novel as a narrative form. But during the 19th century it made a remarkable resurgence, almost simultaneously in the United States, Russia, France, and Germany. Some of the best known short-story writers of this period were Johann Wolfgang von Goethe, E. T. A. Hoffmann, Heinrich von Kleist, Edgar Allan Poe, Washington Irving, Bret Harte, Sarah Orne Jewett, Nathaniel Hawthorne, Prosper Merimée, Alphonse Daudet, Ivan Krylov, Aleksandr Pushkin, Nicolai Gogol, Ivan Turgenev, Anton Chekhov, and the great French master of the form, Guy de Maupassant.

The short story has continued as a popular form in the 20th century. It has been practiced by a great many writers, some few of whom, like O. Henry (William S. Porter), Damon Runyon, and the Frenchman Paul Morand, specialized in the type. Like the novel, the subject matter and techniques of the short story are diverse. (*See also* Short Story.)

Literature for Everyone

Literary works have become available to large numbers of people for two reasons: the profusion of the printed word since the invention of the printing press in the 15th century and the presentation of works in other than printed forms.

The oral literature of the ancient world—poems, tales, songs and other forms—was presented to an audience by speakers and singers. This tradition of the spoken presentation was continued in the West by the development of drama written for the stage. Among the best examples still in existence of ancient theatrical plays are the dramas of the great Greek tragedy writers—Aeschylus, Sophocles, and Euripides—and the comedy writer Aristophanes.

The staging of dramas has continued to the present as an art form in its own right. In the 20th century, because of amazing advances in technology, it has become possible to make available other forms of literature to mass audiences as well. The movies, radio, and television have been responsible for bringing novels, short stories, poetry, and historical documentaries to millions of people at one time. Television has proved an extremely effective means for transforming a literary work into a visual art form because it can allow more time for a full development of a story than is normally feasible on the stage or in a motion picture. Television also permits a much greater audience than would otherwise be possible to see the enactment of a literary work.

Literature has also provided the working material that has served as a basis for some of the world's great musical presentations: oratorios, operas, and ballets. The text for such notable oratorios as Handel's 'Messiah' and Bach's 'Passion According to Saint Matthew' is derived entirely from the Bible. Most operas are based on stories derived from various forms of literature—legends, tales, fairy stories, and short stories. Bizet's 'Carmen', for instance, is based on a short story by Prosper Merimée. Richard Wagner's 'Ring' series of operas, 'Das Rheingold', 'Die Walküre', 'Siegfried', and 'Götterdämmerung', is based on the old Teutonic legend of the Nibelungs (*see* Nibelungs). Verdi's 'La Traviata' is derived from a story by Alexandre Dumas. Victor Hugo's play, 'Le Roi s'amuse', was used by Verdi for another opera, 'Rigoletto'. (*See also* Opera.)

Ballet has drawn from an equally broad array of literary works for its story lines. Prokofiev's 'Cinderella' and Tchaikovsky's 'Sleeping Beauty' come from fairy tales. Prokofiev's 'Romeo and Juliet' is based on the play by Shakespeare. Richard Strauss's 'The Legend of Joseph' is taken from a story in the Old Testament book of Genesis, while Diaghilev's 'Prodigal Son' comes from a New Testament parable. Franz Hilverding based several ballets, including 'Venus and Adonis' and 'Ulysses and Circe', on Greek myths. Cervantes' great novel, 'Don Quixote' was staged as a ballet by Marius Petipa.

The American musical comedy, containing elements of drama, opera, and ballet, has several works based on literature. 'South Pacific' by Rodgers and Hammerstein comes from a collection of stories, 'Tales of the South Pacific' by novelist James Michener. The Lerner and Lowe musical 'My Fair Lady' is a musical adaptation of George Bernard Shaw's play, 'Pygmalion'. The stage musical 'Carmen Jones', with an all-black cast, is based on the opera 'Carmen', in turn based on a short story. One work, 'Auntie Mame', a novel by Patrick Dennis, was adapted as a play, as a movie, and finally as a musical comedy, 'Mame', first on the stage and later on the screen.

BIBLIOGRAPHY FOR LITERATURE

Adler, M. J. and Van Doren, Charles. How to Read a Book (Simon & Schuster, 1972).

Gardiner, J. H. The Forms of Prose Literature (Folcroft, 1973).

Gray, Bennison. The Phenomenon of Literature (Mouton, 1975).

Hess, K. M. Appreciating Literature (Wiley, 1978).

Kennedy, X. J. Literature: an Introduction to Fiction, Poetry, and Drama (Little, 1979).

Moulton, R. G. World Literature (Folcroft, 1973).

Reichert, John. Making Sense of Literature (Univ. of Chicago Press, 1978).

Williams, W. E. The Craft of Literature (Folcroft, 1973).

LITERATURE FOR CHILDREN

LITERATURE FOR CHILDREN. Children's literature is literature that speaks to children. Many stories, poems, and other types of literature were made especially for the young. But a large number of children's favorites were originally aimed at grown-ups. These include 'The Panchatantra', Aesop's fables, 'Arabian Nights', and 'The Pilgrim's Progress'.

Books are an important part of children's literature. But children's literature is more than books. It is magazines, newspapers, tapes, records, TV, films. It is folktales and storytellers, writers and artists and publishers, libraries and librarians—all the things and all the people that bring children and literature together.

THE BACKGROUND

In the beginning there was little literature for children. But there was literature children liked.

All literature began with folklore. Much folklore was probably aimed at a general audience, but children were sometimes a part of that audience. And they adopted many of the stories and songs for their excitement and action and rhythm (*see* Storytelling).

Early books aimed at grown-ups generally. The first books actually aimed at children, or for use with children, were often lesson books. There were also conduct books, which taught manners and morals. These were not typically literature (*see* Literature).

In England of the 600's and 700's, churchmen such as Bede and Alcuin wrote lesson books for students. In Moravia (now Czechoslovakia) in about 1648, Johann Comenius wrote 'Orbis Sensualium Pictus'. 'Orbis Pictus' (The World in Pictures) was a textbook with lots of pictures. Comenius felt these would make it easier for children to learn.

The hornbooks of England and the United States were lesson books. A *hornbook* was not really a book. It was a printed page pasted on a paddle-shaped piece of wood. The page was protected by a see-through sheet of horn, which looked like a clear plastic. On the page were the alphabet, a short prayer, and other material for learning to read.

Primers and battledores followed hornbooks in England. The *battledore* was a sheet of cardboard-like paper folded into several panels.

The first book printed in Burmese, 'First Burmese Reader' (1776), was a lesson book. So was Peter Beron's 'Primer with a Fish' (1824), Bulgaria's first book for children.

CHILDREN'S LITERATURE OF EUROPE

In Europe, written literature for children began in the 1600's. There was little of it at first, and children often turned, as always, to adult literature for adventure.

Scattered Beginnings

In Italy Giambattista Basile's collection of folktales, 'Lo Cunto de li Cunti' (The Tale of Tales), was not written for children. But many of the stories, such as "Sleeping Beauty" and "Cinderella," came to be children's favorites. In Zürich, Switzerland, children who delivered money on New Year's Day were used to getting a treat. But in 1645, each child

More than 800 years ago, the Japanese artist Toba Sojo drew a comic picture story that spoke to children, though it was not intended for them. His scroll showed animals frolicking at a picnic and having such contests as an archery shoot.

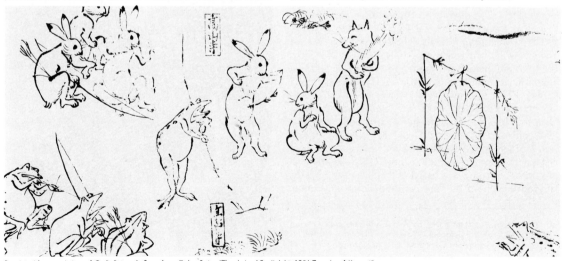

Reprinted by permission of G. P. Putnam's Sons from Toba Sojo, 'The Animal Frolic' (© 1954 Temple of Kazanji)

LITERATURE FOR CHILDREN

Like the hornbook, the battledore was a beginning lesson book, but it was in the form of a sheet of stiff paper, folded.

received a sheet of paper instead. On it was a picture, with some verse underneath. These *Zürcherischen Neujahrsblätter* (Zürich New Year's Sheets) were the beginning of Swiss literature for children.

Children's books of the 1600's were often preachy and dull. But there were exceptions. One of them was Jean de La Fontaine's 'Fables' (1668) (*see* La Fontaine). Another exception was John Bunyan's 'Pilgrim's Progress' (1678) (*see* Bunyan). A third exception was Charles Perrault's French fairy tales, sometimes known as 'Tales of Mother Goose'. Perrault actually rewrote the stories of "Red Riding Hood," "Bluebeard," and others for children.

Another exception to preachy and dull books were the *chapbooks*. They were little paperbacks sold by peddlers, or chapmen, and commonly written for grown-ups. Earlier chapbooks were often sensational versions of medieval romances and other stories. Later chapbooks also contained fairy tales, and many of these appealed to children.

More Children's Books, with Morals

Two outstanding English books of the early 1700's were written for grown-ups. But children claimed the stories as their own—Daniel Defoe's 'Robinson Crusoe' and Jonathan Swift's 'Gulliver's Travels' (*see* Defoe; Swift). In England, publisher John Newbery began to put out a large number of books for children. The first of them was 'A Little Pretty Pocket-Book' (1744). Two of Newbery's most famous books are 'The History of Little Goody Two-Shoes' and 'Mother Goose's Melody'. His Mother Goose book was the first collection of Mother Goose rhymes in English (*see* Mother Goose; Newbery).

Jean Jacques Rousseau's 'Émile' (1762) is about a boy whose learning was based on his interests. Many children's books of the time adopted Rousseau's main

This article was contributed by Augusta Baker, Coordinator of Children's Services, New York Public Library, and by Compton's Encyclopedia Canadian Advisory Board.

characters—the boy and his teacher. In the imitations, however, everything the two did was made to teach a lesson. English engraver Thomas Bewick began to illustrate fine picture books for children. Children's magazines and newspapers appeared. These included Germany's *Leipziger Wochenblatt für Kinder* (Leipzig Children's Weekly) (1772) and Spain's *Gaceta de los Niños* (Children's Magazine) (1798).

Books Get Better

With the 1800's, writing for children became more respectable in Europe. And the quality of both children's writers and children's books improved.

An early book of poems for children was 'Original Poems for Infant Minds' (1804), by Ann and Jane Taylor of England. Jane wrote the famous "Twinkle, Twinkle, Little Star." Charles Lamb and his sister Mary began the retelling of classics for children with their 'Tales from Shakespeare', a version of Shakespeare's plays. Jakob and Wilhelm Grimm collected German folktales (*see* Grimm). In Switzerland, Johann Wyss' 'Swiss Family Robinson' appeared.

Russia's Ivan A. Krylov published his fables in 1825. Sir Walter Scott's 'Tales of a Grandfather'

The English artist John Tenniel gave the Jabberwock horrifying shape and form in Lewis Carroll's 'Alice in Wonderland'.

marked the beginning of Scottish children's literature. Petr P. Ershov's story of a magic horse, 'The Little Humpbacked Horse' (1834), was printed in Russia. In Denmark appeared the first fairy tales by one of the world's great storytellers, Hans Christian Andersen (*see* Andersen).

Charles Dickens' 'Christmas Carol' (1843) gave children Scrooge and Tiny Tim. Peter Asbjörnsen and Jörgen Moe collected Norwegian folktales. Many of these were later retold by a noted Norwegian storyteller, Gudrun Thorne-Thomsen, in 'East o' the Sun and West o' the Moon'. Heinrich Hoffman, a doctor of Frankfurt, Germany, drew humorous pictures for children in his waiting room. The result was 'Struwwelpeter' (Strawhead Peter), later translated as 'Slovenly Peter'. Edward Lear's 'Book of Nonsense' (1846) was pure fun—a taste of things to come in children's literature (*see* Lear).

More Types and Masterpieces

From about the 1850's, children's literature aimed more and more to please rather than teach. Story characters were pictured more like real people. And more types of children's books began to appear.

Aleksandr Afanas'ev collected Russian folktales. Thomas Hughes' 'Tom Brown's School Days' (1857) became one of the best-known school stories in English. 'Cinq Semaines en Ballon' (Five Weeks in a Balloon) (1863) was the first of the Jules Verne science fiction books.

Karel Erben of Czechoslovakia collected folktales, later translated as 'Panslavonic Folk-Lore'. In Germany Wilhelm Busch came out with a picture story, 'Max and Moritz' (1865). It was an ancestor of the comic strip. The outstanding literary event of the time was Lewis Carroll's 'Alice's Adventures in Wonderland' (1865), with illustrations by John Tenniel. It is one of the great fantasies of world literature for children (*see* Carroll).

Among the most important illustrators of the period were Walter Crane, Randolph Caldecott, and Kate Greenaway. These English artists helped develop the colored picture book for the very young.

One children's masterpiece after another began to appear. George MacDonald of Scotland wrote his fantasy 'At the Back of the North Wind' (1871). In 1875 appeared 'Broučci' (The Fireflies) by Jan Karafiát of Czechoslovakia. Retold by Max Bolliger, the book was later translated into English as 'The Fireflies'. Johanna Spyri's 'Heidi' (1880) was written in Switzerland (*see* Spyri). 'Pinocchio', the story of a wooden boy, was written in Italy by Carlo Lorenzini, who used the name Carlo Collodi. Robert Louis Stevenson of Scotland wrote 'Treasure Island' (*see* Stevenson). 'The Heart of a Boy' was written by Edmondo de Amicis of Italy. And Rudyard Kipling wrote 'The Jungle Book' (1894) (*see* Kipling).

Children's Literature Takes a Giant Step

Good books are important. But it's also important to get them into the hands of children. In the early

MGM-EMI Distributors Ltd.

The frog called Mr. Jeremy Fisher leaps out of the pages of Beatrix Potter to dance in the 'Beatrix Potter Ballet'.

1900's, children's libraries opened in many countries of Europe. So did training centers for children's librarians. Children's book councils, book weeks, book reviews, and book awards were organized.

Outstanding children's books appeared in rapid succession. Seumas MacManus' 'Donegal Fairy Stories' (1900) retold Irish tales. Out of England came Beatrix Potter's 'Tale of Peter Rabbit' (1901) and Walter de la Mare's 'Songs of Childhood' (1902). 'Peter Pan', a play by James Barrie of Scotland, was first staged in 1904 (*see* Barrie). From Sweden came Selma Lagerlöf's 'Wonderful Adventures of Nils'. Kenneth Grahame, a Scot, wrote 'The Wind in the Willows' (1908) (*see* Grahame). 'The Blue Bird', by Maurice Maeterlinck of Belgium, was staged in 1908, published 1909 (*see* Maeterlinck). From Sweden came Elsa Beskow's 'Pelle's New Suit'; from Yugoslavia, Ivana Brlić-Mazuranić's 'Brave Adventures of Lapitch'; from Spain, 'Platero and I', by Juan Ramón Jiménez; from Ireland, Padraic Colum's 'King of Ireland's Son'; from England, Hugh Lofting's 'Story of Dr. Dolittle'. In England A. A. Milne's 'Winnie-the-Pooh' (1926) was illustrated by Ernest H. Shepard.

Germany's Erich Kästner wrote 'Emil and the Detectives'. The first of the Babar the elephant series, 'The Story of Babar', was written by Jean de Brunhoff of France. From England came 'Mary Poppins' (1934), by Australian-born Pamela L. Travers; from Russia,

LITERATURE FOR CHILDREN

Illustration © 1958 Tove Jansson, used by permission of Henry Z. Walck, Inc., publishers

A plate of fish soup glides toward an astonished Moomintroll in Tove Jansson's 'Moominland Midwinter'.

Sergei Prokofiev's musical fairy tale 'Peter and the Wolf' (1936) (*see* Prokofiev). Antoine de Saint-Exupéry of France wrote 'The Little Prince'. In Sweden appeared Astrid Lindgren's 'Pippi Longstocking'. Tove Jansson of Finland wrote her first book about the Moomins, 'Comet in Moominland'.

Books Seamy Side Up

From about the 1950's, more and more children's books were realistic. Some began to show the ugly and distasteful side of life. 'Marcelino' by José M. Sanchez-Silva of Spain, is about an orphan boy who kept and killed small animals. 'The Ark', by Margot Benary-Isbert, shows the aftereffects of war on the people of Germany.

But fantasy and folktales continued to flourish. 'The Borrowers' was the first of a charming fantasy series by Mary Norton of England. Gwyn Jones retold 'Welsh Legends and Folk-Tales' (1955). Karl Bruckner of Austria retold the story of Tutankhamen in 'The Golden Pharaoh'. The Scottish folktales of 'Heather and Broom' (1960) were retold from the Gaelic by Leclaire G. Alger, who used the name Sorche Nic Leodhas. She also did 'Always Room for One More'.

More children's literature of Eastern Europe became available in English in the 1960's and 1970's. Stefan Dichev of Bulgaria wrote 'Rali' (1960), a realistic story about Bulgaria when it was ruled by the Turks. 'The Golden Seed' by Poland's Maria Konopnicka was translated in 1962.

Babbis Friis-Baastad, who did her first radio play for Norwegian children in 1957, wrote 'Kristy's Courage', followed by 'Don't Take Teddy'. The first is about a disfigured girl, the second about a retarded child. In England Rosemary Sutcliff wrote 'Dawn Wind', one of the best of her historical novels.

Nada Ćurčija-Prodanović retold Yugoslavian folktales in 'Heroes of Serbia' (1963). 'Koko and the

Ghosts', a mystery story from Yugoslavia by Ivan Kušan, was retold in English. 'The Three Poor Tailors' (1965), a picture book version of a Hungarian folktale, was done by Hungarian-born Victor Ambrus. Alki Zei's 'Wildcat Under Glass', a realistic story of the Greece of the 1930's, was translated in 1968.

Among notable books of the 1970's was 'The Little Chalk Man', by Czechoslovakia's Václav Ctvrtek, the story of a chalk drawing come to life. Denmark's Ib Spang Olsen wrote 'Smoke', about an unorthodox fight against air pollution. Estonian-born Selve Maas retold 'The Moon Painters and Other Estonian Folk Tales' (1971). S. R. van Iterson of the Netherlands wrote 'Pulga', the realistic story of a street child of Bogotá, Colombia. Ioana Sturdza translated 'Fairy Tales and Legends from Romania' (1972).

CHILDREN'S LITERATURE OF THE UNITED STATES

During the colonial period, few children's books were written in the United States. And these were commonly preachy and dull. Not until the 1800's did notable children's writers begin to appear.

The Beginnings

Washington Irving's 'Sketch Book' was not written for children. But the stories "Rip Van Winkle" and "The Legend of Sleepy Hollow" became children's favorites (*see* Irving). In 1822 Clement Moore's 'Visit from St. Nicholas' began a Christmas tradition in the United States. It is commonly known as 'The Night Before Christmas'.

From about the 1850's, story characters were drawn in a more lifelike, less wooden way. An example is

Yesterday's children discover books that speak to them in the children's department of the Cleveland Public Library.

Cleveland Public Library

Peter meets the wolf in Walt Disney's 'Peter and the Wolf', a movie based on Sergei Prokofiev's musical fairy tale.

Mary Mapes Dodge's 'Hans Brinker, or the Silver Skates' (1865). 'Hans Brinker' was also a forerunner of a popular type—stories about other lands. 'Ragged Dick' (1867) was Horatio Alger's first of a series of popular rags-to-riches stories, with morals. Louisa May Alcott's 'Little Women' is a family story with lifelike characters (see Alcott). In 1873 *St. Nicholas* magazine was founded. It greatly influenced writing for children in the United States. Mark Twain's 'Adventures of Tom Sawyer' (1876) shows the seamy side of life and human nature—with humor and understanding (see Twain).

In 1877 Minerva Saunders set aside a corner for children's books at the Pawtucket, R.I., library. It was a giant step for children's literature. Joel Chandler Harris' 'Uncle Remus' (1880) was one of the first folktale collections in the United States (see Harris).

One of the first fine illustrators for children in the United States was Howard Pyle. He wrote and illustrated 'The Merry Adventures of Robin Hood' (1883) (see Pyle). Pratt Institute in Brooklyn, N.Y., began training children's librarians in 1898. A training school for children's librarians was also set up at Carnegie Library in Pittsburgh, Pa. In 1899, story hours began at Carnegie Library. These were crucial steps in the development of children's literature.

Growth in Libraries and Books

The 20th century opened promisingly for children's literature in the United States. L. Frank Baum wrote 'The Wonderful Wizard of Oz' (1900). That same year the American Library Association opened a children's section. A few years later, Effie L. Power set up a children's department in the Cleveland Public Library. And Anne Carroll Moore did the same in the New York Public Library.

In Boston, Mass., Bertha Mahony Miller opened a Bookshop for Boys and Girls in 1916. It was the first bookshop of its kind in the United States. Frederic G.

Melcher helped found Children's Book Week in 1919. Later Melcher and the American Library Association inaugurated the Newbery and Caldecott awards (see Literary Awards). The Macmillan Publishing Company opened the first children's book department in the United States, with Louise Seaman Bechtel as editor.

In 1924 Anne Carroll Moore began reviewing children's books in the *New York Herald Tribune* book section. Her column was called "The Three Owls." *The Horn Book Magazine*, a review of children's books, began the same year. Wanda Gág's 'Millions of Cats' (1928) was one of the first fine picture books for the very young in the United States. In 1928 Walt Disney created Mickey Mouse in a movie cartoon, 'Steamboat Willie' (see Disney).

Types of Books Multiply

From about 1930 to the end of World War II, good children's books of many types became plentiful. In 1932 appeared 'The Dream Keeper and Other Poems', by Langston Hughes (see Hughes). Marjorie Flack's 'Story About Ping' (1933), set in China, was a sign of growing interest in books about other lands. So was Monica Shannon's 'Dobry' (1934), about a Bulgarian peasant boy. Ellis Credle wrote 'Down, Down the Mountain' (1934), a regional story of two Southern mountain children. 'The Good Master' (1934), by Kate Seredy, is set in her native Hungary. Carol Ryrie Brink's 'Caddie Woodlawn' (1935) is historical fiction.

Theodore Seuss Geisel wrote and illustrated his first fantasy for children, 'And to Think That I Saw It on Mulberry Street' in 1937. Geisel used the name Dr. Seuss. In 1938 Augusta Baker compiled 'Books About Negro Life for Children', the first of a series of book lists about the black experience.

Outstanding author-illustrated books of 1939 included Robert Lawson's fantasy 'Ben and Me' and James Daugherty's biography 'Daniel Boone'. Ann Nolan Clark's 'In My Mother's House' (1941) is one of a series of her books about American Indians. A high point in historical fiction for children was Esther Forbes's 'Johnny Tremaine' (1943). Richard Chase's 'Jack Tales' is a collection of Southern mountain legends. Lois Lenski's 'Strawberry Girl' (1945) is one of the best of her regional stories. 'Misty of Chincoteague' (1947), by Marguerite Henry, is an outstanding horse story.

Books About Many Groups—And Some Starkness

From about the 1950's, more and more books about minority-group children and children of other lands began to appear. 'Amos Fortune, Free Man' (1950), by Elizabeth Yates, is the biography of an African prince sold as a slave in the New World. In 1952 appeared E. B. White's outstanding fantasy, 'Charlotte's Web'. 'The Wheel on the School' (1954), by Meindert de Jong, is set in the Netherlands; Taro Yashima's 'Crow Boy' (1955), in Japan. 'Bronzeville Boys and Girls' (1956), by Gwendolyn Brooks, is an outstanding collection of children's poems in a black setting (see Brooks).

In the 1960's and 1970's, realism in children's books was sometimes stark. Paperback books for children appeared, many of them reprints of children's favorites. And there was rapid growth of children's literature in nonbook form—records, films, tapes, and other materials.

Scott O'Dell's 'Island of the Blue Dolphins' (1960) is about an American Indian girl. The author–illustrator Ezra Jack Keats did a series of picture books about a little black boy, beginning with 'The Snowy Day' (1962). 'City Rhythms' (1965), by the author–illustrator Ann Grifalconi, was one of a growing number of books about city life. Isaac Bashevis Singer's 'Zlateh the Goat and Other Stories' (1966) is a collection of Jewish tales filled with humor and wisdom. Realistic stories of ghetto life included "How Many Miles to Babylon?', by Paula Fox, and 'The Jazz Man', by Mary Hays Weik.

Jane Wagner's 'J. T.' (1969) is one of a number of children's books to use photos instead of drawings. 'Who Look at Me' (1969), by the poet June Jordan, expresses the black experience through paintings and poetry. Pura Belpré's 'Santiago' (1969) is about a little Puerto Rican boy in the United States. Traveller Bird's 'Path to Snowbird Mountain' (1972) contains Cherokee legends he heard from his grandmother.

CHILDREN'S LITERATURE OF CANADA

Early Canadian children's literature aimed at "pious feelings and moral lessons." Examples can be found in the first Canadian children's magazine, *The Snow Drop* (1847).

Early writers who put their stories in a Canadian setting include Catherine Parr Traill. Her 'Canadian Crusoes' (1852) was later republished as 'Lost in the Backwoods'. James de Mille wrote the first Canadian series, the Brethren of the White Cross schoolboy stories (1869–73).

'Beautiful Joe' (1894), by Margaret Marshall Saunders, is a sentimental—and very popular—dog story. But Ernest Thompson Seton and Sir Charles G. D. Roberts created the realistic animal story, a unique Canadian contribution to children's literature. 'Wild Animals I Have Known' (1898) was Seton's first collection of animal tales. One of Robert's best is 'The Kindred of the Wild' (1902).

A Canadian regional story, Lucy Maud Montgomery's 'Anne of Green Gables' (1908) became an international best-seller. In 1912 Lillian H. Smith began her work in Boys and Girls Services at the Toronto Public Library. During her almost 40 years there, she greatly influenced selection of children's books in Canada and elsewhere. The year 1922 marked a giant step for Canadian children's books. The Toronto Public Library built Boys and Girls House, the first library building for children in Canada. 'Silver: The Life of an Atlantic Salmon' (1931) is a realistic animal story by one of Canada's outstanding writers for children, Roderick L. Haig-Brown.

There are many romantic stories about the North West Mounted Police (now the Royal Canadian Mounted Police). One of the best known is Muriel Denison's 'Susannah: A Little Girl with the Mounties' (1936). In 1936 *La Bibliothèque des Enfants* (The Children's Library) opened in Montreal to serve the needs of the area's French-speaking children.

The best-illustrated Canadian books of the 1940's are by the author-illustrator Clare Bice. His 'Jory's Cove' (1941) captures the flavor of fishing life in Nova Scotia. In 1941 Mary Grannan's fantasy 'Just Mary' was broadcast over the radio. It was the first of a series, later published in book form. Two of Haig-Brown's best stories of outdoor life are 'Starbuck Valley Winter' (1943) and 'Saltwater Summer' (1948), set in British Columbia.

Bertha Mabel Dunham's 'Kristli's Trees' (1948) is a warm picture of Mennonite farm life in Ontario. In 1948 the Canadian Association of Children's Librarians sponsored the first Young Canada's Book Week. The Canadian Library Association had begun awarding prizes for the best Canadian children's books in 1946. But the awards were confined to books in English. Several years later awards were also established for books in French.

'The Talking Cat' (1952) is a delightful collection of French Canadian folktales retold by Natalie Savage Carlson. A first-class example of history for

The sly thief of Valenciennes outsmarts the people trying to catch him in Marius Barbeau's 'Golden Phoenix'.

Illustration by Arthur Price, reproduced by permission of Oxford University Press, Canadian Branch, from Marius Barbeau, 'The Golden Phoenix', retold by Michael Hornyansky

children is Pierre Berton's 'Golden Trail' (1954), the story of the Klondike Gold Rush. Farley Mowat's prizewinning 'Lost in the Barrens' (1956) was later republished as 'Two Against the North'. Another popular Mowat story is 'The Dog Who Wouldn't Be' (1957).

An outstanding book of 1958 was Marius Barbeau's 'Golden Phoenix, and Other French-Canadian Fairy Tales', a retelling of stories from his 'Contes du Grand-Père Sept-Heures' (Tales of Grandfather Seven O'Clock). Sheila Burnford's 'Incredible Journey' (1960) was made into a movie. Claude Aubry's fantasy 'Les Îles du Roi Maha Maha II' (The Islands of King Maha Maha II) tells the story of how the Thousand Islands came to be. In 1963 it was translated as 'The King of the Thousand Islands'.

Christie Harris' 'Once Upon a Totem' (1963) is a noteworthy retelling of Indian legends. A memorable book based on Eskimo legend is James Houston's 'Tikta'liktak' (1965). Later books by the same author-illustrator include 'The White Archer'.

Claude Aubry's 'Christmas Wolf' (1965), the fanciful story of a Christmas Eve conversion, was translated from 'Le Loup de Noël'. Another outstanding 1965 book is William Stevenson's 'Bushbabies', a story of friendship and adventure set in Kenya. In 1971 the Amelia Frances Howard-Gibbon Medal for illustration was given for the first time. It was awarded to Elizabeth Cleaver, illustrator of the poetry collection 'The Wind Has Wings' (1968).

CHILDREN'S LITERATURE OF LATIN AMERICA

Latin American literature for children began in the late 1800's. It was often moralistic and still is.

Domingo Faustino Sarmiento, president of Argentina, laid the foundation for children's libraries in that country. The Sarmiento Law of 1870 provided for a national library commission and for books. Through his writings, Sarmiento also influenced the development of children's libraries in many other countries of Latin America.

In 1889 José Martí, the Cuban liberator, founded an early children's magazine, *La Edad de Oro* (The Golden Age). Several years later, 'Contos da Carochinha' was published in Brazil. A collection of folktales from several countries, it was the first known book written to entertain children in Latin America. The Biblioteca de Chapulín series of children's books began to appear in Mexico in 1904. Each book was chosen for its literary quality and was illustrated by a noted Mexican artist.

Rafael Pombo of Colombia, one of the first fine children's poets of Latin America, wrote 'Fábulas y verdades' (Fables and True Stories) (1916). 'South American Jungle Tales', by Horacio Quiroga of Uruguay, was translated in 1922. Antonio Robles Soler, who wrote under the name Antoniorrobles, went to Mexico from Spain. His popular children's stories include the books later translated as 'Tales of Living Playthings' and 'Merry Tales from Spain'. 'Perez and Martina' (1932), a Puerto Rican folktale, was

From José Martí, *The Golden Age*

La Edad de Oro, an early Cuban children's magazine, was dedicated to the children of America.

written down by Pura Belpré as she heard it from her grandmother.

In 1936 the National Commission for Children's Literature was founded in Brazil. Two years later, one of Venezuela's outstanding children's magazines came out. It was *Onza, Tigre y Leon*. A later Venezuelan magazine was *Tricolor*. 'Cuentos para Mari-Sol' (Tales for Mari-Sol) (1938), by Chile's Marta Brunet, was a collection of nursery stories. Constancio C. Vigil of Argentina was famous for his animal fantasies. One of his best-loved stories was translated as 'La Hormiguita Viajera/The Adventures of Hormiguita'.

In 1940 Margarida Bandeira Duarte published a Brazilian "why" story, later translated as 'The Legend of the Palm Tree'. Philip M. Sherlock wrote 'Anansi, the Spider Man' (1954), one of the best collections of Jamaican folktales. Costa Rica's María Isabel Carvajal wrote under the name Carmen Lira. Her 'Los Cuentos de mi tía Panchita' (Tales Told by My Aunt Panchita), was published in 1956. 'The Snow and the Sun/La Nieve y el Sol' (1961), a South American folk rhyme in English and Spanish, was done by the author-illustrator Antonio Frasconi, who was born in Uruguay.

Andrew Salkey, a leading Jamaican writer, wrote several exciting children's stories, among them 'The Shark Hunters' (1966). 'Crick-Crack!' (1966), folktales from Trinidad and Tobago, were retold by Eaulin Ashtine. Ricardo E. Alegría of Puerto Rico retold

'The Three Wishes' (1969), a collection of Puerto Rican folktales.

CHILDREN'S LITERATURE OF ASIA

In much of Asia, children's literature has been at least partly to teach. The idea of children's literature for pure fun is not generally accepted.

One of the first to write for children in Asia was Sazanami Iwaya of Japan. In the late 1800's he rewrote old stories, later translated as 'Japanese Fairy Tales'. In 1909 *Phool*, the leading children's magazine in Urdu, appeared in Pakistan. Lu Hsün of China collected old Chinese fairy tales and wrote stories for children. *Akai Tori* (Red Bird), the most important children's magazine in Japan, first came out in 1918. Dhan Gopal Mukerji of India wrote the prizewinning 'Gayneck: The Story of a Pigeon' (1927).

In 1939 a Lahore, Pakistan, publisher began a sort of children's book-of-the-month club called the Paisa Library. For a paisa (about 1½ cents) a day, a member received one children's book at the end of the month. Ch'eng-en Wu's 'Monkey', a popular Chinese story of about 1550, was retold in English for children in 1943. Htin Aung retold 'Burmese Folk-Tales' (1948). In 1949 the Tondo Children's Library opened in Manila. It was the first of its kind in the Philippines.

'The Animal Frolic' (1954) was a reprint, with a few words added, of Toba Sojo's Scroll of Animals. The Japanese artist drew the picture scroll about 1100. So-Un Kim's 'Story Bag' is a collection of Korean folktales. Ashraf Siddiqui of Pakistan wrote 'Bhombal Dass: The Uncle of Lion' (1959).

In the 1960's and 1970's especially, more children's literature of Asia became available in English. This reflected, in part, a growing interest among English speakers in children of other lands. Janice Holland retold a story from 'The Book of Huai Nan Tzu' in 'You Never Can Tell' (1963). The original was written in China before 122 B.C. Miyoko Matsutani's 'Fox Wedding' is a Japanese folktale retold. Mom Dusdi Paribatra retold a Thai legend of love, 'The Reluctant Princess'. 'Blue in the Seed' (1964), by Korea's Yong Ik Kim, is a realistic story about a tormented blue-eyed boy. In 1964 Eliezer Smoli's 'Frontiersmen of Israel' appeared in English. Selma Ekrem retold 'Turkish Fairy Tales' (1964).

Among many excellent translations from Japanese are Momoko Ishii's 'Issun Boshi, the Inchling', a Japanese Tom Thumb story, and Kenji Miyazawa's 'Winds and Wildcat Places' (1967). 'Gilgamesh: Man's First Story' (1967) was retold by Bernarda Bryson. An outstanding book from Iran is Faridah Fardjam's 'Crystal Flower and the Sun'. Devorah Omer's 'Gideonites' is an outstanding book from Israel.

Yasuo Segawa, a top Japanese artist, illustrated Miyoko Matsutani's 'Witch's Magic Cloth' (1969). Vo-Dinh wrote and illustrated 'The Toad Is the Emperor's Uncle' (1970), a collection of animal folktales from Vietnam. 'Juan and the Asuangs' (1970), the story of a little boy and jungle spirits, was done by the author-illustrator José Aruego of the Philippines. Later picture books by Aruego include 'Look What I Can Do' (1971), about two carabaos who are always trying to outdo each other.

CHILDREN'S LITERATURE OF AUSTRALIA AND NEW ZEALAND

Few books for children were written in Australia until the late 1800's. And there has been very little children's literature of New Zealand.

One of the best-known children's writers of Australia, Ethel Sibyl Turner, wrote 'Seven Little Australians' (1894). K. Langloh Parker retold the folktales of the Australian aborigines in 'Australian Legendary Tales' (1896).

Children's services began in the Dunedin Public Library of New Zealand in 1910. That same year, Mary Grant Bruce wrote 'A Little Bush Maid', the first of a popular series about a family who lived on a place called "Billabong." In 1915 the Public Library of South Australia opened a children's department.

May Gibbs's 'Gumnut Babies' (1916) later appeared as a comic strip. Esther Glen, who wrote 'Six Little New Zealanders' (1917), set the standards for children's writing in New Zealand. The author-illustrator Norman Lindsay wrote 'The Magic Pudding' (1918), one of Australia's first fine picture books.

Dorothy Wall's 'Blinky Bill, the Quaint Little Aus-

The Witch of the Mountain tells the villagers to bring her rice cakes in Miyoko Matsutani's 'Witch's Magic Cloth'.

Illustration by Yasuo Segawa, reprinted with the permission of Parents' Magazine Press (© 1969)

tralian' (1933) was the first of a popular series. 'Whalers of the Midnight Sun' (1934), by the Australian Alan John Villiers, is one of the best adventure stories of its time. Mary and Elizabeth Durack wrote 'The Way of the Whirlwind' (1941), a fantasy. 'The Book of Wiremu' (1944), by New Zealand's Stella M. Morice, is a story of Maori life.

The first Children's Book Week in New Zealand was held in 1944. In 1945 the first Children's Book Council was organized in Australia. The Esther Glen awards for the best children's books began in New Zealand in 1945. The following year the Australian Children's Book of the Year awards began. All these helped bring children and good books together.

Recent outstanding books from Australia include Nan Chauncy's 'Tangara' (1960) and Ivan Southall's 'Hills End' (1962) and his dramatic 'To the Wild Sky' (1967). Patricia Wrightson's realistic 'I Own the Racecourse' (1968) is another excellent book.

CHILDREN'S LITERATURE OF AFRICA

Children's literature of Africa is fairly new—from the 1960's and 1970's mostly. Often only small numbers of books by African writers were printed, so that there were few available in United States libraries.

In 1913 the Durban Public Library, South Africa, set aside a children's book section. Six years later the first children's librarian was appointed there. Abayomi Fuja began collecting Yoruba folktales in Nigeria in 1938. There were later published as 'Fourteen Hundred Cowries'. In 1959 the Sierra Leone Library Board began services to children. The Kenya Children's Library opened in Nairobi in 1960.

In 1962 the African Universities Press of Lagos, Nigeria, began to publish a series of children's books called the African Reader's Library. Among these stories by outstanding writers is Cyprian Ekwensi's 'African Night's Entertainment' (1962), set in Moslem Nigeria. J. H. Kwabena Nketia's 'Folk Songs of Ghana' (1963) includes songs about Ananse the spider. In Kola Onadipe's 'Adventures of Souza' (1963), he recalled his childhood adventures in a rural Nigerian village. His 'Sugar Girl' (1964) is a lively fairy tale. In 1964 the Juvenile Book Writers' Group was founded in Nigeria, a giant step in providing more and better books for children.

Ngumbu Njururi's 'Agikuyu Folk Tales' (1966) retells stories from Kenya. 'The Adventures of Coalpot' (1966), about a clay stove and coalpot replaced by an electric stove, was written by Ghana's Nana Adoma. Birago Diop retold Senegal folktales in 'Tales of Amadou Koumba'. J. K. Njoroge's 'Tit for Tat and Other Stories' (1966) is a collection of Kenyan folktales.

'Chike and the River' (1966) was written by Chinua Achebe, one of Nigeria's—and Africa's—best novelists. Nigerian Solomon Irein Wangboje illustrated 'A Crocodile Has Me by the Leg' (1967), a collection of African poems. Mesfin Habte-Mariam's 'Rich Man and the Singer' (1971) is a collection of folktales from Ethiopia.

Illustration © 1967 by Solomon Irein Wangboje, reproduced by permission of the publisher, Walker & Co., Inc. (© 1966, 1967 Leonard W. Doob)

An unlucky man sings a song of problems in 'A Crocodile Has Me by the Leg', a book of African poems.

A PICTURE BOOK

A picture book is not just a book with pictures. Nor is it just a story with pictures added. In a picture book, words and pictures are like peanut butter and jelly. They go well together, and they add to each other. In a picture book, pictures are at least as important as the words.

Some picture books have no words, but they still tell a story. Then the pictures and the unspoken story must do something for each other. Films without words are picture books in a different form.

A GOOD BOOK

A good book is a grabber. It latches onto a child and won't let go. What a child needs is lots of books around to talk to him. And he needs lots of books around to choose from. What he doesn't need is a grown-up forcing a book on him and telling him it's a good book.

Just the same, many adults want to know how to help children find good books. Or how to find good books with which to surround children. There are no sure-fire formulas. Every child is different, and every child is always changing. But a few general guidelines might be of help.

A good book is easy to hold.

A good book is easy to read. Type is large enough, with not too many words on a page. Children from about grade 4 shy away from what looks like a baby book—type that's too large. But most children of any age dislike what looks like a reading chore.

A good book is easy to understand. In a storybook, the plot is clear and easy to follow. As for reading levels of books, children's librarians and children's teachers can offer suggestions, especially if they know the child (see Reading.)

A good book is excitement. Children like interesting characters, lots of action, lively writing. They also appreciate good illustrations (see Reading/Books for Children).

A GIANT STEP

In the history of children's literature, there are many giant steps. The following chart is a selection

Continued on page 258

Giant Steps in Children's Literature

CANADA AND UNITED STATES

CANADA
The Snow Drop, children's magazine 1847
Ernest Thompson Seton *Wild Animals I Have Known* 1898
Lucy Maud Montgomery *Anne of Green Gables* 1908
Boys and Girls House, Toronto, Ont. 1922
Muriel Denison *Susannah, a Little Girl with the Mounties* 1936
Mary Grannan, radio broadcasts for children 1941
Young Canada's Book Week 1948
Farley Mowat *Lost in the Barrens* 1956
Marius Barbeau *The Golden Phoenix* tr. 1958
Claude Aubry *The King of the Thousand Islands* 1960
James Houston *Tikta'liktak* 1965
Elizabeth Cleaver, ill. *The Wind Has Wings* 1968

UNITED STATES
Clement Moore *A Visit from St. Nicholas* 1822
Mary Mapes Dodge *Hans Brinker; or, The Silver Skates* 1865
Louisa May Alcott *Little Women* 1868
St. Nicholas, children's magazine 1873
Mark Twain *The Adventures of Tom Sawyer* 1876
Children's corner, Pawtucket, R.I., library 1877
Pratt Institute, New York City, trains children's librarians 1898
Story hours, Carnegie Library, Pittsburgh, Pa. 1899
L. Frank Baum *The Wonderful Wizard of Oz* 1900
Children's Book Week 1919
Newbery Medal 1922
Anne Carroll Moore, first newspaper column on children's books 1924
Walt Disney creates Mickey Mouse 1928
Caldecott Medal 1938
Gwendolyn Brooks *Bronzeville Boys and Girls* 1956

LATIN AMERICA

ARGENTINA
Sarmiento Law lays foundation for children's libraries 1870
Constancio C. Vigil *La Hormiguita Viajera/The Adventures of Hormiguita* 1940

BRAZIL
Margarida Bandeira Duarte *The Legend of the Palm Tree* 1940

CHILE
Marta Brunet *Cuentos para Mari-Sol* (Tales for Mari-Sol) 1938

COLOMBIA
Rafael Pombo *Fábulas y verdades* (Fables and True Stories) 1916

COSTA RICA
Carmen Lira *Los Cuentos de mi tía Panchita* (Tales Told by My Aunt Panchita) 1956

HUNGARY	Victor Ambrus, ill. *The Three Poor Tailors* 1965
IRELAND	Padraic Colum *The King of Ireland's Son* 1916
ITALY	Giambattista Basile *Il Pentamerone; or, The Tale of Tales* 1634 Carlo Collodi *The Adventures of Pinocchio* about 1881 Edmondo de Amicis *The Heart of a Boy* 1886
NETHERLANDS	S. R. van Iterson *Pulga* tr. 1971
NORWAY	Peter Asbjörnsen and Jörgen Moe *Norwegian Fairy Tales* about 1843 Babbis Friis-Baastad, radio plays for children 1957
POLAND	Maria Konopnicka *The Golden Seed* tr. 1962
RUMANIA	Ioana Sturdza, tr. *Fairy Tales and Legends from Romania* 1972
RUSSIA	Ivan A. Krylov, fables 1825 Alexandr Afanas'ev *Russian Folk-Tales* 1855 Sergei Prokofiev *Peter and the Wolf,* musical fairy tale 1936
SCOTLAND	George MacDonald *At the Back of the North Wind* 1871 Robert Louis Stevenson *Treasure Island* 1883 James Barrie *Peter Pan* 1904 Kenneth Grahame *The Wind in the Willows* 1908
SPAIN	Juan R. Jiménez *Platero and I* 1914 José M. Sanchez-Silva *Marcelino* 1952
SWEDEN	Selma Lagerlöf *The Wonderful Adventures of Nils* 1906 Elsa Beskow *Pelle's New Suit* 1912 Astrid Lindgren *Pippi Longstocking* 1945
SWITZERLAND	*Zürcherischen Neujahrsblätter,* picture-poetry sheets 1645 Johann Wyss *Swiss Family Robinson* 1812 Johanna Spyri *Heidi* 1880
WALES	Gwyn Jones *Welsh Legends and Folk-Tales* 1955
YUGOSLAVIA	Ivana Brlić-Mazuranić *The Brave Adventures of Lapitch* 1913 Ivan Kušan *Koko and the Ghosts* tr. 1966

ASIA

BURMA	Htin Aung *Burmese Folk-Tales* 1948
CHINA	Ch'eng-en Wu *Monkey* about 1550
INDIA	*The Panchatantra* is written down about 200 B.C. Dhan G. Mukerji *Gayneck: The Story of a Pigeon* 1927
IRAN	Faridah Fardjam *Crystal Flower and the Sun* 1968
IRAQ	Sumerians write down Gilgamesh legend about 3000 B.C.

ISRAEL	Devorah Omer *The Gideonites* 1968
JAPAN	Toba Sojo, ill. *The Animal Frolic* about 1100 Sazanami Iwaya *Japanese Fairy Tales* about 1895 *Akai Tori,* children's magazine 1918 Kenji Miyazawa *Winds and Wildcat Places* tr. 1967
KOREA	So-Un Kim *The Story Bag* tr. 1955 Yong Ik Kim *Blue in the Seed* 1964
PAKISTAN	Paisa Library series 1939 Ashraf Siddiqui *Bhombal Dass* 1959
PHILIPPINES	José Aruego *Juan and the Asuangs* 1970
THAILAND	Mom Dusdi Paribatra *The Reluctant Princess* 1963
TURKEY	Selma Ekrem *Turkish Fairy Tales* 1964
VIETNAM	Vo-Dinh *The Toad Is the Emperor's Uncle* 1970

AUSTRALIA AND NEW ZEALAND

AUSTRALIA	Ethel Turner *Seven Little Australians* 1894 K. Langloh Parker *Australian Legendary Tales* 1896 Nan Chauncy *Tangara* 1960 Ivan Southall *Hills End* 1962
NEW ZEALAND	Esther Glen *Six Little New Zealanders* 1917 Stella Morice *The Book of Wiremu* 1944

AFRICA

ETHIOPIA	Mesfin Habte-Mariam *The Rich Man and the Singer* 1971
GHANA	J. H. Kwabena Nketia *Folk Songs of Ghana* 1963 Nana Adoma *The Adventures of Coalpot* 1966
KENYA	J. K. Njoroge *Tit for Tat, and Other Stories* 1966 Ngumbu Njururi *Agikuyu Folk Tales* 1966
NIGERIA	Abayomi Fuja collects Yoruba folktales 1938 Juvenile Book Writers' Group 1964 Chinua Achebe *Chike and the River* 1966
SENEGAL	Birago Diop *Tales of Amadou Koumba* 1966
SOUTH AFRICA	Children's book section, Durban Public Library 1913

Except where preceded by *tr.,* dates give year of publication in the original language. Dates preceded by *tr.* give year translated into English.

eds. = editors   publ. = publisher
ill. = illustrator   tr. = translated into English; translator

of only some of the landmark literature for children that has appeared throughout the world. All titles that are given in English are the titles under which the books were published in English. Titles given in parentheses are free translations of the original titles published in a foreign language.

BIBLIOGRAPHY FOR LITERATURE FOR CHILDREN

Summoned by Books: Essays and Speeches by Frances Clarke Sayers. Compiled by Marjeanne Jensen Blinn. (Penguin, 1968.) A collection of the writings and speeches of a distinguished children's librarian and writer.

Green and Burning Tree. By Eleanor Cameron. (Little, 1969.) A personal approach to the writing of children's books by a well-known writer for children.

Only Connect: Readings on Children's Literature. Edited by Sheila Egoff, G. T. Stubbs, and L. F. Ashley. (Oxford, 1969.) A compilation of critical essays.

Your Child's Reading Today. By Josette Frank. (Doubleday, 1969.) A unique parents' guide to children's reading.

Books in Search of Children: Speeches and Essays by Louise Seaman Bechtel. Selected by Virginia Haviland. (Macmillan, 1969.) Articles and speeches by the editor of the first children's department in a publishing company in the United States.

Books, Children and Men. By Paul Hazard. (Horn Book, 1960.) Universal truths of childhood set forth with wit and wisdom by an eminent French scholar.

Illustrators of Children's Books, 1744–1945. Compiled by Bertha E. Mahony, Louise P. Latimer, Beulah Folmsbee. (Horn Book, 1947.) Essays about illustrators and the graphic arts. Supplemented by **Illustrators of Children's Books, 1946–1956** (Horn Book, 1958) and by **Illustrators of Children's Books, 1957–1966** (Horn Book, 1968).

From Rollo to Tom Sawyer and Other Papers. By Alice M. Jordan. (Horn Book, 1948.) An illuminating discussion of children's books and magazines published in the United States during the 19th century.

A Critical History of Children's Literature. By Cornelia Meigs, Anne Eaton, Elizabeth Nesbitt, and Ruth Hill Viguers. (Macmillan, 1969.) A survey of children's books in English from earliest times to 1968.

My Roads to Childhood. By Anne Carroll Moore. (Horn Book, 1961.) Autobiographical essays with appraisals of children's books and their illustrations.

A Harvest of Russian Children's Literature. Edited by Miriam Morton. Foreword by Ruth Hill Viguers. (Univ. of Calif. Press, 1967.) An anthology in English of Russian children's literature of the past 150 years.

The World of Children's Literature. By Anne Pellowski. (Bowker, 1968.) An outstanding bibliography on children's literature and libraries in 106 countries, compiled by the Director/Librarian of the UNICEF Information Center on Children's Cultures.

The Unreluctant Years: a Critical Approach to Children's Literature. By Lillian H. Smith. (ALA, 1953.) An inspiring guide to the selection of children's books.

A Sense of Story: Essays on Contemporary Writers for Children. By John Rowe Townsend. (Lippincott, 1971.) Critical essays by a well-known British writer.

Margin for Surprise: About Books Children, and Librarians. By Ruth Hill Viguers. (Little, 1964.) Articles and lectures by a distinguished librarian.

That Eager Zest: First Discoveries in the Magic World of Books. Selected by Frances Walsh. (Lippincott, 1961). The reminiscences of different people about their first discoveries as children of the wonderful world that books provide.

LITHOGRAPHY.

LITHOGRAPHY. Offset lithography, also called the planographic method, is a printing process in use throughout the world. It involves a thin metal plate that carries the image area and the non-image area on the same plane; that is, the image and non-image areas are neither raised nor depressed. They are kept separate chemically by the use of the well-known principle that water and oil do not mix. Offset lithography is one of four major printing processes in use today. (*See also* Printing.)

Offset Process

The printing image area on the offset lithographic printing plate is rendered oil- or grease-receptive and water-repellent. Simultaneously the non-image areas of the printing plate are rendered oil-repellent and water-receptive. The oil or grease that will be used on the plate is lithographic ink.

When the lithographic plate is on press, it is wrapped around a steel cylinder that rotates, bringing the plate in contact with rollers that are wet with dampening solution, or water, and rollers wet with ink. The dampening solution prevents ink from depositing on the non-image area of the printing plate. The image area, while repelling water, attracts ink, leaving a plate with ink in the image area only.

After the lithographic plate is sufficiently inked and dampened, it comes into contact with a blanket roller, or cylinder, to which it transfers, or offsets, the inked image. The blanket cylinder, carrying the inked image, comes into contact with and transfers the image to paper. This process is so widely used that the terms lithography and offset are used interchangeably.

Direct Process

Despite the universality of offset lithography, there is another lithographic method called direct lithography. It works on the same principle of oil and water incompatibility, but the blanket cylinder is eliminated, and the paper and inked image carrier contact each other directly. Direct lithography today is most often employed as an art form.

As an art medium, lithography employs a polished stone upon which the artist draws with oil or pen and ink. Stone lithography is unlike other art printing, such as wood engraving or etching, in that the artist can see the work before it is reproduced. It is a tribute to the process that after nearly 200 years of increasing technological sophistication the direct method is still valued as an art form.

History

Lithography was invented in 1796 by Aloys Senefelder. He was working on a method to improve copperplate engraving and was experimenting on Bavarian limestone in place of the more costly copper. His experiments led to the discovery that stone when properly inked and treated with chemicals would transfer its image onto paper. Thus was born stone printing, or, as Senefelder called it, chemical printing,

Neil MacDonald

In the direct lithographic process, the artist (left) draws directly on the image carrier, here a stone. Later an acid bath etches the images into the stone. The stone is then inked with a roller (center). The print is made through direct contact with the stone and is carefully pulled away (right).

the forerunner of lithography. The practical aspects of lithography were immediately apparent, and in 1799 the prince-elector of Bavaria gave Senefelder an exclusive 15-year privilege to exploit his invention. Just one year after Senefelder submitted his model for an automated press in 1817, the first lithograph was published in the United States by Bass Otis.

As an art form lithography enjoyed a wave of popularity throughout Europe. The works of Eugène Delacroix, Jean-Baptiste Isabey, Denis-Auguste-Marie Raffet, and Honoré Daumier in France; Richard Parkes Bonington in England; Francisco Goya in Spain; and Adolph Menzel in Germany were preserved in the medium. Lithographic art fell into disfavor as it grew in popularity as a commercial means of reproduction. Its inherent value as a medium of artistic expression, however, could not be denied, and a second wave of popularity included Édouard Manet, Ignace Fantin-Latour, Henri de Toulouse-Lautrec, and James McNeill Whistler. In the 20th century the Norwegian Edvard Munch; Mexicans José Clemente Orozco, Diego Rivera, and Rufino Tamayo; and United States artists George Bellows and Rockwell Kent have been prominent.

Commercial lithography. Early in the 20th century a misfeed on a press resulted in the back side of a sheet being printed by the rubber blanket. The printer noticed that the accidental print was clearer than the print obtained directly from the imaged litho stone. He then developed a lithographic press that purposely offset the image to the rubber blanket prior to the transfer to paper. Offset lithography was born and hailed as the salvation of the commercial lithographer. By 1916 there were nearly 850 offset presses operating in the United States and Canada.

There are now nearly 50,000 commercial printing plants in the United States employing more than 1.3 million people with an annual payroll in excess of 20 billion dollars and receipts of 76 billion dollars. At least 35,000 of these plants use offset lithography.

A valuable publication for further reading is 'Pocket Pal', which is published by the International Paper Company in New York City.

LITHUANIAN SOVIET SOCIALIST REPUBLIC.

One of the three Baltic states, Lithuania was a major power in Eastern Europe in the Middle Ages, but was partitioned between Russia and Prussia in the 18th century. In 1917 it became an independent country, but,

after Soviet troops occupied it in 1940, it was proclaimed the Lithuanian Soviet Socialist Republic.

The Land and Climate

Lithuania is larger than the other Baltic republics, Estonia and Latvia, which lie to the north. It consists of a coastal plain that gradually rises eastward to the Zhemaiten Hills, a morainic range with summits of more than 650 feet (200 meters). To the east of these uplands, the Central Lithuanian Plain forms a broad belt of lowland stretching from northeast to southwest. The eastern part of the country consists of a second range of hills that rise to more than 800 feet (240 meters) in places. The morainic ranges, which were formed by glacial deposits, contain a number of small lakes.

The major river is the Niemen, or Nemunas. It enters the Baltic Sea in the Kurisches Haff, a lagoon separated from the sea by a long spit of land.

The climate of Lithuania, generally cool and humid, is modified by the Baltic Sea. July temperatures average about 63° F (17° C) and January temperatures about 25° F (−4° C).

The People

With the Latvians, the Lithuanians form the major group of the Baltic peoples. They were among the last of the European peoples to be converted to Christianity, and in the 14th century they became Roman Catholics. Lithuanian folklore and customs still retain some traces of the pagan period. The 14th-centu-

259

ry union between Lithuania and Poland also influenced the culture, especially in the city of Vilna, also called Vilnius, which became a predominantly Polish city with a large Jewish population in the 17th century. After World War II most of Lithuania's Poles emigrated, though some 247,000 still live there. Since the annexation of Lithuania by the Soviet Union, many Russians have settled there and now number about 303,000. About 80 percent of the population of 3,398,000 (1979 census) is Lithuanian.

The major center of cultural life is the capital city of Vilna, with a population of 514,000 (1982). The city has a university, the Lithuanian Academy of Sciences, museums, libraries, and theaters.

Economy and Transportation

When Lithuania was an independent state, the major economic activity was agriculture. Under the Soviet regime agriculture was collectivized and its importance has declined. The republic, still produces grain—especially rye, wheat, oats, and barley—as well as sugar beets, flax, and potatoes. Livestock breeding, particularly cattle and pigs, is the single most important branch of agriculture. The cool climate and areas of poor soils and marshes restrict agricultural output. Much farmland is used as pasture and for haymaking.

Industrial production has increased in spite of the lack of most forms of energy and other raw materials. Peat is virtually the only available fuel, and its uses are limited. A large hydroelectric plant is located on the Niemen River near Kaunas, and there are some thermal power stations, fired by peat or natural gas that is brought by pipeline from the Ukraine. Lithuanian industry produces machine tools, refrigerators, washing machines, radio and television sets, and similar products that require little metal but skilled labor. Other industries include chemicals, textiles, and woodworking. The major industrial centers are Vilna, Kaunas, Klaipeda, and Siauliai.

There is a relatively dense railroad network linked to the rest of the Soviet Union. River vessels can reach Kaunas on the Niemen River. The major port is Klaipeda, which is ice-free in winter. Vilna is linked by air with other Soviet cities.

Government and History

The Lithuanian Soviet Socialist Republic is one of the 15 constituent republics of the Soviet Union. It has its own government and Communist party under the control of the central government in Moscow.

During the Middle Ages Lithuania rose from a small duchy to the largest state in Europe. In 1386 it formed a union with Poland by royal marriage, but the 18th-century partition of Poland resulted in the division of Lithuania between Russia and Prussia. In 1917, after the collapse of the Russian empire, Lithuania gained independence. It was annexed by the Soviet Union in 1940, occupied during World War II by the Germans from 1941 to 1944, and then reconquered by the Soviet Union.

LITTLE ROCK, Ark. Arkansas's capital and largest city, Little Rock, draws its prosperity from an area rich in farmlands, minerals, and timber. Known as the "city of roses," it is the center of government, transportation, culture, medicine, and tourism.

Outside the city cotton, alfalfa, rice, fruits, vegetables, and livestock are raised. Mineral deposits in the vicinity yield coal, petroleum, natural gas, marble, granite, and bauxite (aluminum ore). High-grade timber is cut nearby.

The city is a commercial and industrial center with a diverse base. Its factories process meats and manufacture cotton goods, furniture and other wooden products, fertilizers and insecticides, electrical and electronic apparatus, watches and clocks, roofing materials, data communications equipment, cosmetics, valves, chemicals, and plastic and aluminum products. The separately incorporated city of North Little Rock, which is on the opposite bank of the Arkansas River, has large railroad workshops.

Little Rock is on the south bank of the river, set on the edge of the Gulf Coastal Plain. The foothills of the Ouachita Mountains lie to the west. The business district spreads back from the riverbank.

The Capitol, completed in 1915, is surrounded by a 12-acre (5-hectare) park. Two former Arkansas capitols have been restored—the Old State House and the Territorial Capitol. MacArthur Park contains the Arkansas Arts Center and the birthplace of General Douglas MacArthur, which houses the Museum of Science and History. In Little Rock are also the Arkansas Territorial Restoration (an extended museum of restored buildings of historical significance), Quapaw Quarter Area (the oldest section of the city), state schools for the deaf and blind, and state and federal hospitals. The city is the site of the University of Arkansas at Little Rock (formerly Little Rock University) and the University of Arkansas Medical Center. Little Rock is also the home of Philander Smith College, Arkansas Baptist College, and the University of Arkansas Technical School.

A large rock formation on the riverbank was called "little rock" in 1722 by the French explorer Bernard de la Harpe to distinguish it from a higher rock outcropping ("big rock") two miles (three kilometers) farther up the river. La Harpe built a trading post at a Quapaw Indian settlement near the "little rock." Little Rock's first house was built in 1812 by William Lewis. After the site was surveyed for the territorial capital, the government moved from Arkansas Post in 1821. In early days the town was a busy river port and frontier post. During the Civil War it was taken by Federal forces in 1863. Little Rock was incorporated as a town in 1831 and chartered a city in 1836. It is the seat of Pulaski County and has a council-manager form of government. (*See also* Arkansas.) Population (1980 census), 158,461.

LIVER. The liver is the largest and heaviest organ within the body. It also has the most tasks to perform. Nestled in the upper abdomen behind the right lung, the liver seems to be a uniform blob of reddish-brown tissue, but it is the body's chief chemical factory, blood-purifying and tune-up station, poison detoxification center, and food storage and distribution center as well as a major gland in the digestive system (*see* Digestion). All vertebrates, or animals with backbones, have livers, and all livers perform alike, though they vary in size and shape. The Greek word for liver is *hepar*, and many things pertaining to the liver are called "hepatic."

Structure and function. The human liver is divided into a large right lobe and a smaller left lobe that overhang the stomach and intestine. From the intestine the portal vein transports nutrient-rich blood into the liver through a slit called the porta hepatis (Latin for "door to the liver"). Also entering the portal is the hepatic artery, which carries fresh oxygenated blood to the liver so that it can do its work of processing the substances that arrive from the intestine. As much as 10 percent of all the blood in the body is present in the liver at any one time.

The interior of the liver contains thousands of tall, six-sided spaces called lobules. Inside the lobules are rows of liver cells that converge on a central vein running like a pole through the middle of a room. Branches of the portal vein and hepatic artery tunnel through the lobule walls and flow between the rows of liver cells, depositing their blood into channels called sinusoids. Here special scavenger cells trap and devour worn-out red blood cells, bacteria, and other debris. From the blood, the liver cells take up excess sugar, which is in the form of glucose, and convert it to glycogen for storage. Whenever blood sugar levels drop, glycogen is reconverted to glucose and added to the blood. If the liver uses up its full capacity to store glycogen, it converts glucose to fat for storage in fatty tissue. This fat is reconverted to glucose when glycogen stores are consumed.

Amino acids, the products of digested proteins, are also taken up; some are stored and some processed into new blood proteins. Vitamins and minerals—especially A, D, B_{12}, and iron—are also stored in the liver and added to the blood as needed.

Reprocessed blood flows from the sinusoids to the central vein in the middle of the lobule. All the central veins connect with the hepatic veins, which transport the blood upward through the roof of the liver to a large vein that leads to the heart.

The liver has yet another transport system to carry bile, a yellowish-greenish waste fluid made partly of cholesterol and old blood pigments. Bile contains products that can break down fat into small droplets. This feature is useful to the intestine as an aid in digestion. Cells of the liver secrete bile into tiny intercellular canals that link together to form bile ducts. The ducts merge into one large duct that leaves the liver by the porta hepatis. Outside the liver a branch leads to the gallbladder, a bile storage sac. Below this branch the duct, now called the common bile duct, enters the intestine.

Diseases of the liver. Excess bile pigment in the blood colors the skin and eyeballs yellow, a condition known as jaundice. Causes include a high rate of red blood cell destruction and an obstructed bile duct. Hepatitis, inflammation of the lobules, results from viral or bacterial infection or from injury caused by larger quantities of harmful chemicals than the liver can detoxify. When liver tissue is damaged beyond regeneration, it is replaced by fat and connective tissue. This condition is called cirrhosis, and by far the most common cause is alcoholism. Cancer may also strike the liver. Prospects have improved for prolonging life through liver transplantation, but graft rejection remains a problem.

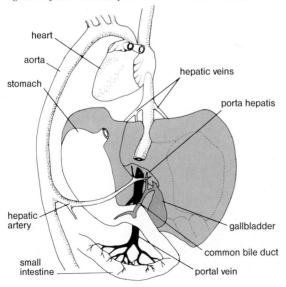

The liver lies near the heart and stomach. It is part of the digestive system and also performs other vital functions.

heart

aorta

stomach

hepatic veins

porta hepatis

hepatic artery

gallbladder

common bile duct

small intestine

portal vein

LIVERPOOL, England. The "city of ships," Liverpool, is one of England's largest ports, located in Merseyside metropolitan county on the Mersey River, three miles (five kilometers) inland from the Irish Sea. It is the natural outlet for the Lancashire industrial region's textiles and machinery. The chief imports are cereals, ores, scrap metal, sugar, wood, and pulp; exports include chemicals, iron, and steel.

One of the interesting sights in Liverpool is the docks. They occupy a river frontage of 7 miles (11 kilometers). The Albert Dock is a distinctive example of early 19th-century architecture. Passenger ships dock at a landing stage in the river—a floating structure 1,148 feet (350 meters) long. Hinged bridges connect the landing stage with the river wall. The western side of the river is lined with the docks of the busy port of Birkenhead, in Cheshire.

· Liverpool's great port owes little to natural advantages. The Mersey estuary has shifting sandbars across the channel and a tide with a range of 26 feet (8 meters). To remove the sand the port authority keeps a fleet of dredges constantly at work maintaining a 30-foot (9-meter) low-water channel. The advantages of a tideless harbor have been secured by a system of wet docks operated like the locks of a canal.

Behind the teeming waterfront, the city spreads out in a rough semicircle covering about 43 square miles (111 square kilometers). The land rises gradually from the riverbank. The commercial section of the city has impressive business buildings. In the residential sections are many well-preserved Georgian houses. The University of Liverpool, established in 1903, is noted for its School of Tropical Medicine. The Walker Art Gallery has many famous pictures. The city has a professional symphony orchestra and two large choirs. The most famous building is Saint George's Hall, completed in 1854, which was built after the style of the Parthenon in Athens.

Two great cathedrals were long in building. The foundation stone of the Anglican Cathedral was laid in 1904. Its central door was opened by Princess Elizabeth, later to become Elizabeth II, in 1949, and it was completed in 1970. It is in neo-Gothic style and is the largest church in the country. A modern Roman Catholic church, the Metropolitan Cathedral of Christ the King, was consecrated in 1967.

Britain's heavy chemical industry is concentrated in and near Liverpool. The Merseyside region is an important flour-milling and agricultural center. Other industries are shipbuilding, ship repairing, engineering works, oil- and seed-crushing mills, tobacco, sugar refining, tanning, rubber, food processing, and clothing. At Birkenhead are the noted Laird shipbuilding yards, which have produced many of Britain's famous battleships and large passenger liners. Birkenhead is connected with Liverpool by the Queensway Road Tunnel. With the completion in 1969 of a new oil terminal at Tranmere, on the Wirral shore south of Birkenhead, crude oil became by far the most important commodity imported.

Liverpool's commercial importance began in the 17th century. In the 18th century the power loom began to make Lancashire the world's greatest cotton-manufacturing center and Liverpool its chief port. The city suffered heavy damage from German air attacks in World War II. Liverpool received a degree of notoriety during the 1960s with the appearance of a singing group, the Beatles, who had a distinctive local sound derived from the rhythm-and-blues musical style. This popular music is called the Mersey Beat, or Liverpool Sound. The Beatles made Liverpool the hub of the international world of popular music. This musical focus on the city had declined by the early 1980s, but folk culture in both music and verse remains a notable Liverpool cultural characteristic. Population (1981 census), 510,306.

262

LIVERWORT. The liverworts look like flat green leaves with rounded lobes. They grow in wet places—on rocks, logs, or damp earth. Their name comes from their shape, which in some varieties looks like that of the human liver. "Wort" comes from an Old English word meaning "plant."

The liverwort is a simple, flowerless plant, one of the first in the Earth's history to grow on land. The plant body, called a thallus, is not differentiated into leaves, stem, and root. On the undersurface are fine white hairs called rhizoids. They anchor the plant and absorb food materials. The organs of reproduction are on the upper surface.

Liverworts have three different ways of reproducing. The most common genus, *Marchantia*, is a typical example. On its upper surface it bears little green cuplike organs called cupules (Latin for "little cups"). Within the cups are tiny greenish balls known as gemmae (Latin for "buds" or "gems"). When gemmae fall to moist ground, they grow into new plants. This is a form of asexual (without sex) reproduction. *Marchantia* may also reproduce by spores, another type of asexual reproduction.

Marchantia does have male and female sex organs with which it can reproduce sexually. The sex organs are on upright umbrella-like stalks that grow from a notch in the upper side of the thallus. At the top of one stalk is the archegonium, which bears egg cells. At the top of another is the antheridium, which contains sperm cells. The two sexes are borne on different plants. During wet weather the sperms swim to the archegonium of a nearby plant to fertilize the eggs. A fertilized egg, or zygote, grows into a spore-bearing plant, or sporophyte. The ripe spores are scattered by wind and water. A germinating spore develops into a new thallus, known as the gametophyte, from which new sex organs grow. Such a life history, in which a plant producing spores alternates with a plant producing sex cells, is called "alternation of generations." (*See also* Spore.)

Liverworts form the group Hepaticae. They are in the Bryophyta division of the Plantae kingdom.

Marchantia is the most common kind of liverwort. The plant's cupules, or "little cups," are too tiny to be seen.

Gottscho—Schleisner

LIVINGSTONE, David

LIVINGSTONE, David (1813–74). For more than 30 years David Livingstone worked in Africa as a medical missionary and traveled the continent from the Equator to the Cape and from the Atlantic to the Indian oceans. In so doing, he gained worldwide fame as an explorer and strongly influenced the way successive generations have thought about Africa. By awakening the interest of the outside world in this then largely unknown continent, he helped pave the way for its European colonization later in the 19th century. Also, through his strong belief that Africans could advance into the modern world, he served as an inspiration for African nationalism.

David Livingstone was born in Blantyre, Scotland, on March 19, 1813. One of seven children in a very poor family, he was already working in a cotton mill by the time he was 10. What education he got came largely through his own efforts and from the determination of his parents, strict Calvinists who believed in hard work and schooling.

In 1834 he heard about an appeal by British and American churches for medical missionaries to go to China. He decided this should be his career, and for two years while continuing to work part-time, he studied theology and medicine. In 1838 he was accepted by the London Missionary Society, but was prevented from going to China by the Opium War. A subsequent meeting with Robert Moffat, the noted missionary to southern Africa, convinced Livingstone that he should take up his work in Africa.

He arrived in Cape Town on March 14, 1841. From the moment he arrived, Livingstone determined to become an explorer to help open up the continent for Christianity and Western civilization. His career can be divided into four fairly distinct phases: the early missionary explorations in the years from 1841 to 1849, during which he traveled to the Transvaal and into the Kalahari region; the expedition from 1850 to 1856 that took him to Luanda on the west coast and to Quelimane on the east coat; the explorations along the Zambezi River from 1858 to 1864; and his determined, but unsuccessful, search for the source of the Nile River from 1866 to 1873.

By mid-1842 he had traveled north into the Kalahari territory, further than any white man had ventured. He established a mission at Mabotsa in 1844. He married Moffat's daughter, Mary, and she accompanied him on his travels until 1852, by which time they had four children. Livingstone then sent them and their mother back to Britain to safeguard her health and to get the children into school.

During his first decade in Africa, Livingstone gained his first measure of fame when he assisted in the discovery of Lake Ngami on Aug. 1, 1849. For this he was awarded a gold medal and a monetary prize by the British Royal Geographical Society.

With his family safely in Scotland, Livingstone was able to set out on his second major journey in November 1853. His first goal was to reach the Atlantic coast to open up an avenue of commerce. He arrived at Luanda, on the Atlantic coast, on May 31, 1854.

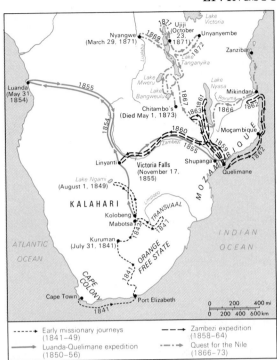

The expeditions of David Livingstone

Four months later he began the return trip, exploring the Zambezi River region along the way. On May 20, 1856, he arrived at Quelimane, on the east coast of Mozambique. The most spectacular result of this trip was the discovery and naming of Victoria Falls on the Zambezi on Nov. 17, 1855. For his accomplishments he was received as a national hero when he returned to England in December 1856. He published a book, 'Missionary Travels and Researches in South Africa' in 1857 and spent six months on a speaking tour in the British Isles. His speeches at Cambridge were published as 'Dr. Livingstone's Cambridge Lectures' in 1858.

Back in Africa early in 1858, Livingstone began extensive explorations of the Zambezi region. On this journey his wife died, in April 1862. The explorations were not successful from a commercial point of view, so the expedition was canceled.

Livingstone's last great venture was the attempt to locate the source of the Nile. This quest, fraught with hardships and dissension among his staff, left him broken in health and—at one point—given up for dead. Henry Morton Stanley, a correspondent for the *New York Herald*, found him in Ujiji on Oct. 23, 1871, and provided him with food and medicine (*see* Stanley). Together they explored the area northeast of Lake Tanganyika. Stanley returned to England in March 1872, but Livingstone refused to accompany him. On May 1, 1873, his servants found him dead in a village in what is now Zambia. His body was taken to England and buried in Westminster Abbey on April 18, 1874. Later that year, 'The Last Journals of David Livingstone' were published.

LIVING THINGS

LIVING THINGS. Living things include plants and animals. They live on the land, in the lakes, rivers, and seas, and billions of tiny microbes live in both water and soil. These many plants, animals, and microbes are very different from one another. Yet all of them have one thing in common: they are *alive*. What is meant by being "alive"? Anyone can think of such tests of living as *eating* and *moving*. But will *all* the tests apply to *every* living thing?

The picture on this page raises some of these questions. It shows, for example, that the test of motion is not easy to apply. Many nonliving things move, and many living things never seem to move. So if motion is a test of being alive, it must be motion *of a certain kind*. We must be able to find this *kind* of motion in moss and other plants that never seem to move. We must be able to say that this kind of motion cannot be found in nonliving things. The same is true of other tests for life. They must be true for all living things and not true for nonliving things.

Tests of Life in Animals

A good way to find answers to questions about life is to study some common animals, such as dogs. They move even when asleep. They also respond to their surroundings. They dodge when we try to catch them but come when we offer them food.

Dogs use food in many ways. Young ones use it to grow. When they are older they use it to repair worn-out parts of their bodies. Dogs get energy from food. They use energy when they run, play, eat, and even while they sleep. Finally, dogs mate and reproduce, which means that they have young ones. Will these same tests apply to plants as well?

Test of Life in Plants

Plants do not try to move when we touch them (except for the "sensitive" plants). But they do change position as they grow. A tree moves its branches and leaves to get sunlight. If a plant starts to grow in a dark spot, it will turn its stem to reach the light. Plants also turn their roots to reach water and minerals in the soil.

Plants therefore move in ways *that are useful to them*, just as animals do. This is the kind of motion that marks living things. Nonliving things move only if an outside force compels them to.

Although plants do not eat, they secure food and use it. Those we know best take water, nitrogen, and minerals from the soil and a gas called carbon dioxide

WHAT MAKES PLANTS AND ANIMALS "ALIVE"?

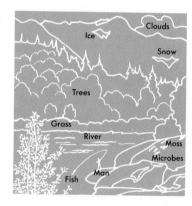

Because they MOVE?
It is easy to say that the *man* is alive because he moves. But the *river* and the *clouds* also move. The *tree* is alive, but moves only in the wind. So movement is not a simple test for life.

Because they EAT?
Fish eat by swallowing food. If eating is a test of being alive, do the *grass* and *moss* "eat"? How do *microbes* in the pool eat? Eating by mouth then is not the only way to take nourishment.

Because they GROW?
Ability to grow may seem to be a good test of being alive. Some lifeless substances, however, expand and take on wonderful shapes. Freezing water forms *ice* or *snow*.

The picture shows various living and nonliving things. We say that the *trees, grass, man, fish, moss,* and *microbes* are alive. On the other hand, we say that the *ice, rivers, clouds,* and *snow* are not alive. The three questions above show that many "easy" tests of being alive are not so easy after all. The real tests of being alive are explained in the article.

from the air. They use these materials to make the foods they need for growth and energy. They also make some foods which can be stored for later use.

Plants reproduce in a number of ways. Many kinds have seeds which grow into new plants. Others grow from roots, pieces of stem, or bulbs. Some kinds even reproduce by means of leaves which grow into new plants when they fall on moist, rich ground.

How Microbes Live

The tests for life described for the larger animals and plants also hold true for smaller and stranger forms of life. Microbes are living things which are too small to be seen clearly with our eyes alone. Enlarged pictures taken through microscopes tell us what they do. Many microbes swim, while others creep or twist to and fro. All respond to conditions around them by going toward things that are good for them and protecting themselves from things that are not.

Microbes get food in various ways. Many capture other tiny creatures. Some make food as large plants do. Other microbes, called germs of decay and disease, get food from dead or living plants and animals. We know that microbes use food when they move about. We can see that they grow and reproduce.

Seven Functions of Living

Thus animals, plants, and microbes perform the *functions of living*. These are the tests of being alive. Here are seven of them:

1. Movement. All living things move *without outside help*. This makes them different from a stone that is thrown, a stream that runs downhill, or an engine which has to be started. No outside force has to start movements of a plant, a dog, or a microbe.

2. Irritability. This means that living things respond to conditions around them. Green plants, for example, grow toward sunshine. Certain microbes shrink into tiny balls when something touches them. Human beings show this kind of irritability by blinking when light shines into their eyes.

3. Feeding. All living things secure food. Some bite, some suck, and some soak up food through membranes ("skins") that cover their bodies. Green plants make food from water, gas, nitrogen, and minerals.

4. Nutrition. This is our name for processes by which food is used. Some food is turned into living material, bones, teeth, or wood. Some is used to provide energy, which living things need to keep going. We may compare this to the process in which an engine burns oil or coal and gets energy to move a train. But no engine can use coal or oil to make itself larger or mend parts, as living things do with food.

5. Growth. We say that snowballs grow when we roll them or that salt crystals grow in salty water as it evaporates. Actually, these lifeless objects only become larger. Living things grow by making new parts and changing old ones. This happens when a seed grows into a plant or a chick grows into a hen. Human beings add new parts, such as teeth, and change the proportions of other parts as they grow.

A special kind of growth heals injuries and replaces worn parts. Shrubs and trees mend injuries by covering them with bark and adding new layers of wood. Crabs grow new legs when old ones are lost. Human beings can heal cut skin and mend broken bones.

6. Reproduction. When living things reproduce, they make new living things. This is true even of simple microbes, which reproduce by dividing into two sections. Each section is able to move, feed, grow, and perform the other functions of living.

7. Excretion. This means getting rid of waste materials. Much waste comes from food. The rest is produced by movement, growth, and other functions of living. If this waste remained in living things, it would soon cause illness and death.

Common lifeless things, such as stones and machines, cannot carry on these seven functions of living. Some lifeless models have been made to perform *some* of these functions. But models are unable to carry on *all* of them.

Living Material, Called Protoplasm

Since all living things perform these functions of life, the urge to do so must come from something within them. Do living things contain some special substance not found in lifeless things? If so, how does this substance form microbes, animals, and plants?

We find part of the answer in a creature known as an *amoeba*. It lives in ponds. To our eyes it looks like a milky speck, but a microscope shows it to be a lump of jelly. This jelly, called *protoplasm*, is the substance which makes up all living things.

When we watch an amoeba closely through a microscope, we see that its protoplasm moves and changes. It streams through the tiny body, especially when the creature changes shape. At one time the living jelly is clear. Then it becomes gray and grainy or

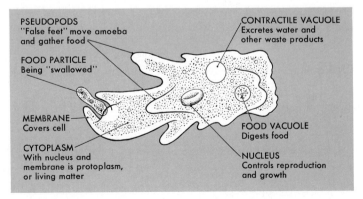

PSEUDOPODS
"False feet" move amoeba and gather food

FOOD PARTICLE
Being "swallowed"

MEMBRANE
Covers cell

CYTOPLASM
With nucleus and membrane is protoplasm, or living matter

CONTRACTILE VACUOLE
Excretes water and other waste products

FOOD VACUOLE
Digests food

NUCLEUS
Controls reproduction and growth

The amoeba consists of a single cell. It crawls by stretching out false feet, or *pseudopods*, and flowing into them. When a pseudopod touches a food particle the creature flows around it. The *food vacuole* then appears and digests it.

seems to fill itself with bubbles or droplets. A clear stiff network may appear too. Its threads are rather like tiny crystals of mineral matter. It serves as a support, or framework, for bubbles, droplets, and thin watery parts of the jelly.

This complex mixture moves and changes according to conditions inside the amoeba as well as around it. The mixture also takes in food, uses it, grows, and finally reproduces. The protoplasm which forms an amoeba also makes the little creature live.

Cells Form Living Things

Although protoplasm is living material, the amoeba is not just a simple lump of protoplasm. It is protoplasm in the form of one definite body called a *cell* (*see* Cell). Several parts fit together, or are organized, in the amoeba's cell. Its surface is a clear, tough membrane which covers and protects a thinner, darker-looking *cytoplasm* inside. The membrane is flexible and permits the amoeba to change shape. By doing so the amoeba can move to get food.

The amoeba shows *irritability* by these movements. It feeds and also excretes waste material by forming little droplets called *vacuoles* in its protoplasm. As it absorbs food, it grows.

All these activities seem to be controlled by a structure called the *nucleus*. The nucleus also performs the function of reproduction. In due time it divides and each half takes its share of the cytoplasm. The two halves of the amoeba become two new amoebas.

Life in a Single-Celled Plant

Another example of life in the form of a single cell may be seen in the tiny green plant known as *Protococcus*. Layers of these plants form green scum on damp trees, rocks, and brick walls.

Each Protococcus cell contains protoplasm, a nucleus, and a thin membrane. The nucleus controls the life of the cell and in time divides for reproduction. Inside the cell is a large structure filled with grains of a green substance termed *chlorophyll*. These grains make food for the plant from water and carbon dioxide. Since the plant can make food in this way,

it does not have to move about like an amoeba. Therefore it can have a stiff, protecting wall, made of a transparent substance called *cellulose*.

These two substances, chlorophyll and cellulose, make plant life quite different from animal life. With them a plant can stay in one place and make its food inside its colorless wall. Since animals do not have chlorophyll, they must get food from other living things or from dead material. To do this they have to move, which means that at least some of their cells must be covered with soft, flexible membrane. In one-celled creatures such as the amoeba, the whole tiny body moves freely.

Simple and Complex Cells

There are many kinds of one-celled plants and animals related to the amoeba. Some one-celled creatures look like slippers, vases, or balls, and have more than one nucleus. Many swim by waving lashes. Others use hairlike structures. One kind has two nuclei, a mouth, and a ring of moving "hairs" that bring in food. It also has a stalk that can stretch or coil up and pull the creature away from danger.

All these parts are organized, which means that they fit and work together. For this reason, we call living things *organisms*. Not all organisms have as many parts as the ones described. Many microbes have no separate nuclei. Their food-making chlorophyll is scattered through the cell. Other microbes, called *bacteria*, have neither nuclei nor green grains. They get their food from other organisms or from dead material.

Bacteria once were said to be the simplest organisms. Then *viruses* and *bacteriophages* were discovered. Bacteriophages are tiny things that kill bacteria. Viruses include the germs that cause colds, yellow fever, and other diseases of animals and plants. Even the largest viruses are too small to be cells. They seem unable to grow or reproduce unless they are in animals or plants. Some scientists think viruses and bacteriophages are almost alive. Others think they are living things that have degenerated, losing most of their parts. The remaining substance gets along by taking material from other organisms.

Many-Celled Organisms

The common plants and animals we know are much larger than viruses and microbes. They also are too big to be formed by a single cell. They therefore are made of many cells that live and work together.

Some of the simplest many-celled organisms are plants that live in ponds and streams. Each plant consists of a chain of cells that drifts to and fro in the water. Most cells in the chain are alike, but the one at the bottom, called a "holdfast," is different. It is long and tough. Its base holds to rocks or pieces of wood to keep the plant from floating away.

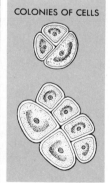

SINGLE CELL

CELLULOSE WALL
Protects cell and makes it rigid

CHLOROPLAST
Contains green chlorophyll for food making

CYTOPLASM
With nucleus and membrane is protoplasm, or living matter

NUCLEUS
Controls reproduction and growth

MEMBRANE
Covers cell

COLONIES OF CELLS

This is Protococcus, a one-celled plant. Inside it is *chloroplast*, which contains *chlorophyll*. The chlorophyll uses energy from sunlight to make food from carbon dioxide and water. Colonies of cells form green scum on mud or moist rocks.

Sea lettuce also has a holdfast. The rest of the plant contains boxlike cells arranged in two layers. These layers are covered and protected by two sheets of clear cellulose that is very tough.

Trees, weeds, and other familiar land plants contain many more cells than sea lettuce and are much more complex. Their cells form organs such as roots, stems, leaves, and flowers. Millions of individual cells are needed to form these complex plants.

No animals consist of chains of cells or of cells arranged in two flat layers like the sea lettuce. But the body of a pond-dwelling creature called *Hydra* has two layers of cells arranged in a tube. The bottom of the tube is closed, but its top contains a mouth. Slender branches of the tube form tentacles that catch food and put it into the mouth.

Great numbers of cells of many kinds form the bodies of such creatures as insects, fish, and horses. Similar

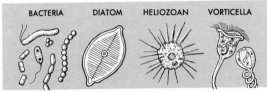

ONE-CELLED PLANTS AND ANIMALS
Bacteria are common single microscopic cells. The *diatom* plant has a glassy shell. The animal *heliozoan* has pseudopods. The animal *vorticella* has a stalk that coils away from danger.

CHAINS AND LAYERS OF CELLS
The plant called *Ulothrix* has its cells joined in a chain. Its bottom cell, called a "holdfast," anchors it. The *sea lettuce* plant and the tubelike animal *Hydra* have cells in two layers.

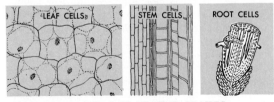

SPECIALIZED CELLS IN HIGHER PLANTS
Higher plants have specialized kinds of cells. Some *leaf cells* have chlorophyll for making food. *Stem cells* stiffen the plant. *Root cells* take in water and minerals.

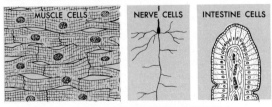

SPECIALIZED CELLS IN HIGHER ANIMALS
Higher animals also have specialized cells. They cannot make food from lifeless materials as plant cells do. *Muscle, nerve,* and *intestine cells* help to secure and use ready-made foods.

cells that work together make up *tissues*. Tissues that work together form *organs*. A dog's heart, for example, is an organ composed of muscle tissue, nerve tissue, connective tissue, and covering tissue. Another kind of tissue, the blood, nourishes them. All tissues work together when the dog's heart contracts.

Parts and Cells Are Controlled

Varied parts and cells work together because they are controlled. In plants, control is carried out by chemical particles called *hormones*. They go directly from cell to cell or are carried about in sap. When something touches a sensitive plant, for instance, the touched cells produce a hormone that goes to countless other cells and makes them lose water and collapse. As cell after cell does this, leaves begin to droop. They will not spread out again until the effect of the hormones is lost.

In many-celled animals, hormones regulate growth, keep muscles in condition, and perform many similar tasks. Other types of control are carried out by nerve cells. They carry impulses to and from various parts of the body. These impulses tell when things are seen, felt, or heard. They also make muscle cells contract or relax, so that animals run, lie down, catch food, and do countless other things. Nerve cells may even deliver the impulses that cause other cells to produce hormones.

Living Things Are Specialized

In the amoeba and Protococcus all parts of the protoplasm—other than structures such as the nucleus—are much alike and can do almost anything. This is not true of one-celled creatures that have lashes, hairs, and other definite parts. The lashes or hairs are used in swimming or in setting up currents that bring food. The food is swallowed through a mouth and digested in droplets that stay in the bubbly body. Special fibers that work like nerves control the hairs and lashes. Several one-celled organisms even possess "eyespots" that are affected by light.

These structures are *specialized*. Each one does its own part in the work of living. Many-celled organisms have tissues and organs that are still more specialized. Roots, leaves, flowers, eyes, and brains are examples of organs that do specialized work.

Specialization is carried from parts to entire living things. Cactus plants, for example, can live well only in dry regions, but cattails must grow in wet places. Herring swim near the surface of the sea, but the deep-sea angler fish lives on the bottom. Certain caterpillars eat only one kind of leaf.

This specialization of whole organisms is called *adaptation*. Every living thing is adapted to its surroundings—to the sea, fresh water, land, or even to living in other organisms. During the ages since life began, organisms have become adapted to all sorts of conditions. Today there are millions of different combinations between organisms and surroundings. With the possible exception of bacteriophages and viruses, however, all the different organisms consist of pro-

267

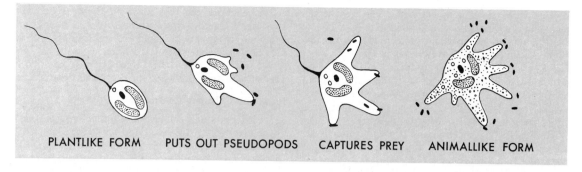

PLANTLIKE FORM   PUTS OUT PSEUDOPODS   CAPTURES PREY   ANIMALLIKE FORM

In its ordinary form the single-celled Chrysamoeba swims with a long lash. It makes food with the two large chloroplasts within its body just as a plant cell does. At times, however, the Chrysamoeba puts out pseudopods, or false feet. It may even absorb its long lash. It then moves about and captures food. It digests its food just as the animal amoeba does.

toplasm that is organized into cells. Cells are the "building blocks" of the living world.

The Elements in Protoplasm

Since protoplasm differs from lifeless materials, people once thought it contained "principles" not to be found in the earth. It is now known that both the earth and protoplasm consist of simple substances called *chemical elements* (*see* Chemistry). These elements may exist alone, as the element carbon does in coal. Generally, however, elements combine into compounds, which may be very complex. Chemists who have studied the compounds in living things have found:

First, that protoplasm contains only elements that are common in the earth.

Second, that only 13 elements are found in *all* kinds of protoplasm. The most important of these "universal" elements are carbon, hydrogen, oxygen, nitrogen, phosphorus, sulfur, magnesium, and iron.

Third, that different varieties of protoplasm contain other elements, such as copper, zinc, and chlorine. These are also plentiful in the earth, which is where plants get them for use in protoplasm. Animals get them by eating plants or other animals.

Atoms in Living Molecules

When elements form compounds, tiny particles called atoms combine and build up molecules. The molecules in protoplasm are complex. A molecule of the substance that makes a horse's blood red contains 2,359 atoms of six different elements. The red material in our blood contains about the same number of atoms.

The complexity is made possible by carbon, which may be called the "framework" element. It links atoms of different kinds in various proportions and arrangements. Carbon atoms also join with each other in long chains, rings, and other arrays.

Oxygen and hydrogen are most important in using energy, while nitrogen enables living things to vary and become specialized. Large amounts of nitrogen are found in protein, or "body-building" compounds. Nitrogen also is used in wood and in the substance called chitin which forms the shells of crustaceans, insects, jointed worms, and related creatures.

How Plants Obtain Food

All living things get food in one of two ways. They make it or they get it ready-made. The one-celled plant Protococcus uses both methods. It combines water, carbon, and mineral matter dissolved in the water by the process called *photosynthesis*. The process requires energy, but the green chlorophyll grains can obtain this from sunlight. After several steps the food-making process results in a kind of sugar called *glucose*.

Protococcus may use glucose molecules almost as fast as it makes them. It also may turn them into starch or droplets of oil, which it stores for use when it cannot get sunlight. Finally, Protococcus may combine atoms from glucose with some ready-made food combinations in the dissolved minerals. In this way it builds up protoplasm and cellulose.

Many-celled plants also get ready-made foods and make glucose. In doing so, however, they use many different cells, tissues, and organs, such as leaves, roots, and sap-carrying channels in the stem.

How Animals Change Food

Although many animals are green, no true animal contains grains of chlorophyll. Therefore no true animal can make food from carbon dioxide and water. This means that animals must get ready-made food from plants or other animals.

Animals, however, can change foods after they are eaten. When a horse eats more grain than it can use, it turns the extra grain into fat and stores the fat in tissues. Animals can turn sugary food into animal starch (*glycogen*) and store it in the liver, ready for use when needed.

Securing Energy from Food

When plants make glucose from water and carbon dioxide, they subtract some atoms of oxygen from the combined materials. More oxygen is lost when glucose is turned into common sugar, starch, fat, or other food substances. As oxygen is lost, more and more energy is stored in the made-over molecules.

When energy is needed for living, the process must be reversed. Food is first digested (dissolved in liquid). Then oxygen is combined with food molecules.

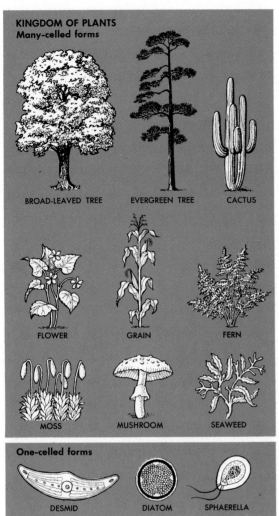

KINGDOM OF PLANTS
Many-celled forms

BROAD-LEAVED TREE   EVERGREEN TREE   CACTUS

FLOWER   GRAIN   FERN

MOSS   MUSHROOM   SEAWEED

One-celled forms

DESMID   DIATOM   SPHAERELLA

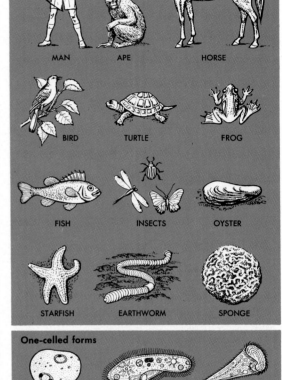

KINGDOM OF ANIMALS
Many-celled forms

MAN   APE   HORSE

BIRD   TURTLE   FROG

FISH   INSECTS   OYSTER

STARFISH   EARTHWORM   SPONGE

One-celled forms

PLASMODIUM   PARAMECIUM   STENTOR

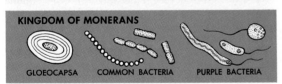

KINGDOM OF MONERANS

GLOEOCAPSA   COMMON BACTERIA   PURPLE BACTERIA

KINGDOM OF PROTISTS

EUGLENA   NOCTILUCA   GONYAULAX

For centuries men thought that all living things were either plants or animals. Today scientists believe that two or more other kingdoms may exist, as the article explains. The draw-ing shows the additional kingdoms of monerans and protists. It should be noted that both the plant and animal kingdoms are further divided into many-celled and one-celled forms.

They are changed into simpler substances and give up energy. This process is called *oxidation*. If oxidation is complete, the food becomes water and carbon dioxide again and gives up all its stored energy. Part of this energy is lost but most of it remains in protoplasm to be used in the work of living.

Some one-celled plants and many parasites or disease germs live where oxygen cannot be had. These organisms secure energy by dividing foods into simpler compounds. Yeast plants in bread dough, for example, turn starch into sugar while they can get oxygen. Later they secure energy by dividing sugar into alcohol and carbon dioxide. These become wastes for the yeast plants. When yeast is used for making bread, this carbon dioxide is what makes the dough rise. The alcohol evaporates as the bread is baked.

Carrying Food and Oxygen

One-celled plants such as Protococcus get food-making substances and energy through the cell wall. In many-celled plants each cell also absorbs and gives out substances through its wall. To provide what every cell needs and to carry off wastes the plant uses a liquid called *sap*, which travels through the

269

cells. The larger many-celled animals provide for the needs of their cells with circulating liquids called *blood* and *lymph*. Blood carries the oxygen needed to release energy from food and it carries away the carbon dioxide and water produced as wastes.

Kingdoms of Living Things

More than a million kinds of organisms are known. For centuries scientists divided them into two kingdoms—plants and animals. Most members of the plant kingdom have chlorophyll and cellulose. Those that do not contain any chlorophyll are supposed to be descended from organisms that lost it long ago. The animal kingdom consists of creatures that never possessed either chlorophyll or cellulose.

These two kingdoms seemed to include all living things until scientists studied one-celled organisms. Some seemed to fit neither kingdom and others seemed to fit both. Bacteria, for example, are too simple to be animals. Yet they contain no cellulose and may never have had chlorophyll. Some organisms swim, crawl, and capture food like animals but contain chlorophyll. Others are also covered with plates of cellulose.

Such "in-betweens" have been called plants by botanists and animals by zoologists. More and more, however, scientists are deciding that these puzzling organisms require a new system of classification. One system divides living things into four kingdoms:

Kingdom 1 – Monerans. These one-celled organisms have no distinct nuclei. They belong to two subkingdoms—bacteria and blue-green algae.

One important group of bacteria is purple and swims by means of lashes. Greenish particles in these purple bacteria can make food from carbon dioxide and water but are not true chlorophyll. Blue-green algae have no swimming lashes and often live together in chains or clumps covered by jelly. They contain true chlorophyll and can make food. They also can soak up ready-made food as many bacteria do.

Kingdom 2 – Protists. Some scientists say that the only protists are the things that have been called both plants and animals. They are one-celled and have definite nuclei. They swim by means of lashes that whip to and fro. They act like animals and may catch other organisms and eat them. In spite of this, they have chlorophyll and can make glucose, as plants and the purple bacteria do.

Other scientists say that the protists include one-celled creatures such as amoebas, which generally are called protozoans, or "first animals." Still others include sponges, seaweeds, and even fungi, such as mushrooms. It seems best to confine the kingdom to one-celled creatures or to "in-betweens."

Kingdom 3 – Plants. Plants probably began as one-celled organisms with nuclei, chlorophyll, and two lashes that were used for swimming. Some plants still drift about, but most do not. Although some of these sessile, or attached, plants are one-celled, most of them have great numbers of cells. Plants such as fungi (which include mushrooms and molds) have

Ron Church

Although they look like flowers, sea anemones are animals. They belong to a group that includes sea fans and corals, both of which are also animals that look like plants. All these animals live in shallow sea waters or in tide pools.

lost their chlorophyll and live on other animals and plants or on dead material.

Kingdom 4 – Animals. Animals are organisms whose cells contain nuclei but no chlorophyll. Except for certain one-celled forms, they also have no cellulose. Most animals move and change shape more freely than plants.

This classification does not include viruses and bacteriophages. If they prove to be living things, one or two kingdoms will have to be provided for them.

LIVY (64? BC–AD 17). Among the great historians of imperial Rome was Livy. His history of Rome from the foundation of the city in 753 BC was particularly hailed for its literary excellence and for the strongly moral viewpoint from which he wrote it. He deplored "the dark dawning of our modern day when we can neither endure our vices nor face the remedies needed to cure them" and urged upon his fellow Romans the moral qualities needed to keep Rome great.

Born Titus Livius in Padua, Italy, in 64 BC, or possibly as late as 59 BC, Livy lived through the turbulent years of the end of the republic and the founding of the empire. Little is known of his early life, but about 29 BC he moved to Rome and conceived the idea of writing his great history. The whole work, in 142 books, tells the story of Rome from the earliest years until 9 AD. Unfortunately books 11 to 20 and 46 to 142 have been lost, and only summaries remain of them. Because he was not active in politics, unusual for a historian of that time, Livy had no access to records and documents that belonged to the government. He had to rely instead on the works of other historians. But he did not see history in political terms. Rather, he emphasized personalities and events and the glories of the past. This technique was his greatest achievement, one that was to influence later historians. Livy died at Padua in AD 17.

LIZARDS. The largest living group of reptiles, the lizards, is made up of more than 3,000 species. They comprise 57 percent of the world's reptiles. Typical of reptiles, lizards have claws, lungs, and a tough outer skin of epidermal scales. Like all reptiles, they do not adjust their own body temperature. They assume the temperature of their environment and cannot live in extreme cold or heat.

Among the reptiles, lizards and snakes are most closely related in a scientific sense, and few characteristics are different between the two groups. Most lizards have four legs, eyelids, and ear openings, in contrast to snakes, which have none of these features. Other differences between snakes and lizards involve bone and tooth structures that are not readily discernible. Lizards and salamanders appear to be similar but are actually different in many ways. Salamanders, for example, have smooth, moist skin without scales and lack claws (*see* Amphibians).

Distribution

Lizards are most common in warm regions of the world, particularly in the wet tropics, but are found also in arid regions. Australia, the driest of the continents, has more than 300 species. The number of species in the South American tropics is even higher, and new varieties are discovered each year. However, lizards do occur in many temperate zone areas, such as northern Europe and central Asia. There is, however, one species found above the Arctic Circle. Lizards are more prevalent on oceanic islands of the temperate and tropic regions than are any other group of reptiles or amphibians.

The United States has about 70 species of lizards, of which only 15 are native east of the Mississippi River. Alabama has 11 species and Georgia has 12. More than 20 species of lizards can be found in Florida, but many of them are non-native tropical species of geckos and anoles that have been accidentally released in the Miami area. Most species of United States lizards live in the arid Southwest. Arizona alone has 44 species of lizards, and more than 30 kinds are found in California.

Appearance

Among the reptiles, lizards vary greatly in size, as do snakes. The smallest lizards in the world belong to the skink and gecko families. Although probably not the smallest, the little brown skink of the southeastern United States reaches a length of only three inches (seven centimeters) and weighs less than a nickel. The largest lizard in the world is the Komodo dragon (scientific name, *Varanus komodoensis*), an impressive creature discovered in the 1800s on islands in the Indonesian region. Komodo dragons reach sizes of

This article was contributed by J. Whitfield Gibbons, Associate Director and Associate Research Ecologist, Savannah River Ecology Laboratory, Aiken, S.C., and Professor, University of Georgia.

greater than ten feet (three meters). They live on land, stalking live prey and eating meat when they can get it. The Komodo dragon belongs to a family of lizards known as the monitors, which are found throughout the Old World tropics and deserts, including Australia.

Lizards do not vary much in shape. Most have four well-developed legs, some are legless, and a few species have only front legs. Some species have flattened bodies. One of the most unusual is the South American flatbellied rock lizard, which escapes predators by slipping into rock crevices and quickly inflating its body so that it cannot be dislodged.

Ornamentation among lizards can be spectacular. Perhaps the most eye-catching example of ornamentation occurs in the true chameleons of Africa. The males of some species have long hornlike extensions on their heads that are used in combat with other males during the mating period. The spiny armor of the American horned lizards and the Australian thorny devil give these animals a bizarre appearance. Although harmless to humans, the spines serve as an effective deterrent to certain would-be predators.

Importance of Color

The role of color is better understood for lizards than for any other group of reptiles. Brilliant color displays are used during courtship by males of some species. The green anole (*Anolis carolinensis*) of the Americas has an enlarged throat sac, called a dewlap, which can be bright red or orange. In defending its territory, the anole inflates the dewlap, warning male anoles or even other animals to back off. The fence lizards of the southern United States are normally drab-colored. But during courtship periods, the males develop brilliant blue patches on their necks and bellies. The bright color is used to threaten other males during courtship or to defend prime territory.

Some lizards can even change color within minutes, from light green to dark brown for instance, in response to their environment. The physiology associated with these color changes is very complex and more research is needed to understand completely how they occur, but certain facts are known. The pigment cells that permit color change are called chromatophores. Within these cells, pigment granules are able to migrate.

The true chameleons of Africa sometimes assume the background color of the site they occupy—a tree trunk or a leaf, for example. Under special circumstances of temperature and surface conditions, a chameleon can even have one half of its body totally brown and the other half green. In the American anole, which is also sometimes called a chameleon, color is related to environmental conditions such as temperature and moisture. An anole sitting on a palmetto plant during a bright, warm day will appear emerald green. One uncovered among dead leaves in the wintertime will be chocolate brown. However, though anoles appear to mimic their surroundings, they are in fact responding to temperature, not color.

Reproduction

Most lizards lay eggs with tough, leathery shells. The eggs are laid in sand or rotting vegetation where they are concealed from predators but can be warmed by the sun. The American anoles lay a single egg each time. Many of the geckos lay two eggs. However, most lizard species lay several eggs at a time. Most lizards lay their eggs in a suitable nest and then abandon them. Females of a few species, such as the blue-tailed skinks of the southern United States, help guard and incubate the eggs in the nest.

Some lizards are viviparous: They bear their young directly without laying eggs. Called "live-bearing," this occurs in representatives of most families of lizards throughout the world. In the United States, certain of the western lizards are live-bearers. These include the desert night lizard (*Xantusia vigilis*), the short-horned lizard (*Phrynosoma douglassi*), northern alligator lizard (*Gerrhonotus coeruleus*), and Yarrow's spiny lizard (*Sceloporus jarrovi*). Females of the live-bearing night lizards, which are in the family Xantusiidae, eat the embryonic membranes that remain after the young are born, a trait which is found primarily among mammals.

A few species of lizards have parthenogenetic reproduction in which females lay eggs that have not been fertilized by a male but produce normal young anyway. In certain species of the whiptail lizards that live in the southwestern United States, populations exist that consist only of females, with no males ever being found.

Behavior

Among the fascinating behavioral features of lizards are the various means of locomotion. Most species run on four legs. Some, such as the large leopard lizards and collared lizards of the Southwest, do their fastest running on their two rear legs, suggesting what some dinosaurs may have looked like. The basilisk lizards of tropical America can actually run rapidly on two legs across small bodies of water.

Some species, such as the glass lizards of America and the slowworm of Europe, have no legs. Legless lizards move by undulating their bodies much as snakes do. A closely related group of legless reptiles known as the amphisbaenids are not true lizards, though they are sometimes called ringed lizards or worm lizards.

The flying dragon of Borneo uses a bizarre form of locomotion. Normally a climber, this lizard occasionally leaps from a tall tree, spreads a flap of skin that is normally tucked between the front and hind legs, and glides to a new site in the manner of a flying squirrel. The flying gecko of Asia glides the same way. Another unusual form of locomotion is that of the Brazilian chameleon. The male mates with the female and then climbs on her back and rides around for the next day, warding off other males anxious to breed.

Lizards have a variety of behavior patterns to protect themselves from predators, including birds, snakes, mammals, and other lizards. Tactics include camouflage, speed, and secretiveness. An interesting defensive behavior of certain large lizards of the American tropics is the use of their long tails like a whip to lash out at any threat. But lizard tails are used most effectively to escape predators through trickery. The tails of many species break off when touched. The broken tail twists and wiggles, diverting the attention of the predator while the lizard escapes. The loss of the tail is only temporary, for tail regeneration, or growing back, is characteristic of most lizards. The new tail may be shorter than the original but is also breakable.

Poisonous Lizards

The only two poisonous lizards in the world are the Gila monster (*Heloderma suspectum*) of the southwestern United States and the beaded lizard (*Heloderma horridum*) of Mexico. Their venom, or poison, can kill a human; however, the lizards are much less effective at getting the poison into their victims than are the poisonous snakes. Lizard venom glands are located in the lower jaw, unlike those of snakes. Also, the fangs of lizards are not hollow hypodermic needles as in snakes. Instead, the fangs have a less effective center groove that channels the venom into the bite.

Both poisonous lizards have impressive reputations, including being tenacious biters that are almost impossible to pry loose. Fortunately, Gila monsters are docile and rarely bite, and deaths from their venom are even rarer. The federal government has declared this species officially "threatened," and its future survival is in far more danger from people than people are from it.

Food

Lizards consume more different kinds of food than do snakes, which ordinarily eat only live animals. Most lizards feed upon live prey, but a few species are strict vegetarians. Some eat seeds. The desert iguana (*Dipsosaurus dorsalis*) of the American Southwest eats insects while young but maintains a vegetarian diet as an adult. The marine iguanas of the Galápagos Islands feed on plants that grow underwater along the rocky shoreline. The horned lizards of the western United States feed on ants.

Techniques to Study Lizards

One of the major challenges for herpetologists who work with lizards is capturing them. Many species are extremely fast and can outrun a person for short distances. Others are adept climbers that can easily escape. Some are difficult to find because they live underground, blend in with their surroundings, or simply because they are rare.

Herpetologists have developed numerous techniques for collecting lizards. For the fleet-of-foot forms, such as the six-lined racerunner (*Cnemidophorus sexlineatus*) of the Southeast and the whiptails of the Southwest, only one approach has proved effective: They must be stopped by something that

Australian Frilled Lizard
(Chlamydosaurus kingii)
Length: 20 cm (8 in)

Family Agamidae

Flying Dragon
(Draco volans)
Length: 18-22 cm (7-9 in)

Family Agamidae

Alligator Lizard
(Gerrhonotus liocephalus)
Length: 16-50 cm (6-20 in)

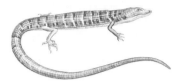

Family Anguidae

Jackson's Chameleon
(Chamaeleo jacksonii)
Length: 11.4 cm (4.5 in)

Family Chamaeleontidae

Tokay
(Gekko gecko)
Length: 26-35 cm (10-14 in)

Family Gekkonidae

Gila Monster
(Heloderma suspectum)
Length: 31-50 cm (12-20 in)

Family Helodermatidae

Desert Iguana
(Dipsosaurus dorsalis)
Length: 10-14 cm (4-5.5 in)

Family Iguanidae

Fence (Swift) Lizard
(Sceloporus undulatus)
Length: 10-18 cm (4-7 in)

Family Iguanidae

Green Anole
(Anolis carolinensis)
Length: 10-20 cm (4-8 in)

Family Iguanidae

Horned Lizard
(Phrynosoma coronatum)
Length: 7-10 cm (2.5-4 in)

Family Iguanidae

Jeweled Lacerta
(Lacerta lepida)
Length: up to .7 m (2.5 ft)

Family Lacertidae

Five-Lined Skink
(Eumeces fasciatus)
Length: 13-20 cm (5-8 in)

Family Scincidae

Sand Skink
(Sphenops sphenopsiformis)
Length: 18 cm (7 in)

Family Scincidae

Six-Lined Racerunner
(Cnemidophorus sexlineatus)
Length: 16-24 cm (6-9.5 in)

Family Teiidae

Monitor Lizard
(Varanus salvator)
Length: 1.3-1.8 m (4-6 ft)

Family Varanidae

moves faster than they do. Dust shot from a .22-caliber pistol has been used to collect museum specimens. A later development, the blowgun, permits live capture of the animals. The technique is an old one, based on the dart guns of African pygmies. The lizard blowgun is a four-foot (one-meter) aluminum tube with corks as projectiles. The accuracy at distances of 30 to 40 feet (10 to 12 meters) is remarkable and results in a fast-moving lizard being stopped in its tracks. The cork stuns the animal but seldom results in serious injury. A recent modification is the use of olives for ammunition instead of corks.

Another lizard-catching technique is noosing. Many lizards can be approached to within a few feet but are intolerant of closer approaches. Yet they do not seem to mind a bamboo pole with a string and tiny lasso at the end waving over their head. With a little adroit manuevering a patient lizard collector can have a lizard dangling in the noose within a few seconds. Because of its light weight, the specimen can then be removed unharmed and in perfect condition.

Life Cycle of a Typical Lizard

The life cycle of the fence lizard (*Sceloporus undulatus*) of the southern United States is typical of those of many small temperate zone lizards. During the colder months of winter, fence lizards are dormant, hiding beneath the bark of trees, under rocks, or in dead vegetation. Although they may make brief appearances on sunny days during warm spells, fence lizards do not become permanently active until springtime when warm days are assured. Even an unusual cold, cloudy period during spring will send them back into hiding.

Once the lizards are active, the males develop strong territorial tendencies, displaying themselves to other males in a threatening manner to drive them away. One form of display is the "push-up," in which a male uses his legs to push his body up and down as a signal that warns another male to stay away. Among many species of lizards, the males will fight if such warnings are ignored.

Courtship and mating occur in the spring. A male may try to mate with several females, but each female usually accepts only one male. Females usually lay 6 to 12 white, oval-shaped eggs in late spring or early summer. Some females lay more than one clutch, or batch of eggs, during the nesting period. The eggs hatch during late summer or early fall. The baby fence lizards look like small replicas of their parents and immediately begin searching for food. The juveniles, along with the adults, begin seeking winter hiding places as soon as cold weather begins in the fall. Fence lizards may live for two or more years.

Lizards as Pets

Lizards make excellent pets. They can be kept in a terrarium with dry soil, sand, or moss on the bottom. Hiding places made of rocks, wood, or live plants should be provided. Many species are climbers and will perch for hours on tree limbs in a cage. Lizards must be kept warm if they are to be active and able to feed readily. However, provisions should be made so that they can escape high temperatures. Many species need direct sunlight or ultraviolet rays during part of each day.

Most lizards will eat insects. Mealworms, crickets, cockroaches, flies, and grasshoppers are eagerly consumed. Some can be trained to eat chopped meat or eggs. Many species will not drink directly from a bowl but will take water that is sprinkled onto leaves or other objects in the cage. Because of the diversity of behavior patterns among lizards of the world, it is advisable to find out the characteristics of a particular species before trying to make a pet of it.

Superstitions

Lizards, like other reptiles, are the subject of several widespread superstitions. The harmless blue-tailed skinks, sometimes mistakenly called scorpions, are dreaded by many people in the eastern United States. Some species are thought to be poisonous, able to bite viciously, or even sting. Many lizards will bite if picked up, but only a few can inflict a bite that is painful. No lizard has a stinger of any sort. Another popular superstition is that a glass snake (actually a legless lizard) will shatter into pieces if hit, and then later the pieces will crawl back together to make a whole animal again. The basis for the story is that a glass lizard is more than half tail. When this long tail breaks off if it is hit or grabbed, it may break into several writhing pieces, plus a body that slithers away. The overworked imagination of a frightened person might easily turn such an event into an almost believable fantasy.

Scientific Classification

Lizards, snakes, and amphisbaenids belong to the order Squamata within the class Reptilia. The suborder Sauria (or Lacertilia) includes only the lizards and is divided into more than a dozen families. Among the most notable families of lizards are the following: Gekkonidae, the geckos, with representatives throughout the world in tropical to warm temperate areas; Iguanidae, the largest family of lizards in the Western Hemisphere, including the fence lizards, American chameleons, iguanas, basilisks, and horned lizards; Agamidae, the Old World counterpart of the Iguanidae; Chamaeleontidae, the true chameleons of Africa; Anguidae, a widespread group of the Americas and Eurasia that includes the legless glass lizards and European slowworms; Helodermatidae, consisting of the Gila monster and Mexican beaded lizard, the only poisonous lizards; Varanidae, the monitors of Africa, Asia, and Australia; Lacertidae, common lizards of Europe, Africa, and Asia; Scincidae, the skinks, the most cosmopolitan of the lizard families; and Teiidae, a primarily Central and South American family that includes the racerunners and whiptails of North America.

LLAMA *see* CAMEL.

LLOYD GEORGE, David (1863–1945). At the age of 17, a small slender Welshman visited the British House of Commons. Afterward he recorded in his diary his hope for a political career. The Welshman, David Lloyd George, in time became the prime minister who guided Great Britain to victory over Germany in World War I.

David Lloyd George was born on Jan. 17, 1863, in Manchester, England, where his Welsh father, William George, had gone to teach school. Soon after David's birth the family returned to Wales. His father died two years later. David was educated by his uncle, Richard Lloyd, the village cobbler. In his honor the boy took the name Lloyd.

At the age of 14 he began to study law and at 21 was admitted to practice as a solicitor. In 1890 he was elected to Parliament as a Liberal from the Welsh district of Carnarvon. "The great little Welshman" held his seat in the Commons for more than 50 years. At no time could public opinion turn him from what he thought was just.

In 1905 Lloyd George accepted a minor office in the Cabinet as head of the Board of Trade. There he put through a shipping act to aid seamen and settled a critical railway strike.

He advanced to the second highest Cabinet post in 1908 when he became chancellor of the exchequer, with Herbert Asquith as prime minister. As manager of British finances, Lloyd George determined to ease the tax burden on the poor. He also planned an Old Age Pension Act. To finance it, he drew up a national budget that put new taxes on the wealthy. These taxes threatened to break up the old landed estates.

The conservative House of Lords rejected Lloyd George's budget. But a general election showed that the mass of the British people favored it. So strong was public support that in 1911 an act of Parliament abolished the power of the House of Lords to reject a money bill such as the budget. Lloyd George at once launched a more extended program of social reform.

When World War I broke out in 1914, many people expected him to resign, as he had long been regarded as a pacifist. After Germany invaded Belgium, however, he denounced the aggression. He was put in charge of the new Ministry of Munitions in 1915. In 1916 he became head of the war office.

The Liberal party at this time was divided. In December 1916 Lloyd George forced Asquith's resignation and became prime minister, heading a coalition government. Before going to the peace conference at Versailles, France, he strengthened his position by winning the "khaki election" of November 1918. At the peace conference he seemed uncertain. Sometimes he sided with France's efforts to destroy Germany. At other times he sided with the United States efforts for a peace based on reconciliation and the rights of nations and people.

After 1919 Lloyd George's leadership weakened, largely as a result of a slump in business that brought on strikes and unemployment. In 1922 the Conservatives withdrew from the coalition and Lloyd George

David Lloyd George in 1908
EB Inc.

at once resigned. He remained in the Commons for the rest of his life, but the influence of the divided Liberal party grew weaker and weaker. His last great effort to return to office came in the general election of 1929, when he made glittering promises to "conquer unemployment." Unimpressed, the voters returned the rising Labor party instead. Lloyd George's later years were given to the writing of his 'War Memoirs'. He died in Wales on March 26, 1945, just as World War II was coming to an end.

LOBACHEVSKI, Nikolai (1792–1856). The co-founder of non-Euclidean geometry, along with his contemporary the Hungarian mathematician János Bolyai, was Nikolai Lobachevski. This geometry was not based on Euclid's geometry of planes, or flat surfaces; it departed from Euclid's parallel postulate which states that through any point in a plane only one line can be drawn that is parallel to another line in the plane. By demonstrating the possibility of a non-Euclidean geometry, Bolyai and Lobachevski were to influence the development of mathematics and physics in the 20th century. (*See also* Geometry, subsection, "Other Kinds of Geometry.")

Nikolai Ivanovich Lobachevski was born on Dec. 1, 1792, in Nizhny Novgorod (now Gorky), Russia. Most of his life was spent at the University of Kazan, where he started his studies at age 14. He began teaching at the university in 1816, became dean of the faculty in 1820, and served as rector of the university from 1827 until his retirement in 1846. He was largely responsible for improving the school's academic standing and generating interest in and respect for the teaching of science and mathematics.

Throughout his career Lobachevski worked in various fields of mathematical theory. His theories were published in his lifetime but were not generally recognized until after his death. He died at Kazan on Feb. 24, 1856. The work on non-Euclidean geometry was taken up by other mathematicians, including Carl Freidrich Gauss, Bernhard Riemann, Eugenio Beltrami, and Felix Klein.

LOBBYING. Attempts to influence the decisions of government are called lobbying. The term comes from the fact that attempts to put pressure on legislators often took place in the vestibule, or lobby, adjacent to the legislative chamber. The activity is most commonly associated with private interest groups, such as representatives of corporations or labor unions, but it may also be carried out by individuals. Legislators themselves, when they try to influence the making of public policy by other officials, are lobbyists.

Governments are composed of competing interest groups and factions. James Madison, in the 10th Federalist paper, states: "By a faction, understand a number of citizens, whether amounting to a majority or minority of the whole, who are united and actuated by some common impulse of passion, or of interest. . . ." Madison realized that the effects of factions could not be prevented, but he believed that they could be controlled by the checks and balances built into the Constitution.

The American experience. In the United States, as well as in other popular democracies, the idea of representative government suggests that elected officials owe service to the people who live in their districts and states. Throughout the 19th century and much of the 20th, however, elected officials were often controlled by private interests whose power and money could, among other things, aid in a political campaign. Thus, in the second half of the 19th century, during a period of rapid industrialization, representatives and senators passed a great deal of legislation favorable to the railroads, steel companies, oil companies, and other industries. These laws were frequently against the public interest.

The power of industry over elected officials became so great that, in 1906, an investigative reporter named David Graham Phillips published a series of articles under the overall title, 'The Treason of the Senate'. In dramatic detail Phillips exposed the alliance between big business and the most influential senators. His articles, combined with a general public outrage over government scandals, led to a movement for reform in campaign financing. Beginning in 1907, a series of laws was passed, culminating in the 1925 Federal Corrupt Practices Act. Unfortunately, the laws were written in such a manner that their intent could easily be evaded.

In 1913 the ratification of the 17th Amendment provided for the direct election of United States senators. Until then they had been elected by the state legislatures and were, therefore, less accountable to the public than to the interests that got them elected. This amendment helped bring the Senate's work more into the spotlight and weaken the strong ties between business interests and the senators.

Demands to curb the excessive influence of pressure groups led to the Federal Regulation of Lobbying Act in 1946. The law requires lobbyists to register and to report contributions and expenditures. The groups they represent must make similar reports.

The assumption behind the law is that lobbyists cannot do much harm if their activities are publicized.

Lobbies. The most effective lobbying in the United States is done by large associations representing single industries, trades, professions, or other interests. Typical national associations have federal, state, and local units capable of operating at every level of government. Representative examples of such associations are the Chamber of Commerce of the United States; the American Fur Industry, Inc.; the American Medical Association; the National Association of Manufacturers; the National Association of Realtors; the American Petroleum Institute; and the Western Cotton Growers Association.

Lobbying is also done directly by corporations, labor groups, and citizens' groups. The citizens' groups are the most recent to emerge, and they represent an effort on the part of a number of organizations to influence legislation on behalf of segments of the general public. Most of the citizens' groups deal with specific matters: the Wilderness Society, for instance, is concerned with environmental issues; and the Citizen/Labor Energy Coalition tries to influence laws on price controls for oil and gas. Two of the best known citizens' groups are Common Cause and Public Citizen, Inc. Common Cause works for general political and social reform, with a goal of making government more responsive to the people. Public Citizen, Inc., started by consumer advocate Ralph Nader, also addresses a broad spectrum of issues, but it emphasizes consumer problems versus the power of the corporations and other private interests.

Lobbying may be done in several ways. Interests may be represented openly before committees of a legislature or before administrative tribunals. Public officials may also have private meetings with lobbyists. Some lobbying organizations organize grass roots campaigns through the media to build support for their causes. In 1983, for example, banks and savings and loan associations campaigned to get people to write senators and congressmen in order to repeal a law requiring these institutions to withhold tax on interest payments for the federal government.

Indirect lobbying. This term denotes group activity designed to influence government by shaping public opinion through the news media and advertising. One of the most notable ways this has been done since the early 1970s is through political action committees, usually called PACs. The comprehensive campaign financing act of 1974 provided for the public financing of presidential campaigns, but it did not make the same provision for congressional campaigns. Business and labor organizations succeeded in having a provision inserted in the law allowing the formation of independent political action committees that could raise funds either to support or defeat particular candidates. By 1983 more than 3,500 such PACs existed. The hundreds of millions of dollars they raised for campaign purposes brought charges that they were unduly trying to influence the legislative process with their contributions.

LOCK AND KEY. A key is nothing more than the solution to a mechanical puzzle, the lock. As with most puzzles there is potentially more than one solution. Substitute solutions range from lock picks to unauthorized duplicate keys. To create the puzzle, four basic methods of keying are used in the construction of mechanical-type locks—warded, lever tumbler, pin tumbler, and wafer, or disc tumbler. The construction of some locks combines more than one of these methods.

Bit key. A lock that incorporates more than a single keying method is the bit key, or "skeleton key," lock popular in America at the turn of the 20th century. It has lever tumblers that require a key with a bit, or projecting part, of proper depth and position cut on the top to cause a lever to rise as the key is rotated. Wards, or protrusions cast into the lock case on either side, require the key to have corresponding cuts on the side of the bit before it can be rotated to engage the lever tumblers. Many such locks also had entering wards cast in the lock case that required a cut running diagonally across the face of the key's bit. Without this cut the key could not enter the keyhole. The bit key lock lost its popularity because of the large cavity that had to be created in the door to hold the lock body and the limited number of possible key changes, or combinations, available.

Lever tumbler. An example of the lever lock in popular use today is that for the safe-deposit box. Perhaps the most dominant use of lever-type locks is on lockers that are found in schools and industry.

Pin tumbler. The keying method used most often on door locks, and in many padlocks, is the pin tumbler lock. This type was invented in the 1860s by Linus Yale, Jr., and is still used extensively on the North American continent. It is not nearly so popular, however, in most other parts of the world. The pin tumbler lock provides almost unlimited quantities of possible combinations and is readily master keyed, a system that allows a single master key to open a number of individually keyed locks. The configuration, or shape, of the keyway is also almost unlimited. This shape is broached, or cut, into the lock cylinder plug and a corresponding shape milled into the blank brass stock that constitutes a key.

In a pin tumbler lock a key with cuts of a proper depth is inserted into a lock cylinder, causing the tumblers in the lock to rise to a "shear line." This line is at the outside diameter of the plug and allows the key to turn. A cam attached to the rear of the plug engages the locking, or retracting, mechanism and moves as the key is rotated.

As lock technology improved in the 1960s, this pin tumbler lock with single action became susceptible to alternative methods of operation such as the use of lock picks and unauthorized duplicate keys. In 1970 a United States patent was issued to Roy Oliver, E. C. Flora, Roy Spain, and Paul Powell for a pin tumbler type with double action known as the Medeco High Security Lock Cylinder. This was the first major variation to improve security and control in the pin

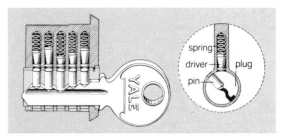

With the correct key, the tops of the tumbler pins in a pin tumbler lock align with the top of the plug, which then turns.

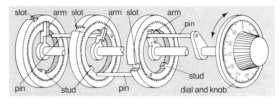

A combination safe lock cannot be opened unless the slots of the three wheels are brought into line by moving the dial.

tumbler lock. The construction of the Medeco lock requires not only proper depth cuts on the key but also proper angles of the cuts. These angles vary, causing the tumblers to rotate to a particular position, which then allows a side bar to operate. Another variation is the Norman High Security Lock Cylinder, patented in 1976 by Norman Epstein. Pins are replaced by balls, and the cylinder has a curved keyhole with a computer-designed key.

Wafer, or disc tumbler, locks came into popular use around the late 1940s. This method of keying requires flat tumblers stamped out of sheet brass. The tumblers are usually incorporated into a die metal cylinder, which results in low-cost manufacture. Wafer tumbler locks are used extensively in desks, cabinets, padlocks, and in some door locks. The possible combinations available in this type are comparatively limited as is the ability to master key.

Combination, or dial, locks are operated by a pattern of movements of a knob or handle over a predetermined set of numbers. A more recent adaptation has a set of push buttons. Such locks are used where extreme precautions are needed. Since they have no keyholes, the lock mechanisms are inaccessible.

Time locks are equipped with clockwork devices that make it impossible to open the lock except at the hour for which the timepiece is set. They are often used on bank vaults.

History. Locks in varying configurations have been employed by mankind since a large stone was first rolled in front of a cave entrance to assure privacy and control over entry. There is evidence that ancient Egyptians used intricate locks 4,000 years ago. The ancient Greeks developed several refinements of bar-and-bolt locks that permitted a door to be unbarred from the outside as well as from the inside. One improvement consisted of a rope attached to a pivoted bar and passed through a hole in the door. A tug on the rope lifted the bar from its cleats.

LOCKE, Alain (1886–1954).

As a writer and teacher, Alain Locke promoted recognition of the contributions of other blacks to American music, art, and literature. He was equally influential in encouraging black Americans to explore their heritage and expand their cultural accomplishments.

Alain LeRoy Locke was born in Philadelphia, Pa., on Sept. 13, 1886. Both his parents were schoolteachers. They wanted their son to enter one of the professions, perhaps medicine, as a means of rising above some of the restrictions that were placed upon his race. But sickness made a career as a doctor impossible, and the parents helped young Locke to prepare himself as a teacher.

After graduating from the Philadelphia School of Pedagogy in 1904, Locke entered Harvard University. There he studied under such great teachers as Barrett Wendell and Charles T. Copeland. Locke's major course of study, philosophy, also brought him under the influence of Josiah Royce, William James, and George Santayana.

Locke won a Rhodes scholarship after graduation from Harvard in 1907. He studied in England at Oxford University for the next three years. After a year at the University of Berlin, he returned home in 1912. He taught at Howard University in Washington, D.C., for nearly 40 years. In the 1920s he was a leader in the Harlem Renaissance. He died in New York City on June 9, 1954.

Locke's books stressed black culture, but he always tried to show how this fitted into the whole of American life. His first book was 'The New Negro' (1925). He acted either as author or editor for a number of others. Among these were 'The Negro in America' (1933), 'The Negro and His Music' (1936), and 'The Negro in Art' (1941). With Bernhard J. Stern he edited 'When Peoples Meet: a Study in Race and Culture Contacts' (1942).

LOCKE, John (1632–1704).

One of the pioneers in modern thinking was the English philosopher John Locke. He made great contributions in studies of politics, government, and psychology.

John Locke was born in Wrington, Somerset, on Aug. 29, 1632. He was the son of a well-to-do Puritan lawyer who fought for Cromwell in the English Civil War. The father, also named John Locke, was a devout, even-tempered man.

The boy was educated at Westminster School and Oxford and later became a tutor at the university. His friends urged him to enter the Church of England, but he decided that he was not fitted for the calling. He had long been interested in meteorology and the experimental sciences, especially chemistry. He turned to medicine and became known as one of the most skilled practitioners of his day.

In 1667 Locke became confidential secretary and personal physician to Anthony Ashley Cooper, later lord chancellor and the first earl of Shaftesbury. Locke's association with Shaftesbury enabled him to meet many of the great men of England, but it also

Courtesy of the Governing Body of Christ Church, Oxford

John Locke

caused him a great deal of trouble. Shaftesbury was indicted for high treason. He was acquitted, but Locke was suspected of disloyalty. In 1683 he left England for Holland and returned only after the revolution of 1688.

Locke is remembered today largely as a political philosopher. He preached the doctrine that men naturally possess certain large rights, the chief being life, liberty, and property. Rulers, he said, derived their power only from the consent of the people. He thought that government should be like a contract between the rulers and his subjects: The people give up certain of their rights in return for just rule, and the ruler should hold his power only so long as he uses it justly. These ideas had a tremendous effect on all future political thinking. The American Declaration of Independence clearly reflects Locke's teachings.

Locke was always very interested in psychology. About 1670, friends urged him to write a paper on the limitations of human judgment. He started to write a few paragraphs, but 20 years passed before he finished. The result was his great and famous 'Essay Concerning Human Understanding'. In this work he stressed the theory that the human mind starts as a *tabula rasa* (smoothed tablet)—that is, a waxed tablet ready to be used for writing. The mind has no inborn ideas, as most men of the time believed. Throughout life it forms its ideas only from impressions (sense experiences) that are made upon its surface.

In discussing education Locke urged the view that character formation is far more important than information and that learning should be pleasant. During his later years he turned more and more to writing about religion.

The principal works by Locke are letters—'On Toleration' (1689, 1690, 1692); 'An Essay Concerning Human Understanding' (1690); two treatises—'On Civil Government' (1690), and 'Some Thoughts Concerning Education' (1693); and 'The Reasonableness of Christianity' (1695). He died in Oates, Essex, on Oct. 28, 1704.

The F40 PH diesel-electric locomotive is a 3,000-horsepower engine. It can travel at speeds of up to 103 miles (165 kilometers) per hour.

LOCOMOTIVE. The "iron horse" that pulls railroad passenger or freight cars is a self-contained power plant on wheels. The term locomotive is used only when the power unit can be uncoupled from the cars. The power plant is part of the passenger cars in self-propelled rail-diesel cars and some streamlined and suburban electric trains. In these the term locomotive is not applicable.

Until after World War II, the reciprocating steam engine locomotive ruled supreme. In North America and Europe, and in much of the rest of the world, it has since been replaced by the diesel-electric locomotive. Modern steam engines are maintained only in countries where coal is much cheaper or more readily available than oil such as in China. In areas of high rail traffic, as along the United States east coast and in central Europe, many rail lines have been electrified and use electric locomotives.

Many a large locomotive actually develops enough power to supply a small city. Most of the time, however, only a small fraction of this power is needed to pull the train, and only a few pounds of tractive effort, or pulling power, is required to keep one ton of the train's weight in motion once it is under way. Full power is needed principally to start the train or to pull it up a steep grade. To start a long train, the locomotive first backs up to loosen the couplings between cars so that in the forward motion one car after the other begins moving.

Steam-Powered Locomotives

The old reciprocating steam locomotive is driven by a steam engine. Steam from the boiler is fed to the cylinders to move pistons back and forth (reciprocating motion). Connecting rods from the pistons then move the driving wheels. The firebox at the rear end of the boiler is fed with coal or oil, which in a large locomotive is stored in a separate tender. The tender also contains the water that is turned into steam. The exhaust from the steam cylinders is directed up the smokestack to create a heavy draft for the boiler fire. The discharge of the used steam from the cylinders is controlled by valves, and the intermittent release of the steam up the stack is responsible for the locomotive's puffing (*see* Steam Engine).

Some steam locomotives weigh 500 tons (450 metric tons) or more and can develop more than 6,000 horsepower. They can pull a long freight train or a passenger train at about 100 miles (160 kilometers) per hour. For extremely heavy loads or steep grades, two or more locomotives may be coupled to a train.

Other Types

Diesel locomotives match steam engines in size and speed. In these an oil-burning diesel engine (*see* Diesel Engine) drives an electric generator that in turn provides power to the wheels through an electric motor. Depending on the load, they may be used in coupled units, each developing about 1,500 to 2,000 horsepower. Better fuel efficiency, more hours of use during a day, and smoother operation—that is, less pounding on the tracks—were largely responsible for the rapid advance of the diesel engine after World War II. Diesel locomotives also require less supporting equipment. The coaling stations and water towers that sprinkled the countryside during the reign of steam could be replaced with oil storage tanks placed much farther apart. Variations of the diesel engine

One of the basic types of steam locomotives is this *American*, which has a four-wheel leading truck and two pairs of driving wheels. This arrangement is called 4–4–0 (the "0" meaning no trailing axle). It was the ancestor of many later types.

For freight service the four-wheel leading truck was replaced by a two-wheel axle and another pair of driving wheels was added. This made the *Mogul* a 2–6–0 type. The locomotive above is the *Show-wa-no*, first placed in service in 1871.

The largest type of steam locomotives was the *Mallet*. This was a 2–6–6–2 (a leading and trailing axle and 12 driving wheels).

An early electric locomotive was this 0–4–4–0. Electric locomotives may also be classified by idle and driving axles.

This 4–8–4 steam locomotive is the *Northern*, *Niagara*, or *Pocono* type. The identification of steam locomotives by counting the wheels in a truck is known as the Whyte system, which may also be illustrated symbolically as oo000000oo for the 4–8–4.

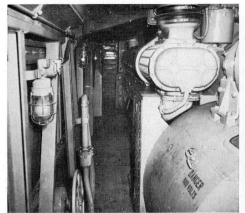

An electric generator on wheels is this power unit of a large diesel-electric locomotive. It can produce 2,000 horsepower.

The engineer (right) and fireman (left) of this fast-moving diesel-electric locomotive see the once-formidable Rockies ahead.

include the *gas turbine* electric locomotives which burn natural gas, oil, or powdered coal. In these types a blast of hot gas drives a turbine which operates the electric generators. (*See also* Electricity; Internal Combustion Engine; Turbine.)

These types of locomotives are all *self-contained;* that is, they carry their power source with them, like a ship at sea. The *electric locomotive,* however, gets its power from the outside, through an overhead wire or third rail. A few main lines use this type of locomotive; but most of them are used in suburban service and in handling through trains near terminals. Another type of electric locomotive, powered by storage batteries, is frequently used in mines.

History of the Locomotive

Like all great inventions, the locomotive grew through the slow accumulation of improvements made by different inventors. Men in England worked on the idea as early as the 1700's. Most of their devices were designed to run on ordinary highways, and so were forerunners of the automobile.

On Feb. 21, 1804, Richard Trevithick ran one of his road engines on rails at Pen-y-darran, in Wales, at five miles an hour. William Hedley improved on this in 1813 with his *Puffing Billy,* so called because it used exhaust steam in the smokestack, as many locomotives do today. This was the first engine to use smooth wheels on smooth track.

George Stephenson built a workable locomotive for the Killingworth colliery in 1815. In 1825 his locomotives ran at the rate of 16 miles an hour on the newly opened Stockton and Darlington Railway. In 1829 Stephenson and his son Robert devised a multi-tubular boiler for the locomotive *Rocket.* This boiler gave power enough to maintain a speed of 25 to 30 miles an hour, and the *Rocket* won a speed, pulling, and endurance contest held by the Liverpool and Manchester Railway. This event is considered the birth of the modern railroad.

The first American-built locomotive was the *Tom Thumb,* constructed by Peter Cooper. In 1830 this locomotive lost a famous race with a horse-drawn

The engineer in this diesel switcher talks to the traffic control tower by means of a two-way radio in his cab.

An electric freight locomotive uses a rectifier to convert the alternating current of the overhead line to direct current.

An 8,500-horsepower gas turbine pulls this freight train. The turbine generates its own electric power.

By courtesy of the Union Pacific Railroad (bottom photo only)

The first locomotive in the world to do actual work was this one built by Richard Trevithick in 1804. It pulled a short train of cars uphill on a coal-mine railway in Wales.

The British *Rocket*, built by George and Robert Stephenson, demonstrated the first really successful use of steam power in the famous locomotive trials at Rainhill, England, in 1829.

The first steam locomotive to operate in America was this British-built *Stourbridge Lion*. It made a trial run in Pennsylvania, but proved to be too heavy for the tracks.

Peter Cooper's *Tom Thumb* was the first American-built locomotive to operate in the United States. Weighing only one ton, it lost a famous race with a horse-drawn car on Aug. 28, 1830.

car on the newly laid tracks of the Baltimore and Ohio Railroad. American-built locomotives that were placed in operation in 1830-31 were the *Best Friend of Charleston*, *West Point*, *York*, and *DeWitt Clinton*. (*See also* Railroads.)

LOCOMOTIVE WHISTLE AND HORN SIGNALS

o indicates short sounds, — longer sounds.

o	Apply brakes. Stop.
oo	Engineer's answer to signal.
ooo	When standing, back.
ooo	When running, stop at next station.
oooo	Call for signals.
oooooooooo . .	Alarm for persons or livestock on track.
——————	Approaching station or junction at grade.
—oo	A second section is following.
—ooo	Flagman protect rear of train.
— —.	Release brakes. Proceed.
— — o — —	Approaching public crossings at grade.

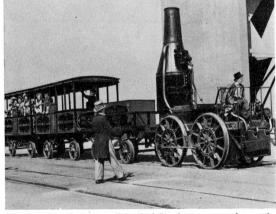

The American-built *Best Friend of Charleston*, operating on the South Carolina Railroad, opened regular service in 1831.

LOCUST. The name locust is popularly given to two different kinds of insects—the short-horned grasshopper and the cicada. Both kinds do great damage to trees and crops when they swarm in huge numbers.

The locusts mentioned in the Bible are short-horned grasshoppers. They belong to the family Acrididae. There is at least one species of these insects on each of the major continents of the Earth. Vast numbers of them, flying in swarms, appear periodically in countries in the Far East and in the western United States. A column of flying locusts seen in India was estimated to be several hundred miles long. The column of insects was so dense that it blocked out the light of the sun.

The 17-year locust is a cicada. It belongs to the family Cicadidae, which has many species. The cicada was called a locust by early settlers of the United States, because the destruction caused during the swarming females resembled that caused during the locust plagues noted in the Bible. (*See also* Cicada.)

A typical North American locust, or grasshopper

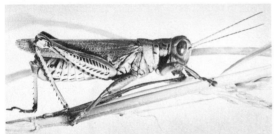

J. M. Conrader—National Audubon Society Collection/Photo Researchers

ŁÓDŹ, Poland. Located in central Poland, Łódź is the nation's second largest city and capital of Łódź province. It is also the center of the Polish motion picture industry and an art community.

Because Łódź developed mainly in the 19th century, it has a modern industrial appearance, characterized by a variety of workers' dwellings. With nearby towns it forms a major center of the nation's textile industry. The city produces more than 40 percent of Poland's cotton goods and processes wool, silk, and synthetic fibers. Agriculture, cattle breeding, electrical engineering, and the manufacture of wood, radio works, and chemical products are other regional industries. Lignite, or brown coal, is mined nearby. Łódź is also a transportation center on the Warsaw-Wrocław railroad line and has an airport. A notable educational center, Łódź houses six institutions of higher learning and maintains a scientific society and a number of research institutes. Łódź is a cultural center with several museums, music centers, theaters, and film studios.

The first recorded information about Łódź is from the 14th century, although the town did not receive municipal rights until 1798. It remained for a long time a small insignificant settlement that in 1820 had only 799 inhabitants. In that year the government made it a center for the textile industry. Foreign weavers and artisans were invited to settle there. Customs barriers that existed between Russia and the kingdom were lifted in 1850, and a great market for Łódź manufactures was opened. By the end of the 19th century, the city had become a leading textile and food-processing center. As a large industrial city, Łódź became a core of working-class movements and of the Polish Communists. Population (1982 estimate), 843,000.

LOG, SHIP'S. An instrument for measuring the speed of a ship through water is called a ship's, or maritime, log. The same word is also applied to the daily record of a ship or aircraft, though it is more properly termed a logbook.

Early Logs

In the years of sailing ships, the Dutchman's log was an early method of calculating ship speed. An object that would float was thrown into the water near the forward part of a ship. In the after, or rear, section, a sailor with a sandglass noted the time taken for the ship to pass the object floating in the water. From the time and the known distance between the two points on the ship, a rough calculation was made of the ship's speed.

The first really practical log was the chip log, a flat, quarter-circle piece of wood. A lead weight on the circular side of the piece, or chip, caused it to float upright and to resist towing. It was tossed overboard attached to a line having knots in it at known distances. The number of knots played out, correlated with a reading from a special sandglass, called a log glass, gave the ship's speed. The term knot, meaning one nautical mile per hour, comes from the knots in the log line.

A later version was the taffrail, or patent, log, which replaced the chip with a propellerlike rotator. Its revolutions were recorded, revealing both the distance covered and the speed at any given time.

Modern Logs

Modern ships use a Pitot-static log, which functions by sensing the difference between static and dynamic water pressures. Static pressure depends on the depth and density of the water; dynamic pressure is proportional to speed. Projecting through the bottom of the ship is a tube with a hole at its forward end to record the dynamic pressure and two other holes at right angles to record the static pressure. When the ship is motionless, the dynamic and static pressure are equal; when the ship moves, dynamic exceeds static. The difference varies as the square of the ship's speed. Aircraft airspeed indicators also operate on the Pitot-static principle (*see* Airplane, subhead "Flight Instruments").

Logbooks

Written accounts of voyages are kept in logbooks, or logs. Entries commonly include such navigational data as the ship's course, speed, and distance traveled as well as weather information. Carefully prepared logbooks may be sources for data used in preparing navigational charts. Dramatic stories of casualties and emergency operations have been found written in the sober language of the logbook.

LOGARITHM *see* INFORMATION THEORY.

LOGIC. One of the more complex disciplines associated with the field of philosophy is logic. The term comes from the Greek word *logos,* which has such a variety of meanings that it becomes difficult to give a precise definition of logic. Among the meanings of *logos* are "reason," "rule," "discourse," "sentence," "word," "ratio," "account," "rational principle," and "definition." Because of the number of possible interpretations, the subject matter of logic has variously been defined as "the laws of thought," "the rules of right reasoning," "the principles of valid argumentation," and "the study of truths (true statements) based solely on the terms they contain."

The last definition, and probably the least known one, implies the curious notion that the "facts" of logic need not necessarily coincide with the everyday realities of life. If a statement, or proposition, is analyzed solely within itself, the statement may be logically true even when contradicted by sense, experience, or knowledge. Or it may be logically true, even if the facts it presents are doubtful or uncertain. This is true because logic depends, first of all, on the ability to move from a premise to a conclusion based on the premise. As an example, the philosopher Aristotle used the following proposition as a simple, logical truth: "If sight is perception, the objects of sight are objects of perception." One can grasp the truth of the statement, regardless what opinions he holds about the relationship of sight and perception. This is a very simple "if-then" proposition. If, within its own terms only, the "if" statement is true, it follows that the "then" statement is true. The proposition is not intended to lead one to inquire into the nature of sight or perception but to demonstrate the process of correct reasoning. Thus even a seemingly ridiculous statement such as "If all animals are purple, then cows are purple," is correct in its reasoning.

Such a use of so-called true statements, without regard for the everyday realities, may seem frivolous and insignificant. In fact, such logic, which moves from premise to premise in a strict and logical sequence, is quite useful in the areas of computer science and mathematics. A computer will execute a program if the statements are in a prescribed order and correctly stated with regard to the capabilities of the computer. The statements themselves may be totally untrue in terms of factual knowledge, or they may be completely true. Among other things, this allows people who use computers to have them answer "what-if" sorts of problems. In mathematics virtually all argumentation is carried out in logical terms. The truth of a mathematical proposition has no necessary relation to the wider world of truth or knowledge. What matters is moving correctly from one premise to the next in precise, sequential order. Only in this way can the abstract statements of mathematics be demonstrated as true. The techniques used in mathematical logic have been adapted by other sciences, particularly physics, chemistry, and astronomy.

Kinds of Logic

The discipline of logic came into use many centuries ago as a branch of philosophy. It has since diversified to the extent that there are now several separate disciplines of logic. Principles of logic have found uses in the natural sciences, physical sciences, statistics, language studies, psychology, law, and education to name a few. In the social sciences, the logic used is borrowed from such fields as probability theory, game theory, utility theory, and operations research, all of which are highly complex areas of study.

The origins of logic, in both East and West, were first associated with an interest in the grammar of language and in the methods of argumentation and discussion in any field of interest, be it law, religion, philosophy, or science. Aristotle, in the 4th century BC, delineated two different types of logic—deductive reasoning and inductive reasoning—each with specific applications.

Deductive reasoning. When a person uses either a general principle or a collection of specific data to draw a specific conclusion, he is using deductive reasoning. A deductive argument is frequently stated in the form of a syllogism. A syllogism consists of three parts: the major premise, the minor premise, and the conclusion. The following example shows the order of the parts:

All men are mortal;
Socrates is a man;
Therefore Socrates is mortal.

Broken down in this way, an argument is far easier to test for fallacies, or errors, than when stated in ordinary conversational form. The conclusion must be valid if the premises are true—true in their own terms, not necessarily in relation to the truth of the world at large.

Inductive reasoning. When a person uses a number of established facts to draw a general conclusion, he uses inductive reasoning. This is the kind of logic normally used in the sciences. For example, a scientist may gather all the facts he can about a certain disease from observation and experiment. Then he draws his inductive conclusion, perhaps that a certain microbe causes the disease. An inductive argument, however, is never final. It is always open to the possibility of being falsified. For instance, the observation of swans over the centuries has led to the conclusion that all swans are white. The discovery of one black swan would falsify this theory, but it would still be true that most swans are white. Inductive reasoning is always subject to revision if new facts are discovered. It is by this process of induction and falsification that progress is made in the sciences.

LOIRE RIVER. The longest river in France, the Loire runs a course of 634 miles (1,020 kilometers). The Loire rises in southeastern France, only 85 miles (137 kilometers) north of the Mediterranean Sea, and flows northward for about half its course. Then it sweeps with a great curve to the southwest and flows into the Atlantic Ocean near Nantes.

The Loire rises in a spur of the Cévennes range some 4,500 feet (1,370 meters) above sea level. Its racing headwaters are fed by melting snows from mountain peaks. Below the mountains it flows through the fertile lowlands of the Paris Basin and the coastal plain.

The Loire Valley is a chief agricultural region of France. Its uplands produce rye and buckwheat, and its great bend near Orléans supports dairying and grazing. Broad stretches of the valley are planted with vegetables and fruit, especially grapes.

The Loire is of little use for navigation, but canals have been built through its valley and connect its estuary with the Seine and the Saône. The scenery along the Loire is very rural, and the castles (*châteaux*) and parks along its course recall the faded glory of the life and landscape of centuries past.

LOMBARDI, Vince (1913–70). An American professional football coach, Vince Lombardi became a national symbol of determination to win. In nine seasons, from 1959 to 1967, he led Wisconsin's Green Bay Packers to five championships of the National Football League (NFL) and, in the last two seasons, to victory in the first two Super Bowl games.

Vincent Thomas Lombardi was born in Brooklyn, in New York City, on June 11, 1913. He attended Fordham University in New York City, where he was a lineman on the football team. After completing his undergraduate education in 1937, he studied law, played minor league professional football briefly, and then in 1939 became an assistant high-school football coach. He then became an assistant coach at Fordham, the United States Military Academy at West Point, and with the NFL New York Giants. He became head coach and general manager of the Packers in 1959, immediately imposing an unusually strict (some called it fanatical) regimen on the players, who had been almost constant losers. In Lombardi's second year, Green Bay led the Western Conference of the NFL. They won the league championship in the 1961, 1962, 1965, 1966, and 1967 seasons, and defeated Kansas City and then Oakland in the Super Bowl games following the 1966 and 1967 seasons.

In 1969 Lombardi left Green Bay and went to the Washington Redskins as head coach and executive vice-president, leading them to their first winning season in 14 years. He died of cancer on Sept. 3, 1970, in Washington, D.C.

LOMBARDS. The most productive region of Italy is Lombardy, the great fertile valley of the Po River. It takes its name from the barbarian Lombard hordes who overran it in the 6th century. These people were the last Germanic invaders of Italy. They pressed down from the north in AD 568 within 15 years after the emperor Justinian had expelled the East Goths. The Lombards soon held most of the peninsula, though Rome, Ravenna, and a few other fortified cities successfully resisted their attack. But the Lombards failed to establish a strong central government. Many small dukedoms grew up and cut Italy into small divisions.

The Lombard kingdom was overthrown in 773 by Charlemagne, who invaded Italy at the request of the pope and dethroned the king. Charlemagne was crowned with an "iron crown," so called because beneath the gold was a circlet of iron, said to be made from one of the nails with which Christ was crucified. After the breakup of Charlemagne's empire the Lombards gradually merged with the other peoples of northern Italy.

LONDON, Jack (1876–1916). The novelist and short-story writer Jack London was, in his lifetime, one of the most popular authors in the world. After World War I his fame was eclipsed in the United States by a new generation of writers, but he remained popular in many other countries, especially in the Soviet Union, for his romantic tales of adventure and survival.

John Griffith London was born in San Francisco on Jan. 12, 1876. His family was poor, and he was forced to go to work early in life to support himself. At 17 he sailed to Japan and Siberia on a seal-hunting voyage. He was largely self-taught, reading voluminously in libraries and spending a year at the University of California. In the late 1890s he joined the gold rush to the Klondike. This experience gave him material for his first book, 'The Son of Wolf', published in 1900, and for 'Call of the Wild' (1903), one of his most popular stories.

In his writing career of 17 years, London produced 50 books and many short stories. He wrote mostly for money, to meet ever-increasing expenses. His fame as a writer gave him a ready audience as a spokesman for a peculiar and inconsistent blend of socialism and racial superiority.

London's works, all hastily written, are of uneven quality. The best books are the Klondike tales, which also include 'White Fang' (1906) and 'Burning Daylight' (1910). His most enduring novel is probably the autobiographical 'Martin Eden' (1909), but the exciting 'Sea Wolf' (1904) continues to have great appeal for young readers.

In 1910 London settled near Glen Ellen, Calif., where he intended to build his dream home, "Wolf House." After the house burned down before completion in 1913, he was a broken and sick man. His death on Nov. 22, 1916, from an overdose of drugs, was probably a suicide.

A broad pedestrian promenade rims the Royal Festival Hall, the center of a music and arts complex that extends along the south bank of the Thames River. The world's great orchestras and ballet troupes appear at the hall, which offers about 450 performances each year.

FPG

LONDON, England.

London is the capital of the United Kingdom and the mother city of the Commonwealth of Nations. It is the seat of one of the world's oldest parliamentary governments, yet it retains all the pomp and ceremony of a medieval kingdom. It is a great industrial city, an international center of finance, and a huge port. Greater London is one of the world's largest metropolitan areas.

The visitor to London usually sees little of its great port and factories. He is more interested in its historic palaces and churches, which link the present with the past. Even the streets of London are memorable. They are well-known through English fiction and biographies of great men of the past who lived and walked on them.

London owes its rise to its location on the Thames River near its mouth on the North Sea (*see* Thames River). This river is the outlet for the English plain and the chief gateway into England from the continent of Europe. When the Romans occupied England—in the 1st century AD—there was already a village on Lud Hill, about 60 miles above the Thames's mouth. Below this point the shores were swampy. At Lud Hill was firm ground on which ships could unload. Here also was the farthest downstream point at which the river could be easily crossed. On Lud Hill the Romans built Londinium, "the City," and ringed it with massive walls reaching down to the Thames. They also built the first London Bridge and laid six roads radiating north and south from it. The City was soon crowded with merchants dealing in tin, cattle, hides, and slaves.

About a mile west of the old walled City of London there grew up on the Thames the City of Westminster. Here the king lived and Parliament met, and here also was Westminster Abbey, the coronation church. The riverside street between the two cities—called the Strand (shore)—became lined with palaces and gardens. Houses spread over the high ground north of the Thames and later over the low ground in Southwark, at the south end of London Bridge.

The City of London became the home of great craft and merchant companies (*see* Guilds). It preserved a degree of independence from the king in Westminster and jealously guarded its privileges. William the Conqueror was compelled to treat with it as with a separate state. He built a strong fortress—the famous Tower of London—to overawe its citizens, but he had to place it outside the city walls.

Throughout the Middle Ages the City kept within the Roman wall. Only a remnant of that wall remains today, but the names of its gates survive in such streets as Newgate, Aldgate, Cripplegate, and Ludgate, as well as in the fish market of Billingsgate. Gradually the City spread west to Temple Bar, at the eastern end of the Strand.

In 1664 and 1665 the Great Plague struck the city and killed 75,000 people. The next year the Great Fire destroyed the City. London quickly recovered from the damage of both calamities. Sir Christopher Wren, genius of church architecture, rebuilt many of the City's ancient churches. His masterpiece is the new St. Paul's Cathedral on Ludgate Hill (the ancient Lud Hill). The dome of this great church is still one of the highest points in London.

In the 18th century London grew from 500,000 to 1 million inhabitants. In the 19th century it became the largest and wealthiest city in the world. Beautiful homes spread over the West End, the area around

Westminster. The old City became a world center of finance. Up the muddy waters of the Thames came ships of all nations, with all kinds of cargo. Most English railways made London their terminal. Highways also radiated from it in all directions. While London owes its importance principally to commerce, it is also a great manufacturing center, turning out clothing, foodstuffs, furniture, machinery, and miscellaneous products.

In World War II London suffered heavily from bombing. From August 1940 to May 1941, German bombers came over night after night. The heaviest attack took place on Dec. 29, 1940, when incendiary bombs ignited London's second Great Fire. In 1944 came the deadly V-bombs, launched from German bases in France. Many Londoners slept in subway stations. Thousands were killed. In the mile-square City, 134 acres were leveled.

Streets, Squares, and Houses

As London grew, it swallowed up more than a hundred towns, villages, and parishes. Many of these communities retained their names and their individual character, along with their irregular street systems. The main east-west thoroughfares follow the windings of the Thames. Others cut across them, making a beeline for one of London's 15 bridges. A wide boulevard, called the Embankment, now borders the north bank of the Thames, hiding London's historic waterfront street, the Strand.

The clay soil made difficult the construction of tall buildings, and the development of transportation encouraged the growth of suburbs. London therefore spread out horizontally and now covers an area about

The Nelson Monument towers high above Trafalgar Square, a famed traffic center and meeting place in the heart of London. St. Martin's-in-the-Fields, a famous 18th-century church, stands to the right.

half the size of Rhode Island. Even in central London most of the buildings are less than six stories high. Blocks of apartment houses are beginning to replace private dwellings; however, the typical London street is still lined with narrow-fronted stone or brick residences that date back to the 18th or 19th

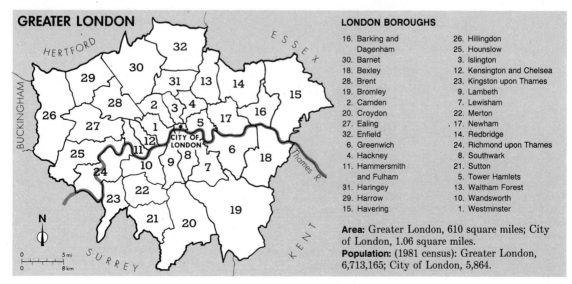

GREATER LONDON

HERTFORD
ESSEX
BUCKINGHAM
SURREY
KENT
Thames R.

N
0 5 mi
0 8 km

LONDON BOROUGHS

16.	Barking and Dagenham	
30.	Barnet	
18.	Bexley	
28.	Brent	
19.	Bromley	
2.	Camden	
20.	Croydon	
27.	Ealing	
32.	Enfield	
6.	Greenwich	
4.	Hackney	
11.	Hammersmith and Fulham	
31.	Haringey	
29.	Harrow	
15.	Havering	

26.	Hillingdon
25.	Hounslow
3.	Islington
12.	Kensington and Chelsea
23.	Kingston upon Thames
9.	Lambeth
7.	Lewisham
22.	Merton
17.	Newham
14.	Redbridge
24.	Richmond upon Thames
8.	Southwark
21.	Sutton
5.	Tower Hamlets
13.	Waltham Forest
10.	Wandsworth
1.	Westminster

Area: Greater London, 610 square miles; City of London, 1.06 square miles.
Population: (1981 census): Greater London, 6,713,165; City of London, 5,864.

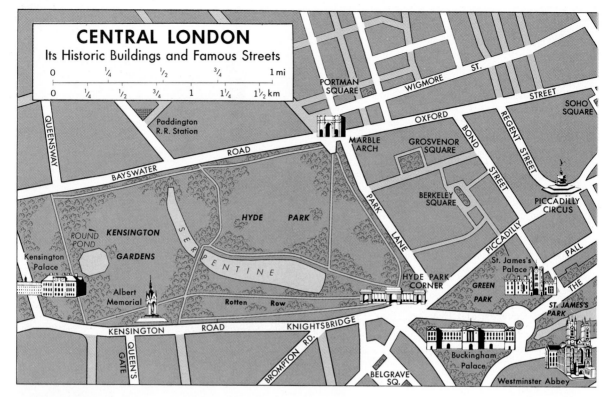

CENTRAL LONDON
Its Historic Buildings and Famous Streets

century. The houses gain in impressiveness by being built in an unbroken row. From every roof rises a cluster of chimney pots. Each chimney pot is the flue of an open fireplace that heats a single room.

The Londoner is seldom far from grass and flowers. Scattered over the city—particularly in the West End—are great parks and dozens of small green squares. The parks are open to the public, but the squares belong to residents of the district and are private.

The open spaces where several streets come together are also called squares, or sometimes circuses. They may be any shape. (Piccadilly Circus is almost a triangle.) When a thoroughfare crosses a square it usually changes its name. Most of London's best-known streets are therefore less than a mile long.

Charing Cross and Trafalgar Square

The center of London is usually regarded as Charing Cross, a small traffic square near the river. Here, until 1647, stood one of the 13 crosses erected in 1291 by Edward I to his queen, Eleanor, marking the stopping places in her funeral procession. A line north from Charing Cross roughly divides the residential West End from the commercial East End.

On the north, Charing Cross opens into Trafalgar Square, named for Lord Nelson's great naval victory (*see* Nelson). From the double open space formed by these two squares, important streets radiate in all directions. Here one may board a bright red two-story bus for any part of London; and here also are three stations of London's extensive subway system, called the Underground. The older subway lines are

shallow and brick-lined. The newer "tubes" are deep metal-lined tunnels.

The Strand Leads to the City

From Charing Cross the wide Strand runs northeast to the old City of London, following the line of the river. This short thoroughfare was once the center of London's night life, and it still has many theaters and restaurants as well as office buildings. Just north of the Strand, on Drury Lane, is the Drury Lane Theater, long famous as the home of drama. Near it, on Bow Street (which runs in the shape of a bent bow), stands Covent Garden, the huge Royal Opera House built more than 200 years ago. The theater takes its name from a space nearby, which was once a quiet garden that belonged to Westminster Abbey. Shops, restaurants, and pubs now occupy this space.

The Strand ends at Temple Bar and enters the City as Fleet Street. In old times Temple Bar was actually a stout wooden bar placed across the street to keep the king and his followers out of the City of London. The last barrier was removed in 1787.

The Temple and Fleet Street

Temple Bar takes its name from the Temple, which lies between Fleet Street and the Embankment. The entrance is a gateway designed by Wren. Inside is a quiet courtyard that takes us back to the Middle Ages. Then the Temple was the headquarters of the Knights Templars, a military religious order dedicated to the protection of the Holy Sepulchre. The Temple Church, dating from the 12th century, is one

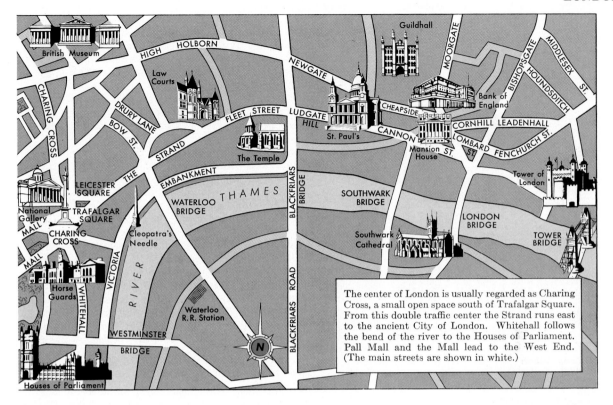

The center of London is usually regarded as Charing Cross, a small open space south of Trafalgar Square. From this double traffic center the Strand runs east to the ancient City of London. Whitehall follows the bend of the river to the Houses of Parliament. Pall Mall and the Mall lead to the West End. (The main streets are shown in white.)

of the finest ancient "round" churches of England.

The Temple has long been part of "legal London." The Inner Temple and the Middle Temple are two of London's "inns of court," which serve as universities for law students. They are called inns because they once furnished permanent residence for their members. They still include dining halls, libraries, chapels, and gardens as well as offices of leading lawyers. The other two inns of court—Lincoln's Inn Fields and Gray's Inn—lie north of Fleet Street. They are reached by Chancery Lane, a curving street on which many lawyers have their offices.

Fleet Street, a narrow, busy thoroughfare, was named for Fleet River (now a sewer). Here newspapers have had their headquarters since newspapers began. On the street are the offices of great London dailies. Printing is done in the maze of small courts and alleys on either side.

St. Paul's and the Bells of Bow

Fleet Street ends at Ludgate Circus, where the east-west thoroughfare changes its name to Ludgate Hill. This short street leads up to St. Paul's Cathedral, the "parish church" of the British Commonwealth and the cathedral of the bishop of London. The church is in the form of a Latin cross, 515 feet in length and 250 feet across the two arms (transepts). The diameter of the dome is 102 feet. The cross on top of the dome is 366 feet above the pavement. The vast interior is crowded with monuments, chiefly of naval and military officers. Tombs lie in the crypt below. In the center of the crypt is the tomb of Admiral Nelson, Britain's great naval hero.

From St. Paul's, Cheapside runs east to the "Wall Street" section of the City. This area suffered heavily in World War II and many of its famous old guildhalls were destroyed. Wren's Bow Church (St. Mary-le-Bow) and its famous bells were badly damaged. According to an old story, the bells called back Dick Whittington to be three times lord mayor of London. Anyone born within the sound of the Bow Bells was said to be a true Cockney—that is, a real Londoner. The bells were restored in 1961.

The Bank of England

Cheapside, after changing its name to Poultry, leads to a small triangular "square" where eight streets meet. Facing this square stands the Bank of England, "the Old Lady of Threadneedle Street." Low, solid, and windowless (for greater security), the bank covers four acres. For centuries it has served the central banks of other countries throughout the world. Though nationalized by the government (in 1946), it still keeps its traditions. Its messengers are known by their pink tail coats and scarlet waistcoats.

East of tho bank is the Stock Exchange and close by, on Leadenhall and Lime Streets, is Lloyd's, the world's largest and most famous insurance company. Lloyd's specializes in marine insurance, but it will insure against almost any calamity except death.

The Lord Mayor of the Mile-Square City

Across from the bank stands Mansion House, the residence of the lord mayor, chief magistrate of the

Perfecta Publications Ltd.; Photograph, Sydney W. Newbery

St. Paul's Cathedral, considered the greatest work of the architect Christopher Wren, escaped serious damage in the second World War when nearby buildings were destroyed.

City of London. The lord mayor is elected yearly by the guilds and corporations of the City, some of which date back to the Middle Ages. The election takes place in the nearby Guildhall, a magnificent 15th-century building. After his election, tradition decrees that the lord mayor must present himself for royal approval. On November 9 he sets out in his lavishly carved and gilded coach, drawn by six horses, to the law courts in the Strand to take his oath before the lord chief justice. The citizens show their approval of their new mayor by accompanying him in gaily decorated trucks or horse-drawn carts. The mayor is always approved. Then he returns to the Guildhall for a banquet that is usually attended by the prime minister and his cabinet.

The king or queen still may not enter the City without permission of the lord mayor. Whenever the sovereign wishes to come, the lord mayor meets him at one of the gates—usually Temple Bar—and hands over a ponderous "key to the City" to open an imaginary gate. Then the sovereign enters and is welcomed by cheering crowds.

The Tower of London

Just east of the City, on the Thames, stands the Tower of London. The ancient fortress is England's most famous historic monument. For centuries it served as a state prison. It is now a museum; but visitors are drawn to it chiefly by the memories it evokes of illustrious prisoners who were confined or executed here.

The Tower of London covers 13 acres and has all the parts of a medieval castle (*see* Castle). The moat, formerly fed by the Thames, is now dry. Inside the moat an outer wall encloses a narrow outer ward. From the inner wall 13 towers rise at intervals. This inner wall surrounds the inner ward, or "bail." In the center stands the White Tower, or Keep, the oldest part of the fortress, which was begun by William the Conqueror in 1078. It is now a museum, in which are displayed old arms, armor, and instruments of torture.

In the outer wall, facing the Thames, is Traitors' Gate, through which state prisoners, brought by way of the river from Westminster, were conveyed to the Tower. Beauchamp Tower, in the west wall, was long the principal prison for persons of rank, but the Bell Tower, the Bloody Tower, the Salt Tower, and the Broad Arrow Tower also have dungeons and other prison chambers in which historic personages were confined. Executions took place both within the Tower and outside the walls on Tower Hill. Many of those executed were buried in the Tower chapel. They included Sir Thomas More; Anne Boleyn; Catherine Howard; and Lady Jane Grey and her husband, Guildford Dudley. Elizabeth I, when a princess, was a prisoner here. Here also Sir Walter Raleigh wrote a history of the world while awaiting his tragic end.

The Crown Jewels

In Wakefield Tower, close to Traitors' Gate, the public may view, glittering under bright lights, the crown jewels, or regalia, of Great Britain. The coronation crown, made for Charles II in 1662, is a copy

Another famous Wren church, St. Clement Danes in the Strand, was badly damaged during World War II. It is part of the rhyme, "Oranges and lemons, say the bells of St. Clement's."

Ewing Galloway

The Houses of Parliament (center) overlook the Thames. The church is Westminster Abbey. In the foreground is Parliament Street, the lower end of Whitehall, lined with government offices. Across the river is London County Hall.

of the ancient crown of Edward the Confessor, which was destroyed by Cromwell. The imperial state crown, made for Victoria's coronation, contains more than 2,700 diamonds, 300 pearls, and the Black Prince's ruby, which is almost as large as a hen's egg.

The yeoman warders who guard the Tower and its collection of valuables are familiarly known as "beef-eaters." They wear colorful doublets, or jackets, and knee breeches, a quaint costume that dates from Tudor times. They are all old soldiers, honorary members of the Yeomen of the Guard.

Whitehall—Heart of the Commonwealth

From Charing Cross, a short, wide street, called Whitehall, follows a bend in the Thames south to the Houses of Parliament. At the north end of Whitehall are the War Office, the Admiralty, the Scottish Office, and the Treasury. Around the corner from the Treasury is No. 10 Downing Street, the modest official residence of the British prime minister. At the south end, called Parliament Street, are huge blocks of government buildings. In the center of Whitehall rises the Cenotaph, a simple square shaft of stone commemorating the "glorious dead" of two world wars.

Whitehall takes its name from the royal palace of Whitehall, formerly the residence of the sovereign. The palace's main buildings burned down in 1698 except for the Banqueting House. This building, erected by Inigo Jones in 1622, houses the Royal United Service Museum. (For picture, see Architecture.)

Opposite the Banqueting House stands the Horse Guards, once a guardhouse for Whitehall Palace and now a military headquarters. Two troopers, in huge sentry boxes, guard the passage to the Horse Guards Parade, a wide graveled space. Every morning a small crowd gathers to watch the half-hour ceremony of the Changing of the Guard. A more elaborate ceremony, Trooping the Color, takes place here on the sovereign's official birthday.

Old Scotland Yard, a short street running east from the north end of Whitehall, was the site of a palace in which the Scottish kings lived when in London. In 1829

Ewing Galloway

No. 10 Downing Street, a modest house on a narrow street, has long been the official residence of British prime ministers.

291

the street became the headquarters of the Metropolitan Police. In 1890 "Scotland Yard" was moved to new buildings, called New Scotland Yard, on the Embankment. In 1967 it moved again, into new quarters on Victoria Street near Westminster Abbey.

Parliament and Westminster Abbey

Parliament Street, at the south end of Whitehall, opens into Parliament Square, one of London's busiest traffic whirlpools. Westminster Abbey and the Houses of Parliament (on the Thames) face this square.

The official name of the Houses of Parliament is the New Palace of Westminster. The old Palace of Westminster was destroyed by fire in 1834 except for Westminster Hall. This beautiful building was the seat of the chief English law courts after the 13th century. Here Richard II was deposed, and here Charles I was condemned to death. Westminster Hall now serves as a spacious vestibule to the Houses of Parliament.

Parliament's "new palace," completed in 1850, was designed by Sir Charles Barry. It covers eight acres and has 1,100 rooms and two miles of passages. The House of Lords is in the southern half. The chamber of the House of Commons, in the northern half, was destroyed during World War II and rebuilt after the war with little change (*see* Parliament, British).

At the north end of the Parliament building rises the Clock Tower, 320 feet high. This is the home of the great bell called Big Ben. The bell weighs 13½ tons; it is 7½ feet high and 9 feet in diameter at its mouth. It was cast in 1858 to replace an earlier bell that cracked (1852) while being tested. The present bell also cracked shortly after it was hung, causing a shrill note, but after the crack had been filed open and smoothed the tone became quite pure. The note is E sharp. The great bell, which rings the hours, is flanked by smaller bells that ring the quarter hours. Big Ben takes its name from Sir Benjamin Hall, who had charge of the work on the first bell. The name is also commonly applied to the tower clock. This has four faces, one on each side of the tower, with dials 23 feet in diameter.

Westminster Abbey, a great Gothic church, is the most historic building in the West End. Here England's kings and queens are crowned and some are buried; and here are tombs, monuments, and tablets commemorating statesmen and priests, scientists and artists, warriors and poets. A slab in the floor marks the tomb of an Unknown Warrior of the first World War. (*See also* Westminster Abbey.)

From Westminster Abbey, Victoria Street leads west to Westminster Cathedral, near the Victoria station. Westminster Cathedral is the most important Roman Catholic church in England. Erected in 1895–1903, it is a huge edifice in Christian Byzantine style.

London's Parks and Palaces

From Charing Cross the Mall runs southwest to Buckingham Palace, the residence of the royal family. The Mall is a wide, tree-lined avenue, about a mile long, used for ceremonial processions. At the Charing Cross end stands Admiralty Arch. In front of Buckingham Palace rises the Queen Victoria Memorial, a white marble statuary group.

On the south side of the Mall is St. James's Park, noted for the ornamental waterfowl on its five-acre lake. On the north side of the Mall stand two palaces. Marlborough House was turned over to the government by Elizabeth II for use as a Commonwealth meeting place. St. James's was the royal residence from the time Whitehall burned down (1698) to the accession of Queen Victoria. It is now set aside for conferences and court functions. The British court is still officially known as the Court of St. James's.

Buckingham Palace, once the residence of the duke of Buckingham, was purchased by George III and rebuilt by John Nash before Queen Victoria chose it for her home in 1837. When the sovereign is in residence the guard at the entrance is changed every day at 10:30 A.M., while a guard's band plays. The palace and its 40-acre gardens are not open to the public. Constitution Hill, a beautiful avenue, runs between the palace

The Poets' Corner in Westminster Abbey honors some of England's literary figures. At left, next to the bust of Henry Wadsworth Longfellow, is Geoffrey Chaucer's tomb. Edmund Spenser is also buried there. Tombs and memorials have overflowed from the original Poets' Corner into the abbey's central aisle.

gardens and Green Park, on the north.

Constitution Hill ends with a great arch at Hyde Park Corner, London's busiest traffic center. On the north side of Hyde Park Corner stands a triple archway that is the principal entrance to Hyde Park.

Hyde Park was once a royal pleasure and hunting ground. After it was opened to the public, crowds used to gather to watch people of fashion ride on horseback or in elegant carriages around the Ring and along Rotten Row. Today the crowds gather near Marble Arch, at the northeast corner of the park, where impromptu orators speak freely on almost every subject.

Only a driveway separates Hyde Park from Kensington Gardens, to the west. Together they form a continuous park of over 600 acres. Kensington Gardens was once the private gardens of Kensington Palace, which stands at the west end of the park.

J. Allan Cash

Buckingham Palace has been the London residence of the reigning monarch of England since Victoria became queen in 1837. Westminster, Whitehall, and St. James's palaces were London homes of England's monarchs in earlier years.

Streets and Districts of the West End

East of Hyde Park lies Mayfair, the traditional home of the English aristocracy. Its western boundary, Park Lane, faces the park. The eastern boundary is Bond Street, famous for its fine shops. Near Bond Street is Savile Row, street of fashionable tailors. High income taxes have driven out many of the former residents of Mayfair. Their stately mansions are being replaced by hotels, shops, and business offices.

Piccadilly, a world-famous street about a mile long, bounds Mayfair on the south. At its western end luxurious clubs overlook Green Park. Farther east are fashionable shops and hotels. Piccadilly ends at Piccadilly Circus, the center of London for the pleasure seeker. To the east is Leicester Square, heart of the theater district. To the north lies Soho, a foreign island in the West End, famous for its restaurants—French, Italian, Spanish, and Chinese.

Mayfair and Soho extend north to Oxford Street, a main east-west thoroughfare, lined with shops and department stores. North of Oxford Street is Bloomsbury, London's intellectual center, site of the British Museum and of the University of London.

South of Mayfair, between Piccadilly and Pall Mall, is a small district called St. James's, after the palace. This is the traditional home of the wealthy bachelor and the center of London's famous clubs, which have played an important part in English social and political life. Pall Mall, lined with palatial clubs, is one of London's finest streets. Both Pall Mall and the Mall take their names from the old French game "paille maille," a kind of croquet, played here in the 17th century.

Belgravia, another fashionable district, lies south of Hyde Park. On the river is Pimlico, a busy working-class neighborhood. West of Kensington Gardens is the well-to-do residential district of Kensington. Chelsea spreads west from Pimlico along the river. It is a charming residential district, the home of artists and writers since the 16th century.

Museums, Art Galleries, and Universities

The British Museum at Bloomsbury is the oldest of national museums and is unrivaled for the richness and variety of its collections. Its exhibits represent the art of all ages. Among its most famous treasures are the beautiful sculptures called the Elgin marbles, which once adorned the Parthenon and other temples in Athens. The museum contains also one of the world's largest libraries.

The National Gallery, on Trafalgar Square, aims to cover the whole range of classical European painting. Here all the important old masters are represented, many of them in great works. Part of the collection is housed in the Tate Gallery, on the Thames, north of the Houses of Parliament. This gallery was originally intended to show only British art, but its scope has been widened, and it is now the National Gallery of British Paintings and of Modern Foreign Art.

The National Portrait Gallery adjoins the National Gallery. Here one may see how the nation's famous men and women looked. Portraits are chosen on the basis of genuine likeness rather than for artistic merit.

In Kensington is the vast Victoria and Albert Museum. It is concerned with arts and crafts of all

293

A winged statue of Eros rises above Piccadilly Circus, the famous hub of entertainment, shopping, and traffic located in the West End of London. Several of the city's major streets—including Piccadilly, Regent, and Shaftsbury—converge at the popular site.

The British Tourist Authority

peoples. Furniture, embroidery, jewels, miniatures, ceramics, and textiles of various periods are displayed. Also in Kensington are the Natural History Museum and the Science Museum.

The headquarters of the University of London is near the British Museum. This university administers more than 60 colleges, specialized schools, and departments scattered over Greater London. The best known of these are University College and King's College.

The East End and the Surrey Side

East of the City and the Tower spreads the East End. It has more slums than any other part of London. The district suffered heavily from bombing in World War II, and rebuilding has been extensive. Back from the wide main thoroughfares are narrow, twisting alleys lined with rows of attached boxlike little houses, each with a door and window on the ground floor and two windows above. The newer buildings are blocks of flats. Whitechapel, one of London's oldest slum districts, is the hub of the clothing industry. Along the waterfront, the life and activity of the people center on the docks. The waterside district of Limehouse, London's Chinatown, once notorious, is now quiet and respectable.

London south of the Thames—the Surrey side—is largely industrial and offers little of historic interest to the tourist. Facing the Houses of Parliament, in Lambeth, is Lambeth Palace, the London residence of the archbishop of Canterbury. Near it, at the end of Westminster Bridge, stands the huge building of the Greater London Council, which governs Greater London. Close to the south end of London Bridge stands Southwark Cathedral, one of London's oldest churches. Southwark was the center of stage life in Shakespeare's time. Now it is an area of drab streets. Theatergoers, however, still go to the Surrey side to see classic drama in the Old Vic repertory theater. This theater stands opposite Waterloo station, the largest railway station in England.

A little farther down the river is the borough of Greenwich. Through the Old Royal Observatory at Greenwich runs the meridian from which longitude and standard time zones are reckoned around the world. The borough's National Maritime Museum contains portraits and relics of England's great seamen. There also is the Royal Naval College, formerly Greenwich Hospital, a complex largely designed by Sir Christopher Wren and opened in 1705.

The Port of London

The Port of London extends 94 miles (151 kilometers) along the Thames River, from its mouth on the North Sea upstream to Teddington, where a dam and lock block further inland penetration by normal tides. Downstream 8 miles (13 kilometers) from London at Woolwich is a floodgate that can be raised when London is threatened with flooding from especially high North Sea tides. There are three enclosed dock systems owned and operated by the Port of London Authority, the main one being the Tilbury Docks, downstream 26 miles (42 kilometers) from the London Bridge. The Tilbury Docks are the largest port facility in the United Kingdom and have a wide range of modern facilities.

The two central London dock facilities—the West India and Milwall Docks and the Royal Docks—have been largely phased out and are being redeveloped for residential, office, and store space. West India, the first commercial dock, was constructed in the 19th century. Before then ships moored midstream in the river and depended on smaller boats to transfer their cargoes to shore. Large oceangoing ships, once a common sight in the Upper and Lower Pools (widenings of the river) downstream from the London Bridge, are now rarely seen upstream as far as London. Pleasure boats regularly ply the Thames, offering views of historic and scenic sites and passing under the 28 bridges spanning the Thames from Teddington Lock to the Tower Bridge. The Woolwich Free Ferry, dating back to the 14th century, provides the last regular ferry service of the several hundred that once crossed the Thames.

BIBLIOGRAPHY FOR LONDON

Clout, H. D. Changing London (State Mutual Book, 1981).
De Mare, Eric. London's River: the Story of a City (Merrimack, 1978).
Menen, Aubrey. London (Time-Life, 1976).
Newman, Robert. The Case of the Baker Street Irregular (Atheneum, 1978).
Williams, Guy. London Walks (State Mutual Book, 1981).

LONDON, Ont. Like the famous city of England from which it takes its name, London, Ont., is situated on a river named the Thames. The Canadian city is in southeastern Ontario—115 miles (185 kilometers) southwest of Toronto and 23 miles (37 kilometers) north of Port Stanley, a harbor on Lake Erie.

Lieutenant governor John Graves Simcoe in 1792 chose this location as the future capital of Upper Canada. His plans went awry, however, and no building was completed until 1826. When London was made the judicial center of the district soon after 1826, its growth was rapid. In 1854 it became a city.

London is now the financial, industrial, marketing, and distributing center for a rich and thickly settled agricultural section. Electric power from Niagara Falls adds to the city's advantages as a manufacturing center. Among its products are diesel locomotives, electrical equipment, chemicals, brass goods, iron, steel, textiles, and paper boxes.

The University of Western Ontario, founded in 1878, is in London. There is also a provincial teachers college. The city is also the seat of Middlesex County. (*See also* Ontario.) Population (1981 census), 254,280.

LONG, Crawford W. (1815–1878). On March 30, 1842, Dr. Crawford W. Long, a young surgeon of Jefferson, Ga., performed the first recorded operation on an anesthetized patient. He administered sulfuric ether before removing a tumor from the neck of James Venable, who felt no pain during the surgery. Long did not make his work public until 1849, after he had used ether in more surgery. Meanwhile the benefits of surgical anesthesia had been proved by others, and Long's delay in reporting his discovery kept him for many years from being recognized as the pioneer anesthetist.

Crawford Williamson Long was born on Nov. 1, 1815, in Danielsville, Ga. He entered Franklin College (now the University of Georgia) at the age of 14 and got his medical degree at the University of Pennsylvania in 1839.

Long's discovery of anesthesia was made as the result of a prank. A few weeks before the famous operation, some of the surgeon's young friends saw a traveling medicine vendor demonstrate a new curiosity, laughing gas (nitrous oxide). Volunteers who inhaled this gas felt extremely exhilarated. Long's friends then asked him for permission to hold a "nitrous oxide frolic" in his room. Since he had no nitrous oxide, he gave them ether. Excited by the gas, the young men became hilariously rowdy and pommeled one another severely. Long noticed that none of them seemed to feel pain. He decided to experiment with ether in his surgical work.

After his achievement Long continued to live the quiet life of a country doctor. In 1850 he moved to Athens, Ga., where he died on June 16, 1878.

LONG, Huey (1893–1935). A flamboyant governor of the state of Louisiana, Huey Long was also a United States senator whose social reforms and radical welfare proposals were ultimately overshadowed by his demagoguery. With the slogan "Every man a king," he gained the nickname "Kingfish."

Huey Pierce Long was born on Aug. 30, 1893, near Winnfield, La. A farm boy with little formal schooling, he managed to pass the state bar examination, becoming a lawyer in 1915. Politically ambitious, he was elected to the state railroad commission at the age of 25 and at 35 won the governorship through the heavy support of the rural districts. Louisiana benefited from his ambitious programs of public works, welfare legislation, improved highways, and expanded educational facilities. Opposed to excessive privileges for the rich, he financed these programs with increased inheritance and income taxes.

Long's folksy manner and sympathy for poor whites masked his ruthless quest for power. Surrounding himself with gangster-like bodyguards, he intimidated members of the legislature and, as both governor and senator, achieved absolute control of state functions. Elected to the United States Senate in 1930, he did not resign as governor until a handpicked successor was chosen in 1932. In 1934 he sought national power with a Share-the-Wealth Society. Long was assassinated on Sept. 10, 1935, in Baton Rouge, La., by Dr. Carl A. Weiss, the son of a political enemy.

LONG BEACH, Calif. Because of farsighted industrial and civic planning and the discovery of large petroleum fields, Long Beach has grown from a small fishing village and seaside resort into one of California's chief cities. It lies 20 miles (32 kilometers) south of Los Angeles on a strip of coastal plain between San Pedro Bay and the snow-crested Sierra Madre mountain range. The city is built on a terrace along miles of white bathing beaches, making it a favorite ocean resort. In its "backyard," however, are thousands of oil derricks.

Petroleum was discovered on nearby Signal Hill in 1921, and again along the shore in 1940. The Los Angeles-Long Beach Harbor is one of the greatest on the coast. It has two ports, one operated by Los Angeles, the other by Long Beach.

The great oil fields and the fine harbor have attracted many industries. They include refineries; aeronautical, shipbuilding, and automobile plants; food processing plants; and marine research and offshore drilling facilities.

Long Beach was founded in 1881 by W. E. Willmore, an Englishman, and named Willmore City. It was incorporated under its present name in 1888. The city has a council-manager form of government. (*See also* California.) Population (1980 census), 361,334.

LONGFELLOW, Henry Wadsworth (1807–82).

Probably the best loved American poet the world over is Henry Wadsworth Longfellow. He was among the first American writers to use native themes. In such memorable works as 'The Song of Hiawatha', 'Evangeline', and 'The Courtship of Miles Standish', he wrote about the American scene and landscape.

The early American settlers had concentrated on carving a place to live out of the wilderness. Their literature, painting, and music came mainly from Europe, especially from England. But the "flowering of New England," as critic Van Wyck Brooks termed the period from 1815 to 1865, took place during Longfellow's lifetime, and he made a great contribution to it. Among his peers in this era of great literary creativity were such notables as Ralph Waldo Emerson, Nathaniel Hawthorne, Henry David Thoreau, Margaret Fuller, Walt Whitman, Oliver Wendell Holmes, William Prescott, John Greenleaf Whittier, Edgar Allan Poe, James Russell Lowell, and Herman Melville. (*See also* American Literature, section "The Flowering of American Literature.")

Henry Wadsworth Longfellow was the son of Stephen Longfellow and Zilpah Wadsworth Longfellow. He was born on Feb. 27, 1807, at Portland, Me. From early childhood it was evident that he was to be drawn to writing and the power of words. His father was eager to have his son become a lawyer. But when Henry was a senior at Bowdoin College, he asserted his ambition in a letter to his father: "I most eagerly aspire after future eminence in literature."

The year after he was graduated from college at age 18, Longfellow set out for Europe to become a scholar and a linguist. He traveled in Spain, Italy, France, Germany, and England before returning to the United States in 1829. At 22 he began his career as a college professor at his alma mater. In 1831 he married Mary Storer Porter, a former schoolmate. While at Bowdoin he expended his energies on translations from old-world literature, contributed travel sketches to the *New-England Magazine,* and served as a professor and librarian.

In 1835 he was appointed to a professorship at Harvard College in Cambridge, Mass., and once more set out for Europe by way of preparation. The trip ended in tragedy when his wife died in Rotterdam. He returned to Massachusetts and took a room at Craigie House, a historic building near the Charles River. In time the ownership of the house passed into his hands. Seven years after he came to Harvard, Longfellow married Frances Appleton, and Craigie House was given to the couple by her father, Nathan Appleton, as a wedding gift.

By this time Longfellow had already published some poetry. From his friend Nathaniel Hawthorne he got the brief outline of a story from which he compiled one of his most famous poems, 'Evangeline, a Tale of Acadie', published in 1847. Feeling that his work as a teacher was a hindrance to his writing, he resigned his post at Harvard in 1854. In June of that year he began 'The Song of Hiawatha'. Its publica-

Henry Wadsworth Longfellow

tion in 1855 caused a literary sensation. For the first time in American literature, Indian themes gained recognition as sources of imagination and originality.

The colonial legend of John Alden and Priscilla Mullins next inspired the poet, and in 1858 'The Courtship of Miles Standish' was published. This romantic ode quickly became one of Longfellow's most popular works.

In 1861 the happy family life of the poet came to an end. His second wife died of burns she received when a package of her children's curls, which she was sealing with matches and wax, burst into flame. Longfellow found solace in translating Dante into English and traveled to Europe for a change of scene.

Longfellow's final years were filled with honors. He was given honorary degrees by the universities at Oxford and Cambridge in England. He was invited to an audience with Queen Victoria. He was chosen a member of the Russian Academy of Science and of the Spanish Academy. Longfellow died at Cambridge on March 24, 1882.

Among his other published works are: 'Outre-Mer' (European travel sketches, 1835), 'Voices of the Night' (his first book of poems, 1839), 'Ballads and Other Poems' (1842), 'The Belfry of Bruges' (1846), 'The Seaside and the Fireside' (1850), 'The Golden Legend' (1851), 'Tales of a Wayside Inn' (1863), 'The Divine Comedy of Dante Alighieri' (a translation, 1865–67), 'The Masque of Pandora' (1875), 'Kéramos and Other Poems' (1878), 'Ultima Thule' (1880), and 'In the Harbor' (1882).

LONG ISLAND. Only nine states of the United States have larger populations than Long Island in New York State. Long Island's great urban centers, Brooklyn and Queens, are

boroughs of New York City. Most of the remainder of the island is residential, with suburbs, farms, and many summer resorts along the coasts. The island is divided into four counties: Kings (which is the borough of Brooklyn), Queens, Nassau, and Suffolk. (*See also* New York, N.Y.)

The island extends from the lower Hudson River about 118 miles (190 kilometers) northeastward. It roughly parallels the Connecticut coast, from which it is separated by Long Island Sound. It is from 12 to 23 miles (19 to 37 kilometers) wide and has an area of 1,723 square miles (4,463 square kilometers) and a population (1980 census) of 6,676,051.

A century and a half ago Long Island was a region of farms, pastures, dunes, and fishing villages except at the Brooklyn end. Sag Harbor and the towns called The Hamptons were whaling ports. Blue Point was an oyster center.

The construction of rail lines connecting to New York City, begun in the 1830s, led to rapid settlement. In recent decades a network of highways, bridges, and tunnels to New York City has speeded the huge flow of automobile traffic and stimulated the island's growth. A ferry connects the eastern end of the island with Connecticut across Long Island Sound. New York City's two airports, La Guardia and John F. Kennedy International, are both situated in Queens County.

The island was formed in the Ice Age, when a glacier that covered New England pushed a moraine into the ocean to rest on an underwater rocky ridge. Many of the scenic areas on the island have been preserved in Gateway National Recreation area (Jamaica Bay), Fire Island National Seashore, and in several state parks. Another tourist attraction is Sagamore Hill National Historic Site, President Theodore Roosevelt's home in Oyster Bay. Beaches, including Coney Island, and marinas provide excellent recreational opportunities.

The early inhabitants were Delaware Indians, whose names remain in many geographical features of the region. Giovanni da Verrazzano, an Italian navigator exploring for France, saw the island in 1524, and Henry Hudson, an Englishman sailing for the Dutch, landed in 1609. Four years later the Dutch navigator Adriaen Block explored the north shore and the Dutch named the island and claimed it. When the English captured New Amsterdam in 1664, renaming it New York, the island became part of the city. The Battle of Long Island on Aug. 27, 1776, was fought on Brooklyn Heights. The British under Gen. William Howe outflanked the colonial troops and drove them from the field. Long Island remained in British hands until 1783.

LÖNNROT, Elias (1802–84). The national epic of Finland, the 'Kalevala', was created by a folklorist-philologist named Elias Lönnrot. He spent years compiling the work from ballads, lyrical songs, and incantations that were part of the Finnish oral tradition. Kalevala, meaning "land of the heroes," is a poetic name for Finland. The times depicted in the epic are pre-Christian, although the last part of the work seems to predict the decline of paganism. Lönnrot published the first edition, in 32 cantos, in 1835; an enlarged edition in 50 cantos was issued in 1849.

Elias Lönnrot was born at Sammatti, Finland, on April 9, 1802. He received a degree in medicine from the University of Helsinki in 1832 and spent the following 20 years as district medical officer at Kajaani, in eastern Finland. He made field trips among the peoples of the region collecting folk poetry and information on the relationship of Baltic branches of the Finno-Ugric languages. He served as professor of Finnish language and literature at the University of Helsinki from 1853 to 1862. His work paved the way for the birth of modern Finnish literature. Lönnrot died at his birthplace on March 19, 1884.

LOON. "As crazy as a loon" is an expression that comes from the strange laughterlike notes that the common loon sends ringing across the waters of North American inland lakes. This bird and three other species make up the family Gaviidae.

During the nesting season loons live near freshwater lakes and ponds. In winter they cruise the seas and large lakes, often living 50 miles (80 kilometers) or more from land. Because their webbed feet are set far back on the body, they are clumsy creatures on land, wobbling along with the assistance of their wings and bill. Although they have some difficulty in rising from the water, they are strong fliers. Fishes, frogs, and aquatic insects are their chief food. Their nests, with two brown eggs, are usually roughly fashioned near the water. The parents are remarkably affectionate, swimming about in company with their young or carrying them on their backs.

The common loon is about 32 inches (81 centimeters) in length. In summer its plumage is beautiful—black-spotted and barred with white, shading to pure white beneath. In winter the upper parts are blackish

Common loon, scientific name *Gavia immer*

Charlie Ott—National Audubon Society Collection/Photo Researchers

without white spots. It breeds from Labrador to Maine and west to northern Illinois and winters from the Great Lakes south.

The red-throated loon, a smaller species about 25 inches (63 centimeters) in length, visits the United States only during winter, when it frequents both the Atlantic and Pacific coasts. The plumage of the back, wings, and tail is a dusky brown slightly spotted with white. Its name is derived from its chestnut-colored throat. The Pacific loon has black upper parts with a band of white streaks on the throat. It is found in the United States mainly in winter, when it ranges along the Pacific coast from Alaska to Lower California. The loon is the state bird of Minnesota.

Loons form the order Gaviiformes, or diving birds. The scientific name of the common loon is *Gavia immer;* of Pacific loon, *G. pacifica;* of red-throated loon, *G. stellata.* Some classifications use the generic name of the closely related grebes, *Colymbus,* for loons.

LORENZ, Konrad (born 1903). An Austrian zoologist, Konrad Lorenz is the founder of modern ethology, the study of comparative animal behavior in natural environments. For discoveries in individual and social behavior patterns, Lorenz shared the 1973 Nobel prize for physiology or medicine.

Konrad Zacharias Lorenz was born on Nov. 7, 1903, in Vienna. He kept all kinds of animals—cats, dogs, monkeys, rabbits, and fishes—many of which he found on his boyhood excursions. He also provided

Konrad Lorenz

Hermann Kacher

nursing care for sick animals from a nearby zoo and kept detailed records of bird behavior in diary form.

Lorenz became a physician in 1928 and earned a Ph.D. in zoology in 1933. The Max Planck Institute built a center for his studies in Seewiesen, West Germany, in 1961. His concepts of how behavioral patterns evolve in a species were later applied to humans. In a popular book, 'On Aggression', he argued that fighting and urban violence were the result of instincts that could be environmentally modified.

LOS ANGELES, Calif. On the Pacific coast of southern California lies a vast, sprawling urban area that is remarkable for the immensity of its population, the diversity of its physical features, its climate, and its economy. The heart of this urban area is the city of Los Angeles. Within its limits live about 3 million people. Another 4.5 million reside outside of the city proper but within the metropolitan area, which is composed entirely of Los Angeles County. One of the nation's fastest-growing places, the county's population increased by almost 1.5 million persons between 1960 and 1980. Los Angeles is also the center of a larger urban region, covering Ventura, Orange, San Bernardino, and Riverside counties, that includes a population of more than 11.5 million people.

The development of Los Angeles is a 20th-century phenomenon. In 1900 the city had only 102,000 people, while New York City had 3.5 million people. According to the 1980 census Los Angeles is the third largest city in the United States, after New York and Chicago, and has the second largest metropolitan area, after that of New York City.

Location and Climate

The city of Los Angeles lies on a gently sloping plain between the Pacific Ocean and the San Gabriel Mountains. It covers an area of 464 square miles (1,202 square kilometers). Los Angeles County spreads out over 4,070 square miles (10,540 square kilometers), an area larger than many whole states. Most of the county's built-up area is in the southern third of its area. Together, with the metropolitan area of San Diego 127 miles (204 kilometers) to the south of Los Angeles, the southern California area now has more than half of the state's population.

The Los Angeles region is notable for the variation of its physical setting. The landscape ranges from extensive beach and shoreline to the moderate heights of the Santa Monica mountains to the higher San Gabriel mountains, which receive considerable snowfall in winter. The Los Angeles area divides rather distinctly into the Los Angeles Basin, which includes most of the city, the surrounding San Gabriel and San Fernando valleys, and the backdrop of high mountain ranges.

The city's mild climate has been one of its most attractive features, although it is beset by occasional periods of severe weather. Its winters are relatively warm and summers almost rainless; annual temperatures average about 64° F (18° C). The surfer on a curling wave or the bikini-clad beach girl have long been symbols of the attractive physical setting and

This article was reviewed and updated in part by William A. V. Clark, Professor of Geography, University of California, Los Angeles, and coauthor of 'Los Angeles: the Metropolitan Experience'.

The commercial center of Los Angeles is set against the beautiful backdrop of the San Gabriel Mountains.

Craig Aurness—West Light

climate of Los Angeles. There are broad variations in the climate within the city, and summer temperatures can range from a cool 68° F (20° C) on the coast to 80° or 90° F (27° to 32° C) only 20 miles (32 kilometers) inland. The rainy season extends from November through April, though rainy days come with considerable irregularity. Heavy rains are not uncommon and a single storm may drop as much as 3 inches (76 millimeters) of rain in an hour. Between rains, the calm blue skies of summer return.

Unfortunately, it is the high levels of sunlight that have contributed to photochemical smog, a type of air pollution that is particularly severe in the city. Smog is caused by the interaction of sunlight with the exhaust from automobiles, oil refineries, and other emitters of hydrocarbons and nitrogen oxides. Recently stringent rules have reduced some of the effect of smog in Los Angeles, but it continues to be a health hazard in the city.

Description of the City

Los Angeles grew from a central core near the present downtown where a Mexican pueblo, or village, had been laid out in 1781. The city expanded rapidly in the 20th century to include numerous independent cities. Unlike many Eastern United States cities, Los Angeles includes large suburban communities within its boundaries. In addition, the city thrusts a finger of land 9 miles (14 kilometers) long and ½ mile (.8 kilometers) wide down to the coast, to include within its limits the communities of San Pedro and Wilmington. Here is Los Angeles Harbor, the nation's third largest port, which accommodates a busy East Asian and Pacific trade.

From the shoreline, the city stretches 44 miles (71 kilometers) inland to residential districts in the foothills of the mountains. Within the city limits are the numerous residential communities of the San Fernando Valley and within the county are the beach cities of Manhattan, Hermosa, and Redondo Beach. In its rapid expansion, Los Angeles has spread beyond and surrounded the independent cities of Santa Monica, Culver City, San Fernando, and Beverly Hills. Other cities such as Pasadena, Glendale, Burbank, Inglewood, and Long Beach fit into the uneven Los Angeles border outline like the pieces of a jigsaw puzzle. It is a city and metropolitan area made up largely of single-family homes. About 50 percent of the housing units are of this type, built on individual residential lots. This is in distinct contrast with the blocks of multilevel apartment buildings found in the cities of the Middle West and Eastern United States and in Europe.

The sprawling area covered by Los Angeles makes it a true city of the motor age. The vast distances to be traveled have made the automobile a necessity for transportation. There are some 5.8 million passenger cars registered in Los Angeles, Orange, and Ventura counties. The metropolitan area has one of the highest ratios of cars to people in the United States. The resulting heavy traffic is carried by one of the world's most extensive networks of freeways and expressways. These high-speed, limited-access roads already total about 650 miles (1,050 kilometers). Further additions have been slowed by environmental concerns, but the Century Freeway, linking the airport and the downtown area, has progressed.

The plaza area near the present central business district was the original heart of Los Angeles. It is still a center of the Mexican-American population and is crowded with shops and restaurants. The local color of this area is surpassed only by that of the New Chinatown, a few blocks to the northeast. Distinguished by modern Oriental architecture, with landscaped courts and narrow arcades, it grew up when old Chinatown was razed to make room for the giant Union Station just east of the plaza.

The Civic Center, which is south of the plaza, includes the 32-story City Hall and several other city and county buildings. Los Angeles is in an earthquake zone, and until 1957 no tall buildings could be constructed in the city. City Hall remained the tallest building until it was deemed safe to build taller buildings and the restriction was removed. Between 1960 and 1975 more than a dozen skyscrapers were constructed with heights ranging up to 62 stories.

299

LOS ANGELES

These new office buildings have become the centers of foreign investment, banking interests, and the Western headquarters of the world's corporations.

The emergence of a major convention center near the downtown area has stimulated the development of the central business district of the Los Angeles metropolitan area. Almost all of the newer buildings have integrated parking structures built within them, often underground. The skyline of Los Angeles has come increasingly to resemble those of other large cities of the United States.

Northwest of the Civic Center, about 7 miles (11 kilometers) away, is the community of Hollywood, with its world-famous crossroads of Hollywood and Vine streets. There are the western headquarters of many national radio and television networks, the Hollywood Bowl, and Mann's (formerly Grauman's) Chinese Theatre. The specialty shops, restaurants, and nightclubs along Sunset Boulevard, from Hollywood to Beverly Hills, make up the Sunset Strip. The Miracle Mile along Wilshire Boulevard, which runs to the ocean in Santa Monica, includes many elegant shops and department stores.

The People

Los Angeles is almost unique in that it is one of the few large United States cities that is still growing. Within the city are numerous distinct communities. They vary in size from Hollywood, which has a population of about 129,000, to Del Rey Palisades, which has fewer than 5,000 inhabitants. Other large communities are Van Nuys, North Hollywood, Westwood, and Boyle Heights.

The people of the region are highly diverse. The largest ethnic minority are the Latinos, who number about 2.8 million in the metropolitan area. They are mainly of Mexican heritage but include many people from other Latin American countries as well. Perhaps 1 million Latino immigrants are in the area without legal status. Asian groups, including Japanese, Chinese, Koreans, Filipinos, Vietnamese, Thai, and Indonesians, contribute almost 500,000 people. The black population amounts to about 1.1 million, a number that changed only slightly through the 1970s. Since about 1900 there has been a large influx of residents from other states.

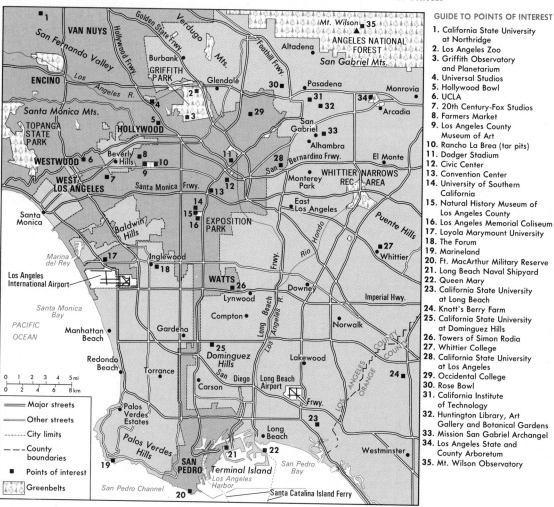

GUIDE TO POINTS OF INTEREST

1. California State University at Northridge
2. Los Angeles Zoo
3. Griffith Observatory and Planetarium
4. Universal Studios
5. Hollywood Bowl
6. UCLA
7. 20th Century-Fox Studios
8. Farmers Market
9. Los Angeles County Museum of Art
10. Rancho La Brea (tar pits)
11. Dodger Stadium
12. Civic Center
13. Convention Center
14. University of Southern California
15. Natural History Museum of Los Angeles County
16. Los Angeles Memorial Coliseum
17. Loyola Marymount University
18. The Forum
19. Marineland
20. Ft. MacArthur Military Reserve
21. Long Beach Naval Shipyard
22. Queen Mary
23. California State University at Long Beach
24. Knott's Berry Farm
25. California State University at Dominguez Hills
26. Towers of Simon Rodia
27. Whittier College
28. California State University at Los Angeles
29. Occidental College
30. Rose Bowl
31. California Institute of Technology
32. Huntington Library, Art Gallery and Botanical Gardens
33. Mission San Gabriel Archangel
34. Los Angeles State and County Arboretum
35. Mt. Wilson Observatory

(Above) Milt & Joan Mann; (right) Michele Burgess—Visualworld

Fisherman's Dock (above) is located at San Pedro near the southern tip of Los Angeles. The George C. Page La Brea Discoveries Museum (right) is situated next to the Rancho La Brea tar pits.

Culture, Education, and Recreation

Because the climate is very mild, Los Angeles is a city that emphasizes outdoor recreation. Picnics, in winter and summer, and outdoor barbecues are popular. The automobile is the most important means of transportation. It accounts for 98 percent of all personal travel trips and 88 percent of all workday commuting trips. Los Angeles sometimes has been characterized as a city of shallow cultural values with little emphasis on the arts. Whether this was ever true, or was an exaggeration from the point of view of Eastern cities, Los Angeles today offers a broad base of educational and cultural activity.

Young people in Los Angeles have a wide range of educational opportunities. Qualified students attend one of the many colleges and universities in the area, including the University of California, Los Angeles (UCLA) and California State University, which has branches at Los Angeles (downtown), Northridge, Fullerton, Dominguez Hills, and elsewhere. There are numerous two-year city and community colleges as well. The University of Southern California (USC) is located near the downtown section and the California Institute of Technology is located in Pasadena. The California Institute of the Arts, in Burbank, and Otis Art Institute specialize in fine and commercial arts. As a noted educational and research center Los Angeles clearly reflects the 20th century and its technological development. A 1982 article in the British magazine *The Economist* states that the Los Angeles area includes "the greatest concentration of Nobel prize winners, scientists, engineers, and technicians in the United States."

In 1969 a new music center was completed in the downtown area and the Los Angeles Philharmonic Orchestra took up residence. The Los Angeles Opera Company, a division of the Joffrey Ballet, the Center Theater Group, and the Los Angeles Master Chorale are also in residence at the center. The city supports two major daily newspapers and the major network television and radio stations as well as many indepen-

dent stations. Broadcasts in Spanish and other languages are quite common.

Los Angeles has more than 200 public parks and playgrounds, totaling about 8,800 acres (3,560 hectares). Within easy driving distance are miles of ocean beaches and the world's largest artificial boating harbor, Marina del Rey. The nearby mountains are the popular site of much winter sports activity. The well-known recreational island of Santa Catalina lies only 25 miles (40 kilometers) from Los Angeles Harbor. Large numbers of tourists also visit the city's old Spanish missions. Among nearby attractions are two of the world's largest telescopes: one at Mount Palomar and the other at Mount Wilson.

Pasadena's Tournament of Roses on New Year's Day is a spectacular flower festival. Its climax is the Rose Bowl football game. The Rose Bowl in Pasadena is the home field for UCLA. Memorial Coliseum (site of the 1932 Olympic Games and designated in 1979 as the site of the 1984 Summer Games) is the USC home football field. The Los Angeles (formerly Oakland) Raiders, who play at the Coliseum, and the Los Angeles Rams, who play at Anaheim Stadium in Orange County, are the city's professional football teams. Anaheim Stadium is also the home of the American League's California Angels. The Los Angeles Dodgers' National League baseball stadium was carved out of a mountainous Chavez Ravine site.

Economic Activities

Although Los Angeles is known for its entertainment industry, it is also an industrial center, a focus of banking, financial, and insurance activity, and an important port city.

Entertainment industry. The motion picture industry settled in Los Angeles in about 1910. It was attracted by the variety of scenery and the clear mild weather. With most films now being made in soundproof enclosures, scenery and climate are no longer so important. Nevertheless, the industry has continued to grow and still produces most of the nation's motion pictures. Radio broadcasting, television, and the

301

recording industries have also flourished in this great center of entertainment.

Hollywood, the traditional name of movieland, is not a suburb but a section of Los Angeles. Culver City, Burbank, and Universal City (unincorporated) also have large television and motion picture studios.

The motion picture industry, together with the mild climate and other attractions, has made Los Angeles an important tourist center. More than 12 million vacationers visit the area each year.

Manufacturing. The economic base of Los Angeles is diversified. Although manufacturing is the dominant industry, it employs fewer than one third of all the workers in the area. Most of the others are engaged in services and wholesale and retail trade.

In the manufacture of aircraft, the Los Angeles area leads the world. Like the movies, this industry was first attracted to southern California by the high percentage of clear days. During World War II the manufacture of aircraft grew enormously. Los Angeles is identified with the production of the B-1 bomber, the Saturn and Apollo space projects, and the Voyager planetary probes. The old line airplane firms have spread into aerospace and electronics and many new firms have entered the field.

Los Angeles is prominent in a number of other industries. Despite recent declines in the United States automobile industry, Los Angeles still assembles a large number of automobiles. It is a leader in oil refining and in the production of oil-well machinery. Food processing and the manufacture of women's clothing are major industries, and the city ranks high in the production of fabricated metal products and as an insurance and banking center.

The waterfront and fisheries. The harbor, 20 miles (32 kilometers) from downtown Los Angeles, was originally an unprotected seaway rimmed by mud flats. In 1909 the city annexed the little coastal villages of San Pedro and Wilmington. With the aid of the federal government, it then constructed one of the world's largest artificial harbors.

An extensive breakwater was built to provide a place where ships could safely anchor. The dredging of channels and slips made an inner harbor with 46 miles (74 kilometers) of waterfront, including Long

The Old Mission Church stands on a site set aside as El Pueblo de Los Angeles State Historical Monument.

Beach, and hundreds of acres of land were reclaimed for terminals, warehouses, and shipyards. Each year the port accommodates thousands of ships.

The harbor is also the home port of one of the world's largest fisheries. The annual commercial catch is about 250,000 tons (227,000 metric tons), with tuna and mackerel predominating.

Government

Since 1925 the city has had a mayor-council form of government. The mayor is popularly elected for a four-year term. The city council consists of 15 members, each representing a separate district. Council members serve four-year terms. Candidates for city public office are not allowed to run as members of a political party.

Much of the work is done by boards of commissioners, who are appointed by the mayor subject to approval of the council. There are more than 20 such boards, including those for city planning, police, fire, health, parks, municipal housing, and the harbor.

The city also serves as the county seat of Los Angeles County. The county is administered by a five-member board of supervisors who serve for four-year

The music center for Los Angeles County was completed in 1969.

terms. Within the county are special governmental units for flood control, lighting, sanitation, and fire protection. The Metropolitan Water District is responsible for administering the water supply of numerous cities in southern California.

History

Los Angeles was founded in 1781 by the Spanish governor of California, Felipe de Neve, near the site of the Indian village of Yang-na. It was named *El Pueblo de la Reina de Los Angeles* (The Town of the Queen of the Angels). At that time it was a small settlement of only 44 people. The community grew, however, and under later Mexican rule it alternated with Monterey as the capital of California. During the Mexican War, the village was captured by Americans in 1846. Only three years later, in 1850, Los Angeles received a city charter.

After the San Francisco gold rush in the late 1840s many miners moved to Los Angeles, then a lawless cow town, and helped it to prosper. The arrival of the Southern Pacific Railroad in 1876 from San Francisco helped the city open up. When the Santa Fe line arrived in 1885 a rate war began with the Southern Pacific. With the resulting lower fares new arrivals poured into the city. The gold rush boom collapsed in 1888, however, and many returned home.

In 1892 oil was discovered and a new boom began. By now irrigation was beginning to turn the semiarid plain into the richest agricultural county in the United States. In 1914 the harbor on the Pacific was opened. Meanwhile an aqueduct about 250 miles (400 kilometers) long had been built and was piping water from the Owens River into the county. The city and its need for water grew, and in 1941 the Colorado River Aqueduct was completed. The system expanded from 1951 to 1959 (*see* Aqueduct). Aqueduct building continued as the community expanded.

The city, with about 102,500 people in 1900, gained almost half a million in population by 1920. With the development of the motion picture, oil, and manufacturing industries the growth rate continued to accelerate. In the next decade the population more than doubled, and it doubled again by 1960. The growth rate slowed after that, though the population grew by another 485,000 people to almost 3 million by 1980. Recent city improvements have included the expansion of Los Angeles International Airport and the construction of a 16-million-dollar passenger and cargo terminal in the harbor area.

Smog has long been a particularly serious problem for Los Angeles, because climate is one of the city's prized assets. The struggle against smog goes on despite stringent rules covering automobile emissions and the burning of industrial wastes. Although smog is a clear and persistent problem, floods and fires are also major concerns in the metropolitan area. The brush-covered hills are attractive, but they are a danger for the community. The chaparral, the major type of brush on the hillsides, is highly flammable, particularly in the fall, when it is dried by the desert Santa Ana winds. While most fires in the area are put out promptly, as recently as 1970 a combination of high temperatures and low humidity resulted in 14 major fires in which three persons died, almost 300 houses were destroyed, and 400,000 acres (161,800 hectares) of brush were burned. In 1983 major coastal storms destroyed several of the piers that provide recreation for the Los Angeles area. Winter rainfall creates mud slides in the coastal and mountain areas of the city. A major earthquake in 1971 killed 65 persons, and the damage reached ½ billion dollars. Earthquakes are an ever-present problem for the coastal region. Strict building and zoning requirements have somewhat lessened the effects of fires, floods, and earthquakes. (*See also* California.) Population (1980 census): city, 2,966,763; county, 7,477,657.

BIBLIOGRAPHY FOR LOS ANGELES

Burnett, William, ed. Views of Los Angeles, rev. ed. (Portriga, 1979).
Caughey, John and LaRee, eds. Los Angeles: Biography of a City (Univ. of Calif. Press, 1976).
Federal Writers' Project. Los Angeles: a Guide to the City and Its Environs (Somerset, 1981).
Kennelley, Joe and Hanky, Roy. Sunset Boulevard: America's Dream Street (Darwin, 1982).
Lantis, D. W., et al,. California: Land of Contrast, 3rd ed. (Kendall-Hunt, 1977).
Nelson, H. J. The Los Angeles Metropolis (Kendall-Hunt, 1983).
Steiner, Rodney. Los Angeles: the Centrifugal City (Kendall-Hunt, 1981).
Weaver, J. D. Los Angeles: the Enormous Village 1781–1981 (Capra Press, 1980).

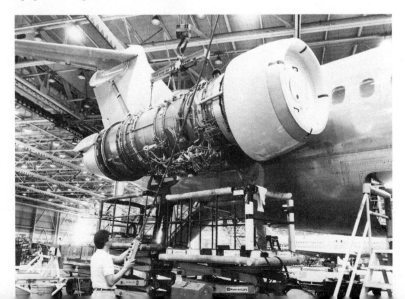

Workmen prepare to mount an engine on a passenger plane at an aircraft assembly plant in Long Beach.

Courtesy of McDonnell Douglas Corp.

LOUIS, Kings of France. The first of the many French kings to bear the name Louis was actually Clovis (*see* Clovis). He ruled from 481 to 511 and founded the kingdom of the Franks. Later the "C" was dropped and the "v" was written as "u," thus making the name Louis. It is the same as the English Lewis and the German Ludwig.

Louis the Pious (born 778, ruled 814–40) is usually reckoned as Louis I. The son of Charlemagne, he succeeded his father as king of the Franks and Holy Roman emperor (*see* Charlemagne). The great empire built up by Charlemagne was divided after Louis I died, and the next four rulers of this name left little mark on the course of history.

Louis VI, the Fat (born 1081, ruled 1108–37), was the first important king of the Capetian line. This line sprang from Hugh Capet, who became king in 987. Louis the Fat was a great fighter, a great hunter, and a great eater. At 46 he became too fat to mount a horse, but he remained the embodiment of warlike energy. His great task was to reduce to order the petty nobles of the royal domain, who could truly be called robber barons. When Louis came to the throne, every lord of a castle robbed at will and it was not safe for even the king to pass along the road. Twenty years of hard fighting were necessary to remedy this condition, but in the end the king triumphed, and law and order prevailed. So that such evils might not recur, every castle that was captured was destroyed or given to faithful followers.

Louis VII (born 1120, ruled 1137–80) was the eldest son of Louis VI. Shortly before his death, Louis VI arranged for his son's marriage to Eleanor of Aquitaine. By this marriage southwest France was added to the domains of the new French king. Unfortunately Louis, who was very religious and prone to be jealous, soon discovered that his beautiful queen was a capricious flirt.

In 1147 Louis departed for the Holy Land on the Second Crusade, taking his queen with him. This Crusade was a miserable failure (*see* Crusades). After they returned, Louis had his marriage annulled in 1152. Eleanor at once sent an embassy to Henry, count of Anjou and duke of Normandy, proposing marriage. Henry was overjoyed because the alliance transferred to him the great duchy of Guienne. Two years later Henry and Eleanor were crowned king and queen of England (*see* Henry, Kings of England, section on Henry II). France thus lost a rich territory to England, its greatest rival.

Louis VIII (born 1187, ruled 1223–26), the son of Philip Augustus, reigned too short a time to accomplish anything of real importance.

Louis IX (born 1214, ruled 1226–70), called Saint Louis, was one of the most virtuous and heroic kings of France. He was the dutiful son of Louis VIII and his queen, Blanche of Castile. Blanche was a remarkable woman who bravely faced numerous revolts of powerful feudal nobles during her son's youth. Louis IX had all the good qualities and few of the bad ones of the age in which he lived. Indeed, his virtues were so remarkable that after his death the Roman Catholic church declared him a saint.

Louis's acts of piety, such as wearing a haircloth shirt, fasting, and waiting on lepers, were usually performed in private. To the world he was a fearless knight, thoroughly trained in the art of war, and a conscientious, just, and able king—usually good-humored and kindly, but at times impatient and angry. He was a strong ruler, who greatly strengthened the royal power. He improved the government by appointing local officials who were responsible to him for the administration of justice, the collection of taxes, and the government of their districts. He encouraged the people to appeal to him if the nobles oppressed them or if his officials were unjust. He improved the administration of justice by abolishing trials by combat and by using in his courts the new lawyers, trained in the Roman law, in place of the churchmen who formerly were the only people who could read and write. These reforms not only benefited the peasants but also checked the power of the no-

Louis IX, called Saint Louis (far left) was canonized by Pope Boniface VIII in 1297. Louis I (left) the Pious was the son of Charlemagne.

Photos, Bibliotheque Nationale, Paris

Although regarded as the greatest monarch of his age, Louis XIV (left), in a 72-year reign, left France economically devastated by his wars and personal extravagance. His successors, Louis XV (center) and Louis XVI (right) were ineffectual rulers who were unable to restore the economy.

bles, who, according to a writer of the time, "undertook nothing against their king, seeing clearly that the hand of the Lord was with him."

Saint Louis made two crusades—to Egypt and the Holy Land, from 1248 to 1254, on which he was captured and held for ransom by Muhammadans; and to Tunis, in 1270, where he died of the plague.

Louis X (born 1289) ruled for only two years, from 1314 to 1316.

Louis XI (born 1423, ruled 1461–83) presented a striking contrast to Louis IX. In appearance Louis XI was ugly and unkingly; in character he was unscrupulous and underhanded. Like his contemporaries, Cesare Borgia and Richard III, he was an embodiment of the principles that are called Machiavellian. He believed that "he who has success has honor" and cared nothing for the way in which he attained success. He made promises only to break them, unless he had sworn by one particular saint: then his word was good. His one ambition seemed to be to extend the boundaries of France. Although he was too stingy to buy a hat to replace the shabby one he wore, he spent large sums in buying back border cities. In his conflicts with the nobles, especially with Charles the Bold, duke of Burgundy, he also acquired much territory, so that by the time of his death most of the land of France was under the direct control of the king. The power of the crown in the latter part of his reign was truly absolute over the territory it held.

Sir Walter Scott, in his novel 'Quentin Durward', gives a fine description of the court of Louis XI, as well as an excellent survey of the customs and traditions of the period.

Louis XII (born 1462, ruled 1498–1515) is chiefly noted for the Italian wars, begun by his predecessor, Charles VIII, and continued after the reign of Louis XII by Francis I.

Louis XIII (born 1601, ruled 1610–43) is chiefly important for the fact that, in spite of all opposition, for 18 years he kept in power his able minister, Richelieu (*see* Richelieu). The first years of the reign were filled with anarchy and disorder. The king was a child, and his mother, who ruled for him, was weak and selfish. When Richelieu came into power, however, all this was changed. The Huguenots were reduced from a powerful political party to a mere religious body, and the nobles were humbled (*see* Huguenots). National unity and religious peace were secured at home, and France was raised to the first position among the powers of Europe.

Louis XIV (born 1638, ruled 1643–1715) inherited this power from his father and carried it further. He was styled the Grand Monarch, and his brilliant court at Versailles became the model and the despair of other less rich and powerful princes, who accepted his theory of absolute monarchy (*L'état c'est moi*, "I am the state"). Until 1661 the government was largely in the hands of the wily Italian Cardinal Mazarin. At the cardinal's death Louis declared that he would be his own prime minister. From then on he worked faithfully at his "trade of a king."

A passion for fame and the desire to increase French territory in Europe were the leading motives of Louis XIV. He neglected the opportunities to gain an empire in America and India and involved France in wars that ruined the country financially and paved the way for the outbreak of the French Revolution.

His first war, fought from 1667 to 1668, was an attempt to enforce flimsy claims to part of the Spanish Netherlands (Belgium). His second (1672–78) was di-

Young Louis XVII was king of France after his father, Louis XVI, was executed in 1793. He himself died two years later of tuberculosis.

Bibliotheque Nationale, Paris

rected against "their High Mightinesses," the States-General of Holland, who had blocked his objective in the first contest. In spite of the great military power of France, the Dutch admiral De Ruyter twice defeated the fleets of the French and their English allies, and Louis XIV failed ingloriously in his attempt to conquer Holland. The third war (1689–97) also was directed chiefly against Holland, whose stadholder had by then become King William III of England. The German province of the Palatinate was terribly wasted, but the Peace of Ryswick brought only slight gains for France. Louis's last and greatest effort was the War of the Spanish Succession (1701–13). In this conflict the English duke of Marlborough (see Marlborough) was the principal leader of the opposing European coalition. The right to seat his grandson Philip V on the throne of Spain was small compensation for the thousands of lives and the millions in treasure that the French king wasted in the struggle.

Millions more were spent by Louis in building the beautiful palace at Versailles, near Paris, and in maintaining his brilliant court. There, etiquette became the "real constitution of France." It required seven persons, some of them the highest princes of the realm, to put the king's shirt on him at his getting up (*levée*) in the morning. A French historian says of Louis XIV: "He was a god in his temple, celebrating his own worship in the midst of his host of priests and faithful." This extravagance of the court meant a heavy burden of taxation for the common people, who were thereby reduced to a misery so great that they eventually rose up in rebellion and drove the Bourbons from the throne.

Louis XIV had the distinction of ruling longer than any other European king: it was 72 years from the time when he ascended the throne, as a child of less than 5, until his death in 1715. The Grand Monarch, who had outlived both his son and his son's son, was succeeded by his 5-year-old great-grandson, Louis XV, the last son of the duke of Burgundy.

Louis XV (born 1710, ruled 1715–74). The luxurious court of Louis XIV was continued under Louis XV. The evils from which the country suffered were clearly recognized, but by the time the king grew up he was too lazy and selfish to try to remedy them. Misgovernment was common at home, and the position of France abroad was lowered by the loss of its colonial possessions in India and America. These misfortunes, however, made little impression on the king, whose attitude was expressed in the phrase, "After me the deluge!"

Louis XVI (born 1754, ruled 1774–92). The storm broke during the reign of Louis XVI. Awkward and timid, no man could have appeared less like a king than did Louis XVI, who was 20 years old when he came to the throne. No man could have seemed more out of place in the brilliant and polished court of which he was the center. Louis realized this and often wished, even before the Revolution, that he were only a common man. He was a good horseman, fond of hunting, and he delighted in making and mending locks. His greatest fault was that he was always ready to listen to and follow the advice of others. When this advice was good, all went well; but in the latter part of Louis's reign the advice was bad and it cost the king his life.

When Louis XVI first came to the throne, he entrusted the management of the finances of the kingdom to Turgot, one of the greatest of statesmen. As long as the king followed his minister's advice, the state of the kingdom was improved. But he was more often under the influence of the beautiful but frivolous and extravagant queen, Marie Antoinette (see Marie Antoinette). He was also swayed by his selfish courtiers, who opposed any financial reforms that would threaten their graft and pensions and life of ease. They soon persuaded the king to dismiss his able minister.

The political climate gradually grew worse, and finally Louis XVI was forced to call the Estates-General, a body that had not met since 1614 (see Estates-General). Its meeting was the first step in the French Revolution (see French Revolution). The members of the Third Estate refused to follow the old method of voting and finally declared themselves a national assembly.

At first the king seemed inclined to work with the revolution and to try to remedy conditions in the country. But the influence of the queen and of the courtiers proved too strong for his weak will. Encouraged by them, he disregarded the promises he had made and sought to flee from France in order to obtain aid against the revolution from Austria.

This attempted flight was the beginning of the end for the court of Louis XVI. The people saw that they could not trust the king and the "Austrian woman," as they called the queen. His disregard of his promises to abide by the constitution led to the storming of the royal palace of the Tuileries on Aug. 10, 1792. The king and his family escaped before the mob arrived and took refuge in the hall of the Legislative Assembly. The assembly declared that the king was suspended from office and ordered that he and his family should be imprisoned. They then 'called a new assembly (the Convention) to decide whether France should continue to be a monarchy.

The Convention first decided against a monarchy and declared the king deposed. They then brought Louis XVI to trial on the charge of conspiring with foreign countries for the invasion of France. Almost unanimously Louis Capet, as he was now called, was declared guilty and was sentenced to death. The next day he was beheaded, meeting his fate with a steadfast courage, and proving greater in death than he had ever been in life. His execution had important consequences for France, because it aroused opinion in other countries against the French Revolution.

Louis XVII, the Dauphin (born 1785), never ruled. He was imprisoned with his parents, Louis XVI and Marie Antoinette, when he was 7. According to the French government, he died at the age of 10.

Louis XVIII (born 1755, ruled 1814–24). When the Bourbons returned to the throne of France in 1814, the younger brother of Louis XVI assumed the crown as Louis XVIII. The difficult task of reconstruction was before the king, but he seemed admirably adapted to meet the situation. He was cold-blooded and cared nothing for revenge; therefore he was satisfied to leave alone those who had driven his family from France. He was a lazy man, and his one ambition was to keep his throne. This ambition at first seemed likely to go unfulfilled, for in 1815 Napoleon returned from exile on the island of Elba, and Louis XVIII fled in a panic from France. At the end of the period known as the Hundred Days, however, Napoleon was again overthrown, at Waterloo, and the Allies entered Paris, "bringing Louis XVIII in their baggage." (*See also* Napoleon I.)

Until 1820 the king was able to resist the demands of the extreme royalists for vengeance and to build up his kingdom, but finally, under the leadership of his brother, they became too strong for him. He yielded to their demands for a reactionary government. This marked the beginning of the end of the Bourbons; ten years later, under his brother, Charles X, they were finally driven from the throne of France.

Louis-Philippe (born 1773, ruled 1830–48). Having disposed of the old Bourbons, the French had to set up a new government. Influenced by Lafayette (*see* Lafayette), they decided to perpetuate the French monarchy with Louis-Philippe, a member of the Orléans family. He accepted the crown on Aug. 9, 1830.

Louis-Philippe was known for his democratic ideas, but his government was not democratic. Demands for a more liberal government were not met.

When the government forbade a banquet organized by supporters of political reform, which was to be held on Feb. 22, 1848, the Republicans of Paris revolted. The prime minister, François Guizot, was forced to resign. This did not satisfy the rioters, however, and Louis-Philippe abdicated on February 24. He fled to England, where he died two years later.

In a fight for the heavyweight title in June 1946, Louis, right, knocked out Bill Conn in eight rounds.

LOUIS, Joe (1914–81). The "Brown Bomber," Joe Louis was the world heavyweight boxing champion for almost 12 years—the longest reign in the history of the heavyweight division. He successfully defended the title 25 times, scoring 21 knockouts.

Joseph Louis Barrow was born on May 13, 1914, in Lexington, Ala. He began his boxing career in Detroit and won the Amateur Athletic Union 175-pound championship in 1934. Three years after his first professional fight, he became the heavyweight champion when he knocked out James J. Braddock in eight rounds in Chicago on June 22, 1937. He was at his peak during the years 1939 to 1942, defending the championship seven times from December 1940 through June 1941. He gave every leading contender a chance at the crown and knocked out five former titleholders in addition to Braddock.

Louis retired in 1949, but, pressured by bills for back taxes, he challenged Ezzard Charles for the championship on Sept. 27, 1950. Louis lost in a 15-round decision. His last fight was against the future champion Rocky Marciano, who knocked Louis out in eight rounds on Oct. 26, 1951.

From 1934 to 1951 Louis had 71 bouts, winning 68 of them, 54 by knockouts. His service in the United States Army during World War II when he was in top physical shape prevented him from defending his title many more times. In later years he worked at a hotel in Las Vegas, Nev., where he died on April 12, 1981. (*See also* Boxing.)

Barely visible through the trees in one of the coastal marshes of Louisiana are the homes of some of the hardy fishermen and fur trappers who make their living in such areas.

LOUISIANA

LOUISIANA. One of the most favorably located states in the Union is Louisiana. It stands on the Gulf of Mexico astride the mouth of the mighty Mississippi River. To the north lies the vast basin of the Mississippi, one of the richest river valleys in the world. To the south, across the Gulf, are the growing markets of Latin America.

This location has made Louisiana one of the great commercial states. Its chief city, New Orleans, is the second-ranked United States port, where much of the nation's petroleum and grain is shipped (*see* New Orleans). In addition to trade Louisiana ranks high in minerals, fish, forest products, furs, and tourism. Its manufactures—of which the most important are chemicals and petroleum—are worth more than 9 billion dollars a year. Its farms produce much rice, cotton, and sweet potatoes. The state ranks third, after Florida and Hawaii, in sugarcane.

For almost a hundred years Louisiana was settled and controlled by France and Spain. This early history is shown in the many French and Spanish names on its map and in the term parish, used instead of county. Louisiana's governmental units were origi-

Population (1980): 4,203,972—rank, 19th state. Urban, 68.6%; rural, 31.4%. Persons per square mile, 94.4 (persons per square kilometer, 36.4)—rank, 21st state.

Extent: Area, 48,523 square miles (125,674 square kilometers), including 3,989 square miles (10,331 square kilometers) of water surface (31st state in size).

Elevation: Highest, Driskill Mountain, 535 feet (163 meters), near Bienville; lowest, New Orleans, 5 feet (2 meters) below sea level; average, 100 feet (30 meters).

Geographic Center: 3 miles (5 kilometers) southeast of Marksville.

Temperature: Extremes—lowest, −16° F (−26° C), Minden, Feb. 13, 1899; highest, 114° F (46° C), Plain Dealing, Aug. 10, 1936. Averages at Alexandria—January, 51.9° F (11.1° C); July, 82.9° F (28.3° C); annual, 67.5° F (19.7° C). Averages at New Orleans—January, 55.2° F (12.9° C); July, 82.7° F (28.2° C); annual, 69.8° F (21°C).

Precipitation: At Alexandria—annual average, 54.6 inches (1,387 millimeters). At New Orleans—annual average, 60.7 inches (1,542 millimeters). At Shreveport—annual average, 46.2 inches (1,173 millimeters).

Land Use: Crops, 23%; pasture, 6%; forest, 51%; other, 20%.

For statistical information about Agriculture, Education, Employment, Finance, Government, Manufacturing, Mining, Population Trends, and Vital Statistics, see LOUISIANA FACT SUMMARY.

nally church units set up by the Spanish in the late 1600s. The state also has a strong French and Spanish heritage in its population, customs, and architecture. Louisiana's civil law is based on that of France and Spain rather than on English common law as in the other states.

Louisiana, meaning "land of Louis," was named by the explorer La Salle in honor of King Louis XIV of France. The nickname Pelican State comes from the pelicans that live along the Gulf coast.

Survey of the Pelican State

Louisiana lies in the southern part of the United States. To the east is the state of Mississippi, separated by three boundaries—the Mississippi River, the 31st parallel, and the Pearl River. Arkansas is to the north. To the west is Texas, separated from Louisiana in part by the Sabine River. Louisiana's southern coastline, 397 miles (639 kilometers) in length, is on the Gulf of Mexico.

The state is shaped somewhat like a boot, with its toe pointing eastward along the Gulf. Its greatest length is 300 miles (483 kilometers) from east to west. Its width is 275 miles (443 kilometers), from north to south. Its area is 48,523 square miles (125,674 square kilometers), including 3,989 square miles (10,331 square kilometers) of inland water.

Louisiana's Three Natural Regions

With an average elevation of about 100 feet (30 meters), Louisiana is one of the lowest and flattest states in the Union. Its surface rises from sea level along the coast to only 400 to 500 feet (120 to 150 meters) in the northwest. The highest point in the state is Driskill Mountain (535 feet, 163 meters), in Bienville Parish. The lowest point is at New Orleans, 5 feet (2 meters) below sea level. The state is divided into three distinct natural regions.

The West Gulf Coastal Plain occupies all western Louisiana. Its eastern boundary is an irregular north-south line running near Monroe, Alexandria, and Lafayette. The plain is wooded with many pine trees. Along the coast is a wide fringe of marshland.

The Mississippi Floodplain covers a 50-mile (80-kilometer) belt west from the river to the boundary of the West Gulf Coastal Plain and some 12,000 square miles (31,000 square kilometers) of swamps in the delta of the Mississippi. The soil is a mixture of clay and fertile silt left by floodwaters of the river. Where the river flows between low ridges it is often higher than the surrounding floodplain. The plain has many oxbow lakes, formed as cutoffs when the Mississippi changed its course.

The East Gulf Coastal Plain occupies most of the area between the Mississippi and Pearl rivers. It is a low, level region similar to the West Gulf Coastal Plain. On the east bank of the Mississippi are bluffs that reach heights of about 300 feet (100 meters) in the Tunica Hills of West Feliciana Parish.

The chief river of Louisiana is the Mississippi (*see* Mississippi River). Its principal tributary is the Red,

which receives the waters of the Ouachita. The junction of the Red and the Mississippi is a short channel called Old River, which connects the Mississippi with the Atchafalaya River. Much of southwestern Louisiana is drained by the Calcasieu River.

Climate and Weather

Louisiana has a moist, near-tropical climate. Warm winds from the Gulf of Mexico keep the temperature fairly even the year around. Average January temperatures range from a low of 48° F (9° C) in the northwest to a high of 55° F (13° C) in the southeast. July temperatures average 82° F (28° C) throughout the state.

The average precipitation varies from 60 inches (1,524 millimeters) a year near Grand Lake to 46 inches (1,168 millimeters) in Caddo and De Soto parishes. The extreme southeast has about 300 growing days a year; the rest of the state about 240.

Natural Resources and Flood Control

Louisiana's chief agricultural resources are fertile soil, plenty of rainfall, and a long growing season. More than half the state is forested. The chief commercial trees are pine in the north-central area and southwest, oak in the northeast, ash in the east and south-central, and cypress in the south swamps. In the damp forests Spanish moss is gathered for mattresses, pillows, and upholstery.

Mineral resources include sulfur, salt, and such fuels as petroleum and natural gas. Waterways on the Mississippi and Red rivers and outlets to the Gulf of Mexico aid commerce. The climate and such festivals as Mardi Gras attract tourists.

Flood control has been aimed at regulating the floodwaters of the Mississippi and its tributaries.

The New Orleans City Hall, part of the Civic Center, was completed in 1959. At the left is the Charity Hospital.

Pix

A map reveals the three natural regions and the surface features of Louisiana. The use that can be made of the land is related to the physical features of each region.

There are extensive levee systems along the Mississippi and along the Red and the upper Atchafalaya. Since 1927, when the Mississippi overflowed hundreds of square miles, there has been considerable improvement of these systems. On the Sabine River is Toledo Bend Dam, a project of Texas and Louisiana. The dam's reservoir supplies municipal, industrial, and irrigation water to the Sabine River basin, but its principal role is to generate power.

The coordination and management of all water-resource activities carried on in the state are handled by the Office of Public Works of the Department of Transportation and Development. Forests are managed by the Office of Forestry in the Department of Resources. The Department of Commerce directs industrial development.

People of the Pelican State

Louisiana's largest tribe of Indians was the Caddo. A few Choctaw lived north of Lake Pontchartrain. In 1835 the Caddo ceded their remaining land in the northwest for $80,000. Most of the Indians had left the state by 1859. (*See also* Indians, American.)

The first white settlers were French, followed by Spaniards. Today the descendants of these colonists are called Creoles. Most of them belong to the Roman Catholic church. From 1760 to 1800 about 5,000 French from Acadia (Nova Scotia) settled in south-central Louisiana (*see* Acadia).

After the Louisiana Purchase of 1803 the center and north were settled by English, Irish, and Scottish from the southeastern United States. Many blacks were brought in as slaves. Today 2 percent of the people are foreign-born. Of the total foreign stock, Italians are the largest group. Blacks make up almost one third of the population.

Manufacturing and Cities

From 1939 to 1947 the value of manufacturing in Louisiana more than tripled. It tripled again between 1947 and 1963 and between 1967 and 1977 when it reached more than 9 billion dollars. New and expanding industries have been aided by a ten-year exemption from certain taxes and other inducements offered by the state.

The chief industry is the production of chemicals and allied products. Next in importance is petroleum refining. The third largest industry is the preparation of food products, such as cane sugar, beverages, and bakery products. Louisiana's forests provide the basis of the state's fourth most valuable industry—paper and allied products. In the late 1970s the state produced about 1 billion board feet (2.4 million cubic meters) of lumber.

Louisiana's largest city is New Orleans, 110 miles (177 kilometers) upstream from the mouth of the Mississippi River. It ships much grain, oil, cotton, and sugar (*see* New Orleans). The second most populous city is Baton Rouge, the capital of the state (*see* Baton Rouge). Shreveport, the third largest city, is a port on the Red River and the industrial center of the oil-rich northwest (*see* Shreveport). Lafayette, the fourth city in size, is a commercial center built on light industry and retail trade. Lake Charles is the chief city of the southwest and an important source of chemicals and petroleum products. Monroe, which is a trade center, lies in a rich gas-producing region in the northeast. Alexandria is a lumbering center on the Red River.

Agriculture in Louisiana

More than one fourth of the land is in crops and nonforested pasture. Most farms are operated by their owners. About one seventh of the commercial farms are occupied by tenants, who are renters or sharecroppers on the land.

The most valuable crop is soybeans. Rice, grown chiefly in marshy lowlands of the southwest, is the second most valuable field crop, and Louisiana is one of the three leading states in rice production. Cotton is grown mainly in the north in the valleys of the Mississippi, Ouachita, and Red rivers.

Louisiana ranks third among the states in the production of sugarcane. For many years the only sugar produced from the cane was a brownish, milky liquid suitable for rum making. Then in 1795 Étienne de Boré, on his plantation near New Orleans, succeeded in refining sugar by boiling the cane juice until it reached the granulation point. From that time on the sugar industry became increasingly important.

Louisiana is second in the nation in the production of sweet potatoes. The state also produces pecans, strawberries, and peaches. Other important agricultural products are cattle, milk, eggs, chickens, hay, corn, hogs, and truck crops.

Minerals, Fish, and Fur

Louisiana is second only to Texas in mineral production in the nation's West South Central region. The most valuable mineral is natural gas. Next in importance is petroleum. The chief sources for these minerals are the parishes on the Gulf of Mexico and the adjacent offshore areas. The third-ranking mineral is sulfur, which is obtained from sources in Jefferson, Lafourche, and Terrebonne parishes. Louisiana and Texas produce most of the nation's sulfur.

Louisiana's fishing industry ranks first in production. Most of the catch comes from the Gulf of Mexico, which yields shrimps, menhaden, oysters, and crabs. Inland waterways supply catches of crayfish, catfish and bullheads, and buffalo fish. Louisiana also ranks first in the value of catch in the Gulf states.

Louisiana is the leading fur-producing state. Nutria provides the bulk of the income. Muskrat, mink, and raccoon are also important.

The Development of Transportation

Flatboats were the first important vessels on the Mississippi River. The steamboat era began in 1812

Sugarcane has been grown in Louisiana since 1742. Cane for sugar is grown in the south, cane for syrup in the north.

when the *New Orleans* made the first trip downriver from Pittsburgh, Pa. The river still carries much barge traffic. Louisiana has up to 7,500 miles (12,000 kilometers) of navigable waterways including the Intracoastal Waterway. New Orleans, Baton Rouge, and Lake Charles are deepwater ports. A large tanker terminal facility, the nation's first offshore crude oil port, was built at Lafourche Parish in 1981.

The first railroad in the state was completed between New Orleans and Lake Pontchartrain in 1831. By 1858 New Orleans was linked to Jackson, Miss., by rail. Through trains began operating between New Orleans and Chicago in 1873. Ten years later a transcontinental line led to the Pacific coast.

An important part of Louisiana's transportation network is the system of state primary and secondary roads. The major north-south routes are US 71, 171, 167, 165, and 61 and Interstate 55 and 59. The chief

A huge oil refinery lights the night sky in Baton Rouge. The refinery uses a special process called alkylation. A major refinery center, Baton Rouge ships much of its processed petroleum down the Mississippi River to the Gulf.

Photographs, Louisiana State Department of Commerce and Industry

Two workmen (left) skin muskrat and hang the furs up to cure. Many fur-bearing animals live in the state's swamps and marshes. The lumber mill at Bogalusa (right) uses logs to make wooden boxes. Lumbering is a significant industry in parts of the state.

east-west highways are US 80, 84, 190, and 90 and Interstate 10, 12, and 20. The state is also served by national and international airlines.

Recreation and Tourist Attractions

The chief tourist attraction is New Orleans. This city is the site of the annual Mardi Gras and of the Mid-Winter Sports Carnival, climaxed by the Sugar Bowl football game. A few miles to the east is Chalmette National Historical Park, the site of Gen. Andrew Jackson's victory over the British in 1815.

The Louisiana Shrimp and Petroleum Festival and Fair draws many visitors to Morgan City. Shreveport is the site of the annual state fair. Old plantation homes along the Mississippi River are popular attractions. The state, advertised as a sportsman's paradise, is noted for its fishing and hunting.

Louisiana's Schools

The first school in the Louisiana Territory, established in New Orleans in 1725 by Father Raphael, had seven students. Education for girls began in August 1727 with the arrival of six Ursuline nuns to establish a school in New Orleans.

Education was hampered by poor transportation, the Civil War, and Reconstruction. The modern school system began in 1877 after passage of a general school act. The system now includes more than 50 vocational centers throughout the state and a vocational curriculum laboratory.

The vessels of shrimp fishermen are blessed by Roman Catholic priests at bayous near Houma, Morgan City, and Golden Meadow every August.

Louisiana State Department of Commerce and Industry

The largest school of higher learning is Louisiana State University, at Baton Rouge. The university also has campuses at Alexandria, Eunice, and Shreveport and a medical center at New Orleans. Other state schools include Grambling State University, at Grambling; Louisiana Tech University, at Ruston; McNeese State University, at Lake Charles; Nicholls State University, at Thibodaux; Northeast Louisiana University, at Monroe; Northwestern State University of Louisiana, at Natchitoches; Southeastern Louisiana University, at Hammond; Southern University and Agricultural and Mechanical College, at Baton Rouge; and The University of Southwestern Louisiana, at Lafayette.

Tulane University of Louisiana and Loyola University, both at New Orleans, are large private schools. Others are Centenary College, at Shreveport; Xavier University and Dillard University, both at New Orleans; and Louisiana College, at Pineville.

Louisiana State Department of Commerce and Industry

The Acadian House Museum, Longfellow-Evangeline State Commemorative Area, displays relics of Acadian life.

Government and Politics

New Orleans served as the seat of government from 1722 until 1849, except for the year 1830, when Donaldsonville served as the capital. Baton Rouge has been the capital since 1849. The state is governed under a constitution adopted in 1974. Louisiana's chief executive officer is the governor. Lawmaking is in the hands of the Senate and the House of Representatives. The Supreme Court heads the judiciary.

The Democratic party dominates Louisiana politics. The state supported the Democratic candidate in most presidential elections since 1876. Exceptions were the elections of 1948, when it voted States' Rights Democratic; 1956, 1964, 1972, and 1980, Republican; and 1968, American Independent.

HISTORY OF LOUISIANA

What is now the Pelican State was part of the Louisiana Purchase of 1803. Its northern boundary, along the 33rd parallel, was fixed by Congress in 1804. Its original eastern boundary followed the Mississippi River and then the 31st parallel as far east as the Perdido River. In 1812 Louisiana's southeastern boundary was cut back to the Pearl River. The western border was in dispute until 1819, when Spain accepted the Sabine River as the basis of the Louisiana-Texas line. The following sections tell the story of Louisiana's development into a modern state.

Exploration and Settlement

The early history of Louisiana was made by three bold explorers. La Salle descended the Mississippi River to its mouth in 1682 and claimed the entire basin for France. The Canadian Iberville made the first thorough exploration of the present New Orleans-Baton Rouge area in 1699. His brother Bienville founded New Orleans in 1718. (*See also* La Salle; Iberville; Bienville.)

In 1762 France ceded the Louisiana region to its ally Spain (*see* French and Indian War). After the Revolutionary War hardy Western boatmen and traders began shipping produce into New Orleans.

Couples stroll on the lawn of the 'Olivier Plantation', a watercolor painted by Adrian Persac in about 1861. This is before the Civil War disrupted the plantation life of the Old South.
Courtesy of the Louisiana State Museum; photo, Jack Beech

LOUISIANA

High customs duties and Spanish threats to close the port angered the Americans.

Spain returned the Louisiana Territory to France by secret treaty in 1800. At that time most of the Louisianans lived along the Red and Mississippi rivers. New Orleans was the chief settlement, with a population of about 10,000.

Louisiana Purchase to the Civil War

The growing tension over trading rights in New Orleans led to the American purchase of Louisiana from France in 1803 (*see* Louisiana Purchase). The following year Congress divided the region into the District of Louisiana (later Missouri Territory), north of latitude 33°, and the Territory of Orleans, south of that parallel. In 1812 the southern section, renamed Louisiana, became the 18th state. In 1815 the British lost the battle of New Orleans near the city (*see* War of 1812). The first street parade of the Mardi Gras in New Orleans was held in 1838.

Louisiana seceded from the Union and joined the Confederacy in 1861. Its control of the mouth of the Mississippi was lost in 1862 when a Federal fleet under David G. Farragut captured New Orleans and Baton Rouge (*see* Farragut; Civil War, American).

Louisiana was readmitted to the Union in 1868 after it had drawn up a new constitution granting equal rights to its black population. P. B. S. Pinchback was one of three blacks who served as lieutenant governor during Reconstruction; he also served for a short time as acting governor. The Reconstruction government was toppled in 1877, when Federal troops were withdrawn (*see* Reconstruction Period).

The Modern State

Louisiana's present commercial importance owes much to the work of two 19th-century men. In the 1830's Capt. Henry M. Shreve opened the Red River to navigation (*see* Shreveport). Another riverman, James B. Eads, completed a system of jetties in the mouth of the Mississippi in 1879 (*see* Jetty).

Much of the state's progress in the 1900's has been due to the development of its rich mineral resources and manufacturing industries. Louisiana's politics were dominated by Huey P. Long, called the Kingfish, from 1928 until his assassination in 1935.

Since 1970 the state's population has increased by about 560,000 persons. (*See also* United States, section "The South"; individual entries in the Fact-Index on Louisiana persons, places, products, and events.)

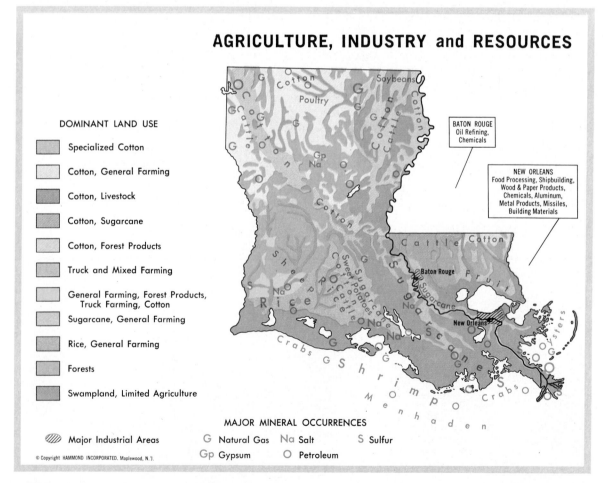

AGRICULTURE, INDUSTRY and RESOURCES

DOMINANT LAND USE

- Specialized Cotton
- Cotton, General Farming
- Cotton, Livestock
- Cotton, Sugarcane
- Cotton, Forest Products
- Truck and Mixed Farming
- General Farming, Forest Products, Truck Farming, Cotton
- Sugarcane, General Farming
- Rice, General Farming
- Forests
- Swampland, Limited Agriculture

BATON ROUGE
Oil Refining, Chemicals

NEW ORLEANS
Food Processing, Shipbuilding, Wood & Paper Products, Chemicals, Aluminum, Metal Products, Missiles, Building Materials

MAJOR MINERAL OCCURRENCES

Major Industrial Areas   G Natural Gas   Na Salt   S Sulfur

© Copyright HAMMOND INCORPORATED. Maplewood, N.J.   Gp Gypsum   O Petroleum

Notable Events in Louisiana History

1541—De Soto explores northern Louisiana.
1682—La Salle descends Mississippi River; names territory Louisiana.
1713–14—Louis St. Denis builds Fort St. Jean Baptiste on site of Natchitoches.
1717—Spaniards establish mission near Natchitoches.
1718—Bienville founds New Orleans; names it for duke of Orléans. Cotton planted near Natchitoches.
1760—Acadians begin arriving from Nova Scotia.
1762—Louis XV gives all Louisiana west of Mississippi River plus "island of New Orleans" to Spain; rest of Louisiana ceded to Britain in 1763.
1768–69—New Orleans revolt against Spain put down.
1779—Spain and Britain at war; Bernardo de Galvez seizes Baton Rouge from British.
1795—Boundary between Louisiana and West Florida set at 31st parallel. Spanish-U. S. treaty permits U. S. navigation on the Mississippi. Étienne de Boré perfects sugarcane refining.
1800—Spain cedes Louisiana Territory to France.
1803—U. S. purchases Louisiana from France.
1804—Territory of Orleans created south of 33d parallel; capital, New Orleans; governor, William Claiborne.
1810—West Floridians rebel; seize Baton Rouge.
1812—Louisiana becomes 18th state, April 30; capital, New Orleans; governor, William Claiborne. First steamboat, 'New Orleans', navigates the Mississippi River from Pittsburgh, Pa., to New Orleans.
1815—Andrew Jackson defeats British at New Orleans.
1819—Spain cedes claim to areas west of Sabine River.
1823—First gas well in state drilled near Natchitoches.
1830—Capital moved to Donaldsonville; New Orleans, in 1831; Baton Rouge, 1849–62 and after 1882.
1835—Caddo Indians cede lands in Louisiana. Capt. Henry M. Shreve founds Shreveport.
1838—First Mardi Gras parade in New Orleans held.
1853—Thousands die in yellow fever epidemic in New Orleans.
1860—Louisiana State University is founded at Baton Rouge.
1861—Louisiana secedes from Union; joins Confederacy.
1862—David G. Farragut takes New Orleans and Baton Rouge.
1864—Confederates retain hold on western Louisiana.
1868—Louisiana readmitted to Union.
1879—James B. Eads builds jetties on Mississippi River.
1894—Federal leprosarium opened at Carville.
1901—Oil discovered near Jennings.
1905—Mining of sulfur begins in Calcasieu Parish.
1927—Mississippi flood causes immense damage.
1928—Huey P. Long, born 1893 in Winnfield, elected governor; elected U. S. senator in 1930; assassinated in 1935.
1932—Present State Capitol completed.
1935—Huey P. Long Bridge across Mississippi River dedicated; Bonnet Carré Spillway constructed.
1946—Second free port in U. S. opened at New Orleans.
1952—Louisiana's Industry Inducement Plan established.
1956—Causeway over Lake Pontchartrain completed.
1958—Longest cantilever bridge in U. S. completed across Mississippi River at New Orleans.
1963—Pontchartrain Expressway completed. Mississippi River-Gulf Outlet completed.
1965—Hurricane Betsy causes 500 million dollars' property damage; 81 persons die in wake of storm.
1974—Present state constitution adopted.
1975—Louisiana Superdome, world's largest indoor stadium, opened in New Orleans.

1682

1795

1812

1838

STATE FLOWER:
Magnolia

STATE TREE:
Bald Cypress

STATE BIRD:
Brown Pelican

STATE SEAL: A pelican feeds its
young; surrounding birds is
state motto.

Louisiana Profile

FLAG: *See* Flags of the United States.
MOTTO: Union, Justice, Confidence.
SONG: 'Give Me Louisiana'—words and
music by Doralice Fontane.

Louisiana is a state in transition—from a rural, agricultural economy to an urban, industrial one. This transition holds great promise for the future of the Pelican State, but it has also created many of the problems and peculiar contrasts that mark Louisiana life today. In colorful New Orleans, a huge facility for the manufacture of Saturn rockets bears witness to Louisiana's commitment to the Space Age. The production of these rockets has made Louisiana vital to the United States space program. Nearby, Cajun trappers still ply the bayous in dugout canoes, hunting fur-bearing animals much as their ancestors did. Agriculture accounts for only about a tenth of the value of the state's annual production, and only 3 percent of the labor force work on farms. Tenant farmers still operate about one sixth of Louisiana's farms, but they are being displaced by the use of modern machinery.

Increasingly, the state's population has come to center upon its cities. New Orleans, perhaps the most genuinely international of United States cities, ranks close to New York City in the value of its foreign trade. The millions of tourists who visit it each year are attracted mainly by the traditional—Mardi Gras, New Orleans jazz, fine antebellum mansions, and Cajun and Creole cooking.

Louisiana has made great progress in attracting new industries, particularly those capable of effectively utilizing the rich mineral resources that are the state's chief source of wealth. Personal income has risen steadily in recent years, and so has the number of available jobs. At the same time Louisiana, like many Northern and Southern states, has suffered serious racial difficulties as school desegregation has extended from the cities into the rural areas and as other branches of Louisiana life have gradually become integrated.

316

Louisiana picture profile

Built before the Civil War, The Shadows is one of the South's many handsome plantation homes. The mansion, in New Iberia, is now owned by the National Trust for Historical Preservation.

The War Memorial Tower, a campanile 175 feet high, dominates the Louisiana State University campus at Baton Rouge. The university opened in 1860 as a seminary and military academy and was given its present name in 1870.

Louisiana has the tallest State Capitol. Its 34 stories rise high over the city of Baton Rouge. Built in 1932, the Capitol stands in a handsome 27-acre park.

The Old State Capitol at Baton Rouge was originally completed in the late 1840's. It was designed in a mixture of styles—Norman, Gothic, and Moorish. The building was reconstructed in 1882.

The facade of St. Louis Cathedral is seen from the lawns of Jackson Square in the French Quarter of New Orleans, Louisiana's largest city. In the foreground is a bronze statue of Gen. Andrew Jackson.

Louisiana picture profile

These Southern belles have gathered at Chalmette National Historical Park to celebrate the anniversary of General Jackson's victory against the British in the battle of New Orleans. The obelisk marks his battle position.

Graceful egrets are characteristic of the varied wildlife of Louisiana. The Jungle Gardens at Avery Island, one of the Salt "islands" of Iberia Parish, is a sanctuary for these and other birds as well as a preserve for rare plants.

Fontainebleau State Park is near Mandeville on Lake Pontchartrain. It is one of nearly 20 picturesque sites that are maintained by the Louisiana State Parks and Recreation Commission.

In the portions of New Orleans that are below sea level, bodies are interred aboveground. In this corner of a New Orleans cemetery, it has not been possible to dig conventional graves.

The Mississippi, which flows through Louisiana and empties into the Gulf of Mexico, is not only one of the great continental waterways but also an inspiration to artists and writers.

Surrounded by the bustle of modern New Orleans, the old French Quarter of the city still preserves a European look. Iron lace, adorned with plants and flowers, is typical of the balconies in the French Quarter.

The Spanish influence on southern Louisiana is noticeable in the St. Joseph Abbey at St. Benedict, a small town 15 miles north of Lake Pontchartrain. The Spanish ruled Louisiana from 1762 to 1800.

At the Cotton Festival, held annually in Ville Platte, Le Tournoi (The Tourney) combines the spirit of a modern American rodeo with that of a medieval joust. The cowboy shown here is riding at full gallop in an attempt to spear a small, dangling ring.

The festival of Mardi Gras, or Shrove Tuesday, is the occasion of a spectacular carnival parade every year in the streets of New Orleans. The festival attracts visitors from all parts of the country.

LOUISIANA FACT SUMMARY

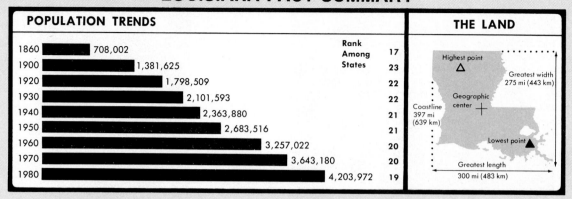

POPULATION TRENDS

Year	Population	Rank Among States
1860	708,002	17
1900	1,381,625	23
1920	1,798,509	22
1930	2,101,593	22
1940	2,363,880	21
1950	2,683,516	21
1960	3,257,022	20
1970	3,643,180	20
1980	4,203,972	19

THE LAND

Highest point △
Greatest width 275 mi (443 km)
Geographic center +
Coastline 397 mi (639 km)
Lowest point ▲
Greatest length 300 mi (483 km)

LARGEST CITIES (1980 census)

New Orleans (557,927): a major U.S. port on the Mississippi River; the commercial center of the South; cotton market; International Trade Mart; New Orleans Museum of Art; Tulane and Loyola universities; Mardi Gras; annual Sugar Bowl football classic; Cabildo, St. Louis Cathedral, and French Market in the French Quarter (*see* New Orleans).

Baton Rouge (219,844): state capital; Mississippi River port and industrial center; petrochemical products; sugar plantations nearby; Louisiana State University; Southern University (*see* Baton Rouge).

Shreveport (205,820): on Red River; oil and natural-gas center; cotton; fabricated metal and lumber products; Louisiana State Fair; Barksdale Air Force Base nearby (*see* Shreveport).

Metairie (164,160): residential area west of New Orleans; Phillips College of Greater New Orleans.

Lafayette (81,961): commercial city; sugar factories; oil company center; The University of Southwestern Louisiana.

Lake Charles (75,226): port; oil refineries; rice; McNeese State University.

Kenner (66,382): suburb of New Orleans; Jefferson Downs Racetrack.

Monroe (57,597): natural-gas field, chemicals, paper, furniture manufactures; Northeast Louisiana University.

Alexandria (51,565): located on Red River; lumbering and trade center; cotton; livestock; state university.

VITAL STATISTICS 1981 (per 1,000 population)

Birthrate:	19.0
Death Rate:	8.4
Marriage Rate:	10.2

GOVERNMENT

Capital: Baton Rouge (became capital in 1849).

Statehood: Became 18th state in the Union on April 30, 1812.

Constitution: Adopted 1974; amendment may be passed by two-thirds vote of Legislature; ratified by majority voting on it in an election.

Representation in U.S. Congress: Senate—2. House of Representatives—8. Electoral votes—10.

Legislature: Senators—39; term, 4 years. Representatives—105; term, 4 years.

Executive Officers: Governor—term, 4 years; may succeed self once. Other officials—lieutenant governor, secretary of state, attorney general; all elected; terms, 4 years.

Judiciary: Supreme Court—7 justices; elected; term, 10 years. Court of Appeals—48 judges; elected; term, 10 years. District courts—167 judges; elected; term, 6 years.

Parish: 64 parishes—53 parishes governed by a police jury of 5 to 15 members; all officials elected; term, 4 years. 11 parishes governed by parish council; officials elected pursuant to their charter.

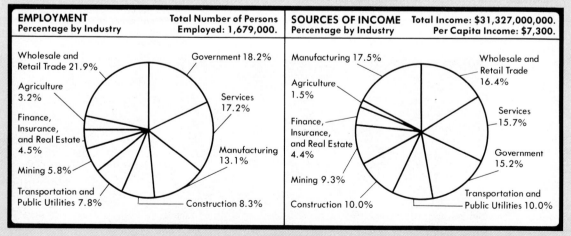

EMPLOYMENT
Percentage by Industry — Total Number of Persons Employed: 1,679,000.

- Wholesale and Retail Trade 21.9%
- Agriculture 3.2%
- Finance, Insurance, and Real Estate 4.5%
- Mining 5.8%
- Transportation and Public Utilities 7.8%
- Construction 8.3%
- Manufacturing 13.1%
- Services 17.2%
- Government 18.2%

SOURCES OF INCOME
Percentage by Industry — Total Income: $31,327,000,000. Per Capita Income: $7,300.

- Manufacturing 17.5%
- Agriculture 1.5%
- Finance, Insurance, and Real Estate 4.4%
- Mining 9.3%
- Construction 10.0%
- Wholesale and Retail Trade 16.4%
- Services 15.7%
- Government 15.2%
- Transportation and Public Utilities 10.0%

MAJOR PRODUCTS

Agricultural: Soybeans, rice, cotton, sugarcane, sweet potatoes, pecans, strawberries, peaches, cattle, milk, eggs, chickens, hay, corn, hogs, truck crops.

Manufactured: Industrial organic and inorganic chemicals, agricultural chemicals, plastics materials and resins, petroleum refining, cane sugar products, beverages, bakery products.

Mined: Natural gas, petroleum, sulfur, salt.

EDUCATION AND CULTURE

Universities and Colleges: Centenary College, Shreveport; Grambling State University, Grambling; Louisiana State University, Baton Rouge; Louisiana Tech University, Ruston; Northeast Louisiana University, Monroe; Northwestern State University of Louisiana, Natchitoches; Southern University and Agricultural and Mechanical College, Baton Rouge; Tulane University of Louisiana, New Orleans; The University of Southwestern Louisiana, Lafayette.

Libraries: East Baton Rouge Parish Library, Baton Rouge; Jefferson Parish Library, Metairie; Louisiana State Library, Baton Rouge; Louisiana State University Medical Center Library, New Orleans; Loyola University Library, New Orleans; New Orleans Public Library, New Orleans; Northeast Louisiana University, Sandel Library, Monroe; Ouachita Parish Public Library, Monroe; Tulane University of Louisiana, Howard-Tilton Memorial Library, New Orleans.

Notable Museums: Gallier House, New Orleans; Louisiana Arts and Science Center, Baton Rouge; Louisiana State Museum, New Orleans; Museum of Art of Centenary College, Saint Martinville; New Orleans Museum of Art, New Orleans; The Historic New Orleans Collection, New Orleans.

PLACES OF INTEREST

Audubon State Commemorative Area: near Saint Francisville; museum housed in Oakley House (1799); naturalist John James Audubon painted and tutored here; formal gardens; nature trails.

Avery Island: near New Iberia; oldest salt mine in Western Hemisphere; Jungle Gardens; McIlhenny Company, producer of famous tabasco sauce.

Chalmette National Historical Park: near Arabi; site where Gen. Andrew Jackson defeated British in battle of New Orleans (1815) in War of 1812; national cemetery.

Chemin-A-Haut State Park: near Bastrop; cabins; water sports.

Crowley: rice capital of state; annual International Rice Festival; Rice Museum.

Fort Jesup State Commemorative Area: near Many; established by Zachary Taylor in 1822; reconstructed officer's quarters, now a museum.

Fort Macomb State Monument: near New Orleans; built to defend New Orleans from 1819 to 1828.

Fort Pike State Commemorative Area: near New Orleans; built to defend New Orleans' waterways in 1819; military museum.

French Quarter: in New Orleans; original settlement of city; Bourbon Street; French Market; Jazz Museum; Preservation Hall; Saint Louis Cathedral.

Hodges Garden: near Florien; 4,700 acres (1,902 hectares) of gardens, greenhouses; lake; wildlife pastures; island memorial to Louisiana Purchase.

Jean Lafitte National Historical Park and Preserve: in New Orleans; 20,000 acres (8,094 hectares); preserves natural and historical resources of Mississippi Delta.

Kent House State Commemorative Area: in Alexandria; late 18th-century restored house of French and Spanish Colonial architecture; period furnishings; gardens.

Kisatchie National Forest: near Natchitoches; 597,661 acres (241,873 hectares); Azalea and Sugar Cane national recreation trails; water sports.

Lake Pontchartrain Causeway: 24-mile (39-kilometer) causeway across Lake Pontchartrain.

Longfellow-Evangeline State Commemorative Area: near St. Martinville; in Acadian country; Acadian House Museum.

Louisiana Arboretum State Preservation Area: near Ville Platte; native flora and herbarium collection; trails.

Marksville State Commemorative Area: near Marksville; prehistoric Indian religious site (AD 1–400); two pyramidal mounds; archaeological museum.

Natchitoches National Fish Hatchery: in Natchitoches; propagation of southeastern United States and Louisiana fishes for pond stocking; reptile tank.

Oak Alley Plantation: near Vacherie; restored Greek revival antebellum home (1837–39); alley of oaks planted in early 1700s.

Opelousas: Confederate capital (1862–63); Louisiana State Arboretum; Louisiana Yambilee Festival.

Poverty Point State Commemorative Area: near Parnell; 400-acre (162-hectare) site of earliest aboriginal group found in lower Mississippi Valley; museum; observation tower.

Rosedown Plantation and Gardens: near Saint Francisville; antebellum house (1835), owned by Daniel Turnbull, typifying Southern aristocratic life-style; gardens.

Saint Martin de Tours Catholic Church: in St. Martinville; Greek Revival church established in 1765 for Acadians; replica of Grotto of Lourdes; historic and religious artifacts.

San Francisco Plantation House: near Garyville; mid-19th century architecture; restored to depict pre-Civil War Creole life-style; Victorian furnishings.

BIBLIOGRAPHY FOR LOUISIANA

Bailey, B. F. Picture Book of Louisiana, rev. ed. (Whitman, 1967).

Carpenter, Allan. Louisiana (Children's, 1978).

Davis, E. A. Louisiana: the Pelican State (La. State Univ. Press, 1975).

Dufour, C. L. Ten Flags in the Wind: the Story of Louisiana (Harper, 1967).

Duplantier, K. B. and Marmillion, Norman. A Child's Louisiana (Pretzel Press, 1981).

Federal Writers' Project. New Orleans: a City Guide (Somerset, 1938).

Feibleman, Peter. The Bayous (Time-Life, 1973).

Kniffen, F. B. Louisiana: Its Land and People (La. State Univ. Press, 1968).

Taylor, J. G. Louisiana: a Bicentennial History (Norton, 1976).

Williams, T. H. Huey Long (Knopf, 1969).

Writers' Program. Louisiana: a Guide to the State, rev. ed. (Hastings, 1971).

All Fact Summary data are based on current government reports.

LOUISIANA

PARISHES

Acadia, 56,427 ... C 3
Allen, 21,390 ... C 3
Ascension, 50,068 ... E 3, E 1
Assumption, 22,084 ... D 4, E 2
Avoyelles, 41,393 ... C 3
Beauregard, 29,692 ... B 3
Bienville, 16,387 ... B 1
Bossier, 80,721 ... B 1
Caddo, 252,437 ... B 1
Calcasieu, 167,223 ... B 3
Caldwell, 10,761 ... C 2
Cameron, 9,336 ... C 4
Catahoula, 12,287 ... D 2
Claiborne, 17,095 ... B 1
Concordia, 22,981 ... D 2
De Soto, 25,727 ... B 1
East Baton Rouge, 366,191 ... D 3, E 1
East Carroll, 11,772 ... D 1
East Feliciana, 19,015 ... D 3
Evangeline, 33,343 ... C 3
Franklin, 24,141 ... D 1
Grant, 16,703 ... C 2
Iberia, 63,752 ... D 4
Iberville, 32,159 ... D 3, E 1
Jackson, 17,321 ... C 1
Jefferson, 454,592 ... E 4, G 2
Jefferson Davis, 32,168 ... C 3
Lafayette, 150,017 ... C 3
Lafourche, 82,483 ... E 4, F 2
La Salle, 17,004 ... C 2
Lincoln, 39,763 ... C 1
Livingston, 58,806 ... E 3, E 1
Madison, 15,682 ... D 1
Morehouse, 34,803 ... B 2
Natchitoches, 39,863 ... B 2
Orleans, 557,927 ... F 3, G 2
Ouachita, 139,241 ... C 1
Plaquemines, 26,049 ... F 4, G 2
Pointe Coupee, 24,045 ... D 3
Rapides, 135,282 ... C 2
Red River, 10,433 ... B 1
Richland, 22,187 ... D 1
Sabine, 25,280 ... B 2
Saint Bernard, 64,097 ... F 4, H 2
Saint Charles, 37,259 ... E 4, F 2
Saint Helena, 9,827 ... E 3
Saint James, 21,495 ... E 3, F 1
Saint John the Baptist, 31,924 ... E 3, F 1
Saint Landry, 84,128 ... C 3
Saint Martin, 40,214 ... D 3
Saint Mary, 64,253 ... D 4
Saint Tammany, 110,869 ... E 3, G 1
Tangipahoa, 80,698 ... E 3, F 1
Tensas, 8,525 ... D 1
Terrebonne, 94,393 ... E 4, E 2
Union, 21,167 ... C 1
Vermilion, 48,458 ... C 4
Vernon, 53,475 ... B 3
Washington, 44,207 ... E 3
Webster, 43,631 ... B 1
West Baton Rouge, 19,086 ... D 3
West Carroll, 12,922 ... D 1
West Feliciana, 12,186 ... D 3
Winn, 17,253 ... C 1

CITIES AND TOWNS

Abbeville, 12,391 ... C 4
Alexandria, 51,565 ... C 2
Alexandria (met. area), 151,985 ... C 2
Amelia, 3,617 ... E 2
Amite, 4,301 ... E 1
Arabi, 10,248 ... G 2
Arcadia, 3,403 ... C 1
Archibald, 425 ... D 1
Arnaudville, 1,679 ... D 3
Baker, 12,865 ... D 3
Baldwin, 2,644 ... D 4
Barataria, 1,123 ... G 2
Basile, 2,635 ... C 3
Bastrop, 15,527 ... D 1
Baton Rouge (cap.), 219,844 ... E 1
Baton Rouge (met. area), 493,973 ... E 1
Bayou Cane, 15,723 ... F 2
Bayou Vista, 5,805 ... D 4
Belle Chasse, 5,412 ... G 2
Benton, 1,864 ... B 1
Bernice, 1,956 ... C 1
Berwick, 4,466 ... E 2
Bogalusa, 16,976 ... E 3
Bossier City, 50,817 ... B 1
Boutte, 950 ... F 2
Boyce, 1,198 ... C 2
Breaux Bridge, 5,922 ... D 3
Broussard, 2,923 ... C 3
Bunkie, 5,364 ... C 3
Buras-Triumph, 4,137 ... F 4
Cameron, 1,736 ... B 4
Campti, 1,069 ... B 2
Carville, 1,037 ... E 1
Chalmette, 33,847 ... G 2
Chatham, 714 ... C 1
Chauvin, 3,338 ... E 4
Cheneyville, 865 ... C 2
Chestnut, 25 ... C 1
Church Point, 4,599 ... C 3
Clarks, 931 ... C 1
Clinton, 1,919 ... E 3
Cloutierville, 100 ... B 2
Colfax, 1,680 ... C 2
Columbia, 687 ... C 1
Convent, 400 ... E 2
Cotton Valley, 1,445 ... B 1
Cottonport, 1,911 ... D 2
Coushatta, 2,084 ... B 1
Covington, 7,892 ... G 1
Crowley, 16,036 ... C 3
Cullen, 1,869 ... B 1
De Quincy, 3,966 ... B 3
De Ridder, 11,057 ... B 3
Delcambre, 2,216 ... C 4
Delhi, 3,290 ... D 1
Denham Springs, 8,563 ... E 1
Des Allemands, 2,920 ... F 2
Donaldsonville, 7,901 ... E 1
Doyline, 801 ... B 1
Dubach, 1,161 ... C 1
Edgard, 400 ... F 2
Effie, 300 ... C 2
Elizabeth, 454 ... C 3
Elton, 1,450 ... C 3
Erath, 2,259 ... C 3
Eunice, 12,479 ... C 3
Farmerville, 3,768 ... C 1
Ferriday, 4,472 ... D 2
Florien, 964 ... B 2
Fort Polk, 14,142 ... B 2
Franklin, 9,584 ... D 4
Franklinton, 4,119 ... E 3
French Settlement, 761 ... F 1
Galliano, 5,159 ... E 4
Garyville, 2,856 ... F 1
Gibsland, 1,354 ... B 1
Gibson, 950 ... E 2
Glenmora, 1,479 ... C 3
Gloster, 780 ... B 1
Golden Meadow, 2,282 ... E 4
Gonzales, 7,287 ... E 1
Grambling, 4,226 ... C 1
Gramercy, 3,211 ... F 1
Grand Chenier, 710 ... C 4
Grand Isle, 1,982 ... F 4
Greensburg, 662 ... E 3
Gretna, 20,615 ... G 2
Gueydan, 1,695 ... C 3
Hackberry, 750 ... B 3
Hahnville, 2,947 ... F 2
Hammond, 15,043 ... F 1
Harahan, 11,384 ... G 2
Harrisonburg, 610 ... C 2
Harvey, 22,709 ... G 2
Haynesville, 3,454 ... B 1
Hodge, 708 ... C 1
Homer, 4,307 ... B 1
Houma, 32,602 ... E 4
Independence, 1,684 ... E 3
Iota, 1,326 ... C 3
Iowa, 2,437 ... C 3
Jackson, 3,878 ... D 3
Jeanerette, 6,511 ... D 4
Jefferson, 15,550 ... G 2
Jena, 4,375 ... C 2
Jennings, 12,401 ... C 3
Jonesboro, 5,061 ... C 1
Jonesville, 2,828 ... D 2
Joyce, 700 ... C 2
Kaplan, 5,016 ... C 3
Kenner, 66,382 ... F 2
Kentwood, 2,667 ... E 3
Kinder, 2,603 ... C 3
Labadieville, 2,138 ... E 2
Lafayette, 81,961 ... D 3
Lafayette (met. area), 150,017 ... D 3
Lake Arthur, 3,615 ... C 3
Lake Charles, 75,226 ... B 3
Lake Charles (met. area), 167,223 ... B 3
Lake Providence, 6,361 ... D 1
LaPlace, 16,112 ... F 1
Larose, 5,234 ... E 4
Lecompte, 1,661 ... C 2
Leesville, 9,054 ... B 2
Livingston, 1,260 ... F 1
Lockport, 2,424 ... F 2
Logansport, 1,565 ... B 2
Longleaf, 80 ... C 2
Longville, 300 ... B 3
Luling, 4,006 ... F 2
Lutcher, 4,730 ... F 2
Madisonville, 799 ... G 1
Mamou, 3,194 ... C 3
Mandeville, 6,076 ... G 1
Mansfield, 6,485 ... B 1
Mansura, 2,074 ... D 2
Many, 3,988 ... B 2
Maringouin, 1,291 ... D 3
Marion, 989 ... C 1
Marksville, 5,113 ... D 2
Marrero, 36,548 ... G 2
Melrose, 500 ... C 2
Melville, 1,764 ... D 3
Mer Rouge, 802 ... D 1
Merryville, 1,286 ... B 3
Metairie, 164,160 ... G 2
Minden, 15,074 ... B 1
Monroe, 57,597 ... D 1
Monroe (met. area), 139,241 ... D 1
Montgomery, 843 ... C 2
Mooringsport, 911 ... A 1
Morgan City, 16,114 ... E 2
Morganza, 846 ... D 3
Napoleonville, 829 ... E 2
Natalbany, 900 ... F 1
Natchez, 527 ... B 2
Natchitoches, 16,664 ... B 2
New Iberia, 32,766 ... D 3
New Orleans, 557,927 ... G 1
New Orleans (met. area), 1,187,073 ... G 1
New Roads, 3,924 ... D 3
Newellton, 1,726 ... D 1
Norco, 4,416 ... F 2
Oak Grove, 2,214 ... D 1
Oakdale, 7,155 ... C 3
Oberlin, 1,764 ... C 3
Oil City, 1,323 ... B 1
Olla, 1,603 ... C 2
Opelousas, 18,903 ... D 3
Paincortville, 2,004 ... E 2
Paradis, 750 ... F 2
Patterson, 4,693 ... D 4
Pearl River, 1,693 ... G 1
Pineville, 12,034 ... C 2
Plain Dealing, 1,213 ... B 1
Plaquemine, 7,521 ... D 3
Pleasant Hill, 776 ... B 2
Pointe a la Hache, 750 ... F 4
Ponchatoula, 5,469 ... F 1
Port Allen, 6,114 ... D 3
Port Barre, 2,625 ... D 3
Port Sulphur, 3,318 ... F 4
Raceland, 6,302 ... F 2
Rayne, 9,066 ... C 3
Rayville, 4,610 ... D 1
Reserve, 7,288 ... F 1
Ringgold, 1,655 ... B 1
Rodessa, 337 ... A 1
Roseland, 1,346 ... E 3
Ruston, 20,585 ... C 1
Saint Francisville, 1,471 ... D 3
Saint Joseph, 1,687 ... D 2
Saint Martinville, 7,965 ... C 3
Schriever, 700 ... E 2
Seymourville, 2,891 ... E 1
Shreveport, 205,820 ... B 1
Shreveport (met. area), 376,710 ... B 1
Simmesport, 2,293 ... D 3
Slidell, 26,718 ... G 1
Sorrento, 1,197 ... F 1
Springhill, 6,516 ... B 1
Starks, 750 ... B 3
Sterlington, 1,400 ... C 1
Sulphur, 19,709 ... B 3
Sunset, 2,300 ... C 3
Sunshine, 900 ... E 1
Supreme, 617 ... E 2
Tallulah, 11,634 ... D 1
Terry Town, 23,548 ... G 2
Theriot, 450 ... E 4
Thibodaux, 15,810 ... F 2
Triumph-Buras, 4,137 ... F 4
Urania, 849 ... C 2
Vacherie, 2,169 ... F 2
Venice, 900 ... F 4
Vidalia, 5,936 ... D 2
Ville Platte, 9,201 ... C 3
Vinton, 3,631 ... B 3
Violet, 11,678 ... G 2
Vivian, 4,225 ... B 1
Walker, 2,957 ... E 1
Washington, 1,266 ... C 3
Waterproof, 1,339 ... D 2
Weeks, 400 ... D 4
Welsh, 3,515 ... C 3
West Monroe, 14,993 ... C 1
Westlake, 5,246 ... B 3
Westwego, 12,663 ... G 2
White Castle, 2,160 ... E 1
Winnfield, 7,311 ... C 2
Winnsboro, 5,921 ... D 1
Wisner, 1,424 ... D 1
Zachary, 7,297 ... D 3
Zwolle, 2,602 ... B 2

OTHER FEATURES

Allemands (lake) ... F 2
Amite (riv.) ... E 3
Anacoco (lake) ... B 2
Atchafalaya (bay) ... D 4
Atchafalaya (riv.) ... D 3
Barataria (bay) ... F 4
Bayou D' Arbonne (lake) ... C 1
Bistineau (lake) ... B 1
Boeuf (riv.) ... D 1
Bonnet Carré (floodway) ... F 1
Borgne (lake) ... H 2
Breton (isls.) ... F 4
Breton (sound) ... F 4
Bundick (lake) ... B 3
Caddo (lake) ... A 1
Caillou (bay) ... D 4
Calcasieu (lake) ... B 4
Calcasieu (riv.) ... C 3
Catahoula (lake) ... C 2
Chandeleur (isls.) ... G 4
Chandeleur (sound) ... F 4
Claiborne (lake) ... B 1
Cocodrie (lake) ... C 2
Cote Blanche (bay) ... D 4
Cross (lake) ... B 1
Curlew (isls.) ... G 4
Dernieres (isls.) ... E 4
Driskill (mt.) ... B 1
East (bay) ... F 4
Eloi (bay) ... F 4
Grand (lake) ... C 4
Grand (lake) ... D 4
Iatt (lake) ... C 2
Intracoastal Waterway ... B 3
Jean Lafitte Nat'l Hist. Park ... G 2
Lafourche (bayou) ... F 2
Little (riv.) ... C 1
Louisiana (point) ... B 4
Macon (bayou) ... D 1
Main Pass (passage) ... F 4
March (isl.) ... D 4
Maurepas (lake) ... F 1
Mississippi (delta) ... F 4
Mississippi (riv.) ... D 2
Mississippi (sound) ... F 3
Mississippi River Gulf Outlet ... F 4
North Pass (passage) ... G 4
Ouachita (riv.) ... C 1
Pass Manchac (passage) ... G 1
Pearl (riv.) ... F 3
Pontchartrain (lake) ... G 1
Red (riv.) ... C 2
Red Chute (bayou) ... B 1
Sabine (lake) ... B 4
Sabine (riv.) ... B 3
Sabine Pass (passage) ... B 4
Saline (lake) ... C 2
Salvador (lake) ... G 2
South Pass (passage) ... F 4
Southwest Pass (passage) ... F 4
Terrebonne (bay) ... E 4
Tickfaw (riv.) ... F 1
Timbalier (bay) ... E 4
Timbalier (isl.) ... E 4
Toledo Bend (dam) ... B 2
Toledo Bend (res.) ... B 2
Turkey Creek (lake) ... D 2
Vermilion (bay) ... C 4
Vernon (lake) ... B 2
Verret (lake) ... E 2
Wallace (lake) ... B 1
West (bay) ... F 4
White (lake) ... C 4

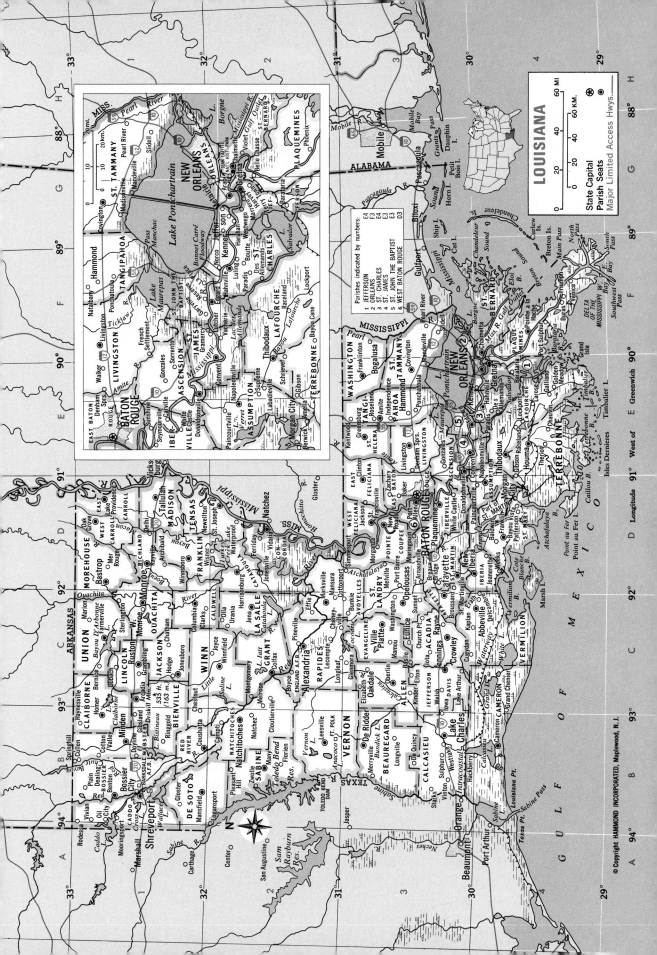

LOUISIANA PURCHASE

LOUISIANA PURCHASE. In 1803 United States President Thomas Jefferson set the example of getting new territory by purchase rather than by war. He did so by buying from France the vast tract of land known as Louisiana. The United States did not differ from Old World countries in wanting to expand its control to its "natural boundaries." It did differ in the method it used to accomplish this.

The city of New Orleans was wanted very much by all the American settlers west of the Appalachians. The nation that controlled New Orleans could control the Mississippi River. Western farmers were eager for this control to be in the hands of the United States. Their grain, hogs, cattle, and other produce were sent to market by flatboats that floated down the great "father of waters."

Spain had held this important gateway to the West since 1762. It was given to Spain by treaty from France. Then suddenly, in 1802, news came that two years earlier Napoleon had forced weak Spain to give New Orleans and the whole Louisiana territory to the French empire. This was bad news for the Western farmer. France was then the most powerful country in the world, and there was no hope of forcing any privileges from it.

Napoleon's dream of a vast colonial empire vanished almost as suddenly as it had come. England in its war against France defeated the French navy. France could hardly hold territory across the Atlantic Ocean while England controlled the seas. Robert Livingston, the American minister to France, pointed out this fact to Napoleon. Napoleon then decided to sell the Louisiana territory.

Cost of Purchase

When James Monroe arrived in France with power from President Jefferson to buy New Orleans and West Florida for not more than 10 million dollars, he was offered the whole of the French territory for approximately 15 million dollars. Although the American agents had no authority to spend such a large sum, they signed the treaty of purchase on April 30, 1803. The area involved was a vast 529,911,680 acres (214,447,647 hectares). In December the Stars and Stripes was raised over New Orleans.

Thus at one stroke the area of the United States was doubled. President Jefferson believed that the annexation and government of so vast a territory was unconstitutional. He wanted an amendment to the Constitution to ratify it. The members of his Cabinet did not think this necessary, and their views prevailed. The New England Federalists were enraged at the prospect of the admission of numerous new states, whose votes in Senate and House would reinforce those of the South and West. Some, such as Josiah Quincy, advocated secession—"amicably, if they can; violently if they must." Thirteen states, either in whole or in part, were carved out of this land between the Mississippi River and the Rockies. The price of the Louisiana Purchase was only a tiny fraction of its value today. (*See also* United States.)

Courtesy of the Louisville Convention & Visitors Bureau

A glass-sheathed atrium highlights the Galleria complex of office towers and shops in the heart of downtown Louisville.

LOUISVILLE, Ky. In pioneer days treacherous rapids interrupted traffic on the Ohio River, forcing the carrying of cargo overland to bypass them. The completion of the Louisville and Portland Canal in 1830 ended this. The Ohio River was from that time on open to through traffic from Pittsburgh, Pa., to the Mississippi River. As a result the port of Louisville grew in commercial importance. Today it is the largest city in Kentucky.

Louisville's industrial growth started soon after the Civil War. Its strategic location was important. To the north and west lay the great grain regions of the United States. To the south were abundant supplies of tobacco, cotton, and minerals.

A hydroelectric plant and steam-electric plants provide abundant power. Oil refining, lumber milling, and photo engraving are important industries. Louisville's factories make electrical appliances, tobacco products, bourbon whiskey, petrochemicals, processed foods, farm machinery and other metal goods, aluminum products, synthetic rubber, paints and varnishes, textiles, and printed matter.

Trunk-line railroads serve the city, which also contains large railroad headquarters and repair shops. Louisville is a major center for livestock and tobacco transactions. There are two airports.

Louisville's parks and playgrounds cover more than 3,300 acres (1,300 hectares). The city is the seat of the University of Louisville, two accredited colleges, and two theological seminaries. The J. B. Speed Art Museum has notable collections. In 1962 the Rauch Memorial Planetarium was opened. The Kentucky Derby is run every May at Churchill Downs, the city's famous racetrack.

Louisville was first called Beargrass Settlement. It was founded in 1778 by George Rogers Clark as a frontier outpost. When it was incorporated as a town in 1780, Clark named it Louisville in honor of Louis

XVI of France. Many of its early settlers came from France, and later a number from Germany.

The city was incorporated in 1828. It has a mayor-council form of government. Population (1980 census), 298,451.

LOURDES, France. Almost 3 million pilgrims—many of them sick or disabled—visit Lourdes each year. Located in southwestern France, the town is primarily important for its religious history. Situated at the foot of the Pyrenees and now on both banks of the  Gave de Pau stream the town and its fortress formed a strategic stronghold in medieval times.

At Lourdes in 1858 in a grotto beside the Gave de Pau, a young girl, Bernadette Soubirous, saw visions of the Virgin Mary. She also found a spring said to have healing powers. Today Roman Catholics from all over the world visit the shrine at Lourdes.

Bernadette, christened Marie Bernard, was born on Jan. 7, 1844, in Lourdes. She was the oldest of nine children in her family.

On Feb. 11, 1858, Bernadette, her sister Marie, and a friend, Jeanne Abadie, went to gather twigs for firewood by the banks of the Gave de Pau. A delicate girl, Bernadette lagged behind her companions. They had waded across a shallow part of the stream that separated them from a grotto on the other side. As she was preparing to cross, Bernadette heard the roar of a great wind; yet the trees were still. Looking up, she saw in the grotto a vision she later described as "a lady, young and beautiful."

Bernadette continued to have visions, always in the grotto. During the ninth vision she uncovered a trickle of water that proved to be a spring. A few days later a blind stonecutter bathed his eyes in the water and reported a miraculous cure.

Twenty thousand people gathered at Lourdes the day of Bernadette's 16th vision. According to various historians, she saw 18 or 19 visions.

Bernadette took final vows as a nun with the Sisters of Charity at Nevers in 1878. On April 16, 1879, Bernadette died of tuberculosis and was buried in the convent chapel. She was beatified in 1925 and canonized on Dec. 8, 1933. Her feast day is February 18.

Today there are three churches near the site of Bernadette's visions: Notre Dame de Lourdes, Saint Pie X (the second largest church in the world), and the Church of the Rosary.

A Way of the Cross with life-size figures mounts the tree-covered hill to the left of Notre Dame de Lourdes. Down by the grotto are three low buildings where the sick can bathe in water from the spring.

Inside the Grotte de Massabielle is an altar. Hundreds of votive candles left by pilgrims burn in and around the grotto. In the grotto and around it hang crutches left by cripples who have visited the shrine.

Candles that burn in the grotto at Lourdes have been left by pilgrims visiting the shrine.

Lourdes is in the department of Hautes-Pyrénées. It is divided into an old town and a new town by the Gave de Pau. The new quarter, of which the grotto is a part, is on the left bank. The old quarter, on the right bank, is famous for its ancient fortress. Population (1975 census), 17,685.

LOW, Juliette (1860–1927). Girl Scouts in the United States celebrate October 31 as Founder's Day. It is the birthday of Juliette Low, who organized the first Girl Guides in the United States at her home in Savannah, Ga., on March 12, 1912. The Girl Guides soon took the name of Girl Scouts. Low became their first president.

Juliette Gordon was born in Savannah on Oct. 31, 1860. Her father was General William Washington Gordon. Her mother is said to have been the first white child born in Chicago. Young Gordon went to private schools in Virginia and in New York City. In 1886 she became married to William Low of Warwickshire, England.

The Lows had houses in England, in Scotland, and in the United States. They were friends of Lord Robert Baden-Powell and of his sister Agnes. Baden-Powell had founded the Boy Scouts and, together with his sister, in 1910 established the Girl Guides in Great Britain.

Juliette Low was a talented artist and helped organize the Savannah Art Club. Her chief interest, however, was the Girl Scouts. Although deaf, she overcame the handicap and traveled widely to interest people in the Girl Scout movement. After retiring as president, she received the title of Founder. She died on Jan. 17, 1927, in England.

LOWELL FAMILY. A prominent and gifted Massachusetts family, the Lowells included, among others, the founder of the first textile mill in the United States, Francis Cabot Lowell; a major literary figure, James Russell Lowell; an astronomer and founder of the Lowell Observatory, Percival Lowell; one of Harvard University's most significant presidents, Abbott Lawrence Lowell; and two renowned 20th-century poets, Amy Lowell and Robert Lowell.

Francis Cabot Lowell (1775–1817). The son of Judge John Lowell, Francis Cabot Lowell was born in Newburyport, Mass., on April 7, 1775. His textile mill performed all operations converting raw cotton into finished cloth. With another inventor he devised an efficient power loom and spinning devices.

The working conditions in his mill and the workers' housing that he built were particularly good for the period. He died on Aug. 10, 1817, in Boston.

James Russell Lowell (1819–91). One of the most imaginative American writers of his generation, James Russell Lowell was born on Feb. 22, 1819, in Cambridge, Mass. After attending classical school in Cambridge, James entered Harvard University. He read a great deal but neglected formal studies. After graduation in 1838, he studied at Harvard Law School and was admitted to the bar in 1840.

By 1844 Lowell had made his start as a poet, editor, critic, and reformer. His literary work had gained him fame that led to the offer of a professorship at Harvard. Lowell accepted but asked to go to Europe for a year to renew his knowledge of modern languages. On his return he married and settled down to a life devoted to teaching and writing.

In 1855 his lectures on English poets before the Lowell Institute led to his appointment as Smith professor of modern languages at Harvard. Longfellow · had held the post before him. In 1857 he became editor of the *Atlantic Monthly,* to which he attracted the major New England authors who ushered in a golden era of American literature. Although he resigned four years later, he continued to contribute most of his poems to that magazine. His prose writings went to the *North American Review.* During the time he was on the Harvard faculty, prose was his usual method of expression. He largely wrote travel pieces, criticisms, and literary and political essays.

In 1877 Lowell was called by the government from his university work to become the United States minister to Spain. He later exchanged this post for that of minister to England. The last years of his life were spent in Cambridge. He died on Aug. 12, 1891, at his family home, Elmwood, in Cambridge. Lowell's prose works include 'Among My Books', published in 1870; 'My Study Windows' (1871); and 'Among My Books, Second Series' (1876).

Percival Lowell (1855–1916). The brother of Abbott Lawrence Lowell and Amy Lowell, Percival was born on March 13, 1855, in Boston. Although he was an astronomer, he devoted himself to literature and travel, much of the time in the Far East. He described his travels in several books. In the 1890s he decided to undertake the study of astronomy, concentrating first on the planet Mars. He eventually predicted the existence of the planet Pluto and initiated the search that ended in its discovery 14 years after his death. He died on Nov. 12, 1916, in Flagstaff, Ariz., where he had built his own observatory.

Abbott Lawrence Lowell (1856–1943). He was born a year after his brother Percival, on Dec. 13, 1856, also in Boston. He was graduated from Harvard University in 1877, received his law degree in 1880, and practiced law in Boston for 17 years before turning to teaching at Harvard. In 1909 he became president of the university, a post he held until 1933. During his administration student enrollment more than doubled, the faculty nearly trebled, endowments increased sixfold, and new professional schools of architecture, business administration, education, and public health were added. Abbott Lowell died in Boston on Jan. 6, 1943.

Amy Lowell (1874–1925). Percival and Abbott's sister, Amy, was born Feb. 9, 1874, in Brookline, Mass. She was the youngest of five children. In 1912 her first book of poems, 'A Dome of Many-Coloured Glass', was published. In 1913 in England she met the imagist poets and was greatly influenced by them. She is most famous for her effective use of free verse.

From 1915 until her death Amy Lowell read and lectured at universities and clubs throughout the United States. She was a contradictory person, radical in her behavior but conservative in her background and in many of her attitudes. She had a vivid personality and a striking appearance. She attracted public attention by her outspokenness and her unusual habits. She smoked cigars most of her life and chose to work at night and sleep during the day. Amy Lowell died on May 12, 1925, at Brookline, in the house where she was born.

Amy Lowell wrote more than 650 poems, few of which are read today. Much of her poetry seems to have suffered from lack of restraint. However, her work has beauty. Perhaps her most famous poem is "Patterns." Her books include 'Men, Women, and Ghosts', 'What's O'Clock' (awarded a Pulitzer prize), and 'John Keats', a biography.

Robert Lowell (1917–77). The 20th-century poet was born March 1, 1917, in Boston. James Russell Lowell was his great-granduncle, and Amy, Percival, and Abbott Lawrence were his distant cousins. He attended Harvard but fell under the influence of the then-flourishing Southern formalist school of poetry and transferred to Kenyon College in Ohio. In 1940 he was graduated and was married to novelist Jean Stafford. He divorced her in 1948 and married writer and critic Elizabeth Hardwick. After some years abroad, the Lowells settled in Boston in 1954. Robert's 'Life Studies', published in 1959, won the National Book Award for poetry. During his lifetime Lowell also won the Pulitzer prize and the Bollingen poetry translation prize. He was active in the American civil rights and antiwar campaigns of the 1960s. He died in New York City on Sept. 12, 1977.

LOYOLA, IGNATIUS OF (1491?–1556). The founder of the Society of Jesus (Jesuits), Saint Ignatius spent the early part of his life as a worldly man. He was born Iñigo de Oñez y Loyola in about 1491 at the castle of Loyola, near Azpeitia in Guipúzcoa province in northern Spain.

Ignatius received only a sketchy education. Interested in games and military matters, he was trained as a soldier. During the siege of Pamplona in 1521, Ignatius broke his leg, thus ending his military career. While convalescing, he had only the lives of the saints to read. This reading moved him deeply and filled him with the desire to serve God. He went in 1522 to Our Lady's shrine at Montserrat and returned to pray and do penance in a cave near Manresa. He gave his worldly garments to the poor and wore a pilgrim's dress of sackcloth and hempen shoes.

In 1523 Ignatius traveled to Jerusalem, but he was not allowed by the authorities to remain. Back in Spain, at the age of 32, he again became a student. He was suspected of heresy, however, and was imprisoned by the Inquisition for teaching before he had completed the prescribed studies.

Meanwhile his plans were taking more definite form. He would found a Society of Jesus—spiritually drilled and disciplined like a military company—to combat heresy and to do missionary work in heathen countries. The members should be bound by the monastic vows of poverty, chastity, and obedience. They should wear no distinctive dress and should not be tied down by minute monastic rules or unusual forms of discipline.

In 1534 Ignatius and six companions formed the beginning of this organization in Paris. In 1540 its members received at Rome the sanction of the pope, and Ignatius became its first "general." The remainder of his life was spent devising the constitution of his order. He also prepared the order for its work in the Counter Reformation, in which the Roman Catholic church was to win back half the lands it had lost through Luther's revolt (*see* Reformation). He died at Rome on July 31, 1556. In 1628 he was canonized.

LUANDA, Angola. Capital of Angola, Luanda is the country's largest city and busiest seaport. Founded by the Portuguese in 1576, it became the administrative center of the colony of Angola in 1627 and was a major outlet for slave traffic to Brazil.

The harbor is situated behind Luanda Island, which forms a natural breakwater from the Atlantic Ocean. It is deep, easily accessible, and has about four square miles (ten square kilometers) suitable for anchoring ships. There are five piers and an offshore tanker terminal equipped with up-to-date loading and unloading equipment. The old fortress of Sao Miguel overlooks the port.

The chief products exported are coffee, cotton, diamonds, iron ore, and salt. Luanda is linked by rail to Malange, 308 miles (496 kilometers) to the east. The city's airport is a port of call for airlines operating between Europe and central and southern Africa.

Petroleum was discovered nearby in 1955, and there is a refinery at the north end of Luanda Bay. In the surrounding region farming is the most important economic activity, and the main crops are coffee, cotton, sisal, palm oil, and palm kernels. Electricity is supplied to the city from the Cambambe Dam on the Kwanza River.

Luanda is the seat of a Roman Catholic archdiocese and the home of the state-controlled University of Angola, founded in 1962. Skyscrapers and wide avenues give the city a modern appearance. Many Mbundu, one of Angola's largest ethnic groups, have migrated to the city over the years, and a sizable Cuban community has largely replaced the Portuguese who left in large numbers prior to independence in 1975. The Cubans supported local Angolan groups in their movement toward independence and they have remained as advisers to the new nation. The higher part of the city consists generally of outlying poverty-ridden residential districts; the lower part is commercial and industrial. (*See also* Angola.) Population (1979 estimate), 475,300.

LUBRICANT. Friction, the rubbing of one object against another, is the worst enemy of machinery. It wears out the metal, wastes power, and generates heat. To reduce friction, substances called lubricants are applied to the bearing surfaces of machinery; that is, the surfaces that rub against each other. The word lubricant comes from the Latin *lubricus*, meaning "slippery." The science of lubrication and friction is called tribology from the Greek *tribein*, "to rub."

Until about 1860 animal and vegetable oils and waxes were the primary lubricants. When petroleum oil was discovered in the United States in 1859, it was used first as a fuel for oil lamps, but soon it was discovered that petroleum oils could be made into high-quality lubricants. Petroleum oil resists degeneration by oxidation and high temperatures. Today other substances, including synthetics, solid lubricants, and even gases, also serve as lubricants.

Several qualities are essential to a good lubricant. It must have "wetting power" so that it will spread easily and penetrate between surfaces in close contact with each other. It must cling so that rubbing motion will not remove it, and it should not evaporate or lose its essential greasiness. Acid and grit should also be absent, as these corrode or scratch surfaces. A lubricant should not catch fire easily at high temperatures or become gummy at low temperatures.

The quality of a lubricant that makes it cling together and resist being squeezed out of the area in which it is working is called its viscosity. Viscosity, however, retards flow. Viscosity and freedom to flow must be balanced: Heavy loads require more viscosity, while high speeds require more freedom of flow. Cold increases the viscosity of liquids, but it reduces it for gases. Petroleum products—ranging from light oils to heavy greases and sometimes modified by additives—are most widely used. For very heavy machinery, greases are often mixed with graphite.

In the United States the viscosities of automotive oils are rated by their SAE (Society of Automotive Engineers) number. The lower the SAE number, the lower the viscosity. A "W" following the number represents winter ratings (at 0° F, or −18° C); otherwise the number is a summer rating at 210° F (99° C). Additives such as small amounts of very viscous synthetic polymers can produce dual-grade oils by increasing the viscosity at high temperatures for a normally low-viscosity oil. Thus an SAE 10W-40 oil is suitable for both winter and summer use; it has a low enough viscosity to allow for cold winter starts and enough viscosity to allow for hot operation.

By 1950 gas bearings were being developed for use in precision tools, dental drills, and high-speed computer memory devices. For low-bearing loads, gas bearings can be used at speeds that are ten times faster than with an oil-lubricated bearing.

LUCITE *see* FIBERS, MAN-MADE; PLASTICS.

LUCKNOW, India. The city of Lucknow is situated in the northern part of the republic of India, 540 miles (870 kilometers) northwest of Calcutta. It lies on the Gomati River, a tributary of the Ganges. It presents a striking appearance with its beautiful domes, cupolas, minarets, and parks.

Lucknow has a fine medical school and hospital, a university, and several colleges. Skilled craftsmen make gold and silver brocades, embroidery, brass and copper objects, pottery, and beaten silver ornaments. The chief industries are food processing, manufacturing, and railroad shops.

The British withstood a famous siege in Lucknow in 1857 during a rebellion of native soldiers (called sepoys) against rule by the British East India Company. At Lucknow on July 1 the rebellious sepoys forced a regiment of British troops under Sir Henry Lawrence to take refuge in the Residency and adjoining grounds of the company's chief commissioner. They were joined by British civilians.

Lawrence died from a wound a few days later. The small garrison, numbering only a few thousand men, held out against 10,000 sepoys for more than four months. At last the defenders saw the signals of Sir Colin Campbell Clyde, commander in chief of a strong relief force. The sepoys lifted the siege immediately, and survivors and rescuers quietly withdrew from the town on November 17. (*See also* India.) Population (1981 census), 895,947.

LÜDA, People's Republic of China. A municipality in Liaoning Province, southern Manchuria, Lüda is located at the southern tip of the Liaodong Peninsula between the Gulf of Bo Hai and the Yellow Sea. Lüda's name is derived from combining the first parts of the names of the naval port of *Lü*shun (for-

merly Port Arthur) and the industrial city and port of *Da*lian (Dairen), both within the municipality.

Dalian is one of China's most important fishing ports and oil tanker terminals. Industrial output has become increasingly diversified and includes machinery, chemicals, textiles, glass, ships, railway equipment and locomotives, steel, refined petroleum products, electronic equipment, and food products. Fruit warehouses and grain elevators store the agricultural products of the surrounding area until they can be loaded for re-transport. The shores of the Yellow Sea are a popular tourist attraction.

Lüshun was an area for military preparation as early as the 2nd century BC, was fortified in the 15th and 16th centuries, and in 1878 became the chief base for the Peiyang fleet. This fleet was China's first modern naval force. In 1898 Russia acquired a lease of the peninsula and the right to build a railway to Harbin. The Russians built a naval base at Port Arthur and began the development of a commercial port at nearby Dalny, now Dalian.

The Japanese occupied the area from the Russo-Japanese War of 1904 and 1905 until the defeat of Japan in World War II. In a treaty of friendship in 1945, the Soviet Union and China shared control until the Soviet forces withdrew in 1955. Population (1980 estimate), 1,927,000.

LULLY, Jean-Baptiste (1632–87). The foremost composer and musician of the 17th-century French court, Jean-Baptiste Lully, was born on Nov. 28, 1632, in Florence, Italy, as Giovanni Battista Lulli. He changed his name to its French form when he became a naturalized Frenchman in 1681.

Little is known of his early life, but in 1652 he joined the court band of Louis XIV as a violinist. His rise in the court was meteoric and was accomplished by intrigue. By 1662 he had gained complete control of all court music and by 1674 had acquired patents of operatic production so that no opera could be performed in France without his permission. He also became one of the king's secretaries, a privilege previously granted only to French nobility.

Lully's early operatic style was similar to that of the Italian masters, but he quickly assimilated the current French idiom and created a new style that was widely imitated. He established the form of the French overture—slow opening with double-dotted rhythm, fast fugal section, and slow dance movement—as an organized work to introduce an opera. He also replaced *recitativo secco* (dry recitative, or free-rhythmic sung recitation with simple chordal accompaniment) with *recitativo stromentato* (accompanied recitative, a more dramatic and involved style with stricter rhythm and more elaborate, often orchestral, accompaniment). His works include some 20 operas and 30 ballets as well as sacred music, including a well-known 'Miserere'.

Lully died in Paris on March 22, 1687, of blood poisoning. The poisoning resulted from a wound in his foot caused by his long conducting stick.

The first step in felling a tree is to saw a notch, or undercut, on one side of the tree. The tree will fall in the direction of the notch when the faller saws straight through the trunk from the other side.

LUMBER

LUMBER. Wood is used to make many things—from homes to furniture to toothpicks. The lumber industry transforms the trees of the forests into the lumber from which other products are made. Its tasks include logging—cutting trees down, sawing them into logs, and carrying the logs to the sawmill to be sawed into boards and timbers, or lumber.

In earlier years the lumber industry of the United States was unable to make use of more than 30 percent of most trees. Small and crooked logs, treetops, branches, limbs, and high stumps were left in the woods to rot. In the sawmill the first slices from logs and the trimmings from sawed planks were burned as fuel or as waste. The present-day lumber industry converts about 70 percent of each tree harvested into useful products. Better equipment permits less wasteful cutting. Thinner saws, for example, reduce the amount of sawdust. Chips that were formerly scrapped are now sold to paper mills.

Improvements in the lumber industry have not been limited to cutting methods. In the United States loggers once stripped forests with no regard for their future regrowth. The men would enter a wooded area, cut down all the valuable trees, and then move on to repeat the performance elsewhere. The early loggers were almost as great a threat to the forests as fire. They destroyed much of America's vast and beautiful virgin forests. Their methods were abandoned only when lumbermen came to realize that America's forests were not inexhaustible and that their industry would eventually run out of trees if the forests were not replanted.

The concept of *forest management* was adopted by the United States lumber industry. The industry now regards forests as farms and trees as crops. Its foresters protect trees from fire, insects, and disease. Many lumber companies maintain tree nurseries. The young trees from these nurseries are transplanted to replace trees that die or are cut down in forest areas. In an effort to keep pace with the growing need for wood, by 1970 the lumber industry was planting 30 percent more trees than were logged or destroyed by fire, insects, disease, and wind.

Modern forest management employs the sustained-yield system. Under this system a forester chooses certain valuable trees for harvest. He also has poor-quality trees removed to improve the composition of the forest. He makes sure that enough valuable trees remain to reseed the forest and may also have nursery seedlings transplanted in it. The forest is never destroyed. It continues to be used for recreation. Wild animals continue to find shelter in it. The roots of the remaining trees continue to retain water and prevent erosion. The management of forests to serve all of these purposes is called the multiple-use system. This approach proved so successful that in 1941 the wood-using industries started the American Tree Farm System, a voluntary program which encourages private owners to use a sustained-yield system. (*See also* Forest and Forestry.)

LOGGING

Before a tree can be sawed or chopped into useful wood, loggers must cut it down and transport it to

329

Large trees are bucked, or cut into shorter logs, so they can be dragged away easily. Only the tops and branches of small trees are removed.

the sawmill. Logging is still rugged work, though power tools and power-driven lifting equipment have eliminated much of the drudgery.

Felling the Tree

Once a tree has been marked for cutting, logging can begin. The person who cuts the tree down is the faller. First he decides the direction in which the tree should fall. He makes sure that other trees will not be damaged when it falls and that it will be easy to move the fallen tree to the loading area.

Having decided the direction of the fall, the faller cuts a large notch, or undercut, on that side of the tree. The undercut is located opposite and below the point where he plans to make the main cut. The exact position of the undercut and the depth to which it is made depend upon the size and the shape of the tree, wind conditions, and other factors. Planning the undercut takes great skill and experience.

When the undercut has been made, the faller makes the main cut on the opposite side. As the saw bites deeper into the trunk, wedges may be driven into the cut behind the saw. The wedges keep the tree from squeezing down on the saw.

Today's loggers use engine-driven chain saws that can be carried by hand. These saws have taken much of the hard labor out of felling. They have helped make the work safer both by reducing fatigue and because they are equipped with protective devices.

Sawing and Assembling the Logs

After a tree is down, the limbs must be removed. A chain saw is generally used to cut off the big limbs. The practice of chopping off smaller limbs with an ax is dying out.

The next step is bucking, or cutting the tree into shorter logs. The length of these logs depends upon the use that will be made of the wood and upon the capability of the equipment that will carry the logs to the sawmill. Ordinarily, small trees are not cut into logs. Only the top is cut off, at the point where the diameter grows too small to be usable.

Whatever their length, the logs must be yarded, or moved to a central collection point called the landing.

Cables run from this 110-foot-tall spar pole (left) to the sites where trees have been cut down. Logs are attached to these cables and reeled in. When the logs arrive at the landing, mechanical loaders (below) hoist them onto the trucks that will transport them to the sawmill.

Many sawmills store logs by floating them in a pond. This helps protect the logs from insect damage and keeps their ends from splitting.

Yarding is done either with cables that lead from the landing or with tractor-type vehicles. Factors that determine which method is used include the size of the timber, the steepness of the terrain, and the need to protect soil, streams, and younger trees.

One frequent cable arrangement is the high-lead system. A tall spar pole is erected at the landing. Cables lead from the pole to the felling areas. Logs are attached to the cables, and an engine reels the cables in. The spar poles are now often made of steel, but very tall trees still serve this purpose.

Helium balloons have been used experimentally to replace the spar pole. They lift the logs completely off the ground and carry them to the landing. Tractors are the most common method of yarding in most

Logs are carried from the storage pond to the upper level of the sawmill on a bull chain, or jack ladder. Jets of water wash dirt and grit from the logs before they are sawed.

parts of the United States. Crawler treads or large tires enable them to operate in rugged logging terrain. They drag, or skid, the logs to the landing.

Moving the Logs to the Sawmill

The landing is the center of logging activity. It receives logs from many directions. The logs are then transported from the landing to the sawmill.

Formerly, logs were brought to the mill by railway or were floated downstream in river drives. Today most logs are transported by large trucks, though the other methods are still used. Mechanical loaders at the landing lift the logs onto the trucks.

Road building has become an important task of the lumber industry. The industry constructs its own roads from the forest logging areas to sawmills or public highways. These roads must be able to support heavy cargoes. They may be relatively simple to build in level country. In rough terrain, however, their construction is very difficult, since steep grades, sharp curves, and narrow roadbeds must be avoided.

After the trip over the forest road, the trucks may still travel many miles by public highway. Sometimes, however, the forest road leads directly to the sawmill. In such cases, vehicles that are too large for public highways can be used to haul the logs.

MILLING

Logs are usually stored at the mill for some time before being sawed up. Often they are sorted by size or species. Some storage areas are on dry land, but frequently the logs are left in ponds. Specialized equipment may be used to unload the trucks and stack the logs. Logs stored in a pond may be moved about by a special boom boat.

Sawing the Logs

When a log is selected for sawing, an endless conveyor, called a bull chain or jack ladder, carries it from the water to the upper levels of the sawmill. The log may be washed clean on the jack ladder, or the bark may be entirely removed before sawing.

331

One type of debarking equipment works something like a pencil sharpener. It follows the configuration of the log and does not cut deeper than the thickness of the bark. In another debarking method, water jets under extreme pressure blast the bark from the log.

Debarking protects the sawing equipment by removing grit and other foreign objects that might damage the saw teeth or cause excessive wear. When the log is sawed into boards, debarked outer pieces can be chopped up into small, clean chips, which are sold to pulp and paper mills. Previously, the outer pieces were burned as fuel or as waste.

After washing or debarking, the log is rolled onto the carriage, a special wheeled platform that rolls on tracks. The carriage has a framework that holds the log securely. The head sawyer, one of the most important men in the mill, controls the carriage. He maneuvers it to the head saw, a high-speed saw that slices the log from end to end.

Small mills usually have a circular head saw. Most large mills, however, use an enormous band saw. The blade may extend from floor to ceiling. The first pass of the saw through the length of the log removes a slab which is flat on one side and round from the curvature of the log on the other. Succeeding passes produce rough-edged boards, some of them enormous because the log is so thick. After each pass, the head sawyer manipulates the controls that move the log into position for the next cut.

Handling the Boards

When the log has been reduced to boards and other wood products, the boards travel to the edger, whose parallel saws remove any irregular shapes and square the edges. Trimmer saws then cut each board to its proper length and square the ends.

The boards then move to the green chain, a conveyor which passes in front of men who grade each piece of lumber. "Green" refers to the moisture in the freshly cut lumber, not to the conveyor color.

The pieces are sorted by grade and by species. Most of them are then dried, or seasoned. Some are stacked in the yard for air-drying. Others are placed in oven-type structures called dry kilns. The heat and humidity control in these kilns permits faster and more precise drying. Many of the larger sawmills have additional equipment, such as the planers which are used to smooth the surface of boards.

Some sawmills have equipment for remanufacturing, or reshaping wood to make specific products. The wood may be converted into a variety of forms. Typical products of remanufacturing include furniture frames, tool handles, wooden dishes, and baseball bats.

Laminated Woods and Plywoods

Logs are sometimes cut into thin sheets of wood. A decorative veneer is a sheet that comes from a valuable wood and is used as the surface of a wood product because of its attractiveness. Other woods are also cut into thin layers. A log may be sliced or sawed into sheets, or sheets may be obtained by a process called rotary cutting. In rotary cutting the log is turned on a lathe against a long, stationary knife.

The sheets are usually glued together to make laminated wood or plywood. Laminated wood consists of thin sheets of wood whose grains run roughly parallel. It can be constructed from lower grades of lumber with a surface layer of decorative veneer. Laminated wood can be made in any size or shape. Its component sheets can be impregnated with a fire retardant and a decay preventive.

The wood in plywood is usually rotary cut. Thin sheets of this wood are glued together at right angles to each other. Plywood does not split and is very strong. (See also Plywood.)

A mechanical debarker (left) may be used to remove bark from the log. A wheeled platform then carries the log to the head saw, which slices it into boards or other forms of lumber. In most large mills the head saw is a band saw (below). The band saw may be a full story tall.

American Forest Institute

Trimmer saws (top) cut lumber into appropriate lengths and square off the ends. The boards are then carried to the green chain (bottom), where they pass in front of men who grade each piece. The green chain gets its name from the newly cut "green" lumber, which has a high moisture content. Seasoning, or drying, reduces the moisture content.

Users

Rough lumber may be shipped from the sawmill to mills that finish and shape the boards and make other lumber products. Wholesalers purchase lumber to sell to large users or to retail lumber yards from which individuals buy it in smaller amounts.

The construction industry, which builds homes and other structures, consumes about three fourths of the lumber produced in the United States. The next largest consumer is the shipping-container industry, which uses about one tenth of the lumber produced. Shipping containers are boxes in which merchandise is shipped or stored. The shipping-container industry also makes pallets, the wooden platforms used to carry materials or merchandise, particularly in the food industry. Somewhat more than a twentieth of United States lumber production goes to the furniture industry, the third largest consumer.

INDUSTRY

Lumber is produced in every section of the United States. Output is measured in board feet. One board foot is represented by a board one foot long, one foot wide, and one inch thick. In other parts of the world,

production is measured in cubic meters—1,000 board feet equal 2.36 cubic meters. The peak year for lumber production in the United States was 1909, when about 45 billion board feet were produced. The demand for lumber lessened when the construction industry began to substitute steel, brick, and concrete for wood and as improved preservatives lengthened the life of wood products. Annual lumber production now hovers at about 37 billion board feet.

The nation's lumber production comes from its commercial forestland. This is land that can grow trees of marketable quality that are available to the lumber industry. Noncommercial forestland includes land too poor to grow good timber, land with too few trees for lumbering to be profitable, and land that has been withdrawn from commercial use to be used for parks, wildlife refuges, and wilderness areas.

The half-billion acres of commercial forestland in the United States provide more than nine tenths of the nation's lumber needs. About three fourths of the domestic output is harvested from land owned by private concerns and individuals.

Government-owned commercial forests—about 28 percent of the total commercial acreage—produce approximately one fourth of the nation's lumber. Most of these woodlands are in 155 national forests located in 43 states, Puerto Rico, and the Virgin Islands. They are administered by the United States Forest Service of the Department of Agriculture. More than 64 percent of the government-owned commercial acreage is concentrated in 12 Western states.

National forests are managed under the multiple-use system to provide watershed protection, lands for recreation, food and shelter for wildlife, and a supply of timber. Private companies bid competitively for timber on government lands. Logging is done under the supervision of government foresters.

Sheets of plywood are nailed to the framework of this barn to form the walls. The framework is made of rough boards. Even rougher boards were used to make the scaffold.

American Forest Institute

333

LUMBER

More than 1,000 species of trees grow in the commercial forests of the United States. About 180 of these have commercial value, and 35 species provide most of the lumber. From the earliest days of American lumbering, the softwoods—pine, spruce, fir, hemlock, cedar, and other conifers—have been harvested in the greatest quantities. The hardwoods—oak, poplar, gum, ash, beech, birch, and other deciduous trees—account for about one fifth of the harvest.

The Western states are the source of nearly half of the nation's lumber production. Oregon has led the country since 1938. In the late 1970s its annual output was about 11½ billion board feet. Washington and California followed, with annual outputs of about 8 billion and 6 billion board feet, respectively. Softwoods—Douglas fir, the Western pines (Ponderosa, Idaho white, and sugar), and the Coast redwoods—form the bulk of Western production.

The great forest of the Southern coastal plain, which includes South Atlantic and Gulf coast states, accounts for about 40 percent of United States production. Much of this is softwood. Important hardwood stands are also scattered through the area. Georgia, Alabama, Mississippi, Louisiana, Arkansas, and North Carolina are major producers.

World Production

The Soviet Union and the United States account for about one fourth of the world's annual production of about 190 billion board feet of lumber. The Soviet Union alone produces some 45 billion board feet per year. Other major producers are Canada, Japan, China, Brazil, Sweden, and West Germany. Northern countries have large softwood forests. Countries nearer the equator contain a greater proportion of deciduous trees. Over a third of the lumber produc-

American Forest Institute

A single piece of laminated wood can be made in any length and can be given many shapes. Structural supports of boats and of modern, curved roofs may be made of laminated wood.

tion in both China and Brazil is hardwood. As the climate becomes hotter and more humid, the trees become more varied. Some tropical countries whose lumber output is small are important sources of rare hardwoods. Burma, for example, exports teak.

LOGGING'S ROUGH AND EXCITING PAST

Most of the early American settlers did some logging. The land they were opening was covered with forests. Each settler began by cutting down enough trees to make a clearing for a house and farm. Some of the timber was used to erect buildings, and the remainder was burned.

As communities grew, local sawmills supplied their needs with wood logged from nearby forests. As long as transportation of logs and lumber over long distances was unprofitable, lumbering remained a local business. New England was the center of this type of lumbering activity during colonial days. The expansion of the United States created greater demands for lumber. At the same time, long-distance transportation was improved to serve the new settlers. Increased demand and improved and cheaper transportation encouraged the nationwide development of the lumber industry.

In the second half of the 19th century the industry's center moved westward. About 1850 New York was the hub of the lumber industry. Ten years later Pennsylvania dominated lumber production. From about 1870 to 1890 the Great Lakes states Michigan, Minnesota, and Wisconsin were the major lumber producers. The South took the lead around 1895, while production rose steadily in the Far West. This was the situation during the peak production years of 1907 to 1910. By 1920 the lead had shifted from the South to the West, where it remained.

Most lumber must be seasoned, or dried, before it can be used. A common method of seasoning is to stack the green lumber in an outside yard to be air-dried.

American Forest Institute

American Forest Institute   Press Associates   Wide World   Wide World

Loggers ate at long tables in a common dining room and slept in double-deck bunk beds in a one-room bunkhouse. Their tools included a two-man saw, a large wedge, and double-bladed axes. The logs were often floated downriver to the sawmill and frequently caused logjams. Men sometimes drowned trying to break logjams.

Life in the Logging Camps

Early loggers led an unsettled life, wandering from one job to another. Many stayed at a logging camp for only a few days or weeks. Their work was hard and long, and they were free only Sundays and evenings. Loggers worked 11 hours a day until their workday was reduced to ten hours in 1910. After 1920 loggers worked eight hours a day, five days a week. Usually they worked even in rain, snow, and freezing cold. If bad weather did stop work, they were not paid for lost time.

A typical logging camp contained a bunkhouse, a cook house, and a dining room; an office; stables and a blacksmith's shop; and perhaps a store, a meat house, and storage sheds. The number of buildings depended on the number of men and on the kind of equipment to be stored and maintained.

The bunkhouses were rude buildings that had tiers of bunks nailed to the walls. There was just room enough between a bunk and the one above it for the men to crawl into bed and roll over. Often double bunks were used. One man would be assigned to each side. Blankets and sometimes a straw mattress were furnished. Otherwise the men made do with spruce boughs. Bedbugs were a common complaint.

Heat was provided by a stove in the middle of the room. After working in the rain or snow, or when they had done their laundry, the loggers hung their clothes around the stove to dry. Smoke from the stove mixed with steam from the wet clothes.

The day began at 5:00 AM when the bull cook (the camp odd-jobs man) woke the loggers. At 5:30 the gong sounded for the huge breakfast that prepared them for the day's work. The cook was one of the most important and best-paid men in the camp. His meals had to satisfy the ravenous appetites of the hardworking loggers. If they did not like their food, they might refuse to work.

At 9:00 PM the lights were turned out. The men immediately went to bed and were quiet. Plenty of rest was as necessary as plenty of food.

Men whose homes were near the camp could leave it on Saturday evening and return on Sunday. The others could not leave until payday. Most evenings were spent playing cards or spinning yarns. The Paul Bunyan legend was one that grew out of these tales (see Folklore).

LUMUMBA, Patrice (1925–61). The first prime minister of the Democratic Republic of the Congo, now Zaire, Patrice Lumumba held office for less than three months and was murdered by his opponents four months after being ejected from office. He is revered as a national hero, more for his courage and ambitions than for his accomplishments.

Patrice Lumumba was born at Onalua, in the Belgian Congo, on July 2, 1925. He failed to complete his schooling before settling in Léopoldville, now Kinshasa, and becoming a postal clerk. While there he became active in the trade union movement and in the Belgian Liberal party. In 1956 he was convicted of embezzlement from the post office and jailed for 12 months. Released, he became a salesman, but he was caught up in the nationalist movements that were burgeoning in Africa. In 1958 he founded the Congolese National Movement. When Belgium granted the Congo its independence on June 30, 1960, his party received the largest number of seats in the legislature, and he became prime minister under President Joseph Kasavubu, a political rival.

In the first year of independence, the new nation was in constant turmoil. The army was rebellious, and Katanga province seceded (see Zaire). Lumumba's efforts to resolve the crises were unsuccessful, and on Sept. 5, 1960, Kasavubu dismissed him from office. Lumumba contested the move, and for months each claimed to head the legal government. In December he was captured by Kasavubu's forces. A month later he was delivered to the secessionist Katanga regime and was killed under circumstances that have never been adequately explained.

LUNGFISH *see* MUDFISH AND LUNGFISH.

LUNGS. All living animals must take in oxygen and get rid of carbon dioxide. In the vertebrates—animals with backbones—that get their oxygen from the air, both tasks are performed by special gas-exchange organs called lungs. The lungs provide a place where oxygen can reach the blood and carbon dioxide can be removed from it. They are equipped with tubes and a bellows system for drawing in air from the outside, while the pulmonary (Latin *pulmo*, "lung") veins and arteries circulate blood through from inside. The lungs also have a cleaning system that traps, ejects, or destroys irritants and other harmful substances that travel in with the air.

In the simpler cold-blooded amphibians and reptiles, the lungs are two balloonlike sacs. In active animals that require large amounts of oxygen, especially the warm-blooded birds and mammals, the lungs are a spongy labyrinth of sacs that supply an enormous surface area for the transfer of gases. In the adult human the total lung surface, if flattened out, would be larger than a badminton court, about 100 square yards (83 square meters).

Human lungs hold about four quarts (3.8 liters) of air. In quiet breathing a person inhales about a pint of air with each breath. When very active, one may inhale six times as much by breathing more deeply and rapidly to supply the increased oxygen demand.

Structure and Function

The somewhat cone-shaped lungs are inside the thorax, or chest, in the cavity framed by the rib cage. One lung is on either side of the heart. The right lung has three lobes, or rounded divisions; the left has two lobes. The lungs are covered by a thin membrane called the pleura. The base of each lung rests on the diaphragm, a strong sheet of muscle that separates the chest and abdominal cavities. In normal breathing the diaphragm and the muscles between the ribs automatically contract and expand in a rhythmic cycle. As the diaphragm contracts, it moves downward and increases the volume of the chest. The chest muscles pull the ribs outward, further increasing the volume. The expanded space creates a partial vacuum that draws in, or inhales, outside air. Then the muscles relax, reversing the process, and the lungs contract, pushing out, or exhaling, the air.

Air inhaled through the nose or mouth enters the trachea, or windpipe. About halfway down the chest, the windpipe divides into a right and left bronchus, or branch. Each enters a lung, where it divides into

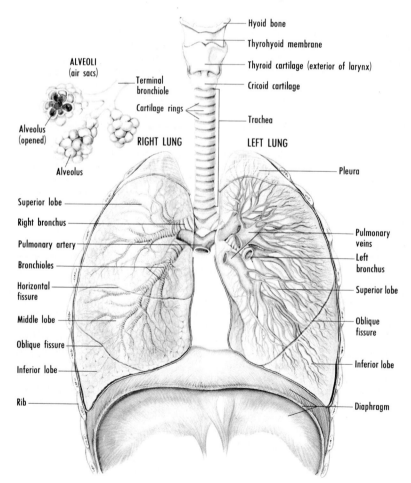

The human lungs have been drawn to appear transparent. The right lung shows how the bronchi divide repeatedly before they end in thin-walled sacs called alveoli, of which there are more than 700 million. Two pulmonary veins from each lung carry oxygen-laden blood to the heart. The pulmonary artery carries venous blood from the heart to the lungs.

smaller and smaller branches called bronchioles. The arrangement resembles an upside-down tree, with the trachea as the trunk.

Each bronchiole ends in a cluster of tiny air sacs called alveoli. The lungs have about 300 million such clusters. Wrapped around each alveolus are pulmonary capillaries, the smallest blood vessels in the lungs. The capillaries are so narrow that red blood cells must pass through in a single line. Here is where gas exchange takes place. Each red blood cell expels carbon dioxide and absorbs oxygen through the thin walls of the capillary and alveolus (*see* Blood).

The cleaning system of the lungs has four main components. Lining the trachea and bronchial tree are cells that secrete mucus, which traps pollutants and bacteria. Also in the bronchi are cells containing tiny hairlike lashes, called cilia, that project into the blanket of mucus and with constant wavelike motions push the mucus up out of the airways. Irritating chemicals, stagnant and excessive mucus, and large bits of foreign matter are forcibly ejected from the bronchi by a cough. This third important cleaning device—like breathing, under partial voluntary control—is a rapid muscle contraction and bronchial-tube constriction that generates a wind force far stronger than a tornado. Small harmful substances that make their way into the alveoli are destroyed by the fourth line of defense, the macrophages. These are patrolling cells that "swallow up" foreign particles or destroy them with enzymes.

Diseases of the Lungs

The leading cause of lung disease is cigarette smoking. Ingredients in smoke paralyze the cilia, change the mucus secretions, and interfere with the work of the macrophages, thus leaving the lungs vulnerable to physical damage and infection. Inflamed and irritated bronchi produce increased and thickened mucus, a condition known as bronchitis. Acute bronchitis often accompanies the common cold and other viral infections. Chronic bronchitis results from constant irritation; the stagnant mucus in the bronchi invites recurring infections and other diseases. Prolonged irritation or infection also causes emphysema, air trapped in the alveoli, resulting in shortness of breath. Chronic bronchitis, emphysema, and several similar diseases, collectively known as chronic obstructive pulmonary disease (COPD), affect 9 million people in the United States and are directly responsible for 45,000 deaths a year. Moreover, they are the fastest rising cause of death. Lung cancer, claiming nearly 120,000 lives a year, is strongly associated with cigarette smoking. Other common diseases are pneumonia, an inflammation with extensive airways congestion from a variety of causes; asthma, an allergic constriction of the bronchi; and pneumoconiosis, a disease category that encompasses chronic irritations from industrial dusts such as those from coal, cotton, and stone.

LUNGWORM *see* WORM.

LUSAKA, Zambia. The capital city of Zambia, Lusaka is located on a limestone plateau 4,198 feet (1,280 meters) above sea level. It lies at the junction of the Great North Road, which runs to Tanzania, and the Great East Road, which goes to Malawi. Lusaka has rail connections to the towns of Livingstone and Ndola and also to Tanzania.

Lusaka is a major marketing center for maize (corn) and tobacco. Its economy depends largely on agricultural trade. Other industry includes cement, shoe manufacture, and food processing. The University of Zambia, founded in 1965, and an international airport are located outside the city limits. The Munda Wanga Botanical Gardens are also nearby.

In 1935 Lusaka became the capital of Northern Rhodesia. It achieved municipal status in 1960. The city and its environs, or immediate surroundings, became a province in 1976. The government is located in a newer section of the city that contrasts with the old town found along the railway line. (*See also* Zambia.) Population (1980), 538,469.

LUTHER, Martin (1483–1546). The Protestant Reformation in Germany was inaugurated by Martin Luther in 1517. It was his intent to reform the medieval Roman Catholic church, but the firm resistance of the church to Luther's challenge led instead to permanent divisions in the structure of Western Christianity (*see* Reformation).

Luther was born in Eisleben in the province of Saxony on Nov. 10, 1483, to Hans and Margaret Ziegler Luther. Shortly thereafter the family moved to Mansfeld, where Hans worked as a miner. The young Luther studied at Magdeburg and Eisenach before attending the University of Erfurt. In 1505, at the urging of his father, he began to study law; but within the year he decided to abandon law and enter the religious life by becoming an Augustinian monk. Later in life, Luther credited this sudden decision to having been caught in a thunderstorm and dashed to the ground by a bolt of lightning. In his fear, he renounced the world and entered the Augustinian monastery at Erfurt in July 1505.

Luther became an outstanding theologian and Biblical scholar. He earned his doctorate in theology in 1512 and became professor of Biblical literature at Wittenberg University.

The seriousness with which Luther took his religious vocation led him into a severe personal crisis: how, he wondered, is it possible to reconcile the demands of God's law with human inability to live up to the law? He found his answer in the New Testament book of Romans: God had, in the obedience of Jesus Christ, reconciled humanity to Himself. What was required of mankind, therefore, was not strict adherence to law or the fulfillment of religious obligations, but a response of faith that accepted what God had done. Such faith would lead to an obedience based on love, not fear.

This belief of Luther's led him into his first major confrontation with the Catholic church in 1517. Pope

Martin Luther, in an oil painting done by Lucas Cranach the Elder in 1526

Courtesy of the Nationalmuseum, Stockholm

Leo X, in order to raise money for the building of Saint Peter's Basilica in Rome, offered indulgences for sale to the people. These offered partial remission of the penalty for sins to those who made donations of money. Luther strongly objected to this practice.

On Oct. 31, 1517, Luther nailed to the door of the church in Wittenberg a list of 95 theses, or propositions. They denied the right of the pope to forgive sins by the sale of indulgences, among other challenges. The theses were widely circulated in Germany and caused a great controversy.

The pope ordered Luther to appear before Cardinal Cajetan in Augsburg. The cardinal demanded that Luther retract all he had said. Luther refused to do this unless it could be proved to him from the Bible that he was wrong.

Early in 1521 the pope issued a Bull of Excommunication against Luther and ordered Emperor Charles V to execute it. Instead, the emperor called a "diet," or council, at Worms and summoned Luther for examination. The diet demanded that Luther recant, but he refused and was outlawed.

With the help of his friend the elector of Saxony, Luther hid in the castle of Wartburg, near Eisenach. There he remained in disguise. During his time at Wartburg he began to translate the New Testament into German.

Finally the emperor's preoccupation with the war he was waging with France made it safe for Luther to return to his work at Wittenberg. While Luther was in concealment some of his followers had carried the reform movement further than he had intended. On Luther's return he tried to correct these excesses but was not successful. In 1524 many of the German peasants used his teachings as a reason for revolting.

In 1525 Luther married a former nun, Katharina von Bora. This emphasized his rejection of monasticism and celibacy for the clergy. The remainder of Luther's life was spent in writing, preaching, and organizing the reformed church in Saxony. He replaced the Latin service of the mass with a service in the German language and wrote many hymns that are still in use, notably the famous 'Ein feste Burg ist unser Gott' (A Mighty Fortress Is Our God). Luther died on Feb. 18, 1546, at Eisleben, his birthplace.

LUTHERANISM.

With more than 68 million members throughout the world, the Lutheran churches today comprise the largest denomination to emerge from the Protestant Reformation that began in Germany in 1517. (*See also* Luther; Reformation.) The greatest number of Lutherans, more than 50 million, live in Europe, and there are more than 9 million in North America. Through foreign missions, large Lutheran contingents have also developed in Latin America, Asia, Africa, and Australia.

Belief and Practice

Luther broke with the Catholic church over the critical issue of how mankind attains salvation. His answer was expressed in the doctrine of justification by faith. This meant that God, in the life, death, and resurrection of Jesus Christ, had accomplished for mankind what it could not do on its own. As the obedient and wholly righteous servant of God, Jesus was unjustly condemned and executed. This undeserved death served as a substitution for mankind's deserved punishment under the rigorous terms of God's law. By this one act, God was able to absolve mankind from the penalty of its disobedience to Him and to declare mankind righteous. This, for Luther, was the gospel ("good news"): Humanity, having been declared just, need no longer live in fear of God's punishment; it could, instead, by acceptance (faith) believe what God had accomplished and live before Him as free and responsible, seeking to obey His will out of love and trust.

This pivotal teaching affected all other aspects of faith and practice as Lutheranism developed. Because this doctrine originated in the free action of God and was testified to solely in the Bible, the Bible became the only source and norm for belief and action. All traditions that were not in accord with it were rejected. Traditions that were helpful for interpretation and for worship were retained, however. It was not Luther's intention to break entirely with the past, but to restructure the church in such a way that it would faithfully reflect the Biblical message.

Lutherans reject the notion that one denomination, the Roman Catholic church, is the single channel of God's message. They reject as well the rule of the popes over the church on Earth. All Christians are regarded as equal before God in one "priesthood of all believers." This means that priests, or the clergy, have no special status, except by virtue of being called to exercise specific ministries based on ability and training.

Instead of the seven sacraments, or means of grace, of the medieval church, the Lutheran churches recognize two: Baptism and the Communion, or Eucharist. They give primacy to the preached message that announces God's word as expressed in the Bible.

The basic order of worship in Lutheran churches is similar to the mass as it developed in the Middle Ages. The service is in two parts. The first, consisting of hymns of praise and prayers in a highly structured format, leads up to the reading of Biblical texts for the day. The second portion consists of the celebration of the Lord's Supper. In some churches, such as the Church of Sweden, the worship may be highly ritualized with ornate vestments used. In others, such as the Lutheran Free Churches, the worship, while retaining the same form, is much plainer and emphasizes preaching.

In addition to the two sacraments, Lutheran churches also use a number of rites: confirmation, marriage, ordination, and burial. Whereas the sacraments were specifically instituted by Jesus during his ministry, rites are traditions, some of which (marriage and burial) need not be performed by a church. The rite of confirmation allows a member who has come of age to confirm belief in the faith into which he or she was baptized. Ordination sets the clergy apart only for the performance of the ministry of preaching, teaching, and administering the sacraments. In recent years, lay people have been playing a greater role even in these ministerial functions. In the late 20th century a number of Lutheran bodies have approved the ordination of women, although this is still a controversial issue in some places.

The official teaching of the Lutheran churches is contained in the 'Book of Concord', first published in complete form in 1580. The book contains the three ancient creeds of the Christian church—the Apostles', the Nicene, and the Athanasian—as well as a number of documents that were composed during the Reformation era. Among these are Luther's Large and Small Catechisms, the Augsburg Confession, the Formula of Concord, and "Treatise on the Power and Primacy of the Pope" by Philipp Melanchthon, one of Luther's associates.

The organization of Lutheran churches varies from country to country. In the early years the churches were closely tied to the state, and there still remain a number of state churches in Europe (Norway, Sweden, Denmark, and Finland). These churches are supported by public funds, as is the Evangelical church in Germany; but in Germany there is no state church—the Catholic church also receives public support.

In the United States and Canada Lutheran congregations are autonomous, private corporations. But local congregations are generally united in regional and national bodies with elected officials. The presiding officials may be called bishops, a practice that has come back into use in the late 20th century—though it has been common in Europe for centuries.

An international cooperative body, the Lutheran World Federation, was established in 1947. It is a free association of churches to which most Lutheran bodies belong. Its purpose is to coordinate the activities of the churches in world missions, refugee relocation, hunger programs, and social missions.

History

The history of Lutheranism may be divided into several distinct, but overlapping, periods: the Reformation and post-Reformation eras in Germany; the spread of Lutheranism to other European nations, particularly the Scandinavian countries; the growth of the churches in North America, beginning in the colonial period; and the spread of the churches throughout the world, beginning with the mission programs of the 19th century.

The Reformation era in Germany coincides generally with Luther's adult life, from 1517 to 1546. For the first Lutherans it was a time of defining their beliefs in opposition to the Catholic church. This was done in an atmosphere of hostility and conflict, because the division of Western Christendom was regarded as a serious matter to both church people and political leaders. At a conclave before Holy Roman Emperor Charles V at Augsburg, Germany, the Lutherans (called Protestants at the time) presented their position in the Augsburg Confession, written by Philipp Melanchthon. Rejection by Charles and the Catholic authorities led to a period of hostilities that was temporarily settled with the Religious Peace of Augsburg in 1555. The final peace between the churches was not attained until the Peace of Westphalia in 1648, which ended the Thirty Years' War (see Thirty Years' War).

The post-Reformation era in Germany was a time of consolidation and theological formulation. From the late 16th to the end of the 17th century, the dominant emphasis was on orthodoxy—adherence to correct doctrine. From 1670 to 1760 orthodoxy gave way to pietism, a movement that emphasized personal Christian living, as well as social and foreign missions. The conflict between orthodoxy and pietism has persisted to the present and has been a frequent source of division among Lutherans.

Lutheranism came to North America with the colonists and immigrants from Europe. Norwegians, Swedes, Danes, Finns, and Germans formed church bodies largely on the basis of their native languages; though the orthodoxy-pietist conflict also influenced the way the American churches developed. English gradually became the language for most American Lutherans, and in the 20th century the several church bodies found they had more in common than they had separating them. While ethnic heritages have not been forgotten, there have been a number of mergers with the result that in the 1980s most American Lutherans belonged to the Lutheran Church in America, the American Lutheran church, the Lutheran Church-Missouri Synod, or the Wisconsin Synod. In 1982 the American Lutheran church, the Lutheran Church in America, and the much smaller Association of Evangelical Lutheran churches each voted to work toward a merger of the three bodies before 1990.

During the latter part of the 20th century, the Lutheran churches became involved in the ecumenical movement, an attempt—particularly through the World Council of Churches—to bring all the Christian denominations into closer working harmony. Interdenominational cooperation has also been encouraged at the local level, in worship services and in social mission efforts.

LUTHULI, Albert (1898–1967). For his efforts in waging a nonviolent campaign against racial discrimination in South Africa, Alfred Luthuli became, in 1960, the first African to be awarded the Nobel peace prize. Ironically, the policy of nonviolence was abandoned by some South Africans within a month of his receiving the award.

Albert Luthuli, a member of Natal's Zulu tribe, was born in 1898 in Rhodesia, now Zimbabwe, where his father was serving as a missionary interpreter. Ten years later when he was 10 he moved to South Africa and learned Zulu traditions. He was educated at a teacher-training college near Durban. After graduation he became one of the school's first African instructors. In 1936 Luthuli left teaching when he was elected chief of the Zulu community at Groutville. Although he ruled a land plagued by poverty and hunger, he was not yet aware of the need for political action to solve the problems of his people.

It was not until 1945 that Luthuli joined an active political organization, the African National Congress. A year later he was elected to the Natives Representative Council. Violence by the army and police against striking African miners prompted his first political protest. In 1948 the Afrikaner Nationalist party came to power, determined to enforce a policy of apartheid—racial separation (*see* Apartheid; South Africa).

At this time Luthuli was elected president of the Natal African National Congress. His opposition to segregation led to a demand that he resign his office or step down from his position as a Zulu chief. He refused and was deposed as chief in 1952, the same year he became president general of the African National Congress. Because of his activism, he and many others were arrested and tried for treason in 1956. He was not convicted, but the government banned his activities and confined him to his neighborhood. After receiving the Nobel prize, he retired from political life and lived in enforced isolation. He died when he was struck by a train on July 21, 1967.

LUXEMBOURG. The Grand Duchy of Luxembourg is a tiny country of only 998 square miles (2,586 square kilometers), surrounded by Belgium, West Germany, and France. Despite its size, Luxembourg is a center of European diplomacy and outranks many larger countries as an iron and steel producer.

The country has two natural regions. The fertile south and center is known as the Good Country: the *Bon Pays* (French) or *Gutland* (German). Luxembourg city, the capital and largest city, is in the Good Country, as is most of the population and industry.

The northern third of the country, called Ösling, lies in the plateau of the Ardennes. Picturesque castles dot the landscape. The highest point (1,834 feet; 559 meters) is near Wemperhardt in the north.

The climate is mild and damp. Temperatures at the capital average 63° F (17° C) in July and 33° F (1° C) in January. It rarely gets hotter than 87° F (31° C) or colder than 15° F (−9° C).

People

Most of Luxembourg's people live in the countryside or in small towns. In 1981 some 78,900 people lived in the capital. Esch-sur-Alzette and Dudelange, in the steel-producing region near the French border, had populations of 25,100 and 14,100 respectively. No other town had as many as 10,000 residents.

One of every four people in the country is a foreigner. The largest numbers are from Portugal and Italy; most of the others are citizens of France, Germany, and The Netherlands. In order to encourage rapid industrial development in the 20th century, the government has actively encouraged workers to come from other countries. This, in combination with a low birthrate, has brought about a population two thirds of which is of working age. Luxembourg owes its high standard of living in part to the fact that the labor force makes up almost half the population.

About 95 percent of the people are Roman Catholic. Religious processions at Echternach carry on a tradition that dates from the Middle Ages.

The everyday language of the Luxembourgers, called Letzeburgesch, is a Germanic dialect influenced by both French and German. French and German are both official languages as well, and are widely used in government, commerce, the press, and cultural life. Schooling is in French and German. Both languages, as well as English, are used at the university in Luxembourg city.

Conservatories train musicians in Luxembourg city and Esch-sur-Alzette. At Vianden, in the Ardennes, a Victor Hugo Museum and a folklore museum feature different facets of local culture. The State Museum in Luxembourg city has exhibits of art, archaeology, local history, and science.

Agriculture and Industry

Over half the land in Luxembourg is used for farming. Cattle graze in the extensive meadows and pastures. Agricultural products grown in the north include barley, oats, and potatoes. Vineyards in the southeast, in the valley of the Moselle River, produce still and sparkling wines. The woodlands that cover about 30 percent of the total land area form the basis for a lumbering industry.

Iron and steel is Luxembourg's leading industry, but rubber tire, plastic, chemical, and machine industries have been introduced. Pig iron, steel, and rolled steel products account for nearly half of the country's exports. Heat from the steel mills is used to generate thermal electric power. A huge dam at Vianden produces hydroelectricity.

Roads, railroads, air service, and waterways link Luxembourg to the main transportation networks of Europe. The canalization of the Moselle River in the 1960s joined Luxembourg to the canal systems of

The Cathedral of Notre Dame stands above the fortress wall in Luxembourg city, the capital of Luxembourg.

France and Germany. Radio-Télévision Luxembourg broadcasts to audiences in France and Germany.

Government and History

In government, too, the grand duchy is an active part of a larger Europe. It is a hereditary and constitutional monarchy, governed by a Chamber of Deputies with the grand duke as chief executive. Luxembourg was a founding member of the European Coal and Steel Community, the European Economic Community (EEC), and the European Atomic Energy Community (EURATOM)—collectively called the European Communities. Many institutions of the European Communities are based in Luxembourg.

History

Luxembourg dates its founding from 963, when Sigefroi, Count of the Ardennes, built a castle—*Lucilinburhuc*, or "little fortress"—on the rock that is now the site of Luxembourg city. The medieval counts of Luxembourg achieved great military prestige and were several times elected king of Germany. In 1354 the county became a duchy, or dukedom.

In 1443, however, it fell to the Burgundians. Through inheritance it passed to the Spanish Hapsburgs, and later, by the Treaty of Utrecht, in 1713, to the Austrian Hapsburgs (*see* Hapsburgs). The French conquered Luxembourg in 1795 and made it a department of the Napoleonic Empire. The Congress of Vienna, which redrew the map of Europe in 1815 after Napoleon's defeat, declared it an independent grand duchy and gave it to the Dutch king. In 1890 Luxembourg became truly independent.

In 1921 Luxembourg joined Belgium in an economic union, which was called Benelux after the addition of The Netherlands in 1944. Luxembourg led in the formation of the European Communities, starting in the 1950s. Population (1981), 365,500.

LUXEMBURG, Rosa (1871–1919). One of the foremost theoreticians of the Socialist and Communist movements in the early 20th century was Rosa Luxemburg. Like Lenin, she believed in the violent overthrow of the capitalist system. Unlike him, however, she was opposed to nationalism and emphasized internationalism, and she argued against his "democratic centralism," which she believed would result in a totalitarian state (*see* Lenin). Instead, she stressed revolutionary mass action, which she believed would lead to more democratic organizations.

Rosa Luxemburg was born in Zamość, Russian Poland (now Poland), on March 5, 1871. While still in high school, she became involved in underground revolutionary activities, a fairly common practice among the educated class in Russia at the time. In 1889 she emigrated to Zurich, Switzerland, where she studied political economy and law. While there, she became a founder of the Polish Social Democratic party, later to become the Polish Communist party.

In 1898 she married Gustav Lübeck, a German national. They settled in Berlin, a center of Socialist activity, where she gradually formulated her own distinct views and became involved in conflicts that divided the party. (*See also* Socialism.)

The major experiences of her life were the Russian Revolution of 1905 and World War I. The first convinced her that the world revolution would start in Russia. She opposed World War I because it undermined Socialist internationalism.

Luxemburg and her associate Karl Liebknecht formed the Spartacus League, dedicated to ending the war through a workers' revolution; in 1918 they founded the German Communist party. Luxemburg was assassinated on Jan. 15, 1919, in Berlin.

LU XUN (1881–1936). Although he died 13 years before the Communist party came to power in China, the writer Lu Xun is considered a revolutionary hero by present-day Chinese Communists. By the 1930s, when his reputation as a writer was established, he hailed Communism as the only means of unifying China and solving its social and economic problems.

Lu Xun was born Chou Shu-jen at Shaoxing in 1881. He attended the School of Railways and Mines of the Kiangnan Military Academy in Nanjing and later studied medicine, literature, and philosophy in Japan. He returned home a committed foe of the Manchu dynasty, and, after the revolution that overthrew the dynasty in 1911, he joined the new republican government in its ministry of education.

Lu Xun's literary activity began in 1918 when, at the urging of friends, he published a short story, "A Madman's Diary." The first Western-style short story written in Chinese, it was a satiric attack on the traditional Confucian culture of China. Its success laid the foundation for acceptance of the short story as a literary vehicle. "The True Story of Ah Q," published in 1921, was also a repudiation of China's old order. In addition to his stories, Lu Xun wrote essays, of which "Outline History of Chinese Fiction" is his best known; made compilations of classical fiction; and translated literature from Russian to Chinese.

His pessimism about the republican government led him to leave Peking in 1926 and settle in Shanghai. There he recruited many fellow writers and countrymen for the Communist party, although he never joined it himself. He died there on Oct. 19, 1936.

LYCURGUS. The legendary lawgiver of the ancient Greek city-state of Sparta was Lycurgus. Nothing is known of him except the traditions that have been handed down about him. Supposedly he lived in the 9th century BC, though many scholars doubt he ever lived at all. The Spartans said that he gave them their laws and institutions. He is credited with having organized Sparta as a nation of soldiers, who lived and ate together (*see* Sparta). Lycurgus created a Council of Elders, gave Spartans their system of education, and instituted a system of iron coinage instead of gold. The laws of Lycurgus, whatever their origin, resulted in Sparta's becoming one of the major military powers in ancient Greece.

After his fellow citizens promised they would obey his laws and not change them until he returned, Lycurgus left Sparta to travel abroad. He had heard from an oracle that the Spartans would prosper as long as they kept their vow. To ensure their good fortune, he decided never to return to the city. His story has been well told by Plutarch in his 'Lives'.

LYELL, Charles (1797–1875). The science of geology owes an enormous debt of gratitude to the Englishman Sir Charles Lyell. It was he who, early in the 19th century, devised the theories, methods, and principles on which the modern science is based. His major contribution was proving that all features of the Earth's surface were produced by natural forces operating for long times. His strong arguments that the Earth's crust was the product of thousands of millions of years of activity did away with the need for unscientific explanations based on the Biblical record or on intermittent natural catastrophes. Lyell's achievements in geology also laid the foundations for evolutionary biology, a field that was to be more fully developed by a young friend, Charles Darwin. (*See also* Darwin; Evolution.)

Charles Lyell was born in eastern Scotland on Nov. 14, 1797, and raised near Southampton, England. He graduated from Oxford University in 1819 and went on to study law in London. He had, however, become an amateur geologist; and as the years passed he devoted more and more time to this pursuit. He made explorations in the British Isles, on the Continent, and in the United States. In 1830 the first volume of his 'Principles of Geology' was published. Eight years later he published 'Elements of Geology'. Both works were hailed as pioneering studies by other scientists, and he was recognized as one of the most eminent scholars in his field. In 1848 he was knighted.

With the publication of Darwin's 'Origin of Species' in 1859, the work of Lyell was overshadowed—even among his colleagues. Yet it was to Lyell that Darwin owed much of the information that was the basis of his own work. Lyell continued his studies and revisions of his books until his death in London on Feb. 22, 1875. He was buried in Westminster Abbey.

LYMPHATIC SYSTEM. The lymphatic, or lymphoid, system consists of tissues and organs designed to protect the body from damage by foreign materials. The major parts of the system are the lymph nodes, tonsils, thymus, spleen, and lymphatic vessels; lymphatic tissue is found in isolated patches in the gastrointestinal tract, lungs, and bone marrow. The system also provides a means of returning liquid that escapes from the blood into the body tissues. Although many animals have a lymphatic system, this article will be confined to the human system.

Lymph Nodes

Lymph nodes are round or kidney-shaped organs usually found in groups distributed throughout the body, both close to the surface and deep. A person has between 500 and 1,500 lymph nodes that range in size from very tiny to about 1 inch (2.5 centimeters) in diameter. Nodes are numerous in the head and neck regions, armpits, chest, abdomen, pelvis, and groin. When nodes in the neck, armpits, or groin are enlarged, they can be felt by an examiner.

Structure. Lymph nodes consist of networks of fibers and cells. The cells may be motile, or able to move about, or fixed. The principal motile cells are called lymphocytes.

Lymph nodes are covered by a thin layer of tissue called the capsule, beneath which is the cortex and then, in turn, the paracortex and the medulla. Cells in the cortex form rounded structures called lymphoid nodules, or lymphoid follicles. The outer portion of such a nodule consists of dense collections of small lymphocytes, while the inside part of the nodule contains larger, activated lymphocytes called immunoblasts. In the medulla of the lymph node, the lymphocytes form branching cords. Lymphocytes play major roles in the protection of the body through immunity (*see* Immune System).

Lymphocytes. Two types of lymphocytes are T cells and B cells. T cells are so named because they are influenced by an organ called the thymus during their development, whereas B cells are so termed because they develop in an organ called the bursa of Fabricius in birds and in the bone marrow in some species. In humans, B cell development appears to occur in the bone marrow and in the lymph nodes and spleen. T and B cells appear similar when viewed through a microscope, but they can be distinguished after certain special treatments.

Most lymphocytes in the bone marrow, blood, and deep in the body are a type called small round lymphocytes, which is a good general description. Lymphocytes that encounter foreign substances in the body may become stimulated and enlarged. Such lymphocytes are called immunoblasts. Mature lymphocytes that produce antibodies to attack the foreign substances they have encountered are called plasma cells. They are large, ovoid B cells.

Lymphatic Vessels and Lymph

Lymph nodes are located along the course of lymphatic vessels, which penetrate the nodes and carry a fluid called lymph. Lymph is composed of water, large protein molecules, salts, glucose, urea, lymphocytes, and other substances. Lymph diffuses from body tissues into lymph capillaries.

Lymph moves much more slowly than blood. Its motion is aided by breathing motion and contractions of the skeletal muscles, which compress adjacent lymph vessels. Valves within the lymphatic vessels prevent backflow of the lymph.

Lymph enters the lymph node and works its way through passages in the node called sinuses. In the process any foreign matter and dead tissue are removed from the lymph. When the lymph leaves the node, it is ready for return to the blood system. The body's major lymphatic vessel is the thoracic duct. It begins near the lower part of the spine and collects the lymph from all the lymphatic vessels from the lower limbs, pelvis, abdomen, and lower chest. It courses up the chest and empties into the central blood circulation through a vein at the base of the left side of the neck. The right lymphatic duct collects lymph from the right side of the neck, right side of the chest, and right arm and empties into a blood vein in the right side of the neck.

Function

The lymph nodes and vessels have multiple functions. First, lymphatic vessels carry some of the tissue liquids back into the bloodstream. This liquid, originally from the blood, leaks out into and bathes the body tissues where it performs a number of vital services. If the liquid were not returned through the lymphatic system, it would eventually accumulate a concentration of protein that would equal that in the blood capillaries. This would interfere with the drawing of tissue fluid into the blood, and edema, or swelling, would result. Examples are found in lymphatics blocked or destroyed by cancer cells or by surgery, or in a disease called elephantiasis in which a parasitic worm blocks the lymph channels.

Second, most digested fats are absorbed by lymph vessels that drain the intestine before they are emptied into the bloodstream. Lymph from the intestines is called chyle and may appear white because of the fat it contains.

Additional functions that occur within the nodes include production of lymphocytes, removal of foreign substances from the lymph (dust particles, microorganisms), and defense of the body from unwanted foreign substances by immune reactions.

Major concentrations of lymphoid tissue that are found outside the lymph nodes occur in the thymus and spleen. They are important in immunity (*see* Immune System).

THE LYMPHATIC SYSTEM

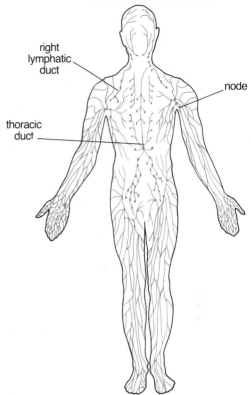

right lymphatic duct

node

thoracic duct

LYMPH NODE

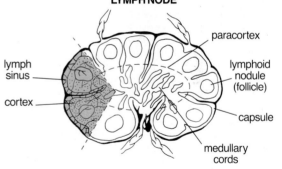

paracortex

lymphoid nodule (follicle)

lymph sinus

cortex

capsule

medullary cords

Disorders

Lymph nodes may become tender or enlarged. Infections and stimulation by foreign materials may cause swelling. Inflammation of a lymph node, called lymphadenitis, may occur when the node receives lymph from an adjacent infected area.

Lymphocytes may become cancerous at various stages of development, causing serious diseases such as certain forms of leukemia, lymphoma, or multiple myeloma. In addition the lymph vessels and nodes play a major role in the spread of cancer within the body. Cancer cells originating in various organs may enter draining lymph vessels and be spread farther.

Sometimes a lymph node is removed and inspected under the microscope. This procedure, called biopsy, may help the physician to determine whether or not the node contains cancer cells. In some circumstances removal of a large number of lymph nodes in an area draining an organ with cancer may prevent further spread of the disease.

It is possible to visualize the lymph nodes and lymphatic vessels on an X-ray film by a procedure called lymphangiography, in which a dye that shows up on X-ray film is injected into the lymphatic vessels of the foot. Some of the dye is retained by each lymph node along the way as it is transported upward. Large lymph nodes may also be seen by specialized X-ray techniques such as computerized axial tomography (CAT scan).

LYNX. So sharp is the sight of the lynx that the people of ancient times believed it could see even through a stone wall. That is why sharp-sighted people are still referred to as "lynx-eyed."

A member of the cat family, the lynx is found in the northern regions of both the New and the Old World. It is smaller than the leopard and larger than the true wildcat, which exists only in Europe. The name wildcat is, however, applied in North America to various species of lynx. All have stumpy tails, long limbs, tufted ears, and eyes that narrow in the daytime to slits. They live in forests and rocky places and are fond of resting stretched out on a tree limb in the sun. By night they hunt their food, which consists of birds and small animals.

The sudden cry of a lynx at night is one of the most frightful sounds in the woods. Usually it consists of a single sharp howl. Then there is silence. The creatures on which the animal preys, such as rabbits or quail, seek to escape notice by lying perfectly still in the darkness. The lynx, unable to distinguish the exact position, crouches down ready for a leap, then emits its piercing cry. The timid victim, startled by the fearful sound, cannot help jumping convulsively. At that instant the lynx strikes and kills.

The Canada lynx has heavy gray fur mottled with brown. The bobcat, also known as the red, or bay, lynx, is common to many parts of the United States and has yellowish-brown fur tinged with red. The European lynx has a restricted range in parts of Europe. The scientific name of the Canada lynx is *Lynx canadensis;* of the bobcat, *Lynx rufus;* and of the European lynx, *Lynx lynx* (see Cat).

LYON, France. The third largest city in France, Lyon became famous as a silk-manufacturing center. Today it has many industries and is a hub of financial and cultural activity.

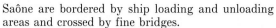

It stands where two great rivers, the Rhône and the Saône, meet. The city spreads back from the slender point between the rivers onto steep hills on both banks. The Rhône and the Saône are bordered by ship loading and unloading areas and crossed by fine bridges.

The silk industry was introduced in the 15th century. At first, hand looms in the weavers' homes turned out the silks, and a few special fabrics are still handwoven. Water power from plunging streams in the nearby Jura Mountains permitted the spread of factories here and in neighboring villages. Today huge hydroelectric plants furnish power. Lyon has become important in chemical and metal manufacturing, food processing, and printing. Each spring an international trade fair for industry is held.

The University of Lyon has schools of letters, law, science, medicine, and pharmacy. The Museum of Textiles has collections of materials of all periods and regions. The old Cathedral of Saint John is outstanding among the city's beautiful buildings.

The town, then called Lugdunum, was founded by the Romans before the Christian era. Augustus made it the capital of Celtic Gaul. Later the town was ravaged by barbarians and abandoned by the Romans. Late in the 5th century it was made the capital of the Burgundians. In 1312 it became part of France.

During the French Revolution a counterrevolutionary uprising did great damage to the city. Napoleon, however, encouraged its rebuilding and improvement. The invention here of the Jacquard loom in 1802 led to increased prosperity in the silk industry. Lyon was damaged again during World War II when it was a center of the resistance movement. (*See also* France.) Population (1975 census), 456,265.

LYREBIRD. A bird whose tail has brought it renown is the lyrebird of Australia. Except for the 16 strange tail feathers of the male, this bird is not unusual. Both male and female are of ordinary form, about the size of a hen, and of a sooty-brown color with a few red markings. The tail feathers are about 2 feet (.6 meter) long. They droop like a peacock's train. When they are raised, however, they take the shape of a lyre. The tail does not reach perfection until the bird is about four years old. It is shed in the fall and renewed in spring.

The male bird seems very proud of his fine feathers. When he is courting his mate, he scratches together a little mound of soil and leaves on which he stands. First he breaks forth into a tuneful song. Then he struts about in a dance, lifting and spreading his gorgeous tail feathers.

The lyrebird is the largest of the singing birds. It has a mellow, liquid note and imitates the songs of other birds and sounds. The female builds a dome-shaped nest on the ground or at the fork in the trunk of a tree. She makes a frame of sticks and a soft lining of fern roots and feathers. A side entrance protects the single dark egg she lays.

The birds are very shy. When approached they escape by running rapidly through the underbrush. They are poor fliers, so they reach nests in trees by jumping from limb to limb. The scientific name of the best-known species is *Menura superba.*

The letter L

probably started as a picture sign of an oxgoad, as in a very early Semitic writing used about 1500 B.C. on the Sinai Peninsula (1). A similar sign (2), denoting a peasant's crook, is found in earlier Egyptian hieroglyphic writing. About 1000 B.C., in Byblos and other Phoenician and Canaanite centers, the sign was given a linear form (3), the source of all later forms. In the Semitic languages the sign was called *lamedh,* meaning "oxgoad."

The Greeks first gave the sign some unbalanced forms (4) and renamed it *lambda.* Later they formed their sign symmetrically (5). The Romans adopted the earlier Greek forms (6). From Latin the capital letter came unchanged into English.

In late Roman times the small handwritten "l" was developed from the capital by rounding the lines. Later a form with an open loop in the vertical stroke was developed (7).

Laaland, Danish island. *see in index* Lolland

Laban, Rudolf von (1879–1958), dancer and teacher of dancing, born Hungary; taught many years in Germany; originated a new system of dance and devised a method of dance notation D-25

La Befana, Italian Christmas character C-329

Label, heraldic charge, *picture* H-142

Label, on clothing C-406

Labiatae, plant family including mint, catnip, and ground ivy M-366

La Boca, artists' district in Buenos Aires, Argentina A-580

Labor L-2. *see also in index* Industrial Revolution; countries by name; *also* topics beginning with Labor
  apprentice system A-510
  banks B-64
  business cycle affects B-518
  child labor C-281
    coal mining C-418
    rugmaking R-313
  civil service C-371
  Communism and C-494a
  convict labor P-505
  economic factors E-56, *table* E-57
  employer's liability E-201
  employment. *see in index* Employment
  forced labor D-131
    Hungary H-275
    Poland P-415
    Russia R-328
    Tibet T-137
  guilds G-256
  Industrial Revolution I-176
  industry I-192
  inflation role I-199
  labor and industrial law L-4
  labor movements L-6
  Lassalle's views L-56
  leisure time L-123
  machinery M-13
  mining M-344, *pictures* M-342–3
  pensions P-188
  railway workers R-75, 83, *pictures* R-85, W-173
  safety S-4
  slavery and serfdom S-212
  Socialism and S-234
  social security S-236
  sweatshop system G-33
  tariff protects T-23
  unemployment. *see in index* Unemployment
  United States U-64, 103, U-179, 186, *chart* U-107
    age trends P-448
    census report C-192
    immigration C-83
    Roosevelt, F. D. R-269
    Roosevelt, T. R-284
    Southern labor C-588
    Truman T-276
  vocations, *picture* V-364
  women W-214, *pictures* W-215, *chart* W-215c
  work efficiency W-235

Labor, in childbirth R-151d

Labor, American Federation of (A.F.L.). *see in index* American Federation of Labor

Labor, Department of, United States U-163, *list* U-157, *table* E-90
  building, *map* W-32
  child labor laws C-281
  secretary in Cabinet C-4

Labor and industrial law L-4
  arbitration A-528
  child labor laws C-281
  Clayton Act M-450
  employers' liability E-201
  England E-247
  industrial health hazards I-175
  labor L-3
  labor movements L-8, 10
  Mexico M-251
  pensions P-188
  social security S-236
  Spain S-356
  United States U-164, U-188, 191
    coal mining C-419
    Kennedy K-202
    Roosevelt, F.D. R-269
    Wilson W-175

Laboratory
  crime, *picture* P-429
  Edison's E-70, 73, *pictures* E-71, N-195
  glass used, *pictures* G-139–40
  medical
    bioengineering B-210
    hormone manufacture H-229
  nuclear energy N-250

Labor Day, International M-177b

Labor-Management Relations Act of 1947, or **Taft-Hartley Act,** United States T-278
  arbitration A-528
  labor and industrial law L-5
  U.S. history U-191

Labor-Management Services Administration, United States U-164

Labor movements L-6
  Industrial Revolution I-181
  Jones, Mother J-140
  labor and industrial law L-4
  Lewis, John L. L-142

Labor party, Great Britain, formed 1906 to represent organized labor and Socialists; cooperated with Liberals, later adopted socialistic program E-247
  Clement Attlee A-758
  Fabian Society F-2
  prime ministers, *table* G-199a
  Socialism S-235

Labor Relations Act, National, U.S. *see in index* National Labor Relations Act of 1935

Labor Relations Board, National, United States, U-166

Labors of Hercules H-143

Labor Statistics, Bureau of, United States U-164
  promotes safety S-6

Labor unions, or **trade unions.** *see also in index* Labor movements; *also* names of labor unions and labor leaders
  apprenticeships A-511
  arbitration A-528
  England E-247
  Industrial Revolution I-181
  labor and industrial law L-4
  labor movements L-6
  lobbying L-276

Mexico M-251
  political activities P-434
  railway brotherhoods R-83
  Russia R-330a, 332c
  socialism S-234
  Spain S-356
  United Nations U-26
  United States U-164, U-191
    Gompers, Samuel G-157
    Jones, Mother J-139
    Lewis, John L. L-142
    postal service P-460c
    Roosevelt, F.D. R-271
    Roosevelt, T. R-284
    Truman T-276, 280

Labouchère, Henry du Pré (1831–1912), English journalist and radical political leader, editor of the weekly *Truth,* noted for exposure of public frauds.

Labouchère, Pierre Antoine (1807–73), French painter, born Nantes, France; known for paintings of the Reformation painting of Calvin, *picture* R-134

Labrador, a peninsula, most easterly part of the North American mainland; area 1,620,000 sq km (625,000 sq mi); e. triangle of Labrador Peninsula (area 292,218 sq km (112,826 sq mi); pop. 188,339; together with Newfoundland Island, forms Province of Newfoundland, Canada L-12
  Cabot discovers C-9
  Canada, *maps* C-73, 99
  Churchill Falls W-73c
  Eskimos E-285
  Newfoundland N-165b, d, *maps* N-165c, k
  Quebec Q-9d, g
  Viking landings E-283
  work of Dr. Grenfell G-239

Labrador Current, or **Arctic Current,** cold ocean current along coast of Labrador; carries ice into important shipping lanes, *charts* O-397h, G-259b

Labrador duck, an extinct black-and-white sea duck closely allied to eider duck; ranged north Atlantic coast of North America as far south as Long Island, N.Y.; believed to have bred in Labrador, Canada B-271

Labrador ice cap, glacial formation I-7, *map* I-8

Labradorite, gem material J-116

Labrador retriever, a dog, *pictures* D-151, 141

Labrador tea, evergreen shrub (*Ledum groenlandicum*) of heath family; found in swamps of Greenland and Labrador, Canada; used for tea.

Labrouste, Henri (1801–1875), French architect A-562

La Bruyère, Jean de (1645–96), French essayist and wit, a moralist, born Paris; one of best writers of classical French L-12, F-395

Labuan, island off n. Borneo; formerly one of Straits Settlements; in 1946 became

part of North Borneo (now Sabah), a part of Malaysia since 1963; 35 sq mi (90 sq km); pop. 14,904, *map* E-36

Laburnum, small tree of pea family native to s. Europe; cultivated for showy yellow flowers, glossy foliage; all parts poisonous; called bean tree or golden chain in U.S.

Labyrinth, a name given by Greeks and Romans to buildings, entirely or partly underground, with intricate winding passages
  Aegean myth A-62
  Theseus T-159

Labyrinth, membranous, of ear, *diagram* E-4

Labyrinthodont, prehistoric amphibian A-461, *picture* A-460, *chart* G-64

'Labyrinth of Solitude, The', work by Paz L-71

'Labyrinths', work by Borges B-367

Lacatan, banana variety B-53

Laccadive Islands, coral islands in Arabian Sea w. of s. India; part of union territory of India, known as Lakshadweep, formerly Laccadive, Minicoy, and Amindivi Islands; pop. 13,109. *see also in index* Lakshadweep.

Laccolith, in geology, *diagram* G-59
  Devils Tower, Wyoming N-35, *maps* N-30, W-327, *picture* W-325

Lace, in textile industry L-13
  dress D-191, *picture* D-192
  producing regions
    Belgium Y-347
    France C-18

Lace-bark tree, tree of the West Indies (*Lagetta lintearia*); inner bark resembles coarse lace; used for collars, frills; also for making whips and rope.

Lacedaemon. *see in index* Laconia

La Ceiba, Honduras, Caribbean port city; pop. 49,900; ships bananas, hides, fruits; brewery; soap and vegetable oil factories, *map* N-309

Lacewing fly. *see in index* Green lacewings

Lacey Act of 1900, United States, on mongoose importation M-436

Lachaise, Gaston (1882–1935), sculptor, born Paris, France; in U.S. after 1906; best known for monumental female figures modeled in large, simple planes L-17, S-91

La Chaux de Fonds, Switzerland. *see in index* Chaux de Fonds, La.

Lachesis, in Greek mythology; one of the Fates F-44

Lachine, Que., Canada, manufacturing city and summer resort on Lake St. Louis connected with Montreal 10 km (6 mi) n.e. by Lachine Canal;

pop. 44,423; structural steel and other metal products. Burned and inhabitants killed by Indians 1689, *maps* M-477, *insets* Q-11, C-99

Lachine Canal, near Montreal M-476a, 477

Lachine Rapids, in St. Lawrence River S-20

Lachish, ancient city in s. Palestine, often mentioned in Tell el-Amarna tablets and in Bible; destroyed by Joshua (Josh. X, 31–3) and assigned to tribe of Judah (Josh. XV, 39).

Lachlan River, in New South Wales, Australia; joins Murrumbidgee River near junction with Murray River; 1,150 km (700 mi) long.

Lachrymal glands, or **lacrimal glands,** the tear-secreting organs E-369

Lachrymator, or **lacrimator,** a tear gas C-230

Lackawanna, N.Y., industrial and railroad city on Lake Erie just s. of Buffalo; pop. 22,701, *map* N-260

Lackland. *see in index* John of England

Laclede, Pierre (1724–78), also called Pierre Laclede Liguest, American fur trader and founder of St. Louis, Mo.; born in Lower Pyrenees, France; emigrated to New Orleans 1755 and established a fur trade with the Indians of the Missouri River area
  founds St. Louis S-21, *picture* M-401

Laclede's Village, old French town on site of St. Louis, Mo. S-22

Lacombe, Albert (1827–1916), Canadian Roman Catholic missionary, born St. Sulpice, Lower Canada; one of first missionaries sent to Northwest Territories; author of grammar and dictionary of Cree Indian language.

La Condamine, Charles Marie de (1701–74), French scientist, born Paris; explored the Amazon R-305

La Condamine, district of Monaco M-425

Laconia, or **Lacedaemon,** in ancient Greece, s.e. district of Peloponnesus of which Sparta was the capital S-369, *map* G-221
  Sparta conquers G-222

Laconia, N.H., resort and industrial city on Winnipesaukee River 28 mi (45 km) n. of Concord in beautiful lake region; pop. 15,575; knitting machines, shoes, hosiery, needles, ball bearings, skis, *map* N-183

La Coruña, Spain, seaport on n.w. coast; pop. 200,955; sailing port of the Spanish Armada (1588); repulse of French by British under Sir John Moore in Peninsular War 1809, *maps* S-350, E-334

Lacquer / Lahn

Lacquer P-73
cellulose, *table* C-184
varnish V-267
Lacquer ware C-295g, *picture* M-248
Lacquerwork, in decorative arts F-456
Lacrimal bone, a small bone within orbit of eye S-210
Lacrimal glands, or **lachrymal glands,** the tear-secreting organs E-369
La Crosse, Wis., city on Mississippi River 120 mi (195 km) s.e. of St. Paul, Minn.; pop. 48,347; center of stock-raising and dairying region and tobacco market; heating and air-conditioning equipment, farm machinery, rubber footwear, beverage coolers, beer; University of Wisconsin–La Crosse; Viterbo College W-194, *maps* W-207, U-41
Lacrosse, guided missile, *picture* G-251d
Lacrosse, sport L-17
Lactarius pergamenus, or **parchment lactarius,** a mushroom, *picture* M-553
Lacteal, any one of lymphatic vessels of intestinal canal.
Lactic acid, the acid formed in sour milk; $C_3H_6O_3$
cheese making C-229, *picture* C-228
fatigue F-45
fermentation F-55
meat M-190
muscle action develops R-160
yeast culture Y-338
Lactobacillus, a bacterium which makes lactic acid B-15
Lactose, or **milk sugar,** a double (disaccharide) sugar ($C_{12}H_{22}O_{11}$), reducible to galactose and glucose; differs from maltose and sucrose in structure of molecule S-508, M-322, D-3
Lacus Juturnae, fountain in Rome, Italy F-335
Ladanum, or **labdanum,** a resin obtained from the plants *Cistus ladaniferus* and *Cistus villosus;* used in the manufacture of heavy perfumes.
Ladd, Edwin Fremont (1859–1925), chemist, born Starks, Me.; on faculty of North Dakota Agricultural College 1890–1920; U.S. senator 1921–25; pioneer in pure food legislation.
Ladd, George Trumbull (1842–1921), philosopher, born Painesville, Ohio; one of first to introduce study of experimental psychology into America; founded Yale University psychological laboratory (translation, Lotze's 'Outlines of Philosophy', 6 vols.).
Ladder
fire fighting F-104
in caisson, *diagram* C-17
safety measures S-7
spacecraft S-346d, *picture* S-347
Ladder dredge D-185
Ladd-Franklin, Christine (1847–1930), scientist, born Windsor, Conn.; first woman student at Johns Hopkins University and at universities of Göttingen and Berlin in Germany; distinguished career in mathematics, physics, and psychology; famous for her theory of color perception.
'Ladies Home Journal', U.S. periodical F-42
Ladies' sorrel. *see in index* Sorrel, wood
Ladies tresses, a wild flower of the genus *Spiranthes* of the orchid family; the flowers are small, white, yellowish- or greenish-white, in twisted spikes.
Lading, bill of. *see in index* Bill of lading
Ladino, a person of mixed Spanish and Indian blood C-195, *charts* C-198, *picture* C-196. *see also in index* Mestizo
Ladislaus, or **Laszlo' I** (1040–95), saint and king of Hungary; obtained Croatia for Hungary and Christianized it; most beloved of Hungarian kings; canonized 1198; festival June 27.
Ladoga, Lake, largest lake of Europe, in n.w. Russia; area about 18,000 sq km (7,000 sq mi), L-19, *maps* R-322, 344, 348, E-335
Ladrone Islands. *see in index* Mariana Islands
Lady, title T-185
'Ladybird, ladybird', nursery rhyme N-381c
Ladybug, or **ladybird,** or **lady beetle,** a small spotted beetle B-138
hibernation H-151
insect, *picture* I-216
scale insects prey S-52f
'Lady Chatterly's Lover', work by D. H. Lawrence L-98
Ladycliff College, at Highland Falls, near West Point, N.Y.; private control; primarily for women; founded 1933; liberal arts and sciences, teacher education.
'Lady Elizabeth Delmé and Her Children', painting by Reynolds P-47
Ladyfinger, banana B-53
'Lady Jean', painting by Bellows P-61, *picture* P-60
Lady Margaret Hall, one of the colleges at Oxford University, England O-515
Lady of Christ's, nickname of John Milton M-327
Lady of the Lake, water fairy and enchantress of Arthurian legend; treacherously imprisoned Merlin in an enchanted tower in the forest of Brécéliande; reared Lancelot in her palace, situated in the middle of an imaginary lake
King Arthur's sword A-655
'Lady of the Lake, The', poem by Sir Walter Scott S-73
Ladysmith, South Africa, trade center, and railroad junction in n. Natal; pop. 22,955; besieged by Boers for 118 days (1899–1900) during Boer War, *map* S-264
siege, *table* W-8d
'Lady's Not for Burning, The', play by Fry F-440
Lady's-slipper, a plant of the orchid type
Minnesota state flower, *pictures* M-356, S-427
Prince Edward Island emblem, *picture* P-497
skin irritant P-409
'Lady with the Unicorn, The', medieval story A-458
Lae, New Guinea, port on e. coast; pop. 4,146; capital of Territory of New Guinea 1941–42; occupied by Japanese 1942–43; reoccupied by Allies Sept. 1943, *maps* E-37, P-4
Laënnec, René (1781–1826), French physician, born Brittany; invented the stethoscope and began practice of auscultation in medicine L-19
medicine M-215c
Laertes, father of Odysseus O-409
Laertes, in Shakespeare's 'Hamlet', son of Polonius H-15
La Farge, John (1835–1910), painter, mural decorator, and designer of first stained glass made in U.S.; born New York City; grandfather of Oliver La Farge; exercised great influence on American art (lunettes, Supreme Court room, Minnesota State Capitol; 'Battle Window', Memorial Hall, Harvard University).
La Farge, Oliver (Hazard Perry) (1901–63), writer, anthropologist; born New York City, grandson of John La Farge; made archaeological and ethnological expeditions to Arizona for Harvard University and to Guatemala and Mexico for Tulane University; wrote with intimate knowledge and understanding of the Indians ('Laughing Boy', novel, won Pulitzer prize 1930; 'All the Young Men', 'A Pause in the Desert', short stories; 'Cochise of Arizona', biography; 'A Pictorial History of the American Indian'; 'Santa Fe', local history).
Lafayette (1757–1834), French general and patriot L-19
American Revolution R-173
De Kalb and D-63
French Revolution F-401
revisits U.S., *picture* M-455
Lafayette, George Washington Motier de (1779–1849), son of Lafayette; aide-de-camp to General Grouchy.
LaFayette, Marie Madeleine, comtesse de (1634–93), French novelist, born Paris; her masterpiece, 'La Princesse de Clèves', is first modern novel of sentiment in which story's interest depends not on the incident but on the character of persons involved F-395
Lafayette, Calif., city 28 mi (45 km) n.e. of Berkeley; pop. 20,879; chiefly residential; settled 1834, incorporated 1968, *map, inset* C-52
Lafayette, Ind., city on Wabash River about 60 mi (95 km) n.w. of Indianapolis; pop. 43,011; aluminum products, prefabricated houses, gears, sponge rubber, meters; r.r. shops; Purdue University at West Lafayette, *map* U-41
Lafayette, La., city about 52 mi (84 km) s.w. of Baton Rouge; pop. 81,961; railroad division point; agricultural and oil center; food products, aluminum products.
'Lafayette', submarine, *pictures* S-496
"Lafayette, we are here," words reportedly uttered by General Pershing when laying wreath on tomb of Lafayette July 4, 1917; actually spoken by Col. Charles E. Stanton.
Lafayette College, at Easton, Pa.; Presbyterian; formerly for men, women admitted 1970; opened 1832 (chartered 1826); arts and sciences, education, engineering, international affairs.
Lafayette Escadrille, World War I, W-257
Lafayette Square, Washington, D.C. public park north of the White House; contains statues of Generals Andrew Jackson, Lafayette, Kosciusko, and Steuben, *map* W-32
La Fère, France, town on Oise River, 25 km (15 mi) n.w. of Laon; pop. 3095; scene of fighting in World Wars I and II.
Lafitte, Jean (1780?–1826?), American pirate, slave trader, and smuggler; born France L-20
blacksmith shop, *map* N-223a
Jackson recruits J-7
La Follette, Philip F(ox) (1897–1965), lawyer and political leader, born Madison, Wis.; son of Robert Marion La Follette; Progressive Republican; governor of Wisconsin 1931–33, 1935–39.
La Follette, Robert M. (1855–1925), political leader, born Primrose, Wis.; called Fighting Bob; father of Philip F. and Robert M. La Follette, Jr.; governor of Wisconsin 1901–5; U.S. senator 1906–25; a Progressive Republican who subordinated party ties to his own principles; opposed U.S. entrance into World War I; many of the reforms he sought incorporated in the "Wisconsin idea"; Progressive party presidential candidate 1924, L-20
heads Progressives P-434, *chart* P-494
Insurgent leader T-8
Seamen's Act (author) S-173
Statuary Hall, *table* S-437b
Wisconsin W-198, *picture* W-204
La Follette, Robert Marion, Jr. (1895–1953), political leader, born Madison, Wis.; son of Robert Marion La Follette; Progressive Republican; U.S. senator from Wisconsin 1925–47; committed suicide.
La Fontaine, Henri (1854–1943), Belgian politician, born Brussels; prolific writer on international arbitration.
La Fontaine, Jean de (1621–95), French storyteller L-21
fables F-3
Lafontaine, Sir Louis Hippolyte (1807–64), Canadian jurist and statesman, premier 1842–44 and 1848–51; chief justice of Lower Canada 1853–64, C-112, B-24
Laforet, Carmen (born 1921), Spanish novelist, born Barcelona S-366, *picture* S-367
Laforgue, Jules (1860–87), French symbolist poet, born Montevideo, Uruguay; one of first to write modern free verse.
LAFTA (Latin American Free Trade Association), Latin American common market L-65
Lagado, in 'Gulliver's Travels', the capital of Balnibarbi; here a celebrated Academy of Projectors engages in extracting sunbeams from cucumbers, in converting ice into gunpowder, and in similar ridiculous ventures.
Lagan, sunken cargo with buoy F-212
Lagash, ancient city-state in Babylonia, one of oldest centers of Sumerian civilization; on site of present Telloh, Iraq; reached peak about 3000 B.C. B-7, *map* B-4
Lager beer, alcoholic beverage B-132
Lagerkvist, Pär (1891–1974), Swedish poet, playwright, and novelist, born Växjö L-21
Lagerlöf, Selma (1858–1940), Swedish writer L-21, S-472
'Wonderful Adventures of Nils, The' R-111a
Lago Argentino, glacial valley, Argentina A-576
Lagomorpha, order of gnawing animals that differ from rodents in having 4 upper cutting teeth (incisors) instead of 2; includes hares, rabbits, and pikas.
Lagoon, a pool or lake, especially one connected with the sea P-13
Lagos, a region (formerly province) of s. Nigeria; in w. Africa; 27,000 sq mi (70,000 sq km); low marshy coast, with countless lagoons; forested interior yields palm oil and kernels, mahogany, rubber; chief cities Ibadan (with surrounding suburban farm district, pop. 459,196) and Lagos N-287
Lagos, Nigeria, capital and chief port, in s.w.; pop. 1,404,000, L-22, N-287, A-119
Lagrange, Joseph-Louis (1736–1813), French mathematician, one of greatest of 18th century, born Turin, Italy; contributed to verification of Newtonian theory of gravitation L-22
La Grange, Ga., industrial city and trade center, 62 mi (100 km) s.w. of Atlanta; pop. 24,204; textiles, lumber products; La Grange College, *maps* G-92, U-41
La Grange, Ill., village 14 mi (22 km) s.w. of Chicago; pop. 15,681; named for Lafayette's home in France; nearby are diesel locomotive plant, aluminum rolling mill, and factory making parts of automobile bodies.
La Grange College, at La Grange, Ga.; Methodist; chartered 1831; opened 1832; arts and sciences, teacher education; graduate studies; quarter system.
La Grange Park, Ill., village 14 mi (22 km) s.w. of Chicago; pop. 13,359; electronic components, plastic products.
La Granja, Spain. *see in index* San Ildefonso
Lagting, in Norway N-368
La Guaira, Venezuela, seaport for Caracas, on Caribbean Sea; artificial inner harbor; pop. 20,681, V-275, *map* S-298
tunnel, *table* T-292
La Guardia, Fiorello (1882–1947), lawyer and public official, born New York City; member of U.S. Congress 1917–21, 1923–33; mayor of New York City 1934–45; director UNRRA 1946, L-22
Civil Air Patrol C-366a
La Guardia Airport, New York, N.Y. N-273, *map* N-271
La Guma, Alex (born 1925), South African writer L-23
African literature A-123
Laguna (Spanish "lagoon"), pueblo 42 mi (68 km) w. of Albuquerque, N.M.; pop. 4,233; founded 1699; Laguna people belong to the Keresan language group of Pueblo Indians, *map* N-220
Laguna Beach, Calif., scenic city on Pacific Ocean about 45 mi (70 km) s.e. of Los Angeles; pop. 17,860, *map* C-53, *picture* U-88
Laguna de Bay, largest lake in Philippines, s.e. of Manila; 344 sq mi (891 sq km), P-256, 259
La Habra, Calif., city 17 mi (27 km) s.e. of Los Angeles; pop. 45,232; electronic components, metal products, processed foods, chemicals, *map, inset* C-53
Lahaina, Hawaii, city on w. coast of Maui; pop. 3,718; exports sugar; first white settlement of Hawaii was here: capital 1810–45, *map* H-71
La Halle, Adam de. *see in index* Adam de la Halle
Lahn River, West Germany, after s.w. course of 215 km (135 mi) joins Rhine opposite Coblenz, *map* G-115

La Hogue / Lambeth

La Hogue, or **La Hogue, Battle of,** fought 1692 near n.e. extremity of peninsula of Cotentin, Normandy, France; English and Dutch fleets under Admiral Russell defeated French fleet under Tourville.

Lahontan, Lake, Nevada N-143

Lahore, Pakistan, capital of Punjab Province, near Ravi River, about 270 mi (435 km) n.w. of New Delhi, India; pop. 2,922,000; transportation center; silk and cotton cloths, carpets, vegetable oils; Punjab University L-23

Laibach, Yugoslavia. *see in index* Ljubljana

Laid paper, paper marked with parallel lines S-405

L'Aiglon, poetic name meaning "eaglet" given by Victor Hugo to duke of Reichstadt, son of Napoleon and Marie Louise; subject of play by Rostand.

Laika, Russian dog, first animal to orbit earth S-345, *table* S-344

Laird, Melvin R(obert) (born 1922), public official, born Omaha, Neb.; to Marshfield, Wis., at early age; member Wisconsin state Senate 1946–52; Republican congressman from Wisconsin 1953–69; U.S. secretary of defense 1969–73; chief adviser on domestic affairs 1973–74.

Laissez faire ("let it be"), the 18th-century (French) way of saying "less government in business"; in contemporary use means unrestricted industrial and commercial competition
- Industrial Revolution I-181
- international trade I-271
- Socialism rejects S-233

Laity, in church C-336

Laius, in Greek mythology, father of Oedipus O-409

Lajoie, Napoleon (Larry) (1875–1959), baseball second baseman, born Woonsocket, R.I.; second baseman chiefly Philadelphia, N.L., 1896–1900, and Cleveland, A.L., 1901–14; in 1901, batted .422, highest in A.L. history; lifetime average .339, B-93

La Jolla, Calif., community in city of San Diego; Scripps Institution of Oceanography; cliffs, caves, and scenic stretches of ocean beach attract many tourists.

La Jonquière, Jacques Pierre Taffanel, marquis de (1680–1753), French naval officer, born near Albi in s. France; fought numerous engagements against British; governor of New France (Canada) 1749–53.

La Junta, Colo., city on Arkansas River 60 mi (100 km) s.e. of Pueblo; pop. 8,338; railroad shops, food processing, livestock sales center; mobile homes, *picture* C-463, *maps* C-467, U-40

Lake, Simon (1866–1945), naval architect and mechanical engineer, born Pleasantville, N.J.; inventor of even-keel type of submarine S-493, *picture* S-495

Lake, asphalt A-702

Lake L-24. For list of greatest lakes. *see table* following. *see also in index* names of individual lakes, as Erie, Lake
- acid rain pollution A-19
- climate affected by G-204
- Earth E-16, *diagram* E-17
- extinct
  - Agassiz M-89a, R-120
  - Bonneville G-208, U-216
- freshwater
  - Superior, Lake S-518
  - Tanganyika, Lake T-15
- part of river R-210
- pollution P-441c, *diagram* P-441d
- salt
  - Caspian Sea C-148
  - Dead Sea D-41
  - Great Salt Lake G-208
  - potassium salts P-465
- seiche O-400a
- water table and G-203

Lake Charles, La., port city in s.w. part of state, on Lake Charles, on direct channel to Gulf of Mexico; pop. 75,226; oil-refinery products, chemicals, synthetic rubber, wood products; meat-packing, rice milling; McNeese State University L-310, *maps* L-323, U-41

Lake Chelan National Recreation Area, in Washington N-40a, *map* N-30

Lake Compounce, amusement park, Bristol, Conn. A-385

Lake District, in n.w. England; has all principal English lakes E-219, 218, *maps* G-199e
- Wordsworth's home, *picture* W-234

Lake dwellers, Stone Age people who built huts on pile foundations along the shores of lakes S-544, *picture* M-78
- shelter S-157
- weaving T-138

Lake Erie, Battle of (1813) P-209, W-13

Lake Erie College, at Painesville, Ohio; private control; for women; chartered 1856; opened 1859; arts and sciences, fine arts; coeducational division Garfield Senior College offers liberal arts, business, education.

Lake Forest, Ill., residential city on Lake Michigan, 30 mi (50 km) n. of Chicago; pop. 15,245; Barat College; Lake Forest College.

Lake Forest College, at Lake Forest, Ill.; private control, Presbyterian related; founded 1857; arts and sciences, teacher education; trimesters.

Lake Geneva, Wis., city in s.e. part of state, on Lake Geneva, 40 mi (65 km) s.w. of Milwaukee; resort; pop. 5,607; Yerkes Observatory of University of Chicago, 6 mi (10 km) w. of city, *map* W-207

Lakehurst, N.J., borough about 55 mi (90 km) s. of New York City; pop. 2,908, *map* N-203

Lake Jackson, Tex., city 50 mi (80 km) s. of Houston; pop. 19,102; metal products, store fixtures; dairy and fruit farms, *map* T-129

Lakeland, Fla., city about 30 mi (50 km) e. of Tampa; pop. 47,406; 12 lakes, resort center; citrus fruit, food-processing, machinery, tile products; phosphate mines, *map* U-41
- Florida Southern College, *picture* U-207

Lakeland College, near Sheboygan, Wis.; United Church of Christ; founded 1862; liberal arts, business administration, education, medical technology, music, science.

Lakeland terrier, dog, native of Lake District of England, *picture* D-148

Lake Mead National Recreation Area, in Arizona and Nevada N-40a, C-470, *maps* N-157, N-30, *picture* N-152

Lake Nasser, reservoir, Egypt A-732

'Lake of Palms, The', work by Dutt I-108

Lake of the Woods, an island-dotted body of water of n. Minnesota and adjacent parts of Ontario, Canada; 1,485 sq mi (3,845 sq km); 105 mi (170 km) long, *maps* M-349, 362, U-70, M-89j, C-73, 98, O-456b. *see also in index* Northwest Angle
- muskellunge fishing P-326

Lake Oswego, Ore., city 8 mi (13 km) s. of Portland; pop. 14,573; cement, infant's wear, wood products; incorporated 1918, *map, inset* O-492

Lake Placid, N.Y., village at s. end of Lake Placid (about 4 mi [6 km] long and ½ mi [1 km] wide); pop. 2,490; a famous winter and summer resort in Adirondack Mts.; hosted 1980 winter Olympics; nearby is the grave of John Brown, the abolitionist, *map* N-261
- Adirondack Mountains A-44
- American Home Economics Association H-205
- bobsled run S-216, *picture* N-254
- Olympic Games O-453

Lake Plains, geographical region, U.S. I-88, *map* I-89

Lake Poets, in England C-432

Lake Regillus, Battle of (496 B.C.) R-242

Lakeshores, National, United States, *map* N-30, *picture* N-42

Lakes-to-Gulf waterway G-205, C-121, *map* G-203
- Illinois Waterway links C-255

Lake Success, on Long Island, N.Y.; pop. 3,254, *map, inset* N-260
- UN headquarters U-22

Lake Superior State College, at Sault Sainte Marie, Mich; founded 1946; arts and social sciences, science and technology; quarter system.

Lake trout T-269
- lamprey as enemy P-114

Lakeview, Mich., community 38 mi (61 km) n.e. of Grand Rapids; pop. 1,139; farm produces, *map* M-285

Lake Washington Floating Bridge, in Washington W-42, S-103, *map* S-103b

Lake Washington Ship Canal, Washington S-103, *map* S-103b

Lakewood, Calif., residential and commercial city 13 mi (21 km) s.e. of Los Angeles; pop. 74,654; incorporated 1954; annual Pan-American festival, *map, inset* C-53

Lakewood, Colo., residential city w. of Denver; pop. 112,860; artificial kidneys, aerospace equipment; Camp George West Military Reservation, *map* C-467

Lakewood, N.J., community 19 mi (30 km) s.w. of Long Branch; pop. 17,874; plastics, cosmetics, woodwork; winter resort, *map* N-203

Lakewood, Ohio, city on Lake Erie, just w. of Cleveland; pop. 61,963; originally East Rockport, took present name 1889, *map, inset* O-429

Lake Worth, Fla., city 9 mi (14 km) s. of Palm Beach, on Lake Worth, which opens into the Atlantic; resort; pop. 27,048; incorporated 1913.

Lakshadweep, or **Laccadive, Minicoy, and Amindivi Islands,** union territory, India; islands and coral reefs; 11 sq mi (28 sq km); pop. 31,810; grain, bananas, copra, fisheries.

Lalande, Saint Jean de (died 1646), Roman Catholic martyr; missionary in Canada and New York; companion of Father Jogues; murdered by Mohawks at Ossernenon, N.Y.; canonized 1930; feasts celebrated Sept. 26 and March 16 (by Jesuits).

Lalande, Joseph Jérôme Le Français de (1732–1807), French astronomer, born Bourg-en-Bresse, France; professor Collège de France, director Paris observatory; popularized astronomy; established annual Prix Lalande for most useful work on astronomy.

Lalemant, Gabriel (1610–49), Canadian saint and Jesuit missionary, born Paris, France; came to Canada 1646; worked with Father Brébeuf among the Huron Indians and was killed by the Iroquois; canonized 1930.

Lalique, René (1860–1945), French jeweler, born Ay, near Reims; famous for carving in jewels and glass.

'Lalla Rookh', Oriental poem by Thomas Moore; an Indian princess, on her way to Sultan Aliris, her betrothed, is entertained by a Persian poet, with whom she falls in love; is later overjoyed to find that the poet was her betrothed in disguise.

'L'Allegro' ("the happy man"), poem by John Milton; companion poem of 'Il Penseroso'; describes quiet pleasures of a contented man E-259

Lalo, Édouard (1823–92), French composer, born Lille, France ('Le Roi d'Ys', opera; 'Symphonie Espagnole', 'Norwegian Rhapsody', orchestral works).

Lamaism, a religion of Tibet and Mongolia T-173, M-432, *pictures* T-172

La Malbaie, also **Murray Bay,** Que., Canada, town on St. Lawrence River at mouth of Malbaie River 124 km (77 mi) n.e. of Quebec (city); pop. 4,307; summer resort, *map* Q-11

La Mama Experimental Theatre Club, forum for creating and performing new plays A-363

Lamar, Lucius Quintus Cincinnatus (1825–93), jurist and statesman, born Putnam County, Ga.; drafted Mississippi ordinance of secession; U.S. senator 1877–85; secretary of interior 1885–88; justice U.S. Supreme Court 1888–93; helped reconciliation between North and South after Civil War, *picture* M-384

Lamar, Mirabeau Buonaparte (1798–1859), soldier, born Louisville, Ga.; participated in Texas revolution and distinguished self at San Jacinto; president Texas Republic 1838–41; major general Mexican War; U.S. minister to Argentina, Nicaragua, Costa Rica.

Lamarck, Jean-Baptiste (1744–1829), French naturalist, born Bazentin, Picardy; in 1802 adopted the word "biologie" as name of new science to be devoted to study of all life considered as the same process whether in plants or animals L-25
- forerunner of Darwin D-35
- heredity theory E-345, G-43a

La Marque, Tex., city s.w. of Texas City; pop. 15,372; chiefly residential; oil production and truck farming; established in 1860's, named 1890, *map* T-129

Lamartine, Alphonse de (1790–1869), French poet, historian, and statesman; born Macon, France L-25
- French literature F-396

Lamar University, at Beaumont, Tex.; established 1923 as junior college; became state-supported senior college 1951; liberal arts, business, education, engineering, fine and applied arts, sciences, vocational training; graduate school.

La Matanza, Argentina, suburb of Buenos Aires; pop. 402,642, *map* S-299

La Mauricie National Park, in Quebec, Canada N-24d, Q-9h, *map* N-24b

Lamb, Charles, or **Elia** (1775–1834), English essayist L-25, E-264
- book annotations B-362
- Coleridge C-432
- essays E-290
- on storytelling S-466
- Shakespeare S-140, 142

Lamb, Mary (1764–1847), English writer, sister of Charles Lamb L-26
- Shakespeare S-140

Lamb, William. *see in index* Melbourne, Viscount

Lamb, Willis E(ugene), Jr. (born 1913), physicist, born Los Angeles, Calif.; professor of physics Stanford University 1951–56, Oxford University 1956–62, and Yale University after 1962.

Lamb, a young sheep S-146
- farming F-29
- furs, *table* F-465
- meat M-189, M-192, *diagrams* M-192b, *tables* M-189–90
- skin G-144d
- wool W-229

Lamballe, Marie Thérèse de (1749–92), French princess, born Turin, Italy; friend of Marie Antoinette; killed by revolutionists; her head carried past queen's prison windows.

Lambaréné, Gabon, town on Ogooué River 95 mi (155 km) s.e. of Libreville; pop. 3,750; Albert Schweitzer's medical center S-56

Lambeau, Earl Louis (Curly) (1898–1965), football halfback and coach, born Green Bay, Wis.; founded Green Bay Packers 1919, halfback and head coach 1919–49.

Lambert, Johann Heinrich (1728–77), German physicist, mathematician, astronomer, and philosopher; born Mulhouse, Alsace; made important contributions to mathematical theory; measured intensity and absorption of light (Lambert, unit of intensity, named for him)
- map projections M-101

Lambert, Louis. *see in index* Gilmore, Patrick S.

Lambert, Richard Stanton (born 1894), Canadian educator and writer, born London, England; promoted educational and cultural films and radio broadcasts; books for children include 'Franklin of the Arctic' (Canadian Book of the Year for Children award 1950) and 'The Adventure of Canadian Painting'; also author of books for adults.

Lambeth, baron of. *see in index* Davidson, Randall Thomas; Fisher, Geoffrey Francis

Lambeth, borough of Greater London, England; pop. 325,070, *map, inset* G-199h
- London, *map* L-287

Lambeth Council (1888), defined essential positions of

Anglican Church in the hope of reconciliation with other Christian denominations A-417

Lambeth Palace, in London, England; begun 1207; heavily damaged by bombing 1940–41, L-294

Lambing Flat, New South Wales, Australia
anti-Chinese riots A-785

Lambkill, or **sheep laurel,** evergreen shrub of heath family; grows to 1 m (3 ft); the flowers, which are purple or crimson, are arranged in flat-topped clusters P-409
laurel L-88

Lambrequin, or **mantling,** heraldic device H-142

Lamb's-ears, a perennial plant (*Stachys lanata*) of the mint family, native to w. Asia. Grows to 46 cm (18 in.), entire plant white, woolly, with oblong leaves and spikes of tiny, tubular, purple flowers; sometimes called woolly woundwort.

Lambskin G-144d
furs, *table* F-463
leather L-108

Lamb's lettuce. see in index Corn salad

Lamb's quarters, or **goosefoot,** an annual herb (*Chenopodium album*) of the goosefoot family with clusters of small greenish flowers and leaves shaped like the foot of a goose; although considered a pest, delicious greens may be made from it.

Lambuth College, at Jackson, Tenn.; affiliated with United Methodist church; established 1843; arts and sciences and education.

Lamb vulture V-388

Lamé, a fabric made of any of various fibers combined with tinsel threads, often of silver or gold; most frequently used for evening wear; also trade name for metallic yarns.

Lame Duck amendment, or **20th Amendment** H-223, U-146, 153

'Lamentation, The', drawing by Dürer D-181, *picture* D-182

Lamentations, book of Old Testament traditionally ascribed to Jeremiah; comprises five dirges bewailing the destruction of Jerusalem B-182

Lamenting bird. see in index Limpkin

Lamer, Antonio (born 1933), Canadian jurist, born Montreal, Que.; justice Superior Court of Quebec 1969–78, Quebec Court of Appeal 1978–80; justice Supreme Court of Canada 1980–.

La Mesa, Calif., residential city 8 mi (13 km) n.e. of San Diego; pop. 50,342; citrus fruit, avocados, poultry; incorporated 1912, *map* C-53

Lamesa, Tex., city 57 mi (92 km) s. of Lubbock; pop. 11,790; cotton and other farming, ranching; poultry; oil fields; cotton gins; garments; *map* T-128

Lamia, in Greek mythology, a beautiful vampire; in John Keats's poem 'Lamia', a serpent that assumes human form to win a man's love.

Laminar Flow Control (LFC), aerodynamics A-80, A-180

Laminated fabric, material consisting of two or more layers of goods put together with adhesive plastic, rubber, or other joining substance; term also applies to fabric joined to plastic sheet, as goods bonded to synthetic foam; used for women's dresses and coats.

Laminating, arranging in thin layers (laminae)
forest products F-316
lumber L-332, *picture* L-334
plastics P-383
plywood P-397
safety glass G-135

La Mirada, Calif., city located on freeway 17 mi (27 km) s.e. of Los Angeles; chiefly residential; pop. 40,986; Biola College; governed by city administrator system.

Lammergeier, or **bearded vulture** V-388

Lamoille River, rises in n. Vermont near Hardwick; cuts w. through Green Mts.; flows into Lake Champlain; dam forms

Lake Lamoille at Morrisville, *maps* V-286, 301

Lamon, Ward Hill (1828–93), law partner, secretary, and biographer of Abraham Lincoln; born Frederick County, Va.; served as marshal of District of Columbia 1861–65, *picture* C-374

Lamona, a breed of poultry P-482

Lamont, Robert Patterson (1867–1948), U.S. secretary of commerce under President Hoover; born Detroit, Mich.; engineer and manufacturer; president American Steel Foundries 1912–29.

La Motte-Fouqué, Friedrich, baron de (1777–1843), German romantic poet and novelist, born Brandenburg; extremely popular in early 19th century G-98

L'Amour, Louis (born 1908?), U.S. writer; pen name Tex Burns for first novel L-26

Lamp L-205. see also in index Lighting
coal mining C-420
Davy, Sir Humphry D-39
design, *picture* I-174
Edison, Thomas E-72
electric light E-157, *picture* E-158
Eskimo E-286
Greece, *picture* G-225
oil P-232
pottery as base, *picture* P-479
signaling S-194
sodium vapor lamps S-247
stereopticon S-444
tungsten T-288

Lampblack, or **carbon black,** a form of carbon G-41, C-132
paint pigment P-73
pencils P-158
tire manufacture G-41, R-303

Lamp-eyed fish, a deep-sea fish having an organ below each eye in which bacteria live; the bacteria secrete a luminous chemical; the fish may draw a lid over the organ when it wishes.

Lampman, Archibald (1861–99), Canadian poet, born Morpeth, Ont. C-113b, 116, *picture* C-114

Lamprey, fish L-26, F-132

animal groups, *chart* Z-366
invades Great Lakes P-114
prehistoric animals A-461

Lampsacus, ancient Greek city of Mysia, Asia Minor, on Hellespont, opposite Gallipoli; settled by Ionian Greeks (654); known for its wines; center of worship of fertility god Priapus.

Lamp shell, bivalve S-151

Län, administrative district in Sweden S-526

Lana, Francesco de, Italian monk A-200

Lanai, island of Hawaii; 139.5 sq mi (361.3 sq km); 18 mi (29 km) long, 10 mi (16 km) wide; pop. 2,204; highest point 3,400 ft (1,035 m); pineapple plantations since 1922; previously pastureland H-53, *maps* H-52, 71, U-98, 117, P-5

Lanao, Lake, second largest lake in Philippines, on island of Mindanao; 134 sq mi (347 sq km) P-259, 255d, 256

La Navidad, in Haiti; Columbus' first settlement in New World C-478, 479, H-7

Lancashire, or **Lancaster,** county of n.w. England; 3,043 sq mi (1,175 sq mi); pop. 5,129,416; cap. Lancaster; iron and coal mines; textiles, machinery, *map* E-218
Liverpool L-261
textile industry M-82

Lancaster, John of Gaunt, duke of. see in index John of Gaunt

Lancaster, Calif., community 45 mi (72 km) n.e. of Los Angeles; in Antelope Valley region of Mojave Desert; pop. 48,027; cotton, citrus fruits, nuts; aircraft, *map* C-53

Lancaster, England, capital of Lancashire, on Lune River, 11 km (7 mi) from sea; pop. 48,170, *map* G-199h

Lancaster, N.Y., village 11 mi (18 km) e. of Buffalo; pop. 13,056; in dairying area; stone quarries, glass products; settled 1810, incorporated 1849, *map* N-260

Lancaster, Ohio, city on Hocking River, 27 mi (43 km) s.e. of Columbus; pop. 34,953;

glassware, machinery, boiler equipment, shoes, foundry products; birthplace of Gen. William Tecumseh Sherman; state industrial school for boys nearby, *map* O-429

Lancaster, Pa., city 34 mi (55 km) s.e. of Harrisburg; pop. 54,725, *maps* P-185, 174, U-41
first chain store C-204
former state capital P-172
Thaddeus Stevens S-445

Lancaster, House of, famous English royal family, *table* R-297. see also in index Roses, Wars of the
Henry IV founded H-136
rulers. see in index England, *table* of kings and queens

Lancaster Turnpike, historical road in United States R-215, T-196, *map* R-219, *pictures* P-175, W-25

Lance, in metalworking I-341

Lance, long-shafted cavalry weapon with spearhead medieval, *picture* M-302

Lance corporal, U.S. military rank, *picture* U-9

Lancelet. see in index Amphioxus

Lancelot, or **Lancelot of the Lake,** in Arthurian legend, bravest and most famous of the Knights of the Round Table; outstanding figure in Tennyson's 'Idylls of the King' R-299a, A-655
quest for Grail G-3

Lancers, a type of quadrille; introduced in 19th century; danced by 8 or 16 couples; also its music. see also in index Quadrille

Lancewood, name given to several trees of family *Annonaceae* native to West Indies and Guiana, and to their highly pliable and tough even-grained wood, which is used for fishing rods and for other articles requiring flexibility and strength.

Lanchow, People's Republic of China, capital of Kansu Province; pop. 732,000; petroleum refining; oil-field equipment, chemicals.

Lanciani, Rodolfo (1846–1929), Italian

LARGEST LAKES OF THE WORLD

Lake	Location	Area sq mi	Area sq km	Elevation Above Sea Level ft	Elevation Above Sea Level m	Maximum Depth ft	Maximum Depth m
Aral Sea	Soviet Union	25,000	64,700	174	53	226	69
Baikal	Soviet Union	12,16	31,494	1,486	453	5,315	1,620
Balkhash	Soviet Union	7,300	18,900	1,115	340	85	26
Caspian Sea	Soviet Union, Iran	143,000	370,000	−94	−29	3,360	1,024
Chad	Chad, Cameroon, Nigeria, Niger	9,950	25,770	922	281	23	7
Chelan	United States	55	142	1,096	334	1,605	489
Crater	United States	21	54	6,176	1,882	1,932	589
Dead Sea	Israel, Jordan	405	1,049	−1,316	−401	1,300	400
Erie	United States, Canada	9,910	25,670	570	174	210	64
Great Bear	Canada	12,275	31,792	512	156	1,356	413
Great Salt	United States	2,000	5,180	4,200	1,280	35	11
Great Slave	Canada	11,170	28,930	512	156	2,015	614
Huron	United States, Canada	23,100	59,830	579	176	750	229
Ladoga	Soviet Union	6,826	17,678	55	17	754	230
Michigan	United States	22,300	57,760	579	176	923	281
Nyasa	Malawi, Tanzania, Mozambique	11,430	29,604	1,550	472	2,310	704
Ontario	United States, Canada	7,550	19,550	245	75	802	244
Rudolph	Kenya, Ethiopia	2,473	6,405	1,230	375	240	73
Superior	United States, Canada	31,700	82,100	600	183	1,333	406
Tanganyika	Tanzania, Zambia, Zaire, Burundi	12,700	32,890	2,534	772	4,710	1,436
Titicaca	Peru, Bolivia	3,200	8,290	12,500	3,810	920	280
Victoria	Kenya, Uganda, Tanzania	26,828	69,484	3,720	1,134	270	82
Winnipeg	Canada	9,465	24,514	713	217	204	62

Lancret / Language

archaeologist, born Rome; professor ancient topography University of Rome; made important discoveries at Ostia, Tivoli, Rome ('Ancient and Modern Rome').
Lancret, Nicolas (1690–1743), French painter, born Paris; greatly influenced by Jean Antoine Watteau; gay portrayals of French society.
Land, Edwin Herbert (born 1909), American inventor and corporation executive L-26, *picture* C-530
Polaroid camera P-300
theory of color vision C-448
Land, Emory S(cott) (1879–1971), U.S. Navy officer, born Canon City, Colo.; chairman U.S. Maritime Commission 1938–46; chief of War Shipping Administration 1942–46; president Air Transport Association of America 1946–53.
Land. *see also in index* Agriculture; Land grant; Lands, public; Land tenure
ancient civilizations A-403
Aztec organization A-892
earth's surface E-16, *chart* E-13
economic factors E-56, 59, *table* E-57
eminent domain C-355
frontier movements F-418
homestead P-340
land use L-28
speculation P-335a
surveying S-520
taxation T-32
U.S. farmlands U-104
Landau, Lev Davidovich (1908–68), Russian physicist, born Baku; head of theoretical physics Vavilov Institute of Physical Problems L-27
Land bridges between continents. *see in index* Geology, *subhead* land bridges between continents
"Land down under" (Australia) A-767
Lander, Richard Lemon (1804–34) and **Lander, John** (1807–39), English explorers, born Cornwall; determined course of Niger River 1830 and published journals; were brothers.
Lander, Wyo., town 120 mi (195 km) w. of Casper on Popo Agie River; pop. 9,126; dairy farming, timber, stock raising, oil and coal mining; popular resort; nearby Wind River Indian Reservation; incorporated 1890, *map* W-326
Lander College, at Greenwood, S.C.; local control; coeducational, formerly for women; founded 1872; arts and sciences, education.
Landes, region of s.w. France, vast tract of sandy marshland bordered by dunes
reclamation S-38
"Land flowing with milk and honey," from Bible, Exod. iii, 8 and Jer., xxxii, 22; place of bounty or unusual fertility; phrase used to describe the abundance of heaven.
Landform C-395d
book about S-64d
evolution G-61
Land grant
educational E-88, *table* E-92
South Dakota S-325
Texas T-115
Vermont V-288
home economics H-205
railroad R-74, N-344
Landing, airplane A-191
Landing craft, in warfare N-99, 94, *pictures* N-97, 100, 106, M-110, W-10
Landing gear
airplane A-184
glider G-144a, *diagram* G-144
Landing net, in fishing, *list* F-146
Landis, James McCauley (1899–1964), public official, born Tokyo, Japan, of American parents, missionaries; taught law, Harvard University, 1926–34; chairman SEC 1935–37; dean Harvard Law School 1937–46; director Office of Civilian Defense 1942–43; director U.S. economic operations in Middle East 1943–45; chairman CAB 1946–47; special assistant to President John F. Kennedy 1961.
Landis, Kenesaw Mountain (1866–1944), jurist and baseball commissioner, born Millville, Ohio; judge U.S. district court of n. Illinois 1905–22; tried Standard Oil rebate case in 1907, B-95
baseball commissioner B-96
Landlord, owner or master of land or of building rented to tenants H-257a
cotton farms C-589
Land Management, Bureau of (BLM), United States, U-161
fire fighting F-107
Land measure, units of, *tables* W-96, 97
Land of Enchantment, popular name for New Mexico N-206
"Land office business, doing a" U-177
Land of Lincoln. *see in index* Illinois
Land of Nod, term used to designate the state of sleep; so called from the unknown land of "wandering," or Nod, to which Cain fled after the murder of Abel (Gen. iv).
Land of the Five Rivers. *see in index* Punjab
Land of the Long White Cloud, Maori name for New Zealand. *see in index* New Zealand
Land of the Midnight Sun
Norway N-363
Sweden S-522
Landon, Alf(red) Mossman (born 1887), political leader, born West Middlesex, Pa.; governor of Kansas 1933–37; Republican candidate for presidency 1936, R-272
Kansas history K-177
Landor, Walter Savage (1775–1864), English author, born Warwick, England; a poet of distinction, also master of English prose style (poetry: 'Gebir', 'Rose Aylmer'; prose: 'Pericles and Aspasia' E-274
Landowska, Wanda (1879–1959), Polish musician, harpsichordist, and educator L-27
Land reform L-29
Landrieu, Moon (born 1930), lawyer and public official, born New Orleans, La.; member Louisiana house of representatives 1960–65; councilman-at-large New Orleans 1966–70, mayor 1970–78; U.S. secretary of housing and urban development 1979–81.
Landrum-Griffin Act (1959), United States L-9
Lands, public
land use by government L-29
Mexico M-250
national parks
Canada N-24a
United States N-22
Rome (ancient) R-244, 246
surveying methods S-520
United States
conservation C-546
Harrison, W.H. H-43–4
Northwest Territory N-362
pioneer movement P-340
railroad land grants R-74
Roosevelt, T. R-285
slave states oppose policy C-372
Taft T-8
Landsats, earth resource satellites, *table* S-344
Landscape B-377
Land's End, or **Lands End,** promontory of Cornwall, forming westernmost point of England, *map* G-199h
Landsgemeinde, in Switzerland S-543, *picture* S-544a
Landshut, West Germany, city on Isar River in Bavaria, 55 km (35 mi) n.e. of Munich; pop. 52,417; 14th- and 15th-century gabled houses; Napoleon defeated Austrians (1809), *map* G-115
Landslide, in U.S. politics
Eisenhower E-130
Nixon N-293, U-196a
Roosevelt, F. D. R-272
Truman T-278
Landsmål, a dialect of Norway N-366
Land snail S-221
Landsteiner, Karl (1868–1943), American bacteriologist and pathologist, born Vienna, Austria; member Rockefeller Institute for Medical Research L-27
blood research B-317
medicine contribution M-215d
physical anthropolgy A-483
Landsting (from Norse *land,* "land," and *ting,* or *thing,* "parliament"), certain legislative bodies in Scandinavian countries; in Sweden, county councils.
Land tenure. *see also in index* Land grant; Lands, public
American pioneers P-340
Canada C-96b
Channel Islands C-207
eminent domain C-355
feudal system basis F-69
Canadian history C-105
Middle Ages, *diagram* M-296
Greece, ancient S-369, S-255
Hungary H-276
Latin America
Central America C-195
Chile C-287
Ecuador E-65
Mexico M-250
Peru P-222
Mongolia M-432
Philippines P-261, 260
Rome, ancient R-244, 246
Sicily S-192
Land use L-28
Canada, *chart* C-88
Central America, *charts* C-199
deserts D-93
drought E-52
Egypt, *chart* E-116
erosion control C-542, E-50, *pictures* C-539, 544, E-49
flood control and F-185
food supply and F-286
Germany, East, *chart* G-108a
Germany, West, *chart* G-112a
grasslands G-193
Great Britain G-198a, E-220, *chart* G-199
Greece, *chart* G-220
location factor H-253
Mexico, *chart* M-257
Netherlands, *chart* N-141
Norway, *chart* N-370
Philippines, *chart* P-255d
Portugal, *chart* P-457b
Russia, *charts* R-334, 336
South America, *chart* S-296
Spain, *chart* S-362
Sweden, *chart* S-528
Switzerland, *chart* S-545
United States U-101, *chart* U-118
Lane, Edward William (1801–76), English Arabic scholar, born Hereford; spent many years between 1825 and 1849 in Egypt; published 'Account of the Manners and Customs of the Modern Egyptians'
'Arabian Nights' A-525
Lane, Joseph (1801–81), statesman, born Buncombe County, N.C.; to Vanderburgh County, Ind., 1820; served as Indiana senator 1844–46; made major general for heroic action in Mexican War; governor of Territory of Oregon 1848–50; Oregon delegate to Congress 1850–58, U.S. senator 1859–61; candidate for vice-president on secession ticket 1860.
Lane, Ralph Norman Angell. *see in index* Angell, Sir Norman
Lane, Richard (Night Train) (born 1928), football player, born Austin, Tex.; defensive back; Los Angeles Rams 1952–53; Chicago Cardinals 1954–59, Detroit Lions 1960–65.
Lane, Sir William Arbuthnot (1856–1943), English physician, born Ft. George, near Inverness, Scotland; consulting surgeon Guy's Hospital, Hospital for Sick Children, French Hospital, London; author books on operative treatment of fractures and of cleft palate.
Lane College, at Jackson, Tenn.; Christian Methodist Episcopal church; founded 1882; liberal arts, teacher education.
Lane Theological Seminary, Cincinnati, Ohio
Beecher family B-131
Lanfranc (1005?–1089), English prelate and scholar, born in Italy; archbishop of Canterbury 1070–89; as chief counselor of William the Conqueror played important part in fixing Norman rule upon English church and people.
Lang, Andrew (1844–1912), Scottish scholar, poet, and writer on many subjects; born Selkirk, Scotland ('Ballads in Blue China'; 'Custom and Myth'; 'History of Scotland'; 'Blue', 'Red', 'Yellow', and other fairy books) S-466, 465, R-111a
'Arabian Nights, The' S-480
Lang, Cosmo Gordon (1864–1945), English divine, archbishop of Canterbury 1928–42; born Aberdeenshire, Scotland; canon of St. Paul's 1901–8; archbishop of York 1908–28.
Langdell, Christopher Columbus (1826–1906), lawyer and educator; born New Boston, N.H.; after 1870 dean of Harvard University Law School; introduced "case system" of teaching, which revolutionized methods of law schools.
Langdon, John (1741–1819), merchant and political leader, born Portsmouth, N.H.; an ardent supporter of the Revolution, he financed Stark's expedition against Burgoyne and built ships for Navy; signed United States Constitution; one of first senators from New Hampshire; governor of New Hampshire 1805–8, 1810–11.
Lange, Christian Louis (1869–1938), Norwegian pacifist and historian, born Stavanger; represented Norway at Hague Peace Conference (1907) and League of Nations.
Lange, Dorothea (1895–1965), U.S. photographer L-29
Langensalza, also **Bad Langensalza,** East Germany, town on Salza River 19 mi (30 km) n.w. of Erfurt; pop. 16,304; Hanoverians defeated Prussians in 1866, but surrendered on arrival of Prussian reinforcements, *map* G-115
Langer, William (1886–1959), attorney and senator, born Everest, N.D.; governor of North Dakota 1933–34 and 1937–39; U.S. senator 1940–59; known for legislation for farmers; Republican, *picture* N-350
Langerhans, Islands of, in pancreas, discovered by Paul L. Langerhans, German pathologist (1849–88).
Langland, William (1330?–1400?), English poet E-255
Langley, Samuel P. (1834–1906), American physicist, astronomer, and inventor L-30
aerospace research A-77
flying machines A-201
'Langley', U.S. aircraft carrier N-105
Langley Air Force Base, Hampton, Va. A-164, N-297, *maps* N-297, V-349
Langley Park, Md., community situated 6 mi (10 km) n.e. of Washington, D.C.; pop. 11,564, *map, inset* M-138
Langmuir, Irving (1881–1957), chemist, born Brooklyn, N.Y.; engaged in research for General Electric Company 1909–50; invented gas-filled tungsten lamp and condensation vacuum pump; helped develop high-vacuum tube used in atomic hydrogen welding ('Atoms and Molecules')
Pupin teaches P-535
Langres, France, ancient town in e. on Plateau of Langres; pop. 8,945; makes cutlery; famous strategic point since time of Roman empire.
Langshan, a breed of poultry P-482, *picture* P-481
Langston, John Mercer (1829–97), public official, born Louisa County, Va.; first Negro elected to public office in United States 1855 (clerk Brownhelm Township, Ohio); elected 1888 for one term in U.S. Congress.
Langston University, at Langston, Okla.; state control; founded 1897; arts and sciences, applied sciences, education, technical and vocational education.
Langton, Stephen (1150?–1228), English cardinal and archbishop of Canterbury, credited with being first to divide Bible into chapters; agitator for Magna Carta J-124
Langtry, Lily (Emily) (1852–1929), English actress, noted for her beauty, born Island of Jersey and known as the "Jersey lily"; first great success in 'She Stoops to Conquer'.
Language L-31. *see also in index* Alphabet; Grammar; Rhetoric; Writing; languages by name, as English language; and language groups, as Indo-European languages
African A-119
art forms A-662
Asian A-682
bilingual education B-191
brain perceives B-402
communication and C-489
computers translate C-503
Europe E-313

Language / La Rochelle

figures of speech F-81
India I-67
Indians, American I-135, 140, *tables* I-138, 139
information theory I-201
Jesperson, Otto J-102
Korzybski, Alfred K-301
Latin America L-61
learning and L-106
linguistics L-229
literature and L-242
logic and L-284
public speaking P-526b
secret C-269
semantics C-488
sign, for deaf D-41b
written W-310

Language arts. *see also in index* Reading for recreation; Spelling
communication skills C-495
reports R-151a, *list* R-151b
writing W-308
writing, creative W-310

Language experience approach, to reading R-103

'Language: Its Nature, Development, and Origin', work by Jesperson J-102

Languedoc, former province in s. France; capital was Toulouse; wine producer.

Languedoc Canal. *see in index* Canal du Midi

Langur, a monkey A-503, M-442, *pictures* A-502, M-443

Lanham Act, United States, *table* E-92

Lanier, Sidney (1842–81), American lyric poet, *picture* G-90
American literature A-350
Hall of Fame, *table* H-11

Laniidae, the shrike family of birds. *see in index* Shrike

Lankester, Sir Edwin Ray (1847–1929), English biologist, born London; widely known as a teacher and as a writer of popular works on science; director of Natural History Museum in London 1898–1907 ('Science from an Easy Chair'; 'Secrets of Earth and Sea').

Lanolin, wool fat W-230

Lansdale, Pa., borough 9 mi (14 km) n.e. of Norristown; pop. 16,526; glue, building products, electronic components, tile, hosiery, *map* P-185

Lansdowne, Henry Charles Keith Petty-Fitzmaurice, 5th **marquis of** (1845–1927), British statesman, born London; governor-general of Canada 1883–88; viceroy of India 1888–93; secretary of foreign affairs 1900–1906, during which time an alliance was made with Japan and friendship cemented with France; leader of Unionist party in House of Lords; favored a moderate peace after World War I.

Lansdowne, Henry Petty-Fitzmaurice, 3d **marquis of** (1780–1863), English statesman, born London; chancellor of the exchequer at 25, a Liberal leader and advocate of parliamentary reform and abolition of slavery.

Lansdowne, Md., community 5 mi (8 km) s.w. of Baltimore; pop. 17,770; metal products, transportation equipment, electronic components, *map* M-139

Lansdowne, Pa., borough, residential suburb about 5 mi (8 km) w. of Philadelphia; pop. 11,891; some small industries; council-manager government; incorporated 1893, *map, inset* P-185

Lansing, Robert (1864–1928), lawyer and authority on international law, born Watertown, N.Y.; counsel for U.S. in Bering Sea and Alaska boundary arbitrations; secretary of state in President Wilson's Cabinet during World War I, W-177

Lansing, Ill., village 24 mi (39 km) s. of Chicago; pop. 29,039; truck farms; aluminum windows and doors; founded in 1860's, incorporated in 1893.

Lansing, Mich., state capital, on Grand River 80 mi (130 km) n.w. of Detroit; pop. 130,414, L-45, *maps* M-285, 270, 276, U-41
Capitol, State, *picture* M-279

Lansknecht, German mercenary band A-640

Lanston, Tolbert (1844–1913), inventor, born Troy, Ohio; patented Monotype in 1887, began production and marketing of machine 1897, M-451

Lantern, lamp
story of Diogenes D-119

Lantern fish, found in almost all seas; some deep-sea and some not; has luminescent organs in groups; family *Myctophidae* F-131

Lanthanide series, of chemicals, *table* P-207

Lanthanum (La), a rare earth metal, *tables* P-207, C-236

Lanuvium, or **Lanuvio,** or **Civita Lavinia,** Italy, city of Latium, 30 km (19 mi) s.e. of Rome; member Latin League; conquered by Rome 338 B.C.; temple of Juno.

Lan Xang, ancient kingdom, Indochina L-48

Laoag, Philippines, city, seaport on Laoag River near n.w. coast of Luzon; pop. 61,727; rice, indigo, sugar, *maps* P-261d, P-4

Lao Bridge, bridge in southern Italy A-447

Laocoön, in Greek mythology, Trojan priest of Apollo, warns countrymen against wooden horse T-267
statue of G-230

'Laocoon', book by Gotthold Ephraim Lessing (1766), in which the functions of poetry and painting are defined and distinguished; an important book in the history of art.

Laodamia, legendary Greek heroine, wife of Protesilaus; celebrated in William Wordsworth's 'Laodamia'. *see also in index* Protesilaus

Laodicea, name of several ancient Asiatic cities in realms extending from Aegean Sea to India; **Laodicea ad Lycum** (modern **Denizli,** Turkey, 120 mi (195 km) s.e. of Smyrna), once wealthy trade center; founded probably 3d century, B.C.; site of one of 7 primitive churches of Asia (Rev. i, 11); **Laodicea ad mare** (modern **Latakia,** Syria), pride of the Caesars, noted for ruins of triumphal arch built possibly by Septimius Severus.

Laoighis, Ireland. *see in index* Leix

Lao-Lu, people L-47

Laomedon, in Greek mythology, founder and king of Troy; father of Priam; lost Troy to Hercules and was killed by him for failure to deliver to Hercules the magic horses promised him.

Laon, France, city 130 km (80 mi) n.e. of Paris; pop. 25,623; fortified by Romans; Blücher defeated Napoleon 1814; captured by Germans 1870, 1914, and 1940, *map* W-252
cathedral, *picture* C-158

Laos, republic in s.e. Asia; area 91,429 sq mi (236,800 sq km); pop. 3,901,000; cap. Vientiane L-46
flag, *picture* F-166
Indochina I-157
Mekong River M-217
national anthem, *table* N-52
neutrality V-321
opium O-471
Vietnam conflict V-321

Lao-Soung, people L-47

Lao-Tai, people L-47

Lao-Theng, or **Mon-Khmer,** people L-47

Lao-tzu, or **Lao-tse** (604?–531? B.C.), legendary founder of Taoism, to whom the 'Lao-Tzu', an important Taoist writing, was traditionally attributed L-48
teachings R-143

'Lao-Tzu', or **'Tao-te Ching',** sacred book of Taoism L-48

Lap-and-lead lever, in steam engine, *diagram* S-442

La Parida, in Venezuela. *see in index* Cerro Bolívar

La Paz, Bolivia, largest city and seat of government; pop. 881,400, L-49, B-335, *map* S-298, *picture* S-281a
Indian dance, *picture* D-18

La Paz, Mexico, port in Lower California, on Bay of La Paz; capital of Baja California Sur; pop. 70,219; in agricultural area; pearl fishing center; silver mines C-55, *map* M-260d

La Peltrie, Marie Madeleine de (1603–71), French Roman Catholic nun, born Alençon; founder of Ursuline convent at Quebec, Canada, 1639; conducted school for Indian and French girls until 1642, when she joined colonists under Maisonneuve and helped to found Montreal, Canada.

La Pérouse, Jean François de Galaup, count de (1741–88), French navigator, born near Albi; in war with England took British forts on Hudson Bay 1782; rounded Cape Horn, explored west coast of the Americas, discovered La Pérouse Strait between Hokushu and Sakhalin, Japan; lost at sea after reaching Australia, 1788; wreckage of his ships found 1826, on coral reef n. of New Hebrides.

Lapham, Silas. *see in index* 'Rise of Silas Lapham, The'

Lapido, Duro, African writer A-121

Lapis lazuli, a semiprecious stone
jewelry and gems J-116
Sumerian culture, *picture* B-6

Lapithae, in Greek mythology, race related to the centaurs, dwelling in Thessaly C-192a

Laplace, Pierre Simon (1749–1827), French mathematician and astronomer L-49
nebular hypothesis P-355

Lapland, region in extreme n. of Norway, Sweden, Finland, and Russia L-49
arctic regions A-571
folk art F-254
Norway, *picture* N-366
reindeer R-139
Sweden S-523

La Plata, Argentina, city 55 km (35 mi) s.e. of Buenos Aires and 8 km (5 mi) inland from Ensenada, its port on Plata estuary; pop. 391,247; National University; meat-packing and petroleum refining, *map* S-299

La Plata, Río de, South America. *see in index* Plata, Río de la

La Plata, Viceroyalty of S-290, 291

La Porte, Ind., city in lake area, 25 mi (40 km) w. of South Bend; pop. 21,796; farm machinery, airplane parts, heaters and radiators, furniture, wood products.

Lappet-faced vulture, bird B-280

Lapping, a polishing operation T-206

Lapp language L-50

Lapps, or **sabme,** people of Lapland L-50
Finland F-89
Norway, *picture* N-366
racial classification, *chart* R-26
reindeer R-139

La Prensa, newspaper, Argentina B-489

'L'Après-midi d'un faune' (The Afternoon of a Faun), tone poem by Debussy D-44
ballet B-31

La Puente, Calif., city 18 mi (29 km) e. of Los Angeles; pop. 30,882; air conditioners, heaters, trailers, chemicals; settled 1841, incorporated 1956, *map, inset* C-53

Laputa, in 'Gulliver's Travels', an island visited by Gulliver G-260

Lapwing, green plover, or **peewit,** an Old World plover (*Vanellus vanellus*) having iridescent bottle-green plumage on upperparts, crested head, and white underparts; noted for its wailing cry; its eggs are esteemed as a delicacy.

Laramide revolution, in geology R-235, *chart* G-64–5

Laramie, Jacques (1785?–1821), Canadian trapper; in Colorado foothills and s.e. Wyoming 1816–20; first explorer of upper Laramie River; killed by Indians.

Laramie, Wyo., city on Laramie River 43 mi (69 km) n.w. of Cheyenne; pop. 24,410; cattle and sheep; railroad shops, tie and timber treating plant; cement, brick W-317, *maps* W-327, U-40
meadow nearby, *picture* P-359
Wyoming, University of W-317, *picture* W-321

Laramie Mountains, in s.e. Wyoming; highest point 9,020 ft (2,750 m), *maps* W-327, 315, U-80

Larboard, old term for the left, or port, side of a boat; perhaps derived from Middle English "ladeborde," the loading side; "port" was substituted for larboard to avoid confusion with "starboard," the right side of a boat.

Larceny, crime, *table* L-93

Larch, a tree, *table* W-218
forest planting, *picture* F-310

Larcom, Lucy (1824–93), poet, born Beverly, Mass. In her youth she was a factory worker, and some of her contributions to the factory magazine won praise of John Greenleaf Whittier, with whom she later compiled two books; editor *Our Young Folks;* outstanding for poems of life in New England ('Childhood Songs'; 'Wild Roses of Cape Ann and Other Poems').

Lard, rendered pork fat
best hog type for H-197

Larder beetle B-140
insects, *picture* I-226

Lardner, Ring(gold Wilmer) (1885–1933), writer of humorous stories showing keen insight and reproducing everyday conversation of ordinary persons; born Niles, Mich.; sportswriter on newspapers ('You Know Me, Al'; 'Gullible's Travels'; 'How to Write Short Stories', which contains character sketch, 'The Champion'; 'Round Up'; 'First and Last'; 'The Portable Ring Lardner') A-360, *picture* M-282

Laredo, Tex., city in s. part of state on Rio Grande opposite Nuevo Laredo, Mexico; pop. 91,449; agriculture, stock raising, oil and gas; vegetable and fruit shipping; hats, garments, antimony smelting, brick; Laredo Air Force Base nearby, *maps* T-129, U-40

Lares, in Roman mythology, protecting deities of the household, associated with the Penates M-577

Laretta, Enrique (1875–1961), Argentine writer and diplomat, born Buenos Aires; minister to France 1910–16.

Large-scale integrated circuit, or **LSI,** computers C-497d

Largetooth aspen, tree (*Populus grandidentata*) of willow family, native from Nova Scotia, Canada, to North Carolina, westward to Manitoba, Canada; grows to 18 m (60 ft); also called large poplar, popple, and large American aspen; wood is soft, weak, light, grayish-white; used for paper pulp, excelsior, matches.

Larghetto, direction in music meaning slow and broad but not quite so slow as largo; term also refers to a passage or movement within a musical composition.

Largo, Fla., town 5 mi (8 km) s. of Clearwater; pop. 58,977; tourist center; citrus groves; incorporated 1905.

Largo, in music, *table* M-566a

Largs, Scotland, yachting center and resort, on Firth of Clyde, 50 km (30 mi) s.w. of Glasgow; pop. 8,908, *map* G-199g
battle of (1263) T-161

Lariat, noosed rope used by cowboys to catch cattle or horses C-176

Laridae, bird family, including gulls and terns. *see in index* Gull; Tern

Lárisa, or **Larissa,** Greece, city in Thessaly on Salambria River; pop. 72,336; transit trade, textiles; important city in ancient times, *maps* G-213, E-335

Lark, bird L-51

Lark bunting, *picture* C-460

Lark sparrow, bird of middle and w. U.S.; abundant in Mississippi valley; head streaked chestnut and white; tail white-edged; good singer; also called lark finch.

Larkspur, or **delphinium,** flower
annual G-21
garden flowers, *picture* F-224
poison in P-408

La Rocca, Dominick James (Nick) (1889–1961), jazz cornetist, born New Orleans, La.; formed Original Dixieland Jazz Band during World War I; credited with composing 'Tiger Rag'.

La Rochefoucauld, François de (1613–80), French courtier and writer, born Paris; engaged in court intrigues against Cardinals Richelieu and Mazarin L-51

La Rochelle, France, historic seaport of w.; pop. 72,075; once great maritime city and

Larreta / Latin

center of French Protestantism, *map* E-334
  Edict of Nantes H-139
  Richelieu besieges R-204
Larreta, Enrique (1875–1961), Argentine writer L-71, *picture* L-73
Larry P. vs. Riles, U.S. court case I-238
Larsa, ancient Sumerian city in s. Mesopotamia, on w. bank of old Euphrates River, 15 mi (25 km) s.e. of ancient Erech; temple libraries and important documents found in the ruins.
Larsen Ice Shelf, Antarctica, in n.w. Weddell Sea along e. coast of Antarctic Peninsula; named for Capt. C.A. Larsen, who sailed along edge of shelf in 1893
Larson, (Lewis) Arthur (born 1910), government official and lawyer, born Sioux Falls, S.D.; professor of law Cornell University 1948–53; dean University of Pittsburgh School of Law 1953–54; undersecretary of labor 1954–56; director U.S. Information Agency 1956–57; director Rule of Law Center, Duke University after 1958; author of 'A Republican Looks at His Party', 'Eisenhower: the President Nobody Knew'.
Larva, in zoology L-51
  amphibians A-378
  animal behavior experiment, *picture* A-440
  ant A-469
  bee B-125
  beetle B-137, *picture* B-139
  caddis fly N-60d
  caterpillar B-525, C-156, *pictures* C-157, B-521 to 523, 525
  clam and mussel C-380
  crab C-598
  eel E-103
  flatfish F-174
  flies F-242
  insects I-220, *picture* I-215
  lamprey L-26
  liver fluke W-298
  marine snail and slug S-222
  mayfly M-183
  mosquito, *pictures* M-497
  oyster O-517
  tadpole T-187
  wasp, *pictures* W-56
Lary, (Robert) Yale (born 1930), football player, born Fort Worth, Tex.; defensive back for Detroit Lions 1952–53, 1956–64.
Laryngitis V-377
Larynx, the organ of voice V-377
  anatomy A-391
La Salle, Sieur de (1643–87), French explorer L-52
  explorations A-338, *map* U-176
    Chicago C-254, 262
    Indiana I-93
    Ohio O-419
    Tennessee T-83
    Texas T-117
  Hennepin and H-133
La Salle, Ill., city on Illinois River, adjacent to Peru and about 13 mi (21 km) w. of Ottawa; pop. 10,347; center of corn area; chemicals, electrical equipment, hydrotransmissions, zinc processing; Starved Rock State Park nearby.
La Salle, Que., Canada, residential city just s. of Montreal, at s. end of island of Montreal, overlooking Lachine Rapids in St. Lawrence River; pop. 76,713; named for La Salle, French explorer Q-9h, *map* M-477, *inset* Q-11
La Salle College, at Philadelphia, Pa.; Roman Catholic; chartered 1863; arts and sciences, business, education; graduate work in theology; Pennyln Biostation.
La Scala, opera house in Milan, Italy M-316
Las Casas, Bartolomé de (1474–1566), Spanish missionary and theologian L-53
  Latin American history L-66
Lascaux Cave, in s. France; Stone Age cave drawings found here A-531, *pictures* A-530, M-72
  'Stag Frieze, The' D-180
Las Cruces, N.M., city 40 mi (65 km) n.w. of El Paso, Tex., in livestock and agricultural region; pop. 45,086; pecans, alfalfa, vegetables; cotton ginning, cottonseed oil; New Mexico State University; White Sands Missile Range nearby, *maps* N-221, 208, U-40
Laser and maser, instruments that produce an intense beam of light L-54
  bibliography S-64d
  book production B-358
  communication S-195b
  eye repair B-312
  holograms C-452
  instrumentation I-229
  medical use S-519a
  platinum used P-384
  reflector, on moon M-479
  supermarket use A-834
La Serena, Chile, iron-shipping center about 360 km (225 mi) n. of Valparaiso; pop. 71,898; historic cathedral, convents; founded in 1544, in 1552 declared a city C-284, *maps* C-282, S-299
Lashio, Burma, town 125 mi (200 km) n.e. of Mandalay; s.w. terminus of Burma Road.
Lashkar, India. *see in index* Gwalior
Lashley, Karl Spencer (1890–1958), psychologist, born Davis, W. Va.; professor of psychology University of Chicago 1929–35; professor of psychology Harvard University 1935–37, research professor of neuropsychology 1937–55.
Lasker, Albert, "the father of modern advertising" A-59
Lasker, Eduard (1829–84), Prussian statesman, born present Poznan, Poland; important service in civil consolidation of German empire.
Lasker, Emanuel (1868–1941), German chess master, born Berlinchen, Germany (now Barlinek, Poland); world chess champion 1894–1921; wrote books on chess, philosophy, and mathematics.
Laski, Harold Joseph (1893–1950), British liberal writer, born Manchester; professor political science (University of London after 1926); visiting lecturer in United States; author of many books, chiefly on contemporary political and social-political trends, also 'Letters, Correspondence, 1916–1935' with Oliver W. Holmes, jurist.
Laskin, Bora (born 1912), Canadian jurist, born Fort Williamson, Ont.; professor University of Toronto 1949–65; judge Supreme Court of Ontario 1965–69; judge Supreme Court of Canada 1970–, chief justice 1973–.
Lasky, Jesse L(ouis) (1880–1958), pioneer motion-picture producer, born San Jose, Calif.; coproducer of Hollywood's first full-length motion picture, 'The Squaw Man'; produced over 1,000 motion pictures; specialized in biographical films ('I Blow My Own Horn', autobiography).
Lasnier, (Marie) Rina (born 1915), Canadian poet, born near Montreal, Que. C-114
Las Palmas, Grand Canary Island, port on n.e. coast; pop. 260,368; largest city of Canary Islands, *inset* S-350
La Spezia, Italy, city 80 km (50 mi) s.e. of Genoa, on Bay of Spezia; pop. 121,923; important naval harbor; shipbuilding; winter resort.
Lassalle, Ferdinand (1825–64), German socialist, founder of German social democratic movement; born Breslau; his life was basis of George Meredith's 'Tragic Comedians' L-56
  Socialism S-234
Lassen Peak, volcanic peak in n. California; erupted 1914–21; vast lava beds; height 10,453 ft (3,186 m), N-40a, *maps* C-52, U-87
Lassen Volcanic National Park, in California N-40a, *maps* C-52, N-30
Lassie, famous dog, *list* D-137
  book about D-154c
Lasso, Orlando di (1532?–94), celebrated composer, forerunner of Palestrina; born Mons, Belgium, where he became choirboy; taken to Italy by patron, viceroy of Sicily; court musician to duke of Bavaria at Munich; composed more than 2,000 works M-556
Lasso, rope or a line of leather with a running noose; used for catching horses and cattle, *picture* C-173
Last, in shoemaking S-180, W-227, *picture* S-181
'Last Communion of St. Jerome, The', painting by Botticelli, *picture* D-93e
'Last Days of Pompeii, The', novel by Bulwer-Lytton giving detailed and vivid picture of life in Pompeii before city was destroyed by eruption of Mount Vesuvius (A.D. 79); realistic description of eruption.
Lastex, trade name for a rubber filament wrapped with cotton, silk, nylon, or rayon fibers; gives great stretch to fabrics woven from it; invented 1931.
'Last Laugh, The' (1925), motion picture, *picture* M-523
'Last Leaf', work by Oliver Wendell Holmes A-347
'Last of the Mohicans, The', novel by James Fenimore Cooper, one of the 'Leatherstocking Tales'; thrilling story of frontier life; romantic idealization of the Indian Uncas A-346, C-562
'Last Picture Show, The', work by McMurty A-362
Last Supper. *see in index* Lord's Supper
'Last Supper, The', painting by Leonardo da Vinci L-132
  Milan, Italy M-316
'Last Tycoon, The', novel by Fitzgerald F-147
Las Vegas, Nev., largest city of state, 23 mi (37 km) n.w. of Hoover Dam; in irrigated agricultural area; pop. 164,674; tourist center; legalized gambling; campus of University of Nevada; Nevada Test Site, Nellis Air Force Base, Lake Mead Base, Las Vegas Air Force Station nearby L-56, N-146, *maps* N-157, 144, U-40, *pictures* N-151
  climate, *list* N-142
  skiing, *picture* N-143
Las Vegas, N.M., livestock center 42 mi (68 km) e. of Santa Fe; composed of modern city (pop. 14,322) and old town (pop. 6,307); livestock center; stone and wood products, garments; tourist trade; New Mexico Highlands University; established by Spanish about 1833, *maps* N-220, U-40
  Fort Union N. Mon. N-37, *map* N-30
Laszlo. *see in index* Ladislaus
Latakia, or **Lattaquié,** Syria, Mediterranean port 115 mi (185 km) n. of Beirut; pop. 67,799; produces famous Latakia tobacco; ancient Laodicea.
Latchstring P-331
Lateen rig, *picture* C-475
'Late George Apley, The', novel (1937) by John P. Marquand; won 1938 Pulitzer prize A-359
Latent heat of fusion W-68, H-112
Latent heat of vaporization W-68, H-112
Lateral line, of fish F-127, *diagram* F-125
Lateran, basilica in Rome, Italy. *see in index* St. John Lateran
Lateran, The, palace in Rome, Italy; original building belonged to Lateranus family; taken from them by Nero; later given to pope by Constantine; used as residence by popes until 14th century; present palace, built in 16th century, now contains two museums.
Lateran Councils, a series of ecumenical church councils held in the Lateran Palace and St. John Lateran at Rome from the 12th to the 16th centuries
  Innocent III, I-208
  Leo X, L-131
Lateran Treaty, or **Concordat of 1929,** between Italy and Vatican V-267–8, 270–1, P-347
Laterite, soil S-253
  jungle J-155
Latex, milky juice secreted by various plants G-266
  guayule G-249
  paints P-72, 76
  rubber R-301, 305, 310, *pictures* R-302, 303
Latham, Hubert, pioneer in aviation A-203
Latham, Jean Lee (born 1902), writer, born Buckhannon, W.Va.; editor in chief Dramatic Publishing Company, Chicago, 1930–36; author of plays presented on radio and television and of children's books ('Carry On, Mr. Bowditch', fictionalized biography awarded Newbery Medal 1956; 'This Dear-Bought Land'; 'On Stage, Mr. Jefferson'; 'Young Man in a Hurry'; 'Man of the Monitor'; 'Retreat to Glory: the Story of Sam Houston').
Lathe, machine tool T-201
  engine lathe, *picture* N-287
Lathing, building material B-377
Lathrop, Dorothy Pulis (1891–1981), writer and illustrator of children's books, born Albany, N.Y.; she illustrated 'Hitty', by Rachel Field, awarded Newbery Medal 1930; in 1938, Dorothy Lathrop's own book 'Animals of the Bible' was awarded the first Caldecott Medal ever given; among the books written and illustrated by her are: 'Who Goes There?'; 'Let Them Live'; 'The Littlest Mouse' R-111a
  Field, Rachel F-78
Lathrop, George Parsons (1851–98), journalist and poet, born Oahu, Hawaiian Islands; married Rose, daughter of Nathaniel Hawthorne; associate editor *Atlantic Monthly;* editor *Boston Courier;* founder American Copyright League.
Lathrop, Julia Clifford (1858–1932), social worker, born Rockford, Ill.; important work at Hull House, Chicago; chief 1912–21 U.S. Children's Bureau, first woman bureau chief; author of articles on child welfare, care of insane, and civil service.
Latifundios, or **latifundia,** large landed estates
  Central America C-195
  Sicily S-192
Latimer, Hugh (1485?–1555), English Protestant reformer and martyr, bishop of Worcester; born Thurcaston, Leicestershire; his homely practical preaching largely drove the English Reformation home to the people; burned at stake (with Nicholas Ridley) exhorting his fellow-martyr, "Be of good cheer, Master Ridley, and play the man; we shall this day light such a candle by God's grace in England as I trust shall never be put out." L-56
Latina, or **Littoria,** Italy, province on land reclaimed from Pontine Marshes s.e. of Rome; fertile farm lands; cap. Latina.
Latin America, collective name for the 20 independent nations of southern North America, Central America, South America, and the West Indies L-57. *see also in index* Central America; South America; and names of separate countries
  arts
    folk art F-254
    music M-561
    painting P-67a, *pictures* P-67b–d
  bibliography S-302–3
  citizenship C-360
  good-neighbor policy R-273
  government
    dictatorship D-112
    republican D-84
  history
    Alliance for Progress S-292
    Bolivar B-332
    Cuban subversion C-628a
    Monroe Doctrine M-457
    Organization of American States O-504
    Peace Corps P-143a
    World War II W-272
  illiteracy P-450
  labor movements L-11
  land use reforms L-29
  literature. *see in index* Latin American literature
Latin American Free Trade Association (LAFTA), Latin American common market L-65
Latin American literature L-68
  children's literature L-251, *charts* L-254, 255
  folklore S-476, *list* S-481c
  Latin America L-62
Latin Empire, established by Crusaders in 1204, C-618
Latin language L-37
  alphabet A-315
  education E-80, 84, *picture* E-82
  influence on
    English E-251
    Romance languages R-239
    Spanish S-353, S-365
  Latin literature L-76
  linguistic analysis L-230
Latin League, confederation of cities of Latium in central Italy, existing from earliest historic times till 338 B.C., R-244
Latin literature L-76
  Augustan Age, *picture* R-241
  Caesar C-14, *picture* R-243
  children's L-245
  Cicero C-341
  drama D-170

Latin / Laval

  Juvenal J-161
  linguistics and grammar L-229
  Livy L-270
  Ovid M-579
  Pliny the Elder R-124
  Renaissance R-146
  Seneca S-108a
  Tacitus T-3
  Virgil V-328

Latin Quarter, in Paris, France P-122, *map* P-120

Latins, in ancient times, inhabitants of Latium; also modern Italians, French, and Spanish
  civilization contribution C-370
  early history R-240, 244

Latinus, in Roman mythology, king of Latium and father of Lavinia, wife of Aeneas; name also given to one of the heroes in Torquato Tasso's 'Jerusalem Delivered'.

Latitude and longitude L-79
  climate control C-392, 395
  geography G-52
  "horse latitudes" W-181, *diagram* W-180
  maps M-97, 103a
  navigation N-88
  time and T-178, 181

Latium, ancient district in middle Italy, inhabited by Latins R-240, 241
  Aeneas ruler of A-63

Latona. *see in index* Leto

La Tour, Charles Amador de (1596–1666), French governor of Acadia 1628–35; quarreled with Charnisay over governorship; regained post after death of Charnisay in 1650.

La Tour, Georges de (1593–1652), French painter; contemporary of Nicolas Poussin; painter to duke of Lorraine.

Latreille, Pierre André (1762–1833), French zoologist, born Brives-la-Gaillarde, Corrèze; noted for his classifications of insects.

Latrobe, Benjamin Henry (1764–1820), American architect and engineer, born Fulneck, Yorkshire, England; to U.S. 1796; surveyor of public buildings, Washington, D.C., 1803; in charge of rebuilding burned Capitol A-568

Latrobe, Pa., borough 33 mi (53 km) s.e. of Pittsburgh in industrial district; pop. 10,799; iron and steel, metal products, building materials, ceramics, die castings, plastics, ingot molds; St. Vincent College, *map* P-184

Latsol, a type of soil, *map* G-61

Lattaquié, Syria. *see in index* Latakia

Latter-day Saints. *see in index* Mormons

Lattice, of crystal C-621, 625, *diagrams* C-134, 623

Lattice, in basketry B-103

Lattice method, in multiplication M-54b, D-135

Latticework, in furniture design. *see in index* Fret

Lattimore, Eleanor Frances (Mrs. Robert Armstrong Andrews) (born 1904), American author and illustrator of children's books, born Shanghai, China; works based on own experiences ('Little Pear' series; 'Peachblossom'; 'Bells for a Chinese Donkey'; 'The Monkey of Crofton'; 'The Journey of Ching Lai'; 'Fisherman's Son').

Lattimore, Owen (born 1900), author and educator, born Washington, D.C.; director Walter Hines Page School of International Relations, Johns Hopkins University 1938–53; political adviser to Chiang Kai-shek 1941–42; deputy director Pacific operations Office of War Information 1942–44 ('High Tartary'; 'Solution in Asia'; 'Situation in Asia'; 'Ordeal by Slander'; 'Nomads and Commissars: Mongolia Revisited'; 'Studies in Frontier History').

La Tuque, Que., Canada, town and lumbering center on St. Maurice River 120 km (75 mi) n. of Trois-Rivières; pop. 13,099; pulp and paper, sashes and doors, *maps* Q-10, C-99

'La Turista', work by Shepard A-363

Latvian Plains, geographic region, U.S.S.R. L-83

Latvians, or **Letts,** people L-83

Latvian Soviet Socialist Republic, Russia, on Baltic Sea; 64,000 sq km (24,710 sq mi); pop. 2,521,000; cap. Riga L-83, U-14, *maps* R-325, 344, 348
  ballet, *picture* R-332f
  folktales, *list* S-480, *picture* S-471
  Lithuanian S.S.R. and L-259
  Riga R-207

Lauan, wood of several species of trees of lauan family (*Dipterocarpaceae*), native to Philippines, nearby islands, and s. Asia; often called Philippine mahogany.

Laubach, Frank Charles (1884–1970), missionary and educator, born Benton, Pa.; ordained Congregational minister 1914; began career as missionary in Philippine Islands 1915; known as founder of worldwide campaign for teaching primitive and illiterate peoples to read, using principle of "each one teach one;" author, 'Toward World Literacy'; autobiography, 'Thirty Years with the Silent Billion'.

Laud, William (1573–1645), English prelate, archbishop of Canterbury; born Reading, England; tried to suppress dissent; beheaded on charge of treason
  Charles I's adviser C-212

Laudanum, tincture of opium antidote P-411

Lauder, Sir Harry Maclennan (1870–1950), Scottish comedian, born Portobello, Scotland; a great favorite for his Scottish songs composed by him and sung in character; knighted 1919.

Laudonnière, René Goulaine de (died 1566), French Huguenot noble; accompanied Jean Ribaut's expedition (1562) to what is now South Carolina; established Fort Caroline colony on St. John's River (1564), but governed badly; wounded in Menéndez' attack, escaped to Europe; wrote memoirs.

Laue, Max (Theodor Felix) von (1879–1960), German physicist, born Pfaffendorf, near Coblenz; professor University of Berlin 1919–43; author of scientific books
  crystals C-624
  solid state physics S-254h
  X-ray spectra X-334

Laugher pigeon P-324

Laughing gas, or **nitrous oxide** (N_2O), an anesthetic A-413
  aerosol propellant A-66
  discovery of properties D-39
  medicine M-215c

Laughing gull G-262

Laughing jackass, or **kookaburra,** an Australian bird A-782

Laughing philosopher. *see in index* Democritus

Laughing Water, or **Minnehaha Falls,** Minneapolis, Minn. M-346

Laughlin, James (1806–82), American manufacturer and philanthropist, born Ireland; one of group which developed Pittsburgh, Pa., as an iron center.

Laughlin, James Laurence (1850–1933), political economist, born Deerfield, Ohio; head of department of political economy, University of Chicago, 1892–1916; prepared monetary reform scheme for Santo Domingo government, 1894–95; author of works on economics.

Laughton, Charles (1899–1962), American actor, born Scarborough, England; first appearance on N.Y. stage 1931 ('Payment Deferred'); in motion pictures from 1932; won Academy award 1933 for his role in 'The Private Life of Henry VIII' ('The Barretts of Wimpole Street'; 'Mutiny on the Bounty'; 'Hunchback of Notre Dame'; 'Rembrandt'; 'The Beachcomber'); popular theatrical dramatic reader; compiler of 'Tell Me a Story' A-27
  Benét and B-161

Launceston, England, quaint old town in Cornwall 34 km (21 mi) n.w. of Plymouth; pop. 4700; George Fox, the Quaker, imprisoned here (1655), *map* G-199h

Launceston, Tasmania, city in n.e. on Tamar River; pop. 62,181, including suburbs; wheat and potatoes grown in area; mining; trade with Victoria and South Australia

Launching, of ship S-172, *picture* S-171
  submarine, *picture* S-495b

Launch vehicles, in space travel S-342b, 346d, *diagrams* S-346c–e, *pictures* S-242c, 341d, 348b

Laundromat L-84

Laundry L-84
  dry-cleaning D-200e
  extractor principle C-200
  soap S-229

Launfal, Sir, knight of the Round Table and steward to King Arthur, in the Arthurian legends; hero of James Russell Lowell's 'Vision of Sir Launfal'.

La Unión, El Salvador, chief port, on gulf of Fonseca at e. end of El Salvador; pop. 11,432; port handles about half of country's foreign trade; railroad terminus.

Laura (1308–48), lady loved by Petrarch and celebrated in his poems R-145

Lauraceae. *see in index* Laurel

Laura Ingalls Wilder Award, established 1954 by Children's Library Association; awarded to authors or illustrators whose books have made "a substantial and lasting contribution to children's literature" L-240.

Laurana, Francesco da (1420?–1502), sculptor and medalist of Dalmatian origin; worked chiefly in Italy and France; stressed design rather than realism.

Laurasia, prehistoric continent G-65a

Laureate, Poet P-402

Laurel, Miss., city 76 mi (122 km) s.e. of Jackson, in yellow pine region; pop. 21,897; petroleum center; Masonite, lumber, garments, poultry M-375, *maps* M-387, U-41
  lignocellulose plant P-379

Laurel, common name for evergreen shrubs and small trees of the genus *Laurus* of the laurel family *Lauraceae* L-88
  camphor tree C-61
  crown of poets, heroes P-402

Laurelwood. *see in index* Madrona

Laurencin, Marie (1885–1956), French painter, born Paris; a modernist with highly individual style; known for female portraits done in soft, pale colors.

Laurens, Henri (1885–1954), French sculptor, born near Paris, France; identified with modernists who emphasized purely plastic forms S-92

Laurens, Henry (1724–92), statesman, born Charleston, S.C.; father of John Laurens; president of Continental Congress 1777–78; one of commissioners to negotiate peace after Revolution R-173

Laurens, John (1754–82), American soldier in Revolutionary War, born Charleston, S.C.; son of Henry Laurens; confidential secretary to George Washington; called the "Bayard of the Revolution"; killed in a skirmish shortly before peace with England was concluded.

Laurens, S.C., city 22 mi (35 km) n. of Greenwood; pop. 10,587; glass, textiles, carpets; cotton and peaches; vermiculite mines; incorporated 1785, *map* S-318

Laurent, Robert (1890–1970), American sculptor, born Concarneau, near Quimper, France; achieved vital beauty in direct carvings in stone, marble, and wood; noted for figures in alabaster and plant forms in wood; elected to National Institute of Arts and Letters 1970.

Laurentian Library, Florence, Italy L-172, *picture* L-174

Laurentian Mountains, or **Laurentides,** in Canada Q-9b, C-71, *picture* C-80
  La Mauricie N.P. N-24d, *map* N-24b

Laurentian Plateau, or **Canadian Shield,** highland area in Canada, extending into n.e. United States L-88
  Canada C-71, 75, *maps* C-72–3, *picture* C-80
    Alberta A-263
    Labrador L-12
    Manitoba M-89a
    Newfoundland N-165b, *map* N-165c
    Ontario O-456c, *map* O-456b
    Quebec Q-9b, *map* Q-9a
    Saskatchewan S-49c
  geologic history G-63
  North America N-300, *picture* N-301
  United States, *map* U-36
    Adirondacks A-44
    Michigan M-269, *map* M-270
    Wisconsin W-193, *map* W-194

Laurentides Provincial Park, in Quebec, Canada, about 50 km (30 mi) n. of Quebec City; 9,358 sq km (3,613 sq mi), 1,500 lakes; trout fishing, *map* Q-11

Laurentius, saint. *see in index* Lawrence

Laurier, Wilfrid (1841–1919), Canadian statesman L-89, C-112d
  King, Mackenzie K-243
  Sir Wilfrid Laurier's House N.H.S. N-24d, *map* N-24b

Lauritsen, Charles Christian (1892–1968), American physicist, born Holstebro, Denmark; professor at California Institute of Technology 1935–62; research on nuclear physics.

Laurium, or **Laurion,** Greece, hill range 30 km (20 mi) below Athens; in ancient times known for silver mines worked until 400 B.C., reopened by French 1864; remains of a Poseidon temple nearby, *map* G-221

Lausanne, Switzerland, historic city on n. shore of Lake Geneva; pop. 137,383; 13th-century cathedral; university S-542, 544a, *maps* S-537, E-334

Lausanne, Treaty of (1912), closed Turko-Italian War; gave Tripoli to Italy; granted Italians right to occupy Dodecanese Islands and Rhodes; settlement made after Balkan states attacked Turkey.

Lausanne, Treaty of (1923), revised Treaty of Sèvres, extending Turkey's territory
  Bosporus B-371
  Dardanelles D-34
  Greece affected G-218
  World War I, W-263

Laut, Agnes Christina (1871–1936), Canadian author, born Stanley, Ont.; authoritative historical books on early explorers and pioneer life in the Northwest ('The Conquest of the Western Empire'; 'Pathfinders of the West'; 'Vikings of the Pacific'; 'Life of Cadillac').

Lauterbrunnen, Switzerland, village 55 km (34 mi) s.e. of Bern; pop. 3,216; lace manufactures, *picture* E-307

Lautrec, Henri de Toulouse. *see in index* Toulouse-Lautrec

Lauzon, Que., Canada, city on St. Lawrence River opposite Quebec (city) and adjoining Lévis; pop. 12,809; shipbuilding center, *map* Q-11

Lava and magma, molten rock discharged from volcanoes or intruded between rock strata under the ground L-89. *see also in index* Lava soil
  basalt B-86
  cave C-178c
  diamonds from D-110, *diagram* D-102
  Earth's features E-25
  Etna lava fields E-303
  geology G-59
  Hawaii, *picture* H-64
  Iceland, *picture* I-16
  igneous rocks formed R-228
  island formation I-368
  minerals M-337
  Vesuvius V-305, P-442
  volcanoes V-378, 383, *diagram* V-379, *picture* V-381

Lava Beds National Monument, in California N-40a, *map* N-30

Laval, Pierre (1883–1945), French political leader, born near Clermont-Ferrand, France; rose in few years from obscurity to dominant position in French politics L-90

Laval, Que., Canada, city comprising island n.w. of Montreal; pop. 228,010, Q-9e, h, *map* M-477, *inset* Q-11

Lavalava, Samoan clothing, *picture* C-398

Lavalleja, Juan Antonio (died 1853), liberator of Uruguay from Brazilian rule 1825–28; dictator 1827–28; insurgent against later governments.

Laval-Montmorency, François Xavier de (1623–1708), first Roman Catholic bishop of

Laval / Lawson

Quebec, Canada, born Montigny-sur-Avre, France; arrived in Quebec 1659 as vicar apostolic of New France; founded Seminary of Quebec 1663; Laval University named for him C-106

Laval University (Université Laval), at Ste-Foy, near Quebec, Que., Canada; Roman Catholic; founded 1852 by the Seminary of Quebec (1663); arts, agriculture, canon law, commerce, law, letters, medicine, nursing, pedagogy, philosophy, sciences, social sciences, surveying and forest engineering, theology; graduate school; affiliated schools; teaching in French Q-15, *pictures* U-210, Q-13, 9e

Lava soil, from volcanoes S-249, V-378
  Central America C-194
  Hawaii H-54
  United States U-84

Lavater, Johann Kaspar (1741–1801), Swiss poet and mystic, born Zurich; founder of physiognomy, the art of reading character, especially from facial features.

Lavatera, a genus of plants and shrubs of the mallow family, native to warm regions of the world. Leaves lobed, often maplelike; flowers, 5 petals, in axils of leaves or in loose clusters, white through red; entire plant somewhat hairy or grayish; tall species used as windbreaks; also called tree mallow.

Lavelli, Dante (Glue Fingers) (born 1923), football player, born Hudson, Ohio; Cleveland Browns 1946–56.

Lavender, an aromatic shrub of the mint family native to s. Europe
  perfume from, *picture* P-204

Lavender laceflower. *see in index* Trachymene

'Lavengro', a semiautobiographical story by George Henry Borrow dealing with his early adventures and his wanderings with the gypsies.

Laver, algae A-284

Laver, Rod(ney George) (born 1938), Australian tennis player, born Gladstone, Queensland; on Australia's Davis Cup team 1959–61; won many top titles; in 1962 and 1969 he won the world's four major singles championships (Australian, French, British, and United States), the first player to achieve this grand slam more than once; professional since 1963 ('The Education of a Tennis Player' with Bud Collins).

Laveran, Charles Louis Alphonse (1845–1922), French physician, born Paris M-498, M-215c

La Vérendrye, Pierre Gaultier de Varennes, sieur de (1685–1749), French Canadian explorer and fur trader, born at Trois-Rivières, Canada; pushed westward in search of the Western Sea; visited Mandan Indian villages on the Missouri; two of his sons, Francois, chevalier de la Vérendrye, and Louis Joseph de la Vérendrye, visted North Dakota and possibly reached the foothills of the Rocky Mts. M-353
  fur trade, *picture* F-469
  Manitoba M-89d, 89f
  North Dakota N-344, *picture* N-345
  route, *map* C-109

La Verne College, at La Verne, Calif.; Church of the Brethren; founded 1891; liberal arts and teacher education; graduate study.

Lavery, Sir John (1856–1941), British painter, born Belfast, Ireland; renowned chiefly for portraits and figure work done in a broad style; also landscape and historical works; knighted 1918.

Lavin, Mary (born 1912), Irish author I-328

Lavinia, in Roman mythology, daughter of Latinus and Amata; betrothed to Turnus but married Aeneas who killed Turnus in single combat (Vergil's 'Aeneid' books 7, 10, and 12).

Lavinium, ancient town of Latium, 27 km (17 mi) s. of Rome, Italy; said to have been founded by Aeneas and named after his wife, Lavinia.

Lavisse, Ernest (1842–1922), French historian, born France; professor at Sorbonne; member of French Academy; wrote and edited histories of Prussia, France, and Europe.

Lavoisier, Antoine Laurent (1743–94), French chemist L-90
  chemistry C-243
  fire research F-93
  head of powder works W-169
  oxygen research O-516
  science contribution S-57j
  theories about heat H-114

Law, Andrew Bonar (1858–1923), British statesman, born New Brunswick, Canada, of Scottish parentage; taken to Scotland as child; made a fortune as iron merchant; began career in Parliament in 1900, becoming leader of Conservative party; helped to form coalition government in World War I; prime minister 1922.

Law, John (1671–1729), Scottish financier, born in Edinburgh; lived in London until convicted of killing a man in a duel; fled to the Continent, where he proposed new government credit systems based on paper money and colonial exploitation; appointed controller-general of French finance (1720); inflation beyond his control followed; escaped to Italy and died in Venice M-379

Law L-91. *see also in index* Government; Government regulation of industry; International law; Labor and industrial law; Social legislation
  administrative A-46
  advertising codes A-60
  air pollution A-147
  apprenticeships A-511
  Arabs A-526
  arbitration A-528
  bankruptcy B-74
  Beccaria's contribution B-122
  bill of rights B-193
  citizenship C-353
  codes, historic
    Greek G-223
    Hammurabi (Babylon) P-506
    Justinian J-161, B-534
    Lycurgus L-342
    Napoleonic N-11
    Solon S-255
    Ten Commandments M-495
  common, defined E-233
  counterfeiting C-592
  courts of justice C-593
  etiquette adapted E-298
  family law F-20
    juvenile delinquency J-162
    marriage M-114
  flotsam, jetsam, and lagan F-212
  foundations regulated F-333
  habeas corpus H-1
  initiative, referendum, and recall I-205
  international law I-255
  Jewish moral law J-149
  jury system J-158
  Kent, James K-207
  labor and industrial law L-4
  local option P-506
  martial C-594
  Mesopotamian B-4
  Mongolian law G-45
  Mosaic law B-181, M-495
  parliamentary law P-132a, *table* P-132b
  purpose of G-163
  state constitutions S-428–9
  United Kingdom U-19
    Edward I, E-100d
    Henry II, H-136, E-233
    Magna Carta M-45
  United States
    Congress C-516, *pictures* C-517
    Constitution U-139
    statehood S-429a
  veto V-308
  wills W-160

Law Enforcement Assistance Administration, United States U-160

Law, merchant, for regulating medieval trade R-149

Law, Scientific. *see in index* name of law, as Ohm's law

Law, The, division of the Old Testament P-509

Lawes, Sir John Bennet (1814–1900), English agriculturist, born Rothamsted, England; there founded experimental farm on family estate; developed a fertilizer by treatment of phosphates with sulfuric acid.

Lawler, Ray, Australian playwright A-799

Lawless, Theodore Kenneth (1892–1971), dermatologist, born in Thibodaux, La.; began practice in Chicago 1924; taught at Northwestern University 1924–41; 1954 Spingarn medal (dermatology).

Law lords, in British Parliament P-131a

Lawn, formerly a fine linen fabric made in Laon, France; now a light thin cotton material, white, dyed, or printed.

Lawn, grass-covered grounds G-189, *picture* H-247
  planting G-24
  power mower noise P-441e
  weeds W-92, *pictures* W-92a–b

Lawn bowling, or **bowls,** outdoor game of ancient origin, played on grass plot, the green; players roll balls (bowls), about 13 centimeters (5 inches) in diameter, at a smaller ball called the jack B-386

Lawndale, Calif., city near Pacific Ocean 12 mi (19 km) s.w. of Los Angeles; pop. 23,460; electronic devices, aircraft parts, candy manufacturing, *map, inset* C-53

Lawn tennis. *see in index* Tennis

Law of comparative advantage, in economics I-266

Law of the Sea Convention, approved by U.N.; established concept of archipelagic waters
  Indonesia I-158

Lawrance, Charles Lanier (1882–1950), aircraft engineer, born Lenox, Mass.; designed and perfected radial, air-cooled engine called "Wright Whirlwind"; organized Lawrance Engineering and Research Corp.

Lawrence, or **Laurentius,** or **Lorenzo** (died 258?), Christian saint and martyr, called "the Deacon," friend of the poor; commemorated August 10; meteorites appearing about that time known as "tears of St. Lawrence" M-120

Lawrence, Abbott (1792–1855), manufacturer and diplomat, born Groton, Mass.; brother of Amos A. Lawrence; minister to Great Britain 1849–52; founded Lawrence Scientific School of Harvard University

Lawrence, Amos Adams (1786–1852), merchant and philanthropist, born Groton, Mass.; brother of Abbott Lawrence; did much to establish cotton textile industry in New England; gave freely to schools and charities. His son **Amos Adams** (1814–86) was chief founder of Lawrence College, now Lawrence University, at Appleton, Wis.

Lawrence, Charles (1709–60), English soldier and statesman, born Portsmouth, England; lieutenant governor of Nova Scotia, Canada, 1754–56, governor 1756–60.

Lawrence, D. H. (1885–1930), English novelist, poet, and painter; born Eastwood, near Nottingham; novels characterized by a sensitive delineation of nature and individual emotion L-98, E-271, 276, W-310b

Lawrence, Ernest O(rlando) (1901–58), physicist, born Canton, S.D.; on faculty University of California 1928–58, director radiation laboratory 1936–58; Fermi award 1957 for invention of cyclotron and other contributions to atomic energy, *picture* S-332

Lawrence, Gertrude (1898–1952), English actress, born London; won first success singing 'Limehouse Blues' 1924; starred in stage shows in England and U.S. ('Private Lives'; 'Tonight at 8:30'; 'Susan and God'; 'Skylark'; 'Pygmalion'; 'The King and I'); author of 'A Star Danced', autobiography.

Lawrence, Sir Henry Montgomery (1806–57), English brigadier general and colonial administrator, brother of John L. M. Lawrence L-328

Lawrence, Jacob (born 1917), artist, teacher, and humanitarian; born Atlantic City, N.J.; paintings on Negro life and history in U.S.; widely represented in permanent collections of American museums; teacher of art at Pratt Institute, Brandeis University, and many other schools; won 1970 Spingarn medal.

Lawrence, James (1781–1813), American naval hero L-98
  New Jersey, *picture* N-200
  slogan on flag F-154, *picture* F-155

Lawrence, John Laird Mair Lawrence, Baron (1811–79), British viceroy and governor-general of India, called "savior of India" because his relief of Delhi during the Mutiny (1857) maintained British dominion; brother of Sir Henry M. Lawrence.

Lawrence, Josephine (1890–1978), author and journalist, born Newark, N.J.; wrote first children's story ever broadcast, 1921; adult books: 'If I Have Four Apples' and 'All Our Tomorrows'.

Lawrence, Sir Thomas (1769–1830), English court painter, born Bristol; supported family with portrait sketches at age of 10; flattering but often superficial likenesses of English beauties and European sovereigns; the successor of Sir Joshua Reynolds as most celebrated portrait painter of his day ('Mrs. Siddons', 'Princess Lieven', 'Calmady Children', 'Pinkie').

Lawrence, T. E. (1888–1935), British soldier, explorer, and scholar; called Lawrence of Arabia L-98.

Lawrence, William (1850–1941), Episcopal bishop, born Boston, Mass.; grandson of Amos and son of Amos Adams Lawrence; bishop of Massachusetts 1893–1926 ('Life of Amos A. Lawrence'; 'Memories of a Happy Life'; 'Life of Phillips Brooks').

Lawrence, Ind., town just n.e. of Indianapolis; pop. 25,591; settled 1849 on site bought from Miami Indians 1783; incorporated 1929.

Lawrence, Kan., city on Kansas River about 35 mi (55 km) s.w. of Kansas City, Kan.; pop. 52,738; chemicals, paper products, pipe organs; Haskell Institute, for Indians: *map* U-41
  attack in 1856, *picture* P-321
  railroad station, *picture* R-73

Lawrence, Mass., manufacturing city on Merrimack River, 30 mi (50 km) from sea; pop. 63,175, *maps* M-161, U-41, M-152
  temperature, *list* M-143

'Lawrence', Perry's flagship, in battle of Lake Erie S-177g, P-209

Lawrence of Arabia. *see in index* Lawrence, T. E.

Lawrence University, at Appleton, Wis.; founded 1847; named for Amos A. Lawrence, a Boston merchant who was its chief founder; arts and sciences, music; quarter system.

Lawrencium (Lw), chemical element, *tables* P-207, C-236

Lawrie, Lee (1877–1963), American sculptor, born Berlin, Germany; instructor Yale University 1908–18; sculptures for Bok Singing Tower, U.S. Military Academy, Nebraska and Louisiana Capitols; Atlas statue, Rockefeller Center
  carving, *picture* P-143d

Lawson, Don (born 1917), writer and editor, born Chicago, Ill.; author of books for young people; editor in chief 'Compton's Encyclopedia' 1965–73; editor American Educator Encyclopedia 1973–74, editor in chief 1974– (adult novel: 'A Brand for the Burning'; history books for young people: 'Young People in the White House', 'The United States in World War I', 'The United States in World War II', 'The United States in the Korean War', 'The War of 1812', 'The Colonial Wars', 'The American Revolution', 'The United States in the Indian Wars', 'The United States in the Spanish-American War', 'The United States in the Mexican War', 'Famous Political Families', 'Frances Perkins: First Lady of the Cabinet', 'The Lion and the Rock: the Story of the Rock of Gibraltar'; anthologies: 'Great Air Battles', 'Youth and War', 'Ten Fighters for Peace').

Lawson, Henry (1867–1922), Australian short-story writer and poet, born near Grenfell, New South Wales A-797

Lawson, John Howard (1895–1977), playwright and motion-picture scriptwriter, born New York City ('Roger

Lawson / Leather

Bloomer' and 'Processional', plays exemplifying expressionism).

Lawson, Robert (1892–1957), author and illustrator of children's books, born New York City; drawings are a fine combination of imagination and humor; illustrated 'The Story of Ferdinand' by Munro Leaf; wrote and illustrated 'They Were Strong and Good' (1941 Caldecott Medal), 'Mr. Revere and I', 'The Tough Winter', 'Captain Kidd's Cat', 'The Great Wheel' R-111a
- 'Ben and Me' R-108, *picture* R-111
- 'Rabbit Hill' R-110a

Lawson, Victor Fremont (1850–1925), editor and newspaper publisher, born Chicago, Ill.; owner of *Chicago Daily News*, which he endeavored to maintain without political bias; president Associated Press 1884–1900; advocacy of government savings bank caused him to be called "the father of the postal savings bank in America."

Lawson quintuplets M-542a

Lawson's cypress. *see in index* Port Orford cedar

Lawton, Henry Ware (1843–99), U.S. Army officer, born Manhattan, Ohio; in Civil War rose from sergeant to brevet colonel; commanded troops which took El Caney in Cuba in 1898; promoted to major general; killed in attack upon Filipinos at San Mateo, Luzon, Philippines.

Lawton, Okla., city about 80 mi (130 km) s.w. of Oklahoma City, in farm district and oil region; pop. 80,054; stock feed, dairy products, meat-packing, cement products, trailer homes, boxes, hats, men's slacks; Museum of the Great Plains; Fort Sill and a wildlife refuge nearby O-436, *maps* O-446, 435, U-40
- wildlife refuge, *picture* O-442

Lawyer, or **attorney,** vocation, V-367, *picture* P-526b
- jury system J-159
- law L-97
- women W-215a

Lawyer, fish. *see in index* Burbot

Laxative, or **physic** H-87, *table* D-200a

Laxness, Halldor (Kiljan) (real name Halldor Gudjonsson) (born 1902), Icelandic novelist, born Reykjavik, Iceland; traveled widely; in U.S. 1927–30 ('Salka Valka'; 'Independent People').

Layamon, English poet and priest, lived about 1200; author of the 'Brut', metrical chronicle of Britain, one of monuments of early English language.

Layard, Sir (Austen) Henry (1817–94), English diplomat, archaeologist, and writer; born Paris; excavated ruins of Nineveh ('Monuments of Nineveh') A-532

Layari River, river, Pakistan, *picture* L-84

Laye, Camara, Francophone author A-122

Layering, in horticulture G-178, P-361

Laying, ropemaking process, *picture* R-293

Layne, Robert (Bobby) (born 1926), football quarterback, born Santa Anna, Tex.; quarterback Chicago Bears 1948; New York Bulldogs 1949; Detroit Lions 1950–58 and Pittsburgh Steelers 1958–62.

'Lay of the Last Minstrel, The', poem by Scott S-73

Layout P-499
- advertising V-365, 370

Laysan Island, small coral island belonging to U.S., in Pacific in group lying n.w. of Hawaiian Islands; breeding place for many birds, *maps* P-5, H-71

'Lays of Ancient Rome', a collection of ballads by Macaulay M-3

Layton, Irving (born 1912), Canadian author and editor C-114, 116

Layton, Utah, city 10 mi (16 km) s. of Ogden; lies between Wasatch Range and Great Salt Lake at altitude of 4,356 ft (1,328 m); pop. 22,862; irrigated farm area; sugar refining, *map* U-232

Lazarus, beggar in parable of the rich man and the poor man (Luke xvi, 19–30); short form of Hebrew name Eleazar meaning "God has helped."

Lazarus, man of Bethany, brother of Martha and Mary; raised from the dead by Christ after four days (John xi); his tomb and house were visited by 4th-century pilgrims.

Lazarus, Emma (1849–87), poet, born New York City; published first poems and translations at 18; did philanthropic work among Jewish refugees from Russia; worked for Jewish nationalism ('Alide'; 'Songs of a Semite')
- Statue of Liberty L-148

Lazear, Jesse William (1866–1900), physician, born Baltimore, Md.; with U.S. Army Yellow Fever Commission in Cuba; for experimental purposes allowed himself to be bitten by mosquito carrying yellow fever germ and died M-499, *picture* R-121

Lazuli bunting, a bird of the finch family B-503

"Lazy heart," in space travel S-346a

L.C.L. (less than carload), freight shipments R-82

LD_{50}, measurement A-449

Lea, Henry Charles (1825–1909), publisher and church historian, born New Orleans, La.; remembered for 'A History of the Inquisition of the Middle Ages' and 'A History of the Inquisition of Spain', the standard books in English in their fields.

Lea, Homer (1876–1912), soldier and author, born Denver, Colo.; although a hunchback, he became a general in the service of Sun Yat-sen in China; author of two prophetic works on Japan's plans for expansion—'The Valor of Ignorance' and 'The Day of the Saxon', *picture* C-464

Lea, Tom (born 1907), painter and writer, born El Paso, Tex.; painted many murals; illustrated J. Frank Dobie's 'Apache Gold & Yaqui Silver' and 'The Longhorns'; wrote and illustrated 'The Brave Bulls', 'The King Ranch'.

Leaching, in metallurgy M-228

Leaching, the draining of minerals and nutrients in a plant environment J-155

Leach's petrel P-227

Leacock, Stephen Butler (1869–1944), Canadian educator and humorist, born Swanmoor, Hampshire, England; professor of political economy at University of Chicago 1899–1903, at McGill University, Montreal, Canada, 1908–36; author of biographies of Charles Dickens and Mark Twain, and of books on history, economics, and political science; won a wider public with nonsensical sketches C-114, *picture* C-115

Lead, S.D., city in Black Hills; pop. 5,420; timber, stock raising; gold mining; tourist center; Homestake Mine, largest gold mine in U.S.; incorporated 1890, *maps* S-334, U-40
- Black Hills B-306
- Homestake Mine S-323, G-150b, *picture* S-331

Lead, a metallic chemical element L-99, *tables* P-207, M-229, C-233, 236
- alchemy A-273
- alloys
  - brass B-410
  - bronze B-463
- automobile exhaust A-848
- cadmium a by-product C-10
- chemical test for, *table* Q-4
- chromate C-335
- electrochemical activity E-167
- end-product of radioactivity R-64, 68, G-62
- gasoline, antiknock G-42
- glassmaking G-137, 142, *picture* G-143
- industrial health hazard I-175
- metalworking M-230
- native form M-332
- ore deposits, *map* O-497
- paints and driers P-73
- radioactive minerals M-335
- red lead (minium), P-73
- silver a by-product S-204
- supercold affects C-620b
- tetraethyl C-239
- United States U-106
  - Missouri M-397, *map* M-400
  - Oklahoma O-436, *map* O-438
- white lead P-73, 76

'Lead, Kindly Light', hymn by Cardinal Newman N-205

Lead azide L-99

Leadbelly. *see in index* Ledbetter, Huddie

Leader, in fishing F-144

Leading, in boxing B-390

Lead line, in navigation N-86

Lead mold, in electrotyping E-173

Lead monoxide, or **litharge** L-99

Lead pencil P-158

Lead sulfide. *see in index* Galena

Leadville, Colo., mining and tourist city in w.-central part of state, about 80 mi (130 km) s.w. of Denver; almost 2 mi (3 km) above sea level; pop. 3,879; gold, silver, molybdenum mines; important center of American mining history C-457, *maps* C-466, U-40
- Tabor, first mayor T-2

Leadwort, a plant. *see in index* Plumbago

Leadwort family, or **Plumbaginaceae,** a family of plants and shrubs including the prickly thrifts, sea lavender, leadwort, and statice, or thrift.

Leaf, Munro (1905–76), author of children's books, born present Baltimore, Md. ('The Story of Ferdinand', 'Wee Gillis', illustrated by R. Lawson; 'Reading Can Be Fun', 'Three Promises to You', 'Science Can Be Fun', 'Who Cares? I Do', illustrated by author).

Leaf, of metal. *see in index* Foil

Leaf, of plant L-100
- adaptation A-39
- carnivorous, or insect eating
  - pitcher plants P-344, *picture* N-60a
  - sundew S-517
  - Venus's-flytrap V-280
- cell structure, *picture* L-267
- clocklike rhythms B-224
- drought resisting G-189
- growth of, *pictures* H-154
- light, response to
  - compass plants C-501
  - eucalyptus E-304
- needlelike (conifers) P-329
- physiology of P-372
- plants P-358, 363c
- reduction by desert plants C-9
- respiration R-159
- transpiration W-69
- tree T-253, *pictures* T-254–7
- water plants W-75

Leaf beetle, *picture* B-141

Leaf butterfly. *see in index* Oriental leaf butterfly

Leaf collecting, hobby L-103

Leaf-cutting ant, ant which cuts and carries away leaves and petals of trees and other plants; found chiefly in tropical America A-468, *picture* N-63

Leaf-cutting bee B-124
- egg, *picture* E-106

Leaf fish, a freshwater fish (*Monocirrhus polyacanthus*) of northern South America; belongs to family *Nandidae*, *picture* F-127

Leafhoppers, a group of insects of the order *Hemiptera;* especially the red-banded leafhopper (*Graphocephala coccinea*) which infests various flowers, vegetables, shrubs, and weeds, *picture* I-214

Leaf insect, an insect of tropical regions, with wings amazingly leaflike in form and color; family *Phasmidae.*

Leaflet bomb, a weapon B-337

Leaf lettuce L-140

Leaf monkey. *see in index* Langur; Guereza

Leaf prints, hobby L-103, *picture* L-102

Leaf rollers, popular name of the *Tortricidae*, a family of small moths, many of whose larvae roll leaves to form a shelter.

Leaf rust, a fungus growth R-363

Leafstalk, or **petiole,** in botany L-100, *picture* L-102

League, an ancient unit of long measure which in modern usage varies in different countries from about 2 to about 4 miles (about 3¼ to about 6½ kilometers), *table* W-96

League Island Navy Yard. *see in index* Philadelphia Navy Yard

'League of American Wheelmen, The', organization B-189

League of Arab States. *see in index* Arab League

League of Nations L-103
- armament limitation P-143c
- Danzig protected by D-33
- Harding's policy H-30
- headquarters at Geneva G-44
- International Labor Organization U-26, C-281
- meeting of, *picture* W-264
- Permanent Court of International Justice H-4, E-322
- supporters
  - Roosevelt, F.D. R-263
  - Taft T-9
  - Wilson W-177
- U. S. rejects U-185
- Versailles, Treaty of W-263

League of Swiss Cantons (1291), *table* T-251a

League of the Three Petticoats, in Seven Years' War S-117

League of Women Voters, nonpartisan association of women interested in the promotion of good citizenship and government C-160, W-215d

'League of Youth, The', work by Ibsen I-15

Leah, elder daughter of Laban and unloved first wife of Jacob (Gen. xxix); from her the tribes of Levi, Simeon, Reuben, Judah, Issachar, and Zebulon descend.

Leahy, William Daniel (1875–1959), U.S. Navy officer, born Hampton, Iowa; chief of naval operations 1937–39; governor of Puerto Rico 1939–40; ambassador to Vichy, France, 1940–42; chief of staff to president of the United States 1942–49; appointed fleet (5-star) admiral 1944.

Leakey, Caroline, Australian writer A-797

Leakey, Louis Seymour Bazett (1903–72), British archaeologist, born Kabete, near Nairobi, Kenya; husband of Mary Leakey; father of Richard Leakey L-104
- fossils F-326
- prehistoric man M-76

Leakey, Mary Nicole (born 1913), British anthropologist; wife of Louis S.B. Leakey L-104

Leakey, Richard Erskine Frere (born 1944), British anthropologist; son of Louis and Mary Leakey L-104

Leamington, England, health resort in Warwickshire, 145 km (90 mi) n.w. of London; pop. 45,090; mineral springs, *map* G-199h

Leander, lover of Hero H-146

Leaning tower of Pisa, in Pisa, Italy P-343
- Galileo's experiment G-195

Lean-to, shelter C-63, *picture* V-241
- Whelan, *diagram* T-105

"Lean-to" fire, *pictures* C-65

Leap year C-28, Y-337

Lear, Edward (1812–88), English humorist L-104

Learning L-105
- animals P-521, *pictures* P-520, 522–3
- child development C-265–80, *pictures* C-265–73, 275–80
- education E-74–100c, *pictures* E-84, 86, 88, *tables* E-76–7
- exceptional children E-346
- expository method S-238
- habit H-2
- inquiry method S-239
- intelligence tests I-238
- memory M-220
- new math concepts M-164f
- play P-386, 390a
- psychological theories P-521
- reading R-101, 102
- study S-491
- teaching machines T-45

Learning center
- alternative schools A-321

Leary, Herbert Fairfax (1885–1957), U.S. Navy officer, born Washington, D.C.; commander of Allied naval forces in s.w. Pacific 1942–43; commander of eastern sea frontier, U.S., 1943–45.

Lease, legal document, *table* L-93

Lease-lend. *see in index* Lend-lease

Leasing system
- shoe manufacturing S-180

Least grebe G-210

Least sandpiper S-40
- silhouette, *picture* B-189

Least tern G-262

Leather L-107
- armor A-630
- clothing labels C-407
- embossing E-191
- gloves G-144d
- Indian clothing I-121
- kinds
  - chamois C-205
  - crocodile C-611

Leatherback / Leeming

goatskin G-147
parchment and vellum D-200e
shagreen
sawfish S-52d
shark S-144
leathercraft, *picture* H-186
shoes S-179, 180–1

Leatherback turtle T-308, 310, *picture* T-309

Leather beetle, *Dermestes vulpinus;* one of family of small, destructive insects sometimes classed as museum beetles; larvae feed on animal substances, especially skins.

Leather carp, fish C-141

Leathernecks, nickname of United States Marines M-109

Leather splits. *see in index* Splits

'Leatherstocking Tales', series of five fast-paced adventure novels by James Fenimore Cooper starring Leatherstocking, the ideal American frontiersman C-562, A-346

Leavening B-428, Y-338

Leavenworth, Henry (1783–1834), U.S. Army officer and Indian fighter, born New Haven, Conn.; built Army posts, later known as Ft. Snelling (1819) and Ft. Leavenworth (1827); stationed at Ft. Atkinson, Neb. (1821–24).

Leavenworth, Kan., city in n.e. on Missouri River; pop. 33,656; steel fabricating and products, paper products, plastics; nearby are state and U.S. penitentiaries and Veterans Administration Hospital; in early days outfitting point for cross-prairie wagon trains, *map* U-41

Leavenworth Prison P-505b

Leaves. *see in index* Leaf

'Leaves of Grass', poems by Walt Whitman W-157, A-349

Leawood, Kan., residential city 15 mi (25 km) s. of Kansas City; pop. 13,360; incorporated in 1948.

Lebanon (from Arabic *laban,* "to be white"), republic on Mediterranean n. of Israel; cap. Beirut; area 4,015 sq mi (10,400 sq km); pop. 3,316,000; cedars of Lebanon supplied by Hiram of Tyre for Solomon's temple (I Kings v) L-111
Arafat's occupation A-527
flag, *picture* F-166
guerrillas, *picture* I-263
money, *table* M-428
national anthem, *table* N-52
railroad mileage, *table* R-85

Lebanon, N.H., city 47 mi (76 km) n.w. of Concord; pop. 11,134; dairy products and poultry, textiles, wood products, machinery, leather goods; founded 1761, *map* N-183

Lebanon, Pa., industrial city 25 mi (50 km) n.e. of Harrisburg; pop. 25,711; in limestone and iron-mining district; chemicals, iron and steel products, textiles, food products, paper boxes, pharmaceuticals, *map* P-185

Lebanon, Tenn., city 30 mi (50 km) n.e. of Nashville; pop. 11,872; livestock, timber, Burley tobacco, and limestone; Sam Houston practiced law here, *map* T-96

Lebanon, Cedar of C-179
Beirut landmark B-144
Lebanon L-111
ships S-164

Lebanon Mountains, range in Lebanon close to the coastal plain; highest point 10,131 ft (3,088 m) L-111, B-143

Lebanon Valley College, at Annville, Pa.; United Methodist church; founded 1866; arts and sciences, education; member cooperative University Center at Harrisburg.

Le Bel, Joseph Achille (1847–1930), French chemist, born Pechelbronn, Alsace; 1874 set forth concept of asymmetric carbon atom independently of his contemporary, Van't Hoff; experiments in organic chemistry.

Lebensraum, German word, meaning "living space," slogan of German imperialism; used by Adolf Hitler to express Germany's demand for new territories and economic self-sufficiency.

Leblanc, Maurice (1864–1941), French writer, born Rouen; wrote stories about Arsène Lupin, gentleman-burglar who turned detective.

Leblanc, Nicolas (1742–1806), French chemist, born Issoudun; in 1789 discovered method of making soda from common salt; lost both property and his patent rights in French Revolution.

Leblanc process, for making soda and by-products S-247

Le Blon, Jacques Christophe (1667–1741), French painter and engraver, born Frankfurt, Germany; the father of modern color printing.

Le Bris, Jean Marie (died 1872), French sea captain and inventor; patterned first glider after albatross G-144b, A-201

Lebrun, Albert François (1871–1950), 14th president of France under the Third Republic, born Mercy-le-Haut, n.e. France; president of the Senate 1931–32; president of France 1932–40.

Le Brun, Charles (1619–90), French artist and designer, born Paris; as one of founders of the Royal Academy of Painting and Sculpture and director of Gobelin tapestry manufactory, he practically directed French art tendencies during his lifetime; court artist under Louis XIV, F-458, 462

Lebrun, Elisabeth Vigée-. *see in index* Vigée-Lebrun

Le Caron, Joseph (1586–1632), French Roman Catholic missionary, born near Paris; pioneered among Huron Indians in Canada; compiler of first Huron dictionary; sent back to France (1629) by British after capture of Quebec, Canada.

Le Carré, John (born 1913), English author L-113

Le Chatelier, Henry Louis (1850–1936), French chemist, born Paris; known for law of chemical equilibrium C-241

Lechfeld, Battle of (955), on plain of Lechfeld in Bavaria; Magyars defeated by Otto I, A-828, H-275

Lechon, Philippine food P-253d

Lech River, rapid and tortuous stream rising in Vorarlberg Alps at height of 1,865 m (6,120 ft); flows n. through Bavaria 290 km (180 mi), joining Danube below Donauwörth, *maps* G-99a, 115, D-32

Lecithin, a fatty substance found in plant and animal cells S-340

Lecky, William Edward Hartpole (1838–1903), Irish historian and publicist, born Newton Park, near Dublin ('A History of European Morals'; 'History of England in the Eighteenth Century')
quoted G-75

Leclaire, Edmé Jean (1801–72), French social scientist; founded system of profit sharing at his interior decorating firm in Paris 1842.

Leclanché, Georges, French inventor B-108

Leclerc, Jacques Philippe, real name Jacques Leclerc de Hauteclocque (1902–47), French army officer, born Belloy-Saint-Léonard, n. France; prisoner of Germans 1940; escaped, joined Free French; led force across Sahara to meet General Montgomery 1943; led French into Paris Aug. 1944; signed for France at Japanese surrender on U.S.S. *Missouri* Sept. 2, 1945.

Lecocq, Alexandre Charles (1832–1918), French composer, born Paris; produced many light operas, melodious, gay, and lively ('La Fille de Madame Angot'; 'Giroflé-Girofla').

Lecompton, Kan., town on Kansas River, 15 mi (25 km) e. of Topeka; pop. 576; settled 1854 by proslavery men and was their headquarters during contest with free-state settlers for control of the state.

Lecompton Constitution, adopted by proslavery faction of Kansas in 1857
Buchanan supports B-476

Le Conte, Joseph (1823–1901), scientist, born Liberty County, Ga.; helped popularize geology ('Elements of Geology'; 'Religion and Science').

Leconte de Lisle, Charles Marie (1818–94), French poet, born island of Bourbon (now Réunion); chief of modern Parnassian school ('Poèmes antiques').

Lecoq de Boisbaudran, Paul Émile, called François (1838–1912), French chemist, discoverer of gallium, samarium, dysprosium, holmium.

Le Corbusier, or **Charles Édouard Jeanneret-Gris** (1887–1965), Swiss architect, born La Chaux-de-Fonds, Switzerland; Visual Arts Center at Harvard University, his first building in U.S., completed 1963, L-113
architecture A-565, 568, *picture* A-564
design D-94

Lecouvreur, Adrienne, French actress A-27

Le Creusot, France, town in e.-center, 120 km (75 mi) n.w. of Lyons; pop. 33,581; famous iron and armaments works.

Lectern, a reading desk
medieval, *picture* M-303

Lectum, Cape. *see in index* Baba, Cape

Lecturer, in college U-206

Lecuona, Ernesto (1895–1963), Cuban composer, conductor, and pianist; born Guanabacoa, Cuba; piano debut at 5; composed first work at 11 ('Malagueña'; 'Andalucía') M-561

Leda, in Greek and Roman mythology, a fair mortal wooed by Zeus (Jupiter) in guise of swan; mother of twins Castor and Pollux, of Helen, and of Clytemnestra.

Ledbetter, Huddie, or **Leadbelly** (1888–1949), folksinger, born Mooringsport, La. B-302
folk music F-273

Lederberg, Joshua (born 1925), geneticist, born Montclair, N.J.; professor University of Wisconsin 1954–59, Stanford University 1959–.

Ledger lines, in musical notation M-564

Ledo Road. *see in index* Stilwell Road

Ledyard, John (1751–89), adventurer, born Groton, Conn.; dreamed of opening up fur trade in Pacific Northwest, glimpsed on voyage (1776–80) with Captain Cook; enlisted interest of John Paul Jones, Thomas Jefferson, Sir Joseph Banks; failed in two attempts to cross Siberia on foot; died during expedition into Africa.

Ledyard, Conn., 7 mi (11 km) n.e. of New London in agricultural area; pop. of township 13,735; plastics; incorporated 1836, *map* C-533

Lee, Ann (1736–84), "Mother Ann," founder of the American Society of Shakers, born Manchester, England; to America 1774; set up first Shaker colony near Albany, N.Y., 1776.

Lee, Arthur (1740–92), diplomat, born Stratford, Va.; brother of Richard Henry Lee; served as American representative in various European countries during Revolutionary War.

Lee, Charles (1731–82), American Revolutionary War general, born Dernhall, Cheshire, England; dismissed for insubordination; involved in treasonable intrigues not discovered until after his death R-168, 172

Lee, Dennis (born 1939), Canadian poet and author, born Toronto (children's poetry: 'Wiggle to the Laundromat'; 'Alligator Pie', won Canadian Book of the Year for Children award 1975; 'Nicholas Knock and Other People'; 'Garbage Delight', won Canadian Book of the Year for Children award 1978).

Lee, Doris (Emrick) (Mrs. Arnold Blanch) (born 1905), modernist painter, muralist, and book illustrator, born Aledo, Mercer County, Ill.; known for rural scenes done with humor and charm; work represented in Metropolitan Museum of Art and major galleries ('Thanksgiving Dinner', 'Country Wedding').

Lee, Fitzhugh (1835–1905), Confederate Civil War general, born Fairfax County, Va.; nephew of Robert E. Lee; military governor of Havana, Cuba, after Spanish-American War.

Lee, Francis Lightfoot (1734–97), signer of Declaration of Independence, born Stratford, Va.; brother of Richard Henry Lee
signature reproduced D-55

Lee, Harper (Nelle Harper Lee) (born 1926), novelist, born Monroeville, Ala.; won 1960 Pulitzer prize for her first novel, 'To Kill a Mockingbird' R-111i

Lee, Isung Dao. *see in index* Tsung Dao-lee

Lee, Jason (1803–45), American Methodist missionary and Oregon pioneer, born Stanstead, Que., Canada, then part of Vermont; went west with Wyeth's expedition (1834) to open mission among Flathead Indians; aided by Dr. McLoughlin in settling in Willamette Valley; established other missions in Clatsop region and at The Dalles O-484, *picture* O-490
Statuary Hall, *table* S-437b

Lee, Joseph (1862–1937), social worker, born Brookline, Mass.; known as "father of American playground movement"; organized and was president of National Recreation Association from 1910; president War Camp Community Service during World War I ('Play in Education'). National Joseph Lee Day celebrated July 28.

Lee, Light-Horse Harry (Henry) (1756–1818), statesman and American Revolutionary War general, born Dumfries, Va.; member of Continental Congress 1785–88; governor of Virginia 1792–95; father of Robert E. Lee L-114
Lee, Robert E. L-115
quoted on Washington W-29

Lee, Manfred B. *see in index* Queen, Ellery

Lee, Richard Henry (1732–94), American Revolutionary War leader L-114, D-51
signature reproduced D-55

Lee, Robert E. (1807–70), Confederate general L-115, *picture* V-342
birthplace, *picture* V-335
Christ Church, *picture* V-334
Civil War C-376, 378
Antietam M-4
Chancellorsville C-206
Gettysburg G-119, *picture* P-178
Grant and G-171, *pictures* C-511, V-337
Custis-Lee Mansion N-35, *map* W-32
Hall of Fame, *table* H-11
horse, Traveller, *list* H-232a
quoted S-490b
Statuary Hall, *table* S-437b
Stone Mountain, *picture* G-82

Lee, Sir Sidney (1859–1926), English author and educator, born London; editor 'Dictionary of National Biography'; works include 'Life of Shakespeare', 'Life of Queen Victoria' S-142

Lee, river in Ireland C-573, *map* G-199h

Leeboard, a slab of wood or metal hung over the leeward side of sailing canoes and other small craft to prevent drifting sideways C-125

Leech, John (1817–64), English caricaturist, whose *Punch* cartoons John Ruskin called "the finest definition and natural history of the classes of our society, the kindest and subtlest analysis of its foibles."

Leech, a bloodsucking worm, *picture* W-298

Leech, nautical, *diagram* B-326

Leechee. *see in index* Litchi

Leech Lake, in n. Minnesota, 20 mi (30 km) long, *maps* M-349, 362

Lee College, at Cleveland, Tenn.; Church of God; founded 1918; arts and sciences, education, religion.

Leeds, England, city on Aire River; pop. 448,528, L-117, *map* G-199h

Leek, herb similar to onion O-455

Leemans, Alphonse (Tuffy) (1912–79), football player, born Superior, Wis.; halfback, fullback; New York Giants 1936–43.

Lee Mansion. *see in index* Custis-Lee Mansion

Leeming, Joseph (1897–1969), author, editor, and publicist, born Brooklyn, N.Y.; writer of books for children, chiefly on making and doing things: 'The Costume Book',

Leesburg / Leigh-Mallory

'Fun with Magic', 'Fun with Clay', 'Fun with Puzzles', 'Fun with Beads'.

Leesburg, Fla., city 36 mi (58 km) n.w. of Orlando; pop. 13,191; citrus fruit and vegetable raising and packing; wood products, mobile homes, plastics.

Lee's Summit, Mo., city 17 mi (27 km) s.e. of Kansas City; pop. 28,741; electric components, chemicals, plastics; incorporated 1865, *map, inset* M-409

Leeuwarden, Netherlands, capital of province of Friesland; pop. 78,247; flourishing trade in cattle, grain, fish, *map* N-133

Leeuwenhoek, Anthony van (1632–1723), Dutch naturalist and microscopist, born Delft; first to describe red corpuscles of the blood; described and illustrated bacteria, yeast plants, hydra, and other microscopic life L-117
- biology B-228
- cell theory C-182
- medicine contribution M-215b
- microscope M-290

Leeuwin, Cape, extreme s.w. point of the continent of Australia

Leeward Islands, n. group of Lesser Antilles, West Indies; includes Virgin Islands of the United States; the island St. Martin (French and Dutch); the islands Saba and St. Eustatius (both Dutch); Guadeloupe and dependencies (French); and the British possessions St. Kitts-Nevis, Anguilla, Antigua, Montserrat, and British Virgin Islands; pop. 566,000, *map* W-105
- name, origin W-102

Lefebvre, Jules Joseph (1836–1912), French painter; eminent as a painter of ideal heads; celebrated also for historical and allegorical paintings ('Lady Godiva'; 'Mignon').

Lefèvre d'Étaples, Jacques (1455?–1537), French theologian and scholar, born Étaples; also known as Jacobus Faber Stapulensis; pioneer of French Protestantism; condemned by Sorbonne for certain critical works on Bible, but protected by Francis I and Margaret of Navarre; translated Bible into French.

Left, in politics, origin P-434

Left and right D-120, *picture* D-122

Left-handedness C-268, H-20, D-120

Leg, in anatomy
- bones S-210, *diagrams* S-208–10
- evolution A-461
- insects I-217

Legacy, gift, *table* L-93

Legal Counsel, Office of, United States U-160

Le Gallienne, Eva (born 1899), American actress, born London, England; daughter of Richard Le Gallienne; educated in France; made American debut at 16; founder and director of Civic Repertory Theatre, New York City, in which she produced plays of high quality and presented them at popular prices ('The Swan'; 'The Master Builder'); author of 'At 33' and 'With a Quiet Heart', autobiographies.

Le Gallienne, Richard (1866–1947), American critic, essayist, and poet; born Liverpool, England; father of Eva Le Gallienne; 'Prose Fancies', 'The Quest of the Golden Girl', 'Pieces of Eight' are imaginative prose sketches; 'Odes from the Divan of Hafiz', 'English Poems', and other volumes of poems include many graceful lyrics.

Legal tender, coins and paper money that may legally be offered in payment of any money debt M-426

Le Gascon (the Gascon), French bookbinder of the 17th century; real name unknown

Legaspi, formerly **Albay,** Philippines, seaport of Luzon on Bay of Albay; pop. of municipality, 84,090; cap. of Albay Province, *maps* P-261d

Legate (from Latin *legare,* "to appoint"), specifically an ecclesiastical or diplomatic representative of the pope; term occasionally used to signify any ambassador or diplomat.

Legato, *table* M-566a

Legend (from Latin *legere,* "to read," originally "to gather"), a fictitious or improbable story based on tradition and some fact, as the legends of King Arthur; originally stories of saints and martyrs F-260. *see also in index* Folklore
- fire and myth F-95
- Fountain of Youth F-336
- Irving influenced by I-358

Legend, the title or description under a picture, diagram, or graph.

'Legend of Sleepy Hollow, The', story by Washington Irving A-345, *picture* S-184
- Irving, Washington I-358

Legendre, Adrien Marie (1752–1833), French mathematician, born Toulouse, France; a leader in introducing the metric system; helped prepare great centesimal trigonometric tables; made important contributions to geodesy.

Léger, Alexis Saint-Léger (1887–1975), pseudonym St.-John Perse, French poet, born on island near Guadeloupe; went to France when 11; general secretary of ministry of foreign affairs 1933–40; in U.S. after 1940 ('Éloges', 'Anabase', 'Exil').

Léger, Fernand (1881–1955), French painter, born Argentan; early work simple abstractions, later turned to cubism and flat-patterned landscapes L-117
- 'Interior' D-178, *picture* D-179
- motion pictures M-527
- United Nations murals U-22

Léger, Jules (1913–80), Canadian political leader, born St. Anicet, Que.; held Canadian government posts from 1940, governor-general 1974–79.

Léger, Paul Émile, Cardinal (born 1904), Canadian prelate, born Valleyfield, Que.; ordained Roman Catholic priest 1929; became archbishop of Montreal 1950, resigned 1967 to do missionary work in African leper colonies; created cardinal 1953.

Legerdemain, sleight of hand M-42–3, *pictures* M-41, 44

Leggings, garment D-190, *picture* D-191

Leghorn, or **Livorno,** Italy, Tuscan port on w. coast; pop. 161,077; Leghorn straw hats; glass, metal products, chemicals; shipbuilding, *map* E-334
- Mascagni's birthplace M-141

Leghorn, a breed of fowls P-482, *pictures* P-480–1

Leghorn, hat H-49

Legion, originally name given to Roman citizen-army, from Latin *legere,* "to gather"; in modern times applied to organizations whose members have performed unusual services either civil or military
- Foreign Legion, of France. *see in index* Foreign Legion
- Roman A-636, W-9, C-535, *diagram* W-8

Legionary ant, or **army ant,** or **driver ant,** insect of the family *Formicidae* A-468

Legion of Honor, French order of merit, reward for civil and military services D-59, *picture* N-8
- knighthood K-259

Legion of Merit Medal, United States D-56

Legion of Valor of the United States of America P-140

Legislative Assembly, body in France during Revolution (1791–92) which succeeded National Assembly of 1789–91.

Legislative assembly, in state government A-804, S-429

Legislative Council, in Australian government A-804

Legislative courts, United States C-594

Legislature, the lawmaking body of a government. *see also in index* Diet; entries beginning Congress and Parliament; *see also* Fact Summary with each state article
- bicameral P-129–30, S-429
- initiative, referendum, and recall I-205
- lobbying influences L-276
- states of United States S-429
- statute law L-94
- United Kingdom, defined U-17

Legitimacy, of children F-18

Legitimate theater T-148

Legitimists, party in France which after Revolution of 1830 supported elder line of Bourbons; now any supporter of monarchy by hereditary right.

Legler, Henry Eduard (1861–1917), American librarian and writer, born Palermo, Italy; came to U.S. in early youth; secretary Wisconsin Library Commission 1904–9; librarian, Chicago Public Library after 1909.

Legnano, Italy, city 26 km (16 mi) n.w. of Milan; pop. 42,460; cotton and silk manufactures; Lombard League defeated Frederick I nearby in 1176, F-390

Legnica, or **Liegnitz,** Poland, former Prussian manufacturing and trade town in Silesia, 60 km (40 mi) n.w. of Wroclaw; pop. 75,900; decisive victory of Frederick the Great over Austrians (1760); included in Poland since 1945.

Legrain, Pierre (1889–1929), French furniture designer F-462

Legree, Simon, a brutal slave driver in Harriet Beecher Stowe's 'Uncle Tom's Cabin'; name later used symbolically for any overbearing and unreasonable taskmaster.

Legros, Alphonse (1837–1911), French painter and etcher, born Dijon, France; for nearly 30 years a teacher in London, where his severe yet dignified realism, simple technique, and respect for European painting traditions exerted a powerful influence on English art.

Legume, plant, pod-bearing plants of pea and bean type; they form the pea family *Leguminosae* or *Fabaceae* L-118
- Australian flora A-783
- clover C-409
- cowpea C-596
- fertilizer type F-58
- mesquite M-227
- nitrogen-fixing bacteria on roots N-291
- pea P-142b
- peanut P-146, *picture* P-147
- plants, uses of P-376
- soybean S-340
- sweet pea S-529
- tamarind T-13
- use as hay H-77
- vetch V-305

Leguminosae. *see in index* Legume

Lehar, Franz (1870–1948), Hungarian composer, born Komarno; fame rests on operetta, 'The Merry Widow'.

Le Havre, France, 2d seaport, at mouth of Seine River; pop. 198,021, L-122, *map* E-334

Lehigh River, tributary of Delaware River, about 120 mi (190 km) long; rises in Wayne County, e. Pa.; empties into the Delaware at Easton; navigable by locks for 84 mi (135 km), *map* P-165

Lehigh University, at Bethlehem, Pa.; private control; formerly for men, women admitted 1971; founded 1865; arts and science, business administration, education, engineering; graduate school.

Lehman, Herbert H(enry) (1878–1963), banker and statesman, born New York City; banker 1908–28; lieutenant governor of New York State 1928–32; governor 1932–42; director general UNRRA 1943–46; U.S. senator, (Democrat) 1949–56; awarded Presidential Medal of Freedom 1963.

Lehman Caves National Monument, in Nevada N-40a, *maps* N-30, N-156, *pictures* C-178a, N-153

Lehmann, Lilli (1848–1929), German dramatic soprano, born Würzburg, Germany; because of superb quality and volume of her voice became famous as Brünnhilde, Isolde, and in other Wagnerian roles; also as interpreter of Mozart.

Lehmann, Liza (1862–1918), English soprano and composer, born London; remarkable success as concert singer; married Herbert Bedford, composer, 1894, and retired, devoting herself to composition of songs and song cycles ('In a Persian Garden').

Lehmann, Lotte (Mrs. Otto Krause) (1888–1976), American soprano, born Perleberg, Brandenburg, Germany; became U.S. citizen 1943; member Vienna State Opera, also of Chicago, New York, and other leading opera companies of U.S.; lieder singer; retired from stage 1951; author of 'Five Operas and Richard Strauss'.

Lehmbruck, Wilhelm (1881–1919), German sculptor, born Meiderich (now Duisburg), Germany; by the use of exaggerated lines attained great esthetic and rhythmic force ('Kneeling Woman') S-91

Lehr, oven, in glassmaking G-138, *picture* G-138

Lei, a rope of flowers worn by Hawaiians; often used as a token of greeting or farewell; also chain or crown of shells, leaves, or flowers given as a sign of friendship by Polynesians, *pictures* H-54, E-136

Lei, monetary unit. *see in index* Leu

Leibnitz, lunar mountain range M-485, *map* M-481

Leibniz, Gottfried Wilhelm (1646–1716), German philosopher, mathematician, and scientist; born Leipzig; a many-sided genius, versed in law, theology, and politics; spent much of his time at courts of German nobles and took part in affairs of state. Most famous for his contributions to philosophy and mathematics; his differential method in calculus prevailed over Newton's earlier system; founder of Academy of Sciences L-122, *picture* C-21
- computer history C-497c
- Newton controversy N-234
- science history S-57h

Leicester, Robert Dudley, earl of (1532?–88), English statesman and soldier; his supposed secret marriage to Amy Robsart is the theme of Sir Walter Scott's 'Kenilworth' E-185

Leicester, Simon de Montfort, earl of. *see in index* Montfort

Leicester, or **Leicestershire,** England, n. midland county; 2,155 sq km (832 sq mi); pop. 682,568; cap. Leicester; on Soar and Wreak rivers; sheep raising; farming; limestone and slate quarries, *map* E-218

Leicester, England, capital of Leicester county, on Soar River, 140 km (90 mi) n.w. of London; pop. 578,470; hosiery, boots and shoes, typewriters; Roman remains, *map* G-199h

Leicester, breed of sheep S-147

Leicester Square, London, England L-293, *map* L-289

Leiden, or **Leyden,** Netherlands, city on Old Rhine River 35 km (22 mi) s.w. of Amsterdam; pop. 95,964; metal products, textiles; printing, food processing; birthplace of Rembrandt, *map* N-133
- bulb industry B-379
- Dutch home of Pilgrims M-181
- siege (1574), *table* W-8d

Leidesdorff, William (1810–48), businessman, born in Danish Virgin Islands; to California 1841; served as American consul in California and city treasurer of San Francisco, *picture* C-48

Leidy, Joseph (1823–91), naturalist, born Philadelphia, Pa.; professor anatomy 1853–91 and director biology dept. 1884–91, University of Pennsylvania; research in vertebrate paleontology of America ('On the Fossil Horse of America').

Leif Ericson. *see in index* Ericson

Leigh, Vivien (1918–67), English actress of stage and screen, born in Darjeeling, India, as Vivian Mary Hartley; twice won Academy award (motion pictures) for acting in 'Gone with the Wind' (1939) and 'A Streetcar Named Desire' (1951); married to Sir Laurence Olivier 1940–60.
- 'Gone with the Wind', *picture* M-527

Leigh, England, town in Lancashire, 30 km (20 mi) n.e. of Liverpool; pop. 46,200; coal mining; textiles, electric cable, *map* G-199g

Leigh-Mallory, Sir Trafford Leigh (1892–1944), British air officer, born Mobberley, near Manchester, England; headed Allied air forces for invasion of

Leighton / Lenôtre

Europe 1944; lost in flight to command in s.e. Asia.
Leighton, Frederick, Baron Leighton of Stretton (1830–96), English painter and sculptor, born Scarborough, England; best known for classical subjects S-90
Leighton, Margaret (born 1896), author, born Oberlin, Ohio; daughter of Thomas Nixon Carver, professor of political economy at Harvard University for many years; books for children: 'The Singing Cave'; 'Judith of France'; 'The Sword and the Compass'; 'Journey for a Princess'.
Leinsdorf, Erich (born 1912), American conductor, born Vienna, Austria; to U.S. 1937, became citizen 1942; chief conductor of German opera Metropolitan Opera House, New York City, 1939–43; conductor Cleveland (Ohio) Orchestra 1943–44, 1945–47, Rochester (N.Y.) Philharmonic Orchestra 1947–56; musical director and conductor Boston Symphony Orchestra 1962–69.
Leinster, one of 4 provinces of Ireland, in middle and s.e. part s. of Ulster and s.e. of Munster provinces; bordered on e. by Irish Sea, on s.e. by St. George's Channel; 19,630 sq km (7,580 sq mi); pop. 1,414,415.
Leipzig, East Germany, city in Saxony, 110 km (70 mi) n.w. of Dresden; pop. 560,012, L-123, *maps* G-115, 99a, E-334
bust of Bach, *picture* M-557
Leipzig, Battle of (1813) N-13
Leipzig, Battle of, or **battle of Breitenfeld** (1631) G-265
Leipzig, University of (renamed Karl Marx University 1953 by East Germany's Communist government), 3d in size and 3d in age of the universities of Germany; established 1409 by 400 teachers and students who seceded from University of Prague as result of Hussite agitations; medicine, law, theology, and liberal arts and sciences.
Leipzig Trade Fair L-123
Leisler, Jacob (1640–91), popular leader in colonial New York, born Frankfurt, Germany; executed for insurrection N-248
Leisure L-123. *see also in index* Hobby; Reading for recreation; Recreation; Sewing
dance, stage D-26, 28
dancing D-16, H-182, *pictures* D-16–17
increase U-103
industry I-184
motion pictures M-504, 524, 529
music M-554, H-183, O-464b, O-474, *pictures* H-182, T-278
outdoor cooking, *picture* H-185
plays D-169, T-148, *picture* T-155
radio R-43, 48, 57
television T-66, 68, 75, P-535
Leith, Scotland, seaport and shipbuilding center on s. shore of Firth of Forth; port for Edinburgh, with which it was incorporated 1920; pop. 51,378, *map* G-199g
Leitmotiv, in music O-463–4, M-559
Leitrim, county in Connaught province, Ireland; 1,526 sq km (589 sq mi); pop. 30,572; lost more by emigration than any other county; beautiful scenery, especially along River Shannon; organized as county 1583.
Leix, or **Laoighis,** or **Queen's,** county in s.e. Ireland, in Leinster Province; 1,720 sq km (664 sq mi); pop. 44,595; farming, dairying, textile manufacturing; county town Port Laoighise (Maryborough).
Le Jeune, Paul (1591–1664), French Jesuit missionary, born Châlons-sur-Marne; 1632–39 was in Quebec, Canada, as superior of Canadian missions.
Lek, monetary unit of Albania, *table* M-428
Leland, Charles Godfrey (1824–1903), poet, ethnologist, traveler, and pioneer educator in art handicraft, born Philadelphia, Pa. ('Hans Breitmann's Ballads', poems in Pennsylvania Dutch dialect).
Leland, Henry Martyn (1843–1932), pioneer automobile manufacturer; founder Cadillac Motor Car Company, Lincoln Motor Company A-858, *profile* A-856
Leland Stanford Junior University. *see in index* Stanford University
Leloir, Luis F(ederico) (born 1906), Argentine biochemist, born Paris, France; director Institute of Biochemical Research, Buenos Aires, 1947–.
Lely, Sir Peter, real name Pieter van der Faes (1618–80), English court painter, born Westphalia, Germany, of Dutch family; portraits of beautiful women of court of Charles II.
Lemaître, Jules (1853–1914), French critic and dramatist, born Vennecy, near Orléans, France ('Impressions of the Theatre' and 'Contemporaries', widely read critical essays; 'The Pardon', 'The Poor Little Thing', plays).
Léman, Lac. *see in index* Geneva, Lake
Le Mans, France, commercial and manufacturing city on Sarthe River, 185 km (115 mi) s.w. of Paris; pop. 140,520; French under General Chanzy defeated 1871 by Germans; again fell to Germans 1940.
Grand Prix auto race A-874
Lemare, Edwin Henry (1866–1934), English organist and composer, born Ventnor, Isle of Wight; organist in London, England, at Carnegie Institute, Pittsburgh, Pa., San Francisco, Calif., Portland, Me., and Chattanooga, Tenn.; composed organ and choral works, and made transcriptions of orchestral works for organ.
LeMay, Curtis E(merson) (born 1906), U.S. Air Force officer, born Columbus, Ohio; Air Force deputy chief of staff for research and development 1945–47; commanding general U.S. Air Forces in Europe 1947–48, Strategic Air Command 1948–57; became 4-star general 1951; Air Force vice-chief of staff 1957–61, chief of staff 1961–65; American Independent vice-presidential candidate 1968; author of 'America Is in Danger' A-159
Lemay, Léon-Pamphile (1837–1918), Canadian poet and novelist, born Lotbinière, near Quebec; educated in theology and law; librarian to Quebec legislature 1867–92 ('Les Vengeances', 'Petits poèmes', 'Les Gouttelettes', 'Reflets d'antan', poetry; 'Le Pèlerin de Sainte Anne', 'L'Affaire Sougraine', fiction) C-113a, b, 116
Lemay, Mo., residential city bordering St. Louis on south; pop. 40,516; stone quarries, *map, inset* M-409
Lemberg, Russia. *see in index* L'vov
Lemelin, Roger (born 1919), French-Canadian writer, born Quebec C-115
Lemke, William (1878–1950), political leader, born Albany, Minn.; attorney general of North Dakota 1921–23; Republican representative from North Dakota 1933–50, *picture* N-350
Lemmon slave case (1854) A-652
Lemnitzer, Lyman L(ouis) (born 1899), U.S. Army officer, born Honesdale, Pa.; commissioned 2d lieutenant 1920, became 4-star general 1955; Army deputy chief of staff (plans and research) 1952–55; commander in chief of Far East command and of UN command 1955–57; Army vice-chief of staff 1957–59, chief of staff 1959–60; chairman Joint Chiefs of Staff 1960–62; supreme allied commander in Europe 1963–69; first person to receive distinguished service medals of Army, Navy, and Air Force at same time (July 1969).
Lemnos, island in n. Aegean; 390 sq km (150 sq mi); held in turn by ancient Greeks, Byzantine Empire, Italians, and Turks; Greek after World War I, *map* G-213
home of Hephaestus H-141
Lemon, Robert Granville (Bob) (born 1920), baseball player, born San Bernardino, Calif.; A.L. infielder-outfielder 1941–42, pitcher 1946–58.
Lemon, a citrus fruit
cultivation of B-178
fruitgrowing F-438
fruit production, *chart* F-430
introduced into Europe C-618
perfume making P-204
pests and diseases S-52e
vitamins V-356
Lemon chrome, a pigment C-335
Lemon Grove, Calif., community just s.e. of San Diego; chiefly residential; pop. 19,690, *map* C-53
Lemonnier, Pierre Charles (1715–99), French astronomer, born Paris; made many observations of Uranus before its discovery as a planet; these led to the discovery of the planet Pluto.
Lemon verbena, a perennial plant (*Lippia citriodora*) related to lantana; flowers white or lilac in a 3-spike cluster; leaves lemon-scented, with glandular dots; native to South America.
Le Moyne, Charles (1626–85), French colonist in Canada; father of famous explorers and soldiers better known by territorial titles. *see also in index* Bienville; Iberville
Le Moyne College, at Syracuse, N.Y.; Roman Catholic; founded 1946; arts and sciences, business administration, and teacher education.
LeMoyne-Owen College, at Memphis, Tenn.; affiliated with United Church of Christ and Tenn. Baptist Convention; founded 1870; liberal arts, education.
Lempira, monetary unit of Honduras, historic value about 50 cents, *table* M-428
Lemur, a fox-faced monkey-like animal L-125, *picture* A-98
Lemur, Flying. *see in index* Flying lemur
Lena Basin, U.S.S.R. L-125
Le Nain, Antoine (1588–1648), **Louis** (1593–1648), and **Mathieu** (1607–77), French painters, brothers, born Laon, France; depicted interiors; also portrayed scenes of everyday life of peasants; pictures grayish and dull in color.
Lenape, Indians. *see in index* Delaware
Lenard, Philipp (1862–1947), Hungarian physicist, born present Bratislava, Czechoslovakia; head of radiological institute at Heidelberg, Germany X-334
Lena River, in n.e. Siberia; empties into Arctic, forming vast delta; length 4,600 km (2,860 mi), L-125, *maps* R-322, *picture* S-190
length, comparative. *see in index* River, *table*
Lenasia, town, South Africa J-122
Lenau, Nikolaus, pseudonym of Nikolaus Franz Edler von Niembsch von Strehlenau (1802–50), Austrian poet, born Hungary; intense melancholia gave his lyrics somber, pessimistic tone; died insane ('Faust'; 'Savonarola'; 'Die Albigenser').
Lenbach, Franz von (1836–1904), German portrait painter, born Schrobenhausen, near Ingolstadt, Germany; called "greatest of his generation"; painted Emperor William I and Bismarck.
Lend-lease, program during World War II, W-270
foreign aid F-307
Roosevelt R-275
Lenepveu, Jules Eugène (1819–98), French painter; best known for classical and historical paintings and for decorative frescoes in theaters, churches, and public buildings ('The Martyrs in the Catacombs'), *picture* H-273
L'Enfant, Pierre Charles (1754–1825), French architect and engineer, who planned Washington, D.C., born Paris; came to fight in American Revolution before Lafayette; served as captain of engineers under Steuben and later was wounded in action at Savannah, Ga., and captured by British at Charleston, S.C. After war, worked as architect in New York City until called (1791) by President Washington to prepare plans for federal capital W-30
Banneker's collaboration B-74
grave N-20
L'Engle, Madeleine (born 1918), actress, teacher, and author; born New York, N.Y.; awarded Newbery Medal 1963 for 'A Wrinkle in Time' ('The Young Unicorns'; 'The Journey with Jonah').
Lenglen, Suzanne (1899–1938), French tennis player, born Compiègne; six-time Wimbledon champion in women's singles, 1919–23 and 1925; also starred in doubles; professional 1926–27.
Length, in physics. *see in index* Measurement; Metric system; Relativity; Weights and measures
Lenin, or **Vladimir Ilich Ulyanov** (1870–1924), Russian Bolshevist leader L-126, R-354, *pictures* U-15, R-355, 356, 357
Communism C-494a
educational system E-99
Khar'kov statue, *picture* K-231
motion pictures M-522
portrait, *pictures* R-326, 328
Socialism S-235
Stalin and S-403
Moscow M-493b, *map* M-493a, *pictures* M-493, 494
Trotsky and T-268
'Lenin', Russian icebreaker S-170
Leninakan, Russia, city in Armenian S.S.R. 140 km (85 mi) s.w. of Tbilisi; pop. 164,000; textile center; much destruction by earthquake 1926, *maps* R-344, 349, E-335
Leningrad, or **St. Petersburg,** or **Petrograd,** Russia, industrial and commercial city, former capital of Russia; pop. 4,719,000, L-127, *maps* R-322, 344, 348, E-335, W-253
cities, world's largest. *see in index* City, *table*
climatic region, *map* R-344, *graph* R-334
flood, *table* F-181
Lenin L-126
New Year's custom N-235
St. Isaac's Cathedral, *picture* R-353
school, *picture* R-332d
siege (1941–44), *table* W-8d
Peter the Great statue, *picture* R-354
Summer Palace, *picture* R-354
Lenin Peak, on border between Kirghiz, S.S.R. and Tadzhik S.S.R.; height 7132 m (23,399 ft); highest point in Trans-Alai Range; former name Mount Kaufman.
Lenin State Library, Moscow, Russia, *map* M-493a
Lennep, Jacob van (1802–68), Dutch poet and novelist, born Amsterdam; wrote patriotic songs and historical romances of which 'De Pleegzoon' (The Adopted Son) is most famous.
Lenni-Lenape, Indians. *see in index* Delaware
Lennon, John (1940–80), British singer B-119
assassination A-703
Lennox, Calif., community 10 mi (16 km) s.w. of Los Angeles; pop. 16,121; industrial and farming area, *map, inset* C-53
Lenoir (Jean Joseph) Étienne (1822–1900), French inventor of practical gas engine, born Mussy-la-Ville, Luxemburg A-858, *profile* A-856
Lenoir, William Benjamin (born 1939), astronaut candidate, born Miami, Fla.; electrical engineer chosen for NASA scientist-astronaut program 1967.
Lenoir, N.C., town 62 mi (100 km) n.w. of Charlotte; resort, set in foothills of Blue Ridge Mountains; pop. 13,748; furniture, textiles, hosiery; incorporated 1851, *map* N-336
Lenoir-Rhyne College, at Hickory, N.C.; affiliated with Lutheran Church in America; established in 1891; arts and sciences, nursing, and teacher education.
Lenormand, Henri René (1882–1951), French dramatist, born Paris; plays deal with psychoanalytical and often abnormal themes ('The Failures'; 'Time Is a Dream').
Lenôtre, or **Le Nôtre, André** (1613–1700), French landscape architect, born Paris; style formal, classical, symmetrical; designed Versailles, Fontainebleau, and other royal gardens for Louis XIV; also English gardens for Charles II, F-335

Lenox / Lessing

Lenox, Walter Scott (1859–1920), potter, born Trenton, N.J. P-477

Lenox porcelain P-477

Lenroot, Katharine Fredrica (born 1891), social worker, born Superior, Wis.; served in Children's Bureau, U.S. Department of Labor, 1915–34, and was chief 1934–51.

Lens, France, coal-mining and iron-manufacturing city 27 km (17 mi) s.w. of Lille; pop. 41,800; victory of French under prince of Condé over Spaniards (1648).

Lens, in optics
camera P-284
contact, for eye S-370
eye, human E-366, 369
fluorite M-335
fused quartz, properties Q-7
field glasses and binoculars F-78
glass employed G-139
light refraction L-196
microscope M-290, 292, L-117
motion picture camera M-504, *diagram* M-505
quartz Q-7
spectacles S-370
stereopticon S-443, *diagrams* S-444
telescopic A-730, T-62, 65

Lenski, Lois (1893–1974), writer and illustrator of books for children, born Springfield, Ohio; historical backgrounds are based on old records and diaries ('Bound Girl of Cobble Hill'; 'Ocean-Born Mary'; 'Indian Captive'); regional stories based on her experiences ('Strawberry Girl', winner of Newbery Medal in 1946; 'Prairie School'; 'San Francisco Boy'); picture books for small children ('Little Airplane'; 'Mr. and Mrs. Noah'; 'Cowboy Small'; 'Papa Small'); awarded Regina Medal 1969; autobiography, 'Journey into Childhood'.

Lent, Blair (born 1930), illustrator, born Boston, Mass.; 1973 Caldecott winner for 'The Funny Little Woman' (author and illustrator 'Pistachio', 'John Tabor's Ride', 'Baba Yaga'; compiler and illustrator 'From King Boggen's Hall to Nothing-at-all'; illustrator 'The Wave') R-106.

Lent, in Christian church E-33
fasting practiced F-44
Mexican festival, *picture* M-246

Lento, *table* M-566a

Lenz's law, of electromagnetic induction E-150, *diagrams* R-59

Leo I (died 461), saint and pope, commemorated as saint April 11, L-130
Attila and H-277

Leo III (died 816), saint and pope, commemorated as saint June 12, L-130, *picture* M-295
crowns Charlemagne C-209, *picture* G-112d

Leo IV (800?–855), saint and pope, commemorated as saint July 17.

Leo IX (1002–54), saint and pope, commemorated as saint April 19, L-130
Great Schism B-536

Leo X (1475–1521), pope L-131
Martin Luther opposes L-338
Medici family M-211

Leo XIII (1810–1903), pope L-131

Leo III, the Isaurian (680?–741), Byzantine emperor 717–41; in 718 saved empire from Saracens; freed serfs and reduced taxation
campaign B-535

Leo VI, the Wise (866–912), Byzantine emperor 886–912; noted for legislative works ('Basilica', revision of Justinian laws; 'Book of Prefect', applied to guilds of Constantinople; 'Tactics', for the army and navy).

Leo, or **Lion,** a constellation, *charts* S-418, 422
Regulus in, *charts* S-418, 422
zodiac Z-356, *chart* A-708

Leofric, earl of Mercia (died 1057), husband of Lady Godiva; in 1051 acted as mediator between Edward the Confessor and Earl Godwin C-596

Leominster, Mass., industrial city about 19 mi (31 km) n. of Worcester; pop. 34,508; plastic and paper products, clothing, furniture, *map* M-160

León, Mexico, city 320 km (200 mi) n.w. of Mexico City; pop. 209,870; center of agricultural and mining district; cereals, potatoes, fruit, livestock; shoes, textiles, *maps* M-241, 260d

León, Nicaragua, city 70 km (45 mi) n.w. of Managua; pop. 55,347; in fertile farming district; corn, coffee, sugarcane, cattle and dairy products; National University; cathedral (completed 1780); city founded 1524 on shore of Lake Managua; after destruction by earthquake, city was moved in 1610 to present site; former capital of Nicaragua, *maps* C-194, N-309

León, Spain, ancient kingdom and modern province in n.w.; cap. León (pop. 73,483)
early history S-358

Leonard, Benny, boxer B-392

Leonard, Walter Fenner (Buck) (born 1907); baseball first baseman, born North Carolina; famed as home run hitter for Homestead Grays; in Negro and Mexican leagues 1933–55.

Leonard, William Ellery (1876–1944), poet and educator, born Plainfield, N.J.; professor of English, University of Wisconsin ('Two Lives', 'A Son of Earth', poems; 'The Locomotive God', autobiography).

Leonardo da Vinci (1452–1519), Italian artist and inventor L-132
aerial screw H-130
anatomical drawings A-875
automation A-833
bicycle design B-187
flying machine A-200
history of biology B-228
invention, *picture* I-277
locks for Venice canals C-119
medical contributions M-251b
'Mona Lisa' P-37, *picture* P-36
parachute idea P-109b

Leoncavallo, Ruggero (1857–1919), Italian composer L-135
opera O-467, *picture* O-462

Leone, monetary unit of Sierra Leone, *table* M-428

Leonidas, king of Sparta, killed 480 B.C. at Thermopylae P-215

'Leonore', work by Beethoven B-136

Leonov, Aleksei Arkhipovich (born 1934), Russian cosmonaut, born near Irkutsk; parachute instructor; copilot of Voskhod II spaceship; Soyuz commander of 1975 Apollo-Soyuz flight S-346f, *picture* U-196b, *table* S-348

Leonov, Leonid Maksimovich (born 1899), Russian novelist, born Moscow R-360b, 361

Leontes, in Shakespeare's 'The Winter's Tale', king of Sicily W-188, 189

Leontief, Wassily (born 1906), American economist, born Leningrad, Russia; came to U.S. 1931, naturalized citizen; did pioneer work in input-output analysis; professor Harvard University 1946–.

Leopard, animal of the cat family L-135
furs, *tables* F-464, 465
protective coloration, *picture* P-513

'Leopard', British warship W-11

'Leopard, The', work by Tomasi I-379

Leopard cat, *picture* C-154c

Leopardi, Giacomo, Count (1798–1837), Italian lyric poet, prose writer, and scholar; born Recanati, near Macerata, Italy; master of finished style and slave of pessimism ('La Ginestra') I-377

Leopard's-bane. *see in index* Doronicum

Leopard seal, or **harbor seal** S-98, 100

Leopold II (1747–92), Holy Roman emperor, A-830

Leopold I (1790–1865), king of Belgium L-136, B-149

Leopold II (1835–1909), king of Belgium L-136, B-149
patron of Stanley S-410

Leopold III (1901–83), king of Belgium; abdicated 1951, L-136, B-149
Baudouin a follower of B-110

Leopold I (died 994), margrave of Austria A-828

Leopold V (1157–94), duke of Austria, succeeded 1177; went on Crusades 1182 and 1190; quarreled with Richard I in Palestine, R-202, A-828

Leopold, Order of, Belgian military decoration D-59

Léopoldville, Republic of Zaire. *see in index* Kinshasa

Lepachys, annual or perennial plants of the composite family, native to North America. Grow 0.6 to 1.5 m (2 to 5 ft); leaves finely cut; flowers solitary, on wiry stems, ray florets, 6 or 7, yellow or purple, droop from the cylindrical thimblelike center of disk florets that are first silver gray, later brown; called yellow, gray-headed, or longheaded coneflower.

Le Pan, Douglas Valentine (born 1914), Canadian poet C-114, 116

Lepanto, Battle of (1571), fought in Gulf of Corinth near Lepanto, Greece T-305
Cervantes at C-201
galleys N-104

Lepaya, Latvian S.S.R. *see in index* Liepaja

Lepidolite, a mineral M-336

Lepidoptera, the order of scaly-winged insects including butterflies, moths, and skippers B-521

Lepidus, Marcus Aemilius (died 13 B.C.), Roman consul and army commander; triumvir with Antony and Octavian (Augustus); his army betrayed him when he attempted a revolt against Octavian A-462, 496

Leporidae, a family of rodents including hares and rabbits. *see in index* Rabbit and hare

Leprechaun, in Irish superstition a pygmy sprite sometimes inhabiting wine cellars, sometimes farmhouses, and aiding in work; possesses treasure which human may get by keeping his eye fixed on sprite F-12

Le Prince de Beaumont, Jeanne Marie (1711–80), French writer, born Rouen, France S-475

Lepromatous leprosy L-136

Leprosy, or **Hansen's disease,** chronic communicable disease of skin, mucous membranes, and peripheral nerves; known since ancient times; bacillus, discovered 1879 by G. H. A. Hansen (1841–1912) of Norway; treatment with sulfones, begun 1943, made possible cure or arrest of disease and eliminated need for traditional isolation of victims from society L-136, *table* D-128e

Leptis Magna, Libya, ancient seaport 100 mi (160 km) e. of Tripoli; founded by Phoenicians; became splendid Roman city; birthplace of Emperor Septimius Severus; ruins of harbor, beautiful sculptures, and buildings have been uncovered.

Lepton, plural **lepta,** a minor coin of ancient times, worth about $\frac{1}{10}$ cent; Jerusalem lepton famed in Bible as "widow's mite"; also a modern bronze Greek coin worth $\frac{1}{100}$ drachma.

Leptons, elementary particles A-750, M-172

Leptospirosis, dog disease D-153

Lepus, or **Hare,** a constellation, *chart* S-421

Le Puy, France, city 225 km (140 mi) n.w. of Marseilles; pop. 22,396; 12th-century cathedral; lace, textiles, spirits.

Lerici, Carlo, Italian archaeologist A-533

Lérida, Spain, walled cathedral city 130 km (80 mi) w. of Barcelona; pop. 50,047; leather, glass, textiles; as a Celtiberian city, **Ilerda,** heroically resisted Romans.

Lérins, Monastery of, on islet of Lérins group in Mediterranean off Cannes, France M-445

Lerma River, rises 29 km (18 mi) w. of Mexico City and flows 560 km (350 mi) w. to Lake Chapala, from which it emerges as Río Grande de Santiago and flows 400 km (250 mi) n.w. to Pacific Ocean; Santiago noted for scenic beauty of its canyon and, near Guadalajara, for the Juanacatlán Falls, which are 15 meters (50 feet) high and 130 meters (430 feet) wide, *map* M-241

Lermontov, Mikhail (1814–42), Russian poet and novelist, born Moscow; ranked next to Pushkin as greatest Russian poet; despised society; felt at home only in Caucasus ('On the Death of a Poet', 'Song of the Merchant Kalashnikov', poems) L-136, R-360, 361

Lerner, Alan Jay (born 1918), author and lyricist, born New York City; collaborated with **Frederick Loewe** (born 1904), Austrian composer, born Vienna ('Brigadoon', 'Camelot', musicals; 'An American in Paris', 'Gigi', films)
'My Fair Lady' O-464a, M-567b

Lerwick, Scotland, capital and chief town of Shetland Islands, on s.e. coast of Mainland Island; pop. 5,919, *maps* E-334, *inset* G-199g

Le Sage, Alain René (1668–1747), French novelist and dramatist, born Sarzeau, near Vannes, France; a satiric realist ('Gil Blas', comic masterpiece of adventurous roguery).

Lesage, Jean (1912–80), Canadian political leader, born Montreal, Que.; crown attorney 1939–44; member House of Commons 1945–58; delegate to UN 1950, 1952; leader Quebec Liberal party 1958–70; prime minister province of Quebec 1960–66.

Les Baux, or **Les Beaux,** France, village in s., near Arles; pop. 87

Lesbos, modern Greek **Mytilini,** Greek island in Aegean Sea off coast of Asia Minor; about 1,680 sq km (650 sq mi); pop. 114,797; important naval and colonizing power in early history of Greece; famed for school of poets (7th century B.C.) and as birthplace of Sappho; passed to Turkey 1462, to Greece 1912; cap. Mytilene; olives, grapes, grain, *maps* G-213, 221, T-299, E-335, *picture* G-212

Lescarbot, Marc (1570?–1630?), Canadian historian C-113

Lescaze, William (1896–1969), American architect, born Geneva, Switzerland; came to U.S. 1920; leader in modernism

Leschetizky, Theodor (1830–1915), Polish teacher of piano, born Lancut, near Rzeszów, Poland; pupil of Czerny, he became eminent pianist; taught in St. Petersburg and Vienna; won chief fame as teacher of Paderewski; composed opera 'Die Erste Falte' and piano numbers.

Leskov, Nikolai Semenovich (1831–95), Russian author, born St. Petersburg R-360a, 361

Leslie, Sir John (1766–1832), Scottish mathematician and physicist, born Fife County, Scotland; inventor of a differential thermometer, photometer, and hygrometer; used air pump and sulfuric acid to freeze water and thus invented a process of artificial refrigeration.

'Les Misérables', novel by Victor Hugo H-268

Lesotho, or **Basutoland,** nation in s. Africa; 11,716 sq mi (30,344 sq km); pop. 1,407,000; cap. Maseru L-137, *map* S-264
flag, *picture* F-166
money, *table* M-428

Lespedeza, a plant C-410

Lespinasse, Julie Jeanne Eléonore de (1732–76), French letter writer and social leader, noted for her love letters C-551

Lesseps, Ferdinand de (1805–94), French engineer, born Versailles; served as consul at Cairo, Rotterdam, and Barcelona L-138, P-92, S-503

Lesser Antilles, eastern islands of West Indies; 5,500 sq mi (14,200 sq km); pop. 2,088,226, W-101, *map* W-105
Latin America L-60

Lesser Himalayas, region of Bhutan B-180

Lesser panda P-97

Lesser Slave Lake, in central Alberta, Canada; about 1,230 sq km (475 sq mi), *map* C-98

Lesser Sunda Islands. *see in index* Sundan Islands

Lessing, Doris (May) (born 1919), Rhodesian writer, born Kermanshah, Persia (now Iran); (novels: 'The Grass is Singing', 'Children of Violence', 'The Golden Notebook'; plays: 'Maria', 'Play With a Tiger'; short stories: 'The Habit of Loving', 'African Stories.').

Lessing, Gotthold Ephraim (1729–81), German critic and dramatist, born Kamenz; famous for 'Laocoon', critical work on poetry and plastic arts ('Minna von Barnhelm',

Lester / Lewis

comedy; 'Emilia Galotti', tragedy; 'Nathan the Wise', noble poetic drama of religious tolerance; 'The Education of the Human Race', religious study) L-138, G-96b, 98, D-173, *picture* G-96a
  Faust legend F-49

Lester, Julius (born 1939), author, musician, singer; born St. Louis, Mo.; ('Black Folktales'; 'Search for the New Land', 'Long Journey Home: Stories from Black History', 'Two Love Stories')
  'To Be a Slave' R-111d

Lesueur, Charles Alexandre (1778–1846), French zoologist and artist; did earliest American work on marine invertebrates and fishes of Great Lakes; called "Raphael of zoological painters"; with Owen's colony at New Harmony, Ind.

Le Sueur, Pierre Charles (1657?–1705?), French explorer and fur trader; in 1700 traveled up Mississippi River, explored Minnesota River, and built fort near site of Mankato, Minn.; town and county in Minnesota named for him.

Lesueur rat kangaroo A-779

Lethal genes H-144

Lethbridge, Alta., Canada, city on Oldman River 174 km (108 mi) s.e. of Calgary; pop. 41,217; cattle ranching; wheat and vegetable farming, the latter under irrigation; coal deposits; flour, beet sugar; food processing C-98
  University of Lethbridge A-266

Lethe, in Greek mythology, river of oblivion H-2

Leto, in Greek mythology, mother of Apollo and Artemis, children of Zeus; goddess of fertility; protected graves; Roman Latona.

LeTourneau College, at Longview, Tex.; private control; founded 1946; liberal arts, engineering, technology.

'Letter from Birmingham Jail', work by Martin Luther King K-244

Lettering, in mechanical drawing M-200, *picture* M-201

Lettering, writing B-346, *picture* B-349
  pencil M-197

Letterpress printing
  color engravings P-278
  halftone engravings P-276, *picture* P-277
  ink I-207
  line engravings P-275

'Letters from an American Farmer', work by Crèvecoeur A-344

Letters of marque, commissions given by a government authorizing private persons to fit out armed vessels and to sail as privateers against the enemy.

Letters of the alphabet. *see in index* Alphabet

'Letters on the Regicide Peace', work by Burke B-507

Letters patent, official, public documents granting specific privileges or authority to an individual or corporation; issued by government or sovereign; typically contains signature and seal; used to confer exclusive rights to inventions and in England to bestow titles of nobility.

Letter writing L-139
  address, forms of, *table* E-297
  dictating machine D-111
  letters as literature
    Gray G-197
    Sévigné, Madame de S-118
  Santa Claus S-46

Letts, or **Latvians,** people L-83

Lettuce, a plant L-140
  farm machinery harvests F-35
  harvesting, *picture* P-191

Letzeburgesch language L-340

Leu, plural **lei,** monetary unit of Rumania; historic value less than 1 cent, *table* M-428

Leucippus, Greek philosopher about 5th century B.C.; regarded as founder of the atomic theory, adopted and improved by Democritus.

Leucite, a rock-forming mineral of potassium and aluminum metasilicate, found in basaltic lavas, and sometimes used as fertilizer.

Leuconostoc, bacteria B-15

Leuctra, Battle of (371 B.C.) named for village of Leuctra in Boeotia T-158

Leukemia, D-129b
  virus, *picture* V-353

Leukocyte. *see in index* White blood cell

Leutze, Emanuel (1816–68), American portrait painter, also painter of historical subjects, born Gmünd, near Stuttgart, Germany; painted the well-known 'Washington Crossing the Delaware' F-156

Leuven, Belgium. *see in index* Louvain

Lev, plural **leva,** monetary unit of Bulgaria since 1928, historic value less than 1 cent; at one time was equal to gold franc, worth 19.3 cents, *table* M-428

Levalloisian culture, from Levallois-Perret, near Paris, France, where remains were found M-75

Levant, Oscar (1906–72), composer, pianist, motion-picture actor; born Pittsburgh, Pa.; author of 'A Smattering of Ignorance', 'The Memoirs of an Amnesiac', 'The Unimportance of Being Oscar'.

Levant, term meaning "rising (of the sun)" applied to the countries along e. Mediterranean; name originated with Italians; includes Greece, Turkey, Syria, Lebanon, Egypt, and Palestine.

Levantine Sea M-216

Levee, an embankment. *see also in index* Dike
  flood control F-183
  Mississippi River M-390, *pictures* U-60, M-391, M-383
  natural formation R-211, *diagram* R-210

Level. *see in index* Spirit level

Levelland, Tex., city 35 mi (55 km) w. of Lubbock; pop. 13,809, in agricultural region; cotton; grain, cattle; oil and gas; incorporated 1926, *map* T-128

Levene, Phoebus Aaron (1869–1940), American biochemist, born Sagor, Russia; member Rockefeller Institute 1907–39; worked out formula for structure of nucleic acids; in 1930 purified and concentrated vitamin B_2.

Lever, a mechanical device M-206, *diagrams* M-207–8
  Archimedes A-541
  brake operation B-405
  voting machine, *picture* V-387
  weighing machines W-93

Leverhulme, William Hesketh Lever, first **Viscount** (1851–1925), English businessman, born Bolton, England; founded soap works (Lever Brothers) with associated companies all over world; model industrial village at Port Sunlight near Liverpool; instituted profit-sharing plans.

Lever lock L-277

Leverrier, Urbain Jean Joseph (1811–77), French astronomer, born Saint-Lô, France; studied motion disturbance of Uranus; calculations indicated presence of then unknown planet Neptune A-714, P-354

Levertov, Denise (b. 1923), American poet A-364

Lever tumbler lock L-277

Lévesque, René (born 1922), Canadian political leader and journalist, born New Carlisle, Que.; member Quebec legislature 1960–70, reelected 1976; premier Quebec 1976–; one of founders and first president of Parti Québécois.

Levey, Barnett, theater developer A-798

Levi, Hebrew patriarch, 3d son of Jacob and Leah, ancestor of tribe of Levi, or Levites, from which came the Jewish priests and keepers of the sanctuary.

Levi, Carlo (1902–75), Italian writer I-379, *picture* I-378

Levi, Edward Hirsch (born 1911), government official, born Chicago, Ill.; dean law school University of Chicago 1950–62, university provost 1962–68, university president 1968–75; U.S. attorney general 1975–77.

Leviathan, Hebrew name for sea monster; also dragon of turmoil which contested against God; mentioned in Job ix, 13 and Isa. xxvii, 1.

'Leviathan', ocean liner; before World War I was German liner *Vaterland;* acquired by United States; scrapped 1937, *picture* W-256

Levin, Harry (Tuchman) (born 1912), writer and educator, born Minneapolis, Minn.; on faculty of Harvard University 1939–('James Joyce: A Critical Introduction', 'Contexts of Criticism') W-310d

Levin, Meyer (born 1905), writer, born Chicago (novels: 'The Old Bunch', 'Citizens', 'Yehuda', 'My Father's House', 'Compulsion', 'The Fanatic', 'The Settlers').

Levine, Charles, aviator A-205, *picture* A-204

Levine, Jack (born 1915), artist, born Boston; gained early fame for expressionistic and satirical works on modern social subjects; rich, glowing colors.

Levine, Philip (born 1900), American bacteriologist and serologist, born Kletsk, Russia; director of biological division, Ortho Research Foundation, Raritan, N.J., from 1944; his research on Rh factors contributed greatly to success of blood transfusions used to save babies at birth.

Levinson, Salmon Oliver (1865–1941), lawyer and advocate of peace, born Noblesville, Ind.; leader of movement to outlaw war; author of plan for readjustment of German reparations, Allied debts, and world peace (1927).

Lévis, Que., Canada, city on St. Lawrence River opposite Quebec (city) and adjoining Lauzon; pop. 15,627; furniture, boilers, tobacco products; base for Wolfe's siege of Quebec, 1759, *map, inset* Q-11

Lévi-Strauss, Claude, French anthropologist L-141
  anthropology A-486

Leviticus, the 3d book of the Old Testament, containing the ceremonial laws of the priests; parts of book (chapters xix–xxii) among oldest surviving fragments of Bible, found with Dead Sea Scrolls 1956
  Golden Rule E-299
  Judaism's laws J-148
  quarantine and sanitation M-215

Levittown, N.J. *see in index* Willingboro

Levittown, N.Y., residential village on Long Island, 6 mi (10 km) e. of Mineola; pop. 65,440; unincorporated housing development of Levitt and Sons, Inc., Manhasset, N.Y., motivated by veterans' housing demands; built by mass production methods 1947–51, *map, inset* N-260

Levittown, Pa., private housing project 8 mi (13 km) from Trenton, N.J.; pop. 68,793; built 1952–58 by Levitt and Sons, Inc., builders of Levittown, N.Y.; more than 17,000 homes in identifiable neighborhoods; conspicuous example of city planning to meet all needs, *map* P-185

Levulose. *see in index* Fructose

Lewes, George Henry (1817–78), English philosopher and critic, born London; founded and edited *Fortnightly Review*
  George Eliot and E-182

Lewes, Del., resort town on Delaware Bay; pop. 2,197; founded 1631 by Dutch as Fort Opdike, first settlement in Delaware; scene of first and last naval battles of Revolution D-69, *maps* D-77, 66
  Zwaanendael Museum D-68, *picture* D-69

Lewes, England, county seat of Sussex, 70 km (45 mi) s. of London; pop. 14,030, *map* G-199h
  battle of (1264) M-475
  Glyndebourne Opera Festival, *picture* O-464a

Lewin, Kurt (1890–1947), German psychologist, born Mogilno, near Inowroclaw, present Poland; to U.S. 1932; professor of child psychology University of Iowa 1935–44; director Research Center for Group Dynamics, Massachusetts Institute of Technology, 1944–47, *table* E-90

Lewis, Andrew (1720?–81), American soldier, born Ireland; brother of Charles Lewis; major in Washington's Virginia regiment; brigadier general Continental army
  victory of Point Pleasant W-112

Lewis, Andrew L., Jr. (Drew) (born 1931), public official, financial and management consultant, born Philadelphia, Pa.; U.S. secretary of transportation 1981–.

Lewis, Sir Arthur (born 1915), British economist, born Castries, Saint Lucia; moved to England as teenager; professor of political economy University of Manchester 1948–58; at University of West Indies 1959–63; professor at Princeton University 1963–; president Caribbean Development Bank 1970–73; Lewis Model describes transition from agrarian to industrialized economy.

Lewis, Cecil Day-. *see in index* Day-Lewis

Lewis, C. S. (1898–1963), writer, born Belfast, Northern Ireland; professor Medieval and Renaissance English, Cambridge University, 1954–63; wrote scholarly, philosophical, and religious books ('Miracles'; 'Mere Christianity'); also children's books ('The Magician's Nephew'; 'The Last Battle'); pseudonym, Clive Hamilton L-141, E-276, R-111b

Lewis, D(ominic) B(evan) Wyndham (1894–1969), English author; of an old Welsh family; columnist on *London Daily Express;* contributor *Daily Mail;* his studies and writings chiefly concerned with Middle Ages ('François Villon'; 'King Spider', on Louis XI of France; 'The World of Goya').

Lewis, Elizabeth Foreman (1892–1958), writer, born Baltimore, Md.; missionary teacher in China; Newbery Medal (1933) for first book 'Young Fu of the Upper Yangtze' ('Ho-ming, Girl of New China'; 'To Beat a Tiger One Needs a Brother's Help').

Lewis, Francis (1713–1802), signer of Declaration of Independence as N.Y. delegate; born Wales; a founder of Sons of Liberty
  signature reproduced D-55

Lewis, Gilbert Newton (1875–1946), chemist, born Weymouth, Mass.; taught chemistry at Harvard University, Massachusetts Institute of Technology, and (after 1912) University of California; proposed (1916) his theory of atomic structure.

Lewis, Isaac Newton (1858–1931), U.S. Army officer and inventor, born New Salem, Pa.; invented Lewis machine gun, which he manufactured in Belgium and supplied to the Allies in World War I.

Lewis, John (born 1920), jazz innovator and pianist, born in La Grange, Ill.; was reared in Albuquerque, N.M.; leader of Modern Jazz Quartet, *picture* N-218

Lewis, John L. (1880–1969), American labor leader L-142
  labor movements L-8
  Roosevelt and R-271
  Truman and T-276

Lewis, Matthew Gregory (1775–1818), English romance writer and dramatist, born London; nicknamed "Monk" after his most popular romance 'Ambrosio, or the Monk', which was suppressed; later reprinted in expurgated form E-264, 274

Lewis, Meade Lux (1905–64), jazz pianist, born in Louisville, Ky.; popularized boogie-woogie upon emerging from obscurity several years after making a memorable record, 'Honky Tonk Train Blues' (1929).

Lewis, Meriwether (1774–1809), American explorer L-142, *picture* M-463
  Lewis and Clark Expedition L-143

Lewis, Sinclair (1885–1951), American novelist L-142, A-359, N-376, *pictures* N-375, M-360

Lewis, William Berkeley (1784–1866), friend, adviser, and campaign manager of Andrew Jackson and member of famous "Kitchen Cabinet."

Lewis, Wyndham (1884–1957), English author and artist, born in Maine; brought up in England; leader of vorticist painters ('Tarr', novel; 'Time and Western Man', philosophy; 'The Revenge for Love', a political satire; 'Rotting Hill', short stories).

Lewis and Clark Centennial Exposition, also called **American Pacific Exposition,** held June l to Oct. 15, 1905, in

Lewis / Library

Portland, Ore., to celebrate 100th anniversary of exploration of the Oregon country; cost about $7,000,000; attendance 2,545,509.

Lewis and Clark College, at Portland, Ore.; private control; chartered 1867; opened as Albany College 1867; name changed 1942; arts and sciences, education, law; graduate studies; quarter system.

Lewis and Clark Expedition (1804–6), in U.S. history L-143, *map* U-176, *picture* E-358
book about R-111c
Clark, William C-381
frontier movements F-419
Idaho I-22, *picture* I-23
Indian council, *picture* N-113
Lewis, Meriwether L-142

Lewis Carroll. *see in index* Carroll, Lewis

Lewis College, or **Lewis University,** at Romeoville, Ill.; private control; founded as technical school 1930, senior college 1950; liberal arts, aviation technology, education, and natural sciences; graduate studies.

Lewis Institute. *see in index* Illinois Institute of Technology

Lewisite, a poison gas C-230

Lewisham, borough, London, England, *map* L-287

Lewisohn, Ludwig (1883–1955), American writer, born Berlin, Germany; to U.S. 1890; books show his attempted complete assimilation in Nordic civilization, his disappointment, and return to identification with Judaism (autobiography, 'Up Stream'; novel, 'The Island Within'; criticism, 'The Story of American Literature').

Lewisohn Stadium, in New York City; belongs to and is on the campus of the City College of the City University of New York; site of summer concerts.

Lewisporte, Newf., Canada, port town on Notre Dame Bay 260 km (160 mi) n.w. of St. John's; pop. 2,892; former names include Big Burnt Bay and Marshallville; present name for English lumberman Lewis Miller who founded business here 1900, *map* N-165l

Lewiston, Idaho, port city on Snake and Clearwater rivers, 90 mi (140 km) s.e. of Spokane, Wash.; pop. 27,986; wheat, livestock, fruit, vegetables; lumber, plywood, cartridges, paper; food processing; first capital of Idaho Territory 1863–64; annual Lewiston Roundup, *map* U-40

Lewiston, Me., 2d city of state, on Androscoggin River opposite Auburn, 30 mi (50 km) n. of Portland; pop. 40,481; textiles, shoes, printing, wire goods, electronic tube and lighting equipment; Bates College M-54, *maps* M-65, 53, U-41
textile plant, *picture* M-54

Lewiston-Queenston International Bridge, over Niagara River between New York and Ontario, *map* N-281

Lewistown, Mont., city at geographic center of state in farming, stock-raising, oil, and mining district; pop. 7,104; brick and tile, lumber, campers; honey, feed, *map* M-471

Lewistown, Pa., borough on Juniata River 43 mi (69 km) n.w. of Harrisburg; pop. 9,830; in farm and dairy area; iron and steel products, clothing, *map* P-184–5

Lewis-with-Harris, island, largest of Outer Hebrides; area 2,135 sq km (825 sq mi), H-121, *map* G-199g

Lex Canuleia, Roman law R-243

Lex Hortensia, Roman law R-244

Lexical meaning, of words G-168

Lexington, Ky. *see in index* Lexington-Fayette

Lexington, Mass., 12 mi (19 km) n.w. of Boston; pop. of township 29,479; scene of first battle of Revolution (Lexington and Concord), *map, inset* M-160
Minute Man N.H.P. N-40b, *map* N-30
minute man statue, *picture* M-150
Revere, Paul, *picture* R-161

Lexington, N.C., city 20 mi (30 km) s. of Winston-Salem; pop. 15,711; furniture, textiles, clothing, electronic and food products, *map* N-336

Lexington, Va., city in farming district 30 mi (50 km) n.w. of Lynchburg; pop. 7,292; Washington and Lee University, Virginia Military Institute; tombs of Stonewall Jackson and Robert E. Lee, *map* V-348

'Lexington', U.S. Navy aircraft carrier W-292, *picture* W-293

Lexington and Concord, Battle of L-144, S-193, *picture* R-168
Revere's ride R-161

Lexington-Fayette, Ky., city and county; in Bluegrass region, about 70 mi (110 km) e. of Louisville; pop. 204,165; horses, livestock, tobacco; machine products, tobacco processing, distilling, food products; Transylvania College; state and federal institutions L-145, *map* U-41

Lexington Plain, or **Bluegrass Plain,** area, Kentucky K-209

Lex Valeria, Roman law R-242

Ley, Robert (1890–1945), German Nazi official, born Niederbreidenbach, Rhine Province; committed suicide when captured at end of war G-105

Ley, Willy (1906–69), American rocket authority and author, born Berlin; to U.S. 1935, became citizen 1944; consultant office of technical services, U.S. Department of Commerce; wrote on space travel ('Conquest of Space'; 'Rockets, Missiles, and Men in Space'; 'The Exploration of Mars', with Wernher von Braun) and natural science ('Dragons in Amber'; 'Salamanders and Other Wonders'; 'Exotic Zoology'; 'Watchers of the Skies'; 'The Dawn of Zoology').

Leyden, Lucas van. *see in index* Lucas van Leyden

Leyden, Netherlands. *see in index* Leiden

Leyden jar, an electrical condenser E-153, *diagrams* E-151
lightning experiments L-207

Leyte, island of the Philippines; 2,786 sq mi (7,216 sq km); pop. 1,223,667; hemp, sugar, sulfur; cap. Tacloban (pop. of municipality, 53,551), P-259, 255d, 256, *maps* P-259a, 261d
population P-253b
MacArthur lands M-2
World War II W-276, 296:

LFC. *see in index* Laminar Flow Control

Lhasa, People's Republic of China, capital of Tibet; in s.e.; pop. 386,200, L-145, T-172, 173

Lhasa apso, terrier, native of Tibet, *table* D-150

Lhévinne, Josef (1874–1944), American pianist, born Russia; U.S. debut 1906; taught in Berlin, Germany, later in New York City.

Liabilities, in accounting A-15

Liability insurance I-233

Liakoura. *see in index* Parnassus, Mount

Liana, a climbing plant P-359
jungle plant life J-155

Liao, river in n.e. part of People's Republic of China; flows e. and s. to Gulf of Liaotung; 900 mi (1,450 km) long M-83, *map* M-84

Liaoning, province in n.e. part of People's Republic of China; area 56,000 sq mi (145,000 sq km); pop. 35,721,693; cap. Mukden L-146, M-83, *maps* M-84
Lüda L-328

Liaotung Peninsula, People's Republic of China, projects s.w. into Yellow Sea between gulfs of Liaotung and Korea; Port Arthur at tip M-84
Dairen. *see in index* Dairen
history M-85
Russo-Japanese War R-362

Liaoyang, People's Republic of China, city in Liaoning Province s.w. of Mukden; pop. 250,000; cotton milling, scene of Russian defeat in Russo-Japanese War R-362

Liard River, Canada, 2d largest tributary of Mackenzie River; rises in s. Yukon Territory and flows through n. British Columbia; enters Mackenzie at Fort Simpson, about 240 km (150 mi) west of Great Slave Lake, *maps* C-72, 98

Liatris, or **blazing star,** a genus of perennial plants of the composite family, native to North America. Tall wandlike flower spikes, purple or white, rise from clusters of narrow, ribbed leaves. Also called gayfeather and button snakeroot.

Libby, W(illard) F(rank) (1908–80), chemist, born Grand Valley, Colo.; professor of chemistry Institute for Nuclear Studies, University of Chicago, 1945–54; member of Atomic Energy Commission 1954–59; professor of chemistry University of California at Los Angeles 1959–80, A-535, M-73, *picture* C-464

Libby Prison, prison for captured Union officers at Richmond, Va., hastily established in Libby and Son's tobacco warehouse during Civil War; moved to Chicago 1889 and became the Libby Prison Museum; razed 1899; Libby Prison bricks used in North Wall of Civil War Room in Chicago Historical Society building.

Libel, in law, *table* L-93

Liberal, Kan., city in s.w. near Oklahoma boundary; pop. 13,789; trade center in agricultural region; oil, natural gas; food products, aircraft; incorporated 1888; International Pancake Race.

Liberal arts U-204–5
history U-209, E-80, 81
Morrill Act, *table* E-92
Russia lacks R-332d

Liberal-Country Coalition, political party, Australia A-816

Liberalism, political viewpoint L-146

Liberal party (Canada) C-112c, g
Brown C-112b
King K-243
Pearson P-150
St. Laurent S-18
Trudeau T-272

Liberal party, or **Whig party** (Great Britain), P-434, E-245, V-313. *see also in index* Whig party (England)
Churchill C-339
conference, *picture* U-17
Gladstone G-133–4
Irish question G-134
Melbourne V-312
prime ministers, *table* G-199a
reforms E-246, 247–8
Russell R-319

Liberal Republican party (U.S.), formed 1872 by Republicans opposed to political abuses under President Grant; nominated candidates 1872 and 1876
Greeley G-236
Schurz a leader G-173

Liberals, or **progressives,** in education E-74, 85, 89, 91, 93, 95, 97, D-98, M-474, *tables* E-76–7, 90

Liberal Unionist party (Great Britain) C-204a

'Liberator', abolitionist paper A-10, A-291, G-34, 35, *picture,* M-153

Liberec, or **Reichenberg,** Czechoslovakia, city in n. Bohemia; pop. 66,365; founded in 13th century; development began when first textile factory was established in 1823.

Liberia, republic on w. coast of Africa; 43,000 sq mi (111,400 sq km); pop. 1,990,000; cap. Monrovia L-146
Africa's independence A-111
anti-slavery movement A-10
flag, *picture* F-166
money, *table* M-428
national anthem, *table* N-52
Peace Corps, *picture* P-143a
political assassination A-704
railroad mileage, *table* R-85
ship tonnage, *table* S-176a

Liberty, Mo., city 13 mi (21 km) n.e. of Kansas City; pop. 16,251; corn, wheat, tobacco; William Jewell College, *map* M-408

Liberty. *see also in index* Freedom; Freedom of speech; Freedom of the press; Religious liberty
Christian doctrine W-247
democracy D-82, W-245
Henry, Patrick H-140
Magna Carta M-45, D-84
Mill, John Stuart, on E-269
Western liberal traditions W-245, 248

'Liberty', sloop belonging to John Hancock H-16

Liberty, Statue of, in New York Harbor L-148, *map* N-271, *pictures* N-263, U-115, U-28
Statue of Liberty N. Mon. N-45, *map* N-30

Liberty Bell D-53, U-115, *pictures* D-52, U-115, P-178

Liberty bonds, United States, in World War W-262

Liberty cap, symbol of freedom; appears on Goddess of Liberty and on many coins and coats of arms H-47

Liberty Island, or **Bedloe's Island,** in New York Harbor, site of Statue of Liberty, *map* N-271. *see also in index* Liberty, Statue of

Liberty Memorial, monument, Kansas City, Mo., *picture* K-188

Liberty party, United States, founded 1839 to oppose slavery; ran James Gillespie Birney for U.S. president 1840 and 1844; joined Free-Soil party 1848, C-373, P-433
presidential vote (1844), *table* P-495a

Liberty Tunnel, at Pittsburgh, Pa., *table* T-292

Libido, in psychology J-152

Libra, unit of weight W-94

Libra, or **Balance,** or **Scales,** a constellation, *charts* S-419
zodiac Z-356, *chart* A-708

Librarian L-149
Middle Ages B-350
reference R-122
vocations V-366, *picture* V-367

Library L-149. *see also in index* Books and bookmaking; Reading for recreation; Storytelling
Africa, *picture* G-121
Australia
Melbourne M-217b
Sydney S-549a
book preservation A-149
Canada C-91
children's literature L-249, *picture* L-248
books R-105, H-182, S-478
home R-101d
storytelling S-461
China T-283, *picture* P-154
England S-140, *pictures* O-515
Germany G-112b
history
Franklin starts F-381
Hittites H-179
Middle Ages M-446
Renaissance R-146
Rome S-212
Italy
Vatican R-254
Mexico, *picture* M-250
microforms M-288
newspaper N-230
Poland C-599
reference books R-122
Russia R-334b
scientific research, *picture* S-59c
state and provincial N-246
United States U-121
Brown University P-516
Carnegie C-138, S-461, *picture* H-40
Chicago, *list* C-260, *map* C-261
City College, *picture* C-433
Cleveland C-390b, S-461
Cornell University *picture* N-247
Delaware, University of, *picture* D-73
Eisenhower, Abilene, Kan. E-137
F.D. Roosevelt, Hyde Park, N.Y., *picture* R-279
Folger Shakespeare, Washington, D.C. S-140. *map* W-32
Hammarskjold, N.Y., N.Y. U-22
Hoover, Calif. and Iowa H-224
Howard University, *pictures* U-208
Library of Hawaii, *picture* H-58
Mount Angel Abbey, Ore., *picture* D-93b
Nebraska at Lincoln, University of, *picture* N-115
Newark, N.J. N-160; reading room, *picture* R-122
New Bedford, Mass. N-160
New Orleans, *picture* N-225
New York Public Library N-270, R-122, *map* N-264, R-123
Oklahoma, University of, *picture* O-441
Peterborough, N.H. N-173
Philadelphia P-251, *map* P-251b, *picture* R-131; Library Company of Philadelphia, *list* P-251d
Pittsburgh S-461, *picture* S-329
San Antonio C-350
South Dakota, University of, *picture* S-329
Tennessee, University of, *picture* T-122

Texas, University of, *picture* T-122

Truman, Independence, Mo. T-280, *picture* M-404

Vermont, University of, *picture* V-293

Washington, University of, *picture* W-47

Wayne State University, *picture* D-96d

Library Company of Philadelphia
Library Hall, *list* P-251d

Library of Congress, Washington, D.C., W-31, 33, *picture* W-31
building, *map* W-32
historic buildings N-27
Jefferson collection J-95

Library of Congress classification, in library science L-156, *diagram* L-157

Library of Parliament, Ottawa, Ont., Canada, O-507

Library science L-168

Libration, in astronomy, an apparent slow balancing movement of a heavenly body on each side of its mean position
moon M-482

Libretto, *table* M-566a

Libreville, Gabon, capital and seaport, on Gulf of Guinea; pop. 57,000; Roman Catholic mission established here 1843; city settled 1849 by blacks from slave ship; site of British and Free French occupation 1940.

Libya, or **Libia,** republic in n. Africa; 679,360 sq mi (1,759,530 sq km); pop. 3,425,000; cap. Tripoli L-188, *map* P-212
earthquakes (1963) E-32
flag, *picture* F-166
money, *table* M-428
railroad mileage, *table* R-85
Sahara S-14, *map* S-15, *picture* S-16
temperature record, *list* W-88
World War II W-271

Libyan Desert, part of the Sahara in Egypt and Libya extending from the Mediterranean to the Sudan, *maps* E-109, D-93
Libyan Erg S-15

Lice. *see in index* Louse

License
dog, *list* D-137
driver S-5
hunting H-279
logging operations Q-9d, O-456e
marriage M-114
merchant ships S-176a, 174
osteopath O-505d
pharmacist P-248a
physician M-212c, a
practical nurse L-383
radio amateurs R-55
radio set owners R-54
radio stations R-53
taxation, form of T-32
teacher E-100a, 100

Lichen L-191, P-370, *pictures* A-474
agent in soil formation S-251
fungi and F-449
Mars supports A-717

Lichfield, England, city in Staffordshire, 25 km (15 mi) n. of Birmingham; pop. 22,930, *map, inset* G-199g

Lichtenstein, Roy (born 1923), artist, born New York, N.Y.; used old-West theme in early paintings; pioneered pop-art movement of 1960's, L-192
painting P-67, *picture* P-69

Licinian laws, six laws of ancient Rome passed 367 B.C. in tribuneship of Gaius Licinius; practically ended the struggle between patricians and plebeians R-244

Licinius (250?–324), Roman emperor 307–323; defeated

Maximinus and became sole ruler in East; married Constantine's half-sister; executed for treason.

Lick, James (1796–1876), philanthropist, born Fredericksburg, Pa.; established Lick Observatory in California; buried in vault under its large telescope.

Licking River, rises in Cumberland Mountains in e. Kentucky and flows n.w. 220 mi (350 km) to Ohio River.

Lick Observatory, California O-392

Licorice, plant; juice used to make licorice candy L-192
Iraq grows I-313

Lictor, official attendant of magistrates in ancient Rome; a dictator had 24 lictors; a consul 12, a propraetor 6, a praetor 2.

Licuri. *see in index* Ouricury

Liddell, Henry George (1811–98), English clergyman, born Binchester, near Bishop Auckland, England; with R. A. Scott prepared 'Greek Lexicon' (1843), still used; dean of Christ Church College, Oxford University, England, 1855–91; his daughter Alice was original of 'Alice in Wonderland'.

Lido, Venice, Italy V-278

Lie, Jonas (1833–1908), Norwegian novelist, born Modum, near Drammen, Norway; friend of Ibsen; insight into character is softened by humor and sympathy ('The Visionary'; 'The Commodore's Daughter'; 'Niobe'; 'The Pilot and His Wife').

Lie, Trygve (1896–1968), Norwegian statesman, born Oslo; legal adviser to Labor party 18 years; minister of foreign affairs 1941–46; secretary-general of the United Nations 1946–53; governor of Oslo and Akershus 1955–63; author of 'In the Cause of Peace' U-22, 24, *picture* U-25

Liebermann, Max (1847–1935), German painter, born Berlin; an exponent of impressionist school in Germany; ('Jesus Among the Scribes'; 'Spinners'; also landscapes and portraits).

Liebig, Justus von (1803–73), German chemist and teacher L-192
mirrors P-370

Liebknecht, Karl (1871–1919), German Socialist leader; son of Wilhelm Liebknecht, friend of Marx and Engels; only member of Reichstag to oppose World War I; shot by soldiers while on his way to prison after Spartacan uprising
Luxemburg, Rosa L-341
Spartacans S-370

Liebknecht, Wilhelm (1826–1900), German socialist and journalist, born Giessen, Germany; father of Karl Liebknecht; with August Bebel helped form German Social Democratic party; writing had great influence S-234

Liebman, Joshua Loth (1907–48), rabbi and writer, born Hamilton, Ohio; rabbi of K.A.M. Temple, Chicago, Ill., 1934–39; rabbi of Temple Israel, Boston, Mass., 1939–48 ('Peace of Mind').

Liechtenstein, principality of Europe on upper Rhine; borders Switzerland s. of Lake Constance; cap. Vaduz; area 158 sq km (61 sq mi); pop. 26,200; L-193, *Fact Summary* E-328, *maps* S-537, E-334
flag, *picture* F-166
money, *table* M-428
national anthem, *table* N-52

Lied, plural **lieder** (from German for "song"), German art song M-558
Mahler M-50
Schubert S-54, 55
Schumann S-55
Wolf M-561

Liège, Belgium, city on Meuse River; pop. 216,604, L-193, *maps* E-334, W-252
Charles the Bold takes C-218

Liegnitz. *see in index* Legnica

Liepaja, or **Lepaya,** Latvian S.S.R., Baltic port, railroad terminus, and manufacturing city; pop. 71,464; ice-free artificial harbor; large export trade; metal-working; maps R-344, 348
Latvia L-83

Lien, in law, *table* L-93

Lieutenant
Canadian Armed Forces, *table* C-100f
U.S. Air Force insignia, *picture* U-8
U.S. Army A-634, *picture* U-8
U.S. Marine Corps insignia, *picture* U-8
U.S. Navy, *table* N-96, *picture* U-8

Lieutenant, junior grade, U.S. Navy
insignia, *picture* U-8

Lieutenant colonel
Canadian Armed Forces, *table* C-100f
U.S. Air Force insignia, *picture* U-8
U.S. Army A-634, *picture* U-8
U.S. Marine Corps insignia, *picture* U-8

Lieutenant commander, in U.S. Navy, *table* N-96
insignia, *picture* U-8

Lieutenant general
Canadian Armed Forces C-100a, c, *table* C-100f
U.S. Air Force insignia, *picture* U-8
U.S. Army A-634, insignia, *picture* U-8
U.S. Marine Corps insignia, *picture* U-8

Lieutenant governor, an officer authorized to perform the duties of a governor during his absence or to take his place if he dies or resigns.

Life. *see in index* Living things

Lifeboat S-177e

Life buoy, or **life preserver,** lifesaving equipment K-190

Life community, in ecology E-46

Life expectancy H-93

Life in many lands P-190–6, *pictures* P-190–6, *Reference-Outline* P-195–6

Life insurance I-234, *chart* I-233
trusts T-282
veterans
Canada C-308
U.S., *table* V-307

'Life of an Amorous Man, The', or 'Koshoku ichidai otoko', novel by Saikaku Ihara J-81

'Life of Samuel Johnson LL.D., The', biography by Boswell B-376
biography B-223
Johnson, Samuel J-136

'Life of Reason', work by Santayana L-242

'Life on the Mississippi', work by Twain A-352

Life preserver, or **life buoy,** lifesaving equipment K-190

Lifesaving, training in emergency medical service for nonprofessional personnel. *see also in index* First aid; Safety devices and measures
Australia A-789

Canada C-100c, *picture* C-100d

Coast Guard C-420a, *picture* C-420b
drowning person S-535
first aid techniques F-115
helicopters, *pictures* H-241a, P-429
MERVAN unit, *picture* H-241c
police P-425, 428
quicksand Q-17
radio used in M-106, R-56
Red Cross R-118
St. Bernards D-140, *picture* D-146

'Life Studies', work by Lowell L-326
American literature A-364

Life support system
bioengineering B-210
first aid F-116

Life zones, or **zoogeographical regions** Z-365
North America N-311
plants, distribution of P-363f, *picture* P-363f

Liffey River, Ireland, 110-kilometer (70-mile)-long stream rising s. of Dublin and flowing w., n., and e. into Dublin Bay, *map* G-199h
Dublin on D-201, *picture* D-201

Lift, in aviation
airplanes A-175
gliders G-144a

Lift bridge, vertical, *picture* M-348

Lifting by one's bootstraps M-209

Ligament (from Latin *ligare*, "to bind"), a tough, fibrous band which connects bones or supports viscera
bones B-342
joints J-137
skeleton S-210

Ligases, enzymes E-281

Ligature, surgical thread used for tying blood vessels; may be absorbable (as catgut) or nonabsorbable (as silk, cotton, nylon, and fine steel wire).

Liggett, Hunter (1857–1935), U.S. Army officer, born Reading, Pa.; in World War I commanded 1st Army, A.E.F. ('Commanding an American Army'; 'Recollections of the World War').

Light, Col. William, South Australian surveyor general A-41

Light L-194. *see also in index* Electric lighting; Gas, for heating and lighting; Lamp; Lighting; and chief topics below
astronomy A-710
black hole B-306
solar system S-254
sun S-512
twilight and dawn T-311
binoculars F-79
circadian rhythm B-226
color C-443, 447, 452, *chart* C-444, *diagrams* C-450–1
diamonds D-100
energy E-206, 211
eye, action on E-366
fibers transmit F-71
glow in electron tubes E-170
illusions caused by I-54
interior design I-243
laser and maser L-54, *picture* L-55
lighting L-205
matter M-169, *diagrams* M-170
microscope uses M-290
mirage M-370
mirrors reflect M-371
phosphorescence P-270
photoelectric devices P-273, *pictures* P-274
photography P-282
cameras P-284
darkroom techniques P-291
photosensitization P-408
physics P-306

polarimeter Q-6, *picture* Q-3
radiation R-33, 37, *table* R-34
rainbow R-88
relativity theories R-140
science history, *picture* S-57g
Einstein E-126
ether theory E-292
Kepler K-228
Michelson M-267
Newton N-234
selenium affected by S-108
solid state physics S-254g
spectrum and spectroscope S-371, *picture* S-372
spectrum of hydrogen N-377c
stereopticon S-443, *pictures* S-444

Light bulb L-205
Edison, Thomas E-72
tungsten filaments T-288

Lighter-than-air craft. *see in index* Airship; Balloon

Light heavyweight, in boxing B-388

Light-Horse Harry. *see in index* Lee, Light-Horse Harry

Lighthouse L-204
ancient, *picture* C-491
Baltimore, *picture* C-420b
Cape Hatteras, N.C., *picture* N-327
Fenwick Island, Del., *picture* D-74
Genoa, Italy, *picture* G-45
Grand Manan Island, *picture* N-162e
light cycle N-86
Marblehead Lighthouse, Ohio, *picture* O-425
Minot's Ledge L-270
Montauk Point, *picture* N-254
nuclear, *picture* C-420b
Pharos of Alexandria S-116
Portland Head Light, Maine, *picture* M-51
Prince Edward Island, *picture* P-497b
Roman ruins at Dover D-164f
Split Rock, Minn., *picture* M-348

'Light in August', work by Faulkner A-360

Lighting L-205. *see also in index* Lamp; Light
airport A-212, *pictures* A-213
aquarium A-515
automobile A-845
electricity E-138
electric light E-157
gas G-38, *picture* M-455
healthful practices H-89
lighthouse L-204
motion pictures M-511, *picture* M-512
photography P-288, *diagram* P-289, *pictures* P-282, 287, 289
pioneer America P-333
sculpture affected by S-80
sodium vapor S-247
solar power S-516
stage T-153, 154
stereopticon S-443, *pictures* S-444
stroboscopic light C-200

Light meter, for photography P-288–9, *diagram* P-289
motion pictures M-511

Lightner Museum of Hobbies, deeded in trust to the city of St. Augustine, Fla., 1947 by Otto C. Lightner (1887–1950), founder-publisher of *Hobbies* magazine, born Norwich, Kan.; museum houses thousands of varied collections from all over the world, including cut glass, metal matchboxes, chandeliers, old musical instruments, and costumes; opened to public 1948.

Lightning L-207
accident prevention S-12
artificial, *picture* P-301
burn cause B-511
electricity E-138, 153
evolution role, *diagram* E-344
forest fires F-314
Franklin's experiment F-382
nitrogen fixation N-291
sound waves S-259
Thor's hammer T-165

Lion / Little Belt

chemicals, footwear, textiles, tobacco products A-826, *maps* D-32, E-334
Lion, animal L-231
cat family C-154a
circus, *pictures* C-346, 351
critical zone, *picture* A-444
distinguished from tiger T-176
food in captivity Z-361d
heraldic device H-142
taxidermy, *pictures* T-36
zoo animal, *picture* Z-358
Lion, or **Leo,** in astronomy. *see in index* Leo
'Lion and the Mouse, The', story by Aesop F-3
Lion dance
Watusi, *picture* D-18
'Lion in Winter, The', play by James Goldman, *picture* T-148
'Lion of Lucerne', sculpture by Thorvaldsen T-166, *picture* T-166
Lion of the North, name sometimes given to Gustavus II, Adolphus, of Sweden; military genius whose forces swept south to save Protestantism in Germany in 1631 and 1632.
Lion Rock Tunnel, in Hong Kong, *table* T-292
Lions, Court of, in Alhambra, *picture* S-358
Lions, Gulf of, wide bay of Mediterranean washing most of s. coast of France, *map* E-334
Lions Clubs International, association founded 1917; more than 995,000 businessmen in over 26,000 clubs in 148 countries; a Lions Club has 11 standing activities: agriculture, boys and girls, citizenship, civic improvement and community betterment, education, health, safety, sight saving and work for blind, work for deaf, international relations, youth exchange; headquarters, Chicago, Ill. F-387
Lions Gate Bridge, over Burrard Inlet, Vancouver, B.C., Canada, *map* V-264, *picture* V-263
Lion's paw (*Pecten nodosus*), clam shell, *picture* S-150
Lion-tailed macaque, a monkey, *picture* M-441
Lipari Islands, or **Aeolian Islands,** Italy, group of volcanic islands in Mediterranean n. of Sicily; 116 sq km (45 sq mi); pop. 11,037; largest Lipari; fruit, olives, pumice stone.
Lipase, an enzyme D-117, E-281, *table* E-281
Lipchitz, Jacques (1891–1973), American sculptor, born near Grodno, present Lithuania; to U.S. 1941, became citizen 1958; early work influenced by cubists L-232
sculpture S-92, *picture* S-93
Lipides, a class of compounds P-312
Lipizzan, or **Lippizan,** horse H-234a, *pictures* H-232i, H-275, *table* H-232f
Lipkind, William (1904–74), pen name Will, anthropologist and author, born New York City; spent 1938–40 in wilds of central Brazil studying Caraja Indians; wrote children's books illustrated by Nicolas Mordvinoff: 'The Two Reds', 'Finders Keepers' (1952 Newbery Medal), 'Circus Ruckus', 'Perry the Imp', 'Four-Leaf Clover' R-108
'Finders Keepers' D-154c
Lipmann, Fritz Albert (born 1899), American biochemist, born Königsberg, Germany (now Kaliningrad, Russia); became U.S. citizen 1944; professor of biological chemistry Harvard University medical school 1949–57; professor Rockefeller University 1957–.
Li Po, or **Li T'ai-po,** (701–62), Chinese poet; wrote of love, wine, and beauties of nature; supposedly drowned kissing the moon's reflection L-232
Lipotropic hormone (LPH) H-225, *table* H-226
Lippe, former state in w. Germany; 1,215 sq km (469 sq mi); after World War II became part of state of North Rhine-Westphalia.
Lippershey, Hans (died 1619), Dutch spectaclemaker, traditionally credited with inventing the telescope 1608, T-62, P-306
Lippi, Filippino (1457?–1504), Italian painter, born Prato, near Florence; son of Fra Filippo Lippi; pupil of Botticelli; masterpieces include 'Vision of Saint Bernard' and 'The Adoration of the Magi', both at Florence.
Lippi, Fra Filippo (1406–69), Italian painter, born Florence; father of Filippino Lippi; probably the greatest colorist of his day; his pictures reveal a strong, naive nature, with a lively and somewhat whimsical observation L-233
Botticelli a pupil B-383
Lippmann, Gabriel (1845–1921), French physicist, born Hollerich, Luxemburg.
Lippmann, Walter (1889–1974), writer, editor, and social philosopher; born New York City; studied at Harvard University under George Santayana and William James; one of founders of *New Republic;* editor *New York World* 1929–31; editorial writer *New York Herald Tribune* 1931–62; syndicated by *Los Angeles Times* and *Washington Post* 1963–69; Pulitzer awards 1958 and 1962; Presidential Medal of Freedom 1964 ('Public Opinion'; 'U.S. Foreign Policy'; 'Essays in the Public Philosophy').
Lippold, Richard (born 1915), sculptor, born Milwaukee, Wis.; professor of art Hunter College 1952–67; commissioned sculpture for architects, Metropolitan Museum of Art, Lincoln Center for the Performing Arts.
Lip reading, aid to deaf D-41b
Lips, *diagrams* T-197
cancer T-190a
speech C-552, V-279
Lipscomb, William N., Jr. (born 1919), chemist, born Cleveland, Ohio; faculty University of Minnesota 1946–59, professor 1954–59; professor Harvard University 1959–; research in chemical bonding of boranes.
Lipstick, cosmetic
color classification C-446
stain removal D-200f
Lipton, Sir Thomas (1850–1931), British merchant and yachtsman, born Glasgow, Scotland; son of poor Irish parents; made start by advertising small provision store; developed business until he amassed great wealth and owned large tea, coffee, and cocoa plantations; also known for yachts (*Shamrock*) entered in America's Cup races.
Liquefaction, of gases G-37
chlorine C-320
cryogenics C-620a, *diagram* C-620b
LP-Gas G-41
nitrogen, *diagram* N-292
Liquefied natural gas (LNG), fuel F-441
Liquefied petroleum gas. *see in index* LP-Gas
Liqueur A-276, L-235
Liquid, in physics. *see also in index* liquids by name, as Gasoline
apparent solids S-254f
boiling point W-68
capillarity C-130b
colloids C-434, *pictures* C-435–7, *table* C-435
crystals C-621
density determined H-288
dew formation D-97
distillation D-132, *diagram* D-132a
emulsions C-435
evaporation E-342
freezing M-167
liquid crystals L-234
liquid-vapor equilibrium C-241
melting M-167
mixtures explained S-256
molecules in, *diagram* M-167
osmosis P-359
siphon S-205, *picture* S-206
sound conductor S-259, *graph* S-260
superfluidity C-620b
surface tension M-167
waves W-81
wetting agents S-231–2
Liquid air, *diagram* N-292
Liquidambar (*Hamamelidaceae*), deciduous trees of witch-hazel family; native to Asia and America; small flowers; spiny, round fruit filled with encapsulated seeds, many of them unsound. *see also in index* Red gum
Liquid crystals, in physics L-234
Liquid Fuels Act, Synthetic (1944), United States P-230
Liquid helium C-620a, b, *diagram* C-620a
Liquid-hydrogen N-377e
Liquid measure, *tables* W-96, 97
Liquid nitrogen C-620a
carbon dating, *picture* C-132
Liquid oxygen, or **lox,** oxygen condensed to a bluish liquid, *diagram* C-620a
explosives E-361
rocket propellant S-342a, 346d, *diagram* R-232
Liquid-propellant rocket J-110, *diagram* J-107
Liquor industry L-234. *see also in index* Alcoholic beverages
Liquor laws
Prohibition P-506
Roosevelt, F.D. R-269
temperance movement T-76
Lira, plural **lire,** (from Latin *libra,* "pound"), monetary unit of Italy and Turkey; historic value of Italian coin 5¼ cents; at one time worth 19.3 cents; name also applied to Turkish gold 100-piaster piece, historic value about $7.45; Turkish lira often called pound, *table* M-428
Liripipe, a headdress D-190
hats and caps H-47
Lisa, Manuel (1772–1820), fur trader, born New Orleans; led first important expedition up the Missouri 1807 and built Fort Manuel at mouth of Bighorn River; with Andrew Henry, Jean Pierre Chouteau, and others founded Missouri Fur Company (1808–9) and built Fort Lisa near mouth of Big Knife River in North Dakota; erected Fort Manuel in n. South Dakota 1812; traveled up and down Missouri at least 12 times
fur trade F-471
South Dakota S-326
Lisboa, Antônio Francisco, or **Aleijadinho** (1730–1814), Brazilian sculptor; crippled, he worked with tools fastened to his arms B-418
Lisbon, or **Lisboa,** Portugal, capital; pop. 812,400, L-238, P-454, 457, *maps* P-455, S-350, E-334, *picture* P-457
cables C-8, *map* C-5
climate P-455, *graph* P-457b
Columbus in C-475
earthquake (1755) E-32
flood, *table* F-181
Lisgar, John Young, Baron (1807–76), English statesman, born Bombay, India; chief secretary for Ireland, lord high commissioner of Ionian Islands, and governor of New South Wales, Australia; governor-general of Canada 1869–72.
Lisle, Leconte de. *see in index* Leconte de Lisle
Lisle, Rouget de. *see in index* Rouget de Lisle
Lisle, a hard, twisted thread originally of linen, now often of specially prepared cotton.
Lisping, in speech C-269
Listening, a learning tool C-496, 495, *picture* C-496
spelling S-376, *picture* S-375
'Listen to Living', painting by Matta P-67d, *picture* P-67d
Lister, Joseph (1827–1912), English surgeon, born Upton, Essex; developed antiseptic surgery; first to use various instruments and to try a number of new operations L-238
medicine contribution M-215c
Listing, in agriculture C-542
Liston, Charles (Sonny) (1932–70), boxer, born Pine Bluff, Ark.
Ali dispute A-306
heavyweight champion B-392, *table* B-391
Lists, in medieval tournament K-258
List system, of voting. *see in index* Proportional representation
Liszt, Franz (1811–86), Hungarian composer L-239
music M-559
piano style P-318
Li T'ai-po. *see in index* Li Po
Litani River, Lebanon L-111
Litany, liturgical prayers in which the clergy leads and the choir or congregation responds (from Latin *litania,* "a prayer"); used in Catholic and in Episcopal and some other Protestant churches.
Litchfield, Conn., borough 23 mi (37 km) w. of Hartford; pop. 1,489; birthplace of Harriet Beecher Stowe, Henry Ward Beecher, and Ethan Allen; first school of law (1784), *map* C-532, *picture* C-519
law school, *picture* C-525
temperance society T-76
Litchi, or **lichee,** or **leechee,** a Chinese tree (*Litchi chinensis*) having leathery pinnate leaves and delicious strawberrylike fruit; also grown in southern Vietnam and Malay Archipelago N-385
Liter, unit in metric system (1.0567 liquid qts.) W-95
conversion equivalents, *table* W-97
Literacy and illiteracy I-239
adult education A-53
American Colonies A-342
India I-72
Latin America L-63
population P-450
Russia E-99
Literacy tests P-450, S-505
Literary agent B-363
Literary awards L-240. *see also tables* following
Literature L-242. *see also in index* Books and bookmaking; Reading for recreation; *also* by languages, e.g. English literature, Latin literature; also chief topics listed below and individual writers by name
art forms A-662
Arthurian legends A-655
autobiography A-831
biography B-222
Buddhist B-484
children's L-245
conversations as C-550
diary D-104
drama D-169
Egypt, ancient E-125
essay E-289
folklore and folktale F-259
humor H-270
magazines M-33
Middle Ages N-375
mythology M-579
naturalism N-376
Northmen N-361
novel N-375
poetry P-403
realism N-376
Renaissance R-145
romance R-239, N-375
romanticism N-376
short story S-183
storytelling S-460
Literature for children L-245
Caldecott, Randolph C-26
Carroll, Lewis C-141
classics retold S-140
educational, *pictures* E-84, 89, 93
hobby books H-182–95
literary awards L-240. *see also tables* following
McGuffey's readers M-8
myths M-579
nature study books N-80
Newbery, John N-161
nursery rhymes N-381a
reading R-104–11e
storytelling S-460, 465
Litharge, or **lead monoxide** L-99
Lithium (Li), an alkali chemical element A-307, *tables* M-229, P-207, C-236
chloride V-255
electrochemical activity E-167
ore M-336
photosensitivity P-274
spectrum, *diagram* S-372
stability R-67
structure, *diagram* C-235
Lithography L-258
cartooning increased C-145c
Currier and Ives prints C-631
photolithography P-277, *pictures* P-278
printing P-500
Lithosphere, the solid body of the earth E-17, *picture* A-749
Lithuanian Soviet Socialist Republic, Russia, area 65,000 sq km (25,100 sq mi); pop. 3,398,000; cap. Vilna L-259, U-14, *maps* R-325, 344, 348–9
Polish history P-413
stamp, *picture* S-409
Litmus, purplish coloring matter; used as an acid-base indicator; turns red in acid, blue in alkali solution Q-6
Litterae humaniores R-146
Little, Arthur Dehon (1863–1935), chemical engineer, born Boston, Mass.; expert on papermaking.
Little America, Admiral Byrd's base in Antarctica B-532, P-423, *map* W-242, *picture* P-418
Little Bear, or **Ursa Minor,** a constellation, *charts* S-416, 419, 422, D-123
Little Belt, strait between Fyn Island and mainland of Denmark D-89, *map* D-91
Baltic Sea B-46
Little Belt Mountains, range of Rocky Mountains, in Lewis and Clark National Forest, Montana, *map* M-460

Little Bighorn River, in s. Montana, flows n. across Crow Indian Reservation for 60 mi (100 km) to Bighorn River, *map* M-471

scene of Custer massacre C-631, *pictures* M-463, 467

Little blue heron H-147

'Little Brown Church in the Vale, The', hymn written 1857 by William S. Pitts, inspired by valley at Bradford, Iowa, *picture* I-293

"Little Church Around the Corner," Church of the Transfiguration (Episcopal), in New York City on 29th St.; founded 1848 by George Hendric Houghton (1820–97); rector 1849–97; received nickname, 1870, when Joseph Jefferson, arranging funeral for an actor friend, was turned away from one church and advised, "There's a little church around the corner that might accommodate you"; nickname persisted and church remained a favorite with theatrical people, *map* N-264

Little Colorado, or **Colorado Chiquito,** river in Arizona, a tributary of Colorado River C-470, *maps* C-470, U-81

Little Corporal, Napoleon N-10

Little Diomede Island. *see in index* Diomede Islands

Little Dipper, seven stars corresponding to constellation Little Bear; tip of handle is North Star. *see also in index* Little Bear

Little Dog, or **Canis Minor,** a constellation, *charts* S-415, 421, 423

'Little Dorrit', novel by Charles Dickens; Little Dorrit is born, brought up, and wed in the prison where her father was confined for debt D-107

Little Entente, alliance between Czechoslovakia, Yugoslavia and Rumania E-322, 323, Y-351

Little Falls, Minn., city on Mississippi River 30 mi (50 km) n.w. of St. Cloud; pop. 7,250; paper, garments, boats; granite quarry nearby, *map* M-363

Little Falls, N.J., 5 mi (8 km) s.w. of Paterson on Passaic River; pop. of township 11,496; ornamental iron, carpets, scissors, *map* N-202

Little Falls, N.Y., manufacturing city on Mohawk River and Barge Canal 18 mi (29 km) e. of Utica; pop. 6,156; waterpower from cascades in river; food-processing equipment, food products, bicycles, footwear, textile products, paper; Gen. Nicholas Herkimer's grave nearby, *map* N-261

Littlefield, Catherine (1908–1951), ballet dancer and choreographer, born Philadelphia, Pa.; première danseuse Philadelphia Grand Opera Co. 1926–33; founded Littlefield Ballet 1935; created several ballets on American themes: 'Barn Dance' and 'Terminal'; restaged 'The Fairy Doll', 'Daphnis and Chloe'.

Little fox mitre (*Mitra vulpecula*), mollusk shell, *picture* S-152

"Little Jack Horner," nursery rhyme N-381a

Little John, a member of Robin Hood's band of outlaws R-225

Little Kanawha River, in West Virginia. *see in index* Kanawha

Little Khingan Mountains, in n.e. part of People's Republic of China; continuation of Great Khingan Mountains; in Heilungkiang Province w. of Amur R.; highest point about 4,665 ft (1,422 m), *map* M-84

Little League, in baseball B-94, *picture* B-96

game, *pictures* H-195, V-239, P-179

'Little Lord Fauntleroy', story by Mrs. Frances Hodgson Burnett of the seven-year-old Little Lord Fauntleroy whose curls and velvet suits set a fashion for small boys.

Little Magician, one of the nicknames of Martin Van Buren V-261

Little Maginot Line, wall, Czechoslovakia F-320

'Little Mermaid', statue C-566, *picture* D-90

Little Miami River, in Ohio, tributary of Ohio River; 140 mi (225 km) long, *map* O-429

'Little Minister, The', novel by Sir James Barrie; Babbie, daughter of a village squire, in the guise of a gypsy, wins the love of Gavin Dishart, the little minister; background of Scottish village life.

Little Missouri River, tributary of the Missouri, rising in Wyoming and flowing 450 mi (720 km) through Montana and North and South Dakota, *maps* N-340, U-40

Bad Lands, *picture* N-341 Theodore Roosevelt N. Mem. P. N-45, *map* N-352, *pictures* N-348

'Little Murders', work by Feiffer A-363

Littleneck. *see in index* Hard-shelled clam

'Little Organum For the Theater, A', work by Brecht B-433

'Little Orphan Annie', comic strip C-145d, *picture* C-145b

Little Pee Dee River, tributary of Pee Dee in e. South Carolina, *map* S-319

'Little Pretty Pocket Book, A', child's book published by John Newbery N-161

'Little Red Lighthouse and the Great Grey Bridge, The', book by Hildegarde Hoyt Swift L-204

Little Rhody, popular name for Rhode Island R-180

Little River Turnpike, historical road in United States R-221

Little Rock, Ark., state capital; largest city of state; on Arkansas River; pop. 158,461, L-260, *map* U-41

Arkansas A-615, *picture* A-619

hospital, *picture* H-239

Little St. Bernard Pass, Alpine pass (2,190 m; 7,180 ft) in Italy s. of Mont Blanc; connects valleys of Dora Baltea and Isère, *map* S-537

Little Sisters of the Poor, founded in France 1840, extended to U.S. 1868; for relief and nursing M-448

Little spotted cat, *picture* C-154d

Little Steel formula, system of U.S. wage increases in smaller steel plants to cover 15 percent rise in living costs between Jan. 1, 1941, and May 1, 1942; adopted by War Labor Board July 1942 to stabilize wages in World War II.

Little theater, a theater in which an amateur group produces dramas T-148, 157

Littleton, Sir Thomas (1422–81), English judge and writer on law; 'Treatise on Tenures', dealing with English land laws of his day, is still used as an authority.

Littleton, Colo., town 8 mi (13 km) s. of Denver on South Platte River; pop. 26,466; missiles, light industry; oil research center, *map* C-467

Little Trianon, or **Petit Trianon,** palace at Versailles, France V-303

Little Turtle (1752?–1812), chief of Miami Indians, born near Fort Wayne, Ind.; kept his people from joining Tecumseh's confederacy I-89

'Little Women', novel by Louisa M. Alcott A-277, R-111c

Littoral nation, a nation with shorelines I-256

Littoral (tidal) zone, area along the shore between the high-tide and low-tide levels Atlantic Ocean A-745

Littoria, Italy. *see in index* Latina

Liturgical music, or **church music** M-555, 562, G-238

Liturgy (from Latin *liturgia*, meaning "a public service"), term applied to any or all of the services used in public worship; especially in Roman Catholic, Eastern Orthodox, and Episcopal churches.

Litvinov, Maxim Maximovich (1876–1951), Russian statesman, born Bialystok, Russia (now Poland); diplomatic agent in England after Bolshevik revolution; commissar for foreign affairs 1930–39; ambassador to the U.S. 1941–43; deputy commissar for foreign affairs March–Aug. 1946.

Liukiu Islands. *see in index* Ryukyu

Liu Shao-ch'i (1898?–1974), Chinese Communist party theorist, born Hunan Province, China: became chairman

LITERARY AWARDS
John Newbery Medal

Awarded	Author	Book
1922	Hendrik Willem Van Loon	The Story of Mankind
1923	Hugh Lofting	Voyages of Dr. Dolittle
1924	Charles B. Hawes	Dark Frigate
1925	Charles J. Finger	Tales from Silver Lands
1926	Arthur B. Chrisman	Shen of the Sea
1927	Will James	Smoky, the Cowhorse
1928	Dhan Gopal Mukerji	Gay-Neck
1929	Eric P. Kelly	The Trumpeter of Krakow
1930	Rachel Field	Hitty, Her First Hundred Years
1931	Elizabeth J. Coatsworth	The Cat Who Went to Heaven
1932	Laura A. Armer	Waterless Mountain
1933	Elizabeth F. Lewis	Young Fu of the Upper Yangtze
1934	Cornelia Meigs	Invincible Louisa
1935	Monica Shannon	Dobry
1936	Carol R. Brink	Caddie Woodlawn
1937	Ruth Sawyer	Roller Skates
1938	Kate Seredy	The White Stag
1939	Elizabeth Enright	Thimble Summer
1940	James Daugherty	Daniel Boone
1941	Armstrong Sperry	Call It Courage
1942	Walter D. Edmonds	The Matchlock Gun
1943	Elizabeth Janet Gray	Adam of the Road
1944	Esther Forbes	Johnny Tremain
1945	Robert Lawson	Rabbit Hill
1946	Lois Lenski	Strawberry Girl
1947	Carolyn S. Bailey	Miss Hickory
1948	William Pène Du Bois	The Twenty-One Balloons
1949	Marguerite Henry	King of the Wind
1950	Marguerite de Angeli	The Door in the Wall
1951	Elizabeth Yates	Amos Fortune: Free Man
1952	Eleanor Estes	Ginger Pye
1953	Ann Nolan Clark	Secret of the Andes
1954	Joseph Krumgold	. . . and now Miguel
1955	Meindert De Jong	The Wheel on the School
1956	Jean Lee Latham	Carry On, Mr. Bowditch
1957	Virginia Eggertsen Sorensen	Miracles on Maple Hill
1958	Harold Keith	Rifles for Watie
1959	Elizabeth George Speare	The Witch of Blackbird Pond
1960	Joseph Krumgold	Onion John
1961	Scott O'Dell	Island of the Blue Dolphins
1962	Elizabeth George Speare	The Bronze Bow
1963	Madeleine L'Engle	A Wrinkle in Time
1964	Emily Cheney Neville	It's Like This, Cat
1965	Maia Wojciechowska	Shadow of a Bull
1966	Elizabeth Borton de Treviño	I, Juan de Pareja
1967	Irene Hunt	Up a Road Slowly
1968	Elaine L. Konigsburg	From the Mixed-up Files of Mrs. Basil E. Frankweiler
1969	Lloyd Alexander	The High King
1970	William H. Armstrong	Sounder
1971	Betsy Byars	Summer of the Swans
1972	Robert C. O'Brien	Mrs. Frisby and the Rats of NIMH
1973	Jean C. George	Julie of the Wolves
1974	Paula Fox	The Slave Dancer
1975	Virginia Hamilton	M. C. Higgins, the Great
1976	Susan Cooper	The Grey King
1977	Mildred D. Taylor	Roll of Thunder, Hear My Cry
1978	Katherine Paterson	Bridge to Terabithia
1979	Ellen Raskin	The Westing Game
1980	Joan W. Blos	A Gathering of Days: a New England Girl's Journal, 1830–32
1981	Katherine Paterson	Jacob Have I Loved
1982	Nancy Willard	A Visit to William Blake's Inn
1983	Cynthia Boigt	Dicey's Song

LITERARY AWARDS
Caldecott Medal

Awarded	Artist	Book
1938	Dorothy P. Lathrop	Animals of the Bible (Text from King James Bible)
1939	Thomas Handforth	Mei Li
1940	Ingri M. and Edgar Parin d'Aulaire	Abraham Lincoln
1941	Robert Lawson	They Were Strong and Good
1942	Robert McCloskey	Make Way for Ducklings
1943	Virginia Lee Burton	The Little House
1944	Louis Slobodkin	Many Moons (Text by James Thurber)
1945	Elizabeth Orton Jones	Prayer for a Child (Text by Rachel Field)
1946	Maud and Miska Petersham	Rooster Crows
1947	Leonard Weisgard	The Little Island (Text by Golden MacDonald)
1948	Roger Duvoisin	White Snow, Bright Snow (Text by Alvin Tresselt)
1949	Berta and Elmer Hader	The Big Snow
1950	Leo Politi	Song of the Swallows
1951	Katherine Milhous	The Egg Tree
1952	Nicolas Mordvinoff	Finders Keepers (Text by William Lipkind)
1953	Lynd Ward	The Biggest Bear
1954	Ludwig Bemelmans	Madeline's Rescue
1955	Marcia Joan Brown	Cinderella
1956	Feodor Rojankovsky	Frog Went A-Courtin'
1957	Marc Simont	A Tree Is Nice
1958	Robert McCloskey	Time of Wonder
1959	Barbara Cooney	Chanticleer and the Fox
1960	Marie Hall Ets	Nine Days to Christmas
1961	Nicolas Sidjakov	Baboushka and the Three Kings
1962	Marcia Joan Brown	Once a Mouse
1963	Ezra Jack Keats	The Snowy Day
1964	Maurice Sendak	Where the Wild Things Are
1965	Beni Montresor	May I Bring a Friend?
1966	Nonny Hogrogian	Always Room for One More
1967	Evaline Ness	Sam, Bangs & Moonshine
1968	Ed Emberley	Drummer Hoff
1969	Uri Shulevitz	The Fool of the World and the Flying Ship
1970	William Steig	Sylvester and the Magic Pebble
1971	Gail E. Haley	A Story—A Story
1972	Nonny Hogrogian	One Fine Day
1973	Blair Lent	The Funny Little Woman
1974	Margot Zemach	Duffy and the Devil
1975	Gerald McDermott	Arrow to the Sun: a Pueblo Indian Tale
1976	Leo and Diane Dillon	Why Mosquitoes Buzz in People's Ears
1977	Leo and Diane Dillon	Ashanti to Zulu
1978	Peter Spier	Noah's Ark
1979	Paul Goble	The Girl Who Loved Wild Horses
1980	Barbara Cooney	Ox-Cart Man (Text by Donald Hall)
1981	Arnold Lobel	Fables
1982	Chris Van Allsburg	Jumanji
1983	Marcia Brown	Shadow

Regina Medal

1959	Eleanor Farjeon	1971	Tasha Tudor
1960	Anne Carroll Moore	1972	Meindert De Jong
1961	Padraic Colum	1973	Frances Clarke Sayers
1962	Frederic Gershom Melcher	1974	Robert McCloskey
1963	Ann Nolan Clark	1975	May McNeer and Lynd Ward
1964	May Hill Arbuthnot	1976	Virginia Haviland
1965	Ruth Sawyer	1977	Marcia Joan Brown
1966	Leo Politi	1978	Scott O'Dell
1967	Bertha Mahony Miller	1979	Morton Schindel
1968	Marguerite de Angeli	1980	Beverly Cleary
1969	Lois Lenski	1981	Augusta Baker
1970	Ingri and Edgar Parin d'Aulaire	1982	Theodor Seuss Geisel
		1983	Tonie De Paola

People's Republic of China 1959; expelled from Chinese Communist party 1969.

Live-forever, or houseleek, or **hen-and-chickens,** perennial plants of the family Crassulaceae; thick, succulent leaves, often in rosettes close to the ground; white, green, rose, or yellow star-shaped flowers.

Live oak, an evergreen oak O-387, 388
  state tree of Georgia, picture G-86

Liver, in human body L-261
  alcohol effects A-276
  anatomy A-391
  blood and B-314
  digestion D-117, diagrams D-114, 115
  hormones, table H-226
  poisoning A-254, M-226

Liver fluke W-298

Liverleaf. see in index Hepatica

Livermore, Mary Ashton Rice (1820–1905), reformer, early advocate of abolition of slavery, prohibition, and woman's suffrage; born Boston, Mass.; won reputation in Civil War as worker for Sanitary Commission.

Livermore, Calif., city 35 mi (55 km) s.e. of San Francisco; pop. 37,703; wine; nuclear research center; annual rodeo; incorporated as town 1876; as city 1930, map, inset C-52

Liverpool, England, seaport of Great Britain; on estuary of Mersey River; pop. 677,450, L-261, maps E-334, inset G-199g
  cathedral C-158
  Queensway Road Tunnel (Mersey Tunnel) T-291, table T-292
  wheat market W-134

Liverpool, N.S., Canada, port town 116 km (72 mi) s.w. of Halifax; pop. 3,607; fishing; papermaking, yeast manufacture; metal products, map N-373k

Liverpool, University of, Liverpool, England L-262

Liverpool and Manchester Railway, England, early railroad R-73
  Stephenson, George S-443

Liverpool Sound, or **Mersey Beat,** in popular music L-262

Liverwort L-262, P-370, pictures P-371, N-54b, 54i
  confused with mosses M-501

Livesay, Dorothy (born 1909), Canadian poet and journalist, born Winnipeg, Man. C-114

'Lives of the English Poets', biographies by Samuel Johnson B-222

Livestock. see also in index Animals, domestic; Breeding, animal; Dairying; Forage crops; Meat; Meat industry
  alligators and crocodiles A-311
  cattle C-161, pictures C-162, 165 to 168
  fair and exposition F-7
  farm machinery F-33
  goats G-146
  hogs H-196
  horses H-232
  improvements A-136
  India I-74
  injurious plants P-408
    weeds W-92
    yew Y-342
  poultry P-480
  reindeer R-139
  sheep S-146, picture S-147
  stock car, pictures R-82, W-257

Living, ways of
  people P-190, pictures P-191 to 194
  world W-238

Living costs
  hospital care H-241b
  inflation I-198
  statistics S-437, P-202
  Truman Administration T-280
  United States U-191

Livingston, Edward (1764–1836), lawyer and statesman, born Clermont, N.Y.; brother of Robert R. Livingston; served as congressman, U.S. senator, secretary of state under President Jackson, and minister to France 1833–35.

Livingston, Philip (1716–78), signer of Declaration of Independence, born Albany, N.Y.

Livingston, Robert R. (1746–1813), statesman, jurist, and experimental farmer; born New York City; brother of Edward Livingston; first chancellor New York State 1777–1801, secretary of foreign affairs 1781–83; minister to France 1801–5
  Declaration of Independence D-51, picture R-162
  defends Constitution U-142
  Fulton aided by F-447
  Statuary Hall, picture S-437b

Livingston, William (1723–90), lawyer, born Albany, N.Y.; attacked English Parliament's interference in provincial matters and Anglican domination of King's College; representative from New Jersey to 1st and 2d Continental Congress; signed United States Constitution; governor of New Jersey 1776–90, N-194

Livingston, Mont., city on Yellowstone River, 45 mi (70 km) n. of Yellowstone Park; pop. 6,994; hunting, fishing, resort area; livestock; timber; mobile homes; railroad shops, maps M-470, U-40

Livingston, N.J., urban township 9 mi (15 km) n.w. of Newark; near Passaic River; pop. 28,040; beverages, poultry, dairy products, map N-202

Livingstone, David (1813–73), Scottish missionary explorer of Africa L-263
  Stanley's search for S-410
  Victoria Falls V-315
  watermelons W-74

Livingstone College, at Salisbury, N.C.; affiliated with African Methodist Episcopal Zion church; chartered 1885; liberal arts, education and theology; graduate studies.

Livingstone Mountains, range in mainland Tanzania bordering n.e. shores of Lake Nyasa.

Livingston University, at Livingston, Ala.; state control; incorporated as private academy 1840; arts and sciences, business education and administration, teacher education; graduate study; quarter system.

Living theater A-363, T-148. see also in index Theater

Living things L-264. see also in index Biology; Embryology; Physiology; Plants; Reproduction
  animals A-126
  bioethical issues B-214
  earth E-6, G-63, P-487
  evolution E-343, diagrams E-344, 345a, pictures E-345b
  group, study of S-242
  human beings P-446, H-93
  Mars P-352
  temperature range for, chart H-111
  trees T-252, 258

Living together, family lifestyle F-19

Livius Andronicus, Lucius (284?–204? B.C.), first known Roman poet, a Greek; enslaved but later freed; became actor and teacher, introducing Greek literature to Rome.

Livonia, district in s. Estonian S.S.R. and n. Latvian S.S.R.; a former Baltic province of imperial Russia with capital at Riga; 45,516 sq km (17,574 sq mi) L-83

Livonia, Mich., city 18 mi (29 km) n.w. of Detroit; pop. 104,814; automobile parts; automotive research laboratory; food processing; horse racing; Madonna College, map M-285

Livorno, Italy. see in index Leghorn

Livre, an old French silver coin worth about 19.3 cents, replaced by franc in 1795; originally equaled English pound in value (from libra, Latin for "pound").

Livy, anglicized name of Titus Livius (59 B.C.–A.D. 17), Roman historian, great prose writer; 35 of the 142 books of his history of Rome still exist L-270
  Latin literature L-77

Livyeres, people L-12

Lizard, The, or **Lizard Head,** a bold promontory of Cornwall; the most southerly point of Great Britain; small bays and hazardous reefs line the coast.

Lizards, the largest living group of reptiles which is made up of more than 3,000 species L-271, R-152
  chameleon C-204b
  embryo, pictures E-194
  flying dragon D-166
  iguana I-32
  legendary, picture S-481b
  monitor, picture P-10
  place in evolution, chart G-64
  prehistoric A-462, picture A-460

LITERARY AWARDS
Canadian Library Association Awards

Awarded	Author or Artist	Book
1947	R. L. H. Haig-Brown	Starbuck Valley Winter
1948	Bertha Mabel Dunham	Kristli's Trees
1950	R. S. Lambert	Franklin of the Arctic (U.S. title, Adventure to the Polar Sea: the Story of Sir John Franklin)
1952	Catherine Anthony Clark	The Sun Horse
1954	Emile Gervais	Monseigneur de Laval (French)
1956	Margaret Louise Riley	Train for Tiger Lily
1957	Cyrus Macmillan	Glooskap's Country, and Other Indian Tales
1958	Farley Mowat	Lost in the Barrens
	Béatrice Clément	Le Chevalier du Roi (French)
1959	John Francis Hayes	The Dangerous Cove
	Hélène Flamme	Un Drôle de Petit Cheval (French)
1960	Marius Barbeau	The Golden Phoenix
	Paule Daveluy	L'Été Enchanté (French)
1961	William Toye	The St. Lawrence
	Marcelle Gauvreau	Plantes Vagabondes (French)
1962	Claude B. Aubry	Les îles du Roi Maha Maha II (French)
1963	Sheila Burnford	The Incredible Journey
	Paule Daveluy	Drôle d'Automne (French)
1964	R. L. H. Haig-Brown	The Whale People
	Cécile Chabot	Férie (French)
1965	Dorothy M. Reid	Tales of Nanabozho
	Claude B. Aubry	Le Loup de Noël (French)
1966	James McNeill	The Double Knights
	James Houston	Tikta'liktak
	Monique Corriveau	Le Wapiti (French)
	Andrée Maillet	Le Chêne des Tempêtes (French)
1967	Christie Harris	Raven's Cry
1968	James Houston	The White Archer: an Eskimo Legend
	Claude Mélançon	Légendes Indiennes du Canada (French)
1969	Kay Hill	And Tomorrow the Stars
1970	Edith Fowke	Sally Go 'Round the Sun
	Lionel Gendron	La Merveilleuse Histoire de la Naissance (French)
1971	William Toye	Cartier Discovers the Saint Lawrence
	Henriette Major	La Surprise de Dame Chenille (French)
1972	Anne Blades	Mary of Mile 18
	S. Takashima	Child in Prison Camp (illustration)
1973	Ruth Nichols	The Marrow of the World
	Simone Bussières	Le Petit Sapin qui a Poussé sur une Étoile (French)
	Jacques de Roussan	Au delà du Soleil (illustration)
1974	Elizabeth Cleaver	The Miraculous Hind
	William Kurelek	A Prairie Boy's Winter (illustration)
1975	Dennis Lee	Alligator Pie
	Carlo Italiano	The Sleighs of My Childhood (illustration)
1976	Mordecai Richler	Jacob Two-Two Meets the Hooded Fang
	William Kurelek	A Prairie Boy's Summer (illustration)
1977	Christie Harris	Mouse Woman and the Vanished Princesses
	Pam Hall	Down by Jim Long's Stage (illustration)
1978	Dennis Lee	Garbage Delight
	Elizabeth Cleaver	The Loon's Necklace (illustration)
1979	Kevin Major	Hold Fast
	Ann Blades	A Salmon for Simon (illustration)
1980	James Houston	River Runners
	Laszlo Gal	The Twelve Dancing Princesses (illustration)
1981	Donn Kushner	The Violin-Maker's Gift
	Douglas Tait	The Trouble with Princesses (illustration)
1982	Janet Lunn	The Root Cellar
	Heather Woodall	Ytek and the Arctic Orchid (illustration)

Laura Ingalls Wilder Award

1954	Laura Ingalls Wilder	1970	Elwyn Brooks White
1960	Clara Ingram Judson	1975	Beverly Cleary
1965	Ruth Sawyer	1980	Theodor Seuss Geisel

Lochner / Logroño

Lochner, Stephan (born 1405–15, died 1451), German painter; birthplace probably Meersburg; his altarpiece is chief treasure of Cologne cathedral.

Loch Ness monster A-462

Loch Raven, Md., community at s.e. end of Loch Raven Reservoir; n.e. suburb of Baltimore; pop. 25,000, *map* M-139

Lochy, Loch, w. Scotland, *map* G-199g

Lock and key L-277

Locke, Alain Le Roy (1886–1954), American author and historian L-278, B-294

Locke, David Ross. *see in index* Nasby, Petroleum V.

Locke, John (1632–1704), English philosopher; father of English empiricism L-278
- bioethical bill of rights B-214
- Carolina constitution S-310
- ideas embodied in Declaration of Independence D-51
- political science P-434
- theory of mind E-82

Locke, William John (1863–1930), English novelist and playwright, born Georgetown, British Guiana; first interest in architecture, secretary of Royal Institute of British Architects 1897–1907; a whimsical romanticist ('The Morals of Marcus Ordeyne'; 'The Beloved Vagabond'; 'Stella Maris'; 'Septimus').

Lockhart, John Gibson (1794–1854), Scottish writer and lawyer, born Cambusnethan, near Glasgow; famous as biographer of his father-in-law, Sir Walter Scott; also wrote life of Burns and novels.

Lock Haven, Pa., city on West Branch of Susquehanna River about 25 mi (40 km) s.w. of Williamsport; pop. 9,617; paper, electronic equipment, aircraft, metal products, dyes, textiles; Lock Haven State College, *map* P-185

Lock Haven State College, at Lock Haven, Pa.; established 1870; formerly a teachers college; liberal arts, education.

Lockheed S-3A, Viking airplane, *picture* A-178

Lockjaw. *see in index* Tetanus

Lockport, N.Y., city on New York State Barge Canal, n.e. of Buffalo; named for two large locks situated there; pop. 25,399; grain and fruit; flour, textiles, wallboard, auto radiators and heaters, air conditioners, plastics, paper, steel products, *map* N-260

Locks, canal C-118, *pictures* C-117, C-119
- Panama Canal, *diagram* P-88, *pictures* P-89, 94
- St. Lawrence Seaway S-20, *pictures* S-19, C-101, U-51
- Sault Sainte Marie Canal S-52b, *pictures* M-277, M-281
- Welland Ship Canal W-98, *picture* O-456d

Lock stitch, sewing machine S-127

Lockwood, Belva Ann Bennett (1830–1917), lawyer, born Royalton, N.Y.; first woman permitted to practice before U.S. Supreme Court; active in woman suffrage movements; nominated for president of U.S. 1884 and 1888 by Equal Rights party.

Lockyer, Sir (Joseph) Norman (1836–1920), English astronomer and physicist, born Rugby, England; pioneer in application of spectroscope to sun and stars; explained sunspots; between 1870 and 1905 conducted eight British expeditions for observing total solar eclipses ('The Sun's Place in Nature'; 'Recent and Coming Eclipses'; 'The Chemistry of the Sun'; 'Inorganic Evolution')
- helium in sun S-372, H-131

Loco-foco, obsolete popular name for friction matches; also applied to a New York City faction of Democratic party, because a meeting at Tammany Hall (1835) was held by the light of candles and matches after a rival faction had turned off the lights.

Locomotive, or **iron horse** L-279
- Civil War, *picture* C-379
- diesel-electric D-113
- mining, *diagram* C-416, *pictures* C-417, V-333
- Panama Canal P-90, *pictures* P-94
- pneumatic P-399
- railroads R-72, *pictures* R-74, 75
- steam engine S-438, *diagrams* S-439 to 441
- Stephenson S-443

Locoweed W-92, *picture* W-92b
- cattle poisoned by C-169
- legume L-118
- poisonous plants P-408

Locris, name for two separate districts of ancient Greece: **East Locris,** on e. coast opposite Euboea; **West Locris,** on Gulf of Corinth, s. of Doris, *map* G-221

Locust, an insect L-283
- animal migration A-452
- beetle parasite B-141
- cicada C-340
- grasshopper G-189

Locust, a rough-barked tree of the pea family
- flower, *picture* T-258
- weight of wood H-155

Locust, honey. *see in index* Honey locust

Lod, Israel. *see in index* Lydda

Lode, or **vein,** of minerals G-150b

Lodestone. *see in index* Magnetite

Lodge, Henry Cabot (1850–1924), political leader and historian, born Boston, Mass.; grandfather of Henry C. Lodge, Jr.; U.S. senator from Massachusetts 1893–1924; led Republican party in blocking U.S. entrance into League of Nations ('The Story of the Revolution'; 'Life of Alexander Hamilton'; 'Life of George Washington'; 'The Senate and the League of Nations') W-177

Lodge, Henry Cabot, Jr. (born 1902), political leader, born Nahant, Mass.; grandson of Henry Cabot Lodge; U.S. senator (Republican) from Massachusetts 1937–53 (resigned 1944 to serve in World War II, reelected 1946); directed campaign which won Republican presidential nomination for Dwight D. Eisenhower 1952; chief U.S. delegate to the United Nations 1953–60; Republican vice-presidential nominee 1960; ambassador to South Vietnam 1963–64, 1965–67, to West Germany 1968–69; chief U.S. negotiator at Vietnam peace talks in Paris 1969; presidential emissary to Vatican 1970–75, N-293d
- Kennedy defeats K-200

Lodge, Sir Oliver Joseph (1851–1940), English physicist, exponent of psychic research, and author; born Penkhull, Staffordshire; did valuable foundation work in electricity and radio; principal of University of Birmingham 1900–1919; in addition to autobiography and many scientific works, wrote 'Raymond, or Life and Death', and other books setting forth his belief in possibility of communication with the dead.

Lodge, Thomas (1558?–1625), English poet, dramatist, and writer of romances; his pastoral romance 'Rosalynde' gave plot to Shakespeare for 'As You Like It'.

Lodgepole pine, slender evergreen tree (*Pinus contorta*) of pine family. Grows 9 to 24 m (30 to 80 ft); thin bark peels off in scales. Leaves in twos, $6\frac{2}{5}$ cm ($2\frac{1}{2}$ in.) long; cones oval; sometimes called jack pine, spruce pine, blackjack, knotty pine, tamarack, scrub pine, and yellow pine, *table* W-218

Lodi, Calif., city 32 mi (52 km) s. of Sacramento; pop. 35,221; wines and brandies, food processing and canning, tire molds; grape festival and national wine show in September, *maps* U-40, *inset* C-53

Lodi, Italy, town 29 km (18 mi) s.e. of Milan on right bank of Adda River; pop. 38,158; French victory over Austrians (1796); founded 5th century B.C.; destroyed in 12th-century wars; reestablished by Frederick I
- Napoleon I at N-10

Lodi, N.J., borough on Saddle River just n.e. of Passaic; pop. 25,213; textile dyeing and finishing, chemicals, plastics, *map, inset* N-202

Łódź, Poland, city 120 km (75 mi) s.w. of Warsaw; pop. 843,000; enormous recent growth due to large textile industry; battle of Lodz (1914) L-283, P-413, *maps* E-334, 335, W-253

Loeb, Jacques (1859–1924), American biologist, born Mayen, near Coblenz, Germany; in U.S. after 1891; fertilized sea-urchin eggs chemically ("artificial parthenogenesis"); developed theory that many so-called "intelligent" actions of animals are physical or chemical in nature ("tropism") A-127

Loeffler, Charles Martin (1861–1935), American composer and violinist, born Mulhouse, Alsace; with Boston Symphony Orchestra 1883–1903; wrote songs, orchestral and chamber music; impressionistic style ('The Death of Tintagiles'; 'La Bonne Chanson'; 'A Pagan Poem'; 'Canticle of the Sun') M-562

Loening, Grover (1888–1976), American aeronautical engineer, born Bremen, Germany; invented first flying boat; designed Loening monoplane and seaplane.

Loess, a type of soil S-249, *picture* S-250
- Argentina A-575
- origin M-337

Loesser, Frank (1910–69), songwriter and playwright, born in New York, N.Y.; won Academy award 1948 for song 'Baby, It's Cold Outside'; New York Drama Critics Circle Award 1950 for 'Guys and Dolls', 1956 for 'The Most Happy Fella', and 1961 for 'How to Succeed in Business Without Really Trying', which also won Pulitzer Prize for drama O-464a

Loewe, Frederick. *see in index* Lerner, Alan Jay

Loewe, Johann Karl Gottfried (1796–1869), German composer, born near Halle, Germany; cantor and teacher in Stettin; one of first to give artistic form to ballad.

Loewi, Otto (1873–1961), American pharmacologist, born Frankfurt, Germany; worked with H. H. Dale on nerve impulses and their chemical transmission; to U.S. 1940, became citizen 1946.

Loewy, Raymond Fernand (born 1893), American industrial designer, born Paris, France; in United States after 1919, became citizen in 1938; designed streamlined trains, ships, and automobiles, also buildings for New York World's Fair 1939–40; author 'The Locomotive—Its Esthetics' D-94d
- industrial design I-169, 174

Löffler, Friedrich August Johannes (1852–1915), German bacteriologist, born Frankfurt-an-der-Oder; discovered causative organism of glanders, of diphtheria (with E. Klebs), and of foot-and-mouth disease (with Paul Frosch).

Lofoten Islands, or **Lofoden Islands,** group of rocky islands off n.w. coast of Norway; 4,040 sq km (1,560 sq mi); pop. 28,980, N-364, *map* N-365

Loft, in golf G-155, *diagram* G-155a

Lofting, Hugh (1886–1947), writer and illustrator, born Maidenhead, Berkshire, England; resident of U.S.; creator of character "Doctor Dolittle" and author of whimsical poetry and stories for young children; awarded Newbery Medal 1923 for 'Voyages of Doctor Dolittle' R-110a

Log, oil-well record P-236

Log, ship's, a device for measuring speed; term also used for ship's record book L-283

Logan, George (1753–1821), statesman, born Stenton, Pa. (now a part of Philadelphia); U.S. senator from Pennsylvania 1801–7; his attempt to settle difficulties between France and United States (1798) without authority from the government led Congress to pass Logan Act, forbidding such activities by nonaccredited persons.

Logan, James (1674–1751), American colonial political leader, born Ireland; a Quaker and secretary to William Penn; chief justice Pennsylvania Supreme Court 1731–39, P-171

Logan, John or **James** (1725?–80), English name of Cayuga Indian chief Tahgahjute; birthplace probably Shamokin, Pa.; friend of the whites until the massacre of his family by the whites 1774; joined English and became a leader in Lord Dunmore's War.

Logan, John Alexander (1826–86), Civil War general and U.S. senator, born Jackson County, Ill.; admitted to bar 1851; distinguished service in Civil War; except for 2-year interval was member of U.S. Senate 1871–86; candidate for presidential nomination on Republican ticket 1884.

Logan, Joshua (born 1908), producer and director, born Texarkana, Tex.; plays: 'Mister Roberts', 'The Wisteria Trees', 'Picnic'; musical plays: 'South Pacific' (awarded 1950 Pulitzer prize), 'Fanny'; also motion-picture adaptations.

Logan, Rayford W(hittingham) (born 1897), educator, born in Washington, D.C.; professor of history Howard University, Washington, D.C., 1938–65, head of department 1942–64; edited 'What the Negro Wants'; author of 'The Negro and the Post-War World: a Primer' and 'The Negro in American Life and Thought'.

Logan, Stephen Trigg (1800–1880), jurist, born in Franklin County, Ky.; judge of circuit court; delegate to Republican convention of 1860, which nominated Lincoln, his former law partner.

Logan, Sir William Edmond (1798–1875), Canadian geologist, born Montreal; mapped coal basin in Wales; first director Geological Survey of Canada 1842–70.

Logan, Utah, city 67 mi (108 km) n. of Salt Lake City; pop. 26,844; dairy products; textiles, pianos, farm machinery; vegetable canning; Utah State University U-218, *maps* U-232, 217, U-40

Logan, Mount, 2d highest peak (6,050 m; 19,850 ft.) of North America, situated in s.w. Yukon Territory C-74, *maps* C-88, 98
- height, comparative. *see in index* Mountain, *table*

Logania family, or **Loganiaceae,** a family of plants, native chiefly to warm regions, including Carolina yellow jessamine, buddleia, pinkroot, ignatius bean, strychnine, natal orange, and summer lilac.

Logansport, Ind., city on Wabash and Eel rivers about 70 mi (110 km) n. of Indianapolis; pop. 17,899; railroad division point; electrical products, hydraulic machinery, springs; state mental hospital and Bunker Hill Air Force Base nearby.

Logarithmic chart G-186, *graph* G-187

Logarithms, in mathematics A-595
- information theory I-202, *table* I-204
- slide rule S-217, C-21

Logbook L-283

Log cabin. *see in index* Shelter, *subhead* log cabin

Log-cabin campaign, of William Henry Harrison H-44

Log-cabin fire C-65

Loggerhead shrike, or **migrant shrike** S-186

Loggerhead turtle (genus *Caretta*) T-310

Loggia dei Lanzi, art gallery of Florence F-189, *picture* F-190

Logging, in lumber industry L-331, 335

Logic L-284
- algebra A-294
- Aristotle's writings A-589
- Boolean principles B-364
- computer hardware C-501
- dialectical, of Hegel H-124
- Frege's contribution F-392
- new math concepts M-164e
- philosophy P-264

Logistics, in military science, details of moving, quartering, and supplying troops.

Logogram, in writing W-306a

Logography, writing W-306a

Logo-syllabic writing. *see in index* Word-syllabic writing

Logrolling. *see in index* Birling

Logroño, Spain, ancient walled city in n., capital of province of same name; on Ebro River; pop. 58,545; wine trade.

Long-tailed / Lost

1880–81; U.S. Railway Commissioner 1898–1904, R-115
  Civil War C-376
  Gettysburg G-119

Long-tailed shrew S-186

Longview, Tex., city about 125 mi (200 km) e. of Dallas; pop. 62,762; oil production; earth-moving equipment, industrial machinery, oil field supplies, chemicals, LeTourneau College, *maps* T-128, U-41

Longview, Wash., port city in s.w. part of state at confluence of Cowlitz and Columbia rivers; pop. 31,052; lumber, paper products, aluminum; incorporated 1924, W-41, *maps* W-52, U-40

Longwall method, in coal mining C-414

Longwood College, at Farmville, Va.; state control; founded 1839; arts and sciences, education; graduate studies.

Longworth, Nicholas (1869–1931), political leader, born Cincinnati, Ohio; Ohio Republican congressman 1903–13, 1915–31; speaker of House 1925–31, *picture* W-153

Lonicera, the honeysuckle genus of plants H-214

Lon Nol (born 1913), premier of Kampuchea (Cambodia) K-170

Lönnrot, Elias (1802–84), Finnish folklorist, philologist, and physician; born Sammatti, s. Finland; best known as compiler of 'Kalevala' L-297
  Finland F-89
  folklore F-259
  storytelling S-470

'Look Back in Anger' (1958), motion picture M-525

'Look Homeward, Angel', autobiographical novel by Thomas Wolfe A-359, W-211

'Looking Backward', novel by Edward Bellamy N-376

'Looking for Mr. Goodbar', work by Rossner A-363

Lookout, Cape, North Carolina, 70 mi (110 km) s.w. of Cape Hatteras N-322, *maps* N-323, 337, U-41
  Cape Lookout N.S. N-32, *map* N-30

Lookout Mountain, ridge in n.w. Georgia extending into Tennessee and Alabama C-221, *maps* T-97, A-223, *picture* T-88

Lookout Mountain, Battle of. *see in index* Battle above the clouds

Loom, machine
  handloom
    England, *picture* E-242
    Guatemala, *picture* G-247
    Mexico, *pictures* M-249
    tapestry T-18
    Turkey, *picture* T-301
  Industrial Revolution I-178
  Jacquard loom J-12
  power loom
    clothing, *picture* C-403
    cotton C-590
    New Hampshire, *list* N-175
    rugs R-316, *picture* R-315
  textiles T-134, *pictures* T-133, T-138
  weaving S-390, *pictures* S-391

Loon, a diving waterbird L-297, *picture* A-426
  state bird, *picture* M-356

Loop, in Chicago, Ill. C-255, 258, *map* C-261

Loop antenna, in radio, *picture* R-55

Looper. *see in index* Cankerworm

Looping pits, in metalworking I-346

Loop of Henle, in kidney anatomy K-235

Loos, Adolf (1870–1933), Austrian architect, *profile* A-569

Loos, Anita (1893–1981), novelist, playwright, and motion-picture scenarist, born Sisson, Calif. (novel, 'Gentlemen Prefer Blondes', later dramatized).

Loos-en-Gohelle, called **Loos** until 1937, town in n. France, about 5 km (3 mi) n.w. of Lens; pop. 3,918; scene of British offensive 1915; town captured but British lost about 70,000 men.

Loosestrife, leafy-stemmed perennial herbs embracing the genus *Lysimachia* of the primrose family; common loosestrife is *L. vulgaris,* a tall coarse plant with large yellow flowers in terminal leafy panicles; *L. nummularia* (creeping Charlie, moneywort, or creeping jenny) is a trailing plant with large yellow flowers which are often used in rock gardens.

Loosestrife family, or **Lythraceae,** a family of plants, shrubs, and trees, native chiefly to tropical America, including swamp loosestrife, loosestrife, henna, crape myrtle, cigar flower, purple loosestrife, and blue waxweed.

Lop-eared rabbit R-22–3

Lope de Vega. *see in index* Vega Carpio

López, Alfonso Ramon (Al) (born 1908), baseball catcher and manager, born Tampa, Fla.; managed A.L. pennant winners, Cleveland Indians 1954, Chicago White Sox 1959.

López, Carlos Antonio (1790–1862), dictator of Paraguay, born near Asunción; teacher and lawyer; established country's first newspaper; rule marked by uneasy relations with U.S. and neighboring countries P-112

López, Francisco Solano (1826–70), dictator of Paraguay P-112

López de Legaspi, Miguel (1524–72), Spanish soldier, born Zumarraga, near Tolosa, Spain; conquered Philippines and founded Manila P-259c

López de Villalobos, Ruy (1500?–46), Spanish navigator; in 1542 attempted conquest of Philippines for Spain and named the islands "Las Filipinas."

López Mateos, Adolfo (1910–69), Mexican lawyer and statesman, born near Mexico City; minister of labor and social welfare 1952–57; president 1958–64, M-256

López Portillo, Josó (born 1920), Mexican political leader, born Mexico City; former professor of law National University of Mexico; finance minister 1973–75; president 1976–82, M-256

López y Fuentes, Gregorio (1897–1966), Mexican writer L-70

Lop Nor, or **Lob Nor,** marshy, salty depression in Sinkiang-Uigur Autonomous Region, People's Republic of China; receives Tarim River.

Loquat, a small evergreen tree or shrub (*Eriobotrya japonica*) of the rose family and its fruit; originated in Asia; now widely cultivated in tropical and subtropical areas; fruit used for jellies, jams, and preserves.

Lorain, Ohio, port and industrial city on Lake Erie, 26 mi (42 km) w. of Cleveland; pop. 75,416; ships steel products, coal, iron ore; steel tubes and pipe, pumps, clothing, chemicals, communications and navigation equipment, toys, gypsum, *maps* O-428, 420

Loran, in radar R-32
  aviation A-886
  fisheries F-134
  navigational equipment N-87, *picture* N-89
  signaling S-194
  submarine S-495a

Loras College, at Dubuque, Iowa; Roman Catholic; established in 1839; arts and sciences, and teacher education; graduate studies.

Lorca, Federico García. *see in index* García Lorca, Federico

Lorca, Spain, ancient city in s.e., on river Sangonera; pop. 19,854; trade center; many battles between Christians and Moors, *map* E-334

Lord, a British title borne by bishops, marquises, earls, viscounts, and barons; also borne as courtesy title by eldest sons of dukes, marquises, and earls, and younger sons of dukes and marquises; title of office borne by lord chancellor T-185

Lord & Thomas, advertising agency A-58

Lord Dunmore's War (1774) named for John Murray, earl of Dunmore, governor of Virginia; expedition by American colonists against Indian coalition formed to check westward expansion of Virginia; ended at battle of Point Pleasant (now Tu-Endie-Wei Park, W. Va.)
  battle W-112: monument, *picture* W-115

Lord Howe Island, dependency of New South Wales, Australia, in Pacific 700 km (435 mi) n.e. of Sydney; resort; 13 sq km (5 sq mi); pop. 223, *map* P-4

'Lord Jim', novel by Joseph Conrad E-270

Lord mayor, English magistrate L-289

Lord of Misrule C-330, *picture* C-331

Lords, House of, upper house of British Parliament P-131, U-18
  appeal court C-595
  Cabinet members C-4
  Reform Bill crisis R-319

Lord's Day S-1

Lord's Prayer, The (Matt. vi, 9–13), commonly used in religious worship; variations exist among denominations; King James version follows:
  "Our Father which art in heaven, Hallowed be thy name.
  Thy kingdom come. Thy will be done in earth as it is in heaven.
  Give us this day our daily bread.
  And forgive us our debts, as we forgive our debtors.
  And lead us not into temptation, but deliver us from evil: For thine is the kingdom, and the power, and the glory, for ever. Amen."
  hornbook contains, *picture* E-84

Lord's Supper, or **Holy Eucharist,** or **Communion,** Christian rite in which bread and wine are taken in commemoration of Christ's death. This sacrament was instituted by Christ at his supper (Lord's Supper, or Last Supper) with his disciples the night before his death (Matt. xxvi, 26–29; Mark xiv, 22–25; Luke xxii, 14–20)
  Anglicans A-417
  Lutheranism L-339
  tabernacle T-1

Lorelei, fabled Rhine siren; legend probably from an echoing rock of that name on the Rhine; in poem by Heine and other literature, also Mendelssohn and Lachner operas F-262, *picture* G-99

Lorentz, Hendrik Antoon (1853–1928), Dutch physicist, born Arnhem, Netherlands; sought consistent theory for magnetism, electricity, and light; explained the Zeeman effect R-140

Lorentz, Pare (born 1905), motion picture producer and director, born Clarksburg, W. Va.; chief of films section U.S. War Department, Civil Affairs Division (1946) M-529, *picture* W-122

Lorenz, Adolf (1854–1946), Austrian orthopedic surgeon; devised bloodless operation (forcible manipulation) for congenital dislocation of hip joint; also operation for clubfoot.

Lorenz, Konrad (born 1903), Austrian naturalist, born Vienna; noted for study of wild animal behavior; head of Max Planck Institute from 1961, L-298

Lorenzetti, Ambrogio (active 1319–48), and **Pietro** (active 1305–48), two Sienese painters, brothers; noted chiefly for religious frescoes; Ambrogio was most gifted, and in vigorous, colorful, and naturalistic works showed influence of Giotto; he painted a series of allegories representing good and bad government.

Lorenzo, saint. *see in index* Lawrence

Lorenzo de' Medici, or **Lorenzo the Magnificent,** (1449–92), Florentine statesman and patron of arts M-211
  Michelangelo M-264, S-87

Lorenzo de' Medici (1492–1519), duke of Urbino, grandson of Lorenzo the Magnificent, father of Catherine; succeeded as ruler of Florence when uncle, Giovanni, became Pope Leo X.

Lorenzo Monaco (1370?–1425), Italian painter A-415

Loreto, town, Mexico C-55

Loretto Heights College, at Denver, Colo.; private control, Catholic related; opened 1918; arts and sciences, nursing, teacher education.

Lorgnette, eyeglass S-370

Loricata. *see in index* Crocodilia

Lorient, France, fortified naval port in n.w. on Bay of Biscay at junction of Scorff and Blavet rivers; pop. 66,023; fisheries, *map* W-277

Lorimer, George Horace (1868–1937), editor, born Louisville, Ky.; editor in chief of *Saturday Evening Post,* 1899–1936; popular books on success ('Letters from a Self-Made Merchant to His Son').

Loring, Eugene, real name LeRoy Kerpestein (1914–1982), dancer and choreographer, born Milwaukee, Wis.; danced with Fokine's ballet, Ballet Caravan, Ballet Theatre; formed company, Dance Players, in New York City, 1941; created ballet 'Billy the Kid'.

Loris, a species of short-tailed lemur; round-eyed with soft fur, poorly formed index fingers; slender type, smaller than squirrel, inhabits forest regions of Sri Lanka and s. India; slow, heavy kind found in other Indo-Malay areas.

'Lorna Doone', novel by Richard Doddridge Blackmore which made the Exmoor country famous B-306

Lorne, marquis of. *see in index* Argyll, duke of

Lorne, Firth of, inlet of Atlantic, w. coast of Scotland; terminus of Caledonian Canal, *maps* G-199g

Lorrain, Claude, real name Claude Gelée or Gellée (1600–82), French landscape painter, born Lorraine; influenced by Italian Renaissance and classical art.

Lorraine, district of n.e. France (also called Lotharingia and Lothringen). *see also in index* Alsace-Lorraine
  Charles the Bold C-218

Lorraine, House of A-830

Lory, or **lorikeet,** any of a large group of parrots, chief genera *Domicella, Lorius, Trichoglossus, Chalcopsitta,* and *Eos;* distinguished from other parrots by its brushlike tongue with which it extracts nectar from flowers; chiefly in Australia and New Guinea.

Los Alamos, N.M., in Los Alamos County, 24 mi (39 km) n.w. of Santa Fe; pop. 11,310; nuclear research and development center; atomic bomb designed and tested in laboratories in this area N-210, *maps* N-220, U-40

Los Altos, Calif., city in Santa Clara County 27 mi (43 km) s.e. of San Francisco; pop. 25,769; chiefly residential, incorporated 1952, *map, inset* C-52

Los Angeles, Victoria de, real name Victoria Gamez Cima (born 1923), Spanish lyric soprano, born Barcelona; appeared in leading opera theaters of world; French, Italian, and German roles.

Los Angeles, Calif., largest city on Pacific coast; pop. 2,966,763, L-298, *maps* U-40, 119
  black youth revolts B-297
  California C-35, 39, *picture* C-36, *maps* C-33, 42, *inset* C-53
  ceramic industry P-477
  earthquake E-32
  motion pictures M-520
  rapid growth, *graphs* G-187
  smog P-441b
  Spanish Americans H-251
  Watts riot U-196

Los Angeles-Long Beach Harbor, harbor, California L-295

Los Angeles Music Center for the Performing Arts, *picture* C-46

Los Gatos, Calif., town 8 mi (13 km) s.w. of San Jose; pop. 29,593; chiefly residential; service industries; incorporated 1887, *map* C-53

Losing checkers, game B-322

Loss, in insurance I-232

Lossing, Benson John (1813–91), historical writer, editor, illustrator, born Beekman, N.Y.; his 'Pictorial Field-Book of the Revolution' a pioneer historical work.

"Lost Battalion, The," 554 men in World War I from the 77th (New York) Division, who were not lost, but cut off during advance and surrounded by

Lost / Louvre

enemy Oct. 2–7, 1918, during Meuse-Argonne battle; under command of Maj. Charles W. Whittlesey, troops refused to surrender in spite of repeated attacks, lack of food, extreme cold, and mistakenly placed artillery barrage from own army; only 194 were rescued
  Meuse-Argonne battle M-237
  pigeon takes message P-324

Lost Colony of Virginia, English colony in what is now North Carolina which disappeared in 1591; the Croatan Indians in North Carolina claim to be descendants of an Indian tribe which these colonists joined; they intermarried with its members; thus an explanation is given for the mixed blood and occasional English names of the Croatans N-327, 332
  pageant about P-20

Lost Ten Tribes, ten of twelve tribes of United Kingdom of Israel which seceded to form separate kingdom of Israel.

Lost-wax process, in casting metals S-81

Lota, Chile, mining town and seaport about 30 km (20 mi) s. of Concepción; pop. 51,548; coal shipping, copper smelting; Cousiño Park nearby, noted for worldwide collection of plants.

Lothair I (795–855), Holy Roman emperor, grandson of Charlemagne; became joint ruler 817 when Louis I, his father, divided the empire among his sons; after years of strife with his brothers received Italy and imperial title together with lands along Rhine and Rhone rivers (Partition of Verdun, 843), A-320

Lothair II, sometimes called Lothair III (1070?–1137), Holy Roman emperor 1133–37; created duke of Saxony 1106, and elected German king 1125; his reign was regarded as a golden age for Germany.

Lothair II (825–869), king of Lorraine, son of Lothair I; received as his kingdom district w. of Rhine between North Sea and Jura Mts., called after him Lotharingia or Lorraine (German *Lothringen*)

Lotharingia, France. *see in index* Lorraine

Lothian, Philip Henry Kerr, 11th marquis of (1882–1940), British statesman; member of Liberal party; secretary of prime minister Lloyd George 1916–22; undersecretary of state for India 1931–32; ambassador to U.S. 1939–40.

Lothringen, France. *see in index* Lorraine

Loti, Pierre, pen name of Louis Marie Julien Viaud (1850–1923), French naval officer and novelist, born Rochefort, France.

Lötschberg Tunnel, in Switzerland, *table* T-292

Lottery, draft C-536, *picture* C-535
  World War I, *pictures* W-260, W-174

Lottery, gambling scheme in which a sum of money is paid for the chance of drawing a prize of greater value than the amount invested; state-sponsored lottery in New Hampshire, first in any state since 1894, adopted 1963.

Lotus, plant W-73d
  Egyptian hieroglyphics N-379

Lotus eaters, in Greek mythology O-406

Lotze, Rudolf Hermann (1817–81), German philosopher, born Bautzen, Saxony; assumed that the orderly functioning of nature implied a motivating, ideal principle; helped to develop physiological psychology.

Loubet, Émile (1838–1929), French statesman, born Marsanne, near Montélimar, France; 7th president of Third Republic 1899–1906; remitted Alfred Dreyfus' sentence.

Loucks, Henry Langford (1846–1928), American farmer and political leader, born Hull, Que., Canada; settled 1884 on homestead in Deuel County, Dakota Territory; founder of *Dakota Ruralist;* president National Farmers' Alliance 1892, leader of successful fight for initiative and referendum in South Dakota.

Loudness, of sound S-260
  noise pollution P-441e

Loudspeaker
  phonograph P-269, *diagram* P-268d
  radio, *diagrams* R-47, 56

Lough, Irish name for lake. *see in index* lakes by name, as Neagh, Lough

Lougheed, Peter (born 1928), Canadian public official and lawyer, born Calgary, Alta.; member Legislative Assembly, Calgary West, 1967–72; premier of Alberta 1972–.

Louis, Saint. *see in index* Louis IX

Louis I, Holy Roman emperor. *see in index* Louis I, the Pious, king of France

Louis II (827–75), Holy Roman emperor (crowned 850) and king of Italy (came to throne 839), son of Lothair I; fought Saracens and restored order in Italy.

Louis III, the Blind (880?–928), Holy Roman emperor (crowned 901) and king of the Lombards (chosen 900), grandson of Louis II; his eyes were put out 905 by Berengar, rival king of the Lombards; exiled to Provence.

Louis IV, the Bavarian (about 1287–1347), Holy Roman emperor (crowned 1328) and king of Germany (elected 1314); despite his being almost constantly at war, first with his brother over Bavaria, then with the pope over Germany, Louis enlarged his domains, and fostered trade and learning.

Louis, kings of Bavaria. *see in index* Ludwig

Louis II, the German (804–76), king of East Franks; 3d son of Louis the Pious and grandson of Charlemagne; his share of Charlemagne's empire after Partition of Verdun (843) formed nucleus of modern Germany J-12

Louis I, the Pious (778–840), king of France and Holy Roman emperor, youngest son of Charlemagne whom he succeeded L-304
  Andorra A-411
  Charlemagne C-210

Louis VI (1081–1137), king of France L-304

Louis VII (1120–80), king of France L-304
  Second Crusade C-616

Louis VIII (1187–1226), king of France L-304

Louis IX, or **Saint Louis** (1214–70), king of France; canonized in 1297; festival August 25 L-304
  Crusades C-618
  Sainte Chapelle P-122

Louis X (1289–1316), king of France, son of Philip IV; ruled 1314–16; nicknamed "the Quarreler"; inherited kingdom of Navarre from mother Joan 1305; resigned to succeed his father to French throne L-305

Louis XI (1423–83), king of France L-305
  Charles the Bold C-218
  silk industry T-140

Louis XII (1462–1515), king of France L-305
  Francis I succeeds F-374

Louis XIII (1601–43), king of France L-305
  dueling in reign S-546
  Richelieu and R-203

Louis XIV (1638–1715), king of France L-305
  architecture A-557
  button adornment B-528
  Cabal affects C-1
  Cadillac in New France C-10
  Canal du Midi C-119
  Colbert aids C-431
  court etiquette E-300
  dance promoted B-33, D-24
  engraving of period E-279
  French Bourbons B-384
  French revolution F-401
  furniture style F-458
  fur trade F-470
  Gobelin tapestries T-20
  hat fashions H-47
  interior design I-248
  King William's War K-247
  Lully's court music L-328
  Marlborough M-112
  Marquise de Maintenon M-67
  marriage V-272
  Netherlands invaded N-139
  Spanish Succession A-829
  Versailles palace V-303
  William III W-164

Louis XV (1710–74), king of France L-306, *picture* L-305
  builds Petit Trianon V-303
  furniture style F-459
  interior design I-249
  Voltaire and V-385

Louis XVI (1754–93), king of France L-306, *picture* L-305
  dress fashions D-192
  Estates-General E-291
  Franklin and F-384
  French Revolution F-402
  Lafayette L-20
  Mirabeau M-369
  popularizes potato P-467
  Robespierre R-223

Louis XVII (1785–95), French Dauphin; son of Louis XVI L-307, *picture* L-306

Louis XVIII (1755–1824), king of France L-307
  Talleyrand T-13

Louis I (1838–89), king of Portugal, born Lisbon; came to throne 1861; abolished slavery in Portuguese colonies; promoted literature, translated Shakespeare and works from French.

Louis II (1870–1949), prince of Monaco, born Baden-Baden, Germany; succeeded to throne of principality of Monaco 1922; son of Albert I; served in French army with rank of major general.

Louis, Joe (1914–81), boxer, born near Lafayette, Ala. L-307
  burial N-21
  heavyweight champion B-392, *table* B-391

Louisbourg, Fortress of, on Cape Breton Island, N.S., Canada C-106
  British capture N-373g
  national historic park N-24c, N-373e, C-130, *map, inset* N-24b, *picture* N-373f
  Wolfe W-211

Louise (1776–1810), queen of Frederick William III of Prussia, born at Hanover; her beauty and goodness and the fortitude with which she bore the hardships of the Napoleonic Wars made her a popular heroine.

Louise, Lake, Alberta, Canada, in Canadian Rocky Mountains, *picture* C-82

Louis-Hippolyte Lafontaine bridge-tunnel complex T-291, 293, M-476a

Louisiade Archipelago, group of islands off s.e. coast of New Guinea, belonging to Papua New Guinea; pop. 11,451, *maps* E-37, P-4

Louisiana, a gulf state of the U.S.; 48,523 sq mi (125,674 sq km); pop. 4,203,972; cap. Baton Rouge L-308
  bird, state, brown pelican P-156, P-441d, *picture* P-155
  Chalmette N.H.P. N-33, *map* N-30
  cities
    New Orleans N-223
    Shreveport S-185
  flags
    French flag F-153
    state, *picture* F-159
  flower, state, magnolia M-49b, *picture* S-427
  geographic region U-56, *map* U-41
  harbors and ports H-24
  history
    Cadillac governs C-10
    Civil War C-509, *map* C-376
    LaSalle L-53, *picture* L-52
    Long, Huey L-295
    Reconstruction R-114, *picture* R-115
  levees M-390
  minerals
    petroleum P-230, *picture* P-234
    salt S-30
    sulfur S-509
  Mississippi river M-389
  Statuary Hall, *table* S-437a
  tree, state, bald cypress C-634, *picture* P-357

Louisiana College, at Pineville, La.; affiliated with Southern Baptist convention; established in 1906; arts and sciences, education, and professional studies.

Louisiana Purchase, in U.S. history L-324
  completion, *picture* U-175, *map* U-177
  frontier expansion F-419
  Iowa region I-293
  Lewis and Clark L-142, 143
  Louisiana L-314
  Monroe negotiates M-456
  New Spain S-339, N-225

Louisiana Purchase Exposition, at St. Louis, Mo., from April 30 to Dec. 1, 1904; recorded admissions were 19,694,855; amusements on the "Pike"; 500 buildings; floral clock with 50-ft (15-m) hands S-22, T-43

Louisiana State University, since 1976 **Louisiana State University and Agricultural and Mechanical College,** at Baton Rouge, La.; opened 1860; arts and sciences, agriculture, business administration, chemistry and physics, education, engineering, environmental design, law, library, music, social welfare, veterinary medicine, and graduate school; four-year branches at Shreveport and New Orleans (University of New Orleans); Louisiana State Medical Center also at New Orleans; two-year branches at Alexandria and Eunice B-106
  War Memorial Tower, *picture* L-317

Louisiana Tech University, at Ruston, La.; state control; founded 1894; formerly called Louisiana Polytechnic Institute; arts and sciences, agriculture and forestry, business administration, education, engineering, home economics; graduate studies; quarter system.

Louisiana Territory. *see in index* Louisiana Purchase

Louis Napoleon. *see in index* Napoleon III

Louis Philippe (1773–1850), "citizen-king" of France L-307
  Bourbon, House of B-384
  Foreign Legion F-308
  Lafayette's support L-20
  Paris improvements P-123

Louisville, Ga., city on Ogeechee R. 40 mi (60 km) s.w. of Augusta; pop. 2,823; capital of Georgia 1796–1805, *picture* G-83, *list* G-77

Louisville, Ky., largest city of state on Ohio River; pop. 298,451, L-324, *pictures* K-209, 210, 217, *map* U-41
  dam D-7

Louisville, University of, at Louisville, Ky.; state control; founded 1798; arts and sciences, business, dentistry, education, law, medicine, music, police administration, science, and social work; graduate school.

Louisville and Portland Canal L-383, *map* C-118

Lounsbury, Thomas Raynesford (1838–1915), scholar, born Ovid, N.Y.; professor English language and literature, Sheffield Scientific School of Yale University, for more than 30 years; distinguished for his studies in development of English language ('History of the English Language'; 'Studies in Chaucer'; 'The Text of Shakespeare').

Lourdes, France, town 132 km (82 mi) s.w. of Toulouse; pop. 17,685, L-325

Lourenço Marques, Mozambique. *see in index* Maputo

Louse, a wingless blood-sucking insect of the order *Siphunculata* (also called *Anoplura*); eggs are called nits
  parasite P-114, *picture* P-115
  crab, V-274
  egg, *picture* E-106
  insect I-224, *picture* I-214
  vaccine source V-251

Louse fly, name for flies of family *Hippoboscidae* that spend adult lives like lice as parasites; some adults wingless, notably the sheep tick (*Melophagus ovinus*); others winged (*Lynchia americana,* which infests owls); still others lose wings during parasitic life (*Lipoptena depressa,* which preys on deer).

Lousma, Jack R. (born 1936), astronaut, born Grand Rapids, Mich.; U.S. Marine Corps officer selected for NASA program 1966; member Skylab 1973, *table* S-348

Louth, agricultural and fishing county in Leinster Province, n.e. Ireland; 821 sq km (317 sq mi) (smallest county in Ireland); pop. 69,519; county seat Dundalk.

Louvain, or **Leuven,** Belgium, city in center; pop. 32,524; bell industry B-156

L'Ouverture, Pierre Dominique Toussaint. *see in index* Toussaint L'Ouverture

Louvois, François Michel Le Tellier, marquis de (1641–91), French statesman, born Paris; Louis XIV's war minister who wasted prosperity of France and destroyed peace of Europe for military "glory."

Louvre, art museum in Paris, France P-121, *map* P-120, *picture* E-324

Louÿs / Lozier

Greek and Roman art G-229
Holbein H-201, *picture* R-148
paintings P-28, 37, 39, 43, *pictures* P-29, 36
sculpture S-83, *pictures* S-81, 86, 89

Louÿs, Pierre, real name Pierre Louis (1870–1925), French poet and novelist, born Ghent, Belgium; competent translator, fooled experts with original poems represented as Greek works ('Chanson de Bilitis').

Lovanium University of Kinshasa, presently the **National University of Zaire** K-248

Love, John Arthur (born 1916), public official, born Gibson City, Ill.; governor of Colorado 1962–73; director U.S. Energy Policy Office 1973.

Love, emotion
child development C-270, 277, 280
Jesus' teachings J-104
motivating force E-198

Lovebird P-135

Love-in-a-mist, a flower. *see in index* Nigella

'Love in a Police Station', motion picture, *picture* M-522

Lovejoy, Elijah Parish (1802–37), abolitionist, born Albion, Me.; editor of an antislavery paper which was published in Alton, Ill.; killed by mob while trying to save his press. His brother **Owen Lovejoy** (1811–64) carried on antislavery movement in Illinois and as member of Congress 1857–64; an early supporter of Abraham Lincoln
Beecher family B-131
Illinois history, *table* I-43
Phillips condemns murder P-263

Lovelace, Maud Hart (born 1892), author, born Mankato, Minn.; known for Betsy-Tacy series of books for girls, also for 'The Tune Is in the Tree', 'The Trees Kneel at Christmas', and 'Early Candlelight'.

Lovelace, Richard (1618–58), English Cavalier poet, born London; immortalized by two lyrics ('To Lucasta, on Going to the Wars'; 'To Althea, from Prison').

Loveland, Colo., city 12 mi (19 km) s. of Fort Collins; pop. 30,244; in farm area; electronic instruments; entrance to Rocky Mountain National Park; incorporated 1881, *map* C-467

Love-lies-bleeding, a hardy annual garden herb (*Amaranthus caudatus*) with clusters of dark purplish flowers; native to the tropics.

Lovell, James Arthur, Jr. (born 1928), business executive, former astronaut, born Cleveland, Ohio; U.S. Navy officer selected for NASA program 1962; resigned from Navy and space program 1973, S-346f, *table* S-348

Lovely fir. *see in index* Silver fir

Loveman, Robert (1864–1923), poet, born Cleveland, Ohio; lived much of life in South; wrote poems of nature ('Songs from a Georgia Garden'; 'On the Way to Willowdale').

'Love of the Three Kings, The'. *see in index* 'Amore dei Tre Re, L' '.

Lover, Samuel (1797–1868), Irish novelist and poet, born Dublin; tendency to caricature Irish life; author of 'Handy Andy', a roaring farce; 'Rory O'More', equally popular as novel and play.

'Love's Labour's Lost', comedy by Shakespeare, written about 1591, in which princess of France and her three ladies cause King Ferdinand of Navarre and his three friends to break vows S-133, 139

'Love Song of J. Alfred Prufrock, The', poem by T. S. Eliot A-355, W-310b

Loves Park, Ill., city 4 mi (6 km) n.w. of Rockford; pop. 13,192; machine tools; incorporated 1947.

Lovett, Robert Abercrombie (born 1895), banker and public official, born Huntsville, Tex.; special assistant to secretary of war 1940–41; assistant secretary of war for air 1941–45; undersecretary of state 1947–49; assistant secretary of defense 1950–51; secretary of defense 1951–53.

Lovett, Robert Morss (1870–1956), educator and writer, born Boston, Mass.; professor of English, University of Chicago 1909–36; government secretary of Virgin Islands 1939–43 ('A History of English Literature', with W. V. Moody; 'Richard Gresham' and 'A Winged Victory', novels; 'Cowards', play).

Lovington, N.M., town near Texas border 20 mi (30 km) n.w. of Hobbs; pop. 9,727; grain, cotton, cattle; in oil-producing region; founded 1908, *map* N-221

Low, Archibald Montgomery (1888–1956), British engineer and writer, born Purley, near London; invented system of radio signaling, television system, and radio controls for torpedoes and rockets.

Low, Sir David (1891–1963), British cartoonist, born Dunedin, New Zealand; created Colonel Blimp as a symbol of stupidity: political cartoonist *Manchester Guardian* 1953–63; autobiography.

Low, Juliette Gordon (1860–1927), founder of Girl Scout movement in the U.S. L-325
Georgia, *pictures* G-89, 90
Girl Scouts G-129

Low, Seth (1850–1916), merchant, educator, and administrator, born Brooklyn, N.Y.; mayor of Brooklyn 1882–86 (enforced first municipal civil-service rules adopted in America); president Columbia University 1890–1901; mayor of Greater New York 1901–3.

Low, Will Hicok (1853–1932), decorative painter, designer of stained glass, and illustrator, born Albany, N.Y. (illustrations for Keats's 'Lamia'; frieze in legislative library, New York State Capitol).

Low, or **low atmospheric pressure center** W-84, *maps* W-86, 87

Low Archipelago, in s. Pacific. *see in index* Tuamotu

Low Countries, name applied to a region in Europe comprising Belgium, Luxemburg, and the Netherlands. *see in index* Belgium; Luxemburg; Netherlands

Lowden, Frank O(rren) (1861–1943), lawyer and political leader, born Sunrise City, Minn.; from poor farm boy became successful lawyer, notable congressman; governor of Illinois 1917–21; also farmer who promoted cooperative marketing.

Lowe, Sir Hudson (1769–1844), English general, born Galway, Ireland; fought in Napoleonic Wars; custodian of Napoleon I on St. Helena.

Lowe, Thaddeus Sobieski Coulincourt (1832–1913), aeronaut and inventor, born Jefferson Mills, now Riverton, N.H.; as chief of aeronautic section of U.S. Army, used balloons for observation in Civil War.

Lowell, Abbott Lawrence (1856–1943), educator and political scientist, born Boston, Mass.; brother of Amy and Percival Lowell; president of Harvard University 1909–33; developed social life among students through freshman dormitories ('The Government of England'; 'Governments and Parties in Continental Europe'; 'Conflicts of Principle') L-326

Lowell, Amy (1874–1925), U.S. writer L-326

Lowell, Francis Cabot (1775–1817), Boston merchant, founder of U.S. cotton manufacturing industry, born Newburyport, Mass.; son of John Lowell L-326
Industrial Revolution I-182
textiles T-135

Lowell, James Russell (1819–91), American poet, essayist, and critic L-326
abolitionist writings C-373
American literature A-348
Cambridge home C-56b
Hall of Fame, *table* H-11

Lowell, John (1743–1802), American jurist, born Newburyport, Mass.; said to have been author of clause in Massachusetts state constitution declaring "all men are born free and equal"; this clause was interpreted in 1783 by the Supreme Court of state to mean that slavery was abolished; father of Francis Cabot Lowell and grandfather of James Russell Lowell.

Lowell, Percival (1855–1916), astronomer, born Boston, Mass.; brother of Amy and Abbott L. Lowell; established Lowell Observatory 1894 near Flagstaff, Ariz.; discovery here of planet Pluto in 1930 direct result of his mathematical prediction ('The Genesis of Planets') L-326, A-714

Lowell, Robert (Traill Spence, Jr.) (1917–77), poet, born Boston, Mass.; great-grandnephew of James Russell Lowell; awarded Pulitzer prize 1947 for 'Lord Weary's Castle' ('For the Union Dead'; 'Near the Ocean'; 'Notebook 1967–68') L-326, A-364

Lowell, Mass., one of the oldest industrial cities of the United States; pop. 92,418, *maps* M-145, 161, 152, U-41
carpet industry R-316

Lowell, University of, at Lowell, Mass.; state control; established 1975 by merger of Lowell State College and Lowell Technological Institute; arts and sciences, education, engineering and technology, music, nursing.

Lowell Observatory, Flagstaff, Ariz. A-601, 604, *picture* A-605
Saturn, *picture* S-52

Lowell State College, at Lowell, Mass.; chartered 1894. *see also in index* Lowell, University of

Lowell Technological Institute, at Lowell, Mass.; state control; established 1895. *see also in index* Lowell, University of

Lower Austria, a province in n.e. Austria; area 19,171 sq km (7,402 sq mi); pop. 1,374,012; wooded hill country; capital Vienna; ruled by Hapsburgs until 1918.

Lower Burrell, Pa., city of Westmoreland county 16 mi (26 km) n.e. of Pittsburgh; in coal-mining area; pop. 13,200; incorporated 1958, *map* P-184

Lower California. *see in index* California, Lower

Lower Canada, name formerly given to province of Quebec C-108, 112, Q-9g, O-456g, *map* C-112a

Lowercase letters, or **small letters** B-356, T-316, 317

Lower Egypt, that part of Egypt north of 30° N. latitude E-108

Lower Fort Garry National Historic Park, in Manitoba, Canada M-89f, N-24d, *map* N-24b

Lower house, in national legislatures P-130
Australia P-131
Canada P-132, C-86
New Zealand N-277a

Lower Merion, Pa., urban township on Schuylkill River just w. of Philadelphia; pop. 63,392; consists of 13 unincorporated communities.

Lower Saxony, or **Niedersachsen,** state in West Germany, former state in British zone, Germany, *map* G-114, *table* G-109

Lower Silesia. *see in index* Silesia

Lower Southampton, Pa., urban township situated in Bucks County just n.e. of Philadelphia; pop. 17,578; largely residential.

Lowes, John Livingston (1867–1945), educator and author, born Decatur, Ind.; professor of English literature Harvard University 1918–39; noted for critical works on Chaucer, Shakespeare, Coleridge ('The Road to Xanadu'; 'Art of Geoffrey Chaucer'; 'Essays in Appreciation').

Lowestoft, England, seaport and resort of Suffolk, 180 km (110 mi) n.e. of London; pop. 50,730; fisheries; captured by Cromwell 1643; Dutch fleet defeated by duke of York 1665, *map* G-199h
porcelain P-476

Low-fat milk M-323, *table* M-322

Low German, dialect G-96

Lowlands, Alberta, Canada A-262

Lowlands, in England E-219

Lowlands, of central Scotland S-67, *picture* S-68

Low latitudes C-392

Lownsbery, Eloise (1888–1967), writer, born Pawpaw, Ill.; brings medieval history to life in her books for boys and girls ('Boy Knight of Reims'; 'Out of the Flame'; 'Marta the Doll').

Low-pressure belt, in meteorology W-83, E-21

Low relief, or **bas-relief,** in sculpture S-80, *picture* P-264

Lowry, Malcolm (1909–57), Canadian novelist, poet, and traveler, born Cheshire County, England C-116

Low wave, *tables* R-34, R-50

Lox. *see in index* Liquid oxygen

Loyalist, or **Tory,** in American Colonies P-432
Revolution R-167, 174, C-107, *pictures* R-166, C-108. *see also in index* United Empire Loyalists

Loyalists, United Empire. *see in index* United Empire Loyalists

Loyal Legion, Military Order of the, patriotic society founded 1865 at Philadelphia, Pa., on the day following Lincoln's assassination; organized by U.S. Army and Navy officers; membership limited to such officers and their direct male descendants; purposes: fellowship among and welfare of U.S. soldiers and sailors, care of widows and orphans of deceased members.

Loyal Order of Moose. *see in index* Moose, Loyal Order of

Loyalty, to one's country. *see in index* Patriotism

Loyalty Day (May 1), designated by Congress in 1958 to reaffirm loyalty to the United States and to acknowledge the heritage of American freedom.

Loyalty Islands, French **Îles Loyauté,** Pacific group 100 km (60 mi) e. of New Caledonia, of which it is a dependency; 2,072 sq km (800 sq mi); pop. 13,378; copra, rubber, *map* P-4

Loyang, People's Republic of China, city in Honan Province 100 mi (160 km) w. of Kaifeng; pop. 580,000; farming, stock raising; trucks, cement, textiles C-293b.

Loyola, Ignatius of (1491?–1556), saint, founder of Jesuit Order; festival July 31, L-327
Counter Reformation R-135, *picture* R-134
Xavier influenced by X-329

Loyola College, at Baltimore, Md.; Roman Catholic; established in 1852; arts and sciences, business administration, and teacher education; graduate division.

Loyola Marymount University, at Los Angeles, Calif.; Roman Catholic; formed 1973 by merger of Marymount College (chartered 1948) and Loyola University of Los Angeles (established 1929); arts and sciences, business administration, education, and engineering; graduate division.

Loyola University in New Orleans, at New Orleans, La.; Roman Catholic; established 1912; arts and sciences, business administration, dentistry, law, music, and teacher education; graduate studies, *map* N-223b

Loyola University of Chicago, at Chicago, Ill.; Roman Catholic; founded 1870; arts and sciences, business administration, education, law, nursing, social work; graduate school; Medical Center (medicine and dentistry) at Maywood; center for humanities at Rome, Italy, *map* C-261

Loyson, Charles (1827–1912), French preacher, born Orléans, France; called "Père Hyacinthe"; eloquent speaker but his unorthodox beliefs caused his excommunication from Roman Catholic church.

Lozeau, Albert (1878–1924), Canadian poet and journalist, born Montreal; an invalid from youth; ranks high for sensitiveness and imagination C-113a

Lozenge, candy C-123

Lozier, Jean Baptiste Charles Bouvet de. *see in index* Bouvet de Lozier

LP-Gas / Luluabourg

LP-Gas, or **liquefied petroleum gas** (LPG) G-41, *chart* P-241a
farm machinery F-31

LSD (lysergic acid diethylamide), a hallucinatory drug synthesized by Dr. Albert Hofmann, Basle, Switzerland, 1938; used to treat terminal cancer patients; may become valuable in psychotherapy; nonmedical use considered dangerous D-200d

LSI, or **large-scale integrated circuit,** computers C-497d

Luanda, or **Loanda,** or **So Paulo de Loanda,** Angola, capital and seaport; pop. 480,613; founded 1575; for about three centuries, a center of slave trade L-327, A-419

Luang Prabang. *see in index* Luoangphrabang

Luau, Hawaiian feast H-57, *picture* H-53

Lubang Islands, small group off s.w. coast of Luzon, in the Philippines; pop. 19,904; largest island Lubang (74 sq mi; 192 sq km) commands entrance to Manila Bay, *map* P-261d

Lubber's knot, or **granny knot** K-262

Lubber's line, on compass C-494d, *diagram* C-500

Lubbock, Sir John. *see in index* Avebury, John Lubbock, Baron

Lubbock, Tex., city about 110 mi (180 km) s. of Amarillo; pop. 173,979; oil wells in area; cotton and cotton products, packed meats, grain sorghums; Texas Tech University; Mackenzie State Park; Reese Air Force Base nearby, *maps* T-128, U-40

Lübeck, West Germany, seaport on Trave River, 19 km (12 mi) from Baltic Sea; pop. 239,339; shipbuilding; machinery, *map* G-114
Hanseatic League H-22

Lubin, David (1849–1919), agricultural organizer, born Klodowa, Russian Poland; brought to U.S. in 1855; founded dry-goods and mail-order business in California, 1874; devoted last part of his life to agricultural problems. *see also in index* International Institute of Agriculture

Lubitsch, Ernst (1892–1947), motion-picture director and producer, born Berlin, Germany; to U.S. 1922; brilliant style and sophisticated humor ('Lady Windermere's Fan'; 'Merry Widow'; 'Ninotchka').

Lübke, Heinrich (1894–1972), West German political leader, born Enkhausen, near Dortmund, Germany; minister of Food, Agriculture, and Forestry, Federal Republic of Germany, 1953–59, president 1959–69.

Lublin, Poland, city 150 km (95 mi) s.e. of Warsaw; pop. 197,100; flourished in 12th century; scene of Russian victory over Austrians in World War I, *maps* P-414, E-335

Lublin, Treaty of (1569), *table* T-251a

Lubricant, oily or greasy substance used to diminish friction L-327
automobile, *picture* A-848
graphite G-178
petroleum, *charts* P-241, 241b

Lubumbashi, or **Elisabethville,** Zaire, city in s.e.; pop. 525,154; copper and tin mining center Z-353a

Luca della Robbia. *see in index* Robbia, Luca della

Lucan (Marcus Annaeus Lucanus) (A.D. 39–65), Roman poet, author of 'Pharsalia', epic on civil war between Caesar and Pompey.

Lucania, region in Italy. *see in index* Basilicata

Lucas, or **Luchich, Anthony Francis** (1855–1921), American mining engineer and geologist, born Dalmatia; to U.S. 1879, became citizen 1885, T-119

Lucas, Edward Verrall (1868–1938), English essayist, novelist, and biographer; born Eltham, Kent; "the modern Charles Lamb"; widely popular for his genial humor and broad sympathies ('The Open Road', anthology; 'The Life of Charles Lamb'; 'Over Bremerton's' and 'London Lavender', novels; 'Pleasure Trove', essays; 'A Wanderer in London' and 'A Wanderer in Paris', travel).

Lucas, Eliza. *see in index* Pinckney, Elizabeth (or Eliza) Lucas

Lucas, Jerry (born 1940), basketball player, born Middletown, Ohio; center, Ohio State University, selected as all-America player 1960, 1961, and 1962; with Cincinnati Royals 1963–69, Golden State Warriors 1969–71; New York Knickerbockers 1971–74.

Lucas, John Seymour (1849–1923), English historical and portrait painter, born London, *picture* W-163

Lucas Van Leyden (1494?–1533), Dutch painter and engraver, born Leiden, Netherlands; superb technician; influenced by Albrecht Dürer, later by Marcantonio.

Lucca, Italy, old and picturesque city 19 km (12 mi) n.e. of Pisa; pop. 88,428; many antiquities; large trade.

Luce, Clare Boothe (Mrs. H. R. Luce) (born 1903), writer and diplomat, born New York City; edited *Vogue* 1930, *Vanity Fair* 1931–34, then turned to writing plays ('The Women'; 'Kiss the Boys Goodbye'); later became a war correspondent; member U.S. Congress 1942–46; U.S. ambassador to Italy 1953–56.

Luce, Henry Robinson (1898–1967), editor and publisher, born Shantung Province, China; son of American missionary; husband of Clare Boothe Luce; in 1923 became co-founder and editor in chief of Time, Inc., editorial chairman 1964–67.

Lucerne, or **Luzern,** Switzerland, capital of canton of Lucerne at n.w. end of Lake Lucerne; pop. 69,879; tourist resort, *picture* S-544, *map* S-537
'Lion of Lucerne' T-166

Lucerne. *see in index* Alfalfa

Lucerne, Lake, or **Luzern (Vierwaldstättersee),** beautiful mountain-rimmed lake in central Switzerland; 39 km (24 mi) long, *map* S-537

Lucia, Santa. *see in index* Lucy, Saint

Lucia Day, in Sweden S-525

'Lucia di Lammermoor', opera by Gaetano Donizetti
story O-465

Lucian (120?–180?), Greek satirist and humorist G-235, S-341c, 348d

Lucifer, a cat that belonged to Cardinal Richelieu, *list* C-152

Lucifer, name of Venus as morning star; applied by Isaiah to king of Babylon ("How art thou fallen from heaven, O Lucifer, son of the morning!"), and, through misunderstanding of this passage by later writers, to Satan.

Luciferase, an enzyme manufactured in the cells of certain animals, the function of which is to control that slow process of oxidation known as bioluminescence or luminescence F-113

Luciferin, a chemical substance occurring in luminescent animals, which, when acted upon by the enzyme luciferase, produces light P-270
firefly and glowworm F-113

Lucilius, (180?–103? B.C.), Roman author L-76

Lucin Cutoff G-208, U-218

Lucite P-383, *picture* P-381

Luckhardt, Arno Benedict (1885–1957), physiologist, born Chicago, Ill.; professor of physiology, University of Chicago 1923–46 (chairman of department 1941–46); with J. Bailey Carter discovered value of ethylene gas as an anesthetic.

Luckman, Sid(ney) (born 1916), football quarterback, born Brooklyn, N.Y.; played for Chicago Bears 1939–50.

Luckner, Felix von, Count (1881–1966), German naval officer and adventurer, born Dresden; sailor at age of 13; gained title "Sea Devil" by daring exploits in World War I; lived in U.S. 1926–34 then returned to Germany; hero of 'The Sea Devil', by Lowell Thomas.

Lucknow, India, manufacturing and rail center, capital of Uttar Pradesh state; pop. 895,947, L-328
siege (1857), *table* W-8d

'Luck of Roaring Camp, The', work by Harte A-351

Lucretia, Roman matron whose suicide because of outrage inflicted by Sextus, son of King Tarquin the Proud, provoked expulsion of the Tarquins.

Lucretius (Titus Lucretius Carus) (96?–55 B.C.), Roman poet-philosopher; preached against the idea of the immortality of the soul P-265

Lucullus, Lucius Licinius (110?–56? B.C.), immensely wealthy Roman noble, helped conquer Mithradates; "Lucullan luxury" has become proverbial.

Lucy, or **Lucia** (283?–304?), saint; noblewoman of Syracuse, Sicily; two attempts at torturing her having failed, she was finally killed by sword; festival December 13, S-525

Lucy, Sir Thomas (1532–1600), English squire, justice of peace, said to have prosecuted Shakespeare; supposedly portrayed in 'Henry IV' as Justice Shallow S-130

Lüda, municipality, People's Republic of China; pop. 1,927,000, L-328

Luddites, bands of workmen organized in England to smash machinery 1812–18 in protest against displacement of hand labor.

Ludendorff, Erich von (1865–1937), German general, born Prussia; expert strategist; worked with Hindenburg in World War I and with him responsible for many successful campaigns; fled to Sweden after Germany's defeat; returned to Munich 1919; supported Hitler for a time; later became a mystic; author of several books about World War I, H-179, *picture* G-104
offensive of 1918 W-258

Lüderitz, South-West Africa, port and health resort in s.w.; pop. 3,604; fish, rock lobsters; center for diamond-producing region, *maps* S-264

Lud Hill, London, England L-286

Ludington, Sybil (1761–1839), Revolutionary War heroine; at age 16 made night ride by horseback to arouse members of her father's volunteer regiment to muster for fight against British; ride was three times longer than Paul Revere's.

Ludington, Mich., commercial city and resort on Lake Michigan and Marquette River 70 mi (110 km) n.w. of Grand Rapids; pop. 8,937; watchcases and jewelry, game boards, furniture, chemicals, vibrator machinery M-287, *map* M-285

Ludlow, England, old town in s. Shropshire; pop. 6,796, *map* G-199h

Ludlow, Mass., community 7 mi (11 km) n.e. of Springfield; pop. of township 18,150; near Westover Air Force Base; plastics; incorporated 1774.

Ludwig I (1786–1868), king of Bavaria, grandfather of Ludwig II; born Strasbourg; munificent patron of art; forced to abdicate by revolution in 1848, M-546

Ludwig II (1845–86), king of Bavaria, grandson of Ludwig I and cousin of Ludwig III; born Nymphenburg, near Munich; succeeded 1864; patron of Richard Wagner; died insane
Neuschwanstein Castle, *picture* G-112
Wagner W-2

Ludwig III (1845–1921), king of Bavaria; cousin of Ludwig II; born Munich; succeeded 1913, abdicated 1918.

Ludwig, Emil (1881–1948), American author, born Breslau, Germany; lived early life in Switzerland; became U.S. citizen 1941; in his youth wrote plays, sketches, and novels but found greatest success in his "humanized" historical biographies, including those of Napoleon I, Bismarck, Goethe, Lincoln.

Ludwig, Otto (1813–65), German dramatist and novelist, born Eisfeld, near Coburg, Germany; one of leading German writers of fiction in middle 19th century G-98

Ludwigia, plants of swamps, ditches, pond margins, and wet pine barrens; a genus of the evening primrose family, *Onagraceae;* used in aquariums N-74

Ludwigshafen, West Germany, city on Rhine opposite Mannheim; pop. 171,510; large chemical works and other manufactures; known for large trade in coal, timber, iron, *map* G-115

Lufbery, Raoul (1884–1918), American aviator, born Clermont, near Beauvais, France; World War I ace; credited with 17 victories; killed in combat.

Luff, *diagram* B-326

Lufkin, Tex., city about 115 mi (185 km) n.e. of Houston; pop. 28,562; livestock, lumbering; oil-field equipment, paper products, machinery; Angelina and Davy Crockett National Forests nearby, *map* T-128

Lufthansa German Airlines G-112

Luftwaffe, German air force, including antiaircraft units, under Hitler. Word means "air weapon" A-158
airplanes A-205
World War II, W-266, 269, 286, 290

Lugano, Lake, deep and narrow lake enclosed by mountains, partly in Switzerland, partly in n. Italy, between Lakes Maggiore and Como; 30 km (20 mi) long, *map* S-537

Lugbait, or **lugworm.** *see in index* Lobworm

Lugdunum. *see in index* Lyon

Lug pole, camp cooking device C-64, *picture* C-69

Luimneach, Ireland. *see in index* Limerick

Luini, Bernardino (1475?–1532?), Italian artist, born Luino, near Varese, Italy; most noted as a fresco painter; excelled at depicting sacred and mythological subjects.

Luke, saint, one of apostolic assistants, traditional author of the Third Gospel and of the Acts; patron of physicians; festival October 18, A-507
Jesus' boyhood, *picture* J-103

Luke, Frank (1897–1918), aviator, born Phoenix, Ariz.; as World War I ace downed 18 or 19 enemy balloons and airplanes; was killed in combat; posthumously awarded the Medal of Honor.

Luke, Gospel of Saint, Third Gospel and third book of New Testament.

Lukeman, (Henry) Augustus (1871–1935), sculptor, born Richmond, Va.; successor to Gutzon Borglum in charge of Confederate memorial, Stone Mountain, Ga.; portrait busts, statues, monuments (portrait statues of William McKinley and Jefferson Davis; equestrian statue of Kit Carson; 'Manu the Law Giver of India').

Luks, George Benjamin (1867–1933), painter, born Williamsport, Pa.; war correspondent and illustrator in Spanish-American War. His paintings of poorer classes, street scenes, portraits, and his interpretations of childhood show free, virile, and spontaneous technique ('The Spielers'; 'Old Clothes Man').

Luleå, Sweden, seaport on Gulf of Bothnia; pop. 30,488; shipbuilding; lumber and iron; chartered 1621, moved 6 km (4 mi) to present site 1648–9, S-523, *maps* S-524, E-335

Lule River, in n. Sweden, flows 320 km (200 mi) to Gulf of Bothnia, *map* S-524

Lully, Jean-Baptiste, or **Giovanni Battista Lulli** (1632–87), French composer and musician, born Italy, called "father of French opera"; taken to Paris, France, as boy, worked as servant; rose to position of court musician to Louis XIV; introduced lively ballets; dominated French opera for almost a century L-328
ballet B-33
opera O-461

Lully, Raymond, or **Ramón Lull,** or **Raymundus Lullius** (1235?–1315), Spanish scientist and missionary, born Palma, Majorca; authority on Arabic; founder of western orientalism
forerunner of modern chemists C-242

Luluabourg. *see in index* Kananga

spreads to its base; reservoir on its side built by Hadrian and Antoninus Pius still in use A-734

Lycaenidae, butterflies B-528

Lycée, French school E-98
U.S. college compared C-433

Lyceum, Aristotle's school in ancient Athens A-14
Aristotle's teaching A-589
Greek language G-235

Lyceum, in United States A-51

Lychnis, scarlet. *see in index* Jerusalem cross

Lycia, ancient division of s.w. Asia Minor on Mediterranean, conquered by Persia 6th century B.C., then subject in turn to Macedon, Egypt, Syria, and Rome, *maps* P-212, M-7

'Lycidas', poem by John Milton commemorating death of his friend Edward King, drowned at sea E-259

Lycoming College, at Williamsport, Pa.; United Methodist; founded as Williamsport Academy 1812, as college 1947; arts and sciences, education.

Lycoperdon bovista, a mushroom, *picture* M-553

Lycopodium, a genus of nonflowering mosslike plants of the club moss family (*Lycopodiaceae*) with trailing stems and numerous small evergreen leaves; the sulfur-yellow, highly inflammable powderlike spores produced by erect fruiting spikes are sometimes used in making fireworks.

Lycoris, a genus of perennial plants of the amaryllis family, native to eastern Asia; root a bulb; leaves long, narrow, disappearing before flowers develop; flowers yellow, red, or rose-lilac, fragrant, grow in cluster at top of tall stem, stamens project beyond flower tube; one species called golden spider lily.

Lycurgus (9th century B.C.), lawgiver of ancient Sparta L-342
legal codes L-91

Lydda, or **Lod,** Israel, ancient town 10 mi (16 km) s.e. of Tel Aviv-Jaffa; pop. 21,000; international airport
St. George legend G-74

Lyddite, an explosive E-361

Lydgate, John (1370?–1451?), English poet, scholar, and monk, born at Lydgate near Newmarket; contemporary of Geoffrey Chaucer and acknowledged him as his "master"; voluminous writer; style rough and verbose; founder of English literary school between Chaucer and Edmund Spenser E-273
Canterbury tale, *picture* C-224

Lydia, ancient kingdom in Asia Minor; early seat of Asiatic

civilization with important influence on Greeks; later part of Roman province of Asia, *maps* G-221, M-7
coins C-430d, *picture* C-430c
King Croesus C-611

Lydian stone. *see in index* Touchstone

Lye, a caustic. *see also in index* Caustic potash
soaps S-229, 231

Lyell, Sir Charles (1797–1875), British geologist, born Kinnordy, near Kirriemuir, Scotland; established James Hutton's "uniformitarian" theory of earth's evolution L-342
evolution E-345

Lyle, David Alexander (1845–1937), U.S. Army officer, born Lancaster, Ohio; attained rank of colonel 1907; inventor of Lyle lifesaving gun.

Lyly, or **Lilly, John** (1554?–1606), English romancer and dramatist, born The Weald; created euphuism, a writing style
drama D-171
English literature E-273

Lyman, Roy (Link) (1898–1972), football tackle; with Canton Bulldogs 1922 and 1924, Cleveland Browns 1923, and Chicago Bears 1925–34.

Lyme grass, or **wild rye,** a coarse perennial grass of erect growth found in temperate climates.

Lyme Regis, England, seaside resort of Dorsetshire, 217 km (135 mi) s.w. of London; pop. 3,310; fine beach, *map* G-199h

Lymph, a colorless liquid exuded through the capillaries to nourish tissues of the body L-343
anatomy A-391
living things L-270

Lymphadenitis, inflammation of lymph nodes L-343

Lymphangiography, diagnostic procedure L-334

Lymphatic system, a system of vessels for collecting lymph and carrying it back into the blood L-342
blood B-314
disease D-128a
immune system I-55

Lymphatic vessel, in anatomy L-343

Lymph node, small glands scattered throughout lymphatic system, but especially in the neck, armpits, groin, thighs, and body organs; produce corpuscular elements of lymph L-342, D-128a

Lymphocyte, one kind of white blood cell L-342
blood B-314, *table* B-317
disease immunity D-128a
immune system I-55
transplant surgery S-519c

Lymphogranuloma venereum, a venereal disease V-274

Lymphoid nodule, or **lymphoid follicle,** in anatomy L-342

Lymphokine, in pathology I-56

Lynbrook, N.Y., resort city on shore of Long Island, near New York City; pop. 23,776; chiefly residential, *map, inset* A-260

Lynch, John Roy (1847–1939), black leader of Reconstruction period, born Concordia Parish, La.; in U.S. Congress 1873–77, 1882–83; in army 1898–1911 B-292

Lynch, Thomas, Jr. (1749–79), signer of Declaration of Independence, born South Carolina S-310

Lynchburg, Va., industrial city on James River, about 95 mi (150 km) s.w. of Richmond; pop. 66,743; foundries, communications products, nuclear reactors; Randolph-Macon Woman's College, Lynchburg College; supply depot for Confederates during Civil War, *maps* V-348, 331, 336, U-41

Lynchburg College, at Lynchburg, Va.; private control; opened 1903; arts and sciences, teacher education; graduate studies.

Lynd, Robert Staughton (1892–1970), sociologist, born New Albany, Ind.; professor of sociology Columbia University 1931–60; with wife, **Helen Merrell Lynd** (1896–1982), wrote 'Middletown' and 'Middletown in Transition', studies of a Middle Western city (Muncie, Ind.).

Lyndhurst, N.J., urban township 6 mi (10 km) n.e. of Newark on the Passaic River; pop. 22,729; incorporated 1852, *map, inset* N-202

Lyndhurst, Ohio, residential city 4 mi (6 km) n.e. of Cleveland Heights; pop. 18,092; incorporated 1917, *map, inset* O-429

Lyndon B. Johnson National Historic Site, Texas, U.S., *picture* J-131

Lyndon B. Johnson Space Center, near Houston, Tex. S-346b, H-262, *map* H-261, *pictures* S-342b, T-123
renamed in 1973 J-135

Lyndon State College, at Lyndonville, Vt.; founded 1911; formerly a teachers college; liberal arts, education; graduate studies.

Lynen, Feodor (1911–79), German biochemist, born Munich; director Max Planck Institute for Cell Chemistry, University of Munich.

Lynn, James Thomas (born 1927), lawyer and government official, born Cleveland, Ohio; general counsel Department of Commerce 1969–71;

undersecretary 1971–73; secretary of housing and urban development 1973–75; director Office of Management and Budget 1975–77.

Lynn, Mass., a city near Boston; pop. 78,471, *map, inset* M-160
early shoe factory S-179

Lynnhaven Bay, on coast of Virginia e. of Norfolk
oysters O-517

Lynnwood, Wash., city 16 mi (26 km) n. of Seattle on Puget Sound; pop. 21,937; prefab homes and panels, *map* W-52

Lynwood, Calif., city 9 mi (15 km) s. of Los Angeles; pop 48,548; metal products, chemicals; incorporated 1921, *map, inset* C-53

Lynx, a member of the cat family L-344, *picture* A-436
furs, *tables* F-464, 465

Lyon, Mary (1797–1849), pioneer in higher education for women, born near Buckland, Mass.; opened Mt. Holyoke Female Seminary (later Mt. Holyoke College) 1837
Hall of Fame, *table* H-11

Lyon, Nathaniel (1818–61), soldier, prominent opponent of states' rights and slavery, born Ashford, Conn.; organized Unionist troops in Missouri; killed at Wilson's Creek M-400

Lyon, or **Lugdunum,** France, city at junction of Rhone and Saône rivers; pop. 456,265 L-344, *map* E-334
Botanic Garden, *table* B-379
Croix Rousse Tunnel, *table* T-292

Lyon, University of, France L-344

Lyonesse, fabled land in Arthurian legends, off s. coast of Cornwall, England; reputedly engulfed by sea.

Lyons, Joseph Aloysius (1879–1939), Australian political leader, born Circular Head, Tasmania; premier, treasurer, and minister for railways 1923–28; prime minister 1932–39; founded United party 1931.

Lyons, Theodore Amar (Ted) (born 1900), baseball pitcher and manager, born Lake Charles, La.; pitcher Chicago, A.L., 1923–42, manager-pitcher 1946, manager 1947–48; won 260 games, lost 230; won over 20 games in each of 3 seasons; pitched no-hit game against Boston, Aug. 21, 1926.

Lyotropic liquid crystal L-234

Lyra, or **Lyre,** constellation across North Pole from Little Bear; represents lyre of Orpheus or of Mercury, *charts* S-419–20, 423

Lyre, form of harp M-568, *picture* M-569
Egyptian, *picture* E-122

Greece, *picture* E-78
legendary invention H-145
Nero's "fiddle" N-128
Orpheus, *picture* O-464

Lyrebird L-344, A-782, *picture* P-110

'Lyrical Ballads' (1798), book of poems by Wordsworth and Coleridge W-234

Lyric poetry P-407
Greek G-234
muse of M-550

Lyrics, in musical comedy M-567a

Lysander (died 395 B.C.), able unscrupulous Spartan admiral; defeated Athens at Aegospotami and terminated Peloponnesian War.

Lysergic acid diethylamide. *see in index* LSD

Lysias (459–380 B.C.), one of great Attic orators; originator of eloquent but plain style in Greek rhetoric.

Lysippus (4th century B.C.), Greek sculptor G-230
Hercules H-144

'Lysistrata', play by Aristophanes A-588

Lysosome, of cell
immune system I-56

Lysozyme, germ-killing enzyme in most body fluids B-234, *table* D-281

Lys River, a tributary of the Scheldt; rises in extreme n. of France and flows n.e. 190 km (120 mi) joining Scheldt at Ghent; scene of terrific fighting in World War I, *map* W-252

Lyster, William, Australian opera director A-800

Lyte, Henry Francis (1793–1847), British divine and hymn writer, born near Kelso, Scotland; author of popular hymns 'Abide with Me', 'Jesus, I My Cross Have Taken'.

Lythraceae. *see in index* Loosestrife family

Lythrum, or **purple loosestrife,** a perennial plant (*L. salicaria*) of the loosestrife family, found from New England to Utah; grows to 1 m (3 ft); leaves narrow, 10 cm (4 in) long; flowers purple, in dense spikes; also called spiked loosestrife.

Lytton, Edward George Earle Bulwer-Lytton, first **Baron** (1803–73), English novelist, playwright, and political leader; born London; member of Parliament 1831–41, 1852–66; made secretary for the colonies 1858; historical novels; known for 'Last Days of Pompeii'.

Lytton, Edward Robert Bulwer-Lytton, first **earl of** (1831–91), pen name Owen Meredith, English statesman and poet, born London; son of Baron Lytton; viceroy of India 1876–80 ('Lucile', novel).